Cognitive Theories in Social Psychology

Papers from Advances in Experimental Social Psychology

EDITED BY

Leonard Berkowitz

Department of Psychology
University of Wisconsin
Madison, Wisconsin

ACADEMIC PRESS   New York   San Francisco   London   1978
A Subsidiary of Harcourt Brace Jovanovich, Publishers

ACADEMIC PRESS, INC.
111 Fifth Avenue, New York, New York 10003

United Kingdom Edition published by
ACADEMIC PRESS, INC. (LONDON) LTD.
24/28 Oval Road, London NW1 7DX

Library of Congress Cataloging in Publication Data

Main entry under title:

Cognitive theories in social psychology.

Includes bibliographies and index.
1. Social psychology--Addresses, essays, lectures.
I. Berkowitz, Leonard, Date   II. Advances in
experimental social psychology.
HM251.C645   301.1   78-4811
ISBN 0-12-091850-1

PRINTED IN THE UNITED STATES OF AMERICA

Cognitive Theories
in Social Psychology

CONTRIBUTORS

Norman H. Anderson

Elliot Aronson

Daryl J. Bem

Leonard Berkowitz

Keith E. Davis

Edward E. Jones

Lee Ross

Stanley Schachter

Percy H. Tannenbaum

Robert A. Wicklund

CONTENTS

Self-Perception Theory   221

DARYL J. BEM

From Acts to Dispositions: The Attribution Process in Person Perception   283

EDWARD E. JONES AND KEITH E. DAVIS

Update of "From Acts to Dispositions: The Attribution Process in Person Perception"   331

EDWARD E. JONES

The Intuitive Psychologist and His Shortcomings: Distortions in the Attribution Process   337

LEE ROSS

CONTENTS

Three Years Later   509

ROBERT A. WICKLUND

LIST OF CONTRIBUTORS

Numbers in parentheses indicate the pages on which the authors' contributions begin.

NORMAN H. ANDERSON (1, 103), Department of Psychology, University of California, San Diego, La Jolla, California 92093

ELLIOT ARONSON (181, 215), University of California at Santa Cruz, Santa Cruz, California 95060

DARYL J. BEM (221), Department of Psychology, Stanford University, Stanford, California 94305

LEONARD BERKOWITZ (455), Psychology Department, University of Wisconsin, Madison, Wisconsin 53706

KEITH E. DAVIS (283), Department of Psychology, University of Colorado, Boulder, Colorado 80309

EDWARD E. JONES (283, 331), Department of Psychology, Princeton University, Princeton, New Jersey 08540

LEE ROSS (337, 385), Department of Social Psychology, Stanford University, Stanford, California 94305

STANLEY SCHACHTER (401, 433), Department of Psychology, Columbia University, New York, New York 10027

PERCY H. TANNENBAUM (127, 177), Graduate School of Public Policy, University of California, Berkeley, California 94720

ROBERT A. WICKLUND (465, 509), Department of Psychology, University of Texas at Austin, Austin, Texas 78712

PREFACE

World War II is a watershed in social psychology as well as in the broader domains of human history. Under the influence of broad cultural changes and the more immediate impetus of writings by psychologists such as Kurt Lewin, Solomon Asch, Robert McLeod, and others, theoretical formulations developed that ended the almost complete prewar domination of social psychology by behavioristic ideas. In one way or another, these writers all insisted that an individual's behavior was usually much more than an unthinking response to external events; action was often determined in important ways by the person's understanding of self and environment. Therefore, it was concluded that any comprehensive account of social conduct is seriously incomplete without due attention to cognitive processes. This argument was then elaborated and extended from the late 1950s on by these postwar psychologists' intellectual heirs and associates. As a result, it is fair to say that most of the research as well as the major systematic analyses in contemporary social psychology are now guided by notions emphasizing cognitive processes. It is simply not possible to discuss social psychology today without focusing on these cognitive formulations.

Since its inception in 1964, the serial publication *Advances in Experimental Social Psychology* has both reflected and contributed to these theoretical developments. To mention only a few examples, one of the seminal papers in the study of person perception and causal attributions, the article by Jones and Davis, was first published in the second volume, and Schachter's exceedingly influential analysis of the role of cognitions in emotional behavior was presented to the social psychological public in the first volume, in 1962.

All sciences modify their concepts and redirect their attention as research continues, but perhaps none does so more rapidly than social psychology. As someone once said, we have a long past but a short history and all too quickly forget the important ideas and studies of earlier years. However, quite a few of the articles from previous decades are still highly relevant to our current interests. This is especially true in the case of the chapters presented in this volume. Although observations have multiplied and theoretical advances have been made since these conceptions were first offered to the field, many of them still pose the questions and issues that confront the latest investigations in this area and provide the constructs that are still employed in the interpretation of the most recent research findings.

This collection of chapters from *Advances in Experimental Social Psychology* has grown out of a firm belief in the importance of these earlier discussions for our current formulations in social psychology—and they are important in various ways. For one, the field does not seem to give as much attention as before to the cognitive consistency models of the 1960s, such as dissonance and congruity theory. And yet the basic phenomena that initially prompted these conceptions still exist, and these phenomena remain significant for social psychology. The analyses that Aronson, Bem, and Tannenbaum had written for earlier volumes on dissonance, self-perception, and congruity theories, respectively, continue to be relevant to present-day social psychology and still warrant our attention.

Consistency formulations, of course, deal with the question of how the person copes with diverse sets of information. Very often, rather than being disturbed by information sets that would result in opposing opinions, the individual integrates much of the information available to him to form a resulting judgment of someone or some object. Anderson's discussion of how these cognitive integrations come about demonstrates the many ways in which these integrative judgments occur and is also as pertinent to social psychology as when it was first published in this series.

In contrast to the apparent decline in the popularity of the consistency theories, there is an abiding interest in person perception and a growing preoccupation with the question of how the average person makes causal judgments. How do most of us arrive at an impression of someone's personality? How do we, given all sorts of information about him, make inferences concerning the kind of person he is? And, furthermore, how do we tend to explain his behavior on the basis of different kinds of information? Questions such as these are now drawing increasing attention. Anyone concerned with these matters would surely do well to read the chapters by Jones and Davis as well as the one by Anderson previously mentioned.

In addition to studying our reactions to and perceptions of other people, social psychologists now have a growing recognition of the importance of the individual's awareness of himself. A person at times makes inferences about his own attitudes from observing his own behavior, as Bem argues, and, according to Schachter, can even experience a particular emotional feeling or display a given kind of emotional behavior because of the way he interprets his bodily sensations. Bem's and Schachter's conceptions surely must be considered by all those who are seriously interested in the analysis of human emotions. The research program mounted by Wicklund and his associates also deals with the consequences of the individual's attention to himself, but in this case it is his awareness of himself as a total being rather than with respect to particular aspects, such as his momentary actions or sensations. This *self*-awareness, Wicklund demonstrates, can stimulate a person so that he "to his own self [is] true." Can any analysis of the role of the self in social behavior be complete if it does not take up this important series of investigations?

I believe that there can be no doubt that the original writings I have just cited are important in their own right. However, we are also fortunate to have many of the writers' latest thoughts on the issues they had faced earlier. In most cases, the original chapter is followed by author comments on recent developments. Anderson tells us of later research bearing on cognitive integrations; Aronson has some remarks about the current state of dissonance theory; Jones briefly summarizes his present views regarding correspondent inference theory; Ross has some additional observations about the attribution process; Wicklund brings us up to date in research on the consequences of self-awareness; and so on. These essays will, no doubt, add to the significance of the writers' earlier conceptions.

COGNITIVE ALGEBRA: INTEGRATION THEORY APPLIED TO SOCIAL ATTRIBUTION[1]

Norman H. Anderson

DEPARTMENT OF PSYCHOLOGY
UNIVERSITY OF CALIFORNIA, SAN DIEGO
LA JOLLA, CALIFORNIA

[1] I wish to thank Nancy Baker, Richard Bowers, Clifford Butzin, Arthur Farkas, Manuel Leon, and Roland Wilhelmy for helpful comments. I also wish to thank R. P. Abelson, M. H. Birnbaum, P. Brickman, J. Clavadetscher, C. C. Graesser, K. R. Hammond, R. Hastie, C. Hendrick, S. Himmelfarb, M. F. Kaplan, G. S. Leventhal, L. L. Lopes, L. A. McArthur, D. M. Messick, J. Mills, G. C. Oden, D. G. Pruitt, and R. S. Wyer for criticism of an earlier draft. I am indebted to Martin Kaplan and Samuel Himmelfarb for the opportunity of presenting some of their unpublished data. This work was supported by NSF Grants GB-21028 and GS-36918, and facilitated by NIMH grants to the Center for Human Information Processing, University of California, San Diego.

Reprinted from *Advances in Experimental Social Psychology*, Volume 7, 1–101.

I. Theoretical Overview

A. Social Judgment

Current developments in social psychology have been increasingly involved with questions of social judgment. Different avenues of investigation have been converging on a common set of problems and, to some degree, on a common conceptual framework.

This article considers some of the interrelations between two of these developments. One is attribution theory as developed by Heider (1958), Jones and Davis (1965), and Kelley (1967, 1971, 1972). The other is the theory of information integration developed by the writer and his colleagues over the past decade (see Anderson, 1962a, 1962b, 1968a, 1970a, 1971a, 1973d, 1973e).

Both integration theory and attribution theory have been much concerned with person perception, but there has been little interaction between them. One reason has been their orientation toward different aspects of the judgment process. Attribution theory has been concerned primarily with questions of valuation, and integration itself has received little attention. In contrast, the first concern of integration theory is how information is combined or integrated. The integration rule, it is true, allows a study of valuation by means of functional measurement methodology, but valuation has so far received secondary attention.

A second reason for the low interaction rate is that much of the work on integration theory has been outside of social psychology, in decision-making and perception. Even within the social area, integration theory has been concerned with problems such as opinion formation that do not involve attribution.

Integration theory gives a unified, general approach to judgment. From this standpoint, there is nothing unique about the interpersonal judgments studied in attribution theory. They should follow the same laws that apply to other kinds of judgments. This is a reasonable working assumption in view of the extensive empirical support that integration theory has received in several different substantive areas. This chapter attempts to illustrate the potential of the integration-theoretical approach to social attribution.

B. INTEGRATION THEORY

1. Valuation and Integration

The two basic operations of integration theory are valuation and integration. Any judgment requires a preliminary evaluation of the meaning and relevance of the stimuli for the task at hand. Clearly, the meaning and relevance of any piece of stimulus information will be different for one judgment than for another. The role of the valuation operation is to process the given information and extract the needed parameters. Once evaluated, the information is ready to be combined in an overall judgment.

A general principle of information integration is assumed to govern the way in which the information is combined into the judgment. This approach differs from the various attempts that have been made to erect a theory on the basis of one or another form of consistency principle such as balance or congruity. As has been noted elsewhere (Anderson, 1971a), a consistency principle is inherently too narrow to provide a basis for a general theory.

To give cogency to the principle of information integration, more explicit formulation is required. For this purpose, the theory makes extensive use of simple algebraic models.

2. Cognitive Algebra

An interesting and important outcome of the experimental work on information integration has been the wide success of simple algebraic models. Applications have been made to attitude change, person perception, psycholinguistics, decision-making, and various problems in psychophysics. Averaging models have played the dominant role, but subtracting and multiplying models have also been useful.

The overall implication of this work is the existence and operation of a general cognitive algebra. Processes for integrating information follow simple rules of ordinary algebra in a wide variety of situations. This cognitive algebra appears to be a general property of the mind, since it is operative in widely different substantive areas.

It is surprising that the applicability of these models was not recognized much earlier. Many previous investigators, especially in psychophysics and decision-making, have attempted to employ algebraic judgment models, but their success has been limited (Anderson, 1973e). The main handicap seems to have been the lack of an adequate theory of measurement. Functional measurement methodology provides a solution to the measurement problem as an integral part of the general theory of information integration.

With functional measurement methodology, it is possible to take a purely verbal expression such as Heider's (1958, p. 83) statement,

$$x = f(\text{trying, power, environment})$$

and treat it in an exact, mathematical manner. Heider suggests that environment should add to the product of trying and power, but that remains a vague, untestable assertion in the absence of any measure of the variables in question. Functional measurement procedure allows a solution to this equation. Exact values can be placed on each stimulus variable in terms of the personal value system of the individual.

3. Functional Measurement

Cognitive algebra is intimately bound up with the theory of functional measurement. The model analyses rest on having interval scales of the stimulus variables, and of the response. Functional measurement methodology provides these scales, as outlined in Section II. As one illustration of its power, functional measurement has provided the first general solution to the long-standing problem of measuring subjective probability and utility (Anderson & Shanteau, 1970; Shanteau, 1970b).

In the functional measurement approach, the algebraic model provides the scaling frame. The stimulus values are those that function in the given integration task. Functional measurement is not a separate theory of scaling, but instead makes scaling an organic part of substantive theory. Measurement theory and substantive theory are thus cofunctional in development.

An important feature of functional measurement is its ability to measure the personal values of the individual. Traditional scaling theories in the Thurstonian tradition have, almost necessarily, employed pooled group data in the scaling procedure. Group scales have their uses, but they average away real individual differences that are often important in the social realm. Further comparative remarks on measurement theory are given in Anderson (1973e).

4. Comment

To date the work on integration theory has placed primary emphasis on the algebraic models themselves. This reflects their fundamental role in the study of the integration processes. However, although this preoccupation with integration models was appropriate in the initial theoretical development, it has resulted in a relative neglect of problems of valuation.

Especially important are stimulus interactions—produced by inconsistency, for example—in which the valuation and integration processes are interwoven. The analysis of these problems is still very rudimentary, although the two-stage integration models are possible tools (Anderson, 1973e). These two-stage models open up the possibility of using functional measurement to scale the stimulus values as these are changed by the stimulus interaction (Section II,D,4).

Also, it must be recognized that algebraic models have only an *as if* status even if they are successful. To show that people average raises the next question of how they do so; possible averaging mechanisms are discussed in Anderson (1973d). Multiplying models have special methodological interest in this regard, as closer consideration has suggested that the operative processes can be quite different from multiplying (Anderson & Weiss, 1971; Sections II,C,3 and III,B,3).

C. RELATION TO OTHER WORK

It will be evident throughout this chapter how much the present approach is indebted to the work of others. Unfortunately, this indebtedness tends to be obscured when one is making critical comparisons between various theoretical approaches. To acknowledge this debt in a short space is not possible, but a few comments may illustrate some of the interrelationships.

Attribution theory means different things to different people, but there is general consensus that it is concerned primarily with interpersonal perception. Heider (1958) has been especially concerned with perceptions of the motivations, intentions, and abilities of other persons. This has had a liberating influence on the traditional approach to person perception which has tended toward a narrow preoccupation with clinical judgment or with evaluative judgments of social desirability. Indeed, the main value of attribution theory has perhaps been in its beneficial effect in calling attention to neglected areas of social judgment rather than in any theoretical structure.

Basic experimental work by Jones and his associates has clustered around the concept of informativeness. The joint action of internal and external causes of behavior has been studied with particular reference to how much information they provide about the internal causes. The concept of informativeness used by Jones is closely related to the concept of weight in integration theory. However, Jones has been concerned mainly with valuation operations and has used experimental designs such that the integration model is not of explicit concern.

In Kelley's approach, the integration processes begin to assume greater importance. Kelley's causal schemata are, in a certain sense, analogous to the algebraic models used in integration theory. However,

Kelley (1972, p. 2) interprets schemata in terms of data from factorial designs rather than as conceptual integration models. Kelley's use of analysis of variance, moreover, remains analogical rather than becoming an analytical tool.

Kelley places considerable emphasis on the role of experience and the external environment in perception of causality. This emphasis parallels that of Brunswik (1956; see also Hammond, 1966), who has given special attention to the probabilistic nature of the environment. Brunswik has attempted to quantify his approach by using multiple regression equations and partial correlations based on observable stimulus and response measures. This approach provides an interesting contrast with integration theory which begins its analysis in terms of the subjective values of the individual, not the objective, physicalistic values of the environment that are required in Brunswik's theoretical framework.

Brunswik's work is in turn related to the attempts by the Bayesians (see Edwards, 1968) to apply statistical decision models to human judgment. An extensive review of these and related approaches has been given by Slovic and Lichtenstein (1971). Related models have been explored by McGuire (1960) and Wyer (1972). These normative statistical models can be useful in practical problems of prediction. However, they seem to be concerned with questions that are peripheral to understanding the psychological processes that underlie behavior (Section III,E; Shanteau, 1972).

The present emphasis on the role of judgment in social affairs carries on the tradition of Sherif and Hovland (1961) and of Helson (1964). Both these approaches relied heavily on the use of assimilation and contrast as explanatory concepts. However, evidence for these two concepts in social judgment is scant, and they do not play an important role in integration theory.

Numerous other workers have made important contributions. The interesting volume by Warr and Knapper (1968) covers a variety of topics in person perception. Smith (1970) gives an overview of speech communication. Byrne (1971) and his associates have produced an extensive collection of experimental studies of interpersonal attraction. The monograph by Slovic and Lichtenstein (1971) gives a detailed, scholarly overview of several currents of work in decision-making. Review chapters by Rosenberg (1968), Tagiuri (1969), and Zajonc (1968) provide useful systematizations of other developments in mathematical models and person perception. Numerous important contributions to integration theory have been made by M. H. Birnbaum, C. Hendrick, M. F. Kaplan, S. Himmelfarb, J. C. Shanteau, and D. J. Weiss, and some of these will be taken up below.

D. Method of Exposition

The method of exposition employed in this chapter deserves a brief remark. A number of published articles have been selected and re-interpreted in terms of information integration theory. This method seemed the most effective for illustrating the same basic principles in operation across a heterogeneous array of experimental situations.

This method, however, has two shortcomings. The first is a tendency toward one-sided presentation. Since the purpose was to illustrate the nature of integration theory, a balanced discussion of other theoretical interpretations was not usually feasible in a brief space. Moreover, many useful contributions in these previous articles did not even come under discussion.

In addition, a heterogeneous collection of particular applications may lack coherence at first sight. Closer consideration should reveal greater unity. To the writer, it has been a pleasure in preparing this chapter to see the same theoretical ideas reappear in quite diverse applications.

II. Integration Models

Three main types of algebraic models have been used in the study of information integration. These are adding, averaging, and multiplying models. Subtracting and dividing models will here be lumped with adding and multiplying models, respectively, to which they are formally similar even though they represent different psychological processes.

Mathematical analyses of these models have been given elsewhere, together with references to a variety of experimental applications (Anderson, 1962b, 1968a, 1970a, 1971a, 1973d, 1973e). This section will accordingly be limited to a brief survey of a few relevant results.

A. Adding Models

1. Qualitative Analyses

A number of experiments (see Section III,A) have employed an adding model in a qualitative form. The basic idea can be illustrated by considering two conditions in which the same overt behavior, R, is the sum of two contributing factors, F and G:

$$
\begin{aligned}
R_1 &= F_1 + G_1 & \text{(Condition 1)} \\
R_2 &= F_2 + G_2 & \text{(Condition 2)}
\end{aligned}
\tag{1}
$$

where the subscripts index the values of the variables in the two conditions.

The typical experiment is designed so that $R_1 = R_2$, and $F_1 > F_2$. Mathematically, it follows at once that $G_1 < G_2$.

Several experiments have shown that subjects do reason by such a model. The main interest in these experiments has been less with the model, which has been taken more or less for granted, than with its application to specific social inferences.

Stating Eq. (1) in explicit form does not add anything new to the essential logic of the experiments in question. It does, however, seem to make the theoretical analysis clearer, and to indicate possible extensions. Some examples are given in Section III,A. Another example from Kelley's (1971) paper will be noted here.

Kelley discussed two response patterns which he termed discounting and augmentation. Both of these can be viewed as special cases of the adding model. Suppose that F_2 is not present or has zero value. If F_1 is positive, then G_1 must be less than G_2. This inference was termed discounting: The value of any factor is reduced if other factors that produce the same effect are added.[2]

On the other hand, if F_1 is negative, then G_1 must be greater than G_2. This inference was called augmentation. From the present standpoint, discounting and augmentation are not special principles but rather special cases of the general adding model.

Qualitative use of an adding model has two great advantages. First, it does not require that subjects be exact in their intuitive calculations. Indeed, the inference may even reduce to a judgment of greater than or less than. Second, the adding model itself need not be completely valid. In particular, certain kinds of interaction among the factors would not affect the qualitative conclusions, although they would complicate an exact analysis. Qualitative applications can be ideal, therefore, for demonstrating the operation of some psychological process in a given situation.

Nevertheless, qualitative applications have limited scope. Ordinarily, the values of all but one variable must be specified so as to leave only one inference open to the subject. For example, most of the applications of Section III,A require that the same overt behavior occur in the two

---

[2] This usage stretches the meaning of discounting which customarily refers to a reduction in the weight parameter by some active cognitive process, in resolving inconsistency, for example (e.g., Anderson & Jacobson, 1965). In the applications in Section III,A, however, it is presumably the scale value rather than the weight that is changed. Weight changes could be operative in the adding models, of course, but not all weight changes represent discounting. Accordingly, the customary meaning of discounting will be employed in this chapter.

conditions, so that $R_1 = R_2$ in model terms. In many situations, such close control might not be feasible.

If subjects follow an adding model in a quantitative manner, then applications of much more general scope would become possible. Accordingly, the quantitative analysis of adding models will be considered next.

2. Quantitative Analysis

Quantitative analysis of adding models is made possible by using the procedures of functional measurement. It is thus possible to take purely verbal assertions such as

$$\text{Response} = \text{Approach} - \text{Avoidance}$$

or

$$\text{Achievement} = \text{Luck} + \text{Skill}$$

and treat them as exact equations. Furthermore, the analysis can be made in terms of the subjective values of the individual.

a. The parallelism test. The simplest tests of the adding model are obtained by using factorial designs. Thus, the rows and columns of a two-way design could represent various levels of Approach and Avoidance factors, respectively (Anderson, 1962b). If the response measure follows a simple adding model, then the data will have the property of parallelism. That is, if the data of each row are plotted as a curve, then these several row–curves will be parallel except for response variability. A numerical example is given in Anderson (1971a, Table 1) and an experimental illustration is given in Section II,B,3,b.

Parallelism thus becomes a key property of the simple adding model. Parallelism can be tested directly by plotting the raw response; it is not necessary to know the values of the stimuli. The traditional approach of beginning with the problem of scaling the stimuli seems more direct but actually has certain disadvantages (Anderson, 1972a, p. 96).

Analysis of variance provides a rigorous statistical test of the adding model. Parallelism is equivalent to lack of a statistical interaction term. If the model is correct, therefore, the statistical interaction term is expected to be nonsignificant. Conversely, a significant statistical interaction casts doubt on the model.

The simple adding model does not allow for psychological interaction among the stimuli. The value of each row stimulus, for example, is assumed to be the same in all columns. Deviations from this assumption would, in general, although not always, cause deviations from parallelism. The subject, of course, might still be adding the changed values within each cell of the design.

The parallelism test also assumes that the observed response is numerical, on an interval scale. A nonlinear response scale would itself cause deviations from parallelism, even without stimulus interaction (Anderson, 1972a). It is possible to rectify nonlinear response scales, although at the expense of considerable complications. Accordingly, experimental precautions to help ensure an interval response may be well worthwhile. Fortunately, there is considerable evidence that ordinary rating methods can, with modest care, yield interval response scales in a variety of situations (Anderson, 1973d, 1973e, Section II,A,7).

b. Functional scales of response and stimuli. If the parallelism test is satisfied, it not only provides support for the model, but also is an indication that the response was indeed on an interval scale. A nonlinear response, as was already noted, would itself tend to cause failure in the parallelism test. Thus the model and the response scale are both tested simultaneously. Success of the parallelism test provides validational evidence that the response is indeed an interval scale.

In addition, it becomes possible to measure the stimulus values on interval scales. These stimulus values are simply the marginal means of the factorial design. In many applications, therefore, subjective values can be measured for the individual person.

c. Experimental evidence. It is an odd fact that there is virtually no evidence for strict adding models. The parallelism prediction, it is true, has been supported in numerous experiments, but in virtually every case the integration process has been shown to follow an averaging rather than an adding model. This question is discussed further in Section II,B,3 (see also Anderson, 1971a, p. 192).

Subtracting models have had more success. Shanteau and Anderson (1969) obtained good support for such a model for preference judgments. Other applications have been made in person perception by Levin, Schmidt, and Norman (1971), and in psychophysical judgment by Birnbaum and Veit (1973). Mathematically, the subtracting model has an additive form and also leads to the parallelism prediction.

Adding-type processes undoubtedly occur in some tasks. The value of a commodity bundle should increase by the addition of even a small good. However, commodity bundles show subadditivity effects and so do not obey a strict adding model (Shanteau, 1970b).

In view of the support for averaging and subtracting models, not to mention multiplying models, there is little doubt that people should be able to use strict adding models. Further work on this question, especially in relation to additive force models, would seem worthwhile (Section III,A).

B. AVERAGING MODELS

Averaging processes are pervasive in information integration, and many experiments gain new meaning when considered from this standpoint. In person perception, the averaging formulation has provided a unified conceptual interpretation of a considerable body of work. In attitude change, several experimental tests have also supported the averaging formulation. The theoretical importance of the weight parameter has been discussed in connection with "resistance" to persuasion by Himmelfarb (1973), and in connection with the "paper tiger" effect of inoculation theory by Farkas and Anderson (1973).

In averaging models, the concept of weight becomes as important as the concept of scale value. The weight parameter of a piece of information reflects its importance in the overall judgment. Weight can be interpreted as amount of information in many situations, and it is often helpful to consider weight in that way.

The averaging model provides a solid theoretical basis for the conceptual distinction between weight and scale value. This distinction is commonly used, to be sure, but it is not always realized that weight estimates may be purely arbitrary. Most theories of measurement are concerned only with scale value, with the consequence that weight is confounded with the scale unit. The averaging model provides a basis for separating and measuring both weight and scale value through functional measurement methodology.

1. General Averaging Model

In the averaging formulation, each stimulus is characterized by a scale value, s, and a weight, w. The scale value is the position of the stimulus on the response dimension, and the weight is the relevance or importance of the stimulus. The response can then be written

$$(2) \qquad R = \Sigma ws$$

where the sum is over all relevant stimuli. The weights are required to add to 1, the condition for an averaging as opposed to an adding model.

The summation of Eq. (2) ordinarily includes an internal state or stimulus that can, in many applications, be considered as the initial opinion. Its value and weight are denoted by s_0 and w_0. The internal state is considered to be averaged in with the externally presented stimuli.

The initial opinion has an important theoretical role. For example, it allows the averaging formulation to account for the set-size effect (Section II,B,5). Considered as an internal state variable, it also allows motivational factors to be taken into account (Kaplan & Anderson, 1973).

2. Distance-Proportional Averaging Model

A special case of the averaging model arises when a single external stimulus is presented. Equation (2) then becomes

$$R = w_0 s_0 + w_1 s_1$$

Since the model requires that $w_0 + w_1 = 1$, this last expression can be rewritten as

$$R = (1 - w_1)s_0 + w_1 s_1$$

or

$$(3) \qquad\qquad R = s_0 + w_1(s_1 - s_0)$$

In this latter form, the new value of the response is seen to equal the initial opinion, s_0, plus the proportion, w_1, of the distance between s_1 and s_0. The change in response is thus proportional to the distance between the initial opinion and the new stimulus. This is the distance-proportional form of the averaging model considered by Anderson and Hovland (1957) in attitude change. In this model, the weight parameter gives a measure of the strength of the stimulus, independent of the base-line value, s_0. Applications are given in Sections III,D,5 and III,E,5.

3. Constant-Weight Averaging Models

a. Model analysis. Under the constant-weight condition, the averaging model has essentially the same properties as the adding model. If the stimuli are combined according to a factorial design, then the constant-weight condition requires that the levels of the row factor all have the same weight, and that the levels of the column factor all have the same weight. The row and column weights, however, need not be equal.

With this constant-weighting condition, the analysis of the averaging model is identical to that for the adding model. The parallelism property applies, and the marginal means yield interval scales of the subjective values of the stimuli.

With constant weighting, however, an estimate of the weights is obtainable only under special conditions. When the subjective stimulus range is the same for each factor of the design, then the weight of each factor can be estimated (e.g., Anderson & Farkas, 1973; Weiss & Anderson, 1969; see also Sections III,F,5 and III,F,8). But in most cases the weight parameter is confounded with the unit of the stimulus scale, as in the adding model. Because of this confounding, great care is needed in speaking about the "importance" of any stimulus factor. A substantial observed effect may reflect either a large weight parameter or a large range in scale value.

b. Experimental illustration. Figure 1 illustrates the constant-weight averaging model in a study designed to scale social desirability of personality-trait adjectives. The adjectives formed a 3 × 10 design as listed in the figure.

The key feature of the figure is the parallelism of the three curves. This parallelism accomplishes three goals simultaneously: (*a*) It validates the integration model. (*b*) It validates the response measure as being on an interval scale. (*c*) It provides social desirability values of the stimulus adjectives on an interval scale. The rationale is the same as that given in the above discussion of adding models. The parallelism test itself does not distinguish between adding and constant-weight averaging models; other data are required to show that person perception obeys an averaging rule (Section II,B,5).

The stimulus values are just the marginal means of the data. The marginal column means are given by the elevation of the mean curve of Fig. 1, and these are listed at the bottom of the figure. The adjectives show a bipolar clustering similar to that in the normative ratings (Anderson, 1968b). The graph shows a jump between *dependent* and *inoffensive* in each curve. If only one curve had been represented in the design,

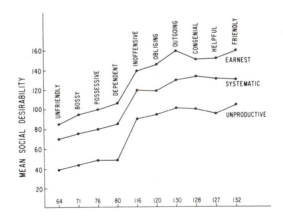

Fig. 1. Social desirability of persons described by two personality traits in a 3 × 10 design using the traits listed in the graph. The parallelism supports the averaging model for trait integration. Each number on the horizontal axis is the functional scale value of the trait listed above it. Adapted from Anderson (1973c).

the jump could have been interpreted as a local nonlinearity in the response scale. But because this jump appears at different places on the response scale, it cannot represent nonlinearity. This illustrates the leverage given by an integration task.

4. Differential-Weight Averaging Models

a. Model analysis. If the weight parameter varies across the levels of, say, the column factor, then systematic deviation from parallelism must be expected. The direction of deviation can be predicted beforehand if a rough idea of the weight values is available. For example, if the weights increase as a function of stimulus value, as would often be expected, then the data curves should converge as a value increases. An experimental illustration is given in the next subsection; see also Anderson (1971a, Fig. 2; 1972a) and Birnbaum (1972a).

A valuable feature of this model is that it makes possible the simultaneous estimation of weight and scale value of each stimulus. However, this requires special design and computation (e.g., Anderson, 1972a; Leon, Oden, & Anderson, 1973). For many purposes, therefore, a directional prediction of deviation from parallelism will be more useful.

b. Experimental illustration. Lampel and Anderson (1968) studied date ratings of boys described by a photograph and two personality-trait adjectives. The rightward divergence of the four solid curves in Fig. 2 deviates from parallelism and implies that neither an adding nor a constant-weight averaging model can account for the data.

However, the averaging model can account for the shape of the data if it is assumed that the weight or importance of the photograph varies inversely with its attractiveness. This assumption makes social sense. If the boy is unattractive, his personality does not make a great deal of

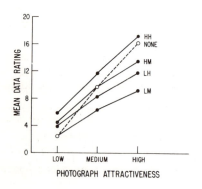

Fig. 2. Date ratings of boys described by a photograph and two (or no) personality traits. The crossover interaction rules out an adding model but agrees with an averaging model. The divergence of the four curves representing adjective pairs implies differential weighting of the photograph, with the less attractive photograph getting greater weight. Adapted from Lampel and Anderson (1968).

difference. As he becomes more attractive physically, it becomes more important how personable he is. This conjunctive type of judgmental process can be interpreted as differential weighted averaging.

It is worthwhile seeing exactly how this works. In the averaging model, the weights must sum to 1. Accordingly, if the Low photograph has higher weight than the High photograph, then the weight of the traits must be lower with the Low than with the High photograph. In Fig. 2, the weight of the traits is proportional to the vertical range of the four solid curves, since the trait scale values are constant along each curve. This inverse variation between vertical range and relative weight is a sign of differential weighted averaging. It appears again in Sections III,B,1, III,C,4, III,C,7, III,D,3, and III,G,3.

The dashed curve for the photograph alone in Fig. 2 has an important methodological value (see also next subsection). If only the four solid curves had been present, it could be argued that the nonparallelism was only a nonlinearity in the response scale that should be eliminated by monotone transformation. But the dashed curve rules out this argument, since the crossover cannot be eliminated by monotone transformation. The lack of significant overall interaction in the Adjective × Adjective component of the design also helped validate the response scale in this experiment.

5. Evidence for the Averaging Hypothesis

The preponderance of evidence has strongly supported the averaging model in the areas of personality impression formation and attitude change. The alternative summation or adding hypothesis has failed in repeated critical tests. Since this issue has generated some confusion, two lines of evidence will be mentioned briefly here.

Several experiments have made a critical test between adding and averaging models by adding the same medium stimulus to both a high stimulus and a low stimulus. In an adding formulation, the response to both should change in the same direction. But an averaging model would imply that the medium stimulus should decrease the response to the high stimulus and increase the response to the low stimulus.

This critical test is illustrated in Fig. 2. The dashed curve is the response to the photograph alone. Adding a near-neutral LH pair of traits pulls up the Low photograph and pulls down the High photograph, exactly as the averaging model requires. The same holds for the HM trait pair. An adding model cannot account for this crossover interaction without introducing assumptions about stimulus interaction.

Table I shows a similar test of the averaging model in attitude formation. The terms H, M^+, M^-, and L denote paragraphs about United

TABLE I
MEAN JUDGED STATESMANSHIP OF UNITED STATES PRESIDENTS
DESCRIBED BY FOUR BIOGRAPHICAL PARAGRAPHS

H H H H	H H M⁻ M⁺	H H L L	H H
7.72	6.61	4.93	7.23
L L H H	L L M⁻ M⁺	L L L L	L L
5.48	4.26	3.14	3.83

Note: H, M^+, M^-, and L denote paragraphs of very favorable, mildly favorable, mildly unfavorable, and very unfavorable information, respectively. The comparison between H H L L and L L H H shows a recency effect from order of presentation. Data from Anderson (1973f).

States Presidents that were highly favorable, mildly favorable, mildly unfavorable, and very unfavorable, respectively. Since the paragraphs were constructed to have equal weight, the 2×3 design in the first three columns of the table should follow the parallelism prediction. That is nearly true, as can be seen.

The second column differs from the last column by the added M^-M^+ information. This pair of paragraphs has a near-neutral value. The averaging hypothesis implies that it should pull down the HH pair, and raise up the LL pair, as indeed it does. Similar results have been obtained in numerous other experiments (e.g., Anderson, 1968c, 1973f; Butzin & Anderson, 1973; Hamilton & Huffman, 1971; Hendrick, 1968; Leon, Oden, & Anderson, 1973; Oden & Anderson, 1971).

The second line of evidence concerns the set-size effect. When all stimuli have the same value, then the response becomes more extreme as the number of pieces of information is increased. Although this incremental "set-size" effect appears to argue for an adding process, it can be accounted for within the averaging model in terms of an initial impression that is averaged in with the overt stimulus information. The model then predicts a negatively accelerated set-size curve that agrees quite well with the data (Anderson, 1965a, 1967a). The set-size effect does not, therefore, necessitate an adding interpretation.

The set-size effect has also given rise to two other interpretations. It might be caused by an increase in confidence with increases in amount of information. Also, it might be a judgmental artifact, since it has been difficult to obtain in between-subjects designs. Both these interpretations seem to be ruled out by Sloan and Ostrom (1974), who obtained a substantial set-size effect on the impression response but no set-size effect on the confidence response in a between-subjects design. Other remarks on this question are given by Anderson (1968c), Kaplan and Anderson (1973), and Weiss and Anderson (1969; Experiment III). An interesting variant of the averaging model has been discussed by Hodges (1973; see also Anderson, 1973b).

C. MULTIPLYING MODELS

1. Qualitative Analysis

Qualitative use of the multiplying model is quite similar to that for the adding model. For simplicity, it is assumed that all quantities are positive on the subjective scale. With the notation of Eq. (1), the model may be written as

(4)
$$R_1 = F_1 \times G_1 \qquad \text{(Condition 1)}$$
$$R_2 = F_2 \times G_2 \qquad \text{(Condition 2)}$$

If $R_1 = R_2$, and $F_1 > F_2$, then it follows that $G_1 < G_2$. This conclusion is identical to that obtained from the adding model above. Many of the same remarks given there apply here as well. For example, if R_1 and R_2 are "medium," then G_1 must be "small" if F_1 is "large," and vice versa.

This qualitative test, it should be noted, does not distinguish between adding and multiplying. It is possible to do so, however, if some subjective values are negative, as in Fig. 3 below.

2. Quantitative Analysis

Functional measurement procedure makes possible a quantitative analysis of multiplying models. Thus it becomes possible to take purely verbal assertions such as

$$\text{Reaction} = \text{Drive} \times \text{Incentive}$$

or

$$\text{Achievement} = \text{Motivation} \times \text{Ability}$$

or

$$\text{Motivation} = \text{Achievement} \times (1/\text{Ability})$$

and treat them mathematically in terms of the individual's own value system.

a. Bilinearity test. Just as parallelism is the key property of the adding model, so bilinearity is the key property of the multiplying model. The first equation implies that Reaction is a straight-line function of Drive for a fixed level of Incentive; the slope of this line is the value of Incentive. In principle, therefore, the data should plot as a diverging fan of straight lines. In practice, the test is not quite so simple because the stimulus values are unknown. However, a fairly straightforward solution is possible, together with an exact statistical test based on analysis of variance. A numerical example is given in Anderson (1971a, Table 2), and experimental illustrations are given just below and in Section III,B,2.

b. Functional scales of response and stimuli. The measurement logic of the multiplying model is identical to that of the adding model. If the model passes the bilinearity test, that provides a concomitant validation of the response measure as an interval scale. Functional scales of the stimulus variable are obtained directly from the marginal means of the data table.

3. Experimental Illustration

Figure 3 illustrates a test of the multiplying model for adverb–adjective combinations proposed by Cliff (1959). Subjects judged social desirability of persons described by a single adverb–adjective combination, and the data for *honest* and *dishonest* are shown in the graph.

The model itself may be written as

$$R = \text{Adjective} \times \text{Adverb}$$

If the adverb values are plotted on the horizontal axis, then the data for each adjective should plot as a straight line with slope equal to the scale value of the adjective.

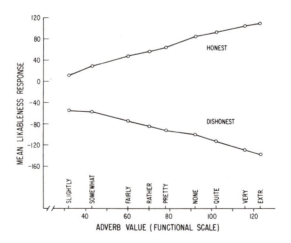

Fig. 3.   Likableness of a person described by an adverb–adjective combination in a 2×9 design as portrayed in the graph. Adverbs are spaced on the horizontal according to their functional scale value. The linearity of the two adjective curves supports the multiplying model of adverb times adjective.

The only drawback is that the adverb values are unknown. However, they can be obtained by spacing out the adverbs on the horizontal so that both curves are simultaneously as straight as possible. The adverb spacing is then an interval scale of adverb value, if the model is correct. A routine procedure is available for doing this, and it was used to construct Fig. 3. If the model is correct, then both curves should be straight except for response variability. The model seems to do reasonably well despite some deviations from linearity in Fig. 3.

The adverb–adjective model illustrates an important aspect of functional measurement, one that differs from the traditional approach in scaling. The traditional approach has been to get the scale values first, and then use these in the substantive inquiry. Thus, previous work on the adverb–adjective model has relied almost entirely on Thurstonian scaling procedures even though they' employ pooled group data that cannot give an adequate test of the model.

Functional measurement methodology, in contrast, makes scaling an integral part of the substantive inquiry. The scale values obtained in this way are those that function in the given situation. Measurement theory and substantive theory are cofunctional aspects of a single theoretical endeavor.

One further methodological point is noteworthy. The multiplying model is only an *as if* model, and a closer conceptual analysis (Anderson, 1973d) indicates that the underlying psychological processes do not involve any multiplying operation. This analysis differs from Cliff's in several aspects. In particular, it predicts a U-shaped curve for words such as *cautious*.

D. OTHER MODELS

More complex integration models can often be handled by extension of the above procedures. A few such applications will be noted briefly here.

1. Multilinear Models

Multilinear models are composite adding–multiplying models for three or more stimulus variables that add or multiply in any combination. For example, consider the model for predicting success, say, in graduate school:

$$\text{Future Achievement} = \text{Past Achievement} + \text{Motivation} \times \text{Ability}$$

Past Achievement combines additively with Motivation and with Ability; both these two-way data plots should exhibit parallelism. The Motivation $\times$ Ability data plot, however, should exhibit the bilinear form.

As a second example, consider the three-factor multiplying model:

Achievement = Motivation × Ability × Opportunity

Here each pair of factors should exhibit the bilinear form. In addition, the data as a whole should exhibit a trilinear form, illustrated in Shanteau and Anderson (1972, Fig. 1).

Experimental applications of multilinear models have been limited mainly to the area of decision-making (Anderson & Shanteau, 1970; Shanteau, 1970b; Shanteau & Anderson, 1972). The last-cited report has special interest, since functional measurement methodology was able to demonstrate the use of variant integration models by different individuals.

2. Comparative Judgment Model

In many situations, the value of a stimulus is relative, depending on its relation to other, contextual stimuli. Contrast effects are one example. Integration theory includes a comparative judgment model that can account for such relative judgments. The response is considered as a sum of both absolute and relative factors. In its simplest form, the comparative judgment model can be treated in the same way as the multilinear models of the previous subsection.

The comparative judgment model has special interest as an alternative to Helson's (1964) theory of adaptation level. Applications in perception have been promising (Anderson, 1970b, 1972b, 1973e; Massaro & Anderson, 1971), and the little available direct evidence shows some advantage for the comparative judgment model over adaptation-level theory (Anderson, 1973e, Section III,B,5; see also Sections II,B,8 and III,B,4). However, no applications to social judgment have been made.

3. Ratio Models

Ratio models of the form,

$$R = F/(F + G)$$

arise in a variety of situations. One example is in equity theory (Section III,C,8). Another example is averaging theory which also implies a ratio rule, based on the weight parameters, in dichotomous decision tasks in which the scale values can be set at 0 and 1 (Section III,E,1,c; Leon & Anderson, 1973).

This ratio rule can be rewritten as

$$1/R = 1 + G/F$$

in which form it is possible to apply the bilinear analysis. However, that requires that the response be measured on a ratio scale. Moreover, inverting the observed response could introduce undesirable statistical properties when R is very small or very large.

An alternative is to apply Chandler's (1969) STEPIT program to estimate the model parameters. This procedure is very fast and has the advantage of applying even to designs with empty cells. Owing to the nonlinearity, however, a proper statistical test of fit is not ordinarily possible even with a complete factorial design.

A potentially useful adaptation of the STEPIT method may be possible if several replications of data are available. Several subjects might be run through all cells of the design, for example, or a single subject might be run through several times to get the several replications. Parameters would be estimated and used to predict values within each replication. Each replication would then yield a set of discrepancy scores, obtained minus predicted. These several sets of scores would then be used in a repeated measurements design with replications as a random factor. The discrepancy scores within each replication are correlated through their dependence on common parameter estimates, but that is allowed for in the repeated measurements design. If the data obey the model, then all main effects and interactions would be expected to be zero. This statistical test should be used cautiously, however, as its statistical properties have not been studied adequately.

4. Two-Stage Integration Model

The two-stage approach provides a method of using a simple model to help analyze a complex process. Particularly important examples are stimulus interaction and valuation of complex stimuli, problems about which relatively little is known. In clinical judgment, for example, a concentrated search for configurality has been notably unsuccessful (Goldberg, 1968; Meehl, 1954). Some information is available in this and other areas of judgment (see Anderson, 1969a, 1971a, 1972a; Slovic & Lichtenstein, 1971), but the overall picture is not very satisfying. One major difficulty is that of getting a validated response measure.

The essential idea of the two-stage model is to cascade two integration tasks; the first is expected to involve stimulus interaction or complex valuation, and the second is expected to obey a simple model (Anderson, 1973e). From the viewpoint of the second stage, the integration in the first stage constitutes a valuation operation. Accordingly, functional measurement based on the second stage can yield a validated scaling of the output from the first stage. This method could also validate the overt judgment in the first stage if one was obtained.

To illustrate the two-stage idea, consider schematic faces described by three features—mouth curvature, nose length, and eye–nose separation. The main interest is in how subjects integrate these three features into a judgment of physical attractiveness. Patterning and configuration must be expected, and a simple adding or averaging model would not apply. Direct judgments of the single faces would yield interaction in the analysis of variance.

It is well known, however, that such interactions are difficult to interpret. The problem is that they may reflect nonlinearity in the response scale, not true configural effects (Anderson, 1972a). Since there is usually no great reason to think that the ratings used in social judgment are more than ordinal scales, any interpretation of such statistical interactions will be touched with uncertainty.

This difficulty can be surmounted by adding a second integration task, based on a simple algebraic model. For example, the subjects could be asked for preference judgments, rating the difference in physical attractiveness of two such faces. The pairs of faces would be constructed according to a factorial design, and the subtracting model would predict parallelism. Subtracting models have been successful in other work (Birnbaum & Veit, 1973; Shanteau & Anderson, 1969), so there is reason to hope that they would apply in this case too. An averaging task could also be used in the second stage, since it seems likely that the constant-weight assumption would hold.

The two-stage technique deserves consideration because of its potential for the study of valuation and stimulus interaction. It does not describe the nature of the integration process in the first stage, but it would provide a valuable tool for analyzing that process.

III. Experimental Applications

A. Additive Force Models

In certain experiments, a stimulus person is portrayed subject to two or more forces. These forces may be internal or external, and they may be parallel or opposed in direction. The judgments required of the subject typically involve the mediation of a force model imputed by the subject to account for the behavior of the stimulus person.

Force models have been continuously attractive in psychology. Within the attribution area, Heider (1958), Jones and Davis (1965), and Kelley (1971) have been most concerned with force models, although numerous other investigators have used them, implicitly or explicitly. The progenitors of these models seem to be the approach–avoidance and other conflict models discussed by Lewin and by Miller, and quantified by Anderson (1962b). In the present applications, the force model is typically attributed or imputed to another person, so it is a judgmental model rather than a strict behavioral model. Of course, functional measurement methodology applies in either case.

The applications below follow the qualitative analysis of Section II,A. Section III,A,2 illustrates a quantitative test, although it is not very stringent. In some of these applications, an averaging formulation might be more appropriate. For present purposes, however, this problem can be bypassed.

In each of these applications, the qualitative force model is quite similar to the rationale used by the investigators. Even in these simple applications, however, there can be a gain in clarity and precision by making the model explicit. In particular, the model helps clarify how different dependent variables require different theoretical analysis.

1. Mills and Jellison (1967)

This experiment gives a nice illustration of the additive force model and its relation to two dependent variables. Subjects read a speech by an electoral candidate who advocated higher taxes on truck trailers. The same speech was represented as being given to one of two audiences— a railway union which would be sympathetic to the speech, and a trucker's union which would be unsympathetic. Subjects judged the sincerity of the candidate; also, they indicated how much they agreed with his speech.

The force model imputed by the subject must allow for internal forces, I, which reflect the candidate's tendency to express his true opinion, and external forces, E, which represent his desire to please the union. The external forces are positive for the railway union and negative for the trucker's union, and are denoted by E_1^+ and E_2^-, respectively. The corresponding internal forces in the two experimental conditions are denoted by I_1 and I_2. The force model can be written:

$$R = I_1 + E_1^+ \quad \text{(railway union)}$$
$$R = I_2 + E_2^- \quad \text{(trucker's union)}$$

Clearly, I_2 must be greater than I_1, because E_2 is negative and E_1 is positive. The internal force is seen as greater when the same speech is given to a hostile than when it is given to a friendly audience. From this imputed model, therefore, the subject would conclude that the candidate was more sincere in the case of the hostile audience. Essentially this same reasoning was used by Mills and Jellison, and the data supported their prediction.

The attitude change data also require interpretation. The simplest information-theoretical view would assign a scale value to the communication and a weight to the source (Anderson, 1971a, Application 3). This piece of information would then be integrated with the subject's initial opinion. The more sincere candidate would correspond to a greater weight and hence produce more attitude change (Section II,B,2; Eq. 3). This argument is similar to that of Mills and Jellison, and the data followed their prediction.

This interpretation is attractive because of its directness, and it may have wider applicability. However, it should be recognized that other interpretations are possible, especially for the election framework used in this experiment.

It is entirely possible, for example, that the subjects actively discounted the arguments in the speech to the railway union; there the speaker was judged as being more cynical and opportunistic. Such discounting would produce a lower weight parameter. This interpretation cannot be distinguished from the first without added conditions, as Mills and Jellison point out.

2. Jones, Davis, and Gergen (1961)

This experiment provides a second example of the opposed forces paradigm. All subjects heard a taped interview of an applicant who desired a certain job. Only two conditions need be considered here. In both, the interview was identical and portrayed an inner-directed, nonsocial personality. Only the job opening was different. In one condition, an astronaut position was open which, the subjects had been told, required an inner-directed personality. In the other condition, a submariner position was open for which an outer-directed personality was said to be most suitable. The subjects rated the stimulus person on degree of inner-directedness, and also gave their confidence in their judgments.

The force model imputed by the subject must allow for internal forces, I, which reflect the stimulus person's tendency to answer honestly, and external forces, E, which represent his desire to act congruent with the job-interview requirements. These two sets of forces coact to produce the interview. Since an inner-directed interview was given in both cases, the job-interview force is positive in the astronaut condition, negative in the submariner condition. These forces may be denoted by E_1^+ and E_2^-, respectively, and the corresponding internal forces by I_1 and I_2.

The model can then be written:

$$R = I_1 + E_1^+ \qquad \text{(astronaut)}$$
$$R = I_2 + E_2^- \qquad \text{(submariner)}$$

It follows immediately that $I_2 > I_1$; a greater internal force is required to produce the same response in the face of an opposing external force. The assumption that subjects judge on the basis of an imputed force model leads directly to the first obtained result: The stimulus person is seen as more inner-directed when his behavior is opposed to the external force.

The second obtained result, that greater confidence is felt in the judgment of out-role behavior, also needs explanation. Jones and Davis (1965) and Kelley (1971) interpret the confidence judgments in terms of number of plausible causes. Various reasons could account for in-role behavior, but almost the only plausible reason for out-role behavior is that it represents the true personality of the stimulus person.

Their interpretation is attractive, and it can readily be related to the model analysis. The confidence judgments would be interpreted in terms of confidence intervals around the estimated value of I. With only one plausible cause for out-role behavior, the confidence interval around I_2 would be narrower than that around I_1. Another way of looking at this is to note that many pairs of I–E values will add up to any given value of R. Since $I = R - E$, and since R is known, the confidence interval around I will be equivalent to that around E. The given result then follows from the plausible assumption that the external force for going against the role requirements is more sharply defined than the external force for obeying the role requirements.

The present theoretical analysis makes a clear distinction between the judgment of the applicant's personality, and the confidence in that judgment. The theoretical discussion of this experiment by Jones and Davis (1965) was concerned primarily with the confidence judgments, and they seem to have felt that the confidence data accounted for the judgments of inner-directedness. In the present view, these two judgments are conceptually distinct.

Jones *et al.* had two other conditions, similar to the above except that the interview portrayed an outer-directed personality. The complete set of four conditions formed a 2×2 design for which the additive force model implies parallelism (Section II,A). The observed data support this parallelism prediction. This particular test, unfortunately, is not very powerful, since symmetry alone would tend to produce zero two-way interaction.

3. Strickland (1958)

This experiment provides an interesting but somewhat speculative application of the parallel forces paradigm. The subject supervised two (fictitious) subordinates, A and B, with the goal of maintaining high output in a dull task. The subject was required to check exactly nine times on A and twice on B in the first block of 10 trials, and this monitoring schedule was known to the subordinates. It was arranged that A and B clearly did equally well overall. The result was that the subject rated A as less trustworthy than B and checked up on him more in the subsequent work period.

From the subject's view, each worker is under two forces: an internal force, I, which stems from the overall task situation, and an external force, E, which reflects his surveillance. It is assumed that the external force is greater for the worker who was supervised more: $E_A > E_B$. The observed output, R, which was the same for both workers, A and B, is the sum of these two forces:

$$R = I_A + E_A$$
$$R = I_B + E_B$$

The critical result, that $I_A < I_B$, follows at once from the assumption that $E_A > E_B$. This analysis is similar to that of Kelley (1971), except that Kelley appears to assume that $E_B = 0$, which is stronger than necessary. An interesting aspect of this experiment is that the judged trust related directly to the supervisory behavior in the subsequent work period.

Kruglanski (1970; Experiment II) replicated Strickland's results, and also added a condition in which the subject could not determine how well the two subordinates had done. In this condition, A was actually seen as more trustworthy than B just following the first work period, but was monitored more often in the subsequent work period.

This is an inconsistent pattern of results that is difficult to interpret. However, the model does suggest a line of attack. Since the output of the subordinates is unknown, the model must be written

$$R_A = I_A + E_A$$
$$R_B = I_B + E_B$$

As above, it can be assumed that $E_A > E_B$. To compensate, at least one of the two inequalities $R_A > R_B$ and $I_A < I_B$ must hold, and it seems psychologically reasonable that both would hold. Kruglanski's pattern of results is then consistent with the interpretation that the judgment of trustworthiness immediately after the first work period is determined more by R, as might happen because of confounding between judgments of output and of trustworthiness, whereas the monitoring behavior in the subsequent work period is determined more by I. Unfortunately, judgments of output, which would shed light on this interpretation, were not obtained.

This interpretation is speculative, of course, but the odd pattern in

Kruglanski's data may warrant the speculation. At the same time, Strickland's original interpretation, in terms of the subject's lack of information about A's motivational state, deserves more detailed consideration. Although this interpretation is most easily represented in terms of the force model, it could also be represented in terms of confidence intervals around otherwise equal forces. A serial integration paradigm, in which each trial constitutes a piece of information about A and B, may be useful in further study of this problem.

4. Bem (1967)

In Festinger and Carlsmith's (1959) experiment on forced compliance, subjects performed a dull motor task, and then were promised $1 or $20 to persuade another subject that the task was interesting. Subsequently, the motor tasks were rated more interesting by $1 subjects than by $20 subjects. In Bem's (1967, Table 1) "interpersonal replication," each condition used by Festinger and Carlsmith was described to a group of subjects. A tape recording that was said to be the persuasive speech was included. Bem's subjects then judged how they thought Festinger and Carlsmith's subjects would rate the motor task.

The task confronting Bem's subjects can be represented as an additive force model. There is an internal force, I, for Festinger and Carlsmith's subjects to express their true opinions. Two external forces also operate: E_0, which represents the experimenter's request to persuade, and $E_\$$, which represents the money force. It is assumed that a greater sum of money constitutes a greater force. The observed attitude, R, can then be expressed as

$$R = I_{\$1} + E_0 + E_{\$1} \qquad (\$1 \text{ condition})$$
$$R = I_{\$20} + E_0 + E_{\$20} \qquad (\$20 \text{ condition})$$

It follows immediately that $I_{\$20} < I_{\$1}$.

To deduce the true opinion itself requires one further integration. The internal force is assumed to correspond to source credibility, as in Bem's discussion, so that the $1 condition represents greater credibility. In the integration model, source credibility corresponds to the weight parameter and so would multiply the scale value of the speech to yield a larger product for the $1 condition (Anderson, 1971a, Application 3). Integration with the initial expectation would then yield the obtained result. This theoretical argument thus parallels that of Mills and Jellison in Section III,A,1, who obtained measures of both dependent variables.

To this main analysis, several remarks should be added. First, the force model implies that the same pattern of results should be obtained if the dull motor task is replaced by an interesting task, although perhaps at a reduced level because of causal redundancy. In contrast, dissonance theory would presumably imply no effect; when the task is interesting, there is no dissonance between the subjects' perception of the task and their behavior toward their fellow subject. A similar analysis has been given by Nisbett and Valins (1971).

Second, it is necessary to account for the negative response that Bem obtained in the $20 condition. Since the task was uninteresting, Bem's subjects would have an initial expectation that was negative in value. Since this initial expectation is integrated in with the external stimulus information, the resultant could also be negative.

Third, Bem (1967, Table 2) reports a follow-up experiment that used a shorter, less persuasive speech, with the expectation that the difference between the $1 and $20 conditions would diminish and perhaps even reverse in direction. A diminished effect follows at once from the integration model because the less persuasive speech should have lower scale value, as well as lower weight. However, a reversal would require that the scale values of the two speeches bracket the initial opinion or expectation, and that the averaging model apply to the final integration. Although Bem did obtain a reversal, it did not approach significance. Calculations based on Bem's tabled data show an F ratio of less than 1 between these two conditions.

Fourth, if $1 exerts a positive force, as would be expected, then the inferred value of I will be lower in the $1 condition than in a control condition that was not paid. Bem's control condition is not relevant to this point, unfortunately, because it did not hear the speech.

Finally, the possibility of a dual role for the internal force should be noted. In the above analysis, it has an indirect, mediational effect through the weight parameter. It is also possible, however, that it constitutes an independent piece of information bearing directly on the judgment. Care is needed, therefore, in defining the dependent variable, and in assessing how the subjects actually interpret it.

The present analysis is similar to Bem's in several respects, especially in its emphasis on judgmental processes. The integration model has certain advantages in explicitness and simplicity. It also avoids Bem's reliance on untestable speculation about the past reinforcement history of the organism.

B. JUDGMENTS OF MOTIVATION AND ABILITY

The general idea that motivation should act as an amplifier or multiplier is one of long standing. A glance through Hilgard's *Theories of Learning* (1956) shows this idea appearing in one or another form in writers as diverse as Freud, Lewin, Tolman, and Hull. It is implicit in the idea of tension used by Freud and by Lewin, and takes a more specific form in Lewin's argument that associationism lacks a "motor." Tolman's emphasis on the learning–performance distinction embodies a similar idea.

In Hull's hands, this general idea began to assume explicit quantitative form:

$$\text{Reaction Potential} = \text{Drive} \times \text{Habit}$$

Similar formulations have been used in discussions of achievement motivation by Atkinson and by Feather (see Atkinson & Feather, 1966; Weiner, 1972) and in social attribution by Heider (1958).

In Heider's approach, the multiplying model is ordinarily judgmental, imputed to another person, rather than behavioral as in Hull. An intermediate case of self-judgment is also frequent (see Section III,B,5). It is quite possible, of course, that the multiplying model would hold at the behavioral but not the judgmental level, or conversely. However, except for the work inspired by Hull, there is not much evidence on the validity of the multiplying rule. Indeed, Prokasy (1967) has argued that a considerable array of evidence in human conditioning is not consistent with Hull's equation.

The basic difficulty in making an exact analysis of the multiplying rule has been the lack of a theory of measurement. Hull was particularly concerned with this problem because he took the algebraic models seriously. However, his attempts to adapt Thurstonian scaling procedures have not worked out very well.

Functional measurement methodology yields a new approach to the measurement problem, opening up, for example, the possibility of scaling drive within the context of approach–avoidance conflict models (Anderson, 1962b). Under fairly general conditions, it is possible to obtain the stimulus values that are functional in the given behavior.

However, the functional measurement procedure does require the operation of some algebraic model. Qualitative applications may be useful in various respects, as noted in Section II,A, but a quantitative model is needed for actual scaling.

In social judgment, there is very little evidence for multiplying as an exact rule of cognitive algebra. Most of the applications below are essentially qualitative. Beyond their inherent interest, however, they point to possible quantitative analysis. The one exact test, in Section III,B,2, finds some limited evidence for the multiplying rule, but suggests that subjects may instead adopt a simpler adding rule. It should be noted, therefore, that considerable evidence for a multiplying rule has been obtained in decision making (e.g., Shanteau, 1970b; Shanteau & Anderson, 1972).

1. Kepka and Brickman (1971)

This paper has special interest as one of the very few in the attributional framework that was designed with reference to a specific algebraic model. Indeed, the design allowed tests both of an adding model and of a multiplying model within the same judgmental context. Stimulus persons were described as being high, medium, or low on college grades, and as high, medium, or low on ability (Scholastic Aptitude Test). Subjects judged them on intelligence and also on motivation.

a. Judgments of intelligence. The two cues have the same quality and carry comparable information for the judgment of intelligence. The subject should, as Kepka and Brickman argued, average them in reaching his judgment. Their report supports the simple averaging model, since the interaction of the two cues was not significant. Nevertheless, a plot of their data suggests a systematic deviation from parallelism, with grades having a decreasing effect as ability increased.

Such a pattern of nonparallelism can be interpreted in terms of differential weighting. High grades are more diagnostic than low grades and hence should carry greater weight (Section II,B,4). The weighting of the ability cue, however, should be constant. This model has considerable interest because a special test of fit is available for this case (Anderson, 1971a, Equation 9).

b. Judgments of motivation. The other response, judged motivation, would be expected to follow a dividing model as in Section II,C,2:

$$\text{Motivation} = \text{Achievement} \div \text{Ability}$$

These judgments should, accordingly, show an interaction concentrated in the bilinear component. The interaction was significant, although it did not follow the bilinear patterning very well. This experiment, unfortunately, used different subjects in every judgment condition so that the variability was markedly higher than in corresponding repeated measurements designs.

Kepka and Brickman, it should be noted, were concerned only with a qualitative test of the model. And, in fact, judged motivation did vary inversely with ability, just as they predicted. This makes sense because of the presence of the achievement cue. For a fixed level of achievement, the subjects are simply saying that motivation and ability have compensatory effects (see also Section III,B,2).

A subsidiary result of this report is also of interest. Judged motivation varied directly with the ability cue when it was given alone, just opposite from the trend in the two-cue task. This may reflect a more or less accurate perception of the environment, or merely a halo effect. Unfortunately, their ability cue (Scholastic Aptitude Test) is not "pure" and could easily be taken to represent or to measure motivational forces in the stimulus person. This also raises the possibility that the ability cue had a dual effect, additive and multiplicative, in the two-cue case (see also Section III,B,2).

The subjects also rated the confidence that they had in each judgment. These data are difficult to interpret because the levels of each cue were unequal in diagnosticity. "Far above average" and "Far below average" are far more specific than "Average." One would expect, therefore, that confidence ratings would be lowest for cue values of "Average," and that was predominantly the case.

2. Anderson and Butzin (1974)

This experiment was designed as an extension of the just-cited experiment by Kepka and Brickman. A primary goal was to obtain an exact, quantitative test of the multiplying model.

Subjects received information on two qualities about a hypothetical athlete trying out for college track, and made a judgment about a third quality. The three qualities were Performance, Motivation, and Ability. Each pair was combined as given information for judgments of the third, so that there were three different judgment conditions. Each of these may be characterized by the equation that was postulated to apply.

a. Judgments of Performance. In this case, the subject was given information about Motivation and Ability. Judgments of Performance were expected to follow the multiplying model assumed by Heider (1958):

$$\text{Performance} = \text{Motivation} \times \text{Ability}$$

The data, plotted in the left panel of Fig. 4, form a diverging fan of lines, in agreement with the multiplying model. The upward sweep of the curves represents the main effect of the Ability cue listed on the horizontal. The slope of each line represents the value of the Motivation cue listed by each line; higher levels of Motivation produce higher slopes.

The bilinear fan form of these data supports the multiplying model. The extent of the divergence may appear to be less than expected, but measuring the vertical spread shows an increase of 60% over the given range of Ability. Theoretically, the curves should intersect at the zero of Ability which, by extrapolation, would be located about six steps

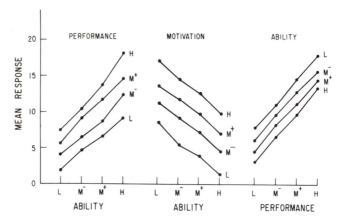

Fig. 4. Judgments of stimulus persons trying out for college track. Each panel plots one judgment dimension—Performance, Motivation, or Ability—as listed above the plot. The values of one of the two stimulus cues are listed on the horizontal, and the values of the other are listed by each curve. The divergence in the left panel supports a Motivation × Ability model. The parallelism in the other two panels supports an additive-type interpretation. From Anderson and Butzin (1974).

leftward. That would imply that the given range of Ability represented the upper third of the total range. Since that seems not unreasonable, the observed extent of divergence may be theoretically appropriate.

Nevertheless, the possibility that some subjects add rather than multiply may need to be checked out (Shanteau & Anderson, 1972; see also Anderson, 1970a, Eq. 18). Partial operation of an adding model would dilute the divergence without affecting the bilinear form. In addition, the alternative conjunctive averaging model cannot be ruled out (Anderson & Butzin, 1974).

b. Judgments of Motivation. The above equation for Performance may be rewritten as

$$\text{Motivation} = \text{Performance} \div \text{Ability}$$

Since dividing can be represented mathematically as multiplying, judged Motivation should form a fan of straight lines.

These data are shown in the center panel of Fig. 4. The downward sweep of the curves means that judged Motivation does vary inversely with Ability. And, since each curve represents a fixed level of Performance, the relative elevations of the four curves means that judged Motivation varies directly with Performance. Qualitatively, therefore, the main effects of both stimulus cues are thus in the direction required by the model and by common sense.

Nevertheless, the subjects do not obey the Motivation equation as stated. It implies that the curves of the center panel of Fig. 4 should converge to the right. Instead, the curves are essentially parallel; the subjects seem to follow some kind of adding rule.

The exact nature of this integration rule is uncertain. One possibility is that the subject begins with a provisional judgment based on the Performance cue, and then makes a subtractive correction for the Ability cue. A related possibility is that the Ability cue is rescaled by reversing the sign relative to a zero at an average level of Ability. A simple adding model would then account for the obtained parallelism.

c. Judgments of Ability. The remaining form of the Performance equation is

$$\text{Ability} = \text{Performance} \div \text{Motivation}$$

The judgments of Ability in the right panel of Fig. 4 show the same basic pattern as in the center panel. Judged Ability is a direct function of the Performance cue, and an inverse function of the Motivation cue, as required by the Ability equation, as well as by common sense. But again, instead of forming a converging fan, the curves are parallel. Apparently, subjects are able to revalue the Motivation cue as required by the contextual Performance cue, but, having gone that far, they make use of a simpler adding strategy instead of going on to the multiplying rule.

d. Comment. These three judgments appear to obey simple algebraic models. Essentially the same pattern of results was obtained in a companion condition that required judgments of performance in graduate school. The cognitive algebra is not exactly as originally hypothesized, however, since it seems to be predominantly based on adding rather than multiplying. The difference between judgments of Performance, and of Motivation and Ability, presumably is related to the need for contextual cue revaluation in the latter two judgments. The exact nature of the adding rule for cue integration requires further study.

3. McArthur (1972)

In this provocative experiment, subjects received sentences of the form "Lola is afraid of the dog" and chose one of four possible explanations: Lola's reaction was due to (1) something about Lola; (2) something about the dog; (3) something about the particular circumstances; (4) some combination of 1, 2, and 3.

a. Theoretical analysis. From the present theoretical standpoint, the Motivation × Valence model of Section II,C should apply. Lola's fear of this particular dog should be the product of her general fear of dogs, multiplied by the fearfulness of this particular dog:

$$\text{Reaction} = \text{Motivation} \times \text{Valence}$$

This multiplying model appears to provide a simple framework for McArthur's results, as will be shown below.

It is also important to recognize the influence of communicational constraints in this kind of judgment. The subject is, in effect, answering a question. A question generally seeks information, and the answerer responds in part to his perception of the questioner's need.

Both Lola and the dog enter into the equation. Both are necessary causes for the reaction. A choice of either one as "the" cause must therefore reflect such communicational constraints.

b. Control subjects. It is instructive to begin by considering the problem from the viewpoint of the control subjects who received single sentences of the given type, but no further information. The main determinant of their response choices is assumed to be the base rates of the two simple causes. The base rates refer to the subject's general impression of the frequencies of the two events in the general environmental context set up by the experiment.

The role of the base rates can be seen by considering alternative sentences. A mailman's fear of the dog would suggest a threatening action by the dog. On the other hand, Lola's fear of a mouse would be attributed more to Lola than to a hostile action by the mouse. When one base rate is high and the other is low, the subject will presumably tend to pick the higher base rate as "the" cause if required to choose between the two. He is simply choosing the more probable answer.

Of course, this experiment allowed four response choices, and 58% of the control data fell in categories 3 and 4 above. In fact, 23% were joint attributions to the person and the object—Lola and the dog, respectively, in the example. This is certainly consistent with the Motivation × Valence model which represents a joint determination as already noted. Moreover, as McArthur (1972, p. 181) suggests, joint attribution would be especially likely if both base rates were low, and perhaps also if both base rates were high. In McArthur's terms, the former case represents dual causality, whereas the latter case represents shared causality. In the former case, neither single cause would be strong enough to exceed an implicit threshold so that summation or interaction of the two would be felt necessary. In the latter case, both single causes would exceed the threshold producing attributional ambiguity.

c. Experimental subjects. These subjects received three pieces of auxiliary information bearing on each sentence. These were Consensus, Distinctiveness, and Consistency information, each of which could be high or low in value. All possible combinations were used in a 2^3 design. These will be discussed in turn for the illustrative sentence used above.

The Distinctiveness statement said that Lola was, or was not, afraid of almost all other dogs. Theoretically, this piece of information is averaged in with the Motivation base rate which represents the initial opinion (Section II,B). Thus, this information acts to increase or decrease the effective value of Motivation. Since the Valence of the object is unaffected, frequency of attributing the cause to something in the person will increase or decrease in accord with the increase or decrease in Motivation.

The Consensus statement said either that almost everyone, or that hardly anyone, was afraid of the dog. The theoretical analysis is the same as for Distinctiveness. The given information is integrated with the Valence base rate to produce the effective Valence. By the assumed choice process, that leads directly to an increase or decrease, respectively, of causal attributions to the object.

The Consistency statement said either that Lola had almost always, or had almost never, been afraid of this same dog in the past. At the risk of oversimplifying, it may be said that this information raises or lowers both Motivation and Valence together. That Lola has almost never before been afraid of this dog is information both that this dog is not generally threatening, and that Lola is not afraid of dogs in general. Simple attributions to the person or the object both become unlikely, and a more complex explanation must be sought. On the other hand, information that Lola has almost always been afraid of this particular dog tends to raise both Motivation and Valence so that more complex explanations should decrease in frequency.

These three predictions were derived by McArthur in a somewhat different way from Kelley's attribution theory. All three were confirmed.

McArthur also made the interesting empirical observation that the three variables appeared to combine by multiplication. This multiplying rule follows directly from integration theory. The Consensus and Distinctiveness cues multiply because each affects one term of the basic Motivation × Valence model.

The Consistency cue also acts as a multiplier, but for a different reason, and only in an *as if* way. It is assumed to leave unchanged the relative frequency of simple person and stimulus attributions, but it does affect their absolute frequency. In so doing, it acts as if it were a multiplier of both Motivation and Valence. If the Consistency cue affected Motivation alone, then it would average with Motivation and multiply with Valence (Section II,D,1).

It should be noted that the above example represents only one of McArthur's four verb categories. The others were accomplishment

(Manuel translates the sentence incorrectly), opinion (John thinks his teacher is unfair), and action (Cheryl contributes a large sum of money to an automobile-safety fund). Although less obvious than in the fear example, each of these also corresponds to a multiplying model. Thus, the accomplishment example corresponds to an Ability × Difficulty model.

d. Methodological comments. McArthur's experiment has a number of other interesting results which cannot be discussed here. However, three methodological points deserve a brief remark, as they represent problems that occur fairly often.

The present analysis helps to clarify McArthur's finding of more person than object choices. As the discussion of base rates indicates, any obtained results will depend heavily on the particular set of sentences. McArthur apparently chose a set of sentences in which the base rates favored person choices.

There may, of course, be a real bias toward person choices. However, there are two distinct ways in which such bias could exist. First, the population of all admissible sentences would be unlikely to split 50:50 between person and stimulus. Bias could refer to this split in the overall population or in a representative sample. Such a linguistic-environmental fact might be interesting, but it is uncertain that it would reflect any basic psychological process. On the other hand, bias could refer to preference for one choice among two that are "equally strong." Unfortunately, there does not seem to be any general way to show that two choices do have equal strength. To demonstrate a true bias, independent of an adventitious choice of stimulus materials, may not be easy.

McArthur also made two dubious comparisons. The first attempted to compare the relative importance of the three information variables. Thus, McArthur claimed that Consistency information accounted for more of the total variance than Consensus information. Although such statements are often made, they are seldom meaningful because they depend so strongly on the particular stimulus materials. A different set of sentences, or a different wording of the three informational cues, could lead to a different picture. Even if it were known that the stimulus materials were representative of some universe, the comparison would still lack precision because of the confounding of importance (weight) and scale value (Section II,B,3,a).

McArthur also attempted to compare response generalization ("How likely do you think Lola would be to warn a mailman about that dog") with stimulus generalization ("How likely do you think Lola would be to be afraid of a cat"). Such comparisons are completely dependent on the particular choice of generalization questions; that can be seen by substituting butterfly and lion for cat in the stimulus generalization question. The problem of generalization is certainly of interest, but it is not simple to handle. Leverage on this problem might be obtainable by studying the effects of the independent variables on the complete generalization gradient, in line with McArthur's (pp. 189–190) discussion of two-step inference processes.

In further work on this kind of problem it may be useful to get numerical response measures. Choice responses tend to obscure the underlying processes. Separate estimates of the likelihood or satisfactoriness of each single cause would seem useful. Use of such numerical response measures would allow direct application of functional measurement methodology.

4. Weiner and Kukla (1970)

In one of the experiments in this report, subjects were told that a stimulus person had succeeded on a task on which $X\%$ of a group had succeeded. They rated the stimulus person on how much his performance was due to his "ability or effort." Since the given value of X is a measure of task easiness, the ratings would be expected to be an ogival decreasing function of X, and that was found to be the case. An interesting feature of the data (Weiner & Kukla, Fig. 7) is that the rating response was approximately a linear function of X expressed in normal deviate form. It is an interesting speculation that people intuitively use percentile scores in this statistical manner. To prove this, however, would require showing that the response was an interval scale, as might be done by using a functional measurement procedure.

The main interest in this particular experiment is its possible extension to multiple-cue integration tasks. One extension would be to add more cues of the same kind. For example, the stimulus person could be said to have succeeded on two different tasks for which $X_1\%$ and $X_2\%$ of the group had succeeded. Since these two cues have a similar quality, they would be expected to combine according to the averaging model. However, the more difficult task would probably be weighted more heavily. Systematic, predictable deviations from parallelism would then be expected as discussed in Section II,B,4.

Another extension, of greater theoretical interest, would be to vary how well the stimulus person did on the task. This would allow an analysis of how the performance cue and the difficulty cue are combined. There are two main theoretical possibilities. Both take the stimulus person's performance to be a scale value; they differ in the role of the difficulty cue.

In the first interpretation, performance is weighted directly by task difficulty. This is just a multiplying model:

$$\text{Judgment} = \text{Difficulty} \times \text{Performance}$$

In the second interpretation, task difficulty corresponds to a reference point on the judgment dimension. Performance is then measured as distance from this reference point. For convenience, task difficulty may be expressed in terms of its complement, task easiness. The model then has a subtracting form:

$$\text{Judgment} = \text{Performance} - \text{Easiness}$$

These two models can be tested by varying difficulty and performance in a two-cue design. The weighting model implies a bilinear pattern in the data, whereas the reference point model implies parallelism. This issue is important, since many social evaluations are made similarly, relative to a standard of others' performance.

5. Karabenick (1972)

This experiment was designed to test certain implications of Atkinson's (1964) theory of achievement motivation. Subjects received preliminary experience with solving 20 anagrams or substitutions that could be varied in difficulty. They then were asked to imagine working on 11 similar tasks that varied from 0 to 100 in terms of their probability of succeeding. For each of these 11 cases, they rated how satisfied they thought they would feel if they succeeded, and also how dissatisfied they thought they would feel if they failed.

According to Atkinson's theory, the incentive value of a task depends on its difficulty. Indeed, the theory postulates a linear relation for this particular experiment. Anticipated satisfaction with success is assumed to be $M_s(1 - P_s)$, where M_s is a personality factor representing the motive to approach success (need for achievement), and P_s is the probability of success. Similarly, anticipated dissatisfaction with failure is assumed to be $M_f(1 - P_f)$, where M_f is a personality factor representing the motive to avoid failure, and P_f is the probability of failure. Thus the satisfaction and dissatisfaction functions should be linear in terms of the probability of success variable. Further, the slopes of these functions should be correlated with the standard measures of motivation used in Atkinson's theory, the TAT assessment of need for achievement (M_s), and the Mandler-Sarason Test Anxiety Questionnaire (M_f).

Karabenick's data gave little support to Atkinson's theory. The most serious difficulty was the lack of correlation between the slopes of the functions and the two above measures of motivation, as in previous work by Feather (1967). The same was true of two additional measures of motivation proposed by Atkinson. On the other hand, there was a correlation between the slopes of the satisfaction and dissatisfaction functions. As Karabenick comments, this is contrary to the theoretical assumption that M_s and M_f are independent.

In addition, the satisfaction and dissatisfaction functions were non-linear, contrary to the theory. The group data, it is true, were approximately linear, but that appeared to be an averaging artifact. Karabenick's careful, detailed analyses showed that 86% of all those individual functions that had a significant linear trend also had a significant nonlinear trend.

Unfortunately, the interpretation of this observed nonlinearity rests on the assumption that the response is on an interval scale, and presumably on the assumption that objective and subjective probability are linearly related. Failure of either of these scaling assumptions could generate apparent nonlinearity where none existed (Anderson, 1972a; Birnbaum, 1973). Karabenick's results are important because they show that linearity in the group data is not sufficient to establish the model. A quantitative test of the model requires a scaling procedure that can operate at the level of the individual. Since functional measurement methodology can do that, it may be useful in further work on motivation.

6. Atkinson (1964)

The work discussed in the two previous subsections is related to Atkinson's (1964) theory of achievement motivation (see also Weiner, 1972). It may be useful, therefore, to add a brief discussion on the analysis of motivation within integration theory and how this might relate to Atkinson's theory.

Integration theory begins at essentially the same starting point as Atkinson's theory—namely, with a simple algebraic model. Examples would be the addition of approach and avoidance tendencies, or the multiplication of motivation and incentive values (see also Kaplan & Anderson, 1973).

From this starting point, integration theory aims to establish the model in an exact, quantitative manner. Unless the model is valid, it cannot form the basis for a valid theory. Previous work on motivation theory has not been able to obtain adequate tests of the basic model. Similar difficulties trouble the Hull-Spence theory, which employs a similar algebraic model (Anderson, 1962b, p. 411). The main difficulty has been the lack of an adequate theory of measurement. Without methods for scaling the response and stimulus variables, a satisfactory test of the model is hardly possible. Functional measurement methodology provides a potential solution to the measurement problems as noted in Sections I and II.

Experimentally, emphasis is placed on situations that involve stimulus integration. The essential requirement is to get two or more stimulus variables that have independent effects in the algebraic model. Incorporation of these variables in a factorial design allows simple tests of the model, together with interval scales of the response and stimulus variables.

One approach would be to manipulate the approach and avoidance tendencies as outlined in an analysis of conflict theory (Anderson, 1962b). Another approach, simpler in certain respects, would be to manipulate the expectancy and incentive values of a goal object, w and s, respectively, in present notation. This approach, based on a multiplying model, has worked well in utility theory (Anderson & Shanteau, 1970; Shanteau & Anderson, 1972). These same methods should generalize to the cognitive algebra of motivation.

C. MORAL JUDGMENT

Daily existence is pervaded by moral feelings—of pride, fairness, guilt and shame, responsibility, and many others. Recent work in social psychology has given increasing attention to the experimental study of moral judgment. A few illustrative experiments are considered here.

From the standpoint of integration theory, moral judgments should be open to attack in much the same way as other judgments. Moral judgments typically rest on several coacting pieces of information, so that integration tasks become a key experimental tool. The expectation is that moral judgment will follow the same cognitive algebra that operates in other kinds of judgment. In this approach, the focus is on how moral judgments operate in daily life, not on any special moral quality they might have. Nevertheless, if this approach is successful, then functional measurement can be applied to scale the stimuli along the given moral dimension.

1. Leventhal and Michaels (1971)

An extended series of studies by Leventhal has centered on problems of fairness and equity in the allocation of reward. Leventhal (personal communication, 1971) has suggested that algebraic models may be helpful, since many of the experimental situations involve information integration. A provisional application to one experiment will illustrate how the matter might be pursued.

A fair reward will depend, in particular, on the "deservingness" of the person's performance. Deservingness will depend on the actual accomplishment and on other factors, such as effort. Teachers experience this when giving grades; favorable treatment of a borderline case is more probable when it represents an earnest effort than when it does not.

  a. Linear model for deservingness. Leventhal and Michaels asked athletics students to judge deservingness of vertical jumps from four pieces of information. Judged deservingness should vary directly with the actual height jumped, and also directly with the effort made by the jumper. The scale values of both the Jump and Effort variables are presumably obtained by comparison to an average or other standard; in this experiment the two levels of each variable were simply specified as above average and below average.

Two other stimulus variables were also used, but these seem to operate by a different process. The person's Height would contribute directly to his performance simply because of the way that the jump was scored. A taller person would make a better score, and his actual performance would need to be evaluated relative to that advantage. Deservingness should, therefore, vary inversely with Height. The same reasoning applies to the Training program, which was either helpful or irrelevant to the jumping task.

Under a linear integration rule, the four stimulus variables would be combined as follows to obtain the deservingness judgment:

$$\text{Deservingness} = \text{Jump} + \text{Effort} - \text{Height} - \text{Training}$$

The four stimulus variables were combined by Leventhal and Michaels in a 2^4 design. The 11 interactions are all zero according to the above model, and the data supported this prediction reasonably well. Only the Jump × Training interaction was significant, and it was small. The test of the model was quite powerful, since the main effects were very large and each subject served as his own control. These data, therefore, provide considerable support for the linear model for deservingness.

The above Deservingness equation is essentially a quantitative transcription of the qualitative analysis given by Leventhal and Michaels and in one sense is no more than a shorthand form of their conceptual analysis. When the equation is viewed quantitatively, however, it takes on added meaning and leads directly to the test of goodness of fit. This test suggests that the model may hold in an exact manner and opens up the possibility of functional scaling of the stimulus variables.

  b. Judgments of ability. Leventhal and Michaels also obtained judgments of ability. These seemed to follow an analogous integration model. This test was not very powerful, however, since only two of the stimulus variables had reliable main effects. As far as they go, however, these data support the integration-theoretical analysis of ability attribution (Section III,B).

2. Weiner and Kukla (1970)

The first experiment in this report studied a complex judgment based on a three-cue task. Subjects were told to imagine themselves as grade-school teachers who had just given an exam and now had to give feedback to their pupils in the form of rewarding gold stars or punishing red stars. The pupils were defined by a 5 × 2 × 2 design with five levels of test performance, two levels (Yes, No) of motivation, and two levels (Yes, No) of ability.

It is instructive to apply a simple linear model to this task even though it has certain inadequacies. The essential reasoning parallels that of the equity experiment by Leventhal and Michaels discussed in the previous subsection. People are rewarded both for their achievements and for their efforts. And since a given achievement is easier with high than with low ability, deservingness will vary inversely with ability. A linear integration rule would then read:

$$\text{Reward} = \text{Achievement} + \text{Motivation} + \text{Ability}^*$$

The asterisk on Ability indicates that it refers to an evaluation based on an expectancy, so that high Ability has a negative scale value.

This linear model does account for the major trends. The judgment was a direct function of Achievement and Motivation, and an inverse function of Ability. Furthermore, the four curves of Fig. 1 of Weiner and Kukla are at least roughly parallel, in agreement with a linear model. This is a little surprising, perhaps, although it is consistent with the apparent success of the linear model for Leventhal and Michael's experiment on equity noted above.

The main deviation from parallelism in Weiner and Kukla's Fig. 1 is a tendency for the Ability curves to converge as Achievement increases. This could reflect a comparative judgment relation between these two cues (Anderson, 1973d). However, other factors, such as weighted averaging, cannot be ruled out. A more detailed experimental analysis would be needed to assess the situation.

The gold star–red star response measure in this experiment has the disadvantage of confounding deservingness with reward strategies. Thus, there might be a tendency to reward a person with high ability but low motivation in order to induce action despite a felt lack of deservingness. However, Weiner and Kukla obtained a similar pattern of results with a pride–shame judgment in a later experiment in this same report. A very similar experiment is discussed in the next subsection.

3. Zander, Fuller, and Armstrong (1972)

This experiment was based on the report of Weiner and Kukla discussed in the previous subsection. It also used a 5 × 2 × 2 design, with five levels of performance, two levels of competence, and two levels of trying. However, these stimulus variables were all intended to apply to a group of which the subject was to consider himself a member. Apparently, the two levels of competence and of trying were intended to apply to the subject as well as to the group, although that might not have been entirely clear in the written instructions in this casual classroom experiment. The subjects rated how much pride or shame they would have in the group, and also in themselves.

Application of the linear integration model is based on much the same reasoning as in the two previous subsections. Deservingness should vary directly with Achievement and with Effort, but inversely with Ability within the context of the first two cues.

The linear model implies parallelism, and in fact the data follow the parallelism pattern rather well, with one main exception. Plotted as a function of Achievement, the curve for High Ability lay below the curve for Low Ability at all points except the very highest level of Achievement. At that point, there was actually a slight crossover. The data of Weiner and Kukla (1970, Fig. 3) are quite similar.

The data of Zander et al. show essentially the same pattern for judgments of self and of the group. There was, however, a tendency for judgments of the group to be more extreme, in pride or shame, than the judgments of self.

This last comparison, between judgments of self and of the group, raises an interesting methodological question. The difficulty arises more clearly in the attempt to interpret differences between ratings made by males and females. Females gave lower ratings than males when the group had failed and the members had not tried. But this does not, of course, allow any inference that females felt more shame. Such comparisons have no validity because there is no way to compare subjective feelings across systematic pre-experimental differences. The overt behavior may be compared, to be sure, but in general the underlying processes can be compared only across conditions equated by random assignment. Even if the response was on a ratio scale with the same zero point for both sexes, a valid comparison would still require that both sexes have the same unit.

4. Pruitt (1968)

Pruitt studied how a person reciprocates past treatment when it comes his turn to allocate resources between himself and another person.

In the initial trials of this experiment, the subject's partner had controlled the resources under one of three different conditions in which the total resources and the amount sent out by the partner to the subject were: 80% of $1, 20% of $1, and 20% of $4.

On the subsequent test trials, the subject controlled the resources, which was $3 in every case. A second independent variable was also used—namely, the amount of resources (50¢ or $2) on the last block of trials when it again became the partner's turn to control the resources. The response measure was the amount of resources that the subject sent out to his partner on the test trials.

Two sets of forces act on the subject—one localized around the previous experience variable, the other around the future resources variable. If these two sets of forces average to produce the behavior, then the data should follow the parallelism prediction. That this happened can be seen in Fig. 5.

The divergence of the Control condition, although not significant, also accords with averaging theory. In this condition, there was no previous interaction with partner, and that stimulus variable would of course have zero weight. That would increase the weight for the future resources variable, since the weights must add to unity, and hence produce a spreading of the two curves in Fig. 5 (see Section II,B). Somewhat similar results were obtained with a second response measure—namely, how much the subject expected the partner to send him on the last block of trials.

In agreement with Pruitt's hypotheses, Fig. 5 shows that the amount

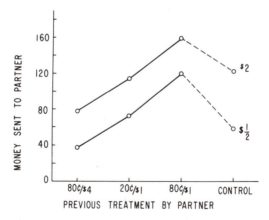

Fig. 5. Amount of money sent by subject to his partner as a function of previous treatment by partner (on horizontal axis) and future resources to be controlled by partner (listed by each curve). Adapted from Pruitt (1968).

allocated to the partner depended both on the absolute and on the proportionate amounts of resources that the partner had previously allocated to the subject (Conditions 20¢/$1 versus 80¢/$1, and Conditions 80¢/$4 versus 80¢/$1, respectively).

Of no less interest is the fact that Condition 20¢/$1 was apparently considered more generous than Condition 80¢/$4, although the subject had received four times as much in the latter condition. Of course, the real value of the money was small, only one-twentieth of its nominal value, so that a proportionate standard would be more appropriate. Nevertheless, a simple proportionate model is inadequate, since the proportion was 20% in both cases. A comparative judgment model (Section II,D,2) might be able to account for the behavior. The judgment of generosity would be a composite of the absolute and proportionate amounts allocated by the partner. At least three levels of the total resources variable would be necessary, and more would be desirable to get a functional scale of the social norms for sharing.

Some question might be raised whether the future resources variable really should obey an averaging principle. Pruitt, following an analysis by Gouldner (see Pruitt, 1968), hypothesized an interaction in Fig. 5 on the ground that the subject uses his allocation procedure to build up future favors. The present model analysis is strictly post hoc. Although it agrees with general averaging theory, it is mainly intended to illustrate a potential method of analysis.

5. Kaplan and Kemmerick (1972)

This study examined some determinants of judgments of guilt and punishment in traffic felony cases. The main piece of information about the defendant was his culpability as established in the case summary. Each case was based on an actual trial but altered so as to yield two versions—one high, one low in culpability. In addition, some personal traits of the defendant were given, of low, medium, or high social desirability. The theoretical hypothesis was that the defendant's personality and the case summary should be averaged to obtain judged guilt.

The data are shown in Fig. 6. The upper pair of curves plots judged guilt on a 1–20 scale. The lower pair of curves plots judged amount of deserved punishment on a 1–7 scale; a rating scale has an advantage over a sentence in months and years which probably would be nonlinear as a function of perceived guilt. Both sets of data obey the parallelism prediction; the interaction term did not approach significance in either case. The data thus support a linear integration rule, although an auxiliary test of adding versus averaging yielded equivocal results.

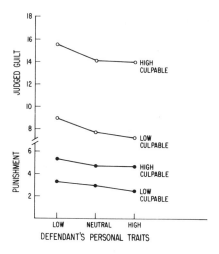

Fig. 6.   Open circles plot judged guilt, and closed circles plot deserved punishment of defendants who were high or low in culpability for a criminal offense. The downward slope of the curves shows that the more likable defendant is seen as less guilty and deserving of less punishment. Data courtesy of M. F. Kaplan.

These graphs show a highly reliable effect of the presumably irrelevant information about the defendant's personality on his perceived guilt: $F(2,186) = 11.60$ and 23.01 for the guilt and punishment judgments. However, the effect is not large, and therefore the data do not provide a very severe test of the integration model itself. For that purpose, Kaplan has suggested that it would probably be desirable to amplify the personality information, with photographs, life history, or a videotape presentation. Also, it might be useful to include other direct evidence such as testimony of witnesses as an added factor in the design.

6. Leon, Oden, and Anderson (1973)

In this experiment, subjects judged the overall badness of hypothetical groups of one, two, or three criminals as a group. Each criminal was defined by one offense from the list of social offenses scaled by Thurstone (1927) and Coombs (1967). Each member of a group was considered as a piece of information to be integrated into one overall judgment.

Three main results were obtained. First, the group judgments followed an averaging model as shown by critical tests of the form described in Section II. This agreed with previous work on judgments of criminal groups (Oden & Anderson, 1971), as well as other kinds of groups (e.g., Levy & Richter, 1963; Rosnow & Arms, 1968). A contrary report by Willis (1960) can be interpreted in terms of the set-size effect of averaging theory.

Second, the averaging model provided a basis for functional measurement of the scale values of the various offenses. These scale values agreed reasonably well with the Coombs-Thurstone paired-comparison values. In addition, the averaging model provided a functional scale of the weight parameter. Weights are not given by traditional scaling procedures, yet they are important in virtually any form of social judgment that requires integration of various pieces of information.

Third, the weight parameter showed extreme variation, from 7.6 for Homicide to 1 for Vagrancy in the main subgroup of subjects. A smaller subgroup carried this differential weighting scheme to the limit and adopted a configural weighting in which the worst member of the group was weighted 1, and the other members were weighted 0. This pattern of results is like the stereotyping found in social attitudes in which a group is judged by a few extreme cases. The appearance of this response strategy in a very simple judgment task suggests that social stereotyping may, unfortunately, be a rather natural form of judgment.

7. Birnbaum (1972a)

Subjects made morality judgments of stimulus persons described by two behavior items (e.g., cheating at solitaire and stealing towels from a hotel). Factorial designs were used to construct the stimulus persons in each of two experiments. In both experiments, the two-way graphs showed a substantial convergence interaction, with the data curves coming closer together as the seriousness of the behavior increased.

These data may be interpreted within an averaging formulation in the same way as in the previous section. It is assumed that the weight of each item was an increasing function of its scale value. The averaging model then implies a convergence interaction (Section II,B,4) similar to that obtained by Birnbaum. The weighting assumption seems reasonable, since the more serious items should also be more diagnostic or informative, as in judgments of behavior of disturbed mental patients (Anderson, 1972a).

Birnbaum favored an alternative range model in which the difference between the scale values of the two items functions as an additional stimulus. This range term is then added onto the simple average of the two stimuli. The range model makes predictions that are qualitatively similar to the differential weighted averaging model for this particular experiment. However, no plausible reason is given why the range between the stimuli should itself function as an effective stimulus. Moreover, Birnbaum (1972b) obtained evidence that suggests possible bidirectional convergence in person perception when both positive and negative stimuli are used. Such bidirectional convergence is expected from the differential-weight averaging model (Anderson, 1971a, p. 184). The range model, in contrast, predicts unidirectional convergence.

8. Adams (1965)

Adams' discussion of inequity in social exchange is built around a concept of proportionate return. A situation is just or equitable when the outcome of a person's efforts is proportional to his input. Relative to another person, or group, equity will obtain when

$$O/I = O'/I'$$

where O and I are the outcome and input of the person, and O' and I' are the outcome and input of the other person or group.

Each term in the above expression can be considered as a composite of various elements. Thus, the input might be a weighted composite that included family or educational background as well as actual job product. Similarly, the outcome would include various status symbols as well as actual pay. Furthermore, all these terms must be considered subjectively, in terms of the person's own value system.

In Adams' discussion, the equity model is essentially schematic or quasi-mathematical. Adams deals mainly with the components of input and outcome, and with mechanisms for resolving inequity. These are interesting and important questions that can be studied without reference to the exact form of the model.

Nevertheless, a mathematical analysis may have considerable value. In particular, if feelings of equity follow an exact cognitive algebra, then functional measurement can be applied to measure the subjective values of inputs and outcomes. Two experimental approaches will be mentioned here. Both depend on experimental manipulation of inputs and outcomes in factorial designs.

In the first approach, all four terms in the above equation are independent. The equation may then be rewritten as

$$O = O'I(I')^{-1}$$

In applications, the three terms on the right would be manipulated experimentally, and the subject would adjust O to the point of equity. The model is then a three-factor multiplying model and can be analyzed in exactly the manner used by Shanteau and Anderson (1972).

The second approach allows the constraint that there is a fixed amount to be divided so that $O + O'$ equals a constant, c. It is easy to show that the model then takes the ratio form,

$$O = cI/(I + I')$$

in which the equitable outcome is proportional to the ratio of the person's input to the total input. This ratio rule for equity also applies when more than two people are involved as long as the total outcome is fixed.

The mathematical analysis of ratio models is discussed in Section II,D,3. It may also be useful to consider equity as comparative judgment (Section II,D,2) which also follows a ratio-type model. It is, of course, an empirical question whether or not a ratio-type model holds, as emphasized by the outcome of the experiment on multiplying models of Section III,B,2.

Two technical points about the equity model should perhaps be added. First, the inputs and outputs are to be considered as subjective values so that, in particular, a value of I that is objectively zero may be subjectively nonzero. Second, if I is negative, I' positive, then the equity equation has two solutions, only one of which makes psychological sense. The solution, O negative, O' positive, is admissible, whereas the other solution, O positive, O' negative, is inadmissible.

D. Attitudes and Opinions

1. Theoretical Overview

What a person says and what he does are usually no more than clues to his real opinions. His statements and actions on a given issue will vary because of other forces that act on various particular occasions. An inference about his true opinion thus requires an integration of the various pieces of available information.

In a previous article (Anderson, 1971a), it was argued that attitude change follows a principle of information integration. One's own attitude is thus an integrated resultant of relevant informational stimuli. Tendencies toward balance and congruity were shown to be derivable from the general principle of information integration. This same approach should hold for the somewhat different judgmental task of determining the opinion held by another.

According to integration theory, therefore, the inferred opinion should be a weighted average of the available information. Each statement or act needs to be evaluated for its relevance (w) and its position (s) with respect to the specified dimension of judgment. The inferred opinion is then the weighted average, possibly including a neutral impression.

Two somewhat different experimental paradigms can be used to study such inferences. The simplest is that in which the person description is a set of statements or actions that are equivalent with respect to the situations in which they originated. For example, the subject might see a list of statements that had been endorsed by the target person as representing his opinion. The weight parameter might be manipulated by varying the degree of endorsement.

If the statements do not interact, then the inferred opinion will be just their weighted average. In many cases, however, the weights and scale value of any one statement will depend on the configuration of statements. For example, an "outlier" statement may be discounted owing to its inconsistency with the other statements. Such discounting effects have been observed in personality impressions (Anderson & Jacobson, 1965) and decision-making (Anderson, 1968d), as well as in attitude change (see Anderson, 1971a, pp. 189–190).

The analysis of configural effects involves certain methodological difficulties (Anderson, 1972a), especially when the scale values are not known. It may be useful, therefore, to use issues such that each statement specifies its own scale value numerically. For example, Rhine and Severance (1970) used communications in which the desired size of the city park was given in acres, and the desired tuition increase was given in dollars.

A somewhat different paradigm has been emphasized by workers in attribution theory. In this paradigm, each statement or action is embedded in some situational context. The weight parameter will then depend on the context, and the principal findings of many of the attribution experiments can be interpreted as showing contextual influences on the weight parameter. Theoretically, however, the inferred opinion should still be a weighted average of the available information, as illustrated in Sections III,D,3 and III,D,6.

2. Weiss (1963)

In this experiment, subjects rated the opinion of target persons on the issue of capital punishment. Each target person was said to have chosen three statements that best characterized his opinion on capital punishment. These opinion triplets were constructed from a 5 × 5 design in which each factor varied from Strong Pro to Strong Con in five steps. The column factor was a single statement, whereas the row factor was a pair of statements of equal value. This is a useful device to combine three pieces of information in a two-way design.

To a fair approximation, Weiss' data appear to follow a linear integration rule; a plot of the data shows that the five curves are roughly parallel. Weiss reached this same conclusion in a somewhat different way, by finding high correlations between the rating of the opinion triplet and the mean value of the three single statements obtained in a separate study.

Weiss also argued for the presence of configural or patterning effects, but on this point the evidence is not very definite. The row × column interaction was statistically significant, it is true, but statistical interaction does not imply psychological interaction (Anderson, 1961, Fig. 1; 1972a). Inspection of Weiss' data suggests that the interaction may be no more than an end effect in rating scale usage, similar to that observed in Anderson (1967a).

Weiss also noted that the response to each nonneutral homogeneous triplet was more extreme than the mean value of its component statements. This extremity effect does not imply patterned response or contrast, however. Instead, it would seem to be just the standard set-size effect, and interpretable as an averaging in of the initial opinion (Section II,B,5).

The lack of a clear discounting effect in Weiss' data is surprising, since some of the opinion triplets contained very inconsistent statements. Certainly, this inconsistency had a definite effect on the confidence ratings (Weiss' Table 4). Possibly different subjects discounted in different directions, leaving a small net effect. Such differences in discounting strategy would seem likely in a casual classroom experiment with instructions that all statements were accurate. Accordingly, it might be advisable to do more extended work with single subjects, and also to obtain weight ratings of the components. Such weight ratings might also allow a better analysis of the effect of the initial impression.

Weiss' experimental paradigm for opinion attribution is interesting and deserves further exploration. A variation is considered in the next section. It is worth noting that the paradigm relates back to scaling studies in which a person's opinion would be taken as an average of the statements that he endorses, a view due to Thurstone (1928). That view might be true in fact, even though the role of the initial impression complicates the averaging model in the attribution task.

3. Himmelfarb and Anderson (1971)

The purpose of this experiment was to unify ideas from information integration theory and the attributional framework developed by Jones and his colleagues (Jones & Davis, 1965; Jones et al., 1971). Subjects judged stimulus persons on a pacifism–militarism dimension. Each person was characterized by a pair of militaristic statements of equal value, plus a single pacifistic statement. The values of the pairs and singles were Mild, Moderate, and Extreme, and the triplets were constructed from a 3 × 3 design. Each statement was said to have come from a different essay written by high-school students under different instructions over the course of the term.

Three different instruction conditions were used. According to the attributional framework developed by Jones and Davis (1965), the weight of the single pacifist essay should vary systematically across the instruction conditions. According to integration theory, this variation in the weight parameter should be reflected in the detailed pattern of the data.

In the *Own Feelings* condition, the target person was said to have written all the essays under instructions to express his own feelings. The simplest expectation from the averaging model would be a set of three parallel curves, with each statement receiving equal weight in the average. Essentially this picture can be seen in the center panel of Fig. 7.

In the *Own Feelings Plus One Pacifistic Essay* condition, one of the essays was said to have been written under instructions to write an essay expressing the pacifistic view. Jones' theory implies that the single pacifistic statement, since it was presumably written under situational constraint, should receive lower weight. The pair of militaristic statements should then exert greater effect, and the inferred opinion should be more militaristic, as indeed is the case in the left panel of Fig. 7.

In the *Militaristic Essays* condition, all three essays were said to have been written under instructions to write expressing the militaristic view. Here the pair of militaristic statements should receive lowered weight, since they were written under situational constraint. At the same time, the single pacifistic essay should receive increased weight because it was written counter to the situational constraint. Accordingly, the in-

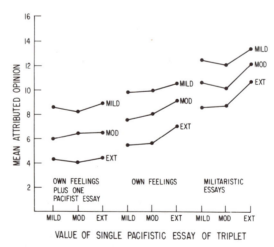

Fig. 7. Judged opinion of stimulus person characterized by three statements about militarism and pacifism. Label by each curve represents the value of the pair of militaristic statements in each set of three. Adapted from Himmelfarb and Anderson (1971).

ferred opinion should be most pacifistic in this condition, as is indeed the case in the right panel of Fig. 7.

Integration theory goes beyond these simple directional predictions to look more closely at the quantitative aspects of the data. The first of these is that the three curves in each panel are approximately parallel, with nonsignificant row × column interaction. That accords with an equal-weight averaging formulation. The parallelism implies a lack of discounting which might have been expected owing to inconsistency in certain combinations. Possibly the instructional context provided enough plausibility for apparent inconsistency to minimize any discounting tendencies. In any case, the parallelism property was verified in two separate experiments.

Three other interrelated aspects of Fig. 7 also deserve notice. These are the elevation, the slope, and the vertical spread, all of which are controlled by the weight parameter of the single pacifistic statement. The relation of this weight parameter to the mean elevation across the three instruction conditions has already been pointed out.

According to averaging theory, the slope of each curve is proportional to the weight times the range in scale value of the pacifistic statement. Since this range is constant in all conditions, the slopes should correlate directly with the elevations. Thus, the curves should be flattest in the left-hand panel and steepest in the right-hand panel. That is at least approximately true, as can be seen in Fig. 7.

According to averaging theory, the vertical spread of the three curves in each panel is directly proportional to the weight of the pair of militaristic statements, and hence inversely proportional to the weight of the pacifistic statement. The mean vertical spread is 4.35, 4.09, and 3.28, across the three panels in Fig. 7, in the prescribed inverse relation to elevation.

These data thus provide detailed support for the averaging formulation. They also illustrate how integration theory links up to other approaches that study valuational processes that control the stimulus parameters.

4. Kiesler, Nisbett, and Zanna (1969)

In this experiment, a subject and a confederate were assigned to give "reliable and valid" factual arguments about an issue in order to collect signatures for a petition in downtown New Haven. The issues were air pollution for the subject, and auto safety for the confederate. The total experimental situation was elaborate, but the difference between the two experimental conditions lay in a single sentence. After the subject and the confederate had been assigned their respective topics, the confederate said to the experimenter, "You said this was reliable, right?," to which the experimenter answered, "Yes." The confederate then said either "Okay, I wouldn't mind convincing people about something I really *believe in*. I guess that's the important thing," or else, "Okay, it would be good to be in a study that really *shows something*. I guess that's the important thing," in the two respective experimental conditions.

The main dependent variable, collected directly after the subject heard the confederate's sentence, was a measure of opposition to air pollution. Subjects who heard the first "believe in" sentence were significantly more opposed to air pollution than subjects who heard the second "shows something" sentence. The subjects who heard the second sentence were little different from a control condition. Also the subjects who heard the first sentence did not change much on auto safety, the issue of the confederate's petition.

The authors interpreted this result to mean that people infer their beliefs from their behavior, or, more exactly in this case, from their behavioral intention of going out on the streets to persuade people to sign their petitions. Their argument was that the subjects who heard the confederate say that he was motivated by his beliefs "apparently assumed that they were similarly motivated by their beliefs." But once this causal attribution is made, their belief must be seen as more extreme in order to account for their own behavior. This interpretation was considered to be in accord with the views of Bem (1967) and Kelley (1967).

Reinterpretation of this experiment in informational terms is straightforward. Consider what the confederate said. He began by reemphasizing the experimenter's statement that the arguments were reliable and then, in the first condition, indicated that he had been persuaded by them. The confederate thus acts as a source weight and implies directly that the subject also should be persuaded by the arguments that he himself is going to use. This interpretation is in line with general knowledge in attitude change, and it is considerably simpler than the attributional interpretation of Kiesler *et al.*

At the same time, the reliability of the result also needs to be considered. It is surprising that one single sentence amidst an elaborate experimental procedure could create a significant effect, even when measured directly after the sentence. If the effect is indeed real, it no doubt depended closely on numerous unreportable procedural details such as the manner and voice of the confederate. Furthermore, if the data are taken at face value, a power analysis (Cohen, 1969) shows that the probability of a significant result in an exact replication is only .58. Since such power estimates are subject to shrinkage, any attempts to follow up this experiment would need to give first attention to increasing power.

5. *Jones and Harris* (1967)

Three experiments were run in which the subject's task was to infer attitude from an essay purportedly written by a stimulus person. The essay itself was pro or anti on the given issue (Castro in Experiments I and II, Segregation in Experiment III), and the stimulus person was said to have had Choice or No-Choice about the pro or anti direction of the essay. These two conditions formed a 2 × 2 design.

Jones and Harris state their crucial hypothesis as: "When a person expresses a modal (high probability) opinion, attribution of underlying attitude will not vary as a function of perceived choice; when an unexpected or unpopular opinion is expressed, correspondent attribution will vary directly with the amount of choice perceived." Thus, Jones and Harris predict no effect of the Choice variable when the essay took the popular side, but greater change in the Choice than the No-Choice condition when the essay took the unpopular side. Essentially these results were obtained.

According to integration theory, the attributed attitude in each condition is simply the weighted average,

$$ws + (1 - w)s_0$$

where w and s are the weight and scale value of the essay, and s_0 is the value of the initial opinion or expectation about the target person's opinion. The weight parameter, w, is assumed to depend on the experimental conditions in a manner analogous to Jones and Harris' hypothesis. Since different weights are expected in Choice and No-Choice conditions, the parallelism prediction of Section II,B does not apply. Instead, the differential weighting should produce nonparallelism as measured by the statistical interaction term in the 2 × 2 design.

To illustrate the application of this averaging model, w values will be estimated for each condition averaged over the first two experiments. The values of s are taken at the scale end points—10 and 70 for anti-Castro and pro-Castro essays, respectively. The value of s_0 is taken as 31.93, the mean value of the subjects' own opinions.

No-Choice, anti-Castro: $w(10) + (1 - w)(31.93) = 23.43; w = .39$

Choice, anti-Castro: $w(10) + (1 - w)(31.93) = 19.63; w = .56$

No-Choice, pro-Castro: $w(70) + (1 - w)(31.93) = 42.44; w = .28$

Choice, pro-Castro: $w(70) + (1 - w)(31.93) = 58.82; w = .71$

These w estimates are intended only to illustrate the direct correspondence between integration theory and the formulation used by Jones and Harris. Since the weight is estimated separately in each condition, no test of the model is available with these data. However, the weights do follow the pattern prescribed by Jones and Harris, and seem to offer a more precise description.

A test of the model is available in Experiment III which used a 2×2 design as just illustrated, but with segregation as the issue. A third factor was added, with the target person being specified as a Northerner or a Southerner. That constitutes an additional piece of information about the target person, and it should, according to integration theory, be averaged in to get the opinion attributed to the target person. That implies that the 2×2 table of means for the Northerner should show the same pattern as for the Southerner, except for being displaced by a constant amount. This pattern of results was obtained, in support of the integration model. Jones and Harris, it may be noted, expected an obverse pattern of results for the Southerner as compared to the Northerner.

Two other aspects of the data are of interest. Jones and Harris noted an irregular tendency for subjects in the No-Choice condition to attribute their own attitudes to the target person. That accords with the integration model: Since the weight of the essay is low under No-Choice, the weight of the initial opinion or prior expectation must be higher. This result was not firmly established, but it agrees with Kaplan's (1970, 1971a) work on the role of the initial impression.

The other remaining aspect of the data is the near-equivalence of the Choice and No-Choice conditions when the essay expressed the modal opinion of the subject population. Jones and Harris claim that this follows from their theoretical analysis, although their reasoning on this point is not entirely clear. The parallel reasoning in the integration model, at any rate, would imply larger w and hence more extreme response for Choice than for No-Choice, regardless of the popularity of the position being advocated. In fact, the data show this directional effect in all four relevant comparisons (Jones & Harris, Tables 1, 3, and 5), although it is significant only in one. The above w estimates reflect this pattern of results. Theoretically, the averaging model predicts a smaller effect for the modal opinion essay, since the initial opinion is closer to the response scale. Thus, the observed results are not too far out of line with integration theory.

There is, however, one additional piece of information in Jones and Harris' Experiment II that is difficult for either of the above analyses to handle. This experiment contained additional conditions in which the essay was ambivalent, being composed by putting the pro and anti essays back to back. In four groups of subjects, there was essentially no difference between a Choice condition, and a No-Choice condition in which the target person had purportedly been told to write an essay favoring the popular view. Both the above theoretical analyses, however, would predict greater change under Choice.

Of course, the ambivalent message may have introduced an added factor of inconsistency, since the pro and anti essays were quite opposed in tone. Under Choice, the effect of the inconsistency would presumably be to reduce the credibility and hence the weight of the essay. That would cause an increase in the weight of s_0 and hence less change in response. This effect would tend to negate the greater expected change under Choice. This line of reasoning is speculative and ad hoc, of course, but it does point up the interest of studying reaction to inconsistent communications in more detail.

6. Lopes (1972)

In this article, Lopes showed how integration theory could provide a unified interpretation of an important experiment on attribution of attitudes by Jones, Worchel, Goethals, and Grumet (1971). These data showed three effects that were originally interpreted in terms of three unrelated processes—"contrast," "footdragging," and "behavior engulfing the field." Lopes showed how all three effects could be related to a single process within an averaging model. Further, the parameters of her model were directly meaningful in terms of attribution theory.

a. Lopes' expectancy–discrepancy model. In the experiment by Jones *et al.*, subjects inferred the attitude of a supposedly real Target person toward the legalization of marijuana. Three variables were combined in a factorial design. *First,* subjects were given the Target's opinion on a related "law-and-order" issue; that implied a corresponding opinion (here called the "prior" opinion) on the marijuana issue as shown by collateral data. *Second,* the Targets were supposed to write an essay on legalization of marijuana under one of two instruction conditions: No-Choice, in which they were arbitrarily assigned to write pro or anti marijuana; Choice, in which they chose their own side of the issue. *Third,* subjects read the actual essay purportedly written by the Target. That could have one of four values—strong or weak pro, or strong or weak anti.

Thus, the subject has two pieces of information about the attitude of the Target toward marijuana. One is the prior opinion as inferred from the related issue; a Target who was strong for "law-and-order" would be presumed to be against legalization of marijuana. The other is the actual essay written by the Target on the marijuana issue.

However, the attributed attitude cannot be an average of just these two pieces of information. Instead, the actual essay must be interpreted in terms of the constraints set up by the instructions. Lopes does this by incorporating a discrepancy or inconsistency term. This discrepancy term plays a key role in her theoretical analysis.

The discrepancy term is the difference between the scale values of the actual essay written by the Target, and the essay that the Target was expected to write. Lopes assumed that the Target would write a strong essay in line with his prior opinion on the related issue, except in one case: No-Choice Targets instructed to write opposite to their opinion would comply with a weak essay.

Lopes' model assumes that the attributed opinion would be an average of the two pieces of information, and the discrepancy term:

$$(5) \qquad R = [w_e s_e + w_r s_r + w_d(s_e - s'_e)]/(w_e + w_r + w_d)$$

Here w_e and s_e are the weight and value of the Target's actual essay, and w_r and s_r are the weight and value of the prior opinion as inferred from the law-and-order issue. The scale value of the expected essay is s'_e, so that $(s_e - s'_e)$ is the discrepancy term, with weight w_d.

Details of the model analysis will not be considered here. The experiment was somewhat complex and needs to be considered cell by cell, both experimentally, and in terms of the theoretical analyses. Lopes' model did fit the data quite well, but, as she notes, the qualitative and conceptual aspects have primary importance. Two main aspects of the analysis will be noted here.

b. Parameter estimates. An interesting outcome of the model analysis is the estimated values of the weight parameters.

First, w_e can be considered as a measure of how informative the subject considers the actual essay. This weight was very high in the Choice condition, near-zero in the No-Choice condition. This result agrees with both common sense and attribution theory, but the model analysis was required to show it. It is necessary to recognize that the actual essay has two effects, one direct, the other indirect via the discrepancy term. These two effects are represented by the weight parameters, w_e and w_d, respectively. Only because the model separates these two effects is it able to show that w_e is a near-zero constant in the No-Choice condition.

Second, consider the weight, w_d, of the discrepancy term. Under the given experimental conditions, the discrepancy term is least informative when it is zero—that is, when the actual essay coincides with the expected essay. It becomes increasingly informative to the degree that the two are inconsistent. To account for this, Lopes allowed the weight of the discrepancy term to depend on its magnitude. A constant w_d would not be able to account for the data.

c. *Conceptual interpretation.* Jones *et al.* required three unrelated processes to interpret the data—"behavior engulfing the field," "foot-dragging," and "contrast." Lopes' analysis gives a unified treatment, based on the discrepancy term.

In the No-Choice condition, a strong essay had considerable influence on the attributed attitudes. To interpret this result, Jones *et al.* had recourse to the Heiderian notion of "behavior engulfing the field," as though the essay behavior should have been, but was not, irrelevant under No-Choice conditions. But behavior did not always engulf the field; the essay had essentially no effect for No-Choice Targets who wrote a weak essay opposite to their prior opinion. To account for this apparent exception, Jones *et al.* introduced the concept of "footdragging."

Both of these effects follow quite naturally from Eq. (5), as Lopes shows in detail. It is important to note that w_e is near-zero in all No-Choice conditions. It is inappropriate, therefore, to say that the behavior engulfs the field because the direct effect of the behavior is negligible. Only if there is an inconsistency between behavior and expectation does the behavior have an effect. But that effect is indirect, via the discrepancy term. Both "behavior engulfing the field" and "footdragging" simply reflect the action of the same discrepancy term under different experimental conditions.

In the Choice condition, a "contrast" effect was observed. Given the same actual anti-marijuana essay, a more extreme anti attitude was attributed when the Target's expected essay was pro than when it was anti. In Lopes' model, this effect also originates in the discrepancy term. When actual and expected essay agree, the discrepancy term has zero weight. But when they disagree, it has considerable weight, and the algebraic direction of the effect is in the same direction as the actual essay.

It should be noted that, in Lopes' analysis, there is no contrast effect in the traditional sense of a change in stimulus values. The "contrast" is produced by changes in the weight parameter while the scale values stay fixed.

d. *Comments.* Lopes' model presents an interesting mixture of agreement and disagreement with attribution theory as used by Jones *et al.* In several respects, some of which were noted above, it supports ideas and conclusions in attribution theory. Yet the overall theoretical orientation is quite different, especially as illustrated in the two previous points.

That Lopes' model gives a unified interpretation argues in its favor, of course, but the interpretation given by Jones *et al.* may nevertheless be correct. But Lopes' model is certainly plausible, and it is a reasonable theoretical candidate. It is clear, therefore, that any theoretical interpretation of the data requires a certain degree of caution.

Finally, it is worth emphasizing that the important processes in Lopes' model center on the concepts of expectancy and inconsistency. Although these have been much discussed, very little quantitative work has been done on them. Lopes' analysis may point the way to further work on these two issues.

E. LOGICAL INFERENCE MODELS

Many judgments are uncertain inferences based on partial, probabilistic evidence. This section considers several approaches to the study of such inferences. The work of McGuire and of the Bayesians places primary conceptual emphasis on a rational standard of correctness. In both of these approaches, the model itself derives from statistical decision theory and prescribes the optimal performance. Although these models allow for subjective probabilities, they require that they obey mathematical probability theory. A rather different approach is used by Abelson and his co-workers. They are concerned with various linguistic aspects of inference judgments and do not employ a quantitative analysis.

Most of this work can be considered as information integration. These kinds of inferences should, therefore, be basically similar to the judgments considered in previous sections. This point of view will be developed by considering some specific experiments.

1. Abelson and Kanouse (1966)

a. Class inference task. Abelson and his co-workers (Abelson & Kanouse, 1966; Gilson & Abelson, 1965; Kanouse, 1971; Kanouse & Abelson, 1967) have studied an interesting inductive inference task that can be illustrated by the following question:

Altogether there are three kinds of women: Southern, Northern, and Central.
     Central women are bad drivers.
     Northern women are bad drivers.
     Southern women are not bad drivers.
Are women bad drivers?

At first reading, this question may seem artificial, but it represents a common kind of judgment. Statements about groups of people, and groups of other things, often refer to a general tendency or opinion, not specifically intended to apply to every member of the group. Further, such statements are often made on a limited base of information.

Four main results emerged from the cited studies. First, "manifest" verbs (e.g., buy, use, have) tended to yield more "yes" responses than "subjective" verbs (e.g., like, trust, hate). That is, "people buy X" is an acceptable generalization from a lower proportion of positive instances than "people like X." Second, affectively positive verbs tended to yield fewer yeses than affectively negative verbs. Third, the verb effects were virtually independent of the specific nouns used for subjects and objects. This result was perhaps due in part to the use of bland, nominal stimulus materials; the above example of women drivers would require consideration of an initial opinion as noted below. Fourth, evidence that particularized the subject population, as in the above example, tended to yield fewer yeses than evidence that particularized the object population. Only a very brief discussion of these and other interesting results will be given.

b. *Verb differences.* Abelson and Kanouse were principally concerned with explaining the above verb differences. Because specific nouns had little effect, they argued that each verb had a natural or implicit degree of quantification. This implicit quantifier corresponds to the minimal amount of evidence needed to justify a generalization based on the given verb. Thus, it would take less evidence to establish that a woman bought magazines than that she liked magazines. Kanouse (1971) suggests that this is a matter of physical availability, as she could easily like more magazines than she could easily buy. Accordingly, "like" would have a higher implicit quantifier than "buy." This explanation is not completely satisfactory, although it probably has part of the truth, as will be seen.

The present interpretation proceeds along a somewhat different line from the Heiderian framework used by Abelson and Kanouse. The basic starting point is that word usage has been shaped by the need to communicate information. Any verb can refer to a considerable range of action, varying in amount or degree. Over a given referent population, it will have some typical or average value. It is assumed that the unquantified verb refers to some small range around that typical value. Lower or higher values would be indicated by adding some specific verbal quantifier. This kind of scheme is efficient, since the single, unquantified word has the modal usage.

Mild negative subjective verbs (e.g., criticize) may help to distinguish between the various explanations of the verb differences. The communicational interpretation would allow, if not imply, low implicit quantifiers for such verbs: If Arthur criticizes a few people, then he criticizes people. That disagrees with Abelson's generalization that subjective verbs have high implicit quantifiers and require more evidence than manifest verbs. Also it disagrees with Kanouse's physical availability hypothesis, since one can easily criticize as many people as one can like. The difference between positive and negative verbs could also be interpreted from this communicational point of view.

The communicational interpretation refers each verb back to its experiential context. In doing so, it would be generally consistent with Kanouse's physical availability hypothesis because availability is an experiential factor which would help shape word usage. However, other factors will also be operative for particular verbs, and it seems doubtful that any simple classification will be completely adequate. More detailed study of the experiential factors that affect verb usage would nevertheless be of considerable interest.

The problems of verb differences will not be pursued further here because integration theory leads to a different attack strategy, illustrated in Section III,E,1,c. However, two minor points that derive from a monopolar–bipolar distinction deserve mention, as they may be important in further work. Verbs like *like* are bipolar, since *does not like* implies *dislike;* but *buy* is monopolar, since *does not buy* does not imply *sell.* Nearly all the positive subjective verbs studied by Abelson and Kanouse were bipolar. They might not be comparable with the manifest verbs for which *no* means something different within their task. Unfortunately, Abelson and Kanouse did not use the negative form of any of their verbs (e.g., *distrust* as well as *trust*). Doing so could also shed light on the positive–negative verb differences.

It is also worth noting that the communicational interpretation can be extended to personality-trait adjectives. Many of these have verb counterparts, like *like* and *likable*. It is assumed that people tend to be described in terms of their distinctive traits, as that transmits information by setting them off from the general population. On this hypothesis, a *likable* person should be one who is liked more than the average. In contrast to verbs, the unquantified adjective should refer to a value somewhat different from the modal value of the trait in the population. There should, therefore, be a systematic difference between adjectives and their corresponding verbs: *Gregg helps people* should be established with less evidence than *Gregg is a helpful person.*

c. Integration-theoretical analysis. The inductive inference task studied by Abelson and Kanouse is one of information integration, and it has a straightforward analysis within the present theoretical framework. Each piece of evidence has a weight and a scale value along the dimension of judgment. In the above example, the scale values would be 1 and 0 (for yes and no), and the weights would presumably be equal for the three pieces of evidence. The weighted average of the evidence yields the judgment; it is referred to a criterion to reach a dichotomous decision. If the judgment value is greater than the criterion, the subject says yes, otherwise no.

The averaging model leads immediately to a simple ratio rule: The proportion of yeses should depend on the ratio of positive to negative information, but be independent of the total amount of information. Some support for this ratio rule can be seen in the preliminary experiment in Gilson and Abelson (1965).

This derivation of the ratio rule from averaging theory depends on the assumption that there is no effect of initial opinion. That assumption seems appropriate for the cited studies in which the items were essentially nominal, and the subject or object population was completely specified. However, the above example of women drivers is not a nominal item like buying magazines. To handle such items, it would be necessary to allow for an initial opinion which is averaged in with the given evidence. The initial opinion would then produce systematic deviations from the simple ratio rule.

The decision criterion corresponds to what Abelson and Kanouse have called the implicit quantifier. Thus, each verb will have its own decision criterion. However, other factors such as instructions or context could also affect the decision criterion, much as in the theory of signal detection (e.g., Green & Swets, 1966; Anderson, 1973e, Section II,B,9).

One technical problem arises in applying integration theory to the particular form of the inference task used by Abelson. Most model analyses assume a numerical response measure, not simply a yes–no response. The percentage of subjects who responded yes might serve, perhaps with a linearizing transformation as in signal detection theory (Anderson, 1973e). However, such group data are not completely satisfactory, since they obscure individual differences.

Accordingly, it would be desirable to seek a direct numerical response measure, such as a rating of degree of belief or agreement. With constant weighting in a factorial design, the parallelism prediction should hold. Success of this prediction would provide a joint validation of the model and the response scale. Further, it would provide interval scales of the stimuli at the level of the individual person. In short, the full capabilities of functional measurement methodology could be brought to bear. Some progress in this direction has been made by Gollob, Rossman, and Abelson (1973).

The integration-theoretical analysis has several advantages. It allows the use of less artificial evidence than in Abelson's task. The evidence need not be all-or-none but can assume any form; it is necessary only that it be meaningful to the subject. Other dimensions of judgment can be handled in the same way as the all-or-none class generalizations studied by Abelson and Kanouse. Finally, prior opinions are included as an integral part of the conceptual and analytical framework. All these capabilities become important in realistic social judgment.

2. McGuire's Logical-Consistency Model

McGuire's (1960) model for logical inference begins with the assumption that probabilistic beliefs obey the laws of mathematical probability. Thus, the belief in two propositions, A and B, would be related by the equation:

$$(6) \quad \text{Prob}(B) = \text{Prob}(A) \times \text{Prob}(B|\text{given } A) + \text{Prob}(\text{not } A) \times \text{Prob}(B|\text{given not } A)$$

where Prob(B) denotes the subjective probability of B, etc. These subjective probabilities need not have any relation to objective fact, but they are required to be consistent among themselves as exemplified by Eq. (6).

This approach to consistency theory specifies a highly interconnected cognitive structure. Information that changes one belief should have multiple, ramified effects throughout the entire belief network. McGuire's goal was to map out the belief network by changing one belief and observing how this change propagated across the network. Some very interesting work has been done from this orientation on Socratic effects and other phenomena of belief change.

Equation (6), it should be noted, represents a syllogism in probabilistic form: (A) and (B|given A) are premises, and B is the conclusion. The probabilistic form requires the two complementary premises, (not A) and (B|given not A). Clearly, the logic model places severe constraints on thought.

Unfortunately, as McGuire points out in his 1968 review, people do not seem to follow the logic model in any exact way. Other factors—wishful thinking, for example, and cognitive inertia—also seem to play a role. Although the logic model could be modified to accommodate such factors, McGuire (1968, pp. 161–162) is doubtful that such a "logic with corrections" strategy will be adequate.

McGuire suggests instead that subjective inference may follow more primitive modes of thought. A unified approach should not need "corrections" but instead should incorporate these modes of thought directly.

The present approach shares this hope. Inference is viewed as information integration. It should obey cognitive algebra much like other forms of judgment. Cognitive inertia can be represented in terms of the weight parameter of the initial opinion. Wishful thinking would be reflected in the valuation processes that yield the weight and scale value of each piece of information. Both of these processes are thus within the theory at the start. The success of integration theory in other areas suggests that it may provide a basis for a unified theory. Additional remarks on logic models are given in Anderson (1971a, pp. 194–195) and in Sections III,E,3 and III,E,4.

3. Wyer's Consistency Model

A series of papers by Wyer have attempted to provide quantitative tests of McGuire's logic model, especially of Eq. (6), which Wyer assumes to hold exactly. A typical experiment provides two kinds of tests. First, ratings are obtained of the five subjective probabilities of Eq. (6) in some specific context. The direct rating of Prob(B) can then be compared to its value as predicted by substituting the other four ratings into the right side of Eq. (6). Second, information is given to the subject that is designed to change, say Prob(A). New ratings of the subjective probabilities are then obtained and used to predict the change in Prob(B).

The net result of this work has been disappointing (e.g., Wyer, 1970, 1972; Wyer & Goldberg, 1970). Direct predictions of Prob(B) range from poor to good in appearance, but the graphs and correlations that are typically reported do not provide a serious test of the model. Substantial correlations are more or less guaranteed by the choice of stimuli, and an adequate test requires an assessment of the deviations from prediction (Anderson, 1962a, 1972a; Birnbaum, 1973).

An appropriate test was made by Wyer (1972), who used an impression task in which the same value of Prob(B) should have been predicted from four different A premises. The predictions were markedly different, contrary to the model.

One simple test of the model seems to have been neglected. Wyer has assumed that Prob(not A) = 1 − Prob(A), although this assumption has long been doubted (Peterson & Beach, 1967). To fulfill this requirement, Wyer and Goldberg (1970) simply omitted all cases in which the sum of ratings of Prob(A) and Prob(not A) was less than .5 or greater than 1.5. That hardly seems satisfactory. If the sum of ratings is reliably different from 1, then the basic model is invalid, or else the ratings themselves are invalid.

As this example suggests, Wyer's method of testing the model, despite its directness and seeming simplicity, suffers technical difficulties. The unreliability of the several ratings needs to be taken into account in the test of fit. Furthermore, the ratings are required to be on an absolute scale, with known zero and unit. As it stands, therefore, Wyer's data do not show whether the discrepancies are in the model itself, or merely in the measurements.

Functional measurement methodology may be able to provide definitive tests of the logic model. A key experimental change is to use two pieces of information instead of only one (Anderson, 1971a). Measurement is required only of Prob(B), not of the other four quantities, and only an interval scale is required. With suitable choice of information, a factorial stimulus design will theoretically yield parallelism or bilinearity in the values of Prob(B). Straightforward tests of the logic model can be obtained in this way, including, in particular, a test of the mediational assumption that changes in Prob(B) occur indirectly, mediated by changes in Prob(A) and the other terms (Anderson, 1971a, p. 195).

4. Bayesian Models

The models of Bayesian statistics are similar in spirit to the logic model used by McGuire and by Wyer. These models have been introduced in psychology as a part of the pioneering work on decision-making by Ward Edwards. The Bayesian approach has been attractive because it is a model for revising beliefs in the light of new information. However, it also is a normative model in that it prescribes the rational or statistically optimal response.

In the case of the Bayesian model, there is no doubt that it is wrong. Indeed, the bulk of the research has been concerned with the so-called "conservatism" effect, a systematic tendency for subjects to be less extreme than the optimal response (Edwards, 1968; Slovic & Lichtenstein, 1971). Unfortunately, "conservatism" has been reified, and various attempts have been made to "explain" it. It is doubtful that there is anything to be explained, since the effect exists only by reference to an admittedly incorrect model.

In applied settings, of course, the Bayesian model may be useful for obtaining optimal predictions. But as a model of psychological processes, it is difficult to see its relevance.

Fundamental work by Shanteau (1970a, 1972) has shown that the integration model is superior to the Bayesian model in the two-urn task that has been the foundation of Bayesian research. Most of the applications of the Bayesian model in social psychology (e.g., DeSwart, 1971; Lovie & Davies, 1970; McNeel & Messick, 1970) seem to be amenable to similar analyses, although no direct comparisons have been made. One particular shortcoming of the Bayesian approach is that it disallows primacy or recency effects. These are statistically suboptimal, of course, and the normative model does not allow for them. In social judgment, however, order effects are ubiquitous (Section III,F).

5. McNeel and Messick (1970)

This paper considered a task introduced by DeSoto and Kuethe (1959) in which subjects estimated the probabilities of various interpersonal relations, such as A likes B, conditional on certain other pieces of information, such as A likes C, and/or C likes B. Since this paradigm has attracted some attention in the attribution literature, it will be briefly considered here in terms of integration theory. From this standpoint, the averaging model for person perception should apply. Each piece of information has a scale value and a weight, and the integration response is just the weighted average value, including the initial impression.

To illustrate how the averaging model could be applied to this situation, one numerical example will be taken from McNeel and Messick's data:

$$\text{Prob(A likes B)} = .54$$
$$\text{Prob(A likes B|A likes C)} = .61$$
$$\text{Prob(A likes B|C likes B)} = .62$$

The first listed value of .54 constitutes an estimate of s_0, the initial impression in the absence of given information.

The weight of the information, A likes C, and C likes B, will be denoted by w_1 and w_2, respectively. The second and third listed values provide estimates of w_1 and w_2 from the averaging equations:

$$\text{Prob(A likes B|A likes C)} = \frac{w_0 s_0 + w_1 s_1}{w_0 + w_1} = .61$$

$$\text{Prob(A likes B|C likes B)} = \frac{w_0 s_0 + w_2 s_2}{w_0 + w_2} = .62$$

The value of w_0 may be set equal to 1 arbitrarily. For simplicity, the values of s_1 and s_2 will be set equal to 1, the end point of the probability scale. Solving the two listed equations yields $w_1 = .179$, $w_2 = .211$.

These estimates allow prediction of the joint effect of the two pieces of information from the equation

$$\text{Prob(A likes B|A likes C, \& C likes B)} = \frac{w_0 s_0 + w_1 s_1 + w_2 s_2}{w_0 + w_1 + w_2}$$

The predicted value is .67, and the observed value was .72. This prediction is intended only to illustrate the operation of the model, as the published data do not allow a test of fit.

As usual, the integration model gets its leverage from responses to combinations of informational stimuli. The present application has methodological interest because the assumption of equal weighting (Section II,B,3) is probably inapplicable. As a consequence, parameter estimation is more laborious and less neat statistically.

McNeel and Messick themselves give a rather different analysis, in terms of Bayesian statistics. In that formulation, the likelihood ratio is analogous to the weight parameter in integration theory. Both can be considered as measures of the informativeness of the given piece of information. McNeel and Messick also note that the likelihood ratio might serve as a measure of change of belief corrected for the base-line belief. The weight parameter of the averaging model serves the same function, of course, since it corresponds to the change parameter in the distance-proportional form of the model (Section II,B,2). This question has been discussed by Anderson and Hovland (1957).

(*Note.* David Messick has pointed out that this analysis would not hold for other relations such as *hates* and *avoids* which were also studied in the given paper. Such cases present difficulties for either theoretical analysis since they involve configural effects, much like the impression-dyads of Section III,G,1.)

F. ORDER EFFECTS

Order effects are important in social judgment for both practical and theoretical reasons. In daily life, information usually arrives a piece at a time, and the order in which it arrives can have considerable importance. "Had I but known," as the saying goes.

Theoretically, also, order effects present important problems. If the same information produces a different response when arranged in a different serial order, then the weights or scale values must be different in the two orders. This issue has central theoretical importance. If the weights or scale values depend on the order of presentation, then this dependence must be taken into account in any quantitative models. An adequate model must allow for such contextual effects. No less important is the nature of the underlying processes that produce the changes in weight and value.

These problems have been studied by the writer and his co-workers in several different substantive areas, including decision-making (e.g., Shanteau, 1972) and psychophysics (e.g., Weiss & Anderson, 1969). In this section only the work on person perception and attitude change will be considered. The main emphasis will be on the integration model, and on the tests designed to delineate the underlying processes. Considerable supportive work has been done, using simultaneous rather than serial presentation (e.g., Anderson, 1971b; Kaplan, 1971b; Himmelfarb & Senn, 1969), but this will not be covered here.

1. Serial Integration Model

Because of its dynamic nature, serial integration is more difficult to analyze than when all the information is effectively present at one time. Under certain conditions, however, a simple analysis can be obtained by treating serial position as a factor in the experimental design. It then becomes possible to get a complete serial curve of the weight parameter. That is, knowing only the response at the end of the sequence of information, it can be dissected into its constituent contributions from each serial position.

The methodology of the serial integration model will not be discussed here. Experimental applications are given by Anderson (1964, 1965b, 1973a), Shanteau (1970a), Weiss and Anderson (1969), and Anderson and Farkas (1973). The last-cited paper gives the first serial position curve of the weight parameter in the attitude change literature (see Section III,F,5).

2. Primacy in Impression Formation

One major line of work on order effects begins with a task and result due to Asch (1946). Asch read a short sequence of personality-trait adjectives to his subjects and asked for their impression of the person so described. A primacy effect was obtained; the impression was more favorable when the words were presented in the good-to-bad order than when they were presented in the opposite bad-to-good order. The effect is replicable and surprisingly large, over a half-point on an eight-step scale (Anderson & Barrios, 1961). That is a substantial effect to get from merely reversing the order of six words presented in 20 seconds.

An extensive research program in the writer's laboratory has studied three explanations of the primacy effect. These are assimilative *change-of-meaning*, due to Asch, *discounting*, and *attention decrement*. The theoretical interest in the primacy effect lies in large part in these explanatory mechanisms. For many reasons, it is important to know whether the trait adjectives do change in meaning as a function of context, or whether they change only in importance or weight. In the latter case, it is important to know whether there is an active discounting process, or a more passive attention decrement. As it has turned out, the evidence clearly eliminates the first two interpretations and supports the attention decrement hypothesis.

Asch's original change-of-meaning explanation of primacy was simple and plausible. The initial adjectives were thought to produce a set ("directed impression") that affected the meanings of the later words. With good traits first, the subject would select more favorable shades of meaning of the later bad traits. In a good person, *stubborn* would mean *determined perseverance;* in a bad person, *stubborn* would mean *dull obstinacy.* Such an assimilation effect provides a direct and simple account of primacy.

Under the discounting hypothesis, the later words do not change meaning (scale value) but instead are given less weight owing to their inconsistency with the earlier words. This hypothesis gains in plausibility, since discounting effects have been demonstrated with simultaneous presentation (Anderson & Jacobson, 1965). However, the one experiment with serial presentation that seemed to provide definite evidence for discounting (Anderson, 1968c) has been shown to be attributable to an attentional factor in a neat demonstration by Hendrick and Costantini (1970); see also Hendrick (1972).

Most of the tests between these three theoretical interpretations of primacy have employed a simple rationale. Change-of-meaning and discounting both imply that primacy should be a robust effect. Increasing the subject's attention to the later words should not much affect the primacy. If anything, primacy should be increased by such attentional manipulations because they would accentuate the affective difference between the earlier and later words. But in fact, the primacy effect is quite sensitive and changes to recency under a variety of such attentional manipulations (see Anderson, 1965b, 1968a). An impressive demonstration of this type is given by Hendrick and Costantini (1970), who showed that merely having the subject pronounce the words caused primacy to change to recency. Other evidence from serial presentation is given by Briscoe, Woodyard, and Shaw (1967) and by Tesser (1968). Supportive evidence from simultaneous presentation is given by Anderson (1971b) and in an important paper by Kaplan (1971b).

All these experiments cause difficulty either for discounting or for Asch's assimilative change-of-meaning hypothesis. However, all are consistent with the attention decrement hypothesis. Decreased attention to the later adjectives causes them to have lower weight in the sequence, and that produces a primacy effect. Manipulations that would eliminate such an attention decrement should also eliminate primacy. This implication has been supported in every one of the cited experiments.

In the integration model, the weight parameter thus becomes a function of serial position, but remains independent of the arrangement of adjectives in the particular sequence. Under certain conditions, the serial weight curve obtained from the integration model shows an almost linear decrease across serial position (Anderson, 1965a, 1973a). Such a serial curve is, of course, consistent with the attention decrement interpretation, but not with the two interactive interpretations.

It is also worth noting that there is no enhancement in recall at the affective juncture between the high and low adjectives in the sequence (Anderson & Hubert, 1963). That also is consistent with attention decrement. In contrast, the interactive interpretation would seem to imply that enhanced recall should result from the salience of the presumed inconsistency reaction.

It should be emphasized that attention decrement provides a unified account of the existing data on order effects in the personality adjective task. Various writers have been concerned because primacy is obtained in some experiments, recency in others. However, it is just this fact, as established by the appropriate experimental manipulations, that supports the attention decrement interpretation. The unity is not in the phenotypic order effect, but in the underlying processes.

Of course, attention decrement itself stands in need of explanation. Gross lapses of attention can be ruled out, at least under the usual experimental conditions. Two other possibilities, not mutually exclusive, may be mentioned. Attention decrement may result from a gradual crystallization of the impression across the sequence. As the impression becomes increasingly solid, new information may be neglected as being unneeded. The other possibility is that the integration mechanism becomes occupied with processing the adjectives already received so that the later adjectives have less influence.

3. Recency in Impression Formation

As was already noted, the standard primacy effect is readily changed to recency by any of several mild changes in procedure. Three explanations of this recency effect have been considered in the writer's research program. These are *contrast, recall memory,* and *overweighting* or *short-term salience.*

Contrast is defined as a shift in value of a focal stimulus away from the value of a contextual stimulus. Contrast effects have been much studied in perception and have been imported into social judgment where they have been quite popular. It is well known, however, that apparent contrast can readily be produced by linguistic artifacts (see e.g., Anderson, 1971a; Upshaw, 1969). At the same time, there is virtually no evidence for true contrast with the usual kinds of social stimuli. At present, therefore, contrast should not be considered as an explanation of recency without clear evidence of its presence.

According to the verbal memory hypothesis, the impression response is based directly on the contents of the verbal memory at the time of the response. However, Anderson and Hubert (1963) obtained evidence for separate memory systems for the impression itself and for the words. They suggested, therefore, that as each word was received, its meaning was extracted and integrated into the current impression. The word itself was no longer necessary and was stored elsewhere. This representation of memory is also consistent with the very low correlations that are typically found in attitude research between verbal recall and attitude change (Insko, 1967; McGuire, 1969).

The remaining explanation of recency is that it is caused by a tendency to overweight the immediately present stimulus relative to the aggregate of previous stimuli. Disproportionate weighting is not surprising; indeed, it would not be easy for the subject to maintain exact proportionate weighting over the course of the sequence. Once the present adjective has been integrated into the impression, the serial integration model implies that its greater weight should be perpetuated through the remainder of the sequence. There is, however, some evidence for a temporary short-term salience effect, at least in attitude change (Section III,F,5).

4. Methodological Comments

A sobering outcome of the above program of research is the apparent failure of the more plausible and glamorous interaction hypotheses. Both discounting and change-of-meaning provide attractive interpretations in terms of cognitive interaction. Indeed, the change-of-meaning hypothesis becomes so compelling in actual examples that it is hard to believe that it is not true. Yet a substantial research effort has uniformly supported the alternative interpretation in terms of attention decrement.

It should be emphasized that the above results have been obtained within one specific experimental situation. It is hoped that the same underlying processes will be found to operate in other situations, but that remains an open question. Certainly, phenotypical primacy and recency will depend considerably on experimental conditions; that holds even within the personality adjective task. As was already noted, just such dependence has provided experimental leverage on the causative process.

In psychophysical judgment, a substantial research program in the writer's laboratory has obtained mainly recency effects (see Weiss & Anderson, 1969; Anderson, 1973e). The same is true for decision-making (Anderson, 1964; Shanteau, 1970a, 1972). This work has been pursued for its substantive interest, not for purposes of comparison with person perception, and it is uncertain whether there is any inconsistency between the two sets of results. Thus, most of the work on psychophysical integration has used continuous responding which produces recency even in the person perception task (Stewart, 1965; Briscoe *et al.*, 1967), in accord with the attention decrement hypothesis. Nevertheless, some of the evidence suggests that there may be a difference in the processes involved in verbal stimuli as compared to psychophysical stimuli.

Order effects have been studied by numerous investigators in attitude change. This work has yielded mixed primacy and recency with no evident pattern (see McGuire, 1969, p. 214; Rosenberg, 1968). In the writer's work on attitude change, recency has typically been obtained (Anderson, 1959, 1973f; Anderson & Farkas, 1973) except when only two messages were used in each sequence (Sawyers & Anderson, 1971). Most work on order effects in attitude change has used only two messages, and that may be one reason that a clear pattern has not emerged. As will be illustrated in Section III,F,5, a serial curve of the weight parameter may be a valuable tool in the analysis of order effects.

5. Two-Component Structure of Attitudes

An interesting outcome of the work on order effects in attitude change (Anderson, 1959; Anderson & Farkas, 1973) is the evidence that there are two components, basal and surface, to attitude structure. With stimulus materials from a jury trial (Anderson, 1959), a basal component appeared to develop in mid-sequence, as though the opinion began to crystallize at that point. Once developed, the basal component was quite resistant to change. However, even after the basal component had developed, there was still a surface component, quite reactive to immediate testimony, but decaying fairly rapidly after being formed. An interesting outcome of the joint action of the two components was the appearance of a hidden primacy effect, produced by the basal component, but temporarily masked by recency from the surface component.

Further evidence for the two-component hypothesis of attitude structure is given by the serial position curves of Fig. 8. In this experiment, subjects judged statesmanship of United States Presidents from a sequence of informational paragraphs (Anderson, Sawyers, & Farkas, 1972). The judgment was revised after the receipt of each new piece of information. The curve labeled R4 portrays the weight of each serial position in the final judgment. The curve is flat over the first three positions, showing that they have equal influence on the final opinion. The upswing at the last point implies a net recency effect. An interesting aspect of the curve is the lack of any bowing as might be expected from a verbal memory or learning hypothesis.

The comparison of the curves labeled R3 and R4 brings out the distinction between the basal and surface components. The R3 curve

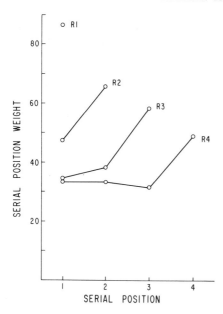

Fig. 8. Serial position curves for attitudes toward United States Presidents. Dependent variable is effective weight of stimulus information as a function of serial position. R1, R2, R3, and R4 represent attitude response at first, second, third, and fourth serial positions. From Anderson and Farkas (1973).

gives the weights of each serial position on the opinion response at the third serial position. It is flat over the first two positions, with a terminal recency component. Since that recency component has completely disappeared in the R4 curve, it is a short-term surface component. The same conclusion is indicated by the comparison of the curves labeled R2 and R3.

The basal component is represented by the flat portions of these serial curves. In this experiment, the basal component builds up at a uniform rate over the sequence. The surface component, however, would almost seem to be an artifact, since it disappears so rapidly under the impact of new information.

This experiment suggests the usefulness of complete serial curves in attitude change experiments. Most work in this area has used only two messages, which does not yield an adequate serial curve. Indeed, Fig. 8 seems to be the only complete serial curve in the attitude literature. The methodology of the serial integration model, as well as the jury trial and president stimulus materials developed for the cited experiments, should be helpful in the further study of attitude structure.

Although the two-component representation of attitude change is attractive, not much other evidence seems to be available. However, it is consistent with the finding that it is hard to get opinion change outside the laboratory. Everyday social opinions would presumably be largely developed in their basal component, and any changes effected in the surface component would have limited duration.

6. Jones and Goethals (1971)

Jones and Goethals give a general discussion of order effects in impression formation, but only three points will be considered here.

Jones and Goethals emphasize that judgmental context can have an important influence on order effects. Their main concern is with judgments of ability, and they point out the relevance of sequence-related hypotheses. For example, a steadily decreasing level of performance could be interpreted to imply high ability together with a gradual decline in motivation. On the other hand, a steadily increasing level of performance could reflect learning. Such judgments will clearly depend heavily on experimental specifics. Judgments of ability and motivation have great social importance, and Jones and Goethals' paper is valuable in bringing these problems to the focus of attention.

In their theoretical discussion, however, Jones and Goethals are less felicitous. Aside from noting the potential importance of sequence-related hypotheses, they consider essentially the same set of explanatory processes listed in Sections III,F,2 and III,F,3. However, they seem to prefer those explanations for which there is least evidence. Their reliance on concepts of contrast and assimilation is especially doubtful in view of the prevailing lack of evidence for either assimilation or contrast in social judgment.

Observed contrast effects in social judgment are often no more than response artifacts. That was clear in the results of Campbell, Lewis, and Hunt (1958), and the same point has been made repeatedly since then (see Anderson, 1971a; Upshaw, 1969). Despite considerable effort, there is virtually no clear evidence for true contrast effects with social stimuli.[3]

---

[3] A recent report by Dawes, Singer, and Lemons (1972) showed that "Hawks" imagine that the typical "Dove" holds a considerably more extreme view than in fact obtains, and vice versa. This is an interesting and important kind of inaccuracy in social judgment. However, it seems doubtful that it should be considered as a contrast effect, which, by definition, is a shift in the value of a focal stimulus produced by a contextual stimulus. In the given example, the focal stimulus would be opinion statements made by the typical Dove. Since the focal stimulus was never present, no contrast could occur. To demonstrate contrast would require showing that Hawks distort the statements actually made by the typical Doves. The data do not show that, because the Doves in fact rejected as too extreme the statements that the Hawks imagined they would make. It seems evident, and could easily be tested, that the Hawks would view the statements actually made by the typical Dove as less extreme than those statements they imagined that the typical Dove would make. If so, then the cited data would not demonstrate contrast.

The result of Dawes et al. is important because it represents a presumably common form of inaccuracy in social judgment. However, inaccuracy need not be distortion, since it can result, for example, from mere ignorance. And "distortion" need not be contrast, since it can be produced by simple averaging processes (see Anderson, 1971a, p. 190; also Sections III,C,6 and III,D,6).

Assimilation can occur in more than one way. Psychophysical assimilation is typically a weak effect, and there is little reason to believe that it plays any significant role with social stimuli. Asch's assimilative change-of-meaning hypothesis has great face plausibility, but repeated attempts have failed to find supportive evidence. Other effects that might seem to represent assimilation can be more readily interpreted in other terms as illustrated in Section III,F,9.

It is quite possible that assimilation and contrast are important in certain social situations. But with so meager a footing in evidence, they cannot be considered as freely available explanatory concepts. On the contrary, each application would seem to require specific justification.

7. Jones, Rock, Shaver, Goethals, and Ward (1968)

Jones and Goethals also discuss a set of six experiments on ability attribution by Jones, Rock, Shaver, Goethals, and Ward (1968). Subjects first observed a stimulus person who worked on a series of 30 problems under one of three prespecified patterns of success and failure. In each case, the stimulus person was seen to get 15 correct out of 30, but the frequency of successes followed a Descending, Random, or Ascending pattern. The subjects next predicted the trial by trial performance of the stimulus person on a second series of 30 similar problems, this time with no information about the correct response. Finally, they judged the intelligence of the stimulus person and recalled how many correct responses she had made in the first series.

The general result of these experiments was a primacy effect. The Descending stimulus person, whose successes were more frequent early in the sequence, was predicted to have most successes in the second series, was judged to be most intelligent, and was estimated to have had most successes in the first series. The Ascending stimulus person, who had the reverse order of successes and failures, was seen as poorer in all three respects.

Although a variety of explanations of this primacy effect were considered, Jones and Goethals' "favored explanation" was in terms of memory distortion. Since the problems were specified to be equally difficult, the subject should expect a uniform distribution of successes and failures across the 30 trials of the first series. At the same time, performance in the initial block of trials should set up an expectation about the level of performance on the later trials. It was assumed that the actual performance on the later trials was distorted to fit the initial expectation. This explanation would, of course, account for the primacy effect.

The attention decrement hypothesis discussed above provides an equally plausible explanation. In this view, less attention is given the later trials, quite possibly because the initial block of trials does establish a directed impression or expectancy, as Jones and Goethals suggest. Decreasing attention would correspond to decreasing values of the weight parameter, and that would produce primacy in the serial integration model. Memory distortion would be a consequence, not a cause as Jones and Goethals claim. Jones and Goethals acknowledge this possibility, but feel that their memory distortion explanation is "much more likely." On the present view, the recall difference, like the difference in judged intelligence, would be a generalized halo effect. Attention decrement provides a more parsimonious interpretation than memory distortion, but the data of Jones *et al.* do not allow a distinction between them. However, Anderson and Hubert (Section III,F,3) found evidence for two memory systems, which argues against memory distortion.

One alternative interpretation also needs to be considered. These ability attribution experiments differ in one possibly important respect from the usual experiments on order effects. As Jones *et al.* point out, the Ascending stimulus person has fewer cumulative successes at every trial from the second to the twenty-eighth. Judged probability that the stimulus person would succeed on the next trial would, therefore, be markedly lower for the Ascending than for the Descending stimulus person over most of the sequence. Indeed, just such judgments were obtained in Experiments IV and V. Since this judgment task is similar to the standard probability learning task, the serial integration model would be expected to apply (Anderson, 1969b; Anderson & Whalen, 1960; Friedman, Carterette, & Anderson, 1968). Jones *et al.* consider an analogous model which can be considered as a special case of the serial integration model. However, it requires that the weight parameter be equal over trials, and that disallows the order effects that are typical of such work.

Judgments of ability may be made, not simply on the basis of the sequence of successes and failures per se, but also on the basis of the sequence of explicit or implicit judgments of probability of success. In effect, two stages of information integration would be involved. The first would operate on the successes and failures to reach a judgment of probability of success for each trial of the sequence. The second would operate on the sequence of judgments of probability of success to reach an overall attribution of ability. If such a process is operative, then a primacy effect would be almost inevitable. This two-stage interpretation is speculative, but it seems useful to keep it in mind.

All the above explanations have a common shortcoming. They all imply that the Ascending target person should be seen as less able than the Random target person for whom the 15 successes were spread uniformly over the sequence. In fact, however, the observed differences between these two conditions were small. Resolution of this theoretical difficulty evidently has primary importance.

Further study of this problem will probably require an experimental design that allows a complete serial position curve of the weight parameter. This would be feasible, for example, if the trials were blocked by fives or tens to yield a 2^6 or 2^3 serial-factor design. Methods for getting such serial position curves are illustrated in Anderson (1964), Anderson and Farkas (1973), Shanteau (1970a, 1972), and Weiss and Anderson (1969). Such results would show how the judgment of ability developed over the course of the sequence.

8. Himmelfarb and Charash (1972)

Since the above was written, such an experiment has been reported by Himmelfarb and Charash (personal communication, 1972). Their subjects saw a sequence of six numbers which represented the performance of a stimulus person on successive examinations in a mathematics course. Subjects were told that all examinations were equally difficult and so constructed that luck could not affect performance. Stimulus sequences were constructed in a 2^6 design so that all possible sequences of High and Low scores were used. The High and Low scores were different at each serial position, but their difference was constant, as in Anderson (1964).

After viewing the sequence of scores, subjects made three responses: They judged the ability and the motivation of the stimulus person, and also predicted how well he would do on a seventh examination. For each response, the serial integration model yielded a complete serial curve that exhibited the effect of the information at each serial position upon the response.

The serial curves for the three response measures are shown in Table II. Each entry is a weight parameter estimated from the serial

TABLE II

WEIGHT PARAMETERS AS A FUNCTION OF SERIAL POSITION FOR THREE
RESPONSE MEASURES[a]

Response measure	Serial position					
	1	2	3	4	5	6
Ability	.21	.16	.16	.14	.15	.18
Motivation	.00	.06	.13	.20	.26	.35
Performance	.07	.10	.14	.17	.23	.29

[a] After Himmelfarb and Charash (1972).

integration model. It measures the effect of the given serial position on the integrated response.

Judgments of ability show a mild primacy, in agreement with the data of Jones *et al.* (1968). It is interesting that the main contribution to the primacy comes at the very first serial position. Thereafter, the serial curve is nearly flat except perhaps for a slight upturn at the end.

In contrast, the judgments of motivation and performance show very strong recency effects. Indeed, for motivation, the very first examination has zero weight. This is a striking difference from the judgments of ability.

A noteworthy and important feature of this experiment is the use of more than one response measure. In view of the marked differences among the serial curves of Table II, the use of only one response measure may be quite misleading. Even for two response measures that show overall recency, the serial pattern may be rather different, as in the comparison between judgments of motivation and performance.

The methodology and results of Himmelfarb and Charash appear to be quite important for the study of order effects. Besides their use of three response measures, their procedure of simultaneous presentation of the stimulus information has special interest. Since the subjects could see all the information at one time, certain factors should operate differently than in the usual procedure in which only one piece of information is present at a time. Simultaneous presentation should effectively eliminate memory effects and amplify the effect of any cognitive factors that may be present. For example, any sequence-related hypotheses of the kind conjectured by Jones and Goethals would be expected to increase in importance because the simultaneous presentation would increase the salience of patterning in the sequence. It is surprising, therefore, that the evidence failed to show any sequence-related hypotheses. Under other experimental conditions, they might well play a major role. The value of the methodology of integration theory is that it provides a direct attack on this problem.

9. *Thibaut and Ross* (1969)

This experiment obtained both recency and primacy effects under specified experimental conditions, and these were interpreted as contrast and assimilation effects, respectively. The purpose of the present discussion is to point out that other interpretations are possible and that the contrast–assimilation framework is inconsistent with direct tests that have been made in related areas.

The subjects in this experiment saw a series of 20 slides, each a 16×16 matrix of 0's and 1's. In the Ascending series, the proportion of

1's increased irregularly from $\frac{3}{16}$ to $\frac{13}{16}$ over the successive slides of the series. In the Descending series, the slides were in the reverse order. Each subject judged two series, either in Ascending–Descending order, or vice versa.

In the Preference condition, subjects were told that each matrix in a series represented judgments by 16 nonexperts on 16 attributes of one of 20 pictures by an unknown artist, with 1 and 0 corresponding to good and bad judgments, respectively. As they saw each slide, the subjects made a rating of the goodness of the particular picture that that slide was supposed to represent. The mean judgments averaged over the 20 slides was higher for the Ascending than for the Descending series, on both a within-subject and a between-subject basis. This recency effect was not due simply to the integration requirement; similar results were obtained in the Attribute condition in which each slide was judged individually in terms of its proportion of 1's.

Thibaut and Ross noted that contrast effects, such as are assumed in Helson's (1964) adaptation-level theory, could account for the recency effect. However, there are two serious difficulties with the contrast interpretation. First, contrast can be produced by response language effects without any perceptual distortion. Thibaut and Ross recognized this difficulty and attempted to avoid it. However, there is no guarantee that they succeeded.

Second, when direct tests are made for the contrast effects, they are not obtained. With simultaneous presentation of a set of unrelated personality-trait adjectives, no context effect is obtained (Anderson & Lampel, 1965; Condition W; Takahashi, 1971; Wyer & Watson, 1969). With serial presentation, a very small assimilation effect is obtained for verbal stimuli (Anderson, 1972a) and for lifted weights (Anderson, 1971c). Similar results have been obtained for other stimulus dimensions (see Ward, 1972). For these reasons, then, the contrast interpretation does not seem applicable.

Thibaut and Ross also ran a third condition in which apparent primacy was obtained. In this Commitment condition, subjects were given collateral information about and judged the quality of the artist before seeing and judging each series of slides. The arrangement was such that each Ascending series was preceded by collateral information that the artist was bad, while each Descending series was preceded by collateral information that the artist was good. The mean judgment was greater for the Descending than for the Ascending series. This apparent primacy effect was interpreted in terms of assimilation, analogous to the contrast interpretation of the recency already discussed.

The essential idea and importance of this assimilation interpretation is that the commitment manipulation causes the subjects to distort the subsequent information. However, a simpler interpretation is possible in terms of information integration. The subject begins each series with an initial opinion about the artist induced by the collateral information. The judgment of the first slide is then the average of two pieces of information: the initial opinion, and the slide itself. Similar reasoning holds for the later slides. Because of the confounding in the design, the initial opinion was always high for the Descending series, low for the Ascending series. Consequently, the serial integration model implies a shift from recency toward primacy as a result of information averaging. On this view, the apparent primacy would not represent true assimilation, but only straightforward information integration.

G. Other Applications

1. Anderson (1967b)

This experiment used an impression-dyad paradigm (Anderson, 1968a) to test between balance and congruity theories on the one hand, and the principle of information integration on the other. Each person in the dyad was described by three favorable personality-trait adjectives, all of equal value, and the two persons were connected by a relation— Like, Dislike, or Doesn't Know. These three dyads are shown in Table III together with the mean rating of likableness of each member of the dyad. The rightmost two columns list the change scores relative to the Doesn't Know control. Three of the four change scores are highly significant, the −.06 value excepted.

Neither balance theory nor congruity theory accounts for these results, although for somewhat different reasons. The first dyad contains no incongruity. Congruity theory predicts zero change, except perhaps for an "assertion constant" effect on liking for B. This prediction is con-

TABLE III
LIKABLENESS OF BOTH MEMBERS OF IMPRESSION-DYADS

	Impression-dyad		Mean liking		Change in liking	
			A	B	A	B
A	Likes	B	7.72	7.75	.50	.57
A	Doesn't Know	B	7.22	7.18		
A	Dislikes	B	6.62	7.12	− .60	− .06

Note: Response on a 0–10 scale, with 10 = most liked. Means averaged over 2 stimulus replications and 30 subjects. Data from Anderson (1967b).

tradicted by the significant change for A. In the last dyad, pressure toward congruity implies that A and B should change equally toward zero, except for a possible "assertion constant" effect on B. This prediction is contradicted by the near-zero change in B.

Balance theory is ineffectual. It makes no prediction for the first, balanced dyad; extra-theoretical reasons would be required to account for any changes that might occur. The last dyad is unbalanced, so balance theory predicts that something will change, but it does not say what.

Integration theory provides a straightforward conceptualization. For each person, the relation word and the other member of the dyad provide relevant information that should be averaged in with the three personality-trait adjectives to determine the overall impression. Thus, the results for the first dyad seem straightforward. That A likes B is a favorable piece of information about A and B alike; it should be integrated into the impression along with the traits describing A or B.

The last dyad is interesting because disliking has its effect almost entirely on the disliker in this dyad. As the last dyad suggests, the value of the relational information may be configural (Anderson, 1968a), depending on the likableness of the two persons. Disliking a good person may be bad, as Table III indicates, but the same would not be expected to hold for a bad person. In fact, the effect was near zero, perhaps a net resultant of two opposed tendencies. Integration theory does not actually predict the value of the relational information in such cases. As yet, there is relatively little theory of configural valuation (Anderson, 1971a, pp. 198–201; 1972a, pp. 99–101). However, integration theory does have the conceptual breadth to study the configural problem in a detailed way. A more extensive experimental and theoretical analysis of the impression-dyad paradigm has been given by Lindner (1970, 1971).

2. Himmelfarb (1972)

In this report, Himmelfarb illustrated how complementary ideas from attribution theory and integration theory could be combined in an analysis of person perception. Subjects judged likableness of persons described by one, three, or six isovalent personality traits which reflected their behavior as judged by certain observers. There were two observer variables, representing source and situation. The sets of three and six traits were said to be contributed either by the same observer, or by different observers; also they were said to have been observed in similar situations, or in dissimilar situations.

In attribution theory, the source and situation variables would affect the confidence with which the trait was attributed to the person. In any one situation, the behavior might be caused primarily by situational constraints. Hence confidence should be greater when the person is observed in several different situations. Similarly, the description given by any one observer might reflect in part that observer's biases. Hence confidence should be greater when the traits are contributed by different observers than when they are contributed by the same observer.

In terms of integration theory, the degree of confidence would manifest itself in the weight parameter. A more confident trait attribution would produce greater weight for that trait in forming the impression of the person. Theoretically, therefore, the impression should reflect this differential weighting.

Himmelfarb's two main theoretical predictions were that the impression should be more extreme for multiple sources than for a single source, and also more extreme for different situations than for single situations. Both predictions were verified. It should perhaps be noted that the theoretical analysis rested on the use of the concept of initial impression which also accounted, in much the same way, for the set-size effect in Himmelfarb's data (see Section II,B,5).

Himmelfarb's analysis is not restricted to the person perception task but should apply more generally, even outside the field of social judgment. However, the effects in his data were not large, and it might be useful to amplify them in further work. One way to do that would be to make the stimulus items moderately redundant in their semantic relations. The effective redundancy in the judgment task itself is communicational, dependent on source and situation characteristics as well as on the semantic relations among the traits. Repetition of one trait by the same observer could be completely redundant and have zero weight. In contrast, repetition of the same trait by a second observer might carry as much weight as for the first observer.

3. Anderson, Lindner, and Lopes (1973)

Judgments about groups are common in social life, and the study of groups has been one of the main themes of social psychology. However, as Collins and Raven (1969) observe, very little has emerged in the form of useful theory.

From the integration-theoretical standpoint, judgments about groups should obey the same models as judgments about other objects. There is nothing essentially different about a group as an object of judgment. Integration theory does not cover all aspects of group theory, but it does provide a unified conceptual framework and methodology for attacking a large class of judgments about groups.

Judgments of groups have special interest within integration theory because they typically involve more complex integration processes than in person perception. Indeed, as illustrated in the present experiment, two successive integration stages may be involved—first, of the separate members of the group, and second, of the group itself.

Subjects in this experiment judged attractiveness of groups of three members, each described by two personality traits. These judgments require two successive integration stages. First, the traits in each person description must be integrated to form an impression of that person. Second, the three person impressions must be integrated to form an impression of the group. Both types of judgments were obtained, and both appeared to follow an averaging formulation (see also Section III,C,6).

Of special interest in this experiment was the leader manipulation. In half the groups, all three members had equivalent roles, but in half the groups, one member was designated as leader. This manipulation produced two extremity effects, both directly interpretable in terms of averaging theory. First, the impression of the leader was more extreme than that of a nonleader described by the same personality traits. Second, the impression of a group in which one member had been designated leader was more extreme than that of the same group in which there was no designated leader. In both cases, an attractive person or group became more attractive, whereas an unattractive person or group became less attractive.

The theoretical interpretation is based on the assumption that designating a person as leader increases a corresponding weight parameter in each of the two judgment tasks. In the person impression, therefore, increased weight is given to the trait adjectives. Consequently, the initial, neutral impression receives lower relative weight and the judgment becomes more extreme. The same logic applies to the group impression, although the informational stimuli are now the group members themselves.

IV. Concluding Comments

A. COGNITIVE ALGEBRA

The present survey has yielded considerable support for the operation of a general cognitive algebra in social judgment. Cognitive integration seems to follow simple averaging, subtracting, and multiplying rules far more commonly than has been recognized.

This conclusion is not entirely surprising. In fact, algebraic models have been suggested by numerous investigators in a variety of particular applications. When these begin to be aggregated, it is impressive how many such attempts have appeared. Many of these applications have remained at a verbal level, it is true, but they still reflect the same basic intuitions that are seen in the more precise formulations.

Furthermore, rigorous tests have given firm quantitative support for algebraic models in numerous experiments. Many such applications are outside of social judgment, of course, in decision-making, psychophysics, and other areas. The work of Shanteau in decision-making and that of Weiss and Birnbaum in psychophysics are especially notable. Although such applications are only indirectly relevant to social judgment, they do support the conception of a general cognitive algebra.

B. Integration Theory

The present approach to social judgment begins from a principle of information integration. This principle, coupled with a systematic use of algebraic models, provides a unified, general approach to the study of judgment.

The integration-theoretical approach involves a new way of getting hold of many traditional problems. Despite its basic simplicity, it often takes time to come into focus because it has a somewhat different emphasis. Its leverage, both experimental and theoretical, derives from the use of tasks that require integration of information. This has a continuing influence on the investigation, from the pilot work to the theoretical interpretation of the data.

This point can be illustrated by reference to Atkinson's work on achievement motivation (Section III,B,6). Atkinson begins with an attempt to find a test that measures achievement motivation. This measure is then employed in the substantive work—in particular, on the algebraic model that Atkinson postulates. This method of attack is typical of the traditional approach to measurement.

Integration theory is more direct. It makes the measurement of motivation an organic part of the study of the model itself, not a separate preliminary. Functional measurement methodology finds the best possible scaling of motivation. If the model fails, it is not simply because the measure of motivation is at fault. If the model succeeds, it yields a validated functional scale of motivation, measured as it functions in the behavior under study.

C. Role of Algebraic Models

A frequent complaint against mathematical models is that numerous models are available, and that some model can be found to fit any given set of data with a suitable choice of parameters. Those who work with models, however, find that they impose a far tighter conceptual discipline than the more verbal formulations. Indeed, the attractiveness of verbal theories sometimes seems to reflect the verbal glitter of surplus meaning in the theoretical terms rather than any implicational power in the theoretical structure. Balance theory is a good example of unfilled promise (Abelson & Kanouse, 1966; Collins & Raven, 1969, p. 118; Rosenberg, 1968, p. 198; Zajonc, 1968, pp. 345, 353), and recent work on social attribution often seems to place undue weight on a clever theoretical story.

Nevertheless, the complaint against mathematical models does have some basis, and a few comments may help to clarify the matter. The first is that the complete array of simple algebraic models is clearly necessary to handle the variety of possible judgment tasks. Preference judgments, for example, call for a subtracting model. Adding and averaging models are natural candidates for serial integration. Multiplying and ratio models also arise quite naturally in various situations (Section II,B; Anderson, 1973e, Section III). It is clear, therefore, that a variety of models will be required. In most cases, of course, the appropriate model to test in a given situation is not in great doubt. Averaging or multiplying models would not make much sense for preference judgments, for example.

When the simple model fits the data, no great problem ordinarily arises. One test only goes so far, of course, and confirmation is always needed. Also the power of the test needs to be considered, though the methods of functional measurement have been found to be very powerful at picking up discrepancies from the model (e.g., Anderson, 1972b, Fig. 1).

A more serious question arises when more than one model can fit the data. For example, the adding model and the constant-weight averaging model both predict parallelism. In this particular case, tests to distinguish between the two models are easily devised. In other cases, the matter may not be so easy (Section III,B,2; Anderson, 1972b). On the whole, however, the situation is fairly straightforward when the simple model does fit the data.

It should be emphasized, therefore, that simple models have been shown to hold in numerous studies. Such applications have been made in a variety of substantive areas, and each of the simple models has been verified repeatedly, excepting only the strict adding model (Section II,A). This work provides a firm basis for the important role of cognitive algebra. This point deserves emphasis because there are many situations in which a simple model does not hold. In psychophysics, for example, the multiplying models for fractionation and ratio setting have not had much success (Anderson, 1973e, Section III,B).

In social judgment, the most frequent source of failure of a simple model has been nonparallelism in integration tasks to which an adding or averaging model might be expected to apply. That rules out adding or summation models, but the averaging model has typically been able to account for the nonparallelism in terms of differential weighting (Section II,B,4). This interpretation is reasonable, in part because of the substantial support that has been obtained for the constant-weight averaging model, in part because differential weighting must be expected to be quite prevalent. However, the differential-weighted averaging model does require added weight parameters, and that raises a natural fear that the model could hardly fail when so many parameters are allowed.

It is important to recognize, therefore, that the weight parameters are not arbitrary constants. They must make empirical sense (see, e.g., Sections II,D,3,5,6). Furthermore, independent evaluation of the rank order of the stimulus weights permits prior predictions of the deviations from parallelism. The differential-weight averaging model derives its support not so much from being able to fit the data as from its base in the constant-weight averaging model, from its congruence with collateral information about the weight parameters, and from critical tests of the averaging hypothesis (Section II,B,5).

In general, to be sure, the situation is always somewhat uncertain when the simple model does not fit the data. When these discrepancies can be given a substantive interpretation (e.g., Anderson, 1972a; Anderson & Jacobson, 1965; Lampel & Anderson, 1968; Sidowski & Anderson, 1967), the model may have served its purpose. Unfortunately, the interpretation of model discrepancies is often in doubt. They may reflect a basic shortcoming in the model itself. They may also reflect complicating factors of no great interest. These would include floor or ceiling effects, or number preferences, which produce minor nonlinearity in the response scale, as well as extraneous response tendencies not allowed for in the model. Such discrepancies might have negligible effects on qualitative, directional predictions, but they can be troublesome in exact quantitative tests. For this reason, caution and forethought are desirable when algebraic models are being used.

A final point which should be recognized is that many questions that seem at first glance to be empirical turn out, on closer consideration, to be answerable only within a model framework. A pertinent example is the frequent claim that negative information carries more weight than positive information. This is not a simple question of fact. As most investigators have realized, it requires controlling for the scale values so that the observed differences reflect only the weight parameter. But that already involves the conceptual distinction between the weight and value parameters, as well as some assumptions about measurement. A model analysis can be useful for conceptual clarification by requiring precise statements of implicit assumptions, even though the model may not be used in a quantitative way.

D. Process Analysis

The main reason for studying algebraic models is to penetrate beneath surface appearances to the processes that underly the behavior. When several forces act together to produce a given response, it may not be feasible to dissect their separate influences without the aid of a model. The serial integration model (Section III,F) and Lopes' expectancy-discrepancy model (Section III,D,6) illustrate this point. In both cases, evaluation of the weight parameters depends on using the model.

However, success of a model is not a final goal. It gets down one level in the analysis of the underlying processes. The next one or two levels are no less interesting. A few problems will be mentioned briefly to illustrate possible directions of attack.

1. "As If" Models

It has been emphasized at several points that some of the algebraic models may be only formal, *as if* models. Cliff's multiplying model for adverb–adjective combinations (Section II,C,3) illustrates this point, since the cognitive processing appears to have little to do with any kind of multiplication. A formal model may be very useful—as a basis for functional scaling, for example—but the exact nature of the integration mechanism is also of interest.

For averaging models, simple physical mechanisms exist which may have psychological counterparts. For example, stimuli can be represented as point masses on a massless plank, whose locations are their scale values, and whose masses are their weights. From introductory physics, the fulcrum or balance point is at the weighted mean. Intuitively, it seems likely that such a balancing operation is at work in certain averaging tasks. A chemical or statistical analogy, in terms of combining solutions or samples, may also be useful (Anderson, 1973d).

2. Valuation and Knowledge

In certain judgment tasks, the weight and value parameters can seemingly be considered as givens. For example, in judging the likableness of a person described by common trait adjectives, no thought process seems necessary to get the values of the adjectives. They have already been learned and need only be retrieved from storage.

However, many, if not most, judgments would seem to require a chain or net of thought to get the stimulus values. In stimulus interactions, for example, the effective values of each stimulus will depend specifically on the other stimuli that are present. Since the number of such stimulus combinations is virtually unlimited, it seems unlikely that the appropriate response or the stimulus values are located in a passive memory store. In general, they cannot have been learned beforehand, but instead must be computed on the spot.

In a very real sense, therefore, people do not know their own minds. Instead, they are continuously making them up. Knowledge and belief are not static memories but typically involve active, momentary cognitive processing. In a computer analogy, both data storage and computational subroutines are needed for judgment. Two aspects of this analogy need comment.

First, valuation subroutines are necessary in a variety of different conditions. In person perception, for example, discounting of inconsistent or redundant information has received considerable study (e.g., Sections III,D,3, III,F,2; Anderson, 1972a). Lopes' expectancy–discrepancy model (Section III,D,6) illustrates a somewhat different kind of stimulus interaction. Somewhat less interactive in nature is the task in Mills and Jellison (Section III,A,1) in which the force model governs the valuation of the weight parameter that is then operative in the attitude change. Further discussion of valuation operations is given in Anderson and Lopes (1973), who consider judgments of various adjective–noun combinations. In all these cases, the integration model provides a useful but insufficient hold on the problem. More detailed process analysis is desirable.

Second, information search will be necessary in general. In many experiments, this problem is effectively avoided by restricting the judgment task, and by presenting the effective stimuli experimentally. In general, however, that is not possible. In many decisions, for example, a choice among several courses of action will require envisaging, evaluating, and integrating the various imagined consequences of each course of action (Anderson, 1973d). Additional external information may be sought out, of course, but typically some sort of internal scenario will be needed for each course of action.

This same view applies to attitudes and beliefs. Certain salient beliefs will no doubt be stored as data. But in many cases a person asked about his attitude toward some entity has to stop and think. Presumably, he is engaged in searching for, evaluating, and integrating stored data information that bears on the judgment in question. In such cases, therefore, it can be misleading to say that the person has such and such an attitude, since he is, in effect, constructing it on the spot. This view, it should be noted, implies that the observed attitude will be somewhat variable, since it will also be affected by external stimulus information that happens to prevail on any given occasion.

This view has certain affinities with that of Bem (1967) and others that people infer their beliefs from their behavior (Section III,A). In the present view, such inferences fall under the general principle of information integration. The behavior, or strictly its internal representation, constitutes one piece of information that can be integrated in with other information such as the initial attitude, other internal stimuli (Kaplan & Anderson, 1973), and stimuli presented by the experimenter. According to the averaging model, the role of the behavior per se should be strongest when the absolute weights of the other pieces of information are small.

The information integration view is also consistent with the means–ends formulation used by Peak (1955) and by Rosenberg (1960). These investigators used an additive or summation model which Fishbein (e.g., 1967) has attempted to develop in a more quantitative fashion. Extensive evidence has ruled out the summation model in favor of an averaging model (Section II,B,5; Anderson, 1971a, p. 192). However, the basic conception that attitude can be represented as an integrated resultant of weighted values remains valid within averaging theory.

The concept of knowledge, as can be seen, has a complex structure from the integration-theoretical view. Knowledge consists only in small part of stored data, or even of subroutines for retrieving from storage. More important are the dynamic judgmental processes, including the subroutines for evaluating and integrating the information. Much the same view has been used in various philosophies of education, of course, but it is interesting to see it arise from psychological theory.

3. Response Structure

Related to the valuation problem is the fact that the same set of stimuli may be judged on a variety of different dimensions. This is especially true in person perception as noted in Section IV,D,4. In terms of integration theory, the weight and value parameters of a given stimulus will depend on the dimension of judgment. Conversely, different integrated resultants may be obtained for different dimensions of response. A one-dimensional approach may not provide an adequate representation of the cognitive structure (Anderson, 1971a, p. 173).

The usefulness of obtaining response measures on more than one dimension has appeared in several articles discussed above (Mills & Jellison, Section III,A,1; Anderson & Butzin, Section III,B,2; Anderson &

Hubert, Section III,F,3; Himmelfarb & Charash, Section III,F,8). In each case, different information was provided by the different response measures.

A similar analysis is given by Anderson and Lopes (1973) in a study of adjective–noun combinations in person perception. As that article makes clear, the generalized evaluative dimension provided by the semantic differential is an agglomerate of three distinct dimensions that should be kept separate. Other articles that give a more detailed analysis of cognitive structure include those of Cohen and Schümer (1968), Edwards and Ostrom (1971), Hamilton and Huffman (1971), Posavac and McKillip (1972), and Rywick (1971). However, the most extensive work on this question has been done in connection with implicit personality theories as noted next.

4. Implicit Personality Theories

The so-called "implicit personality theories" refer to the network of relations among personality traits. Given some traits of a stimulus person, inferences are readily made about other traits of the same person. The most commonly studied case is that of judgments of likableness, of course. However, other dimensions of judgment can be studied in exactly the same manner. The network of such interrelations clearly reflects a cognitive structure about the nature of people in general. Most attempts to study this cognitive network have relied, naturally enough, on some form of multidimensional analysis (see Hastorf, Schneider, & Polefka, 1970; Rosenberg & Sedlak, 1972). Despite their interest and potential usefulness, these analyses are descriptive and static and give limited information about process. For example, most discussions of implicit personality theories seem to assume that the network of trait interrelations already exists and is present for study. In many cases, however, one would expect that a train of inferential thought would be needed to produce a judgment. It is pertinent, therefore, to note three main bases of the network of interrelations.

The first base is semantic. A person described as *honest* will be seen as *sincere* or *dependable* simply because of the relations among the verbal meanings of these terms. The relation to person perception may be merely fortuitous, a reflection of the fact that these terms apply only to people. The second base is judgmental. A person described as *warm* may be seen as *honest* because of a mediating judgment of likableness. This halo-type effect could be substantial despite a probable near-zero correlation in the real world. The final base is experiential. Traits may be seen as correlated because experience has shown them to be correlated in fact. It deserves to be doubted that experience plays a large role. People do not come with trait labels on them, and the evidence (Mischel, 1968) indicates that real-world correlations are quite small. Work on partial reinforcement and probability learning suggests that such correlations would never be learned on an actuarial basis. Implicit personality theory, therefore, may be largely a judgmental and linguistic matter.

5. Psycholinguistics

In many applications, social judgment merges into psycholinguistics, as was just illustrated in the discussion of implicit personality theories. Several other instances have been covered in earlier sections, the most notable being the change-of-meaning question (Section III,F). The influence of communicational constraints was important in the discussions of the work of Abelson and Kanouse (Section III,E,1), and of McArthur (Section III,B,3). In both cases, the conceptual analysis seemed to require explicit allowance for decision criteria established by social expectations. Other relations between psycholinguistics and person perception are discussed in Sections II,C,3, III,B,2, and III,F,3, in Anderson and Lopes (1973), and in Oden and Anderson (1974).

Information integration theory may have a special value in the study of certain problems in psycholinguistics. Implicit personality theory provides an illustration. The main change from previous experiments on person perception would be to obtain judgments along several trait dimensions at once. Each such trait defines its own dimension of judgment, and each judgment reflects an integration of several informational stimuli. Each informational stimulus has a weight and a scale value along each dimension of judgment, and these may, at least in principle, be evaluated by applying the averaging model with differential weighting. Theoretically, the resultant matrix of weights and values represents the effective network of trait interrelations. It would correspond to the intercorrelation or similarity matrices ordinarily used in the multidimensional analyses of implicit personality theory.

A unique aspect of this approach is that two parameters, w and s, are required to represent the relation between two traits. In contrast, multidimensional analyses have typically used a single parameter for that purpose. The w-s representation is more complex, of course, and it is unclear how it might be handled. Nevertheless, the evidence for the averaging hypothesis suggests that the w-s representation is psychologically valid. Accordingly, it would seem desirable, if not necessary, to employ it in the study of implicit personality theory, as well as in the semantic base of general judgment theory.

REFERENCES

Abelson, R. P., & Kanouse, D. E. Subjective acceptance of verbal generalizations. In S. Feldman (Ed.), *Cognitive consistency.* New York: Academic Press, 1966.

Adams, J. S. Inequity in social exchange. In L. Berkowitz (Ed.), *Advances in experimental social psychology,* Vol. 2. New York: Academic Press, 1965.

Anderson, N. H. Test of a model for opinion change. *Journal of Abnormal and Social Psychology,* 1959, **59**, 371–381.

Anderson, N. H. Scales and statistics: parametric and nonparametric. *Psychological Bulletin,* 1961, **58**, 305–316.

Anderson, N. H. Application of an additive model to impression formation. *Science,* 1962, **138**, 817–818. (a)

Anderson, N. H. On the quantification of Miller's conflict theory. *Psychological Review,* 1962, **69**, 400–414. (b)

Anderson, N. H. Test of a model for number-averaging behavior. *Psychonomic Science,* 1964, **1**, 191–192.

Anderson, N. H. Averaging versus adding as a stimulus-combination rule in impression formation. *Journal of Experimental Psychology,* 1965, **70**, 394–400. (a)

Anderson, N. H. Primacy effects in personality impression formation using a generalized order effect paradigm. *Journal of Personality and Social Psychology,* 1965, **2**, 1–9. (b)

Anderson, N. H. Averaging model analysis of set size effect in impression formation. *Journal of Experimental Psychology,* 1967, **75**, 158–165. (a)

Anderson, N. H. Test of averaging, balance, and congruity theories. Paper presented at summer conference on mathematical models in social psychology. Kent, Connecticut, 1967. (b)

Anderson, N. H. A simple model for information integration. In R. P. Abelson, E. Aronson, W. J. McGuire, T. M. Newcomb, M. J. Rosenberg, & P. H. Tannenbaum (Eds.), *Theories of cognitive consistency: A sourcebook.* Chicago: Rand McNally, 1968. (a)

Anderson, N. H. Likableness ratings of 555 personality-trait words. *Journal of Personality and Social Psychology,* 1968, **9**, 272–279. (b)

Anderson, N. H. Application of a linear-serial model to a personality-impression task using serial presentation. *Journal of Personality and Social Psychology,* 1968, **10**, 354–362. (c)

Anderson, N. H. Averaging of space and number stimuli with simultaneous presentation. *Journal of Experimental Psychology,* 1968, **77**, 383–392. (d)

Anderson, N. H. Comment on "An analysis-of-variance model for the assessment of configural cue utilization in clinical judgment." *Psychological Bulletin,* 1969, **72**, 63–65. (a)

Anderson, N. H. Application of a model for numerical response to a probability learning situation. *Journal of Experimental Psychology,* 1969, **80**, 19–27. (b)

Anderson, N. H. Functional measurement and psychophysical judgment. *Psychological Review,* 1970, **77**, 153–170. (a)

Anderson, N. H. Averaging model applied to the size-weight illusion. *Perception & Psychophysics,* 1970, **8**, 1–4. (b)

Anderson, N. H. Integration theory and attitude change. *Psychological Review,* 1971, **78**, 171–206. (a)

Anderson, N. H. Two more tests against change of meaning in adjective combinations. *Journal of Verbal Learning and Verbal Behavior*, 1971, **10**, 75–85. (b)

Anderson, N. H. Test of adaptation-level theory as an explanation of a recency effect in psychophysical integration. *Journal of Experimental Psychology*, 1971, **87**, 57–63. (c)

Anderson, N. H. Looking for configurality in clinical judgment. *Psychological Bulletin*, 1972, **78**, 93–102. (a)

Anderson, N. H. Cross-task validation of functional measurement. *Perception & Psychophysics*, 1972, **12**, 389–395. (b)

Anderson, N. H. Serial position curves in impression formation. *Journal of Experimental Psychology*, 1973, **97**, 8–12. (a)

Anderson, N. H. Comment on the articles of Hodges, and of Schonemann, Cafferty, and Rotton. *Psychological Review*, 1973, **80**, 88–92. (b)

Anderson, N. H. Functional measurement of social desirability. *Sociometry*, 1973, **36**, 89–98. (c)

Anderson, N. H. Information integration theory: A brief survey. In D. H. Krantz, R. C. Atkinson, R. D. Luce, & P. Suppes (Eds.), *Contemporary developments in mathematical psychology*. San Francisco: Freeman, 1974. (d)

Anderson, N. H. Algebraic models in perception. In E. C. Carterette & M. P. Friedman (Eds.), *Handbook of perception*, Vol. 2. New York: Academic Press, 1973. (e)

Anderson, N. H. Information integration theory applied to attitudes about U. S. Presidents. *Journal of Educational Psychology*, 1973, **64**, 1–8. (f)

Anderson, N. H., & Barrios, A. A. Primacy effects in personality impression formation. *Journal of Abnormal and Social Psychology*, 1961, **63**, 346–350.

Anderson, N. H., & Butzin, C. A. Performance = Motivation × Ability: An integration-theoretical analysis. *Journal of Personality and Social Psychology*, 1974, in press.

Anderson, N. H., & Farkas, A. J. New light on order effects in attitude change. *Journal of Personality and Social Psychology*, 1973, in press.

Anderson, N. H., & Hovland, C. I. The representation of order effects in communication research. In C. I. Hovland (Ed.), *The order of presentation in persuasion*. New Haven: Yale University Press, 1957.

Anderson, N. H., & Hubert, S. Effects of concomitant verbal recall on order effects in personality impression formation. *Journal of Verbal Learning and Verbal Behavior*, 1963, **2**, 379–391.

Anderson, N. H., & Jacobson, A. Effect of stimulus inconsistency and discounting instructions in personality impression formation. *Journal of Personality and Social Psychology*, 1965, **2**, 531–539.

Anderson, N. H., & Lampel, A. K. Effect of context on ratings of personality traits. *Psychonomic Science*, 1965, **3**, 433–434.

Anderson, N. H., Lindner, R., & Lopes, L. L. Integration theory applied to judgments of groups. *Journal of Personality and Social Psychology*, 1973, **26**, 400–408.

Anderson, N. H., & Lopes, L. L. Some psycholinguistic aspects of person perception. *Memory and Cognition*, 1973, in press.

Anderson, N. H., Sawyers, B. K., & Farkas, A. J. President paragraphs. *Behavior Research Methods and Instrumentation*, 1972, **4**, 177–192.

Anderson, N. H., & Shanteau, J. C. Information integration in risky decision making. *Journal of Experimental Psychology*, 1970, **84**, 441–451.

Anderson, N. H., & Weiss, D. J. Test of a multiplying model for estimated area of rectangles. *American Journal of Psychology*, 1971, **84**, 543–548.

Anderson, N. H., & Whalen, R. E. Likelihood judgments and sequential effects in a two-choice probability learning situation. *Journal of Experimental Psychology,* 1960, **60,** 111–120.

Asch, S. E. Forming impressions of personality. *Journal of Abnormal and Social Psychology,* 1946, **41,** 258–290.

Atkinson, J. W. *An introduction to motivation.* Princeton, N. J.: Van Nostrand, 1964.

Atkinson, J. W., & Feather, N. T. (Eds.) *A theory of achievement motivation.* New York: Wiley, 1966.

Bem, D. J. Self-perception: An alternative interpretation of cognitive dissonance phenomena. *Psychological Review,* 1967, **74,** 183–200.

Birnbaum, M. H. Morality judgments: Tests of an averaging model. *Journal of Experimental Psychology,* 1972, **93,** 35–42. (a)

Birnbaum, M. H. The nonadditivity of impressions. Unpublished PhD dissertation, University of California, Los Angeles, 1972. (b)

Birnbaum, M. H. The Devil rides again: Correlation as an index of fit. *Psychological Bulletin,* 1973, **79,** 239–242.

Birnbaum, M. H., & Veit, C. T. Scale convergence as a criterion for rescaling: Information integration with difference, ratio, and averaging tasks. *Perception & Psychophysics,* 1973, in press.

Briscoe, M. E., Woodyard, H. D., & Shaw, M. E. Personality impression change as a function of the favorableness of first impressions. *Journal of Personality,* 1967, **35,** 343–357.

Brunswik, E. *Perception and the representative design of psychological experiments.* Berkeley, Calif.: University of California Press, 1956.

Butzin, C. A., & Anderson, N. H. Functional measurement of children's judgments. *Child Development,* 1973, in press.

Byrne, D. *The attraction paradigm.* New York: Academic Press, 1971.

Campbell, D. T., Lewis, N. A., & Hunt, W. A. Context effects with judgmental language that is absolute, extensive, and extra-experimentally anchored. *Journal of Experimental Psychology,* 1958, **55,** 220–228.

Chandler, J. P. STEPIT—Finds local minima of a smooth function of several parameters. *Behavioral Science,* 1969, **14,** 81–82.

Cliff, N. Adverbs as multipliers. *Psychological Review,* 1959, **66,** 27–44.

Cohen, J. *Statistical power analysis for the behavioral sciences.* New York: Academic Press, 1969.

Cohen, R., & Schümer, R. Eine Untersuchung zur sozialen Urteilsbildung. I. Die Verarbeitung von Informationen unterschiedlicher Konsonanz. *Archiv für die gesamte Psychologie,* 1968, **120,** 151–179.

Collins, B. E., & Raven, B. H. Group structure. In G. Lindzey & E. Aronson (Eds.), *The handbook of social psychology,* Vol. 4 (2nd ed.). Reading, Mass.: Addison-Wesley, 1969.

Coombs, C. H. Thurstone's measurement of social values revisited forty years later. *Journal of Personality and Social Psychology,* 1967, **6,** 85–91.

Dawes, R. M., Singer, D., & Lemons, F. An experimental analysis of the contrast effect and its implications for intergroup communication and the indirect assessment of attitude. *Journal of Personality and Social Psychology,* 1972, **21,** 281–295.

DeSoto, C. B., & Kuethe, J. L. Subjective probabilities of interpersonal relationships. *Journal of Abnormal and Social Psychology,* 1959, **59,** 290–294.

DeSwart, J. H. Opinion revision and the influence of corresponding and conflicting adjectives. *Acta Psychologica,* 1971, **35,** 198–206.

Edwards, J. D., & Ostrom, T. M. Cognitive structure of neutral attitudes. *Journal of Experimental Social Psychology*, 1971, **7**, 36–47.

Edwards, W. Conservatism in human information processing. In B. Kleinmuntz (Ed.), *Formal representation of human judgment*. New York: Wiley, 1968.

Farkas, A. J., & Anderson, N. H. Inoculation theory and integration theory as explanations of the "paper tiger" effect. Unpublished paper, 1973.

Feather, N. T. Valence of outcome and expectation of success in relation to task difficulty and perceived locus of control. *Journal of Personality and Social Psychology*, 1967, **7**, 372–386.

Festinger, L., & Carlsmith, J. M. Cognitive consequences of forced compliance. *Journal of Abnormal and Social Psychology*, 1959, **58**, 203–210.

Fishbein, M. A behavior theory approach to the relations between beliefs about an object and the attitude toward the object. In M. Fishbein (Ed.), *Readings in attitude theory and measurement*. New York: Wiley, 1967.

Friedman, M. P., Carterette, E. C., & Anderson, N. H. Long-term probability learning with a random schedule of reinforcement. *Journal of Experimental Psychology*, 1968, **78**, 442–455.

Gilson, C., & Abelson, R. P. The subjective use of inductive evidence. *Journal of Personality and Social Psychology*, 1965, **2**, 301–310.

Goldberg, L. R. Simple models or simple processes? Some research on clinical judgments. *American Psychologist*, 1968, **23**, 483–496.

Gollob, H. F., Rossman, B. B., & Abelson, R. P. Social inference as a function of the number of instances and consistency of information presented. *Journal of Personality and Social Psychology*, 1973, **27**, 19–33.

Green, D. M., & Swets, J. A. *Signal detection theory and psychophysics*. New York: Wiley, 1966.

Hamilton, D. L., & Huffman, L. J. Generality of impression-formation processes for evaluative and nonevaluative judgments. *Journal of Personality and Social Psychology*, 1971, **20**, 200–207.

Hammond, K. R. (Ed.) *The psychology of Egon Brunswik*. New York: Holt, 1966.

Hastorf, A. H., Schneider, D. J., & Polefka, J. *Person perception*. Reading, Mass.: Addison-Wesley, 1970.

Heider, F. *The psychology of interpersonal relations*. New York: Wiley, 1958.

Helson, H. *Adaptation-level theory*. New York: Harper & Row, 1964.

Hendrick, C. Averaging vs summation in impression formation. *Perceptual and Motor Skills*, 1968, **27**, 1295–1302.

Hendrick, C. Effects of salience of stimulus inconsistency on impression formation. *Journal of Personality and Social Psychology*, 1972, **22**, 219–222.

Hendrick, C., & Costantini, A. F. Effects of varying trait inconsistency and response requirements on the primacy effect in impression formation. *Journal of Personality and Social Psychology*, 1970, **15**, 158–164.

Hilgard, E. R. *Theories of learning*. (2nd ed.) New York: Appleton, 1956.

Himmelfarb, S. Integration and attribution theories in personality impression formation. *Journal of Personality and Social Psychology*, 1972, **23**, 309–313.

Himmelfarb, S. "Resistance" to persuasion induced by information integration. In S. Himmelfarb & A. H. Eagly (Eds.), *Readings in attitude change*. New York: Wiley, 1973.

Himmelfarb, S., & Anderson, N. H. Integration theory analysis of opinion attribution. Unpublished paper, 1971.

Himmelfarb, S., & Charash, B. Unpublished paper, 1972.

Himmelfarb, S., & Senn, D. J. Forming impressions of social class: Two tests of an averaging model. *Journal of Personality and Social Psychology*, 1969, **12**, 38–51.

Hodges, B. H. Adding and averaging models for information integration. *Psychological Review*, 1973, **80**, 80–84.

Insko, C. A. *Theories of attitude change.* New York: Appleton, 1967.

Jones, E. E., & Davis, K. E. From acts to dispositions: The attribution process in person perception. In L. Berkowitz (Ed.), *Advances in experimental social psychology*, Vol. 2. New York: Academic Press, 1965.

Jones, E. E., Davis, K. E., & Gergen, K. J. Role playing variations and their informational value for person perception. *Journal of Abnormal and Social Psychology*, 1961, **63**, 302–310.

Jones, E. E., & Goethals, G. R. *Order effects in impression formation: Attribution context and the nature of the entity.* New York: General Learning Press, 1971.

Jones, E. E., & Harris, V. A. The attribution of attitudes. *Journal of Experimental Social Psychology*, 1967, **3**, 1–24.

Jones, E. E., Rock, L., Shaver, K. G., Goethals, G. R., & Ward, L. M. Pattern of performance and ability attribution: An unexpected primacy effect. *Journal of Personality and Social Psychology*, 1968, **10**, 317–340.

Jones, E. E., Worchel, S., Goethals, G. R., & Grumet, J. F. Prior expectancy and behavioral extremity as determinants of attitude attribution. *Journal of Experimental Social Psychology*, 1971, **7**, 59–80.

Kanouse, D. E. *Language, labeling, and attribution.* New York: General Learning Press, 1971.

Kanouse, D. E., & Abelson, R. P. Language variables affecting the persuasiveness of simple communications. *Journal of Personality and Social Psychology*, 1967, **7**, 158–163.

Kaplan, M. F. Forming impressions of personality: The effect of the initial impression. *Psychonomic Science*, 1970, **18**, 255–256.

Kaplan, M. F. Dispositional effects and the weight of information in impression formation. *Journal of Personality and Social Psychology*, 1971, **18**, 279–284. (a)

Kaplan, M. F. Context effects in impression formation: The weighted average versus the meaning-change formulation. *Journal of Personality and Social Psychology*, 1971, **19**, 92–99. (b)

Kaplan, M. F., & Anderson, N. H. Information integration theory and reinforcement theory as approaches to interpersonal attraction. *Journal of Personality and Social Psychology*, 1973, in press. (a)

Kaplan, M. F., & Anderson, N. H. Comment on "When research paradigms converge: Confrontation or integration?" *Journal of Personality and Social Psychology*, 1973, in press. (b)

Kaplan, M. F., & Kemmerick, G. D. Jury judgment as information integration. Paper presented at Psychonomic Society, St. Louis, November, 1972.

Karabenick, S. A. Valence of success and failure as a function of achievement motives and locus of control. *Journal of Personality and Social Psychology*, 1972, **21**, 101–110.

Kelley, H. H. Attribution theory in social psychology. In D. Levine (Ed.), *Nebraska Symposium on Motivation*. Lincoln, Nebraska: University of Nebraska Press, 1967.

Kelley, H. H. *Attribution in social interaction.* New York: General Learning Press, 1971.

Kelley, H. H. *Causal schemata and the attribution process.* New York: General Learning Press, 1972.

Kepka, E. J., & Brickman, P. Consistency versus discrepancy as clues in the attribution of intelligence and motivation. *Journal of Personality and Social Psychology,* 1971, **20,** 223–229.

Kiesler, C. A., Nisbett, R. E., & Zanna, M. P. On inferring one's beliefs from one's behavior. *Journal of Personality and Social Psychology,* 1969, **11,** 321–327.

Kruglanski, A. W. Attributing trustworthiness in supervisor-worker relations. *Journal of Experimental Social Psychology,* 1970, **6,** 214–232.

Lampel, A. K., & Anderson, N. H. Combining visual and verbal information in an impression-formation task. *Journal of Personality and Social Psychology,* 1968, **9,** 1–6.

Leon, M., & Anderson, N. H. A ratio rule from integration theory applied to inference judgments. *Journal of Experimental Psychology,* 1973, in press.

Leon, M., Oden, G. C., & Anderson, N. H. Functional measurement of social values. *Journal of Personality and Social Psychology,* 1973, in press.

Leventhal, G. S., & Michaels, J. W. Locus of cause and equity motivation as determinants of reward allocation. *Journal of Personality and Social Psychology,* 1971, **17,** 229–235.

Levin, I. P., Schmidt, C. F., & Norman, K. L. Person preference choices: Tests of a subtractive averaging model. *Journal of Experimental Psychology,* 1971, **90,** 258–261.

Levy, L. H., & Richter, M. L. Impressions of groups as a function of the stimulus values of their individual members. *Journal of Abnormal and Social Psychology,* 1963, **67,** 349–354.

Lindner, R. Associative and dissociative bonds in personality impression formation. In R. G. Smith, *Speech-communication: Theory and models.* New York: Harper, 1970.

Lindner, R. Congruity, balance and information integration in personality impressions. Unpublished PhD dissertation, Indiana University, 1971.

Lopes, L. L. A unified integration model for "Prior expectancy and behavioral extremity as determinants of attitude attribution." *Journal of Experimental Social Psychology,* 1972, **8,** 156–160.

Lovie, A. D., & Davies, A. D. M. An application of Bayes' theorem to person perception. *Acta Psychologica,* 1970, **34,** 322–327.

Massaro, D. W., & Anderson, N. H. Judgmental model of the Ebbinghaus illusion. *Journal of Experimental Psychology,* 1971, **89,** 147–151.

McArthur, L. A. The how and what of why: Some determinants and consequences of causal attribution. *Journal of Personality and Social Psychology,* 1972, **22,** 171–193.

McGuire, W. J. A syllogistic analysis of cognitive relationships. In M. J. Rosenberg et al., *Attitude organization and change.* New Haven: Yale University Press, 1960.

McGuire, W. J. Theory of the structure of human thought. In R. P. Abelson, E. Aronson, W. J. McGuire, T. M. Newcomb, M. J. Rosenberg, & P. H. Tannenbaum (Eds.), *Theories of cognitive consistency: A sourcebook.* Chicago: Rand McNally, 1968.

McGuire, W. J. The nature of attitudes and attitude change. In G. Lindzey & E. Aronson (Eds.), *The handbook of social psychology,* Vol. 3 (2nd ed.). Reading, Mass.: Addison-Wesley, 1969.

McNeel, S. P., & Messick, D. M. A Bayesian analysis of subjective probabilities of interpersonal relationships. *Acta Psychologica,* 1970, **34,** 311–321.

Meehl, P. E. *Clinical versus statistical prediction.* Minneapolis: University of Minnesota Press, 1954.

Mills, J., & Jellison, J. M. Effect on opinion change of how desirable the communication is to the audience the communicator addressed. *Journal of Personality and Social Psychology,* 1967, **6,** 98–101.

Mischel, W. *Personality and assessment.* New York: Wiley, 1968.

Nisbett, R. E., & Valins, S. *Perceiving the causes of one's own behavior.* New York: General Learning Press, 1971.

Oden, G. C., & Anderson, N. H. Differential weighting in integration theory. *Journal of Experimental Psychology,* 1971, **89,** 152–161.

Oden, G. C., & Anderson, N. H. Integration of semantic constraints. *Journal of Verbal Learning and Verbal Behavior,* 1974, in press.

Peak, H. Attitude and motivation. *Nebraska Symposium on Motivation,* 1955, **3,** 149–189.

Peterson, C. R., & Beach, L. R. Man as an intuitive statistician. *Psychological Bulletin,* 1967, **68,** 29–46.

Posavac, E. J., & McKillip, J. The set size effect and confidence in reports of behavioral intentions. *Psychonomic Science,* 1972, **29,** 94–96.

Prokasy, W. F. Do *D* and *H* multiply to determine performance in human conditioning? *Psychological Bulletin,* 1967, **67,** 368–377.

Pruitt, D. G. Reciprocity and credit building in a laboratory dyad. *Journal of Personality and Social Psychology,* 1968, **8,** 143–147.

Rhine, R. J., & Severance, L. J. Ego-involvement, discrepancy, source credibility, and attitude change. *Journal of Personality and Social Psychology,* 1970, **16,** 175–190.

Rosenberg, M. J. An analysis of affective-cognitive consistency. In M. J. Rosenberg et al., *Attitude organization and change.* New Haven: Yale University Press, 1960.

Rosenberg, S. Mathematical models of social behavior. In G. Lindzey & E. Aronson (Eds.), *The handbook of social psychology,* Vol. 1 (2nd ed.). Reading, Mass.: Addison-Wesley, 1968.

Rosenberg, S., & Sedlak, A. Structural representations of implicit personality theory. In L. Berkowitz (Ed.), *Advances in experimental social psychology,* Vol. 6. New York: Academic Press, 1972.

Rosnow, R. L., & Arms, R. L. Adding versus averaging as a stimulus-combination rule in forming impressions of groups. *Journal of Personality and Social Psychology,* 1968, **10,** 363–369.

Rywick, T. Primacy effects in impression formation as a function of type of impression. *Psychonomic Science,* 1971, **25,** 195–196.

Sawyers, B. K., & Anderson, N. H. Test of integration theory in attitude change. *Journal of Personality and Social Psychology,* 1971, **18,** 230–233.

Shanteau, J. C. An additive model for sequential decision making. *Journal of Experimental Psychology,* 1970, **85,** 181–191. (a)

Shanteau, J. C. Component processes in risky decision judgments. Unpublished PhD dissertation, University of California, San Diego, 1970. (b)

Shanteau, J. C. Descriptive versus normative models of sequential inference judgment. *Journal of Experimental Psychology,* 1972, **93,** 63–68.

Shanteau, J. C., & Anderson, N. H. Test of a conflict model for preference judgment. *Journal of Mathematical Psychology,* 1969, **6,** 312–325.

Shanteau, J. C., & Anderson, N. H. Integration theory applied to judgments of the value of information. *Journal of Experimental Psychology,* 1972, **92,** 266–275.

Sherif, M., & Hovland, C. I. *Social judgment.* New Haven, Conn.: Yale University Press, 1961.

Sidowski, J. B., & Anderson, N. H. Judgments of city-occupation combinations. *Psychonomic Science,* 1967, **7,** 279–280.

Sloan, L. R., & Ostrom, T. M. Amount of information and interpersonal judgment. *Journal of Personality and Social Psychology,* 1974, in press.

Slovic, P., & Lichtenstein, S. Comparison of Bayesian and regression approaches to the study of information processing in judgment. *Organizational Behavior and Human Performance,* 1971, **6,** 649–744.

Smith, R. G. *Speech-communication: Theory and models.* New York: Harper & Row, 1970.

Stewart, R. H. Effect of continuous responding on the order effect in personality impression formation. *Journal of Personality and Social Psychology,* 1965, **1,** 161–165.

Strickland, L. H. Surveillance and trust. *Journal of Personality,* 1958, **26,** 200–215.

Tagiuri, R. Person perception. In G. Lindzey and E. Aronson (Eds.), *The handbook of social psychology,* Vol. 3 (2nd ed.). Reading, Mass.: Addison-Wesley, 1969.

Takahashi, S. Effect of the context upon personality-impression formation. *Japanese Journal of Psychology,* 1971, **41,** 307–313.

Tesser, A. Differential weighting and directed meaning as explanations of primacy in impression formation. *Psychonomic Science,* 1968, **11,** 299–300.

Thibaut, J., & Ross, M. Commitment and experience as determinants of assimilation and contrast. *Journal of Personality and Social Psychology,* 1969, **13,** 322–329.

Thurstone, L. L. The method of paired comparisons for social values. *Journal of Abnormal and Social Psychology,* 1927, **21,** 384–400.

Thurstone, L. L. Attitudes can be measured. *American Journal of Sociology,* 1928, **33,** 529–554. Reprinted in L. L. Thurstone, *The measurement of values.* Chicago: University of Chicago Press, 1959.

Upshaw, H. S. The personal reference scale: An approach to social judgment. In L. Berkowitz (Ed.), *Advances in experimental social psychology,* Vol. 4. New York: Academic Press, 1969.

Ward, L. M. Category judgments of loudnesses in the absence of an experimenter-induced identification function: sequential effects and power-function fit. *Journal of Experimental Psychology,* 1972, **94,** 179–184.

Warr, P. B., & Knapper, C. *The perception of people and events.* New York: Wiley, 1968.

Weiner, B. *Theories of motivation.* Chicago: Markham, 1972.

Weiner, B., & Kukla, A. An attributional analysis of achievement motivation. *Journal of Personality and Social Psychology,* 1970, **15,** 1–20.

Weiss, D. J., & Anderson, N. H. Subjective averaging of length with serial presentation. *Journal of Experimental Psychology,* 1969, **82,** 52–63.

Weiss, W. Scale judgments of triplets of opinion statements. *Journal of Abnormal and Social Psychology,* 1963, **66,** 471–479.

Willis, R. H. Stimulus pooling and social perception. *Journal of Abnormal and Social Psychology,* 1960, **60,** 365–373.

Wyer, R. S. Quantitative prediction of belief and opinion change: A further test of a subjective probability model. *Journal of Personality and Social Psychology,* 1970, **16,** 559–570.

Wyer, R. S. Test of a subjective probability model of social evaluation processes. *Journal of Personality and Social Psychology,* 1972, **22,** 279–286.

Wyer, R. S., & Goldberg, L. A probabilistic analysis of the relationships among beliefs and attitudes. *Psychological Review,* 1970, **77,** 100–120.

Wyer, R. S., & Watson, S. F. Context effects in impression formation. *Journal of Personality and Social Psychology,* 1969, **12,** 22–33.

Zajonc, R. B. Cognitive theories in social psychology. In G. Lindzey & E. Aronson (Eds.), *The handbook of social psychology,* Vol. 1 (2nd ed.). Reading, Mass.: Addison-Wesley, 1968.

Zander, A., Fuller, R., & Armstrong, W. Attributed pride or shame in group and self. *Journal of Personality and Social Psychology,* 1972, **23,** 346–352.

Progress in Cognitive Algebra

Norman H. Anderson
UNIVERSITY OF CALIFORNIA,
SAN DIEGO

The following supplement to the chapter by Anderson (1974b) has two main sections. The first applies information integration theory to causal attribution. This discussion unifies and extends the earlier treatment and includes additional brief theoretical comparisons. The second main section gives a brief overview of progress on cognitive algebra since the cited chapter was written.

A. Causal Inference

1. INFERENCE AS INFORMATION INTEGRATION

a. Qualitative Attribution Model

Suppose that two causes, F and G, give rise to some action or event A. This causal dependence may be symbolized as

$$A = F * G. \tag{1a}$$

Here $*$ denotes a generalized integration operation, the exact nature of which is not of immediate concern. For certain purposes, it is only necessary that A be a monotone function of the two variables, F and G. This model may be called a *qualitative causal model,* useful for conceptual and directional predictions.

Cognitive Theories in Social Psychology

To illustrate qualitative predictions, suppose that the same action A occurs in two situations, indexed by subscripts 1 and 2. Thus, $A = F_1 * G_1 = F_2 * G_2$. Then, if $F_1 > F_2$, it follows that $G_1 < G_2$. This simple principle has been put to effective use by a number of investigators (e.g., see Sections III,A,1 and III,A,2). Similarly, the response patterns that Kelley (1972a) has called discounting and augmentation can be viewed as special cases of the qualitative model (Section II,A,1).

b. Forward and Inverse Inference

In forward inference, information is given about the causal forces, F and G in Eq. (1a). The problem is to infer something about the consequence, A. Forward inference is thus part of the general problem of prediction.

In inverse inference, information is given about the consequence, A, and the problem is to infer something about, say, the causal force, G. That can only be done if something is known or assumed about F. This problem of inverse inference can be schematized analogously to Eq. (1a) as:

$$G = A *' F. \tag{1b}$$

Inverse causal inference is central in attribution theory.

c. Two Illustrative Tasks

Two experimental tasks will be used for illustration. The first concerns the relations among judgments of performance, motivation, and ability (Section III,B,2). It has been found that

$$\text{Performance} = \text{Motivation} \times \text{Ability}, \tag{2a}$$
$$\text{Motivation} = \text{Performance} - \text{Ability}, \tag{2b}$$
$$\text{Ability} = \text{Performance} - \text{Motivation}. \tag{2c}$$

This trio of empirical relations illustrates not merely the pervasiveness of cognitive algebra but also its difference from mathematical algebra. Mathematical consistency would require either a plus sign in Eq. (2a) or a division sign in Eqs. (2b) and (2c). In general, therefore, forward and inverse inference, or Eq. (1a) and (1b), are not reversible.

In the second task, fear of animals depends on fearfulness of the person and frightfulness of the animal (Section III,B,3; Anderson, 1978):

$$\text{Fear} = \begin{cases} \text{Fearfulness} \times \text{Frightfulness}, & \text{(3a)} \\ \text{Motivation} \times \text{Valence}, & \text{(3b)} \\ \text{Person} \times \text{Environment}. & \text{(3c)} \end{cases}$$

2. First and Second Integration Problems

Two distinct integration problems are involved in causal inference. First, various information may be given about, say, the Motivation term in Eq. (2b). How does the person integrate this information in order to obtain the effective value of Motivation? This is the *first integration problem.*

Surprisingly, this first integration problem has been virtually ignored within the attribution area. However, it has been extensively studied in applications of integration theory to other areas. It may be expected, therefore, that the first integration problem will exhibit averaging processes, set–size effects, positive context effects, etc. (Anderson, 1974d).

The *second integration problem* concerns the nature of the inference model. This corresponds to determining the algebraic nature of $*$ for forward inference [Eq. (1a)] and of $*'$ for inverse inference [Eq. (1b)].

Three algebraic models for the second integration problem have shown promise in different situations. Most prominent to date is the multiplying model. In motivation theory, a multiplicative rule has long been rationalized on the idea that motivation acts as an energizer or amplifier of a basic capability factor. Since motivation or intention is a common type of causal attribution, multiplying models arise quite naturally in attribution theory, as in Eq. (2a) and (3). In addition, linear-type models have also appeared, as in the causal attributions of Eq. (2b) and (2c).

Recent studies have also suggested that the ratio model

$$A = \text{Force}_1/(\text{Force}_1 + \text{Force}_2) \tag{4}$$

may have wide applicability. This model, which can be derived from a general averaging theorem (Section B,1,g), would be expected to apply when there are two mutually exclusive causal forces. No tests have yet been conducted in social attribution, but the model has done well in the analogous Bayesian two-urn task (Leon & Anderson, 1974).

3. Distinctiveness, Consensus, and Consistency

Integration theory provides a straightforward analysis of the concepts of distinctiveness, consensus, and consistency used by Kelley (1972b). Consider Eq. (3c): Fear = Person × Environment. Distinctiveness, consensus, and consistency refer to different kinds of information; each has its effect on the Person or the Environment term of the model. These three concepts, therefore, relate directly to the first integration problem.

a. Distinctiveness

Distinctiveness information concerns past reactions of the person to similar environmental objects. Such information is obviously relevant to person characteristics. Theoretically, each such piece of information has a scale value and a weight along the relevant dimension, here the judged fearfulness of the person. This information, including base rate or initial impression (Section III,B,3), would be integrated in accord with averaging theory to determine the effective value of Person in Eq. (3c).

· b. Consensus

Consensus information concerns past reactions of other persons to the same environment object. That several other persons have been afraid of the animal, for example, is evidence for the frightfulness of the animal. Theoretically, this information is integrated by an averaging rule to determine the value of the Environment term in Eq. (3c).

c. Consistency

Consistency information concerns reactions of the same person to the same object in the past. It would seem (Section III,B,3,c) that such information should affect both Person and Environment terms of the qualitative model. If the person has already been afraid of this animal a number of times, that provides joint support for the hypotheses that the person is fearful and that the animal is frightening. Theoretically, therefore, consistency information has two scale values and two weights, one for each term of the model. This proposition can easily be tested by obtaining quantified judgments of the separate Person and Environment terms.

This analysis of consistency information shows a basic difference between integration theory and Kelley's formulation. Kelley has assumed that high consistency causes an increase in attributions to the person. But if consistency information can affect both Person and Environment, then it can, at least in principle, increase attributions to the environment and decrease attributions to the person. If the mailman was afraid of the dog (Section III,B,3), for example, that might suggest that the dog was agressive, rather than that the mailman was timid. As this example indicates, consistency is probably not a basic theoretical concept.

d. Averaging Hypothesis for Attribution

There is little evidence on the validity of the averaging hypothesis for the integration of distinctiveness, consensus, and consistency information. Indeed, the first integration problem has been largely overlooked in attribution theory. Orvis, Cunningham, and Kelley (1975) attempted to study inferences about missing information, but their methods were not adequate, not to say obsolete. The averaging assumption seems a sound generalization from integration theory. It can readily be tested using standard procedures and obtaining quantified judgments of the Person and Environment terms.

The present approach can allow for any kind of information, not merely Kelley's three types. For example, knowing whether the dog was loose or penned would have a definite bearing on the causal attribution. As this example illustrates, the restriction to distinctiveness, consensus, and consistency information is too narrow a base for theory construction.

4. INTEGRATION MODELS AS CAUSAL SCHEMAS

A model for causal attribution can be viewed as a representation of the person's causal world. Such integration models are analogous to Kelley's (1972b) causal schemas, but the two conceptualizations have basic differences. One such difference will be taken up here. The concepts of distinctiveness, consensus, and consistency appear as basic constructs in Kelley's formulation but not in the present approach, as already noted. Kelley's experimental study (Orvis, Cunningham, & Kelley, 1975) provides a basis for further comparison.

In this report, three specified patterns of high and low values of distinctiveness, consensus, and consistency information were taken as "causal schemata": "As such, the three patterns enter into the inferential process itself. Information is compared with them and is interpreted in terms of the pattern(s) with which it is consistent [p. 606]."

In Kelley's view, therefore, the HHH pattern, in which all three kinds of stimulus information have high value, constitutes one causal schema. This particular schema is said to lead to an environment attribution. Any given pattern of stimulus information is compared to this standard pattern and, to the degree that it is similar, it will lead to a similar attribution.

In the present theory, in contrast, the causal schema is the integration rule itself, not a single pattern of specific values of three kinds of stimulus information. Further, the attribution itself does not result from comparison with standard patterns of these three kinds of information, but from the second integration operation, augmented by communicational constraints.

5. COMMUNICATIONAL CONSTRAINTS ON ATTRIBUTIONS

Making an attribution involves a variety of processes. Valuation operations are needed to obtain the meanings or implications of each piece of information (Section IV,D). Integration operations are needed to combine these implications, as already outlined.

Associated with these valuation and integration operations is a set of factors that may be called communicational constraints. These may be illustrated by considering the canonical question of attribution theory, "Why did the person act that way?" Such questions frequently occur as requests for information, and the attribution is an answer. As an answer, it is constrained in various ways by the communicational context.

In the first place, the very format of an attribution question may tend to constrain the answer to certain response categories. "Why was the person afraid of the dog?" explicitly points to two causal factors, the person and the dog. Other questions such as "Why did the person write a bad paper?" also seem to set up a cultural hierarchy of answer categories, including motivation, ability, and extenuation. These answer categories may be reflected directly in the attribution model, as in the above equations.

Related to the answer categories is the concept of threshold criterion: A cause must have some minimal strength to be an adequate explanation. When one cause is below criterion and the other above criterion, no great problem arises. Choosing the stronger cause would generally be an adequate rule.

However, when both causes are weak or below criterion, a choice of one or the other is not satisfactory. Two obvious resolutions of this problem are to assume some unknown third causal force or to appeal to summation effects of the two given causes. On the other hand, when both causes are strong, a choice between them may also miscommunicate. One obvious resolution is to make a joint causal attribution. The results of McArthur (1972; see Section III,B,3) provide some support for this analysis.

Response to an attributional question will also be influenced by assumptions about what the questioner knows already (see, e.g., Sections III,B,3; III,E,1,b; Lindsay & Norman, 1977), as well as about what the questioner seeks to learn. If the animal in the preceding example was already understood to be dangerous, the attribution question would normally be understood as a request for some particular kind of information about the person.

One final communicational constraint is that of social demand. Some answers may be unacceptable because, for example, they would violate politeness norms. Other answers may be inadvisable because they could produce social or material loss. Thus, a teacher might hesitate to publicly attribute a student's poor performance to stupidity or bad upbringing.

The needed theoretical amplification of this process issue cannot be given here. However, this overview does serve to reemphasize the complex of cognitive processes that are involved in attributional judgments. Previous work on social attribution has to a surprising degree neglected the study of cognitive process and general theory (Section I,C). The present theory offers a unified approach to a number of problems of social attribution. It is hoped that it will help in the development of new directions in attribution theory.

6. Responsibility and Blaming

In a typical experiment on attribution of responsibility, an actor is involved in some unpleasant event, and the subject judges responsibility. An obvious informational model (Anderson, 1976c) is

$$\text{Blame} = \text{Intent} + \text{Consequence} - \text{Extenuation} - \text{Personal Goodness.} \tag{5}$$

This approach contrasts with previous formulations based on motivation.

According to Walster's (1966) self-protection hypothesis, the subject interprets the situation so as to avoid the unpleasant thought that similar events could befall himself. Assigning responsibility to chance implies a capricious, uncontrollable world. For self-protection, therefore, the person will attribute responsibility to the actor and also try to accentuate differences between the actor and himself. Both tendencies will be increased by a more severe event because that creates greater threat and greater need for self-protection.

According to Shaver's (1970) defensive attribution hypothesis, the subject will interpret the situation so as to reduce its threat. Threat may be reduced by attributing responsibility to the actor and denying personal similarity, just as with Walster's self-protection hypothesis.

But when personal similarity cannot be denied, then responsibility will be assigned to chance because that would avoid blame if the person found himself in a similar situation.

The information-integration approach seeks first for an explanation in terms of informational factors rather than in terms of indirect threats to the self. Thus, the more similar actor is seen as a more likable person (Byrne, 1971; Kaplan & Anderson, 1973). The blame model, Eq. (5), implies that integration of this information reduces blame, in accord with the data (see Brooks & Doob, 1975).

Severity of event affects the Consequence term in the model: Greater blame is assigned when greater harm occurs. However, this Consequence term also requires a relevance weight parameter that is nonzero to the degree that the actor is lax, careless, or otherwise culpable, but zero when the event is an act of God, beyond the actor's control. This weighting interpretation accounts for the lack of effect of event seriousness in Walster's (1967) experiment, in which the event was an act either of God or of the U.S. Government.

An informational view also seems to account for most results of Chaikin and Darley (1973). Subjects role-played supervisors or workers and are accordingly assumed to evaluate information from their respective role-views. The primitive blaming postulate then implies that the subject–supervisors will tend to blame chance or the equipment, whereas subject–workers will tend to blame the supervisors. And by the weighting argument of the previous paragraph, both classes of subjects will assign less chance responsibility when the consequences are more severe. Other results obtained by Chaikin and Darley also seem more readily interpretable in informational terms than in their motivational framework. Similar informational analyses may account for Lerner's (1971) "just world" formulation (see also Anderson, 1976c; Brewer, 1977; Godfrey & Lowe, 1975).

7. Self-Perception as Information Integration

Self-perception can be viewed within the same theoretical framework as other perception (Anderson, 1976c). Indeed, most perception is self-perception. Loudness and pain, for example, are as much properties of the self as are ability and sorrow; and all typically involve stimulus integration. The same holds true for the formation and development of social attitudes and self-attributions for which the integration may be viewed as informational learning over time (Section III,F; Anderson, 1974d, Section 6). Even a judgment of one's present attitude typically requires integration of internal information, according to the constructivist view (Section IV,D,2; Anderson, 1978).

The present approach to self-perception may be contrasted with that of Bem (1972). One major difference is that motivational constructs are important to the present theory, whereas Bem explicitly disallows them. A second difference is that Bem's basic self-perception postulate has been severely qualified to state that self-attitudes and emotions are "partially" inferred from observations of one's own behavior when internal cues are "weak, ambiguous, or uninterpretable [p. 2]." By this qualification, Bem puts his theory outside the realm of strong or unambiguous internal cues that play a vital role in the integration-theoretical analysis.

Perhaps the major difference is that integration theory is centrally concerned with underlying structures, processes, and internal states. These are explicitly disallowed and have only a Cinderella role in Bem's behavioristic approach. From the present standpoint, therefore, Bem's theory ceases before the basic theoretical problems have been reached.

8. BAYESIAN FORMULATION

Besides information integration theory, only the Bayesian approach from mathematical statistics has attempted a general attack on the second integration problem of inverse inference. These two approaches have many similarities. Both are concerned with integration of evidence to form or change beliefs. Both also make extensive use of algebraic models. Thus, the ratio model of Eq. (4) is analogous to a ratio model from Bayesian theory.

Of course, the two approaches have fundamental differences. Integration theory is concerned with psychological processes and actual behavior. Bayesian theory, as part of mathematical statistics, prescribes statistically optimal behavior. Not surprisingly, people are far from optimal, and Bayesian theory has fared poorly in comparison (e.g., Sections III,E,4–5; Anderson, 1974d, Section 7.2; Leon & Anderson, 1974; Shanteau, 1970, 1975a, 1977; Slovic & Lichtenstein, 1971). The Bayesian approach has now been generally abandoned as a psychological model of decision processes.

Despite these difficulties, attempts have been made to revive the Bayesian approach and apply it to social attribution (e.g., Ajzen & Fishbein, 1975; Trope & Brickman, 1975; see also Fischoff & Lichtenstein, 1978). But for social attribution, the Bayesian model seems even less suitable than it was for decision theory, a fact that has been obscured by "weak inference" methodology (Anderson & Shanteau, 1977). One particularly troublesome limitation of the Bayesian approach is its requirement that the causal hypotheses be mutually exclusive, and that exactly one be correct. In much social attribution, several causes are coactive, as in Performance = Motivation × Ability. Such attributions seem outside the scope of Bayesian theory but are readily treated within information integration theory.

B. Experimental Studies of Cognitive Algebra: A Quick Glance

1. SOCIAL JUDGMENT

a. Equity

A new theoretical approach to social equity has developed around algebraic models (Section III,C,8). Anderson (1976a) found that the standard form of the ratio model failed badly, but that a different form for fixed-sum division did quite well. Farkas and Anderson (1974) found failures of the input integration, that multiple dimensions of input are integrated to yield a unitary input value. Instead, the data supported equity integration's alternative structural hypothesis that an equity ratio is calculated for each input dimension, followed by integration of these separate equity ratios. Children give similar results (Anderson & Butzin, 1978).

Equity judgments involve two comparison processes, one between inputs and outcomes, the other between persons. An equity model dating back to Aristotle and a common modern form (Adams, 1965) differ in their assumptions about the comparison structure but, unfortunately, are mathematically equivalent. However, judgments of inequity provide a clean test (Anderson & Farkas, 1975). Aristotle's model did better than Adams' but not as well as a ratio model from integration theory derivable from the social averaging theorem of Section B,1,g.

Farkas (1977) studied generalizations of the equity models to handle over–underpayment, outcome summation, and interpersonal salience. Theoretical analyses of negative input and other problems are given in Anderson (1976c).

b. Attitudes

Conceptual developments in integration theory of attitudes (Anderson, 1976c, 1978) include informational interpretations of group discussion, group polarization, and implicit personality theory. An informational analysis of Festinger and Maccoby's (1964) distraction effect dispensed with the popular assumption of belief threat, as was also done in Farkas and Anderson's (1976) study of "inoculation."

A successful test of the integration model for attitudes developed in group discussion (Anderson & Graesser, 1976) is notable also for its use of cognitive unitization that allows a complex interpersonal interaction to be validly treated as a single informational unit. The two-memory hypothesis of Anderson and Hubert (1963) that the attitude produced by a verbal message is stored in a different memory system than the verbal material itself received further support from Brink (1974, p. 564) and Rywick and Schaye (1974). Simms' (1976) study of attitudes toward outstanding U.S. women yielded a nearly exact replication of Anderson's (1973) study of attitudes towards U.S. presidents. Myers and Kaplan (1976) showed that group discussion of jury cases produced attitude polarization. Himmelfarb and Anderson (1975) extended the integration model to attribution of attitudes, though not without one theoretical discrepancy (see p. 1068).

Fishbein's (1967) central assumption of classical conditioning of attitudes was put to the test in four experiments by Anderson and Clavadetscher (1976). Fishbein's theory received no support; the results reaffirmed the theoretical critique by Kaplan and Anderson (1973) of the classical conditioning approach to attitudes. Fortunately, Fishbein seems to be changing over to an information-integration approach (Fishbein & Ajzen, 1975, p. 235).

c. Legal Psychology

Cognitive algebra in the courtroom has been studied in seminal work by Ebbesen and Konečni (1974, 1975). Averaging theory was used to explain a paradoxical, unjust interaction in which persons accused of more serious crimes had to post much higher bail when they had stronger community ties. This ground-breaking study also illustrates the usefulness of controlled experiments in conjunction with field studies (Anderson, 1976c, 1978).

d. Attribution

A neat study by Nelson (1975) found that responsibility for a harmful act was an additive function of the intent of the actor and the consequences of the action. But judged intent was the sum of responsibility and consequence, not the difference that formal mathematical consistency would require. Since the information about responsibility was specified by a grand jury finding, it could imply intent and so account for the result (Anderson, 1976c). Aside from evidence on cognitive algebra, Nelson's work suggests interesting studies of implicit inference.

Graesser and Anderson (1974) verified Eq. (2) in two experiments on Gift Size = Generosity × Income. Lane and Anderson (1976) found that gratitude follows an averaging rule for intent and consequence.

e. Person Perception

Numerous contributions by Birnbaum include important support for the averaging hypothesis of integration theory (Birnbaum, Wong, & Wong, 1976). T. Anderson and Birnbaum (1976) extended averaging theory to a task of social inference for which Gollob, Rossman, and Abelson (1973) had claimed support for an adding model. For integration of bad deeds, however, Riskey and Birnbaum (1974) found a configural effect, somewhat similar to that of Leon, Oden, and Anderson (1973) for criminal groups, that does not seem amenable to any simple model.

Multiple dimensions of judgment were studied by Anderson and Lopes (1974), who showed how the valuation operation depended on judgment dimension and on similarity. This work provides another illustration of the capability of integration theory to provide a validated representation of implicit personality theory (Section IV,D,4; Anderson, 1977b, p. 155, 1978).

f. Individual Differences

Kaplan (1975) reviewed an extensive experimental and theoretical analysis of personality predispositions in terms of integration theory. Lopes' (1976a) study of level of aspiration showed how integration theory allows for a joint, nomothetic–ideographic approach to personality.

g. Social Averaging Theorem

Many social situations involve conflicting forces, and the final action represents some compromise among these forces. Under fairly general conditions, this compromise obeys a social averaging theorem. Each force is assumed to represent a preferred or focus point, X_i for Force i. For any proposed decision X, the effective value of Force i, $F_i(X)$, is assumed to be proportional to the distance $(X_i - X)$ from the focus point:

$$F_i(X) = w_i(X_i - X).$$

Here F_i is a directed force, being positive or negative, that is, pushing left or right, according to whether X is greater or less than X_i.

The social decision, denoted by X^*, is that value of X for which the several forces sum to zero net force:

$$\Sigma F_i(X) = \Sigma w_i(X_i - X^*) = 0.$$

Solving for the social decision yields

$$X^* = \Sigma w_i X_i / \Sigma w_i.$$

Thus, the social decision is a weighted average of the force foci, with weight parameters w_i that represent social power coefficients. Anderson (1976c) discusses implications for social power, conformity, and group cohesiveness.

Graesser (1977) presents three experimental tests of the social averaging theorem to group bargaining. The first experiment provided good quantitative support for the model for two-person groups. Similar results were obtained in the second experiment, in which coalitions were used in groups of two to six members. The final experiment provided a critical test between social averaging and Davis's (1973) social decision schemes. Although the results were not definitive, they favored social averaging.

2. DEVELOPMENTAL STUDIES

The judgmental orientation of integration theory leads to a different research direction, both in conception and in methodology, than does the Piagetian operational orientation. Promising initial applications suggest a new orientation to the study of children's thought.

a. Moral Judgment

In an impressive thesis, Leon (1976, 1977) studied integration rules for intent and consequence information in judgments of harmful acts. When intent was explicitly stated, most subjects from second grade up followed an averaging rule. The main alternative rule was accident-configural: Consequences were completely ignored when they were accidental, but otherwise the averaging model applied. When intent was not explicit, as in the standard Piagetian stories, the younger children did not use it. This appears to be a failure of inference, since they did use explicitly stated intent, a result that tends to vitiate the Piagetian moral objective–subjective classification. These and related results illustrate how integration-theoretical methods can diagnose integration strategies for the individual child.

b. Equity

Children divided a fixed reward between two stimulus children on the basis of their need and of how hard they had worked (Anderson

& Butzin, 1978). Capacity to integrate the four pieces of information increased with age to essentially adult performance by the 8-year-olds. However, even some 4-year-olds could handle all four pieces of information, striking testimony both to the cognitive capacity of young children and to the usefulness of the experimental methodology to reveal processing operations. The data supported a ratio rule, together with the hypothesis of equity integration, just as with adults. Implications for new research directions were discussed.

c. Quantity

For judged area of rectangles, 5-year-olds showed a simple, surprising Height + Width pattern (Anderson & Cuneo, 1978). This additive rule was experimentally robust and was interpreted as a manifestation of a general purpose additive rule in young children.

For liquids in glasses, these same 5-year-olds used a Height-only rule, consistent with Piagetian claims of "centration" but inconsistent with the two-dimensional rule for area. This Height-only rule may not be a basic cognitive limitation but may merely transfer from everyday drinking experience. This hypothesis was supported by showing that judged amount of wax cylinders exhibited the Height-only rule when they were inside glasses but exhibited the Height + Width rule when they stood alone. It was suggested that conservation is a derivative from perceptual judgment, independently of and probably causal in the development of Piaget's operation of compensation.

d. Attribution

Developmental changes in integration rules were studied by Kun, Parsons, and Ruble (1974) in predictions of performance from information about effort and ability [Eq. (2a)]. The data suggested shifts from an Effort + Ability rule in younger children to the adult Effort × Ability rule in older children. Since the same trend was previously noted for area judgments, the rules may reflect general purpose cognitive operations.

Kun (1977) presented information about performance and ability (or effort) and obtained judgments of effort (or ability). Both judgments were direct functions of performance, with little developmental trend from 6 to 12 years. As a function of ability, however, judgments of effort developed from a halo-type rule, in which greater ability implies greater effort, to the inverse compensation rule that characterizes adult thought. Surprisingly, judgments of ability as a function of effort showed a mild halo effect at all ages. This fascinating study, notable for its focus on qualitative integration rules, points to a fertile field for further work.

e. Other Applications

Singh and his associates have applied integration theory to children's perceptions of playgroups (Singh, Sidana, & Saluja, 1978) and family groups (Singh, Sidana, & Srivastava, 1978), with good results. Verge and Bogartz (1978) present an important and novel application of integration theory to an area matching task. Anderson and Cuneo (1978) give an extensive theoretical treatment of perceptual judgment as a complement to Piaget's operational view, and discuss numerous research possibilities.

3. DECISION MAKING

a. Decision Theory

Fundamental contributions by Shanteau accumulate apace. Studies of risky decision making (Shanteau, 1974, 1975a) confirm the multiplying rule for subjective probability and utility, thus providing a functional measurement solution to the classical problem of joint measurement of these two concepts. These same studies, however, find pervasive subadditivity, contrary to the basic postulate of traditional utility models.

Developments in self-estimated parameters by Shanteau and Nagy (1976) bring new theoretical capability to the cognitive algebra of dating. Shanteau (1975b) and Troutman and Shanteau (1977) find effects of nondiagnostic and irrelevant information in the Bayesian two-urn task. This poses serious difficulties for subjective versions of the Bayesian models. On a more homey level, Troutman and Shanteau (1976) confirm the averaging hypothesis for judgments of diapers by expectant couples, and Shanteau, Troutman, and Ptacek (1977) extend this approach to husband–wife decision making. Even the unprepossessing task of livestock judging is put to basic use (Phelps & Shanteau, 1976).

b. Probability Models

Lopes's (1976b) poker experiments found remarkable support for the multiplying rule of independent probabilities. Strikingly, amount of bet was proportional to subjective probability of winning, a money-losing strategy that was maintained by sophisticated cardplayers over a long-term experiment. In this case, verbal attitudes did predict behavior.

It is an attractive speculation that the algebraic models from mathematical probability theory also apply to human judgment (Section III,E). But tests of this hypothesis have long been stymied owing to lack of methods that allow for subjective values of probability. Thus, Wyer's (1975b) valiant efforts have been mostly inconclusive because of reliance on "weak inference" (Anderson & Shanteau, 1977). Wyer reported failure of the multiplying rule for conjunctive events, whereas this probability model, as well as the probability model for disjunctive events, received good support in a functional measurement analysis (Anderson, 1975b). Using like procedures, Wyer (1975a) did find support for an averaging-type probability model, a result that has been replicated by Anderson (1975b).

c. Applied Decision Making

Integration processes pervade practical decisions, and initial studies have shown considerable promise for integration theory in this area. The simple averaging model has done well in judgments of job satisfaction (Singh, 1975) and in evaluations of job applicants (Norman, 1976c). The latter report is notable for showing the power of the theory to solve the long-standing problem of measuring importance weights that are truly comparable across qualitatively different stimulus variables. A differentially weighted arithmetic mean for judgments about bus transportation may be preferable to the geometric mean used by Norman and Louviere (1974), which does not allow negative values. A number of studies using integration theory are included in Louviere's (1977) special issue of the *Great Plains–Rocky Mountain Geographical Journal*. Numerous studies by Levin (e.g., 1975; Levin, King, & Cory, 1976) and an important paper by Birnbaum (1976) have brought new light to "intuitive statistics."

4 OTHER AREAS

a. Psycholinguistics

Fundamental work by Oden has attacked the critical psycholinguistic problem of representing truth value as a continuous quantity. The concepts and methods of information integration theory are ideal for this purpose and provide a natural replacement for the traditional, two-valued true-or-false propositional representation. The utility and validity of this approach are shown in studies of multiplying rules for subjective degree of truthfulness of conjunctions and disjunctions of "fuzzy" propositions (Oden, 1977a). A successful ratio model for ambiguity (Oden, 1974) and for "fuzzy" class membership (Oden, 1977b) help provide construct validity for this current trend in psycholinguistics. An earlier study of continuous semantic constraints

(Oden & Anderson, 1974) has also been of use in social balance theory (Anderson, 1977b). In related work, Oden (1977c) has applied his fuzzy logic model to phoneme identification.

b. Learning

Information integration theory provides a natural cognitive approach to learning (Anderson, 1974d, Sections 6, 8.3). This is a Tolmanian view in which reinforcement is essentially informational in nature, and learning is serial integration of information.

Studies by Norman have assessed effects of feedback on weights and scale values in a simulated personnel selection task (Norman, 1976b) as well as in motor skills (Norman, 1974a). An interesting extension of the latter study considered learning of rules rather than discrete movements (Norman, 1974b). Learning of cue validities was studied by Levin (1973) and Birnbaum (1976), who demonstrated the ubiquity of averaging processes, a result that undercuts previous theoretical interpretations that have mainly relied on additive assumptions. Lopes (1976a) has applied sequential dependency analysis to study integration of success–failure experiences in level of aspiration. Somewhat more afield, Farley and Fantino (1978) apply functional measurement to test the matching law in operant work.

c. Psychophysics

The classical problem of bisection leads to a simple averaging model that has long resisted analysis because the response is measured in the physical metric, whereas the bisection process takes place in the psychological metric. A complete solution to this bisection problem is given by Weiss (1975) and Anderson (1976d, 1977a, 1977c), who found that the simple model held for grayness but not for length.

Other studies have applied integration theory and functional measurement to geometrical illusions (Clavadetscher, 1978; Clavadetscher & Anderson, 1977), to study feature integration for acoustic cues to the dimension of voicing in phoneme identification (Massaro & Cohen, 1976), to verify a multiplying model for number quantifiers (Borges & Sawyers, 1974), for theoretical analysis of context effects and range–frequency theory (Anderson, 1975a), to get cross-task validation of the psychophysical law using heterogeneous stimuli in a "total magnitude" task (Anderson, 1974c), and to determine the psychophysical law for subjective time (Blankenship & Anderson, 1976). Numerous contributions by Birnbaum include analyses of context effects in range–frequency theory (Birnbaum, 1974), studies of expectancy-contrast effects (e.g., Birnbaum, Kobernick, & Veit, 1974), as well as attempts to resolve the vexing problem of discriminating ratio from difference models (Birnbaum & Elmasian, 1977; Rose & Birnbaum, 1975).

d. Motivation

Functional measurement of motivation and incentive is discussed by Anderson (1977), and a successful experimental test of the MEV (Motivation × Expectancy × Value) model from cognitive theory is given by Klitzner and Anderson (1977). Applications to behavioral measures in snake phobics by Klitzner (1978) were also promising. An interesting byproduct concerned the use of the model to yield a functional scale of motivation considered as an individual difference, a behavioral measure. In other work, Klitzner (1975) applied a two-stage linear model to hedonic integration.

e. Methodology

Methodology continues as a basic theme. The long-known but ill-appreciated fact that correlation coefficients are inadequate for model tests is amply documented in a discussion of "weak inference" (Anderson & Shanteau, 1977). Difficulties in using analysis of variance in balance theory are noted by Anderson (1977b), who also discusses an alternative informational view. Methodological and conceptual problems in measurement of cognitive responses, especially the problem of the generalized halo effect, are included in a theoretical chapter on attitudes (Anderson, 1978). Work by Norman (1976a, 1976c) takes up statistical problems in estimation of weights and scale values. The inherent dependence of certain data analyses on theoretical assumptions of adding versus averaging are reemphasized in discussions of the proportional change model for attitudes by Harris (1976) and for developmental by Bogartz (1976). Within-subject design, which has been basic in work on integration theory, has also been espoused by Ronis, Baumgardner, and Greenwald (1977), who employed the collection of "president paragraphs" developed by Anderson, Sawyers, and Farkas (1972) to facilitate within-subject studies of attitudes. Two papers give elementary expositions of functional measurement and discuss problems of data analysis (Anderson, 1976b, 1977a). The latter paper is notable for presenting the first general error theory for ordinal data in algebraic models.

f. Comment

This cursory glance at recent experimental studies of cognitive algebra cannot do justice to the many contributions. Brief as it is, however, this summary should indicate something of the penetration and scope of this theoretical approach. It has shed important new light on some old problems and has also led to a variety of interesting new problems. Although the work to date is but a bare beginning, it shows a conceptual coherence and power that give it much excitement and promise.

REFERENCES

Adams, J. S. Inequity in social exchange. In L. Berkowitz (Ed.), *Advances in experimental social psychology*, Vol. 2. New York: Academic Press, 1965, Pp. 267–299.

Ajzen, I., & Fishbein, M. A Bayesian analysis of attribution processes. *Psychological Bulletin*, 1975, **82**, 261–277.

Anderson, N. H. Information integration theory applied to attitudes about U.S. Presidents. *Journal of Educational Psychology*, 1973, **64**, 1–8.

Anderson, N. H. Algebraic models in perception. In E. C. Carterette & M. P. Friedman (Eds.), *Handbook of perception*, Vol. 2. New York: Academic Press, 1974, Pp. 215–298. (a)

Anderson, N. H. Cognitive algebra. In L. Berkowitz (Ed.), *Advances in experimental social psychology*, Vol. 7. New York: Academic Press, 1974, Pp. 1–101. (b)

Anderson, N. H. Cross-task validation of functional measurement using judgments of total magnitude. *Journal of Experimental Psychology*, 1974, **102**, 226–233. (c)

Anderson, N. H. Information integration theory: A brief survey. In D. H. Krantz, R. C. Atkinson, R. D. Luce, & P. Suppes (Eds.), *Contemporary developments in mathematical psychology*, Vol. 2. San Francisco: W. H. Freeman, 1974, Pp. 236–305. (d)

Anderson, N. H. On the role of context effects in psychophysical judgment. *Psychological Review*, 1975, **82**, 462–482. (a)

Anderson, N. H. Unpublished experiments. La Jolla, California: University of California, 1975. (b)

Anderson, N. H. Equity judgments as information integration. *Journal of Personality and Social Psychology*, 1976, **33**, 291–299. (a)

Anderson, N. H. How functional measurement can yield validated interval scales of mental quantities. *Journal of Applied Psychology*, 1976, **61**, 677–692. (b)

Anderson, N. H. *Social perception and cognition* (Tech. Rep. CHIP 62). La Jolla, Calif.: University of California, San Diego, Center for Human Information Processing, July, 1976. (c)

Anderson, N. H. Integration theory, functional measurement, and the psychophysical law. In H. G. Geissler & Yu M. Zabrodin (Eds.), *Advances in psychophysics*. Berlin: VEB Deutscher Verlag, 1976, Pp. 93–130. (d)

Anderson, N. H. Note on functional measurement and data analysis. *Perception & Psychophysics*, 1977, **21**, 201–215. (a)

Anderson, N. H. Some problems in using analysis of variance in balance theory. *Journal of Personality and Social Psychology*, 1977, **35**, 140–158. (b)

Anderson, N. H. Failure of additivity in bisection of length. *Perception & Psychophysics*, 1977, **22**, 213–222. (c)

Anderson, N. H. Integration theory applied to cognitive responses and attitudes. In R. Petty, T. Ostrom, & T. Brock (Eds.), *Cognitive responses in persuasion.* McGraw-Hill, 1978, in press.

Anderson, N. H. Measurement of motivation. *Behavior Research Methods and Instrumentation,* 1978, in press.

Anderson, N. H., & Butzin, C. A. *Integration theory applied to children's judgments of equity. Developmental Psychology,* 1978, in press.

Anderson, N. H., & Clavadetscher, J. Tests of a conditioning hypothesis with adjective combinations. *Journal of Experimental Psychology: Human Learning and Memory,* 1976, **2**, 11–20.

Anderson, N. H., & Cuneo, D. O. The height + width rule in children's judgments of quantity. *Journal of Experimental Psychology: General,* 1978, in press.

Anderson, N. H., & Farkas, A. J. Integration theory applied to models of inequity. *Personality and Social Psychology Bulletin,* 1975, **1**, 588–591.

Anderson, N. H., & Graesser, C. C. An information integration analysis of attitude change in group discussion. *Journal of Personality and Social Psychology,* 1976, **34**, 210–222.

Anderson, N. H., & Hubert, S. Effects of concomitant verbal recall on order effects in personality impression formation. *Journal of Verbal Learning and Verbal Behavior,* 1963, **2**, 379–391.

Anderson, N. H., & Lopes, L. L. Some psycholinguistic aspects of person perception. *Memory & Cognition,* 1974, **2**, 67–74.

Anderson, N. H., Sawyers, B. K., & Farkas, A. J. President paragraphs. *Behavior Research Methods and Instrumentation,* 1972, **4**, 177–192.

Anderson, N. H., & Shanteau, J. Weak inference with linear models. *Psychological Bulletin,* 1977, **84**, 1155–1170.

Anderson, T., & Birnbaum, M. H. Test of an additive model of social inference. *Journal of Personality and Social Psychology,* 1976, **33**, 655–662.

Bem, D. J. Self-perception theory. In L. Berkowitz (Ed.), *Advances in experimental social psychology,* Vol. 6. New York: Academic Press, 1972, Pp. 1–62.

Birnbaum, M. H. Using contextual effects to derive psychophysical scales. *Perception & Psychophysics,* 1974, **15**, 89–96.

Birnbaum, M. H. Intuitive numerical prediction. *American Journal of Psychology,* 1976, **89**, 417–429.

Birnbaum, M. H., & Elmasian, R. Loudness "ratios" and "differences" involve the same psychophysical operation. *Perception & Psychophysics,* 1977, **22**, 383–391.

Birnbaum, M. H., Kobernick, M., & Veit, C. T. Subjective correlation and the size–numerosity illusion. *Journal of Experimental Psychology,* 1974, **102**, 537–539.

Birnbaum, M. H., Wong, R., & Wong, L. Combining information from sources that vary in credibility. *Memory & Cognition,* 1976, **4**, 330–336.

Blankenship, D. A., & Anderson, N. H. Subjective duration: A functional measurement analysis. *Perception & Psychophysics,* 1976, **20**, 168–172.

Bogartz, R. S. On the meaning of statistical interactions. *Journal of Experimental Child Psychology,* 1976, **22**, 178–183.

Borges, M. A., & Sawyers, B. K. Common verbal quantifiers: Usage and interpretation. *Journal of Experimental Psychology,* 1974, **102**, 335–338.

Brewer, M. B. An information-processing approach to attribution of responsibility. *Journal of Experimental Social Psychology,* 1977, **13**, 58–69.

Brink, J. H. Impression order effects as a function of the personal relevance of the object of description. *Memory & Cognition*, 1974, **2**, 561–565.

Brooks, W. N., & Doob, A. N. Justice and the jury. *Journal of Social Issues*, 1975, **31**, 171–182.

Byrne, D. *The attraction paradigm.* New York: Academic Press, 1971.

Chaikin, A. L., & Darley, J. M. Victim or perpetrator: Defensive attribution of responsibility and the need for order and justice. *Journal of Personality and Social Psychology*, 1973, **25**, 268–275.

Clavadetscher, J. E. Unpublished Ph.D. dissertation. University of California, San Diego, 1978.

Davis, J. H. Group decision and social interaction: A theory of social decision schemes. *Psychological Review*, 1973, **80**, 97–125.

Ebbesen, E. B., & Konečni, V. J. *Cognitive algebra in legal decision making* (Tech. Rep. CHIP 46). La Jolla, California: University of California, San Diego, Center for Human Information Processing, October, 1974.

Ebbesen, E. B., & Konečni, V. J. Decision making and information integration in the courts: The setting of bail. *Journal of Personality and Social Psychology*, 1975, **32**, 805–821.

Farkas, A. J. *A cognitive algebra for bystander judgments of interpersonal unfairness.* Unpublished doctoral dissertation, University of California, San Diego, 1977.

Farkas, A. J., & Anderson, N. H. *Input summation and equity summation in multi-cue equity judgments* (Tech. Rep. CHIP 47). La Jolla, California: University of California, San Diego, Center for Human Information Processing, December, 1974.

Farkas, A. J., & Anderson, N. H. Inoculation theory and integration theory as explanations of the "paper tiger" effect. *Journal of Social Psychology*, 1976, **98**, 253–268.

Farley, J., & Fantino, E. The symmetrical law of effect and the matching relation in choice behavior. *Journal of the Experimental Analysis of Behavior*, 1978, **29**, 37–60.

Festinger, L., & Maccoby, N. On resistance to persuasive communication. *Journal of Abnormal and Social Psychology*, 1964, **68**, 359–366.

Fischoff, B., & Lichtenstein, S. Don't attribute this to Reverend Bayes. *Psychological Bulletin*, 1978, **85**, 239–243.

Fishbein, M. A behavior theory approach to the relations between beliefs about an object and the attitude toward the object. In M. Fishbein (Ed.), *Readings in attitude theory and measurement.* New York: Wiley, 1967, Pp. 389–400.

Fishbein, M., & Ajzen, I. *Belief, attitude, intention and behavior.* Reading, Massachusetts: Addison-Wesley, 1975.

Godfrey, B. W., & Lowe, C. A. Devaluation of innocent victims: An attribution analysis within the just world paradigm. *Journal of Personality and Social Psychology*, 1975, **31**, 944–951.

Gollob, H. F., Rossman, B. B., & Abelson, R. P. Social inference as a function of the number of instances and consistency of information presented. *Journal of Personality and Social Psychology*, 1973, **27**, 19–33.

Graesser, C. C. *A social averaging theorem for group decision making.* Unpublished Ph.D. dissertation, University of California, San Diego, 1977.

Graesser, C. C., & Anderson, N. H. Cognitive algebra of the equation: Gift Size = Generosity × Income. *Journal of Experimental Psychology*, 1974, **103**, 692–699.

Harris, R. J. The uncertain connection between verbal theories and research hypotheses in social psychology. *Journal of Experimental Social Psychology*, 1976, **12**, 210–219.

Himmelfarb, S., & Anderson, N. H. Integration theory applied to opinion attribution. *Journal of Personality and Social Psychology*, 1975, **31**, 1064–1072.

Kaplan, M. F. Information integration in social judgment: Interaction of judge and informational components. In M. F. Kaplan & S. Schwartz (Eds.), *Human judgment and decision processes*. New York: Academic Press, 1975.

Kaplan, M. F., & Anderson, N. H. Information integration theory and reinforcement theory as approaches to interpersonal attraction. *Journal of Personality and Social Psychology*, 1973, **28**, 301–312.

Kelley, H. H. *Attribution in social interaction*. New York: General Learning Press, 1972. (a)

Kelley, H. H. *Causal schemata and the attribution process*. New York: General Learning Press, 1972. (b)

Klitzner, M. D. Hedonic integration: Test of a linear model. *Perception & Psychophysics*, 1975, **18**, 49–54.

Klitzner, M. D. *Small animal fear: An integration-theoretical analysis*. Unpublished doctoral dissertation, University of California, San Diego, 1978.

Klitzner, M. D., & Anderson, N. H. Motivation × Expectancy × Value: A functional measurement approach. *Motivation and Emotion*, 1977, **1**, 347–365.

Kun, A. Development of the magnitude-covariation and compensation causal schemata in ability and effort attributions of performance. *Child Development*, 1977, **48**, 862–873.

Kun, A., Parsons, J. E., & Ruble, D. N. Development of integration processes using ability and effort information to predict outcome. *Developmental Psychology*, 1974, **10**, 721–732.

Lane, J., & Anderson, N. H. Integration of intention and outcome in moral judgment. *Memory & Cognition*, 1976, **4**, 1–5.

Leon, M. *Coordination of intent and consequence information in children's moral judgments*. Unpublished doctoral dissertation, University of California, San Diego, 1976.

Leon, M. *Coordination of intent and consequence information in children's moral judgments* (Tech. Rep. CHIP 72). La Jolla, California: University of California, San Diego, Center for Human Information Processing, 1977.

Leon, M., & Anderson, N. H. A ratio rule from integration theory applied to inference judgments. *Journal of Experimental Psychology*, 1974, **102**, 27–36.

Leon, M., Oden, G. C., & Anderson, N. H. Functional measurement of social values. *Journal of Personality and Social Psychology*, 1973, **27**, 301–310.

Lerner, M. J. Observer's evaluation of a victim: Justice, guilt, and veridical perception. *Journal of Personality and Social Psychology*, 1971, **20**, 127–135.

Levin, I. P. Learning effects in information integration: Manipulation of cue validity in an impression formation task. *Memory & Cognition*, 1973, **1**, 236–240.

Levin, I. P. Information integration in numerical judgments and decision processes. *Journal of Experimental Psychology: General*, 1975, **104**, 39–53.

Levin, I. P., Kim, K. J., & Corry, F. A. Invariance of the weight parameter in information integration. *Memory & Cognition*, 1976, **4**, 43–47.

Lindsay, P. H., & Norman, D. A. *Human information processing* (2nd ed.). New York: Academic Press, 1977.

Lopes, L. L. Individual strategies in goal-setting. *Organizational Behavior and Human Performance*, 1976, **15**, 268–277. (a)

Lopes, L. L. Model-based decision and inference in stud poker. *Journal of Experimental Psychology: General*, 1976, **105**, 217–239. (b)

Louviere, J. J. Note from the session chairman. *Great Plains–Rocky Mountain Geographical Journal,* 1977, **6,** 2–3.

Massaro, D. W., & Cohen, M. M. The contribution of fundamental frequency and voice onset time to the /zi/ - /si/ distinction. *Journal of the Acoustical Society of America,* 1976, **60,** 704–717.

Myers, D. G., & Kaplan, M. F. Group-induced polarization in simulated juries. *Personality and Social Psychology Bulletin,* 1976, **2,** 63–66.

Nelson, C. *A cognitive algebra approach to judgments of responsibility, intention, and consequences.* Unpublished doctoral dissertation, Kent State University, Kent, Ohio, 1975.

Norman, K. L. Dynamic processes in stimulus integration theory. *Journal of Experimental Psychology,* 1974, **102,** 399–408. (a)

Norman, K. L. Rule learning in a stimulus integration task. *Journal of Experimental Psychology,* 1974, **103,** 941–947. (b)

Norman, K. L. A solution for weights and scale values in functional measurement. *Psychological Review,* 1976, **83,** 80–84. (a)

Norman, K. L. Effects of feedback on the weights and subjective values in an information integration model. *Organizational Behavior and Human Performance,* 1976, **17,** 367–387. (b)

Norman, K. L. Weight and value in an information integration model: Subjective rating of job applicants. *Organizational Behavior and Human Performance,* 1976, **16,** 193–204. (c)

Norman, K. L., & Louviere, J. J. Integration of attributes in bus transportation. *Journal of Applied Psychology,* 1974, **59,** 753–758.

Oden, G. C. *Semantic constraints and ambiguity resolution.* Unpublished doctoral dissertation, University of California, San Diego, 1974.

Oden, G. C. Fuzziness in semantic memory: Choosing exemplars of semantic categories. *Memory & Cognition,* 1977, **5,** 198–204. (a)

Oden, G. C. Integration of fuzzy logical information. *Journal of Experimental Psychology: Human Perception and Performance,* 1977, **3,** 565–575. (b)

Oden, G. C. Integration of place and voicing information in the identification of synthetic stop consonants. *Journal of Phonetics,* 1978, in press.

Oden, G. C., & Anderson, N. H. Integration of semantic constraints. *Journal of Verbal Learning and Verbal Behavior,* 1974, **13,** 138–148.

Orvis, B. R., Cunningham, J. D., & Kelley, H. H. A closer examination of causal inference: The role of consensus, distinctiveness, and consistency information. *Journal of Personality and Social Psychology,* 1975, **32,** 605–616.

Phelps, R. H., & Shanteau, J. Livestock judges: How much information can an expert use? *Organizational Behavior and Human Performance,* 1978, in press.

Riskey, D. R., & Birnbaum, M. H. Compensatory effects in moral judgment: Two rights don't make up for a wrong. *Journal of Experimental Psychology,* 1974, **103,** 171–173.

Ronis, D. L., Baumgardner, M. H., Leippe, M. R., Cacioppo, J. T., & Greenwald, A. G. In search of reliable persuasion effects. *Journal of Personality and Social Psychology,* 1977, **35,** 548–569.

Rose, B. J., & Birnbaum, M. H. Judgments of differences and ratios of numerals. *Perception & Psychophysics,* 1975, **18,** 194–200.

Rywick, T., & Schaye, P. Use of long-term memory in impression formation. *Psychological Reports,* 1974, **34,** 939–945.

Shanteau, J. C. An additive model for sequential decision making. *Journal of Experimental Psychology,* 1970, **85,** 181–191. (a)

Shanteau, J. Component processes in risky decision making. *Journal of Experimental Psychology,* 1974, **103**, 680–691.

Shanteau, J. An information-integration analysis of risky decision making. In M. F. Kaplan & S. Schwartz (Eds.), *Human judgment and decision processes.* New York: Academic Press, 1975, Pp. 109–137. (a)

Shanteau, J. Averaging versus multiplying combination rules of inference judgment. *Acta Psychologica,* 1975, **39**, 83–89. (b)

Shanteau, J., & Nagy, G. Decisions made about other people. A human judgment analysis of dating choice. In J. Carroll & J. Payne (Eds.), *Cognition and social judgment.* Potomac, Maryland: Erlbaum, 1976, Pp. 221–242.

Shanteau, J., Troutman, C. M., & Ptacek, C. H. Averaging processes in consumer decision-making. *Great Plains–Rocky Mountain Geographical Journal,* 1977, **6**, 86–99.

Shaver, K. G. Defensive attribution: Effects of severity and relevance on the responsibility assigned for an accident. *Journal of Personality and Social Psychology,* 1970, **14**, 101–113.

Simms, E. S. *Information integration theory and attitude change applied to classroom situations.* Unpublished doctoral dissertation, University of Arizona, Tucson, 1976.

Singh, R. Information integration theory applied to expected job attractiveness and satisfaction. *Journal of Applied Psychology,* 1975, **60**, 621–623.

Singh, R., Sidana, U. R., & Saluja, S. K. Playgroup attractiveness studied with information integration theory. *Journal of Experimental Child Psychology,* 1978, in press.

Singh, R., Sidana, U. R., & Srivastava, P. Averaging processes in children's judgments of happiness. *Journal of Social Psychology,* 1978, **104**, 123–132.

Slovic, P., & Lichtenstein, S. Comparison of Bayesian and regression approaches to the study of information processing in judgment. *Organizational Behavior and Human Performance,* 1971, **6**, 649–744.

Trope, Y., & Brickman, P. Difficulty and diagnosticity as determinants of choice among tasks. *Journal of Personality and Social Psychology,* 1975, **31**, 918–925.

Troutman, C. M., & Shanteau, J. Do consumers evaluate products by adding or averaging attribute information? *The Journal of Consumer Research,* 1976, 3, 101–106.

Troutman, C. M., & Shanteau, J. Inferences based on nondiagnostic information. *Organizational Behavior and Human Performance,* 1977, **19**, 43–55.

Verge, C. G., & Bogartz, R. S. A functional measurement analysis of the development of dimensional coordination in children. *Journal of Experimental Child Psychology,* 1978, **25**, 337–353.

Walster, E. Assignment of responsibility for an accident. *Journal of Personality and Social Psychology,* 1966, 3, 73–79.

Walster, E. "Second-guessing" important events. *Human Relations,* 1967, **20**, 239–250.

Weiss, D. J. Quantifying private events: A functional measurement analysis of equisection. *Perception & Psychophysics,* 1975, **17**, 351–357.

Wilkening, F. Combining of stimulus dimensions in children's and adults' judgments of area: An information integration analysis. *Developmental Psychology,* in press.

Wyer, R. S., Jr. Functional measurement methodology applied to a subjective probability model of cognitive functioning. *Journal of Personality and Social Psychology,* 1975, **31**, 94–100. (a)

Wyer, R. S., Jr. The role of probabilistic and syllogistic reasoning in cognitive organization and social inference. In M. F. Kaplan & S. Schwartz (Eds.), *Human judgment and decision processes.* New York: Academic Press, 1975, Pp. 229–269. (b)

THE CONGRUITY PRINCIPLE REVISITED: STUDIES IN THE REDUCTION, INDUCTION, AND GENERALIZATION OF PERSUASION[1]

Percy H. Tannenbaum
MASS COMMUNICATIONS RESEARCH CENTER
UNIVERSITY OF WISCONSIN
MADISON, WISCONSIN

[1]The research reported in this chapter was conducted largely under Grant G-23963 from the National Science Foundation, Division of Social Science. Some of the preliminary work was supported by grants from the Graduate Research Committee of the University of Wisconsin from funds supplied by the Wisconsin Alumni Research Foundation. The present chapter was written while the author was a fellow at the Center for Advanced Study in the Behavioral Sciences, Stanford, California. He is grateful for the support of these various institutions, and for the liberal manner in which such support was provided and administered. He also acknowledges the assistance of several graduate students who participated in this research, principally Jacqueline Macaulay, Eleanor Norris, Kjell Nowak, and Stephen Schleifer.

Reprinted from *Advances in Experimental Social Psychology*, Volume 3, 271–320.

I. Introduction

As is amply testified in previous volumes of this series and other such recent publications, social psychology has made substantial and rapid strides in its development as a bona fide behavioral science. Leading this trend has been the emergence, within the last decade or so, of a number of apparently independently developed but highly related theoretical principles which generally fall under the rubric of *balance* or *consistency* theories. One thinks immediately of the tremendous influence of cognitive dissonance theory (cf. Festinger, 1957, 1964; Brehm and Cohen, 1962). In the realm of interpersonal behavior, there is Heider's (1958) pioneering balance theory, and its elaborations by Newcomb (1953, 1959) and by Cartwright and Harary (1956). While the foregoing formulations also deal extensively with attitudinal phenomena, more specific attitude models are those based on cognitive-affective balance (Abelson and Rosenberg, 1958; Rosenberg, 1960; Rosenberg and Abelson, 1960) and, of particular interest to us here, the principle of congruity (Osgood and Tannenbaum, 1955; Osgood *et al.*, 1957).

There are, to be sure, some important differences among these theoretical schemes—for example, in range of application, degree of elaboration and specification, and for that matter, in the definition of the basic motivational state. More to the point, however, particularly considering their more or less independent development, is their common characteristic: the basic premise of a tendency within the human organism to minimize cognitive inconsistency and to strive toward consistency. Such a basic postulate and its attendant assumptions within the various theories have generated a wide variety of theoretical considerations and research undertakings, as the contemporary literature of social psychology attests. Collectively, these approaches have lead at least one authority to characterize them as representing "the first truly general ... and compelling theoretical system in social psychology" (Brown, 1962).[2]

[2] It is not our function here to present a complete review of the current status, the similarities and differences, of the cognitive consistency theories. Such reviews have been

One of the main areas of application of these consistency models has been that of the formation and modification of attitudes. Indeed, the congruity principle was initially developed for just this problem (Osgood and Tannenbaum, 1955)—to account for the attitude change resulting from a given communication situation—although it has since been extended to other cognitive areas, such as word mixture studies (cf. Osgood *et al.*, 1957), color and shape connotations (Tannenbaum, 1966a), interpersonal impression formation (e.g., Willis, 1960; Triandis and Fishbein, 1963), and other complex social stimuli (e.g., Podell and Podell, 1963; Manis *et al.*, 1966).

The simple and not atypical communication situation to which the congruity principle was originally applied is one in which an identifiable *source* makes an *assertion* about some *concept* or object. Prior to exposure to such a message, the individual has attitudes toward any number of potential sources or concepts, which he can maintain without any problems. The issue of congruity arises with the assertion of the message; it is only then that the particular source and the particular concept are brought into an evaluational relationship to each other as the source assumes a position favorable or unfavorable to the concept. Under certain conditions—for example, where the preexposure attitudes toward the source and toward the concept are both favorable and the direction of the assertion is also favorable—there is no incongruity, and no pressure toward change is generated. Under other defined circumstances—for example, when one initially favorable source makes a favorable assertion about a decidedly negative concept—incongruity obtains and, according to the theory, pressure is generated to change the attitudes toward the objects of judgment involved in order to achieve congruity.

The principle of congruity can be applied in this manner to account for conditions under which attitudes toward the source, the concept, or both, will be expected to change; the change always depends on the pre-communication attitudes toward both objects and on the nature of the assertion linking them. The theory further predicts the *direction* of attitude change for the source and for the concept: always toward increased congruity. The theoretical postulates also allow the derivation of a set of specific formulas to account for the respective *magnitudes* of change, although there are, as one might expect, a number of qualifying conditions and corrective factors involved in applying such formulas. [See Osgood and Tannenbaum

---

offered in the past by, for example, Zajonc (1960), Osgood (1960), and Brown (1962), and more recently by McGuire (1966b). At the time of this writing, a group (consisting of R. P. Abelson, E. Aronson, W. J. McGuire, T. M. Newcomb, M. J. Rosenberg, and P. H. Tannenbaum) is periodically convening at the Center for Advanced Study in the Behavioral Sciences to explore this general area in more detail.

(1955) for a more detailed account of the underlying assumptions, development of the predictive formulas, and the limiting conditions.] While the original experimental findings (Osgood and Tannenbaum, 1955) show substantial support for the predictive formulas (for example, correlations between predicted and obtained attitude changes on the order of .90 or better), their accuracy and underlying logic have recently been called into question (cf. Triandis and Fishbein, 1963; Fishbein and Hunter, 1964; Rokeach and Rothman, 1965).

Our concern here, however, is not so much with the derived formulas and other such details of the theory as it is with the more general theoretical premise that attitude change, at least in the communication situation we have posed, is a direct consequence of the condition of incongruity. The attitude change occurs in response to the incongruity, and functions to reduce it. This reasoning amounts to an essentially self-regulative, automatic, homeostatic model—perhaps more so than any of the other consistency or balance theories—in which the upsetting of a condition of equilibrium elicits a state of disequilibrium which provides the impetus for its own reduction. Such a homeostatic principle has long been considered a fundamental mechanism for the regulation of a variety of bodily functions (such as the balance of oxygen and carbon dioxide in the blood and internal temperature control). Although not originally derived from such general homeostatic considerations, the various consistency theories, and particularly the congruity principle, have much in common with other homeostatic models. One distinction, however, is that whereas physiological homeostasis usually involves the maintenance of an existing level of equilibrium, the congruity principle allows for balance at a variety of levels, mostly different from the original state of affairs. That is, what is important is not the maintenance or restoration of a predetermined ideal level, but the notion of a tendency toward any consistent or balanced situation.

In the decade or so since its introduction, the congruity principle has not been applied to attitude change issues beyond the kind of problems to which its original formulation referred. Recently, however, we have used the basic model to attempt to deal with several additional theoretical issues that have arisen in the persuasion area. This chapter is a report of current applications of the congruity model.

The main impetus to this recent research was a concern with the opposite side of the attitude change coin. We sought to account not so much for the modification of attitudes but rather for the reduction of such change. Accordingly, we will consider several strategies suggested by the theory to accomplish such reduction of persuasion. We will also report on the results of various combinations of these strategies. Our work in this area closely parallels that derived from another approach to the development of resistance to persuasion (cf. McGuire, 1964). In our studies we have used the experimental procedures developed by McGuire but have hypothesized different mechanisms to account for the results. Thus, we also have several studies to report which were designed to test these alternative hypotheses.

As so often happens, embarking on this program of research led to the consideration of related phenomena. For one thing, it raised anew the question of the relative efficacy of different modes of *inducing*, as well as reducing, attitude change. Because of the close theoretical affinity between promoting and reducing attitude change, this chapter will include several such investigations. Another, possibly serendipitous, consequence of this research was a closer look at the problem of the *generalization* of attitude change, also considered within the framework of congruity theory.

II. Strategies for the Reduction of Persuasion

The advent of the various consistency theories, along with other recent findings in the attitude and opinion change area, has not been without untoward implications. By providing a theoretical base and generating research on specific persuasion strategies, the theories have raised the specter of a public increasingly vulnerable to a variety of persuasive manipulations. Cohen (1960) was led to such a gloomy view in his summary of relevant studies. But he also saw a possible silver lining to this Orwellian cloud: "On the positive side, let us hope that any principles derived ... are equally applicable for developing resistance to persuasive inducements [and] may provide a basis for inoculation of the individual against manipulation" (Cohen, 1960, p. 318). While Cohen may have been more concerned with the social and political values of such a situation, his comments have an important theoretical relevance in that theories of how attitudes are formed and changed also carry implications for the *reduction* of such change.

In a previous contribution to the *Advances in Experimental Social Psychology*, McGuire (1964) has, in his typically thorough and scholarly manner, provided a comprehensive review of a variety of investigations dealing with this general problem of resistance to persuasion. Several distinctive approaches and many specific studies are described (although many were not necessarily originally conceived of in that context). Additional references, including some of the work reported here, can be found in the 1966 *Annual Review* (McGuire, 1966a). For the most part, the earlier research in this area did not stem from consistency theory. More recent work, including that dealing with the effects of warnings of coming belief attacks (Allyn and Festinger, 1961; Festinger and Maccoby, 1964; Kiesler and Kiesler, 1964) and perceived choice in exposure to the persuasive communication (Freedman and Steinbruner, 1964), has involved dissonance theory applications.

By far the most ambitious and systematic approach to the problem of inducing resistance to persuasion has been McGuire's own *inoculation theory*.[3] While having some roots in the so-called selective exposure postulate of dissonance theory—that people tend to defend their beliefs by avoiding information contrary to their viewpoints—inoculation theory can be treated independently of this generally accepted (cf. Festinger, 1957; Klapper, 1960) but still questionable (Steiner, 1962; Freedman and Sears, 1966) premise. McGuire deliberately focuses on "cultural truisms"— various widely held beliefs about health practices, on the assumption that such unquestioned beliefs are maintained in a noncontroversial, ideologically aseptic environment, and hence are highly susceptible to attack since the individual is both unmotivated and unpracticed in defending them. He reasons that prior messages which merely offer support for the initial belief fail to induce resistance to the subsequent attack since they merely "belabor the obvious." If anything, the supporting messages make the individual overconfident but no less vulnerable. McGuire proposes that a prior treatment, such as a refutation of the attack, can serve as a threat to the existing belief by alerting the recipient to the possibility of attack. This threat should stimulate the individual to muster defenses for the opinion and make him less vulnerable to the coming massive attack— a procedure quite analogous to biological immunization, such as that of a person raised in a germ-free environment who is inoculated with a weakened virus.

In a systematic series of experiments, McGuire has marshalled considerable support for such a theoretical position. Not only does he find the foregoing prediction regarding the superiority of the refutational over the supportive treatments to hold (McGuire and Papageorgis, 1961); he also finds that the refutation of one set of arguments generalizes to provide immunization against a different set of arguments (Papageorgis and McGuire, 1961). Furthermore, he noted that the supportive treatment gains in efficacy when combined with the refutational (McGuire, 1961b), and that both treatments, more particularly the supportive, confer more resistance when preceded by a warning of the impending attack (McGuire and Papageorgis, 1962). These results, along with an assortment of other evidence, are in accord with the threat-provoking, defense-arousing rationale of inoculation theory.

[3] The most comprehensive statement of the theory and the supporting evidence is contained in McGuire's chapter in the first volume of this series McGuire, 1964). Earlier versions may be found in McGuire's earlier writings (e.g., McGuire and Papageorgis, 1961; McGuire, 1961a).

The congruity principle has also recently been applied to the problem of reducing the effect of persuasion. This work has dealt with a basic communication setting in which the main attack on the belief consists of a favorably evaluated source making a strongly negative assertion against a favorably evaluated concept. This is an intrinsically incongruous situation, and the theory predicts, among other things, a resultant negative shift in attitude toward the concept. The problem posed, then, is how to eliminate, or at least significantly reduce, this unfavorable attitude change.

Application of the principle of congruity to such a situation stems from its central postulate that the existence of an incongruity directly generates the pressure toward change, and that such pressure is absent when the situation is a congruous one. Accordingly, any means of reducing the prevailing degree of incongruity should render the situation more congruous and thus serve to reduce the degree of attitude change.

Four such strategies for reducing the degree of persuasion were derived from congruity theory. These strategies were first tested in an original study designed for just that purpose (Tannenbaum et al., 1966). In the present section, we shall describe the results of this initial investigation, along with the findings from replications of the four treatments which were conducted in somewhat different settings as parts of other studies. Since each strategy has its own particular theoretical basis, and since the four were manifested in somewhat different forms, we will consider them individually at this stage. Our immediate purpose is to present the rationale for each treatment and to consider the experimental results in terms of that rationale. We want first to determine if each treatment works as intended before we proceed to other considerations.

A. GENERAL METHODOLOGICAL CONSIDERATIONS

To allow for comparison of our results with McGuire's, the belief issues used in the original and in most of the subsequent studies were similar to those employed by McGuire: various health measures, such as frequent toothbrushing to prevent dental decay, regular medical checkups in the absence of specific illness, and the use of X rays for the detection of tuberculosis. The main attack on such beliefs in the initial study consisted of a message purporting to be an official statement from the United States Public Health Service (USPHS). According to pretesting, this agency was a clearly favorable source for the undergraduate student subjects. In subsequent studies, the source was usually identified by name as a professor of medicine, for reasons that will become clearer later. In either case, the attack message first stated generally, and then argued specifically, four separate and seemingly telling points against the particular health practice.

The various belief-defense messages representing the persuasion-reduction strategies were given to subjects to read either before or after the belief-attack message. The sequence in which a defense message is read *before* an attack message will be referred to as *immunization*. In this situation, the subject's belief is assumed to be at least partially "immunized" against the effects of later attacks. The reverse sequence, where the attack message is read before the defense message, will be termed *restoration*. In the latter situation, the attack message presumably has some initial success and thus the defense message in effect "restores" the belief to something like its initial state. In addition to the main experimental treatments, two control groups were usually included, one that read no messages (that received no treatment) at all, the other that read only the main attack.

Attitudes toward the particular health practice were assessed on a set of 15-point scales similar to those employed by McGuire (1964), sometimes using only one such scale, sometimes using several, which were then averaged to a single score. Both after-only and before-after designs were employed. In the latter, the beliefs measures were administered at the very outset of a testing session (that is, before any message exposure) and after the full experimental treatments (that is, after both defensive and attack messages); on a few occasions, however, intermediary measures were taken after individual message treatments. Because earlier research (cf. Tannenbaum, 1956; Hovland *et al.*, 1957) has shown the degree of attitude change to be related to initial attitudinal position, we have usually employed analysis of covariance, with the dependent variable being either the after-scores or the before-after change scores, adjusting for the before-scores. In general, independent groups of subjects were used in the various testing conditions, with each experimental group receiving both a defense treatment and the main attack in either the immunization or restoration sequence. Where more than one health topic was employed in a single design, we have preferred to expose subjects to messages on only one topic—a preference which is underlined for us by the findings of other studies (see Section VI) indicating a generalization of change from one manipulated topic to another. Thus, different subjects are used in each condition.

B. DENIAL TREATMENT

Basic to the congruity principle is the premise that incongruity arises only when the cognitive elements involved are brought into evaluative relationship to one another via an assertion (Osgood and Tannenbaum, 1955, p. 43). The communication situation we have posed has a negative assertion being made by an initially favorable source about a favorable concept. Thus, if the particular source and concept can be dissociated by severing the negative linkage between them in the main attack message, then the degree of incongruity, and hence the pressure toward change, should accordingly be reduced.

In our main study, this strategy was made manifest in a message purporting to be a press release from the source of the main attack (USPHS) denying any connection with the "recent statements erroneously attributed" to it. The message carefully avoided taking any side on the issue, nor did it comment at all on the major points of argumentation contained in the main attack. This form of the denial treatment was not effective in lessening attitude change, either in the immunization (denial-then-attack [DA] mean = 9.06) or restoration (attack-then-denial [AD] mean = 9.96) conditions; both means being significantly less ($p < .05$) than the mean in the no-treatment control group ($0 = 11.77$) group but not significantly higher than the mean in the attack-only ($A = 8.56$) group. A similar finding was obtained in a subsequent replication, with the denial strategy again not reducing the negative belief change to a significant degree. Both results are in keeping with the journalistic adage that "a denial never catches up with a false story" (cf. Hall, 1965).

In more recent investigations, some variation in the messages operationalizing this treatment have been introduced, with some noteworthy consequences. One particularly critical addition was that the source not only denied making the attributed assertion but also expressed a stand in favor of the specific health practice. In such cases, the denial treatment turned out to be quite effective in reducing the degree of persuasion. In one such study (Macaulay, 1965), both the denial-attack and attack-denial conditions were significantly ($p < .02$ and $p < .01$, respectively) different from the attack-only control group. In another investigation using only the X-ray issue and only the immunization sequence, this new form of the denial strategy resulted in significantly ($p < .05$) less attitude change (-4.79 from initial belief level) than in the attack-only condition (-8.44). However, attitude change in this denial condition was significantly ($p < .02$) greater than in the no-message condition ($+.30$).

The fact that the source in this procedure disclaims responsibility for the main attack on the truism and takes a position contrary to that attributed to him is entirely consistent with the theoretical rationale offered for this treatment. The essence of the denial strategy is to negate the impression that *that* source was against *that* concept. Mere denial may help weaken the linkage, but some doubt may linger and hence some incongruity may remain. To restore an appreciable degree of congruity the favorable source must actively be in favor of the favorable concept. He erases all doubt of his position by asserting an opinion directly contrary to that of the main attack. It is not at all surprising, then, that the initial, relatively naive, versions of the denial treatment failed in producing their intended effect, and that its more recent manifestations, incorporating this critical element of a positive stance toward the concept, succeeded.

C. Source Derogation Treatment

The communication situation we have posed involves a favorable source making a negative assertion about a favorable concept. A less incongruous situation would prevail in this case if the source were negatively evaluated. Thus, another indicated strategy was to derogate the source of the main attack in a separate message, either before (immunization sequence, SA) or after (restoration sequence, AS) subjects read the belief attack. Hopefully, this message would result in subjects adopting a negative attitude toward the source.

In our main study, this treatment took the form of the USPHS being attacked as "incompetently staffed (and) riddled with political appointees." In this study the strategy was found to be effective only in the immunization sequence; there was significantly ($p < .05$) less attitude change in the SA condition (mean = 10.62) than in the attack-only condition (A mean = 8.30). This SA change was not significantly greater than in the no-message control condition (0 mean = 11.86). The AS mean was 8.54, not appreciably higher than the A mean. When evaluation of the source was examined, it was found that the intended negative shift in attitude toward the USPHS source did not take place in either the SA or AS conditions.

Again, we introduced some variations designed to make this strategy more effective, and more pronounced results were obtained. For one thing, the institutional USPHS was dropped as the main source and was replaced by a single individual who was identified as "Dr. William J. McGuire, Professor of Medicine (or Dentistry) at Columbia University" (the real Dr. McGuire, who of course authored the original materials, was in the department of social psychology at Columbia and kindly consented to allow us the use of his name). The source derogation treatment in these cases consisted of a faculty committee report recommending dismissal of their colleague on grounds of "unethical and unprofessional behavior," including the issuing of "unjustified statements to the public." In one study in which all the messages were delivered orally, the manipulation was very successful in downgrading the source and showed very clearly significant differences in final belief level between the 0 (13.26), SA (10.43), and A (5.19) conditions. In another study, an increase in the relative efficiency of the restoration condition was noted—AS (6.60) was still not significantly higher than A (5.96), but was not significantly lower than SA (7.88).

D. REFUTATION TREATMENT

The change in attitude toward the concept in the communication context we posed can be considered to derive from at least two factors. One is the basic incongruity of a positive source taking a negative position vis-à-vis a positive concept. (It is primarily to reduce this inconsistency that the denial and source derogation treatments were directed.) The second factor involves the assertion itself. It not only serves to link source and concept, but also carries the argumentation and reasoning against a favorable evaluation of the concept. The assertions were particularly important in this series of experiments; they were rather detailed and really quite convincing arguments against the health practice. The fact that our data reflect such pronounced attitude change in the attack-only treatments— roughly, from above 12.00 to lower than 6.00 on the 15-point scale—cannot be attributed simply to the source-concept inconsistency. The force of the assertion itself must also be reckoned with.

In the initial formulation of the congruity theory, Osgood and Tannenbaum (1955) explicitly recognized such a factor, referring to it as the *assertion constant*. This was taken as the impact of the message per se on the concept, and was conceived of as being absorbed totally by the concept rather than the source. The assertion constant was recognized as being separate from the pure source-concept congruity relationships involved. Its value was estimated in the original data (Osgood and Tannenbaum, 1955) by assessing the relative difference between source and concept change within similar conditions. In a subsequent elaboration of the congruity principle, however, it was further speculated that the degree of incongruity, and hence the pressure toward change, was related to the intensity of the assertion—more incongruity with more intense messages (Osgood *et al.*, 1957, p. 213). To our knowledge, however, such hypothesis has not undergone appropriate empirical testing.

In terms of our present concerns, it is clear from the foregoing line of reasoning that an appropriate way to lessen attitude change would be to *weaken* the assertion as such. This could be accomplished if the subject were made to question the validity of the attack arguments. The procedure would be even more effective if such a manipulation were totally to rebut, and perhaps even reverse, the salient points of the attack.

We reasoned that a detailed and explicit refutation of the attack message would best accomplish such an assertion-weakening goal. In our original study, such a refutation was attributed to a special professional (medical or dental, depending on the issue) committee without mentioning USPHS or otherwise specifically identifying the main attack. In each case, the message clearly stated each argument offered against the health practice and then offered a point-by-point rebuttal. The specific materials used here were adapted from McGuire's messages. But while this treatment is given the same "refutation" label and utilized highly similar materials in McGuire's investigations and ours, it should be noted that the fundamental theoretical rationales are quite different—an important point to which we shall return later in this chapter.

The results of this refutation treatment show it to be the most effective strategy for reducing persuasion in both the immunization (RA) and restoration (AR) sequences. In the original study, the refutation mean for the immunization sequence (12.46) was not only significantly ($p < .02$) higher than the attack-only mean (8.82), but it was higher, although not significantly so, than the no-message control mean (11.70). Similarly, the AR (10.45) restoration condition was significantly ($p < .01$) higher than A, but not significantly lower than 0. These general results have held uniformly, in more than a half-dozen assorted replications, usually with the RA condition somewhat if not significantly superior to the AR sequence.

E.   CONCEPT BOOST TREATMENT

In developing the predictive implications of the basic postulate of a pressure toward change stemming from an incongruous situation, Osgood and Tannenbaum (1955) argued that this total pressure is not necessarily equal for the source and the concept; the total pressure toward change is distributed between source and concept in inverse proportion to the respective intensities of the original attitudes toward source and concept. In so doing, Osgood and Tannenbaum invoked one of the more widely accepted empirical generalizations in attitude theory: that more intense attitudes are less susceptible to change than weaker ones (cf. Tannenbaum, 1956; Klapper, 1960).

This general rule has direct application to the present situation. That is, if the initial attitude toward the concept can be boosted and made even more intensely favorable, it should be less susceptible to subsequent persuasion attempts in a negative direction.

The strategy is similar to McGuire's so-called supportive treatment, and again the messages used were adapted from his materials. In our versions, these messages were identified as coming from a professional committee (as in the refutation treatments). They merely offered the supportive evidence for the particular health practice without any direct reference to the main attack arguments.

For a variety of reasons, the concept boost treatment was used only in the immunization sequence (BA) in the original and subsequent studies. The BA mean (10.85) proved to be significantly ($p < .05$) higher than the attack-only mean (8.39) and very close to the no-message control group mean (11.22), even though there was no indication that the treatment had created the expected favorable attitude change. In an additional study, however, a significant ($p < .001$) strengthening of the concept belief (from 11.91 to 13.29) was noted. McGuire (1961b), too, found a significant strengthening of belief after exposure to the supportive manipulation. Contrary to our findings above, however, he claims that this strengthening is not effective in conferring a significant degree of resistance to the belief attack (McGuire, 1964, pp. 206–207).

III. Combinations of Congruity Strategies

We have seen that when the conditions were right each of the four strategies derived from congruity theory considerations was successful in accomplishing a reduction in attitude change, at least in the immunization sequence. It would also appear that there are differences in relative efficacy between treatments. While it is tempting to accept such differences at face value and attribute them to the differences in respective theoretical mechanisms, there are other factors present that might also be important. For example, in order to make the various strategies operational in their own ways, there were differences in length of the treatment messages; the refutation generally was longer than the others. Similarly, it is difficult to estimate the comparative effects of such factors as reality of the presentation or acceptability to subjects—all quite apart from the relative effects of the strategies as such.

Nevertheless, it is possible to study such relative effects by investigating various pairings of the individual treatments. This approach stems from the fundamental theoretical consideration that if two treatments are independent of one another in the manner in which they achieve their effect, they should be nonredundant in their combined effect. More specifically, independence of the effects of two treatments, each of which produces some degree of reduction of attitude change, implies that the two in combination should be superior to either of the component treatments alone.

Such comparisons have another theoretical implication. When two treatments are independent, their combination should yield an *additive* effect: Two significant and mutually exclusive treatments in union should be equal to the simple summation of their independent effects. If, however, such an additivity model does not hold—that is, if the combination is significantly greater or less than the addition of the component effects—then some kind of *interactive* model is indicated. If the combination is greater than additivity, a *facilitative* model, in which the strategies enhance each other's effects, is suggested. If the combination is significantly less than that expected from pure additivity, then a *redundant* model, whereby the effects overlap somewhat, is suggested.

We can thus examine the various pairings in terms of independence and nonindependence of the component strategies. Examination of the six possible pairings resulting from the four main strategies suggests that the components of four of the combinations appear to be independent. For these we expect the combination to be superior to either of the components and for additivity to obtain. Although we were able to test the first hypothesis for each, the assessment of the additivity model was not possible to accomplish in precise terms. The two remaining combinations are theoretically nonindependent and some degree of redundancy of effect is indicated such that the effect of combination should not equal the summed effects of the components. In addition, for one of the independent combinations we were able to ascertain whether an additional variation—having both treatments emanate from the same or different sources—produced an expected facilitative effect.

A. COMBINATIONS OF INDEPENDENT TREATMENTS

1. Source-Refutation Combination

Clearly, among the more successful single treatments uncovered in the original set of studies were the source derogation and refutation strategies. Clearly, too, the mode of operation of each as a persuasion reducer, at least in terms of the congruity model, suggests that these strategies are quite independent in their effect. The source attack involves a simple congruity mechanism. It is directed at the particular cognitive relationship involved in the given communication situation, and has little if anything to do with the nature of the argument against the health practice involved. The refutation treatment, on the other hand, is specifically directed at this argument attacking the concept. It is concerned with invalidating the attacking assertion itself. Although this may possibly lead to a less incongruous situation, its main focus is on reducing the weight of argumentation rather than on the particular source-concept relationship.

Because of such obvious nonredundancy in their respective mechanisms, these two treatments were selected in a test of some of the predictions made earlier involving a variety of combinations of the two strategies (Tannenbaum and Norris, 1965). Four single treatments were employed: the source derogation in both the immunization (SA) and the restoration (AS) sequence, and the refutation treatment in the same sequences (AR and RA). There also were four combined treatments: two "massed" versions with both strategies either before (SRA) or after (ASR) the main attack; and two "distributed" versions, one with the source treatment preceding the attack and the refutation following (SAR), and the other in the reverse sequence (RAS). In this manner, each combination could be compared with its respective components: for example, SRA with SA and RA; RAS with RA and AS; and so on. Only the X-ray issue was employed in this study, and belief toward the topic was assessed on a single 15-point scale used in the earlier research.

  a. *Single versus combined treatments.* Table I presents the results of the comparisons between each combination and its respective components. (The higher the score, the greater the resistance is to the persuasion attempt.) A significant superiority for the combined treatment is indicated in each of the comparisons involved, in perfect keeping with the theoretical predictions. Each strategy is enhanced by the addition of the other, suggesting that the two do indeed function in separate and independent ways. In terms of relative enhancement, we find the refutation to contribute significantly ($p < .05$) more when added to the source derogation treatment than vice versa, suggesting that the refutation is indeed the superior of the two as a persuasion reducer.

TABLE I

RESISTANCE TO PERSUASION COMPARISON OF COMBINED WITH COMPONENT
TREATMENTS FOR THE SOURCE DEROGATION AND REFUTATION CONDITION[a]

Combination		Components		diff.	p[b]
SRA	(13.20)	SA	(8.00)	6.78	.001
		RA	(10.60)	3.39	.002
ASR	(11.30)	AS	(7.30)	5.22	.001
		AR	(9.40)	2.48	.02
SAR	(11.50)	SA	(8.00)	4.56	.001
		AR	(9.40)	2.74	.01
RAS	(12.10)	RA	(10.60)	1.97	.05
		AS	(7.30)	5.61	.001

[a] Data from Tannenbaum and Norris (1965).

[b] Based on the within-group error term from a one-way analysis of variance across all ten test groups. The higher the score, the greater the resistance to the attack-persuasion attempt.

  Comparisons among the four combined treatments themselves indicate that SRA was significantly ($p < .05$) more effective in lessening persuasion than the other three, with no differences among the latter. Further detailed examination of the data revealed this SRA superiority was not due to a general massed versus distributed superiority. The two massed conditions taken together (SRA + ASR, mean = 12.25) were not significantly more effective than the two distributed conditions taken together (SAR + RAS, mean = 11.80). Rather, the SRA superiority arises from the fact that both component treatments appeared in their maximized form as immunizers. That is, both the source derogation and refutation strategies by themselves were more effective in the immunization than in the restoration sequence. Hence, when both are combined in the immunization version, as in the SRA treatment, their joint effect is greater.

b. *Additivity assessment.* Our data do not allow for a totally adequate test of the additivity model implied by the independence of the two component treatments. It was possible, however, to evaluate the obtained results in terms of those expected purely on the basis of additivity (see footnote 16, Tannenbaum and Norris, 1965, p. 154, for the method of calculating the expected values). Even though only four such instances are available, we found the relationship between obtained and expected values to be just short of the 5% level $[r = .951; Nr^2(X^2) = 3.62; .05 < p < .06 (1 df)]$—not enough to suggest any real departure from the additivity assumption.

Another implication of additivity is that the interaction between the two treatments is not significant. Appropriately, no such significant interaction was found in four specific analyses of variance conducted for this purpose (see Table VI, Tannenbaum and Norris, 1965, p. 155). Although the additivity hypothesis is a null hypothesis and so cannot be disproved, these results do provide a basis for rejecting the alternative facilitative or redundancy models—both of which imply a significant interaction effect—thus leaving additivity as the best available explanation for the obtained findings.

2. *Refutation-Denial Combination*

It can also be reasoned from our earlier discussion that the refutation and denial treatments should also be independent in their locus of effect. Again, the refutation is presumed to operate on the assertion itself, weakening its impact on the concept. As with the source derogation, the denial treatment is essentially aimed at reducing the incongruity in the source-concept relationship. It seeks to break the linkage between the source and concept by having the source strongly deny authorship of the main attack. In so doing, he may invalidate the specific relationship between source and concept, but he does not invalidate the force of the assertion itself, which the subject may now ascribe to some other unnamed source.

a. *Single versus combined treatments.* As part of another investigation in this program of research, Macaulay (1965) was able to compare combinations of the denial and refutation strategies with each by itself, again under both immunization and restoration conditions. Because of other purposes in the study, certain special conditions obtained. As we have noted before (see Section II, B), the denial treatment here had the source both disclaiming any connection with the attack statement and taking a firm position in favor of the health practice (X-ray diagnosis for TB detection). Furthermore, in the combined condition the denial and refutation were more directly associated than in the previous source refutation study. Here, the two treatments were issued in a single message and were, moreover, identified as emanating from the same source: that is, from the very source to which the attack was attributed. The source, then, not only denied making the attack statements but also attacked the attack, as it were, by issuing the specific point-by-point refutation of the arguments against the X-ray issue. This, it should be noted, is not an implausible situation; for instance, it is not uncommon for public officials both to deny and refute rumors attributed to them in the public media. We expected that such a situation would enhance the efficacy of the combined treatments, possibly producing a facilitative effect beyond pure additivity.

Eight independent groups of subjects were employed: the denial and refutation singly in immunization and restoration sequences (DA, AD, RA, AR), and the combinations in immunization (DRA) and restoration (ADR) sequences as well, along with the usual A and 0 control groups. This particular study (Macaulay, 1965) employed a wider variety of measures than before—largely aimed at providing a more direct assessment of the refutation mechanisms (see Section IV)—including four of the 15-point belief items similar to those used in the previous work with the X-ray issue.

The main findings relevant to our present interests are shown in Table II. Earlier analysis had indicated that each of the single treatments induced a significant amount of resistance to change (as compared with the A control group), and it is apparent that each of the combinations is significantly superior to its respective components taken singly, as predicted. That is, the addition of either the refutation or the denial treatment does contribute significantly to the presence of the other. The relative contribution of the refutation to the denial is significantly (by roughly a 2:1 ratio, $p < .02$) more than the denial adds to the refutation, again indicating refutation is the best single resistance-creating treatment.

In checking for departure from additivity, it was found that the obtained ADR mean (10.61) was somewhat higher than that expected from pure additivity (9.86), suggestive of a facilitative effect. In the immunization sequence, however, DRA (10.65) was somewhat less than expected (11.16). Moreover, when evaluated by the interaction test, these departures from additivity were considerably short of significance, so that we are again left with the additivity model as being the most parsimonious to account for the obtained data.

b. Same versus different sources. In the preceding study, the cards were stacked, as it were, in favor of a strong combined effect since the

TABLE II

RESISTANCE TO PERSUASION MEANS FOR INDIVIDUAL AND
COMBINED DENIAL AND REFUTATION TREATMENT[a,b]

	Treatments					
Sequence	Refutation		Denial		Combined	
Immunization	(RA)	9.60_b	(DA)	8.17_{cd}	(DRA)	10.65_a
Restoration	(AR)	8.96_{bc}	(AD)	7.51_d	(ADR)	10.61_a

[a] Means showing the same subscript are not significantly different at the .05 level by Duncan range test.
[b] Data from Macaulay (1965).

refutation and denial both came from the same source. What would happen if we had different sources for each of the defense treatments? It was possible to examine the effect of this differentiation in a separate study in which the two critical conditions (both in the immunization sequence only) were: (1) where the source of the attack issued the denial but another source offered the refutation ($R_y D_x A_x$), and (2) where the source of all three was the same ($R_x D_x A_x$). Indexed in terms of the before-after change score, the same-sources $R_x D_x A_x$ condition actually yielded a net increase in the concept belief score (adjusted mean = + .33 on a 15-point scale), whereas the $R_y D_x A_x$ condition showed a net negative change (-1.82). The difference between the two conditions is significant at the .05 level. Thus, there was a significant increment in immunization when the source who denies the statements attributed to him actually contradicts those statements. One possible explanation here—and one supported by some incidental findings in still another separate investigation—is that by issuing the refutation the alleged source of the attack removes any possible semblance of a source-concept incongruity that might otherwise still linger, even with the denial condition present. There is not only a repealing of the assertion itself and a lessening of the incongruity, but also as complete a repudiation of the attack and its attendant implications of incongruity as can be provided.

3. Source-Boost Combination

Similar to the earlier lines of reasoning, another apparently independent combination is provided by the pairing of the source derogation and the concept boost strategies. As before, the former is aimed at reducing the inherent source-concept incongruity and is focused on the source element. On the other hand, the boost strategy is not directly concerned with the incongruous relationship as such, being directed only at strengthening and intensifying belief in the concept itself.

These two strategies were examined in their separate and combined states in the immunizing sequence as part of an investigation trying various pairs of treatments on the X-ray issue. The results clearly showed the SBA combination (11.05) to be significantly superior ($p < .05$ and $p < .02$, respectively) to the SA (8.95) and BA (7.75) treatments in conferring resistance to persuasion. Both treatments apparently add significantly to the presence of the other. There is also an indication that the source attack adds somewhat more to the boost than vice versa. With only single cases available, the interaction test is even more limited, but again no real departure from additivity is obtained.

4. Denial-Boost Combination

The same study included conditions to allow for an assessment of still another presumably independent combination: the denial, which deals with the incongruous relationship, and the boost, focused on strengthening the concept. These too were studied on the X-ray issue and only in the immunization sequence.

The results again support the general prediction of the DBA combination (9.95) being superior to either the DA (8.05) or BA (7.75) components. There is a suggestion in the data that the addition of the denial strategy helps the boost treatment somewhat more than the reversed situation, though the difference is not quite significant ($p = .15$ approximately). This is not totally unexpected, since it can be argued that the denial treatment by itself already contains some aspects of the boost; the source, in this situation, not only dissociates himself from the attack but actually expresses strong support in favor of the X-ray procedure. Even though actual arguments for such support are not offered directly, it is conceivable that this would in itself help intensify the concept attitude (a possibility which was, unfortunately, not specifically assessed in the study).

B. COMBINATIONS OF NONINDEPENDENT TREATMENTS

1. Refutation-Boost Combination

The foregoing discussion of the denial and boost strategies suggests that the concept boost may overlap with other treatments. This is not readily expected in the combination between boost and source attack, since the latter would not be at all expected to affect the concept attitude itself, and our earlier results (see Section III, A,3) tend to support this. In the case of the refutation and boost treatments, however, we might well expect a quite substantial degree of overlap or redundancy. As we shall see subsequently (Section III), a number of somewhat differing mechanisms might conceivably account for the immunizing effect of the refutation. Our previous reasoning has suggested that the main function of the refutation is to weaken the force of the assertion. As this strategy has been manifested in the actual messages, however, the very act of refuting the attack arguments also involves making both general and specific assertions in favor of the concept, much as does the boost treatment. Indeed, the messages representing these two strategies were deliberately prepared to be quite similar—the boost uses much the same statements as the refutation but it does not define the specific arguments against the health practice, and thus does not engage in any explicit counterargumentation.

McGuire (1962) studied combinations of similar versions of the refutation and supportive treatments. He found that while the refutation considerably abetted the efficacy of the concept-supporting boost, the latter did little to raise the resistance offered by the refutation alone. Although his interpretation of such a finding is in terms of the inoculation theory of resistance to persuasion, the result is to be expected from the present reasoning as well. To McGuire, the boost is insufficient because it does not contain the alerting and defense-provoking threat to a person's belief, but can achieve this added critical factor when the refutation is added. In the terminology of the present theoretical framework, on the other hand, the two treatments are nonindependent, and hence should be nonadditive in their effect. Furthermore, since the refutation contains most of the boost and then some, we would expect it to gain less from the addition of the somewhat redundant boost than the latter would gain from the somewhat novel refutation.

This was investigated as part of the above-mentioned study of different strategy pairings, again dealing only with the X-ray issue in the immunization condition. In general agreement with McGuire's earlier findings and with the present predictions, the combined RBA treatment (11.20) was significantly ($p < .01$) superior to the BA (7.75) in creating resistance to the attack, but not significantly different from the refutation-only RA (10.80) group. Such a finding also suggests a significant departure from additivity in the direction of a lower or somewhat redundant combined effect, a suggestion that is supported by a significant interaction effect ($F = 4.64$; 1/76 df; $p < .05$).

Although the boost strategy gains significantly from the addition of the refutation, there is no reciprocation in the reverse direction. Whether this finding results from the processes emphasized in McGuire's inoculation theory or from those specified by the somewhat different reasoning provided here—or, for that matter, from some third set of factors—is something we cannot determine at present. Furthermore, since the theories are not logically incompatible, it is even possible that both theoretical positions are correct.

2. *Denial-Source Derogation Combination*

Having two treatments that are partly or completely redundant is one way of achieving nonadditivity of combined effect. What about the situation where the presence of one treatment appears to violate or operate contrary to the functioning of another? In such instances, one would expect to find that the combination of the two is *less* effective than one or the other component alone.

Such a possibility could occur in the remaining one of the six possible combinations, that of the source derogation and denial treatments. Both of these treatments are intended to reduce the inconsistency of a favorable source taking a position against a favorable concept, but they do so by somewhat different means. In the source derogation, the intent is to discredit the source, to make him negative and of low credibility. The denial does not seek to alter the source attitude in any way, but rather to sever the alleged relationship. The success of this treatment depends on the source's being regarded as trustworthy and favorable, for otherwise the source would not be trusted and his denial would not be taken seriously. But this is just the sort of negative reaction the source attack procedure is designed to elicit. Accordingly, the two treatments, while seemingly appropriate each on its own, become incompatible when brought together.

In order to explore the consequences of such a situation, the separate and combined versions of the denial and source attack strategies were compared (again, on the X-ray issue in the immunization sequence). The combined strategies (SDA mean = 7.60) provided significantly ($p < .05$) *less* resistance to the persuasion attempt than the source attack (SA mean = 8.95) and also less, but not significantly, than the denial (DA mean = 8.05). The SDA mean was, however, still significantly ($p < .05$) higher than the attack-only control mean (5.60). That the denial does not gain (in fact, it loses somewhat) in effectiveness when the source attack is added is to be expected since its operation depends on the source's remaining in a favorable light, which the source manipulation clearly contradicts. Similarly, the significant decrement in the source attack treatment when the denial is added is also to be expected. The denial presumably works by creating an accepted, more congruous situation from the incongruous one established by having a negative source making an unfavorable assertion about a positive concept; the denial treatment essentially contends that the incongruous relationship does not really exist.

IV. Mechanisms of the Refutation Treatment

One of the more consistent findings emerging from the foregoing data is the clear superiority of the refutation treatment as a persuasion reducer. In none of our studies has it failed to produce a significant lessening of attitude change, whether in the immunization or restoration sequences. Further, it has generally produced more resistance to persuasion than any of the other single treatments under more or less similar circumstances, a relative efficacy that is further attested to in the combined treatment studies.

These findings tend to corroborate those of McGuire in pointing to the power of the refutation manipulation, although it must again be recognized that while McGuire's and our messages representing this strategy are quite similar, they are not identical. Indeed, the refutation treatment lies at the very heart of McGuire's inoculation theory, which maintains that the individual is both unmotivated and unpracticed in defending his belief in the kind of "cultural truisms" being dealt with. Accordingly, the indicated strategy is to provide the motivation and material for defense "by making him aware of the vulnerability of the truism ... [and by giving] careful guidance in developing defensive material" (McGuire, 1964, pp. 201–202). The refutation treatment is designed to perform both these functions. By first raising the arguments to be encountered in the attack, it presumably is a threat that alerts the individual to muster his defenses. Then, by providing a specific rebuttal of the attack, it theoretically supplies the useful information with which to construct those defenses.

The position we have adopted emphasizes the assertion-weakening attributes of the refutation treatment. This, in fact, is what use of the term *refutation* implies—a point-by-point explicit countering of the attack arguments, rendering the attack invalid. Although this hypothesized mechanism is derived from general congruity principle considerations, the conjecture is surely not unique to our theoretical position. Indeed, McGuire himself apparently recognized this probable process when he referred to the refutation defense as serving to "weaken the plausibility of the [attack arguments]" (McGuire, 1961b, pp. 193–194).

As we noted in our consideration of the combination of the refutation and concept boost treatments (Section III, B, 1), there is an additional resistance-inducing mechanism that may be attributed to the refutation strategy: Both explicitly (by actually stating so outright) and implicitly (in the act of providing counterarguments to those raised in the attack), the refutation may serve to strengthen and intensify the belief, much in the manner suggested for the boost strategy itself. Such opinion intensification (or similar effects on other possible components of the attitude; cf. Guttman, 1954) may then help blunt the impact of the subsequent attack.

Thus, four principal mechanisms by which the refutation treatment may accomplish reduction of persuasion are indicated: the threatening, defense-alerting and defense-providing aspects emphasized in inoculation theory, and the attack-weakening and concept-boosting attributes we have tended to accentuate. The evidence in favor of inoculation theory is quite formidable, but it is also rather circumstantial (cf. Macaulay, 1965). This position is, to be sure, not unique in social psychology, largely because we lack *direct* measures of many of the postulated theoretical mechanisms, but it does raise the issue of alternative explanations. In most of the experiments cited by McGuire, the assertion-weakening characteristic of the refutation could account for the obtained data just as readily as does the threat-providing aspect underlined by inoculation theory. Similarly, it is possible to explain the results of the studies reported in this chapter employing inoculation theory considerations.

Within the context of our over-all research program we have conducted a number of investigations over the past few years which relate directly to the mechanisms posited for the refutation treatment. Some of these have already been described. Several additional analyses will be reported in this section. In so doing, we will consider both the inoculation and congruity approaches to the refutation treatment.

A. ALERTING DEVICES

McGuire's earlier versions of inoculation theory tended to emphasize the critical role of the refutation in alerting the individual to the possibility of attack, with less attention being given to the actual content of the refutation message. Thus, the relative superiority of the refutation over the supportive condition (McGuire, 1961a; McGuire and Papageorgis, 1961) was attributed to the former's having the crucial threat component. The increase in efficiency of the supportive defense when the refutation was added to it (McGuire, 1961b) is similarly explained by postulating the addition of a threat-arousing motivation created by the refutation. It was also found that although the supportive treatment did more to strengthen belief prior to the attack than did the refutation, it elicited even less resistance to persuasion (McGuire and Papageorgis, 1961), tending to rule out the concept-strengthening mechanism as an important immunizing consideration. More impressive evidence for the defense-alerting character of the refutation came from the demonstration that the refutation of one set of arguments apparently generalized to confer resistance to another set of arguments (Papageorgis and McGuire, 1961). Not least, an independent threat, in the form of a warning of the impending attack, was shown to enhance the effectiveness of both refutation and supportive defenses, but particularly of the latter, which presumably did not have the necessary threat component to begin with (McGuire and Papageorgis, 1962; McGuire, 1964).

In one of our earlier studies, conducted some time before McGuire's later work became available, several alerting devices were studied to determine whether they alone would provoke resistance to the subsequent attack. There were five different levels of alert, varying from a general alert, which merely indicated that various health practices, including toothbrushing (the key single issue in this study), were worthy of periodic evaluation and discussion, to one that specifically singled out toothbrushing and explicitly presented the four main points against the practice to be encountered in the attack. The intermediate steps varied in terms of explicitness of the details of the arguments to be raised against toothbrushing. An additional condition included a warning of a "severely critical" attack. The purpose of these variations on the alerting theme was to attempt a more specific location of the source of the alerting mechanism—if, indeed, such a mechanism were to be found.

The results indicated that none of the alerting conditions produced a final belief score that was significantly different from the attack-only group. Indeed, only one condition, which merely mentioned the toothbrushing issue as specifically deserving of reevaluation and discussion, had a score higher than the control condition, all others scoring even below the attack mean. If anything, then, there is some evidence that presumable alerting or threatening conditions facilitate the attack (although the differences fall far short of significance), but no evidence for any alert-created resistance.

It is obvious from this and other studies that alerting the subject that his belief is not all that secure, or even directly threatening his belief, is insufficient for producing resistance to persuasion. For one thing, if it were true, the attack itself could be considered such a threat, but it obviously fails to stimulate defense on the belief. More to the point, as the foregoing results showed, McGuire and Papageorgis (1962) also found a warning to be inadequate by itself.

But, although it emphasizes the threat component, inoculation theory does not maintain it is sufficient. The individual must also have the material from which to construct defenses. The refutation treatment apparently contains both these necessary elements. Additional highly convincing support for the theory is that when both elements are presented separately, by providing a threatening warning along with the supportive message, the resistance was greater than in the supportive condition and not less than that noted for the refutation condition (McGuire and Papageorgis, 1962). (However, when our versions of these two conditions, that is, a warning with the boost treatment, were attempted in a recent study, we found the combination to be less effective than the refutation.) In any case, while the data supporting inoculation theory are indeed impressive, it is still not clear how the refutation works. The lack of a difference between refutation and supportive-plus-warning does not necessarily prove that the two conditions work by the same means. Barring an independent message of threat as such, it is just as reasonable to assume that a warning weakens the attack rather than threatens or motivates the individual. Similarly, the results of another study in which the threat factor was manipulated by varying the number of arguments against the belief (McGuire, 1964) can be accounted for in terms of relative weakness of the attack.

B. EFFECTS OF DIFFERENT MESSAGE SOURCES

1. Varying Source of Refutation

Another of our earlier studies was undertaken to determine whether the influence of the refutation treatment was constant or whether it would vary as a function of the kind of source with which it was identified. In terms of congruity theory, we would expect attitude toward the source to influence the acceptability of a message. Thus, if the refutation were identified as coming from a favorable source, its impact should be more pronounced and hence the resistance it may confer should be enhanced. On the other hand, if the refutation were issued by an unfavorably regarded source, the subject should tend to discount it, and its influence in reducing the attack's impact would be lessened.

A study was undertaken in which the same refutational message for the X-ray issue was assigned to both a favorable (a fictitious Dr. John A. Schmidt, Professor of Clinical Medicine at Johns Hopkins Medical School) and an unfavorable (a fictitious *Truth and Health* magazine, distributed through health food stores) source. A third group read an irrelevant story dealing with food for astronauts. All three groups were subsequently exposed to the main attack message, in all cases identified as coming from our generally favorable Dr. William J. McGuire.

The results were clear-cut, showing that although both refutation treatments conferred significant degrees of resistance to subsequent persuasion, the one with the negative source conferred significantly less ($p < .01$). (Means: refutation–positive source, 11.33; refutation–negative source, 8.37; attack-only, 6.38.)

Just what inoculation theory would predict in such a situation is difficult to ascertain, largely because it does not address itself to such variables as message sources and the like. One could argue that, regardless of the source of the refutation, the two ingredients specified by inoculation theory as necessary and sufficient for the induction of immunization—the motivating threat and the defensive information—are present in both the favorable and unfavorable source conditions, and thus equal degrees of resistance should be induced.

It can also be argued, however, that a refutation emanating from a negative source provokes less threat than one from a positive source, and that there is therefore less motivation to utilize the defensive information.

By the same token, it cannot be said that the results demonstrate that the refutation operates as an assertion-weakening device. Although the findings are clearly in accord with congruity theory predictions, they do not prove anything about the refutation mechanism per se. They do indicate that the refutation effect is not uniform, but is itself subject to other influences.

2. Varying Attack Source

In a subsequent study, some variations on the design just described were introduced. In this case, there were two versions of the attack treatment: one with a favorable (Schmidt), the other with an unfavorable (the health fad magazine), source. The only source of the refutation was favorable (McGuire). The two main attacks appeared either as attack-only conditions, or with each preceded by the refutation, subjects being randomly assigned to the four experimental conditions.

The findings are summarized in Table III, which presents the mean before-after change scores resulting from the attack adjusted by convariance for variations in initial (preexposure) attitudinal position. We find that when the two attacks are presented by themselves, the attack from the negative source leads to significantly ($p < .02$) less opinion change, a finding similar to those of many earlier studies on differential source effects and in perfect keeping with the usual congruity theory predictions. When the refutation is

TABLE III

MEAN CHANGES FOR DIFFERENT ATTACK SOURCES
WITH AND WITHOUT REFUTATION TREATMENT[a]

Attack source	Refutation treatment			
	None		Positive source	
Positive	(A +)	− 6.00	(R + A +)	− 1.48
Negative	(A −)	− 3.76	(R + A −)	+ .92

[a]All means are significantly ($p < .05$) different from one another by Duncan range test. Negative scores signify changes in accord with the attack.

presented prior to the positive-source attack, there is a marked ($p < .01$) diminution in the effect of the attack, as we have found repeatedly in several earlier studies. When the refutation from the favorable source is combined with the subsequent attack from a negative source, there is an actual increase in favorability of attitude toward the concept. Such a strengthening of belief is also in keeping with congruity principle predictions. Both a negative attack source and a positive refutation source would bring about such a favorable opinion change, in this case apparently enough to overcome a fairly strong negative assertion. Thus, we find a significant effect due to the attack source, and a significant influence of the refutation treatment, with the interaction between the two being nonsignificant.

A key comparison here, and the main reason the study was conducted, is between the refutation-plus-positive-attack $(R+A+)$ and the negative-source, attack-only $(A-)$ conditions. The former condition represents the usual application of the refutation treatment, the effect of which we have ascribed to its weakening the impact of the attack. It was reasoned that the $A-$ treatment also represents a way of weakening the assertion's impact. Thus, if the two conditions produced the same reduction of persuasion, this finding would constitute support (but not confirmation) of the hypothesis of an assertion-weakening mechanism. In fact, as shown in Table III, there is a differential reduction of persuasion, with the $R+A+$ condition producing significantly $(p < .05)$ more resistance than $A-$. Again, there is no way of guaranteeing that the two conjectured means of weakening the assertion indeed function that way. But even assuming that they do, the relatively greater efficacy of the $R+A+$ condition implies that the refutation does something that a negative attack source does not do, something beyond their common weakening of the attack. It is quite possible that this additional element is made up of the threat- and defense-arousing characteristics inoculation theory attributes to the refutation treatment.

C. IMMUNIZATION VERSUS RESTORATION

One of the less successful predictions derived from inoculation theory has concerned possible order of effects in the presentation of various defense treatments. In particular, McGuire has argued that, with the refutation treatment, the restoration sequence should preserve the belief better than the immunization sequence. The assumption here is that the attack itself serves as a stronger motivating threat than the refutation. Thus, in the restoration sequence, subjects should make more appropriate use of the defense materials provided by the refutation since they will be highly motivated in this direction by the preceding attack—more so, at least, than in the reverse sequence.

No such difference showed up, however, in McGuire's (1961a) study bearing on this point. McGuire felt at the time that this could be explained by an insufficient time lag between attack and defense, and that a longer period might result in a superior restoration sequence effect. This reasoning paralleled his belief that a longer time period was necessary for the refutation to make its effect manifest as an immunizer (McGuire, 1962). It happened that in one of our studies (Tannenbaum *et al.*, 1966), a full week was allowed between messages. There was indeed a difference between sequences, but it was significantly $(p < .05)$ in favor of the *immunization* condition.

As a matter of fact, in a number of additional comparisons of the two sequences, with the refutation strategy appearing both by itself and in combination with other treatments, the results have consistently favored immunization over restoration, though not always to a statistically significant degree. The same results obtain in the case of the source derogation treatment and, to a somewhat lesser degree, with the denial strategy. (We never did employ the concept boost manipulation as a restorative condition.)

There are a variety of possibilities to account for this greater effectiveness of the immunization sequence. For example, one can derive a prediction from inoculation theory opposite to that of McGuire's prediction. In the immunization sequence, the refutation is viewed as threatening but not overwhelming the belief, thus stimulating defense for the coming attack, much in the manner that inoculation with a weakened virus can stimulate the production of defensive antibodies. Continuing the biological analogy, introducing the inoculation after the strong attack is futile since the unalerted defenses have already—as in the case of the barn door that is closed after the horse has been stolen—been overcome. In the same manner, the rather powerful nature of the main attack may have already subdued the defenses provided by the refutation in restoration conditions. While this reasoning, if extended far enough, could lead us to predict no reductive effect for the restoration sequence, which is clearly not the case, it does allow for a superior immunization influence.

Alternatively, one can just as readily attribute the differential effect to a more pronounced weakening of the attack, in keeping with our theoretical emphasis. The attack, according to our rationale, is directly weakened by the refutation. The attack may also be indirectly weakened by other strategies: derogation of the attack source (as we have argued earlier) and denial. If such attack weakening takes place, it should be more effective if done before the attack has had a chance to take maximum effect, that is, in the immunization sequence.

Some empirical support for this position is contained in the study by Macaulay (1965), to be described in more detail later. This study involved the refutation and denial treatments, and included a judgment of the quality of the attack message as a separate (from the belief measures as such) dependent variable. Subjects in the immunization condition rated the attack (6.73 on a 15-point scale) as being less fair and believable than did those in the restoration sequence (8.30), the difference being sufficient at beyond the .02 level.

Such an interpretation, it should be noted, has some of the earmarks of the general hypothesis of the superiority of primacy over recency in persuasion, a problem that is still not fully resolved (e.g., Insko, 1964; Anderson and Barrios, 1965; Lana, 1964). Another possibility is that, in the restoration sequence, the attack produces a change in attitude such that the subsequent defense treatment is then dissonant (Keisler and Keisler, 1964) or incongruous (Tannenbaum and Norris, 1965) with the new belief. The defense therefore loses some of its effectiveness. As with the other possible explanations, this is purely speculative at present. In the absence of more direct measures of the possible mechanisms involved, we must allow for alternative explanations, although Macaulay's above-mentioned findings provide some more direct support for the attack-weakening process.

D. GENERALIZATION VERSUS SPECIFICITY OF DEFENSE

A rather telling point in favor of inoculation theory has been the demonstration that the refutation of one set of arguments against a belief generalizes to induce immunity to an attack composed of a somewhat different set of agruments (Papageorgis and McGuire, 1961; McGuire, 1961a). Such a finding is in perfect accord with the position that the refutation, by threatening the belief, stimulates the building of defenses which should then reduce the impact of any subsequent attack. The finding also runs counter to the analysis of the refutation as essentially an attack-weakener, since the latter position argues that the refutation contradicts the specific attack arguments, and hence should be effective only against such an attack. It is also possible, however, that the refutation of one set of arguments implies that the originally favorable position was indeed the proper one and that refutation thus serves to diminish the influence of *all* subsequent attacks. Further, while the demonstration of any degree of generalized resistance is impressive in itself, the results do indicate more resistance when the attack arguments are the same as those refuted rather than novel ones (Papageorgis and McGuire, 1961; McGuire, 1961b). Moreover, in one case (McGuire, 1961b), the refutation failed to produce any significant degree of generalization.

A separate investigation of our own focused directly on this issue of generality versus specificity of the refutation mechanism by utilizing a design in which all subjects were exposed to two related but separately focused attacks on the belief, with variations in the degree of relevance to these different attacks of an intervening refutational condition. The particular belief concerned the benefits of regular toothbrushing. The general attack on this practice used by both McGuire and ourselves in earlier research was divided into two separate attack messages. One (A_a) argued that toothbrushing does not really do any good in promoting dental hygiene, that it is an unnecessary practice as far as health is concerned. The second attack (A_b) argued that toothbrushing was not only futile but that it was positively dangerous in that it could induce damaging effects to dental and general health. Four experimental groups were employed, each receiving both the A_a and A_b attacks, in that order, but receiving different treatments between the two attacks. One group received only a refutation of the first attack (R_a); another group received only a refutation of the second attack arguments (R_b); a third group received refutations of both attacks (R_{ab}), while the fourth group, serving as a control condition, received no intervening treatment at all (R_o). Ratings were obtained on a set of three 15-point scales, each administered at three points in the procedure: a base-line measure prior to any exposure at all (T_1); after the first A_a attack and the particular refutation treatment (T_2); and the last after the second A_b attack (T_3).

This design allowed assessment of several effects of interest in determining the mechanism of the refutation strategy. Of direct concern is whether there is a differential effectiveness of the various refutation treatments, as the notion of specificity of effect would maintain, or if they all are more or less equally effective, as inoculation theory would hold. The various refutation treatments have three different loci of effect: in terms of reducing the impact of attack A_a, of attack A_b, or of both attacks combined.

Table IV summarizes the various findings. The first column presents the T_2-T_1 change scores, and thus reflects the impact of attack A_a along with the refutation treatments, which of course serve as restoration conditions in this respect. Here we find rather marked evidence for specificity of effect: Where the refutation treatments contain specific counterarguments relative to the A_a attack arguments (that is, in conditions R_a and R_{ab}), there is a significant and equal reduction of persuasion. In the case of R_b, however, where the refutation counterarguments are not directly relevant, there is more negative attitude change, not significantly less than that in the attack-only control.

TABLE IV

MEAN BELIEF CHANGE ACCORDING TO TYPE OF REFUTATION TREATMENT
AND LOCUS OF EFFECT[a]

| Refutation treatment | Effect | | |
	First attack (A_a) (T_2-T_1 change)	Second attack (A_b) (T_3-T_2)	Total (T_3-T_1)
R_a	-0.21_a	-4.98_d	-5.19_y
R_b	-5.45_b	-1.98_c	-7.43_y
R_{ab}	-0.21_a	-1.02_c	-1.24_x
R_o	-8.02_b	-7.86_e	-15.88_z

[a] *Within the same column only*, means with the same alphabetical subscript do not differ from each other at the .05 level by Duncan multiple range test. The greater the negative score the more effective was the attack.

The data on T_3-T_2 change reflect the impact of the A_b attack. In this case, the different refutation treatments act as immunizers. Again, there is evidence for specificity in that the more relevant conditions—R_b and R_{ab}, both containing rebuttals of the specific A_b arguments—confer the most resistance, with the difference between them being nonsignificant. However, here we also find some evidence for generalization, since R_a treatment, where the refutation materials are not directly relevant, does show less T_3-T_2 change than the attack-only control group. It is to be noted, however, that this reduction of change is significantly less than when the information is directly appropriate, as in the R_b and R_{ab} conditions.

The last column reflects the over-all change accruing from both attacks. As expected, the condition where the arguments from both attacks are refuted, R_{ab}, shows the most resistance. The groups that get only partial refutation, R_a and R_b, each change more, but still significantly less than the attack-only control. The R_a condition exhibits somewhat less change than R_b but the difference falls short of significance ($p = .15$).

Thus, the findings offer strong support for the specificity hypothesis implied by the congruity principle notion of an assertion-weakening mechanism. There is also some evidence for a generalization effect, however, particularly in terms of the significant degree of resistance provided by the R_a treatment to the A_b attack. As we pointed out at the beginning of this section, though, this can be interpreted in terms other than the arousal of defense from the R_a treatment.

Further support for the specificity model is obtained when the data are analyzed separately for each of the belief items, instead of across all three at once. The three items were prepared so that one reflected the main focus of the A_a attack, another of the A_b attack, and the third was a general evaluative statement not particularly linked to either attack. The detailed analysis indicates that these items are indeed sensitive to the respective treatments. There was a substantial degree of specificity rather than generalization in the refutation treatments. Thus, the R_a and R_{ab} groups show substantial change at T_2 on the relevant A_a attack item, with relatively little effect on the nonrelevant item reflecting attack A_b. Conversely, groups R_b and R_{ab} show more change on the second item than the first at T_3. For the most part, the general item changes along with the directly relevant one in each case.

E. DIRECT ASSESSMENT OF MECHANISMS

Mention has already been made of the study of Macaulay (1965), especially in reference to the combination of the refutation and denial treatments (Section III, A, 2) and in terms of the immunization versus restoration comparisons (Section IV, C). In addition to such aims, a major purpose of this study was to attempt a more direct assessment of the various mechanisms suggested for the refutation treatment through the use of specific question-naire items. Although there are some recognized weaknesses in employing these items, the data are of some use since the main dependent variable in this and other studies, the actual belief measures, were inadequate for the purpose of discriminating among the several possible mechanisms.

In this study, it will be recalled, there were four single treatments—denial and refutation in both immunization and restoration sequence (DA, AD, RA, AR)—and two combined DRA and ADR conditions, along with the usual A and 0 control groups. In addition to the regular belief items, subjects were asked to express their reactions to various aspects of the messages on a set of 9-point scales; all, including the belief items, were administered on an after-only basis. Analysis on such items is focused on the various refutation groups in comparison with those receiving either the denial or no defense treatment at all.

1. Defense Arousal

A number of items were included to get at factors presumed to underlie the stimulation of defense mechanisms by the refutation strategy. One concerned the subjects' interest in receiving more information on the X-ray topic; inoculation theory implies that the refutation subjects would be more interested in having such information. In general, a relatively high degree of interest (6.73 on the 9-point scale) in this information was found across all groups, with no differences to speak of between groups.

A similar prediction was made for expressed certainty of belief in the X-ray practice; the notion was that those people feeling threatened would feel less certain, and those stimulated to develop defenses would feel more confident. Again, however, there were no differences between groups; all conditions, including the no-message control, showed only moderate certainty (mean = 5.50 on 9-point scale). This measure relates somewhat to one employed by Papageorgis and McGuire (1961) where their subjects were asked to record as many individual arguments as they could in support of the various truisms employed. Although there was a slight tendency for the refutation subjects to list more supportive statements than those in the no-defense treatment, the difference also failed to reach significance.

Macaulay also included an item assessing the perceived position of the attack message, in order to test the hypothesis advanced by Manis and Blake (1963) that the belief threat would lead those subjects who had not been immunized to assimilate the message to their own position. Again, however, there was no support in the data, with subjects in all conditions generally judging the attack message to be equally strong against the practice.

2. Belief Strengthening

As we have noted, another mechanism suggested for refutation to function is that it strengthens and intensifies the belief. McGuire and Papageorgis (1961), however, reported that while there was such a slight strengthening effect for the refutation, it was less than for the supportive treatment, although the refutation then turned out to be by far the more effective immunizer. McGuire has further elaborated upon such an apparent "paper tiger" phenomenon, pointing to "the peril of assuming the immunizing effectiveness of a defense to be a direct function of its apparent strengthening effect" (McGuire, 1964, pp. 207–208).

Macaulay included two statements concerning supportive points for the main belief in her inventory of belief measures, and found the refutation-only treatment led to stronger endorsement of these items (8.66) than the denial-only (6.99) group, although the difference falls just short of statistical significance ($p = .06$). In addition, there is a significant difference for these items between the combined DRA and ADR groups (10.10) and the no-message control group (8.45), indicating some strengthening of belief. Macaulay concluded, from these and other correlational data, that "observed differences tend to support the prediction that refutation works at least in part by belief strengthening, but these differences are not all statistically significant ... the hypothesis has not been strongly confirmed but has received enough support not to be dismissed" (Macaulay, 1965, p. 53).

3. Assertion Weakening

Reference has already been made to judgments of the fairness and believability of the attack message in connection with the earlier discussion of immunization and restoration sequences. Such an index is of obvious interest here since it relates directly to the mechanism suggested by congruity theory as being most responsible for the effectiveness of the refutation.

The findings across all conditions were unequivocal. There was a significant ($p < .01$) difference in attack rating between conditions where the refutation treatment was present (6.83) and when it was absent (9.20). This difference existed under both immunization and restoration conditions, more so in the former, as we noted earlier.

In this connection, it should also be mentioned that Papageorgis and McGuire (1961) included such an index in their attempt to identify the mechanism for the refutation condition. They used a set of ten semantic differential-type scales designed to measure the judged quality of the attack arguments. Their results also pointed to a weakening in the credibility of the attack when it was preceded by a refutation defense. And, in connection with our earlier comment of what it may be that generalizes from a refutation of one set of arguments conferring immunity against a different set, it was also found that such a weakening of the attack was equally apparent in the refutation-same and refutation-different conditions.

It is clear that the refutation condition, whatever else it might do, substantially alters the force of the assertion. Given the fact that we are generally dealing with fairly strong assertions to begin with, such assertion weakening is clearly one factor that must be considered in determining how the refutation treatment effects resistance to persuasion. There is evidence from a number of studies reported here that this is indeed the case, and that such a mechanism provides a quite parsimonious accounting of the various findings. But there is evidence, too, that the mechanisms suggested by McGuire's inoculation theory are also at work.

As we have indicated before, these two major approaches are not natural enemies. The main difference between them is one of emphasis rather than contradiction. It is more than possible that both theoretical positions are valid and that both may be operative in a given application of the refutation strategy. As McGuire has noted in a somewhat different context, inoculation theory does "not rule out the possibility that other components of the refutational defense also would contribute to resistance to persuasion, any more than Boyle's law implies the invalidity of Charles' law" (McGuire, 1964, p. 215). Macaulay (1965) has taken a similar stance, offering an "additive multifactor model" representing contributions from both congruity and inoculation theory, and we here advocate a corresponding position.

V. Persuasion via Congruity and Information Processes

It is apparent that underlying much of our work in developing resistance to persuasion are two general and quite different processes by which persuasion, and hence its reduction, may be accomplished. On the one hand, we have relied heavily on rather straightforward congruity principle procedures whereby the elements involved in a cognitive relationship are in a congruous or balanced state, or where the existence of incongruity generates pressures toward attitude change. This type of reasoning is best exemplified by the rationale for the source derogation treatment as a means of inducing immunization, and this rationale, in turn, stems directly from the earlier work on the congruity principle in situations involving the induction, rather than reduction, of attitude change. Mechanisms of this type generally belong in the realm of "psycho-logic," to use Abelson and Rosenberg's (1958) most apt term.

On the other hand, there is the position that much attitude change, or lack of it, stems from the inherent informational content of a message. Katz, for example, speaks of attitude change occurring when, among other things, an individual "finds his old attitudes in conflict with new information and new experiences, and proceeds to modify his beliefs" (Katz, 1960, p. 190). Similarly, Brehm and Cohen (1962) refer to the "information processing" that goes on upon exposure to a message, with the incoming information being weighed and considered against existing cognitions, and there are numerous other such conceptualizations. In the present context, such an approach would attribute much of belief change in the various attack conditions of our research to the novel (for the subject, at least) information being presented against the particular health practice. By the same reasoning, the refutational defense confers resistance to persuasion largely because it provides direct information that refutes or contradicts the arguments in the attack.

The basic dichotomy referred to here can take many different forms, and both can be present in different or even the same situations (cf. Kelman and Eagly, 1965). In some ways, the contrast is reminiscent of earlier research in the field of persuasion comparing between so-called rational versus emotional appeals. The accumulated evidence on this issue is rather spotty and divided, with some studies purporting to demonstrate superiority for the emotional appeal (e.g., Hartmann, 1936; Menefee and Granneberg, 1940; Lewan and Stotland, 1961), others claiming more or less equal effectiveness (e.g., Knower, 1935; Weiss and Lieberman, 1959) and at least one (Weiss, 1960) indicating a stronger rational effect. Other factors, however, were rarely equivalent between the critical experimental conditions, and it is more than likely that the relative effectiveness of the two approaches interacts highly with personality (cf. Hovland et al., 1949) and situational characteristics.

Although most of out attention in this chapter has been directed to the problems of reduction of persuasion, such concerns led us to a reexamination of the relative efficacy of the congruity and informational approaches as inducers of attitude change. Two studies on this theme were conducted, and these in turn led to an additional study on the reduction of attitude change.

A. VARYING SOURCES OR INFORMATION INPUTS

The basic method we adopted, one calculated to reduce the possible contamination of factors other than the theoretical mechanisms, was to use the double-attack paradigm similar to that employed in the study of the specificity of refutation (Section IV.D). The belief area selected was the use of X rays for the detection of TB. As with the toothbrushing issue used earlier, it was possible to divide the arguments of the attack into two separate messages, one supporting the contention that X rays are unnecessary (A_a) and a second featuring information that X rays are positively damaging to a person's health (A_b). Similarly, two different sources, both judged as highly favorable on pretests, were employed; one was a professor of radiology (S_x), the other the Surgeon General's Office (S_y).

Four basic groups of subjects were used, each group receiving two message exposures. All groups were first exposed to the A_a attack from either S_x or S_y, the four groups varying in terms of the redundancy of the second message relative to the first. For Group I, the situation was totally redundant, that is, the same source issued essentially the same statement in the second message as in the first. For Group II, the second message was also identified as coming from the same source, but contained new information in the form of A_b attack. For Group III, a different source issued the same A_a attack. Group IV had both sources and information nonredundant, with a different source issuing a different attack. Belief measures were assessed on three of the usual 15-point scales prior to the first message and after the second, the analysis being conducted on the change scores, covarying for initial belief score.

Table V presents the relevant data. The covariance analysis revealed a significant ($p < .01$) difference between the two source treatments, and somewhat less but still significant ($p < .05$) between the two attack treatments, with the interaction effect being negligible ($F < 1$). This testifies that both mechanisms are effective in their own right, but more so for the congruity strategy. This is seen more clearly in the comparison between the

TABLE V

ADJUSTED MEAN CHANGE SCORES ACCORDING TO SOURCE AND ATTACK CONDITIONS[a]

	Same sources	Different sources	Marginals
Same attacks	-3.21_a	-5.68_c	-4.45
Different attacks	-4.45_b	-6.55_c	-5.50
Marginals	-3.83	-6.12	

[a] Means with different subscripts are significantly different from one another at the .05 level.

individual cell means. Both theories predict that the least total change would occur in the totally redundant (Group I) condition and the largest change in the totally nonredundant (Group IV) condition, which is plainly the case. The new information, redundant source condition (Group II) is superior to the Group I mean, as expected from the information-processing approach. However, the main congruity strategy reflected in Group III (redundant information, different sources) produces significantly more change than the corresponding Group II mean, and is, moreover, not significantly less than the maximum Group IV mean. Thus, although there is evidence that both treatments—varying the information content, or varying the identified sources—produce significant increments of persuasion, the latter procedure is relatively more effective.

B. CONGRUITY VERSUS INFORMATIONAL CONSISTENCY

A similar means of investigating the differences between the two persuasion processes was utilized in another study involving the two-message paradigm. In this case, the topic was a relatively neutral concept, teaching machines, and two messages were prepared, one with information favorable to the concept (I +), the other with unfavorable information (I −). Similarly, two different sources were employed, one favorable (S +), the other unfavorable (S −). Four groups were employed, each one getting two messages from the two different sources, but in different combinations.

Group I received the S + I − and the S − 1 + messages, while Group II received the S + I + and the S − I − messages. In both cases, the pair of messages are consistent with one another in the congruity principle sense but are inconsistent in terms of only the informational content. Thus, in Group I, a favorable source being against the concept is perfectly congruous with an unfavorable source being for the concept, both conditions creating pressure toward a negative shift in attitude toward the concept. From a purely informational standpoint, however, the message contents are contradictory and, assuming that the I + and I − effects are roughly equal, they should cancel one another. Similarly, in the Group II situation, congruity theory would predict a substantial positive attitude change toward the concept, both messages being consistent in that direction, while the inconsistent information would again predict a minimal change in one direction or the other.

The two remaining conditions present the opposite prediction situation. In Group III, the S + I + and S − 1 + messages were used. In terms of the informational approach, these messages are consistent in a favorable direction, and a substantial positive change is indicated. From a congruity position, however, the messages are inconsistent. But the congruity principle does recognize an assertion constant and would thus allow for some positive attitude change, but less than in the Group II situation. Similarly, Group IV had the S + I − and S − I − messages, again representing informational consistency but congruity inconsistency. The former position would here predict a strong negative shift, whereas congruity, again mindful of some assertion effect, would allow for only a slight change in a negative direction.

Within each group, the order of presentation of the two messages was alternated across subjects to control for any possible order effects. In this study, judgments of the concept were obtained on a set of semantic differential scales, with ratings across four scales, which had high loadings on the evaluative factor, constituting the attitudinal measure. These scales were administered before and after the two-message exposure, the covariance analysis being conducted on the change scores.

The results, presented in Table VI, completely confirm the congruity theory predictions. In the two instances where the theory predicts favorable changes, such changes occur, but significantly ($p < .02$) more so for Group II than for Group III, also as predicted. Groups I and IV also exhibit the anticipated unfavorable changes, the former significantly ($p < .05$) more than the latter. There is almost a complete washout of the informational effect as such, with the congruity theory providing by far the most parsimonious accounting for the obtained results.

TABLE VI

ADJUSTED MEAN CHANGE FOR VARIOUS CONDITIONS OF
CONGRUITY AND INFORMATIONAL CONSISTENCY

Condition	Messages		Group	Mean change
Congruity consistency, informational inconsistency	S+I−	S−I+	I	−4.16
	S+I+	S−I−	II	+5.36
Congruity inconsistency, informational consistency	S+I+	S−I+	III	+2.30
	S+I−	S−I−	IV	−2.42

A recent study by David Sears at UCLA (personal communication) yielded somewhat similar findings. A political situation in the state of California during a recent gubernatorial election campaign was utilized. In one condition, partisan Democrats were told that both their own candidate and the Republican candidate agreed on an issue (as in Groups III or IV in the experiment just described) while another such group was told only the position of the Democratic candidate. Contrary to what might be expected in such a situation, but consistent with congruity theory, there was actually less change in the advocated direction in the condition where both candidates agreed. However, subjects in that condition apparently felt more confident in their belief, an added variable that we unfortunately did not include in our own study.

C. APPROPRIATENESS OF DEFENSE TO ATTACK

Given two basic and somewhat different processes to account for the induction of attitude change, there are also two corresponding processes for eliciting resistance to persuasion. An interesting question for research is thus presented when we contrast the two defensive with the two attacking strategies. In keeping with the general theoretical position we have adopted earlier, we would predict that the more appropriate and directly relevant a given defensive treatment is to the attacking strategy, the more effective that defense should be.

To examine this proposition, an experiment was conducted in which two main attacks on the X-ray belief were administered. One attack merely consisted of a statement by a respected source (an alleged dean of medicine at a well-known university and chairman of the "National Medical Research Board") condemning the practice as "useless and even dangerous... almost criminal to use for the detection of TB considering the presence of much safer, more advanced techniques." This attack (A_s) merely established that the source was strongly against the practice but did not give any information as such regarding the specific points of contention. The second attack (A_I) was not identified as coming from any particular source, but featured in detail the four arguments against the practice, much as in earlier versions of the main attack.

Within each attack condition, there were three variations of pre-attack defensive treatment. One consisted of a derogation of the source (D_s) of the A_s attack. This was considered to be a defense more appropriate to the A_s than to the A_I attack. The second defense was a detailed refutation of the A_I attack arguments, without any mention of the source as such (R). This was considered to be a more appropriate defense for the A_I attack than for the A_s attack. To provide a baseline control, subgroups within each attack version did not get any defensive pretreatment at all. Pretreatment and posttreatment belief measures were obtained, the analysis being conducted on the change scores covarying for initial position.

Table VII contains the adjusted mean change scores for each experimental condition. Both attack versions produced substantial degrees of persuasion, significantly more for A_I than for A_s. When the A_I attack was preceded by the directly relevant refutation defense (R), a very significant $(p < .001)$ reduction of change was noted. When the inappropriate source derogation defense was used with A_I, however, no such diminution in impact of the attack resulted.

For the A_s attack, the more relevant D_s defense induced a significant degree of resistance, although not nearly as marked as the D_R defense for the A_I attack. It is also apparent, however, that the refutation does confer some degree of immunity of the attack. Although the difference between the A_s attack by itself and the less appropriate refutational defense is not quite significant $(.15 > p > .10)$, the D_R change is not significantly more than that for the D_s defense.

TABLE VII

ADJUSTED MEAN CHANGES FOR DIFFERENT DEFENSE AND ATTACK TREATMENTS[a]

	Defensive treatment		
Attack treatment	None (D_0)	Source derogation (D_S)	Refutation (D_R)
Source statement (A_S)	-4.60_b	-3.14_{cd}	-3.72_{bc}
Informational (A_I)	-6.43_a	-6.06_a	-1.98_d

[a] Means with the same subscript are not different from one another at the .05 level.

Thus, while we generally find that the defense that is directly relevant to the attack's mechanism is most effective in reducing the persuasive impact of that attack, the D_R treatment demonstrates some generalization in its influence—certainly more than the D_S defense. A similar phenomenon was noted earlier (Section IV, D) when it was found that although the refutation was more effective when it coped with the same arguments as the attack, it also showed some ability to immunize against novel arguments. Again, the present data do not allow us to determine the instrumentality of such apparent generalization; it may be because the refutation stimulates defense building, or because it causes one to be suspicious of any forthcoming attack, or because of both. For that matter, it may be the result of some quite different factor.

VI. Generalization of Attitude Change

It sometimes happens that in the course of pursuing one line of research other areas of equal or even more theoretical interest present themselves. Such a case occurred in our program of research, where work on the reduction of persuasion uncovered some findings involving the generalization of attitude change from one concept, toward which attitude had been manipulated, to others where no specific manipulation had taken place. This, in turn, led to some more deliberate efforts to apply the congruity principle to the area of persuasion research.

A. AFFECTIVE SIMILARITY

Our original interest in this phenomenon was stimulated by a more or less chance set of consequences in our original investigation of the various congruity theory strategies for resistance to persuasion (see Section II). In that study, three separate belief issues were employed (X rays for the detection of TB; regular toothbrushing; and regular medical checkups) in a before-after testing design. Independent groups were used, such that subjects in any one group were experimentally manipulated on only one of the belief issues. To facilitate administration of the testing, however, both pre- and posttreatment belief measures were obtained from all subjects on all three issues; that is, for any given group or subject, there was one manipulated concept (MC) and two nonmanipulated "filler" concepts (NMCs). Although our main concern in the study was the change on the manipulated concepts, change scores were also available for the filler items.

There was little basis to expect any substantial change within each group on the nonmanipulated concepts. There was no mention of the filler issues in any of the experimental messages and no information at all about them was conveyed. However, examination of the data revealed slight, generally negative shifts in the change scores, and it was decided to subject these data to somewhat closer scrutiny.

The particular focus selected was to examine the change scores for a particular pair of NMCs in terms of their respective similarity to the particular MC for that subject. For each of the three concepts, the pre-exposure attitude scores on a 15-point scale were available, and it was thus possible to divide the two NMCs, in a given case, in terms of their proximity in these initial ratings vis-à-vis the MC in that case. The rationale for such a focus stems from the repeated demonstration in learning theory research (cf. Mostofsky, 1965) of the generalization of some conditioned response as a function of similarity of the unconditioned stimuli. It was similarly reasoned here that if there were any spread of persuasion from the manipulated to the nonmanipulated concepts it would be systematically related to the similarity in initial (preexposure) attitude—the more similar the initial ratings between MC and NMC, the greater the degree of generalization.

In the first analysis the two NMCs for a given subject (these, of course, varied across the three concepts, since the MCs also varied) were cast into two categories of relative closeness in preexposure attitude scores to the MC. Such allocation was made regardless of direction or magnitude of the differences involved: the NMC closer to the MC in either direction was put in the "closer" category, the other NMC into the "further" category. In the event of a tie, the data for that subject were discarded.

The results supported the similarity model. Most changes were in a negative direction, in accord with the generally negative shifts for the MC in the various experimental conditions, but significantly ($p < .02$, Wilcoxon paired replicates test) more so for the more similar preexposure attitudes (mean change $= -2.24$) than the less similar attitudes ($+0.36$). Moreover, when the data were subsequently analyzed in terms of the magnitude of the MC-NMC differences, the usual negatively decelerating generalization gradient was obtained—the greatest negative change found where the NMCs were minimally different from the MC, this change becoming increasingly less as the difference became greater.

These findings, along with highly similar ones in another study, which involved both positive and negative attitude changes, are consistent with the view that attitudes are learned responses (cf. Doob, 1947; Hovland *et al.*, 1953) and, as such, may be acquired and altered through indirect as well as direct means. Earlier studies have demonstrated that the affective components of highly evaluated words and concepts could be transferred on other verbal stimuli through classical conditioning procedures (e.g., Staats and Staats, 1958; Staats *et al.*, 1959; Das and Nanda, 1963), and we now find a similar phenomenon for the transfer of attitude change. The findings are also consistent with the view that attitudinal objects tend to be structured and clustered on the basis of perceived attributes or relationships, and that change in one element of a related structure tends to precipitate changes in the other elements. McGuire (1960) demonstrated such a transference between logically related elements of a syllogism, and the present data tend to support a similar position in terms of pure attitudinal similarity (cf. Osgood and Tannenbaum, 1955).

B.   GENERALIZATION FROM CONCEPT TO SOURCE

The foregoing findings, obtained mainly as by-products to an experiment directed along quite different lines, led to a reconsideration of the earlier work on the congruity principle in terms of a generalization paradigm. In the initial studies (Osgood and Tannenbaum, 1955; Tannenbaum, 1956), communication messages were used in which an identifiable source made an assertion for or against a given concept, but with the bulk of the argumentation directed at the concept. In addition to the expected change in attitude toward the concept, the results supported the prediction of appropriate change in attitude toward the source. Since the source was merely mentioned in the message and not specifically manipulated, this situation can also be viewed as an instance of generalization of change in the concept to the source. In this case, however, the relationship between manipulated and nonmanipulated elements is in terms of a directed evaluative association and not, as in the foregoing, of mere affective similarity.

In terms of the generalization paradigm, there are two main cognitive operations involved: the establishment of the directed relationship between source and concept, and the manipulation of the attitude toward the concept. In the original experiments, these two operations were accomplished in the same message and thus it was impossible to have the two operations in contrast to one another; for instance, the source could not be against the concept and yet have the concept supported.

These two steps were independently manipulated in a recent study (Tannenbaum and Gengel, 1966), thus allowing for a more complete test of the congruity theory predictions. The source-concept linkage was established first, then the concept attitude was altered without any reference to the source, the main dependent variable being the change in attitude toward the source. On the basis of pretesting, three psychologists, two fictitious and one actual, were selected as being essentially neutral sources. Each was subsequently linked with a neutral concept (teaching machines), one source being in favor of the concept (S+), another adopting an unfavorable position (S−), and the third being in a neutral relationship (S$_0$). A separate message was subsequently administered, half the subjects getting information designed to create a favorable attitude toward teaching machines, the other half getting negative information. Attitude measures were obtained on four semantic differential scales before and after the messages.

Predictions for change in attitude toward the sources can be readily derived from congruity theory. Where the concept changes favorably, we would expect S+ to change in a favorable direction too, and we would expect S− to change negatively. Conversely, when the concept changes unfavorably, S+ should change unfavorably, but S− favorably. In both cases, S$_0$ should not change appreciably one way or the other.

TABLE VIII

MEAN ATTITUDE CHANGE TOWARD SOURCES
ACCORDING TO TYPE OF CONCEPT MANIPULATION [a,b]

Concept manipulation	Source linkage		
	Favorable (S+)	Neutral (S$_0$)	Unfavorable (S−)
Positive ($n = 57$)	+4.75$_a$	+4.08$_a$	+1.87$_{bc}$
Negative ($n = 67$)	+1.44$_b$	+3.59$_a$	+3.61$_{ac}$

[a]Means with the same subscript are not significantly different from one another at the .05 level (by one-tailed Dunn Test). The comparisons apply only within a given row or column, but not across both simultaneously.

[b]Data from Tannenbaum and Gengel (1966).

The fit of the experimental data to the theoretical predictions may be seen in Table VIII. One immediate discrepancy is readily apparent: all changes are in a favorable direction. Further, S$_0$ shows substantial positive change under both concept manipulation conditions. A plausible explanation is that a general halo effect accrued to all sources as a function of the setting of the various messages. In order to make the situation appear realistic, subjects were informed in the first message that the three psychologists appeared at a symposium on the topic of teaching machines at a meeting of the American Psychological Association. It is possible that for our subjects (undergraduate students) any psychologist appearing at such a symposium must be an authoritative and favorably regarded person. Further, S_0 was identified as the chairman of the symposium, but was referred to as a "principal authority on learning theory," and this statement may have contributed to the favorable impression of him.

In any case, even if all differences are in a positive direction, the relative changes may still be examined, and here there is general support for the congruity theory predictions. Within the positive manipulation condition, $S+$ shows significantly ($p < .01$) more favorable shift than $S-$, as predicted. Also as predicted, $S-$ shows significantly more favorable shift than $S+$ when the concept is negatively manipulated. Looking at a specific source across the two manipulations, we found the predicted greater favorable change on $S+$ in the positive rather than the negative manipulation; no difference on S_0; but, contrary to the prediction, lack of a significant difference for $S-$. On this last comparison, however, a t test, which is also appropriate here, was significant ($t = 1.98$; 122 df; $p < .05$).

Thus, although the findings were not entirely as predicted, the results generally conform to congruity theory expectations. As Tannenbaum and Gengel (1966) point out in their fuller report on this study, the predicted differences are sharpened when the analysis is conducted with control for actual change in attitude toward the manipulated concept, rather than in terms of expected change, with all differences at $p < .01$.

Further evidence on such concept-to-source generalization of persuasion was obtained as part of the study reported in the following section, this time using a single source differentially associated (for different groups) with the same concept and omitting the neutral linkage condition. In this case, with somewhat "cleaner" experimental conditions obtaining, the results more clearly support the theoretical predictions. All changes in source attitude were in the predicted directions, including anticipated negative shifts, and all predicted differences were highly significant (see Table 2 in Tannenbaum, 1966b).

C. MEDIATED GENERALIZATION

A further extension of the congruity principle as a model for the generalization of attitude change is readily apparent. A source may be evaluatively linked to more than one concept, each such linkage constituting a specific cognitive relationship. Change in attitude toward one concept influences that particular source-concept relationship, and may result, as we have seen, in change in attitude toward the source in order to put that relationship on a congruous basis. But this modification in the source introduces an incongruity in its relationship with a second concept (even though the latter concept is not specifically manipulated) and attitude toward the second concept should change in order to resolve that new incongruity. Thus, generalization of persuasion from one concept to another may be effected in the absence of any direct linkage between the two conepts and mediated through their association with a common source.

Materials similar to those used in the preceding experiment were employed in a new study designed to examine this phenomenon (Tannenbaum, 1966b). Pretesting allowed for the selection of two neutral concepts—teaching machines (TM) and "Spence learning theory" (LT)—and a single neutral source. All subjects were first exposed to a message in which the source's position on both concepts was established. Four such conditions being used were: one in which the source stated positive positions on both concepts (*pp* condition); another with the source favoring TM but negative to LT (*pn* condition); a third with the source against TM but in favor of LT (*np* condition), and the fourth with the source being against both concepts (*nn* condition). After a half-hour interval of irrelevant activity, all subjects were exposed to a message designed to manipulate the attitude toward only the TM concept, without any mention at all of either the source or the LT concept. Half the subjects in each linkage condition received a message favorable to TM (*P* treatment), the other half an attack against TM (*N* treatment). Attitudes were again assessed (with semantic differential evaluative factor scales) before and after the exposures, the analysis being conducted on the appropriate change scores.

By tracing the expected patterns, from the manipulated TM change to corresponding change in the source attitude and hence to LT change, one could test the congruity theory predictions. For example, in the *Pnp* condition, the experimental manipulation should lead to a favorable TM attitude. Since here the source was originally against what is now a positive object, the source attitude should change negatively. As this newly negative source is favorable to the LT concept, according to the theory, the subjects' attitude toward LT should shift in an unfavorable direction. Similarly, the congruity principle predicts favorable LT changes in the *Ppp*, *Nnp*, *Npn*, and *Pnn* conditions, and unfavorable LT changes in the *Ppn*, *Nnn*, *Npp*, and *Pnp* conditions.

Table IX presents the appropriate data, and indicates that all observed changes are in the predicted direction, without exception. The four cells in which a positive LT change is predicted all change in that direction, with the differences among them being nonsignificant. Similarly, the four predicted negative changes all obtain, again without differences between them. However, the differences between matched pairs of positive and negative changes (that is, within each linkage column) are all significant.

These data provide impressive support for the congruity principle

TABLE IX

MEAN ATTITUDE CHANGE ON NONMANIPULATED (LT) CONCEPT[a,b]

TM concept manipulation	Source-concept linkages			
	pp	pn	np	nn
Positive (P)	$+2.84_a$	-1.92_c	$-.76_{bc}$	$+1.56_a$
Negative (N)	-2.72_c	$+.60_{ab}$	$+2.12_a$	-2.52_c

[a] Means with the same subscript are not significantly different at the .05 level by Newman-Keuls test.

[b] Data from Tannenbaum (1966b).

formulations. In this connection, it is important to note what conditions would differentiate between predictions based on the mediated generalization model suggested by congruity theory and predictions based on the assumption of direct transfer of persuasion from concept to concept, without the mediating source. One theoretical basis for such differentiation is suggested by our earlier findings on direct generalization (Section VI, A), as well as by demonstrations of attitude generalizations by mediated conditioning procedures (Staats *et al.*, 1959; Das and Nanda, 1963). However, we would then expect LT changes to generally follow the direction of TM changes, but this is clearly not the case: the *Ppn* and *Pnp* conditions show negative rather than positive change, and the *Npn* and *Nnp* conditions show positive rather than negative change. In all four critical cases the results confirm the congruity predictions, but are contrary to what would be expected from the direct transfer notion.

VII. Concluding Remarks

Our central concern in this chapter was with a recent program of research involving theoretical considerations based on the principle of congruity in persuasion. In general, the findings to date offer fairly strong support for the congruity principle as a model for attitude change, and hence for the reduction of the generalization of attitude change. Strategies suggested by the theory for diminishing the impact of messages fared quite well singly and in combination, and the theory was found to supplement McGuire's inoculation theory by suggesting an additional, if not necessarily alternative, set of mechanisms to induce resistance to persuasive inducements. Similarly, congruity theory held up most favorably in contrast to a rather straightforward integration-of-information approach in producing appropriate attitude change. It also proved to be a powerful predictive model to account for generalization of persuasion in given communication situations.

While the research reported here stemmed from congruity principle considerations, it is likely that many of the findings could be quite readily explained by one or another of the other consistency models. In part, this is due to a basic similarity between these various models, at least in their central premise of a tendency toward cognitive consistency. It may also be partly due to the generally vague nature of some of the basic mechanisms involved in the several theories, which tends to inhibit clear-cut comparisons between them.

Perhaps one point of distinction between congruity and the other consistency models is its lack of specification of an intervening stress or discomfort variable to mediate between the existence of inconsistency as such and behavior for its resolution. It is in this sense that congruity theory assumes more the characteristics of a semiautonomous, self-regulating process for the maintenance of psychological harmony. One of our current research interests lies in questions concerning stress states: Does stress indeed accompany the presence of inconsistency? Are there different modes for the reduction of the stress state? Does the reduction of the discomfort as such also effect the inconsistency? And so on. There are some major methodological problems involved in such undertakings, but the theoretical significance of the problem warrants continuing efforts. Space limitations prohibit a complete presentation of such efforts here.

The fundamental homeostatic mechanism attributed to congruity theory is perhaps most apparent in the generalization studies where changes in evaluation of an object of judgment occur without any direct manipulation of that object. It is more than likely that many of our "real-life" attitudes are formed and modified along just such lines. Political attitudes constitute a prime example. Most of us rarely have any direct contact or experience with a political personality, but we often develop quite intense attitudes for or against him as a result of the stands he assumes on a number of issues toward which we already have some well-defined attitudes. Once formed, such attitudes toward this politician become factors around which other opinions are developed as he continues to take positions pro or con a number of novel political issues. To be sure, such opinion formation does not always take place in a complete vacuum of factual information, but quite often such information considerations occupy a secondary role.

In this connection, it is possible to suppose that individuals differ in terms of relative susceptibility to persuasion via pure congruity manipulations, involving the use of more distinctively "psycho-logical" inducements as against more "logical" information, or reasoning, or both. This represents another area of research that has begun to occupy our attention, but we are prevented from reporting it in detail in this chapter, not only by limitations of space but also by the preliminary nature of some of the findings. However preliminary, the evidence to date suggests a range of individual differences in this regard. Moreover, there appears to be a relationship between a person's relative vulnerability to a particular type of inducement to change and his susceptibility to the same type of resistance-to-change manipulation. On the assumption that these are acquired predespositions, we are probing for possible antecedent learning conditions that make for such differential susceptibility. In addition, we are exploring situational factors that may influence susceptibility to one or another mode of persuasion within the same individual.

REFERENCES

Abelson, R.P., and Rosenberg, M.J. (1958). Symbolic psycho-logic: a model of attitudinal cognition. *Behav. Sci.* **3**, 1–13.

Allyn, Jane, and Festinger, L. (1961). The effectiveness of unanticipated persuasive communication. *J. abnorm. soc. Psychol.* **62**, 35–40.

Anderson, N.H., and Barrios, A.A. (1965). Primary effects in personality impression formation. *J. abnorm. soc. Psychol.* **63**, 346–350.

Brehm, J.W., and Cohen, A.R. (1962). *Explorations in cognitive dissonance.* New York: Wiley.

Brown, R.W. (1962). Models of attitude change. In R.W. Brown, E. Galanter, E.H. Hess, and G. Maudler (Eds.) *New directions in psychology.* New York: Holt, Rinehart & Winston, pp. 3–85.

Cartwright, D., and Harary, F. (1956). Structural balance: a generalization of Heider's theory. *Psychol. Rev.* **63**, 277–293.

Cohen, A.R. (1960). Attitudinal consequences of induced discrepancies between cognition and behavior. *Publ. Opin. Quart.* **24**, 297–318.

Das, J.P., and Nanda, P.C. (1963). Mediated transfer of attitudes. *J. abnorm. soc. Psychol.* **66**, 12–16.

Doob, L.W. (1947). The behavior of attitudes. *Psychol. Rev.* **54**, 135–156.

Festinger, L. (1957). *A theory of cognitive dissonance.* New York: Harper & Row.

Festinger, L. (Ed.) (1964). *Conflict, decision, and dissonance.* Stanford, California: Stanford Univ. Press.

Festinger, L., and Maccoby, N. (1964). On resistance to persuasive communications. *J. abnorm. soc. Psychol.* **68**, 367–380.

Fishbein, M., and Hunter, Ronda (1964). Summation versus balance in attitude organization and change. *J. abnorm. soc. Psychol.* **69**, 505–510.

Freedman, J. L., and Sears, D. O. (1966). Selective exposure. *Advance. Exp. Soc. Psychol.* **2**, 58–97.

Freedman, J. L., and Steinbruner, J. D. (1964). Perceived choice and resistance to persuasion. *J. abnorm. soc. Psychol.* **68**, 678–681.

Guttman, L. (1954). The principal components of scalable attitudes. In P. Lazersfeld (Ed.) *Mathematical thinking in the social sciences.* New York: Free Press.

Hall, M. (1965). The great cabbage hoax. *J. pers. soc. Psychol.* **2**, 563–569.

Hartmann, G. W. (1936). A field experiment on the comparative effectiveness of "emotional" and "rational" political leaflets in determining election results. *J. abnorm. soc. Psychol.* **31**, 99–114.

Heider, F. (1958). *The psychology of interpersonal relations.* New York: Wiley.

Hovland, C. I., Lumsdaine, A. A., and Sheffield, F. (1949). *Experiments on mass communication.* Princeton, New Jersey: Princeton Univ. Press.

Hovland, C. I., Janis, I. L., and Kelley, H. H. (1953). *Communication and persuasion.* New Haven, Connecticut: Yale Univ. Press.

Hovland, C. I., Harvey, O. J., and Sherif, M. (1957). Assimilation and contrast effects in reactions to communication and attitude change. *J. abnorm. soc. Psychol.* **55**, 244–252.

Insko, C. A. (1964). Primacy versus recency in persuasion as a function of the timing of arguments and measures. *J. abnorm. soc. Psychol.* **69**, 381–391.

Katz, D. (1960). The functional approach to the study of attitudes. *Publ. Opin. Quart.* **24**, 163–205.

Kelman, H. C., and Eagly, Alice H. (1965). Attitude toward the communicator, perception of communication content, and attitude change. *J. abnorm. soc. Psychol.* **1**, 63–78.

Kiesler, C. A., and Kiesler, Sara B. (1964). Role of forewarning in persuasive communication. *J. abnorm. soc. Psychol.* **68**, 547–549.

Klapper, J. (1960). *The effects of mass communication.* New York: Free Press.

Knower, F. H. (1935). A study of the effect of oral argument on changes of attitude. *J. soc. Psychol.* **6**, 315–344.

Lana, R. E. (1964). Three theoretical interpretations of order effects in persuasive communications. *Psychol. Bull.* **61**, 314–320.

Lewan, P. C., and Stotland, E. (1961). The effects of prior information on susceptibility to an emotional appeal. *J. abnorm. soc. Psychol.* **62**, 450–453.

Macaulay, Jacqueline R. (1965). A study of independent and additive modes of producing resistance to persuasion derived from congruity and inoculation models. Unpublished doctoral dissertation, Univ. of Wisconsin.

Manis, M., and Blake, J. R. (1963). Interpretation of persuasive messages as a function of prior immunization. *J. abnorm. soc. Psychol.* **66**, 225–230.

Manis, M., Gleason, T. C., and Dawes, R. M. (1966). The evaluation of complex social stimuli. *J. pers. soc. Psychol.* **3**, 404–419.

McGuire, W. J. (1960). A syllogistic analysis of cognitive relationships. In C. I. Hovland and M. J. Rosenberg (Eds.), *Attitude organization and change.* New Haven, Connecticut: Yale Univ. Press, pp. 65–111.

McGuire, W. J. (1961a). Resistance to persuasion conferred by active and passive prior refutation of the same and alternative counterarguments. *J. abnorm. soc. Psychol.* **63**, 326–332.

McGuire, W. J. (1961b). The effectiveness of supportive and refutational defenses in immunizing against persuasion. *Sociometry* **24**, 184–197.

McGuire, W. J. (1962). Persistence of the resistance to persuasion induced by various types of prior belief defenses. *J. abnorm. soc. Psychol.* **64**, 241–248.

McGuire, W. J. (1964). Inducing resistance to persuasion: some contemporary approaches. *Advanc. exp. soc. Psychol.* **1**, 191–229.

McGuire, W. J. (1966a). Attitudes and opinions. *Annu. Rev. Psychol.* **17**, 475–514.

McGuire, W. J. (1966b). The current status of cognitive consistency theories. In S. Feldman (Ed.), *The consistency motive.*

McGuire, W. J., and Papageorgis, D. (1961). The relative efficacy of various types of prior belief-defense in producing immunity against persuasion. *J. abnorm. soc. Psychol.* **62**, 327–337.

McGuire, W. J., and Papageorgis, D. (1962). Effectiveness of forewarning in developing resistance to persuasion. *Publ. Opin. Quart.* **26**, 24–34.

Menefee, S. C., and Granneberg, A. G. (1940). Propaganda and opinions on foreign policy. *J. soc. Psychol.* **11**, 393–404.

Mostofsky, D. I. (Ed.) (1965). *Stimulus generalization.* Stanford, California: Stanford Univ. Press.

Newcomb, T. M. (1953). An approach to the study of communicative acts. *Psychol. Rev.* **60**, 393–404.

Newcomb, T. M. (1959). Individual systems of orientation. In *Psychology: a study of a science*. Vol. 3. New York: McGraw-Hill.

Osgood, C. E. (1960). Cognitive dynamics in human affairs. *Publ. Opin. Quart.* **24**, 341–365.

Osgood, C. E., and Tannenbaum, P. H. (1955). The principle of congruity in the prediction of attitude change. *Psychol. Rev.* **62**, 42–55.

Osgood, C. E., Suci, G. J., and Tannenbaum, P. H. (1957). *The measurement of meaning.* Urbana, Illinois: Univ. of Illinois Press.

Papageorgis, D., and McGuire, W. J. (1961). The generality of immunity to persuasion produced by pre-exposure to weakened counterarguments. *J. abnorm. soc. Psychol.* **62**, 475–481.

Podell, Harriet A., and Podell, J. E. (1963). Quantitative connotation of a concept. *J. abnorm. soc. Psychol.* **67**, 509–513.

Rokeach, M., and Rothman, G. (1965). The principle of belief congruence and the congruity principle as models of cognitive interaction. *Psychol. Rev.* **72**, 128–142.

Rosenberg, M. J. (1960). An analysis of affective-cognitive consistency. In C. I. Hovland and M. J. Rosenberg (Eds.), *Attitude organization and change.* New Haven, Connecticut: Yale Univ. Press, pp. 15–64.

Rosenberg, M. J., and Abelson, R. P. (1960). An analysis of cognitive balancing. In C. I. Hovland and M. J. Rosenberg (Eds.), *Attitude organization and change.* New Haven, Connecticut: Yale Univ. Press, pp. 112–163.

Staats, A. W., and Staats, Carolyn K. (1958). Attitudes established by classical conditioning. *J. abnorm. soc. Psychol.* **57**, 37–40.

Staats, A. W., Staats, Carolyn K., and Heard, W. G. (1959). Language conditioning of meaning using a semantic generalization paradigm. *J. exp. Psychol.* **57**, 187–192.

Steiner, I. D. (1962). Receptivity to supportive versus nonsupportive communications. *J. abnorm. soc. Psychol.* **65**, 266–267.

Tannenbaum, P. H. (1956). Initial attitude toward source and concept as factors in attitude change through communication. *Publ. Opin. Quart.* **20**, 413–425.

Tannenbaum, P. H. (1966a). Colour as a code for connotative communication. In H. Spencer (Ed.), *The Penrose annual.* London: Lund, Humphries, pp. 115–121.

Tannenbaum, P. H. (1966b). Mediated generalization of attitude change via the principle of congruity. *J. pers. soc. Psychol.* **3**, 493–499.

Tannenbaum, P. H., and Gengel, R. W. (1966). Generalization of attitude change through congruity principle relationships. *J. pers. soc. Psychol.* **3**, 299–304.

Tannenbaum, P. H., and Norris, Eleanor L. (1965). Effects of combining congruity principle strategies for the reduction of persuasion. *Sociometry* **28**, 145–157.

Tannenbaum, P. H., Macaulay, Jacqueline R., and Norris, Eleanor L. (1966). The principle of congruity and reduction of persuasion. *J. pers. soc. Psychol.* **3**, 233–238.

Triandis, H. C., and Fishbein, M. (1963). Cognitive interaction in person perception. *J. abnorm. soc. Psychol.* **67**, 446–453.

Weiss, W. (1960). Emotional arousal and attitude change. *Psychol. Rep.* **6**, 267–280.

Weiss, W., and Lieberman, B. (1959). The effects of "emotional" language on the induction of change of opinions. *J. soc. Psychol.* **50**, 129–141.

Willis, R. H. (1960). Stimulus pooling and social perception. *J. abnorm. soc. Psychol.* **60**, 365–373.

Zajonc, R. B. (1960). Balance, congruity, and dissonance. *Publ. Opin. Quart.* **24**, 280–297.

A *Personal Addendum*

Percy H. Tannenbaum
GRADUATE SCHOOL OF PUBLIC
POLICY
UNIVERSITY OF CALIFORNIA,
BERKELEY

I keep telling myself I will get back to it some day, but it has not yet happened. When I wrote this article more than a decade ago, I was imbued with the study of persuasion, of how individuals form, modify, and reshape their attitudes toward objects and others in their environment. As the chapter ending testifies, I still had some unfinished business along this line on my research agenda. But that petered out within a few years as I changed institutions (from the University of Wisconsin to the University of Pennsylvania) and, a few years later, another change (from Penn to Berkeley) involved a more substantial alteration in my main field of teaching and research.

But I still feel a yearn to return to the kind of research reported in this chapter. If it was not the most innovative, it was some of the most rewarding in my personal experience. There are several reasons for this, and they may be worth contemplating in this current, somewhat jaded era of social psychology.

There was, from the very outset, the alluring attraction of the basic consistency theory formulation. Although it has fallen into some disfavor in the interval (there are, however, some encouraging signs of revival recently), it was and remains possibly the most compelling theoretical system introduced into social psychology. True enough, some of the experiments got to be a bit belabored, even overly contrived, but the cumulative research yielded an impressive and consis-

Cognitive Theories in Social Psychology

tent array of evidence of the basic conceptual system. Moreover, it did so without doing too much violence to the essentially simple basic conceptual scheme. The revisions that were introduced as a result offered tantalizing possibilities for further research, as is abundantly attested to in the handbook that was published not long after this article (Abelson *et al.*, 1968). I retain my own roster of such "unresolved dilemmas" on hand for any students who lament that they cannot find "interesting problems to work on," but in this era of "socially relevant" research the takers are few and far between.

If research on the more general consistency theory has abated, that dealing with implications of the particular congruity principle has been even less apparent. Though activity in the area of the integrated judgment of complex stimuli continues, it does not address the congruity principle formulation directly. In the attitude change arena, my mail does testify to a perceptible level of activity— there are periodic replications of one or another study conducted by a graduate student as a term project, occasionally a paper testing one or another of the theoretical propositions, and, of course, the usual set of requests for some of the experimental materials employed. But precious little of this gets into print, at least not in the journals I scan. Earlier on, I did have a number of students who were interested in the area for thesis or even dissertation work, but that has abated as my own research has changed focus.

I nevertheless remain impressed by the congruity principle findings, particularly several of the studies reported here. One reason is undoubtedly that I was never a committed believer in the theory in the first place, and nothing impresses the true skeptic more than findings disconfirming his expectations. From the very beginning, the congruity notion seemed far too simplistic to account for the kind of attitude-change behavior it sought to address. Though it had a ring of truth about it—that is, it seemed to "fit" familiar situations in others and in ourselves—it tolled rather thinly. Could people really behave according to such a simple, nonrational (if not irrational) set of premises? The initial findings helped convince us that there was something in it after all, especially when some nonobvious implications of the pure formalized theory held up rather well. But the skepticism persisted—not only the healthy scientific kind we are all supposed to carry around with us, but a more nagging personal doubt that the original formulation just could not hold up under real scrutiny. It was this sense of disbelief that motivated the various studies reported in this chapter.

A particular case in point was the set of studies dealing with the generalization of persuasion. It is this notion of generalization, as the term is used and operationalized in the paper, that lies at the heart of the congruity concept. Not to be confused with the concept of stimulus (or response) generalization in the conventional sense, the reference here is to cognitive linkages between two or more belief elements, such that a change introduced in one of the elements tends to affect the others. It is not too far a leap beyond the bilateral, or even tri-element, link to the notion of belief systems, of clusters of attitudes in more or less stable equilibrium within and between the clusters but vulnerable to external pressures that indirectly introduce change in the configuration through modification of one of its key components. That such changes can be specified as to direction or relative magnitude or both, and in somewhat intricate combinations, is a rare enough occurrence in social psychological theory as to warrant attention. That such theoretical predictions are borne out so well by the data I considered remarkable then, and still do. The impetus to design such experiments in the first place was not to find situations in which the theory was likely to be supported by (or, what is more often the case, not contradicted by) the data, but to put the theory to more of an acid test. The predicted patterns of change were logical extensions of the theory, and if there was anything to it, it should stand up to them. This it did so surprisingly well that I almost became skeptical of my skepticism (how is that for a definition of a true cynic?)—almost, but not quite, because I still do not believe people should really behave that way.

At that, there is obvious functional utility for people to behave according to such a principle, if for no other reason than that it embraces a least-effort principle in its operation. It takes less energy, time, etc. to maintain a finite set of belief clusters than an almost infinite number of individual items—a condition which inherent limitations of the memory system encourage. In the more limited case of applying the congruity principle to attitude change stemming from source-identified messages, there is some value in relying on source estimations in order to form an opinion or judgment. This is particularly true, of course, when there is little other basis on which to form an impression, when other, more objective evidence is lacking, and when the source has proven to be a reliable "belief barometer" in the past. When decisions have to be made—whom to vote for, what product or brand to buy, etc.—one tends to use whatever basis of judgment available, and often a judgment based on an apparent source's credibility, or lack of it, is as good a basis as any.

By the same token, the experiments reported in Section V of the chapter, contrasting congruity and so-called informational processes for attitude change, sought to address my doubts about the viability of the theory as a model of behavior. This series of studies tests the readiness of an individual to go along with the simple calculus of valences that the congruity principle postulates, as against a more factual basis for change. Although the data do not deny modification due to factual information, they do support the congruity-based processes rather well.

The experiments dealing with preparing an individual to be relatively immune from persuasion represent still another—and uncommon—tactic for testing the theory. Here, the theory is reversed, so to speak, by having it address the "other side" of the very issues for which it was originally developed. This results in a variety of strategies for reducing the subsequent impact of a highly persuasive message, strategies that can be employed individually or in combination. Again, as the various reported studies attest, the theory stands up in this respect as well.

So, what of the current status of the congruity principle? Although it remains somewhat in limbo for the present, it did test out rather well in a variety of situations and through a variety of experimental strategies—possibly as thoroughly as any social psychological theory to date. To be sure, each of the studies has its methodological measurement problem, since this continues to be among the less assured measurement areas in the field. However, whatever the weakness of measurement, experimenter expecting effects, etc., they are for the most part constant throughout the various experimental conditions and hence cannot readily account for the *differences* between conditions, which should remain as the primary focus for experimentally assessing any theory.

One is, in all humility, tempted to suggest a similar multi-faceted strategy to be employed in the testing of other social psychological theories—a continuing attempt, as I have said earlier, to push a theory to its limits, rather than the more common, often redundant, testing within the same limited sphere of action. In this respect, the various immunization treatments of the present program of research are a particular case in point, since they do represent a good theory-testing strategy that is all too often ignored: A theory that predicts when certain kinds of effects take place should also predict (and hence be tested for) conditions in which those effects should either be reduced or not occur at all.

REFERENCE

Abelson, R. P., Aronson, E., McGuire, W. J., Newcomb, T. M., Rosenberg, M. J., & Tannenbaum, P. H. (Eds.). *Theories of cognitive consistency: A sourcebook.* Chicago: Rand-McNally, 1968.

THE THEORY OF
COGNITIVE DISSONANCE:
A CURRENT PERSPECTIVE[1]

1969

Elliot Aronson
DEPARTMENT OF PSYCHOLOGY
UNIVERSITY OF TEXAS
AUSTIN, TEXAS

[1]Slightly revised from a chapter entitled "Dissonance Theory: Progress and Problems," in *The Cognitive Consistency Theories: a Source Book,* edited by R. Abelson, E. Aronson, W. McGuire, T. Newcomb, M. Rosenberg, and P. Tannenbaum; Chicago: Rand McNally, 1968; reprinted by permission of the author, editors, and publisher. This paper was prepared while the author's research was being supported by the National Institute of Mental Health, grant MH 12357.

181

I. Introduction

As a formal statement, Festinger's theory of cognitive dissonance (1957) is quite primitive; it lacks the elegance and precision that are commonly associated with scientific theorizing. Yet its impact has been great. As McGuire has observed in his recent survey in the *Annual Review of Psychology* (1966, p. 492), "Over the past three years, dissonance theory continued to generate more research and more hostility than any other one approach." We will allude to the "hostility" part of this statement from time to time throughout this article; but first, let us discuss the research.

The research has been as diverse as it has been plentiful; its range extends from maze running in rats (Lawrence and Festinger, 1962) to the development of values in children (Aronson and Carlsmith, 1963); from the hunger of college sophomores (Brehm *et al.*, 1964) to the proselytizing behavior of religious zealots (Festinger *et al.*, 1956). For descriptive summaries of dissonance experiments, the reader is referred to Festinger (1957); Festinger and Aronson (1960); Brehm and Cohen (1962); Festinger and Bramel (1962); Festinger and Freedman (1964).

The proliferation of research testing and extending dissonance theory results for the most part from the generality and simplicity of the theory. Although it has been applied primarily in social psychological settings, it is not limited to social psychological phenomena such as interpersonal relations or feelings toward a communicator and his communication. Rather, its domain is in the widest of places—the skull of an individual organism.[2]

A. The Theory

The core notion of the theory is extremely simple: Dissonance is a negative drive state which occurs whenever an individual simultaneously holds two cognitions (ideas, beliefs, opinions) which are psychologically inconsistent. Stated differently, two cognitions are dissonant if, considering these two cognitions alone, the opposite of one follows from the other. Since the occurrence of dissonance is presumed to be unpleasant, individuals strive to reduce it by adding "consonant" cognitions or by changing one or both cognitions to make them "fit togeth-

---

[2]An additional reason for the great number of experiments on dissonance theory is completely *ad hominem;* Leon Festinger has an unmatched genius for translating interesting hypotheses into workable experimental operations and for inspiring others to do so. He has produced a great deal of research irrespective of any particular theoretical approach.

er" better; i.e., so that they become more consonant with each other.[3] To use Festinger's time-worn (but still cogent) example, if a person believes that cigarette smoking causes cancer and simultaneously knows that he himself smokes cigarettes, he experiences dissonance. Assuming that the person would rather not have cancer, his cognition "I smoke cigarettes" is psychologically inconsistent with his cognition "Cigarette smoking produces cancer." Perhaps the most efficient way to reduce dissonance in such a situation is to stop smoking. But, as many of us have discovered, this is by no means easy. Thus, a person will usually work on the other cognition. There are several ways in which a person can make cigarette smoking seem less absurd. He might belittle the evidence linking cigarette smoking to cancer ("Most of the data are clinical rather than experimental"); or he might associate with other cigarette smokers ("If Sam, Jack, and Harry smoke, then it can't be very dangerous"); or he might smoke filter-tipped cigarettes and delude himself that the filter traps the cancer-producing materials; or he might convince himself that smoking is an important and highly pleasurable activity ("I'd rather have a shorter but more enjoyable life than a longer, unenjoyable one"); or he might actually make a virtue out of smoking by developing a romantic, devil-may-care image of himself, flaunting danger by smoking. All of these behaviors reduce dissonance, in effect, by reducing the absurdity involved in going out of one's way to contract cancer. Thus, dissonance theory does not rest upon the assumption that man is a *rational* animal; rather, it suggests that man is a rationa*lizing* animal—that he attempts to appear rational, both to others and to himself. To clarify the theoretical statement and to illustrate the kind of research generated by the theory a few experiments will be briefly described.

B.   DISSONANCE FOLLOWING A DECISION

One of the earliest experiments testing derivations from dissonance theory was performed by Brehm (1956). Brehm gave individuals their choice between two appliances which they had previously evaluated. He found that following the decision, when the subjects reevaluated the alternatives, they enhanced their liking for the chosen appliance and downgraded their evaluation of the unchosen one. The derivation is

[3]Although dissonance theory is an incredibly simple statement, it is not quite as simple as a reading of this article will indicate. Many aspects of the theory (for example, the propositions relevant to the magnitude of dissonance) will not be discussed here because they are peripheral to the major focus of this essay.

clear: Following a difficult choice, people experience dissonance. Cognitions about any negative attributes of the preferred object are dissonant with having chosen it; cognitions about positive attributes of the unchosen object are dissonant with *not* having chosen it. To reduce dissonance, people emphasize the positive aspects and deemphasize the negative aspects of the chosen objects while emphasizing the negative and deemphasizing the positive aspects of the unchosen object (see also Festinger, 1964).

C.   DISSONANCE RESULTING FROM EFFORT

Aronson and Mills (1959) reasoned that if people undergo a great deal of trouble in order to gain admission to a group which turns out to be dull and uninteresting they will experience dissonance. The cognition that they worked hard in order to become a member of the group is dissonant with cognitions concerning the negative aspects of the group. One does not work hard for nothing. To reduce dissonance, they will distort their perception of the group in a positive direction. In the Aronson-Mills experiment, college women underwent an initiation in order to become a member of a group discussion on the psychology of sex. For some of the girls the initiation was very embarrassing—it consisted of reciting a list of obscene words in the presence of the male experimenter. For others the initiation was a mild one. For still others there was no initiation at all. All of the subjects then listened to the same tape recording of a discussion being held by the group they had just joined. As predicted, the girls in the Severe Initiation condition rated the discussion much more favorably than did those in the other two conditions [see also Aronson (1961); Zimbardo (1965); Lewis (1964); Gerard and Mathewson (1966)].

D.   INSUFFICIENT JUSTIFICATION

Aronson and Carlsmith (1963) predicted that if threats are used to prevent people from performing a desired activity, the *smaller* the threat, the greater will be the tendency for people to derogate the activity. If an individual refrains from performing a desired activity, he experiences dissonance: The cognition that he likes the activity is dissonant with the cognition that he is not performing it. One way to reduce dissonance is by derogating the activity—in that way he can justify the fact that he is not performing it. However, any threat provides cognitions that are consonant with not performing the activity; and the more severe the threat, the greater the consonance. In short, a severe threat provides ample justification for not performing the activity; a mild threat provides less justification, leading the individual to add justifications of his own in the form of convincing himself that he *does not like* to perform the activity. In their experiment, Aronson and Carlsmith found that children who were threatened with *mild* punishment for playing with a desired toy *decreased* their liking for the toy to a greater extent than did children who were severely threatened (see also Turner and Wright, 1965; Freedman, 1965).

II. What Is Psychological Inconsistency?

The very simplicity of the core of the theory is at once its greatest strength and its most serious weakness. We have already discussed the heuristic value of its simplicity. It should be emphasized that many of the hypotheses which are obvious derivations from the theory are *unique* to that theory; i.e., they could not be derived from any other theory. This increases our confidence in dissonance theory as an explanation of an important aspect of human behavior. The weakness occurs primarily in the difficulty involved with defining the limits of the theoretical statement. While at the "center" of the theory it is relatively easy to generate hypotheses that are clear and direct, at its "fringes" it is not always clear whether or not a prediction can be made from the theory and, if so, exactly what that prediction will be.[4] Although investigators who have had experience working with the theory seem to have little difficulty intuiting its boundary conditions, they have had considerable difficulty communicating this to other people; indeed, a situation has evolved which can best be described by the statement: "If you want to be sure, ask Leon." This has proved to be both a source of embarrassment for the proponents of the theory as well as a source of annoyance and exasperation to its critics.

Why is it so difficult to make a more precise theoretical statement? Perhaps the most basic reason has to do with the nature of the inconsistency involved in the core definition of dissonance theory. It would be easy to specify dissonant situations if the theory were limited to *logical* inconsistencies. There exist relatively unequivocal rules of logic which can be applied without ambiguity or fear of contradiction. But recall that the inconsistency that produces dissonance, although it can be logical inconsistency, is not necessarily logical. Rather, it is *psychological* inconsistency. While this aspect of the theory increases its

---

[4]Later in this article some attempt will be made to specify exactly what is meant by "center" and "fringes."

power, range, and degree of interest, at the same time it also causes
some serious problems. Thus, returning to our friend, the cigarette
smoker, the cognition regarding smoking cigarettes is not logically inconsistent with the cognition linking cigarette smoking to cancer; i.e.,
strictly speaking, having information that cigarette smoking causes cancer does not make it illogical to smoke cigarettes. But these cognitions
do produce dissonance because, taken together, they do not make
sense psychologically. Assuming that the smoker does not want cancer,
the knowledge that cigarettes cause cancer should lead to *not* smoking
cigarettes. Similarly, none of the research examples mentioned above
deals with logical inconsistency; e.g., it is not illogical to go through
hell and high water to gain admission to a dull discussion group; it is
not illogical to choose to own an appliance that one considers slightly
more attractive than the unchosen alternative; it is not illogical to refrain from playing with a toy at the request of an adult.

Festinger (1957) lists four kinds of situations in which dissonance
can arise: (1) logical inconsistency; (2) inconsistency with cultural mores;
(3) inconsistency between one cognition and a more general, more encompassing cognition; and (4) past experience.

(1) Logical inconsistency: Suppose a person believed that all men
are mortal but also held the belief that he, as a man, would live forever.
These two cognitions are dissonant because they are logically inconsistent. The obverse of one follows from the other on strict logical grounds.

(2) Cultural mores: If a college professor loses his patience with one
of his students and shouts at him angrily, his knowledge of what he is
doing is dissonant with his idea about what is the proper, acceptable behavior of a professor toward his students — in our culture. In some other
cultures this might be appropriate behavior and, therefore, would not
arouse dissonance.

(3) Inconsistency between a cognition and a more encompassing
cognition: In a given election, if a person who has always considered himself to be a Democrat votes for the Republican candidate, he should experience dissonance. The concept "I am a Democrat" encompasses the
concept "I vote for Democratic candidates."

(4) Past experience: If a person stepped on a tack while barefoot and
felt no pain, he would experience dissonance because he knows from experience that pain follows from stepping on tacks. If he had never had
experience with tacks or other sharp objects, he would *not* experience
dissonance.

The illustrations presented above are clear examples of dissonance.
Similarly, the situations investigated in the experiments described above
are clearly dissonant. But there *are* situations where for all practical pur-

poses it is not perfectly clear whether two cognitions are dissonant or merely irrelevant. Because dissonance is *not* limited to logical inconsistencies, it is occasionally difficult to specify *a priori* whether or not a cultural more is being violated, whether or not an event is markedly different from past experience, or whether or not it is different from a more general cognition. Recall the basic theoretical statement: Two cognitions are dissonant if, considering these two cognitions alone, the obverse of one follows from the other. The major source of conceptual ambiguity rests upon the fact that Festinger has not clarified the meaning of the words "follows from."

For example, if I learn that my favorite novelist beats his wife, does this arouse dissonance? It is difficult to be certain. Strictly speaking, being a wife-beater is not incompatible with being a great novelist.[5] However, there may be a sense in which the term "great novelist" implies that such a person is wise, sensitive, empathic, and compassionate — and wise, sensitive, empathic, and compassionate people do not go around beating their wives. This is not a logical inconsistency; nor is it a clear violation of a cultural more; moreover, it may have nothing to do with past experience — and it is not *necessarily* embedded in a more general cognition. Thus, a knowledge of the kinds of situations in which dissonance *can* occur is not always useful in determining whether dissonance *does* occur.

A rule of thumb which we have found useful is to state the situation in terms of the violation of an expectancy. For example, one might issue the following instructions: "Consider Mr. Roy Wilkins of the National Association for the Advancement of Colored People. I'm going to tell you something about his beliefs about the native IQ of Negroes relative to that of Caucasians. What do you expect these beliefs to be?" No doubt most people would have a firm expectancy that Mr. Wilkins would say that there are no innate differences. Consequently, one could then conclude that if individuals were exposed to a statement by Mr. Wilkins to the effect that Negroes were innately stupider than Caucasians, most would experience dissonance. Let's try our difficult example. Suppose we confronted a large number of people with the following proposition: "Consider the great novelist, X. I am about to tell you something about whether or not he beats his wife. What do you expect me to say?" Probably most people would shrug; i.e., they would not have a strong expectancy (but, again, this is an empirical question; there is no certainty that

---

[5]If *I* had beaten my wife I might experience dissonance because of *my* violation of a cultural more. But since I know that many people beat their wives, discovering that a particular person beats his wife is not necessarily inconsistent with my cognition about the world and human nature. More will be said about this later.

it would come out this way). If this occurred, one could conclude that X's wife-beating behavior is irrelevant to his status as a novelist. An empirical rule of thumb may be of practical utility but is, of course, no substitute for a clearer, less ambiguous, more precise theoretical statement. Near the end of the article this rule of thumb will be elaborated upon and it will be indicated how it might be used conceptually.

III. Methodological Problems

Some critics have pointed to the ambiguities inherent in the theoretical statement and have concluded that they make the theory impossible to disprove and, consequently, worthless. As stated above, some conceptual ambiguities do exist and will be elaborated on shortly. But first, we should make it clear that these conceptual ambiguities exist in a very small part of the domain in which the theory has continued to make clear and precise predictions; these predictions have been validated a number of times in a number of different ways. Why, then, does the theory inspire what McGuire (1966) referred to as ". . . more hostility than any other one approach"? We feel that a good deal of the hostility is misdirected — stemming from a confusion between conceptual and methodological ambiguities. Much of the difficulty in disproving dissonance theory arises from weaknesses in the method of social psychological experimentation. These weaknesses are hardly the fault of the theory. Moreover, these methodological problems are not peculiar to research on dissonance theory but are shared by research on all theories that predict social psychological phenomena. They tend to have been associated with dissonance theory precisely because of the great quantity of research generated (and, therefore, of methodological problems unearthed) by that theory. The major methodological problems stem from the lack of tried and true, standardized techniques for operationalizing conceptual variables in social psychology. Consequently, any single failure in a given experiment can be attributed to a failure in the experimental operations rather than an error of conceptualization. At the same time, repeated failures across a wide variety of techniques would spell the end of dissonance theory or any theory.

The Problem of Alternative Explanations

The lack of a standardized method in social psychology has contributed to another major difficulty with research in this area: It is frequently possible to come up with alternative explanations for empirical results. Thus, like experiments testing other theories in social psychology, many of the experiments testing dissonance theory are subject to alternative explanations. If some of the data can be explained without recourse to dissonance theory, our confidence in the theory is weakened. At the same time, dissonance theory does provide the most parsimonious explanation for the data taken as a whole—as McGuire has argued: "The whole set of dissonance studies would require accepting a tremendous variety of alternative explanations, whereas dissonance theory alone explains a large subset of them" (1966, p. 493). Although this is some recommendation, it is not wholly sufficient. One still wants to be able to determine which explanation is more nearly correct. The best way to distinguish among plausible alternative explanations is through a series of well-controlled systematic experiments which are essentially conceptual replications using markedly different sets of operations to test the same hypothesis. This technique has been referred to as "purification"; the necessity for such procedures as well as a fuller description is provided elsewhere (Aronson and Carlsmith, 1968).

Let us take, as an illustration, the initiation experiment by Aronson and Mills (1959). Recall that the investigators predicted the results on the basis of dissonance theory; specifically, the cognition that one has gone through an unpleasant and embarrassing initiation in order to get into a group was dissonant with the cognition that the discussion group was dull and dreary. In order to reduce dissonance, subjects in the Severe Initiation condition (but not in the Mild Initiation condition) convinced themselves that the "dull" group was really quite exciting. In order to maximize credibility and impact, the investigators constructed a rather novel method for operationalizing "unpleasant effort"; they had the girls in the Severe Initiation condition recite a list of obscene words and some lurid passages from contemporary novels in the presence of a male experimenter. This procedure made sense in terms of the over-all "scenario" of the experiment, thus effectively masking the true purpose of the experiment and reducing the possibility of suspicion. It also seemed to be effective in the sense that the girls appeared to be embarrassed—they tended to hesitate, blush, cast their eyes downward, etc. Nevertheless, the use of sexually related material opened the door for at least two plausible alternative explanations, both offered by Chapanis and Chapanis (1964). One is that while reciting the material the girls did not become embarrassed, but, rather, became sexually aroused; this could have produced pleasure or the expectation of pleasure which supposedly would increase the attractiveness of the discussion group. The second is quite the reverse: The subjects in the Severe Initiation condition felt relief (from sexual anxiety?) when they found the group discussion banal instead of embarrassing. Supposedly, this could lead them to rate the discussion as not banal at all.

Whether these explanations are more or less plausible than the dissonance explanation is not important. The important point is that they are at
least possible. In order to distinguish between the dissonance explanation
and these alternative explanations, the same hypothesis should be tested
using an operational definition of "unpleasant effort" which has nothing to
do with the pleasantness of sexual arousal or relief from sexual anxiety.
Such an experiment has been performed by Gerard and Mathewson
(1966), who replicated the Aronson-Mills (1959) experiment conceptually. In their experiment they advertised their group discussions as
being on the topic of college morals; the actual discussion was a rather
pallid one involving cheating on examinations. The initiation procedure
consisted of electric shocks instead of obscene words as used by Aronson
and Mills. The results paralleled those of Aronson and Mills and confirmed the prediction from dissonance theory: Those subjects who underwent a series of severe electric shocks in order to gain admission to a dull
discussion group came to rate that group more favorably than those who
gained admission after having undergone mild electric shocks.

This single procedure, of course, does not eliminate all alternative
explanations. Let us return to the critique of the Aronson-Mills (1959)
experiment. To quote Chapanis and Chapanis:

> It is interesting to speculate what would have happened if the girls had
> been 'initiated' into the group by the use of a more generally accepted painful
> procedure, such as using electric shock. Somehow it seems doubtful that this
> group would appreciate the group discussion more than the control group, unless
> — and here is the crucial point — the conditions were so manipulated that Ss expe-
> rienced a feeling of successful accomplishment in overcoming the painful obsta-
> cle. It seems to us that if there is anything to the relationship between severity of
> initiation and liking for the group, it lies in this feeling of successful accomplish-
> ment. The more severe the test, the stronger is the pleasurable feeling of success
> in overcoming the obstacle. There is no need to postulate a drive due to disso-
> nance if a *pleasure principle* can account for the results quite successfully
> (1964, p. 5).

Thus, while Chapanis and Chapanis would appear to have been
wrong in their conviction that the effect demonstrated by Aronson and
Mills would *not* replicate if electric shock had been used, they have apparently left themselves an escape hatch. Fortunately, however, there are
some data on this issue also. According to Chapanis and Chapanis (1964),
the more painful the situation one overcomes, the greater the feeling of
successful accomplishment. Although they do not explain how this feeling
of pleasure would make subjects like the discussion group better, one assumes that they are using a rather simple contiguity model: If a person
feels good, contiguous stimuli (e.g., the discussion group) look and feel

good. Dissonance theory, of course, does not make use of such a contiguity explanation; i.e., the group discussion looks good *not* because it is contiguous with pain reduction (dissonance reduction)—rather, it comes to look good as a *means of reducing* dissonance. The crucial aspect of dissonance arousal in this situation is that getting into a group was contingent upon going through a severe initiation; that is, it was an initiation, not simply a stimulus that was contiguous with a pleasant feeling. Consequently, if one simply hears a group discussion after having successfully undergone a severe shock, dissonance theory would make no prediction regarding the attractiveness of the group. It would make a prediction only if the person had experienced dissonance; i.e., if the person had undergone a severe initiation *in order to* get into a dull group.

Thus, a test between the Chapanis and Chapanis "successful accomplishment" explanation and the dissonance explanation can be arranged simply by comparing an initiation (i.e., an "in order to" situation) with a contiguous situation. Such a test was built into the Gerard-Mathewson (1966) study. In this experiment some subjects underwent a severe shock in order to get into a group (Initiation condition) while other subjects simply underwent severe shock (No Initiation condition). If a feeling of success is aroused by getting through the shock situation, both groups had it. All subjects were then exposed to a taped group discussion. Thus, for subjects in both conditions the discussion was contiguous with feelings of "successful accomplishment"; but only those in the Initiation condition experienced dissonance. The results clearly support dissonance theory. Those who went through severe electric shock in order to get into a dull group rated the taped group discussion as more attractive than a "mild shock" control condition. Those who went through a severe shock (without dissonance) and then listened to the same tape rated the discussion as less attractive than those in the Initiation condition—indeed, they tended to rate the taped discussion as *less* attractive than subjects in the parallel (No Initiation) condition who underwent mild electric shock. This latter finding suggests that even in the absence of dissonance, "a feeling of successful accomplishment" does not operate—but something else does; more will be made of this later.[6]

To sum up this point, it should be made clear that neither the receiving of electric shock nor the recitation of obscene words is a perfect empirical realization of the conception "unpleasant effort." Neither, by it-

[6]One additional piece of data is of relevance. One-half of the subjects in the Initiation condition were told they passed the test and one-half were not told. The "told—not told" manipulation did not interact with the severity of shock. This provides further evidence against the "successful accomplishment" explanation.

self, is free of alternative explanations. The recitation of obscene words is open to alternative explanations involving sexual matters — electric shock is open to alternative explanations involving pain, fear, pain reduction, and fear reduction. But taken together, they eliminate most possible alternative explanations. Accordingly, many of the results supporting dissonance theory have been and can continue to be strengthened by eliminating alternative explanations through the purification of operations afforded by conceptual replications. As this process continues, our confidence in the validity and viability of the theory increases — in spite of its simplicity and inelegance as a conceptual statement.[7]

Of course, as indicated, not all the problems of dissonance theory are methodological. Several additional conceptual problems will be discussed in a moment.

IV. The "Nothing But" Critique

Scientists tend to be conservative, parsimonious creatures. This is generally a healthy attitude which most frequently manifests itself in a reluctance to accept a new theory or a novel explanation for a phenomenon if the phenomenon can be squeezed (even with great difficulty) into an existing approach. In this regard, dissonance theory has been referred to as "warmed-over soup"; i.e., as nothing but a new name for an old explanation. This has been most persistently stated in regard to that aspect of the theory related to decision making. In this context dissonance theory has been referred to as nothing but another name for conflict theory.

A.   DISSONANCE OR CONFLICT?

In fact, there are several differences. Conflict occurs before a decision is made, dissonance occurs after the decision. During conflict it is assumed that an individual will devote his energies to a careful, dispassionate, and sensible evaluation and judgment of the alternatives. He will

---

[7]In struggling toward greater methodological sophistication, investigators working with dissonance theory face the same problems as other experimental social psychologists. Thus, the major critical review of dissonance theory to date (Chapanis and Chapanis, 1964) is largely a methodological critique. Although many of the points made in this review involve reasonable methodological criticisms, the unfortunate illusion is created that, somehow, "dissonance theorists" commit more methodological blunders than the rest of us. In articulating this point, Chapanis and Chapanis attempt to cite examples of good (i.e., nondissonance) methodology in this area. Ironically, their principal example of good methodology is an experiment where the subjects were allowed to assign *themselves* to experimental conditions (p. 19), thus negating the major defining characteristic of an experiment.

gather all of the information, pro and con, about all of the alternatives in order to make a reasonable decision. Following the decision, a person is in a state of dissonance – all negative aspects of X are dissonant with having chosen X; all positive aspects of Y are dissonant with *not* having chosen Y. Far from evaluating the alternatives impartially (as in conflict), the individual experiencing dissonance will seek biased information and evaluations designed to make his decision appear more reasonable. As in Brehm's (1956) experiment, he will seek to spread the alternatives apart. The more difficulty a person had making a decision, the greater the tendency toward this kind of behavior as a means of justifying his decision.

But how can we be certain that the "spreading apart" of the alternatives in Brehm's experiment occurred after the decision? Could it not have occurred during the conflict stage? That is, it is conceivable that, in order to make their decision easier, subjects in Brehm's experiment began to reevaluate the appliances in a biased manner *before* the decision. If this were the case, then there is no essential difference between predecisional and postdecisional processes; if so, this behavior can be considered part of conflict – and there is, indeed, no need to complicate matters by bringing in additional terminology.

Brehm's experiment does not allow us to determine whether the evaluation of chosen and unchosen alternatives was spread apart before or after the decision. Experiments by Davidson and Kiesler (1964) and by Jecker (1964) serve to clarify this issue. In Jecker's experiment, subjects were offered their choice between two phonograph records. In three conditions there was *low conflict*; i.e., subjects were told that there was a very good chance that they would receive *both* records no matter which they chose. In three other conditions, *high conflict* was produced by telling them that the probability was high that they would be given only the record that they chose. All of the subjects rated the records before the instructions; in each of the conflict conditions subjects rerated the records either (*a*) after they discovered that they received both records, (*b*) after they discovered that they received only the one record they chose, or (*c*) before they were certain whether they would get one or both. The results are quite clear: No spreading apart occurred when there was no dissonance; i.e., when the subject actually received both records or when he was not certain whether he would receive one or both, he did *not* reevaluate the alternatives systematically. Where dissonance did occur there was a systematic reevaluation; i.e., subjects spread their evaluation of the alternatives when they received only one record – this occurred independently of the degree of conflict. This experiment provides clear evidence that conflict and dissonance are different processes; whatever else dissonance theory might be, it is *not* "nothing but conflict theory."

B. DISSONANCE OR SELF-JUDGMENT?

An intriguing variation on the "nothing but" theme is Bem's (1965, 1967) analysis of the insufficient justification phenomenon. Speaking from the point of view of "a radical behaviorist," Bem suggested that the experiments involving insufficient justification can be accounted for by a self-judgment model. Accordingly, an aversive motivational state (dissonance) is superfluous to an understanding of these phenomena. Bem's model was based upon an individual's ability to infer what his real attitudes are by merely discriminating the circumstances which control his behavior. According to Bem, each person is the observer of his own behavior. The individual, then, in effect asks himself what the reinforcements were which guided his actions. If the person observes that he performed for a large reward, he is *less* apt to believe that the behavior was a reflection of his real attitudes than if he performed it for a small reward.

To clarify the different approaches, let us examine the experiment by Cohen (1962) in which Yale students were induced to write an essay favoring the repressive actions of the New Haven Police Department in quelling a student riot. Cohen found that those students who were paid 50¢ came to believe in the truth of their statements to a greater extent than did those who were paid $1.00

According to dissonance theory, the cognition that one has written an essay is dissonant with the cognition that one disagrees with the point of view of the essay. The smaller the compensation, the greater the dissonance; the greater the dissonance, the greater the tendency to agree with what one has written.

Bem suggested that what is called "dissonance" is really an instance of self-judgment based upon the subject's simple discrimination of the reinforcement contingencies. According to Bem, the subject says, in effect, "If I wrote the essay for only 50¢, then I must really believe it, whereas if it required $1.00 to get me to write it, then I probably don't believe it as much." This reasoning, in and of itself, is not really different from the way a dissonance theorist would conceptualize the process. But Bem carried his reasoning one step further: He reasoned that an aversive motivational state is unnecessary. Consequently, an observer should be able to arrive at the same inference as the subject himself — if the observer has knowledge of the incentive offered to the subject to induce him to perform a given behavior. Bem tested this prediction by describing to each of his subjects one of the conditions in Cohen's (1962) experiment. He found that these observers could estimate the attitude of Cohen's subjects — even though these observers, of course, were not experiencing dissonance. In short, Bem's observer-subjects estimated that Cohen's subjects who wrote the essay for 50¢ were more favorably disposed to the actions of the New Haven police than those who wrote the essay for $1.00.

But the events experienced by a "real" subject and those experienced by an observer are very different. Taking this position, Jones *et al.* (1968, in press) argue that Bem's results are misleading. Picture the situation: Yale students are asked to write an essay favoring police suppression of Yale students. It seems reasonable to assume that Bem's observers would infer that a typical Yale student would be unwilling to comply with the experimenter's request. But the subject Bem described to an observer *did*, in fact, comply. Because of this, Bem's observers in the 50¢ condition are likely to infer that the behavior of that specific subject was not typical; i.e., since he was quite willing to express an obviously unpopular point of view for such a small sum of money, he must have been more willing to comply than most Yale students. Consequently, it is possible that he favored the actions of the New Haven police in the first place. In Cohen's original experiment, of course, since the subject was himself the complier, if he complied reluctantly and was initially opposed to the actions of the New Haven police, it is more likely that he was aware of it.

This is a subtle distinction, but it may be an important one. In a set of factorial experiments, Jones *et al.* demonstrated that they can replicate Bem's results under Bem's conditions; i.e., observers felt that subjects who wrote the essay for 50¢ were more favorably disposed to the New Haven police than those who wrote the essay for $1.00. But under conditions which effectively eliminated the possibility of observers attributing *a priori* differences to the subjects, the results were opposite to Bem's. Here observers estimated that the original subjects in the $1.00 condition were more favorable to the actions of the New Haven police than were the original subjects in the 50¢ condition. These results, then, cast serious doubt on the contention that the observer (who, of course, is not experiencing dissonance) can effectively infer the attitudes of a subject in a dissonance experiment.

However, this experiment is not completely conclusive because it involves a change in the conditions of Cohen's original experiment. The possibility remains that Cohen's subjects *did* come to feel that they *initially* favored the actions of the New Haven police. Thus, Bem's results may, indeed, be an accurate translation of the Cohen experiment. What must be established in future experiments is whether or not the subject's behavior (writing a counter-attitudinal essay) becomes so very salient that it overwhelms his memory about his original position. This seems unlikely when the issue is as personally involving for the Yale students as the actions of the New Haven police. Nevertheless, the question remains an open one; at this time the most that can be said is that there is no compelling evidence that dissonance-like phenomena can occur in the absence of an aversive motivational state.

V. The Multiple Mode Problem

As indicated earlier, several problems are central to the theoretical statement. One of the knottiest and most interesting conceptual problems in dissonance theory involves the fact that in a given situation there is usually more than one way for a person to reduce dissonance. For example, the cigarette smoker has several techniques at his disposal. He may use any one, or several simultaneously. Experimentally, this problem can be eliminated by the simple device of blocking alternative techniques of dissonance reduction. This is part of the definition of experimental control; any experimenter worth his salt will attempt to control the environment so that the behavior elicited by his independent variable will occur in a manner which is measurable and at a time and place where the measuring instruments have been set up. To illustrate: In a typical communication – persuasion experiment, if a highly credible communicator states a position which is discrepant from the position of the recipient, the recipient experiences dissonance. He can reduce dissonance in one of four ways: (1) he can change his opinion to make it coincide with the communicator's, (2) he can attempt to change the communicator's opinion, (3) he can seek social support from other members of the audience, or (4) he can derogate the communicator. If one is interested in measuring opinion change (1), one can eliminate (2) and (3) by making it impossible for the subject to interact either with the communicator or his fellow subjects. Furthermore, one can reduce the subject's ability to derogate the communicator by assigning the latter high enough prestige so that he becomes virtually nonderogatable. Thus, if these four techniques exhaust the universe, the only way that a subject can reduce dissonance is by changing his attitude on the issue. The prudent experimenter will have built his experiment to make it appear reasonable to measure the subject's attitudes after the communication, and he will use the most sensitive measuring instrument he can construct.

Thus, if the question one asks is "Does dissonance occur in such a situation and does it get reduced?" the answer can be easily determined experimentally. But we may have a different question in mind: "In a given situation, how do people generally reduce dissonance?" And the answer to this question may be strikingly different from the mode found in the laboratory experiment. To illustrate, in the above example, most people might prefer to argue with the communicator rather than change their opinion.

The above argument suggests that the results from carefully controlled laboratory experiments, on occasion, may be somewhat misleading. For example, suppose a young Ph.D. is being considered for a teaching position in a major department at a prestigeous Ivy League university. What happens if the members of that department decide not to hire him? If he feels that he is a good and worthy scholar, he will experience cognitive dissonance: His cognition that he is a good scholar is dissonant with his cognition that he was rejected by members of a good department. Thus, he can reduce dissonance in at least two ways: (1) he can convince himself that his rejectors are, in reality, stupid, defensive, unprofessional, and/or senile people who cannot or will not recognize a good man when they see one; (2) he can convince himself that if they can reject him (as good as he is), then their standards must be astronomically high and therefore they are a fine group of nonsenile professionals. Both of these techniques succeed in reducing dissonance; moreover, they both protect the individual's ego—he leaves for his job at East Podunk State Teacher's College with the conviction that he is a good scholar. But note that the results of his dissonance-reducing behavior can leave him with totally opposite opinions about the members of the staff at the Ivy League university. Thus, if one wanted to arouse dissonance in an individual for the specific purpose of enhancing his impressions of the people at Ivy University, one had better be careful. The same dissonance-producing situation can result in quite the opposite dissonance-reducing behavior.

A. CONSISTENCY WITH OTHER EVENTS

This is a serious conceptual problem. One way that it can be solved is by coming up with a set of specific propositions that can lead one to state the conditions under which one mode or the other is more likely to occur. A possible solution was previously outlined in a specific situation (Aronson, 1961). The situation was one involving alternative modes of dissonance reduction following the unsuccessful expenditure of effort. If a person struggles to reach a goal and fails, he experiences dissonance. His cognition that he exerted effort to attain the goal is dissonant with his cognition that he did not reach it. He could reduce dissonance by convincing himself that the goal was not worth it anyway; recall that this was the way that Aesop's fox reduced dissonance in the fable of the sour grapes. There is another reasonable way to reduce dissonance: by the person's finding something else in the situation to which he can attach value in order to justify his expenditure of effort without achieving his avowed goal. Thus, the fox might convince himself that he got some much-needed exercise while leaping for the grapes, and that even though he failed to get those luscious, sweet grapes, it was worth the effort because of the muscles he developed while trying.

Under what conditions will an individual take one path rather than the other? The first solution (Aronson, 1961) is probably easier, but only in a situation where the effort expended is of short duration. However, if the situation consists of a long and repeated expenditure of effort, it becomes a less viable solution. To use the previous illustration, if the fox made a few leaps at the grapes and failed, he could convince himself that they were probably sour anyway; but if he spent the entire afternoon struggling to reach the grapes, it would not effectively reduce dissonance to maintain that the grapes were sour—for if that were the case, why in the world did he try to reach them over and over and over again? The data from the above-mentioned experiment indicated that after the repeated expenditure of effort people *do* attach value to an incidental stimulus; however, the definitive factorial experiment remains to be done.

It is encouraging to note that experimenters are beginning to focus their efforts on this kind of problem. A good example of this trend is described in a very recent article by Walster *et al.* (1967), who hypothesize that individuals will choose that mode of dissonance reduction which is least likely to be challenged by future events. In their experiment, children were given their choice between two toys. In a situation like this, individuals can reduce dissonance in two ways: by cognitively increasing the attractiveness of the chosen alternative and/or by cognitively decreasing the attractiveness of the unchosen alternative. One-half of the children were led to expect that they would subsequently hear objective information about the toy they chose; one-half of the children were led to expect that they would hear objective information about the rejected toy. The investigators found, as predicted, that individuals reduced dissonance by distorting the attractiveness of that toy which they were not going to hear information about; that is, they opted to reduce dissonance in a manner which was less likely to run up against objective reality.

B. COMMITMENT AND VOLITION

In order to be of maximum use, such specific solutions should be restated into more general propositions, where possible, and incorporated into the theory. An important step in this direction was taken by Brehm and Cohen (1962) in emphasizing the importance of commitment and volition in determining not only the strength of the dissonance involved, but also, perhaps more important, in determining the nature of the dissonance and, hence, the nature of the mechanisms needed to reduce dissonance. Whether or not a high degree of volition is present can change the nature of the prediction even though both situations may involve cognitive dissonance. For example, in a minor part of their experiment, Aronson *et al.* (1963) reasoned that disagreement with a highly credible source produces more dissonance then disagreement with a source having low credibility. The cognition that a highly sentient person believes X is dissonant with the cognition that I believe *not X*. The higher the credibility of the source, the greater the dissonance — because the less sense it makes to be in disagreement with him. This should lead to greater attitude change in the Highly Credible condition — to reduce dissonance. The results of their experiment were consistent with this reasoning. On the other hand, Zimbardo (1960) and Brehm and Cohen (1962) reasoned that under certain conditions a source having low credibility would produce greater attitude change than one having high credibility. Specifically, if a person had chosen of his own volition to go to hear a speech by a low credibility source, he would experience a great deal of dissonance. The cognition involving volition and commitment is dissonant with the cognition that the credibility of the communicator is low; after all, it is absurd to choose to go out of one's way to hear a low prestige source make a speech which is discrepant with one's own opinion. In order to reduce dissonance, one might convince oneself that there was no essential discrepancy — that one always held the position espoused by the low credibility source. Thus, Zimbardo and Brehm and Cohen suggested that under conditions of high commitment one might get greater agreement with a low credibility source than with a high credibility source. This prediction made by Zimbardo and by Brehm and Cohen is consistent with other data involving choice and commitment. For example, Smith (1961) found that soldiers who volunteered to eat grasshoppers when induced by an unpleasant leader, came to like the grasshoppers better than did those who volunteered to eat them when induced by an affable leader. Similar results are reported by Zimbardo (1964a,b).

It should be clear that the prediction made by Aronson *et al.* and that made by Zimbardo and by Brehm and Cohen are not mutually exclusive; rather, they apply to a crucially different set of circumstances. Although both predictions are derived from dissonance theory, they involve different aspects of the theory; the crucial distinction is whether or not a high degree of volition is present. Nonetheless, to avoid confusion, these distinctions should be articulated with even greater clarity.

To sum up this section, dissonance theory, as originally stated, *does* have some areas of conceptual fuzziness. Much of this fuzziness can be eliminated by empirical research. Again, this research should be focused

on the conditions and variables which maximize and minimize the occurrence of dissonance and dissonance reduction as well as the conditions
which lead to one or another mode of dissonance reduction. This position
will be elaborated upon in a moment.

VI. Dissonance Theory and Reward-Incentive Theory

A. Not Which but When

One of the intriguing aspects of dissonance theory is that it frequently
leads to predictions which stand in apparent contradiction to those made
by other theoretical approaches, most notably, to a general reward-incentive theory. The words "stand in apparent contradiction" were carefully
chosen, for as we shall see, these theories are not mutually exclusive on a
conceptual level. No advocate of dissonance theory would take issue with
the fact that people frequently perform behaviors in order to obtain rewards or that activities associated with rewards tend to be repeated. What
they would suggest is that under certain carefully prescribed conditions,
cognitive events are set in motion which result in behaviors quite different
from what one would expect from reward-incentive theories. Moreover,
they might also suggest that such situations are not rare and, therefore,
such behaviors are not flukey. Rather, they are quite common; one reason
that they seem strange or "uncommonsensical" to us is that total reliance
on other theoretical approaches (explicitly or implicitly) have blinded us
to alternative possiblities or have made us disinclined to look beyond the
obvious events generated by reward-reinforcement theories. The much
discussed "nonobvious" predictions generated by dissonance theory are
nonobvious only in an apparent sense; they become obvious and make
sense once we gain an understanding of the dissonance-reducing process.

In the previous section, when discussing alternative ways of reducing
dissonance, the author tried to make the point that it is not very fruitful to
ask what the mode of dissonance reduction is; rather, it is far more meaningful and instructive to isolate the various modes of reducing dissonance
and to ask what the optimum conditions are for each. Similarly, rather
than ask whether dissonance theory or reward-incentive theory is the
more valid, one should attempt to determine the optimal conditions for
the occurrence of processes and behaviors predicted by each theory.

One example of this approach has already been discussed. Recall
that in the Gerard and Mathewson (1966) conceptual replication of the
Aronson-Mills (1959) experiment, they found that when dissonance was
eliminated from the experimental situation (in the No Initiation condition)

subjects tended to rate the group discussion as being less attractive if it followed severe electric shock. Recall also that this is opposite to the feelings of "successful accomplishment" interpretation proposed by Chapanis and Chapanis (1964); rather, it can be considered as consistent with a general reward theory; i.e., stimuli contiguous with severe shock are considered to be unattractive. Similar findings relevant to reward theory are reported by Aronson (1961).

Another example of this approach can be found in an experiment by Freedman (1963), who had subjects perform a dull task after first informing them that either (*a*) the data would definitely be of no value to the experimenter since his experiment was already complete, or (*b*) the data would be of *great* value to the experimenter. According to dissonance theory, performing a dull task is dissonant with the fact that it is not very valuable; in order to reduce dissonance, subjects should attempt to convince themselves that they actually enjoyed performing the task for its own sake. However, if the data are valuable, there is little dissonance, hence, little need to convince one's self that the task was enjoyable. Freedman's results confirmed his prediction: Subjects in the No-Value condition enjoyed the task to a greater extent than did subjects in the High-Value condition. In addition, he ran a parallel set of conditions except that he withheld information about how valuable the task performance was for the experimenter until *after* the subjects had completed the task. With this modification he found the opposite effect: Those who were told the task was valuable enjoyed it more than those who were told it was useless.

A moment's reflection should indicate that there is little or no dissonance in the above situation. No subject can have any reason to suspect that an experimenter is observing him for no reason at all. If the subject performed the task in good faith, he had no way of knowing his data would not be used by the experimenter; that is, experimenters do not generally collect data that they have no intention of using. Accordingly, the subject does not need to seek justification for performing the task—the fact that his performance turned out to be futile was nothing that he could have possibly foreseen. On the other hand, if, in advance, he had some reason for believing that his efforts might be futile (as in the previous condition), he *does* need additional justification—he must convince himself that he chose to do it for its own sake. The point stressed here is that where little or no dissonance exists, an incentive effect emerges: The more valuable the task, the "better" it is; the "better" it is, the more the subjects enjoyed doing it. This experiment clearly demonstrates that dissonance effects and incentive effects can exist side by side. Moreover, it helps define some of the limiting conditions of each.

In a similar vein, a recent experiment by Carlsmith *et al.* (1966) has taken us a long way toward an understanding of the conditions optimal for the emergence of incentive and dissonance phenomena following counter-attitudinal advocacy. According to dissonance theory, if a person says something he feels is untrue, he experiences dissonance: The cognition "I said X" is dissonant with the cognition "I believe not X." In order to reduce dissonance, he might attempt to convince himself that what he said was not so very untrue. Thus, dissonance theory suggests that advocating an opposite position increases one's tendency to believe in that position. However, if one is provided with a great deal of justification for advocating an opposite position (for example, if one is paid a great deal of money for telling a lie), one experiences less dissonance; that is, if I told a small lie for \$53,000, I would have ample justification for having lied: The cognition that I received \$53,000 is consonant with having lied. Consequently, I would have less need to justify my action by convincing myself that I really believed what I said than if I had been paid a mere 53¢ for lying. This general prediction has been confirmed by several experiments (e.g., Festinger and Carlsmith, 1959; Cohen, 1962; Nuttin, 1964; Lependorf, 1964). These experiments have shown greater attitude change for less reward across a wide range of topics; moreover, it has been confirmed across a wide range of rewards, from \$20.00 (high) and \$1.00 (low) in the Festinger-Carlsmith experiment, to 50¢ (high)[8] and 5¢ (low) in the Lependorf experiment. Thus, it would appear that this is a sturdy finding. On the other hand, there is some evidence that under certain conditions the opposite effect might emerge (Janis and Gilmore, 1965; Elms and Janis, 1965; Rosenberg, 1965).[9] Briefly, under certain conditions, offering a high incentive for advocating a given position may lead to a better performance, i.e., thinking up more and better arguments. This could lead to greater attitude change; i.e., a person changes his attitude *because* he has exposed himself to more arguments *because* he has looked harder *because* he was paid more money.

B. COMMITMENT AND COMPLEXITY

But what are these conditions? Or, better still, what conditions are optimum for the dissonance effect and what conditions are optimum for the incentive effect? The experiment by Carlsmith *et al.* (1966) provides

---

[8]"High" and "low" means, of course, relative to the other conditions; thus, 50¢ is high because it is higher than 5¢.

[9]For a more detailed critical analysis of all of these experiments, see Aronson (1966).

us with a solid clue. In their experiment subjects were put through a dull task and were then asked to describe the task as interesting. The dependent variable was the extent to which the subjects convinced themselves that the task really was interesting. The results showed a dissonance effect (the smaller the reward, the greater the opinion change) only under conditions where subjects lied to another person in a highly committing face-to-face situation. In other conditions, subjects wrote an essay, were assured complete anonymity, and were told that only bits and pieces of their argument would be used. Here an incentive effect emerged: The greater the reward, the greater the opinion change. In the early experiments (e.g., Festinger and Carlsmith, 1959) the importance of the face-to-face situation was not fully appreciated by the investigators because this variable was not systematically manipulated. In a recent analysis of this area (Aronson, 1966) it was suggested that the important distinction between the above conditions is "degree of commitment"; i.e., in the face-to-face situation the subject was saying things to a person which he himself believed were untrue. In our opinion, this situation involves much more commitment and, hence, arouses much more dissonance than the writing of an anonymous essay which the subject has been told would not be used in its original form.

At the same time, it should be noted that the complexity of the experimental operations employed by Carlsmith et al. (1966) allow for alternative explanations. One of the most serious of these alternative explanations is in terms of the complexity of the counter-attitudinal task involved. Rosenberg (1966) has argued that dissonance theory may be limited to situations where not much cognitive elaboration is required; he contended that where the task is more complex, incentive effects might occur. In analyzing the study by Carlsmith et al., Rosenberg made the reasonable point that writing an essay and telling a lie not only differ in degree of commitment but also may differ in the degree of cognitive complexity required. Consequently, this experiment cannot be taken as offering unambiguous support for our suggestion that degree of commitment is the decisive factor.

Two very recent experiments shed some additional light on this problem. In one, Linder et al. (1967) were careful to hold the complexity of the task constant. The task was a complex one in all conditions: College students were asked to write an essay favoring more stringent paternalistic supervision of students by the college administration. The experimenters varied (a) the degree of commitment (in terms of whether or not the subjects were allowed to feel that they had a clear choice as to whether or not to write the essay) and (b) the magnitude of monetary incentive for writing the essay. The results are quite clear: When commitment was high there was a dissonance effect; i.e., the smaller the incentive, the greater the opinion change. When commitment was relatively low there was an incentive effect. A different experiment (Helmreich and Collins, 1968) produced similar results. Here the task was also held constant, but instead of being complex (as in the study by Linder *et al.*) it was a simple one. Subjects were asked to record a statement which would be played to a large classroom of other students. In two relatively high commitment conditions the subject's simple statement was put on *video* tape along with his name, class, major, and hometown. In a low-commitment condition the subjects made statements anonymously on *audio* tape. The results paralleled those obtained by Linder *et al.* In the high-commitment conditions the smaller the incentive, the greater the opinion change (dissonance effect); in the low-commitment condition the greater the incentive, the greater the opinion change (incentive effect).

VII. The "Underlying Cognition" Problem

The importance of commitment emerges most clearly when we scrutinize the phenomenon of the white lie more thoroughly. Clearly, every time we say something that we do not believe, we do *not* experience dissonance. Under certain conditions there are some underlying cognitions which serve to prevent the occurrence of dissonance. For example, if we stated a counter-attitudinal position in the context of a formal debate, we would not experience dissonance (see Scott, 1957, 1959; Aronson, 1966). It is clearly understood both by the speaker and the audience that a debater's own personal views have nothing to do with the opinions he expresses. The rules of the game of debating are an underlying cognition which prevents the occurrence of dissonance. Similarly, as teachers we frequently get exposed to a great many stupid ideas from our students. Unless we know the student well—know that he is capable of better ideas and know that he is capable of "taking it"—most teachers refrain from tearing the idea to pieces. Instead, we tend to give the student our attention, nod and smile, and suggest that it is not such a bad idea. We do this because we have a general underlying cognition that we should not discourage students early in their careers and that it is wrong to be unkind to people who are relatively powerless to fight back. It would be ludicrous to suggest that teachers begin to believe that a student's poor idea is really a pretty good one simply because the teacher had said "pretty good idea" to the student. The underlying cognition prevents the occurrence of dissonance. But observe how commitment can make it a dissonant situation: If, on the basis of the teacher's statement, the student had decided to read his paper at an APA convention, the teacher might begin to convince himself that it was not such a bad idea—because the teacher has now been committed—he has misled the student into taking some action. This increases the teacher's commitment to the situation and is probably more powerful than the underlying consonant cognition "this is how we treat students." The teacher now seeks additional justification for having misled the student, perhaps by convincing himself that it was not such a bad idea after all.

The general point to be made here is an important one. Inconsistency is said to arise between two cognitive elements if "considering these two alone, the obverse of one element follows from the other" (Festinger, 1957, pp. 260–261). But we know that in most situations two cognitions are almost never taken by themselves. Occasionally, two cognitions, which in the abstract would appear to be dissonant, fail to arouse dissonance because of the existence of a "neutralizing" underlying cognition. For example, suppose I know a brilliant fellow who is married to an incredibly stupid woman. These cognitions are inconsistent but I would contend that they do not necessarily produce dissonance; i.e., I can tolerate this inconsistency—it does not cause me pain, it does not necessarily lead me to change my opinion about the brilliant fellow or his wife. I do not conclude that he is dumber than I thought or that she is smarter. Why? Because I have a general, underlying, pervasive cognition that there are a multitude of factors which determine mate selection—similarities of intelligence being only one of them. Moreover, I know that it is extremely rare for all of these to be matched in a marital relationship. Therefore, although taken by themselves, the above two cognitions are incompatible, I simply do not ever take them by themselves.

Festinger suggested that one way to reduce dissonance is to martial consonant cognitions; thus, he might say that the above reasoning is one way of reducing dissonance. But it is a moot yet important point whether I martialed the above cognitions as a result of the inconsistency, or whether I walked around with these cognitions about mate selection before the fact. If the latter is the case, then it can hardly be said that I dredged up this overriding cognition as a means of reducing dissonance. For example, let us look at the finding (Aronson and Carlsmith, 1963; Turner and Wright, 1965; Freedman, 1965) that children threatened with mild punishment for playing with a toy tend to derogate that toy after refraining from playing with it. Suppose that many children entered the situation with the strong feeling that adults must be obeyed always, even when commands are arbitrary and threats are nonexistent ("My mother, right or wrong!"). Put another way (which will become important in a moment), suppose that part of the self-concept of these children involved "obedience to adult authority." If this were the case there would have been no dissonance even though, *taken by itself,* the cognition "I like that toy" is dissonant with the cognition "I'm not playing with it." If this were *not* already a part of the person's self-concept, it might have become one as a function of the experiment; i.e., developing a belief in the importance of obedience is one way of reducing dissonance in the above situation. But if it were already there, there would have been no dissonance to begin with.

This added complexity should not lead us to throw up our hands in despair. Rather, it should lead us to a more careful analysis of the situations we are dealing with and perhaps even to a greater concern with individual differences.

VIII. The Importance of the Self-Concept and Other Expectancies

In discussing the difficulties involved in making precise predictions from dissonance theory in some situations, we have purposely tiptoed around the problem of individual differences. The fact that all people are not the same presents intriguing problems for dissonance theory as it does for all general motivational theories. Of course, one man's problem is another man's primary datum; i.e., psychologists who are interested in personality regard individual differences as being of great interest. For those who are primarily interested in establishing nomothetic laws, individual differences usually constitute nothing more than an annoying source of error variance. Nevertheless, whether or not we are interested in individual differences per se, an understanding of the way people differ in dissonant situations can be an important means of clarifying and strengthening the theory. Basically, there are three ways that individuals differ which should be of concern to people investigating dissonance theory:

(1) People differ in their ability to tolerate dissonance. It seems reasonable to assume that some people are simply better than others at shrugging off dissonance; i.e., it may take a greater *amount* of dissonance to bring about dissonance-reducing behavior in some people than in others.

(2) People probably differ in their preferred mode of dissonance reduction; e.g., some people may find it easier to derogate the source of a communication than to change their own opinion. Others may find the reverse resolution easier.

(3) What is dissonant for one person may be consonant for someone else; i.e., people may be so different that certain events are regarded as dissonant for some but not for others.

The first two possibilities are covered in depth elsewhere (see Abelson *et al.*, 1968). We shall not dwell on them here except to say that earlier in this article we underscored the difficulty of ascertaining the proper conditions for establishing whether or not dissonance exists for *most people* and the conditions for determining which mode of dissonance reduction *most people* will use; the existence of individual differences complicates matters further by adding another important dimension which should eventually be specified. The third case will be discussed here because it is of great relevance for the general theory. Furthermore, it is prior to the other two, for before one can determine whether (*a*) an individual is experiencing *enough* dissonance to reduce it or (*b*) *how* he will reduce it, we must first determine whether the events are indeed dissonant, consonant, or irrelevant to him.

Dissonant or consonant with what? Recall the earlier discussion wherein a rule of thumb based upon an expectancy was described (e.g., the Mr. Roy Wilkins of the NAACP and wife-beating novelist illustrations). Dissonance theory makes a clear prediction when a firm expectancy is involved as one of the cognitions in question. Thus, our cognition about Roy Wilkin's *behavior* can be dissonant with our expectancy about how he *will* behave. Dissonance theory is clearer still when that firm expectancy involves the individual's self-concept, for—almost by definition—our expectancies about our own behavior are firmer than our expectancies about the behavior of another person. Thus, at the very heart of dissonance theory, where it makes its clearest and neatest prediction, we are not dealing with any two cognitions; rather, we are usually dealing with the self-concept and cognitions about some behavior. If dissonance exists it is because the individual's behavior is inconsistent with his self-concept.

As we suggested several years ago (Aronson, 1960), this point has been elusive because almost all of the experiments testing dissonance theory have made predictions based upon the tacit assumption that people have a high self-concept. Why do people who buy new cars selectively expose themselves to advertisements about their own make of car (Ehrlich *et al.*, 1957) and try to convince themselves that they made the right choice? Because the knowledge that one has bought a junky car is dissonant with a high self-concept. But suppose a person had a low self-concept? Then the cognition that he bought a junky car would *not* be dissonant. Indeed, if the theory holds, such a person should engage in all kinds of "bizarre" behavior such as exposing himself to advertisements about other cars, hearing squeaks and rattles that are not even there, and saying, in effect, "Just my luck, I bought a lemon—these things are always happening to me." In short, if a person conceives of himself as a "schnook," he will expect to behave like a "schnook"; consequently, wise, reasonable, successful, "un-schnooky" behavior on his part should arouse dissonance. One of the advantages of this kind of statement is that it allows us to separate the effects of dissonance from other hedonic effects; that is, people with *high* self-concepts who fail *do* experience dissonance, but they experience many other negative feelings as well simply because failure is unpleasant. No one can deny that success brings pleasant consequences for people with high and low self-concepts alike; that is, regardless of a person's self-concept, successful achievement is often accompanied by such pleasant things as acclaim, money, fame, admiration, and popularity. But dissonance theory allows us to predict that for people with low self-concepts the "good feelings" aroused by the products of success will be tempered by the discomfort caused by dissonance – the dissonance between a low self-concept and cognitions about high performance. Several experiments have demonstrated that people who expect failure are somewhat discomforted by success (Aronson and Carlsmith, 1962; Cottrell, 1965; Brock *et al.*, 1965), but the data are by no means unequivocal (see Abelson *et al.*, 1968).

Thus, although we were not fully aware of it at the time, in the clearest experiments performed to test dissonance theory, the dissonance involved was between a self-concept and cognitions about a behavior that violated this self-concept. In the experiments on counter-attitudinal advocacy, for example, we maintain that it is incorrect to say that dissonance existed between the cognition "I believe the task is dull" and "I told someone that the task was interesting." This is not dissonant for a psychopathic liar – indeed, it is perfectly consonant. What is dissonant is the cognition "I am a decent, truthful human being" and the cognition "I have misled a person; I have conned him into believing something which just isn't true; he thinks that I really believe it and I cannot set him straight because I probably won't see him again." In the initiation experiment, in our opinion dissonance does not exist between the cognition "I worked hard to get into a group" and the cognition "The group is dull and stupid." Recall that for a "schnook" these cognitions are not at all dissonant. What is dissonant in this situation is the cognition "I am a reasonable and intelligent person" and the cognition "I have worked hard for nothing." Reasonable, intelligent people usually get a fair return for their investment – they usually do not buy a pig in a poke (unless there is some reasonably implicit guarantee, as in Freedman's [1963] experiment discussed above).

As an empirical refinement this self-concept notion is probably trivial. Experimenters have made the tacit assumption that people have high self-concepts – and these experimenters achieved positive results; this implies that the assumption is valid for most people in these situations.

But the self-concept notion may constitute a valuable and interesting *theoretical* refinement. A theory becomes infinitely more meaningful when its domain is clearly demarcated; i.e., when it states clearly where it does not apply. If it is the case that dissonance theory makes unequivocal predictions only when the self-concept or another strong expectancy is involved, then an important set of boundary conditions has been drawn. What we have described earlier as a rule of thumb may actually be a conceptual clarification.

It was stated early in this article that "at the center of the theory" predictions are unequivocal, but at the "fringes" they are somewhat fuzzy. At this point, we can assert that "at the center" means situations in which the self-concept or other firm expectancies are involved—and in which most people share the same self-concepts or other firm expectancies. Thus, most people have self-concepts about being truthful and honest so that we can make clear predictions intuitively, as in the Carlsmith *et al.* (1966) experiment. Most people have self-concepts involving making reasonable and wise decisions so that we can intuit clear predictions, as in the Brehm (1956) or Jecker (1964) experiments. Also, most people have firm expectancies about what Mr. Wilkins might say about Negro intelligence, so that a dissonance theory prediction makes sense and can be made clearly, even though a self-concept is not involved. The prediction about the great novelist who beats his wife gives the theory trouble precisely because people differ tremendously with regard to whether or not they expect a particular novelist to be a gentle and considerate man. In a specific instance, the knowledge of whether or not individual X has this expectancy would increase the accuracy of the prediction. In our opinion, this is of no great importance. What we consider important is the recognition of the fact that dissonance theory may be best suited for making general predictions in situations where expectancies are firm and nearly universal.

Several years ago, Zajonc (1960) raised a very interesting and reasonable question: If dissonance is bothersome, why do we enjoy magicians? That is, magicians can be thought of as people who arouse dissonance. Should we not experience pain and discomfort when we see rabbits pulled from hats, women sawed in half, or dimes turned into quarters? Perhaps the reason that we are not upset by magicians is because the behavior of a magician is consonant with our expectancy regarding magicians. That is, since we know in advance that a magician uses tricks and sleight-of-hand techniques to produce interesting illusions, why should we experience dissonance when we see him do these things? Is this not akin to the "schnook" who expects to purchase an inferior car?

Before the reader dismisses this as mere sophistry, it should be remarked that this is an empirical question. What is suggested is that we enjoy magicians *only* when they are billed as magicians. If they were not billed as magicians, they would cause quite a bit of discomfort. If the fellow sitting next to us at the bar suddenly "became" a fat woman, this would be very upsetting — unless the bartender had forewarned us that we were sitting next to a professional quick-change artist known as "Slippery Sam, the man of a thousand faces." If he then "became" a fat woman, we would be thrilled and delighted. It is interesting to note that the bartender could have produced a similar result if he had forewarned us that he had placed some LSD in our drink. In short, either being told a man is a magician or being told we were fed a halucinogen is consistent with seeing a man "become" a fat woman.

Empirically, this can be tested by finding some young children or some people from a different culture who have never seen or heard of magicians. Without the expectancy regarding magicians that Zajonc and the author share, these subjects might be quite upset by the goings on.

IX. Man Cannot Live by Consonance Alone

The implication of this article is that dissonant situations are ubiquitous and that man expends a great deal of time and energy attempting to reduce dissonance. It should be obvious that man does many other things as well. Festinger never intended dissonance theory to be imperial or monolithic. In 1957, he emphasized the fact that dissonance reduction is only one of many motives and can be counteracted by more powerful drives. We have already discussed how dissonance effects and reward-incentive effects can both occur in the same experimental design. Even more basic is the confrontation that occurs when consonance needs meet utility needs head-on. An extremely high drive to reduce dissonance would lead man to weave a cocoon about himself; he would never admit his mistakes and would distort reality to make it compatible with his behavior. But if a person is ever going to grow, improve, and avoid repeating the same errors, he must sooner or later learn to profit from past mistakes. One cannot profit from one's mistakes without first admitting that one has *made* a mistake. And yet, the admission of error almost always arouses some dissonance. The fact is, people frequently *do* profit from their mistakes; thus, people occasionally do not avoid or reduce dissonance.

To illustrate, if a man spends $50,000 for a home, dissonance theory would suggest that he may be the last to notice that during the rainy season there is water in the basement. Noticing water would arouse dissonance by making his purchase appear to have been a mistake. But to notice the water has great utility — for he must notice it in order to repair it,

or at least to prepare for the flood. Moreover, if he does not take cogniz-
ance of his leaky basement he may walk into the same problem the next
time he purchases a house. Thus, dissonance and utility are in constant
tension by virtue of the fact that under certain conditions dissonant information may be extremely useful and, conversely, useful information can
arouse dissonance. This phenomenon was discussed by Mills *et al.*
(1959), who suggested that one reason why people frequently do not
avoid dissonant information is that it often has great utility. In their experiment, they found that many subjects who had recently committed themselves to taking essay examinations as opposed to multiple-choice examinations opted to read articles explaining why essay examinations were
more difficult, anxiety-provoking, etc. In this situation, apparently, the
utility of the information was considered worth the price to be paid in dissonance. More recent experiments by Canon (1964) and Aronson and
Ross (in preparation) have begun to indicate the requisite conditions for
these effects. Precise predictions can be made by manipulating the
strength of the opposing drive. As utility increases and dissonance becomes weaker, individuals begin to show a preference for dissonance-
arousing but useful information. But as dissonance increases (i.e., immediately after a decision or when commitment is high, etc.), individuals
tend to manifest dissonance-reducing behavior in spite of the fact that the
future consequences of such behavior tend to be unpleasant.

X. Epilogue

The theory of cognitive dissonance is much more complicated than
we thought it was some 10 years ago. A good deal of research has been
done since then. Many of the problems which were specified earlier have
been solved; many new problems have been unearthed, some of which remain to be solved. Hopefully, future research will lead to the emergence
of still new problems, which will lead to still more research, which will
continue to yield an increased understanding of human behavior. Perhaps this is what the scientific enterprise is all about.

In their critique of five years of dissonance theory, Chapanis and
Chapanis (1964) concluded with the pronouncement "Not proven."
Happily, after more than 10 years, it is still not proven; all the theory ever
does is generate research.

212 ELLIOT ARONSON

REFERENCES

Abelson, R., Aronson, E., McGuire, W., Newcomb, T., Rosenberg, M., and Tannenbaum, P. (Eds.), *The cognitive consistency theories: a source book.* Chicago: Rand McNally, 1968.

Aronson, E. The cognitive and behavioral consequences of the confirmation and disconfirmation of expectancies. Proposal to the National Science Foundation, 48 pp., August, 1960.

Aronson, E. The effect of effort on the attractiveness of rewarded and unrewarded stimuli. *Journal of Abnormal and Social Psychology,* 1961, 63, 375-380.

Aronson, E. The psychology of insufficient justification: An analysis of some conflicting data. In S. Feldman (Ed.), *Cognitive consistency.* New York: Academic Press, 1966. Pp. 115-133.

Aronson, E., and Carlsmith, J. M. Performance expectancy as a determinant of actual performance. *Journal of Personality and Social Psychology,* 1962, 65, 178-182.

Aronson, E., and Carlsmith, J. M. Effect of the severity of threat on the devaluation of forbidden behavior. *Journal of Abnormal and Social Psychology,* 1963, 66, 584-588.

Aronson, E., and Carlsmith, J. M. Experimentation in social psychology. In G. Lindzey and E. Aronson (Eds.), *Handbook of social psychology.* (Rev. ed.), Vol. II. Reading, Mass.: Addison-Wesley, 1968.

Aronson, E., and Mills, J. The effect of severity of initiation on liking for a group. *Journal of Abnormal and Social Psychology,* 1959, 59, 177-181.

Aronson, E., and Ross, A. The effect of support and criticism on interpersonal attractiveness. In preparation.

Aronson, E., Turner, Judith, and Carlsmith, J. M. Communicator credibility and communication discrepancy as determinants of opinion change. *Journal of Abnormal and Social Psychology,* 1963, 67, 31-36.

Bem, D. J. An experimental analysis of self-persuasion. *Journal of Experimental Social Psychology,* 1965, 1, 199-218.

Bem, D. J. Self-perception: An alternative interpretation of cognitive dissonance phenomena. *Psychological Review,* 1967, 74, 183-200.

Brehm, J. W. Postdecision changes in the desirability of alternatives. *Journal of Abnormal and Social Psychology,* 1956, 52, 384-389.

Brehm, Mary L., Back, K. W., and Bogdonoff, M. D. A physiological effect of cognitive dissonance under stress and deprivation. *Journal of Abnormal and Social Psychology,* 1964, 69, 303-310.

Brehm, J. W., and Cohen, A. R. *Explorations in cognitive dissonance.* New York: Wiley, 1962.

Brock, T. C., Adelman, S. K., Edwards, D. C., and Schuck, J. R. Seven studies of performance expectancy as a determinant of actual performance. *Journal of Experimental Social Psychology,* 1965, 1, 295-310.

Canon, L. K. Self-confidence and selective exposure to information. In L. Festinger (Ed.) *Conflict, decision and dissonance.* Stanford University Press, 1964. Pp. 83-96.

Carlsmith, J. M., Collins, B. E., and Helmreich, R. L. Studies in forced compliance: I. The effect of pressure for compliance on attitude change produced by face-to-face role playing and anonymous essay writing. *Journal of Personality and Social Psychology,* 1966, 4, 1-3.

Chapanis, Natalia P., and Chapanis, A. Cognitive dissonance: Five years later. *Psychological Bulletin,* 1964, 61, 1-22.

Cohen, A. R. An experiment on small rewards for discrepant compliance and attitude change. In J. W. Brehm and A. R. Cohen, *Explorations in cognitive dissonance.* New York: Wiley, 1962. Pp. 73-78.

Collins, B. E. An experimental study of satisfaction, productivity, turnover, and comparison levels. Unpublished paper, Northwestern University, 1963.

Cottrell, N. B. Performance expectancy as a determinant of actual performance: A replication with a new design. *Journal of Personality and Social Psychology*, 1965, **2**, 685-691.

Davidson, J. R., and Kiesler, Sara B. Cognitive behavior before and after decision. In L. Festinger ,Ed.., *Conflict, decision and dissonance*. Stanford University Press, 1964. Pp. 10-21.

Ehrlich, D., Guttman, I., Schonbach, P., and Mills, J. Post-decision exposure to relevant information. *Journal of Abnormal and Social Psychology*, 1957, **54**, 98-102.

Elms, A. C., and Janis, I. L. Counter-norm attitudes induced by consonant versus dissonant conditions of role-playing. *Journal of Experimental Research in Personality*, 1965, **1**, 50-60.

Festinger, L. *A theory of cognitive dissonance*. Evanston, Ill.: Row, Peterson, 1957.

Festinger, L. (Ed.), *Conflict, decision and dissonance*. Stanford University Press, 1964.

Festinger, L., and Aronson, E. The arousal and reduction of dissonance in social contexts. In D. Cartwright and A. Zander (Eds.), *Group dynamics: research and theory*. Evanston, Ill.: Row, Peterson, 1960. Pp. 214-231.

Festinger, L. and Bramel, D. The reactions of humans to cognitive dissonance. In Bachrach, A. J. (Ed.), *Experimental foundations of clinical psychology*. New York: Basic Books, 1962.

Festinger, L., and Carlsmith, J. M. Cognitive consequences of forced compliance. *Journal of Abnormal and Social Psychology*, 1959, **58**, 203-210.

Festinger, L., and Freedman, J. L. Dissonance reduction and moral values. In P. Worchel and D. Byrne (Eds.), *Personality change*. New York: Wiley, 1964, Pp. 220-243.

Festinger, L., Riecken, H. W., and Schachter, S. *When prophecy fails*. Minneapolis: University of Minnesota Press, 1956.

Freedman, J. L. Attitudinal effects of inadequate justification. *Journal of Personality*, 1963, **31**, 371-385.

Freedman, J. L. Long-term behavioral effects of cognitive dissonance. *Journal of Experimental Social Psychology*, 1965, **1**, 145-155.

Gerard, H. B., and Mathewson, G. C. The effects of severity of initiation on liking for a group: A replication. *Journal of Experimental Social Psychology*, 1966, **2**, 278-287.

Helmreich, R., and Collins, B. E. Studies in forced compliance: IV. Commitment and incentive magnitude as determinants of opinion change. *Journal of Personality and Social Psychology*, in press.

Janis, I. L., and Gilmore, J. B. The influence of incentive conditions on the success of role playing in modifying attitudes. *Journal of Personality and Social Psychology*, 1965, **1**, 17-27.

Jecker, J. D. The cognitive effects of conflict and dissonance. In L. Festinger ,Ed.., *Conflict, decision and dissonance*. Stanford University Press, 1964.

Jones, R. A., Linder, D. E., Kiesler, C. A., Zanna, M., and Brehm, J. W. Internal states or external stimuli: Observers' attitude judgments and the dissonance theory-self-persuasion controversy. *Journal of Experimental Social Psychology*, 1968, in press.

Lawrence, D. H., and Festinger, L. *Deterrents and reinforcement*. Stanford University Press, 1962.

Lependorf, S. The effects of incentive value and expectancy on dissonance resulting from attitude-discrepant behavior and disconfirmation of expectancy. Unpublished doctoral dissertation, State University of New York at Buffalo, 1964.

Lewis, M. Some nondecremental effects of effort. *Journal of Comparative and Physiological Psychology*, 1964, **57**, 367-372.

Linder, D. E., Cooper, J., and Jones, E. E. Decision freedom as a determinant of the role of incentive magnitude in attitude change. *Journal of Personality and Social Psychology,* 1967, 6, 245-254.

McGuire, W. J. Attitudes and opinions. In P. R. Farnsworth, Olga McNemar, and Q. Mc-Nemar (Eds.), *Annual Review of Psychology,* 1966, 17, 475-514.

Mills, J., Aronson, E., and Robinson, H. Selectivity in exposure to information. *Journal of Abnormal and Social Psychology,* 1959, 59, 250-253.

Nuttin, J. M., Jr. Dissonant evidence about dissonance theory. For Second Conference of Experimental Social Psychologists in Europe, Frascati, 1964.

Rosenberg, M. J. When dissonance fails: On eliminating evaluation apprehension from attitude measurement. *Journal of Personality and Social Psychology,* 1965, 1, 28-42.

Rosenberg, M. J. Some limits of dissonance: toward a differential view of counter-attitudinal performance. In S. Feldman ,Ed.., *Cognitive consistency.* New York: Academic Press, 1966. Pp. 135-170.

Scott, W. A. Attitude change through reward of verbal behavior. *Journal of Abnormal and Social Psychology,* 1957, 55, 72-75.

Scott, W. A. Attitude change by response reinforcement: Replication and extension. *Sociometry,* 1959, 22, 328-335.

Smith, E. E. The power of dissonance techniques to change attitudes. *Public Opinion Quarterly,* 1961, 25, 626-639.

Turner, Elizabeth A., and Wright, J. C. Effects of severity of threat and perceived availability on the attractiveness of objects. *Journal of Personality and Social Psychology,* 1965, 2, 128-132.

Walster, Elaine, Berscheid, Ellen, and Barclay, A. M. A determinant of preference among modes of dissonance reduction. *Journal of Personality and Social Psychology,* 1967, 7, 211-216.

Zajonc, R. B. The concepts of balance, congruity, and dissonance. *Public Opinion Quarterly,* 1960, 24, 280-286.

Zimbardo, P. G. Involvement and communication discrepancy as determinants of opinion conformity. *Journal of Abnormal and Social Psychology,* 1960, 60, 86-94.

Zimbardo, P. G. A critical analysis of Smith's "grasshopper" experiment. Dept. Psychol., New York University. 13 pp., 1964. mimeo (a).

Zimbardo, P. G. A reply to Jordan's attack on dissonance theory. *Contemporary Psychology,* 1964, 9, 332-333. (b).

Zimbardo, P. G. The effect of effort and improvisation on self-persuasion produced by role playing. *Journal of Experimental Social Psychology,* 1965, 1, 103-120.

The Theory of Cognitive Dissonance: A Current Perspective

Elliot Aronson

UNIVERSITY OF CALIFORNIA
AT SANTA CRUZ

1978

A great many things have happened in social psychology since the original publication of this article in 1969. One of the major occurrences has been the apparent rise of attribution theory and the apparent decline of dissonance theory as the primary focus of attention, affection, and controversy. This trend has led some observers to conclude that dissonance theory is dead or dying. My own belief is that the theory is very much alive—and aging nicely. Indeed, I would venture to say that dissonance theory has never been healthier. What kills a theory? Thomas Huxley once identified one of the great tragedies of science as the slaying of a beautiful theory by an ugly fact. Although facts (ugly or otherwise) may slay theories in the *natural* sciences, in the *social* sciences, theories are almost never bumped off that easily or clearly. In the social sciences, what generally kills a theory is benign neglect—by its critics as well as by its advocates. And dissonance theory has never lacked for either advocates or critics.

A critic keeps a theory alive by vigorously pointing out areas of conceptual fuzziness and inconsistency as well as methodological sloppiness—the way a good gardener would designate rotten or withered branches on a tree. It is the advocates whose job it is to prune that tree—to keep it healthy as long as it is bearing fruit. (To push the analogy much too far, the "fruit" takes the form of interesting, testable hypotheses.)

215

Cognitive Theories in Social Psychology

As the reader of this essay knows, dissonance theory has inspired an astounding array of interesting, testable hypotheses. It has also produced more than its share of useful and vociferous critics—who have occasionally gone beyond the call of duty into the realm of *ad hominem* aspersion-casting! What I tried to do when I wrote the preceding essay in 1969 was, in effect, to be a good advocate, to be responsive to the major criticisms of the theory by limiting its domain to those areas where it makes the clearest and least ambiguous predictions. Similar attempts have been made by others (Gerard, Connolley, & Wilhelmy, 1974; Wicklund & Brehm, 1976). How successful have we been?

Commenting on an earlier version of this essay, Sears and Abeles (writing in the *Annual Review of Psychology* for 1969) indicated that the restatement of Festinger's theory presented here had marked a major shift in the orientation of dissonance theory:

> The current dissonance Establishment view is available in a paper by Aronson. The youthful brashness of dissonance theory is replaced by well-fed middle-aged generosity; Aronson acknowledges much 'conceptual fuzziness' about dissonance theory, at least around its fringes, and suggests that research focus upon determining the conditions under which dissonance effects obtain as opposed to those under which other (e.g., incentive or conflict) effects obtain—a far cry from the early days when no behavioral phenomenon was safe from the ravages of the imperialistic dissonance hordes.

Theories frequently evolve and change in the same way that humans do. And it is altogether fitting and proper for a theory, in its infancy, to bite off more than it can chew in an "imperialistic" fashion. As a theory matures, one often finds its domain shrinking. This frequently leads to a diminution in the number of studies being done to test it. But, as if in compensation for the loss in numbers, those experiments that do get performed tend to take the form that I called for in 1969—that is, studies testing the "conditions under which." Thus, as a theory moves into middle age it not only becomes less imperialistic, but the research it produces also tends to be less glamorous, less swashbuckling, and *more* focused.

There is no way that I could cover even a small fraction of the truly excellent research done since 1969—for although the quantity of research *has* diminished relative to what it was, it is still considerable. What I would like to do in this section is provide a brief update in three areas: (*a*) the relevance of the self-concept as the core notion of dissonance theory; (*b*) recent research on the "dissonance versus self-judgment" controversy; and (*c*) the concept of selective exposure.

I. Dissonance and the Self-Concept

The notion that the self-concept is important (and perhaps crucial) to the experience of dissonance was put to the test in several experiments performed subsequent to the original publication of this essay. Here I will describe a prototypical study. Nel, Helmreich, and Aronson (1969) reasoned that making a counterattitudinal presentation would not engage the self-concept (and therefore would not arouse dissonance) if no bad consequences resulted from that statement. For example, suppose that Sam were opposed to the use of marijuana and were induced to make a speech on videotape favoring its use—for little reward. So far, it sounds like a dissonance situation. But suppose further that Sam were assured that that tape would only be played to a group of people who were deeply and irrevocably committed not to smoke or deeply and irrevocably committed pot-heads. We predicted that under those conditions there would not be a dissonance effect— that is, that there would be little or no difference between a high reward condition and a low reward condition. Why? Since no one was being influenced, no harm was being done, and, therefore, the self-concept was not much engaged in that operation. But suppose Sam had been told that the tape would be shown to a group of high school students who had not yet made up their minds about whether or not to use marijuana. Here we would expect a dissonance effect; since there is great danger of doing harm, the self-concept comes into play, and the individual will reduce dissonance by changing his attitude in the direction of the speech *in the low reward condition,* in which external justification is minimal. The results of our experiment confirmed these predictions. That is, of all six conditions (high or low reward and influenceable, noninfluenceable–favorable, or noninfluenceable–unfavorable), the only condition that showed a high degree of attitude change was influenceable, low reward. These findings were replicated and extended in experiments by Aronson, Chase, Helmreich, and Ruhnke (1974), Collins and Hoyt (1972), Hoyt, Henle, and Collins (1972), and others.

II. Dissonance Theory versus Self-Judgment Theory

In 1969, we left Daryl Bem and his critics standing in the middle of a controversy focused on whether or not a person is aware of his or her initial position. In subsequent years, investigators have focused more directly on determining whether or not dissonant cognitions produce an aversive state of tension in the individual. One of the more exciting experiments on this issue was performed by Pallak and Pittman in 1972. Pallak and Pittman based their research on the well-known interaction between drive level and complexity of task in the psychology of learning. An example will clarify. Suppose you are performing a task that has several possible responses that compete for your attention (as opposed to a task in which there is one clear response). If you are in a state of high drive (that is, if you are hungry, thirsty, tense, or whatever), you will perform more poorly than if you are in a low-drive state. On the other hand, if the task is a clear and simple one, being in a high-drive state seems to energize a person without causing interference; hence, you will do better at such a task if you are in a high-drive state. Pallak and Pittman simply put some subjects in a highly dissonant situation and others in a situation that produced very little dissonance. The low-dissonance subjects performed better than the high-dissonance subjects in a complex task (one with many competing responses), whereas the high-dissonance subjects performed better than the lows in a simple task (one with few responses). Thus, dissonance arousal seems to act like hunger or thirst or tension. Although these data are not conclusive, they do indicate that something that may be akin to an aversive state of tension is going on inside the subject during dissonance arousal. See also Cooper, Zanna, and Taves (1977), Kiesler and Pallak (1976), and Zanna and Cooper (1974).

Recently, Fazio, Zanna, and Cooper (1976) have taken a close look at the conditions under which dissonance effects and self-judgment effects would be most likely to apply. Briefly, after surveyint the literature, Fazio *et al.* suggested that self-judgment theory predicts attitude change most clearly when one is dealing with attitude-congruent behavior, whereas dissonance theory is best at predicting attitude change in the context of attitude-discrepant behavior—that is, in behavior outside an individual's latitude of acceptance. In their experiment, subjects who were allowed the opportunity to misattribute any potential dissonance arousal to an external stimulus did not change their attitudes (relative to "low choice" subjects) if they were committed to endorsing a position outside of their latitude of acceptance. If, however, the commitment involved an attitude *within* their latitude of acceptance, these subjects *did* show more attitude change than "low choice" subjects.

III. A Brief Look at Selective Exposure

Near the end of the preceding essay, I suggested that people could not live by consonance alone. I specified, as one of the ramifications of that statement, that dissonance and utility are in constant tension simply because dissonant information can be very useful— and useful information can cause dissonance. For example, an experiment by Mills, Aronson, and Robinson (1959) failed to demonstrate selective exposure to information. In that article, we speculated that a likely reason for this failure is the aforementioned tension; that is, individuals will frequently expose themselves to dissonant information if they believe that the utility of the information is worth the pain of dissonance. Subsequently, Wicklund and Brehm (1976) added "novelty" and "attractiveness" to utility as factors that can operate to mask selective exposure. These speculations have now been confirmed in an excellent experiment by Olson and Zanna (1977). Not only have Olsen and Zanna applied the principle of "under what conditions" to the problem of selective exposure, but they have also done it in the form of individual differences—another aspect of human behavior that had proved problematical to the early dissonance researchers. Specifically, Olson and Zanna reasoned that Byrne's (1964) dimensions of "repression-sensitization" might be of relevance to selective exposure. When faced with anxiety-arousing stimuli, repressors generally respond with avoidance strategies (e.g., denial) as a way of coping. Sensitizers, on the other hand, are said to deal with such stimuli by approaching them; their strategy tends to be intellectualization, rumination, etc. To test their position, Olson and Zanna put people in a dissonance-arousing situation involving choice. Specifically, subjects were allowed to choose and keep one of two possible pairs of art reproductions. Each pair contained one painting they liked and one they did not like. After the decision, subjects were allowed to inspect the alternatives for about 75 seconds. The experimenters unobtrusively videotaped the eye gaze of the subjects. The findings were clear: Repressors (but not sensitizers) engaged in selective exposure; that is, repressors tended to spend their time looking at the attractive painting that they chose (consonance) and avoiding the attractive painting that they had rejected.

IV. Conclusion

Rumors to the effect that the theory of cognitive dissonance is dead appear to be grossly exaggerated. Although experiments inspired by the theory are breaking little new ground, they continue to clarify, specify, and strengthen the applicability of the conceptual statement by establishing clear boundaries. The theory seems to have survived its brash infancy and tempestuous adolescence. It has now matured into a much tighter conceptual scheme that accounts for an important set of human social behaviors.

REFERENCES

Aronson, E., Chase, T., Helmreich, R., & Ruhnke, R. A two-factor theory of dissonance reduction: The effect of feeling stupid or feeling "awful" on opinion change. *International Journal of Communication Research,* 1974, **3**.

Collins, B. E., & Hoyt, M. F. Personal responsibility-for-consequences: An integration and extension of the "forced compliance" literature. *Journal of Experimental Social Psychology,* 1972, **8**, 558–593.

Cooper, J., Zanna, M. P., & Taves, P. A. Arousal as a necessary condition for attitude change following induced compliance. Unpublished paper, 1977.

Fazio, R. H., Zanna, M. P., & Cooper, J. Dissonance and self-perception: An integrative view of each theory's proper domain of application. *Journal of Experimental Social Psychology,* 1977, **13**, 464–479.

Gerard, H. B., Connolley, E. S., & Wilhelmy, R. A. Compliance, justification, and cognitive change. In L. Berkowitz (Ed.), *Advances in experimental social psychology,* Vol. 7. New York: Academic Press, 1974, Pp. 217–247.

Hoyt, M. F., Henley, M. D., & Collins, B. E. Studies in forced compliance: Confluence of choice and consequences on attitude change. *Journal of Personality and Social Psychology,* 1972, **23**, 205–210.

Kielser, C. A., & Pallack, M. S. Arousal properties of dissonance manipulations. *Psychological Bulletin,* 1976, **83**, 1014–1025.

Mills, J., Aronson, E., & Robinson, H. Selectivity in exposure to information. *Journal of Abnormal and Social Psychology,* 1959, **59**, 250–253.

Nel, E., Helmreich, R., & Aronson, E. Opinion change in the advocate as a function of the persuasibility of his audience: A clarification of the meaning of dissonance. *Journal of Personality and Social Psychology,* 1969, **12**, 117–124.

Olson, J. M., & Zanna, Mark P. A new look at selective exposure. Paper presented at the Annual Meeting of the American Psychological Association, San Francisco, California, August, 1977.

Pallack, M. S., & Pittman, T. S. General motivational effects of dissonance arousal. *Journal of Personality and Social Psychology,* 1972, **21**, 349–358.

Sears, D. O., & Abeles, R. Attitudes and opinions. In P. H. Mussen & M. Rosenzweig, *Annual Review of Psychology,* 1969, **20**, 253–288.

Wicklund, R. A., & Brehm, J. W. *Perspectives on cognitive dissonance.* New York, John Wiley & Sons, 1976.

Zanna, M. P., & Cooper, J. Dissonance and the pill: An attribution approach to studying the arousal properties of dissonance. *Journal of Personality and Social Psychology,* 1974, **29**, 703–709.

SELF-PERCEPTION THEORY[1]

Daryl J. Bem　　　1972

STANFORD UNIVERSITY
STANFORD, CALIFORNIA

[1] Development of self-perception theory was supported primarily by a grant from the National Science Foundation (GS 1452) awarded to the author during his tenure at Carnegie-Mellon University.

Reprinted from *Advances in Experimental Social Psychology*,
Volume 6, 1–62.

I. Introduction

Individuals come to "know" their own attitudes, emotions, and other internal states partially by inferring them from observations of their own overt behavior and/or the circumstances in which this behavior occurs. Thus, to the extent that internal cues are weak, ambiguous, or uninterpretable, the individual is functionally in the same position as an outside observer, an observer who must necessarily rely upon those same external cues to infer the individual's inner states.

These two propositions constitute the heart of the author's self-perception theory and, accordingly, the central topic of this review. This article will trace the conceptual antecedents and empirical consequences of these propositions, attempt to place the theory in a slightly enlarged frame of reference, and, hopefully, clarify just what phenomena the theory can and cannot account for in the rapidly growing experimental literature of self-attribution phenomena.

Self-perception theory was initially formulated, in part, to address empirically certain questions in the "philosophy of mind" (e.g., Chappell, 1962; Ryle, 1949). When an individual asserts, "I am hungry," how does he know? Is it an observation? An inference? Direct knowledge? Can he be in error, or is that impossible by definition? How does the evidential basis for such a first-person statement (or self-attribution) differ from the evidential basis for the third-person attribution, "He is hungry"?

Such questions have traditionally been subjected to purely analytic rather than empirical analyses, and psychologists have generally been willing to leave such exercises to the philosophers. In earlier times, when debates about introspection were in vogue, psychologists did discuss such matters, but those discussions, too, were primarily philosophical rather than empirical in tone. In fact, it appears that the only discussion in the literature which treats such questions as substantive psychological problems is B. F. Skinner's "radical-behavioral" analysis of "private events" and their role in a science of human behavior (Skinner, 1945, 1953, 1957). It was Skinner's analysis which inspired the present "self-perception theory"; accordingly, it is with Skinner's analysis that this review begins.

A. THE ONTOGENY OF SELF-ATTRIBUTIONS

In order to identify and label things in his environment, a child must initially have someone else around who will play the "original word game" of pointing and naming, someone who will teach the child to distinguish between objects and events that appear similar and to label them with different descriptors. The skills of self-description would appear to emerge from the same procedure, both with respect to overt behavior ("I seem to be eating more today") and to the effects of stimuli on the individual ("It gives me goose pimples"). The problem, of course, arises when the stimuli or events to be described are "private" internal states to which nobody but the individual himself has access, for it then becomes difficult for the verbal community to make differential reinforcement of the appropriate descriptive response directly contingent upon the presence or absence of the stimuli which are to be labeled. What, then, can be done?

As Skinner has noted, there are a few cases when an appropriate descriptor can still be acquired without explicit training. For example, some private stimuli are generated from covert behavior which was at one time overt or which accompanied parallel overt behavior to which descriptors could be attached. Thinking sometimes has this property: "I said to myself said I . . ." A second resource which is sometimes available is metaphor or stimulus generalization. An individual, for example, can easily learn to identify "butterflies in the stomach," and at least one child has generated his own metaphor-by describing a foot which had fallen asleep as "feeling like gingerale when I hold the glass to my face." Some descriptors of emotional states (e.g., "feeling blue" or "down in the mouth") may have similar historical origins. But these special cases cover a very limited domain of self-descriptive statements, and most of the time a child must still be explicitly taught how to describe his internal states in the same way he is taught to describe his outer environment: someone must be able to "point and name." In training a child to describe pain, for example, an observer, at some point, must teach him the correct response at the critical time when the appropriate private stimuli are impinging upon him. But the observer himself must necessarily identify the "critical time" on the basis of observable stimuli or responses and implicitly assume that the private stimuli are, in fact, accompanying these public events. The description "it hurts" may thus be established in a child's repertoire by saying: "Don't cry; I know it hurts to bump your head." The descriptor itself can then generalize to a large class of private "painful" stimuli even though it was originally an observable response (crying) and a public stimulus variable (bumping the head) which set the occasion for the observer's inference that the child was experiencing pain.

If the resources available to the community for setting up descriptions of private events seem inadequate—and it is proposed that this list of resources is exhaustive—it should be recalled that the result is also often inadequate. Not only does the community remain ignorant of whether the complaint of a headache is valid, for example, but the same deficiencies which generate public mistrust lead the individual himself to faulty self-knowledge. "There appears to be no way in which the individual may sharpen the reference of his own verbal repertoire in this respect [Skinner, 1953, p. 261]."

Thus, far from having direct and unerring knowledge of our internal states, Skinner's analysis implies that we have virtually no knowledge at all until we have been explicitly trained. Internal identifications that we have not been taught remain internal identifications that we cannot make. In everyday life we are spared from confronting our incompetence in this regard only because people know better than to call upon us to make internal discriminations which we are typically not taught ("Is it your spleen or your liver which is causing you the discomfort, Mr. Jones?"). It should be noted that Skinner's analysis thus reverses the usual practice in psychology of assuming the existence of awareness *a priori* and then treating any residual unawareness as problematic. For Skinner, awareness, not unawareness, is the phenomenon which normally requires analysis, and the uniqueness of his conceptual contribution resides precisely in his explicit recognition of this fact.

B. THE SELF-PERCEPTION POSTULATES

It was the above analysis which first suggested that many of the self-descriptive statements which appear to be exclusively under the control of private stimuli may in fact still be partially controlled by the same accompanying public events used by the training community to infer the individual's inner states in the first place (Bem, 1964, 1965). Meanwhile, the underlying corollary that private stimuli probably play a smaller role in self-description than we have come to believe—either as self-observers ourselves or as psychologists—was already receiving support from the experimental work on emotional states by Schachter and his colleagues (Schachter, 1964).

For example, in their now classic experiment, Schachter and Singer (1962) manipulated the external cues of the situation and were able to evoke self-descriptions of emotional states as disparate as euphoria and anger from subjects in whom operationally identical states of physiological arousal had been induced. These subjects required the internal stimuli of arousal in order to make the gross discrimination that they were emotional, but the more subtle discrimination of *which* emotion they were experiencing was under the control of the external cues, the "emotional" behavior of a stooge. In another experiment conducted within Schachter's theoretical framework, Valins (1966) was able to manipulate attitudes toward stimulus pictures of seminude females by giving his male subjects false auditory feedback which they could interpret as their heartbeat, thus showing that any internal stimulus control of attitude statements could be overridden by external cues.

The controlling external cues in these and similar experiments have usually resided in the social or physical setting in which the individual was placed or in verbal instructions given to him by the experimenter. But that is not the only possible source of such cues. To us as observers, the most important clues to an individual's inner states are found in his behavior. When we want to know how a person feels, we look to see how he acts. Accordingly, it seemed possible that when an individual himself wants to know how he feels, he may look to see how he acts, a possibility suggested anecdotally by such statements as, "I guess I'm hungrier than I first thought." It was from this line of reasoning that the first postulate of self-perception theory was derived: Individuals come to "know" their own attitudes, emotions, and other internal states partially by inferring them from observations of their own overt behavior and/or the circumstances in which this behavior occurs.

The second postulate of self-perception theory suggests a partial identity between self- and interpersonal perception: To the extent that internal cues are weak, ambiguous, or uninterpretable, the individual is functionally in the same position as an outside observer, an observer who must necessarily rely upon those same external cues to infer the individual's inner states.

Because self-perception theory is conceived of as a "behaviorist's" theory, it is important to emphasize that neither the interpersonal observer nor the individual himself is confined to inferences based upon overt actions only. Social psychologists (e.g., Asch, 1952) have long been critical of behavioral analyses of social interaction (e.g., the Miller-Dollard analysis of imitation; see Miller & Dollard, 1941) precisely because they feel that there is something more to interpersonal perception than responding to the overt behavior of another individual. In particular, so the criticism goes, behavioral analyses fail to explicate how it is that individuals are able to take account of one another's meanings, motives, intentions, and the like.

This criticism is often illustrated by citing cases in which identical behaviors may have different "meanings," meanings which observers have no difficulty discerning. For example, an individual might attribute "suddenly aroused determination" to his friend were he to see him chasing a mouse into the room with a raised broom. But he would attribute "fear" if an identical hasty entrance were to be followed rather than preceded by the mouse. Were no mouse present, he might well classify his friend's action as anger directed at him. In all three cases the overt behaviors observed are the same, and it is not particularly illuminating simply to say that the individual is responding to the "intent" of his friend or to the "meaning" of the action, since it is precisely the intent and meaning which require explication. In this example, it is clear that the meaning of the action resides in the mouse, that is, the intent or meaning is inferred from the stimulus conditions that appear to be controlling the observed behavior. To a radical behaviorist, this *is* the "intent" or "meaning" of the behavior. This, then, is the "something more" of interpersonal perception: the ability to respond not only to the overt behavior of others, but to respond as well to the controlling variables of which their behavior appears to be a function. The first postulate of self-perception theory embraces this observation in its proposal that self-attributions are made from the individual's observations of his "own overt behavior and/or the circumstances in which it occurs," for most important among those "circumstances" are the apparent controlling variables of that behavior.

A less whimsical, more pertinent example of interpersonal perception in which the apparent controlling variables of the behavior can provide a basis of inference is provided by the individual who attempts to infer the actual beliefs or attitudes of a persuasive communicator. Is the communicator being paid? If so, how much? Did the communicator have a free choice in what to say, or was he coerced? To the extent that the communicator appears to be free from the control of these kinds of explicit reinforcement contingencies, that is, to the extent that he does not appear to be "manding" reinforcement (Skinner, 1957), he will be judged to be a credible communicator, and his statements will typically be described as his "actual" beliefs and attitudes.

If one now applies the postulates of self-perception theory to this same example, one arrives at the hypothesis that the communicator himself might infer his own beliefs and attitudes from his behavior if that behavior appears to be free from the control of explicit reinforcement contingencies. This hypothesis was, in fact, the first prediction to be derived from self-perception theory (Bem, 1964, 1965), and tentative evidence for its validity appeared to reside already in the forced-compliance experiments conducted within Festinger's (1957) theory of cognitive dissonance.

Consider, for example, the classic experiment by Festinger and Carlsmith (1959). In this experiment, 60 undergraduates were randomly assigned to one of three experimental conditions. In the $1 condition, the subject was first required to perform long repetitive laboratory tasks in an individual experimental session. He was then hired by the experimenter as an "assistant" and paid $1 to tell a waiting fellow student (a stooge) that the tasks were enjoyable and interesting. In the $20 condition, each subject was hired for $20 to do the same thing. Control subjects simply engaged in the repetitive tasks. After the experiment each subject indicated how much he had enjoyed the tasks. The results show that the subjects paid $1 evaluated the tasks as significantly more enjoyable than did subjects who had been paid $20. Subjects paid $20 did not express attitudes significantly different from those expressed by the control subjects. This phenomenon is now known as the reverse-incentive effect.

As implied above, self-perception theory interprets such results by considering the viewpoint of an outside observer who hears the individual making favorable statements about the tasks to a fellow student, and who further knows that the individual was paid $1 [$20] to do so. This hypothetical observer is then asked to state the actual attitude of the individual he has heard. If the observer had seen an individual making such statements for little compensation ($1), he can rule out financial incentive as a motivating factor and infer something about the individual's attitudes. He can use an implicit self-selection rule and ask: "What must this man's attitude be if he is willing to behave in this fashion in this situation?" Accordingly, he can conclude that the individual holds an attitude consistent with the view that is expressed in the behavior: He must have actually enjoyed the tasks. On the other hand, if an observer sees an individual making such statements for a large compensation (e.g., $20), he can infer little or nothing about the actual attitude of that individual, because such an incentive appears sufficient to evoke the behavior regardless of the individual's private views. The subject paid $20 is not credible in the sense that his behavior cannot be used as a guide for inferring his private views. The observer's best guess, then, is to suppose that the individual's attitude is similar to that which would be expressed by anybody who was selected at random and asked for his opinion—the attitude of a control subject, in other words.

Self-perception theory asserts that subjects in the Festinger-Carlsmith experiment (and other experiments utilizing this paradigm) are themselves behaving just like these hypothetical observers. They survey their own behavior of making favorable statements about the task and then essentially ask themselves (implicitly): "What must my attitude be if I am willing to behave in this fashion in this situation?" Accordingly, they produce the same pattern of results as the outside observers: low-compensation subjects infer that they must agree with the arguments in their communication, whereas high-compensation subjects discard their behavior as a relevant guide to their "actual" attitudes and express the same attitudes as the control subjects. In short, if one places the hypothetical observer and the communicator into the same skin, the findings obtained by Festinger and Carlsmith are the result. The final attitudes of the actual subjects in the experiment are thus viewed as a set of self-attributions made by the individual on the basis of his own behavior in the light of the contextual constraints in which this behavior appeared to be occurring.

Judges made blind ratings of the persuasive communications delivered by subjects in the Festinger-Carlsmith experiment and found that $1 communications were no more persuasive than $20 communications; in fact, the trend was in the other direction. This illustrates again that it is not the behavior *per se*, but the behavior in conjunction with its apparent controlling variables which provides the crucial information for either interpersonal or self-attributions.

The crux of the self-perception interpretation in such studies is that the individual's own behavior will be used by him as a source of evidence for his beliefs and attitudes to the extent that the contingencies of reinforcement for engaging in the behavior are made more subtle or less discriminable. Monetary inducement is not the only way of manipulating this parameter of self-credibility. For example, several cognitive dissonance studies have manipulated the degree to which the individual appears to have the choice of engaging in the behavior or refusing to do so. Thus if an outside observer sees an individual freely choosing to make opinion statements (e.g., "the tasks were fun and interesting"), he is more likely to take such statements at face value, to infer that they reflect the individual's true opinions, than if the individual was required or coerced into making such statements. The same analysis applies to the amount of justification given a subject for engaging in the counter-attitudinal behavior: The more justification given, the less likely it is that the behavior will be used by an observer or the individual himself to infer what he believes. When the operations of forced-compliance studies are submitted to a careful analysis in terms of the discriminative stimuli presented to the subject, then those conditions in which outside observers would base an inference of the individual's attitudes on the overt behavior are found to be the same conditions in which the individual's own attitudes are affected.

II. Experimental Evidence for the Theory

As we shall see in Section III, several other experiments and paradigms from the cognitive dissonance literature are amenable to self-perception interpretations. But precisely because such experiments are subject to alternative interpretations, they cannot be used as unequivocal evidence for self-perception theory. In particular, the stimulus operations in such studies have several functional properties. For example, monetary compensation not only manipulates the parameter of self-credibility (according to self-perception theory), but that of incentive and reinforcement as well, a fact which has led to replication failures, replication reversals, and a profusion of interpretations. [For several discussions, see Abelson, Aronson, McGuire, Newcomb, Rosenberg, and Tannenbaum (1968, pp. 801–833).] Similarly, manipulations of justification, choice, commitment, and so forth involve a veritable jungle of complex and ambiguous stimulus operations, a feature of dissonance studies which has been a major target of criticism (e.g., Chapanis & Chapanis, 1964). It thus seemed desirable to design a "self-credibility" experiment in which the controlling stimuli would be "raised from birth" in the laboratory so that they would have no functional properties other than those postulated by the theory to be relevant to the self-credibility of the induced behavior. Secondly, it seemed desirable to eliminate the variance in the overt behavior which arises from permitting the subject to compose his own persuasive communications. Finally, reflecting the author's Skinnerian bias, it was decided to design experiments for testing self-perception theory in which every subject is his own control and provides a complete replication of the entire design. The cartoon experiment (Bem, 1964, 1965) was the first of these studies.

A. The Cartoon Experiment

The dependent variable in the cartoon study was the subjects' attitudes toward a series of magazine cartoons. The induced behavior which served as the source of self-attribution was the overt statement, "This cartoon is very funny" or, "This cartoon is very unfunny." The self-credibility parameter was manipulated with two colored lights whose functional properties were established through the preliminary training procedure described below.

The experimental session was disguised as a tape-recording session for the preparation of experimental stimulus materials. Each subject first underwent a training procedure in which he answered simple questions about himself. After each question was asked, a tape recorder was turned on, automatically illuminating a colored light. The subject was instructed to answer the question truthfully whenever the light was amber. Whenever the light was green, he was to make up a false answer to the question and say it aloud into the tape recorder. In this way, the subject learned that he could believe himself whenever he spoke in the presence of the amber light, but could not believe himself in the presence of the green light. The lights were reversed for half the subjects. After this training procedure, the subject was shown a series of magazine cartoons which he had rated as "neutral," that is, as neither funny nor unfunny in a previous session. For each cartoon, he was instructed by the experimenter either to say, "This cartoon is very funny," or, "This cartoon is very unfunny." The tape recorder was turned on just before he made each statement so that one of the colored lights was on while he spoke, even though he was not instructed to attend to the lights in this portion of the session. Sometimes the "truth" light was illuminated, other times the "lie" light. After the subject had made each statement and the recorder (and light) had been turned off, he was asked to indicate his actual attitude toward the cartoon on an attitude scale. An awareness questionnaire was administered at the end of the session.

As the self-perception hypothesis predicted, the subjects changed their attitudes significantly more when they made their statements in the presence of the "truth" light than when they made their statements in the presence of the "lie" light. For example, if a subject had said "This is a very funny cartoon" in the presence of the "truth" light, then he subsequently rated this cartoon to be funnier than if he had made the statement in the presence of the "lie" light. As a parallel to the Festinger-Carlsmith dissonance experiment, the "truth" light replicated the controlling functional property of the $1 inducement, signifying to the individual that his behavior could be used as a guide to his "true" attitude; the "lie" light abstracted the function of the $20 inducement, signifying to the individual that his behavior was irrelevant to his true attitude. It should also be noted that no subject was aware of any attitude change nor of any effects of the two lights on his subsequent cartoon ratings.

B. The False Confession Experiment

The cartoon study demonstrated that the self-attributions known as attitude statements could be brought directly under the control of an individual's own verbal behavior and the accompanying stimulus conditions in which that behavior occurs. The false confession experiment (Bem, 1966) was an attempt to retain the same independent variables, but to extend the evidence for the theory to a different kind of dependent variable: the recall of prior events. In particular, the false confession study attempted to verify the possibility that a false confession can effectively distort an individual's recall of his past behavior if the confession is made in the presence of cues previously associated with telling the truth. A second possibility tested was that cues previously associated with lying can create self-disbelief in *true* statements, leading again to distortions in recall of the actual behavior.

The experiment utilized the same experimental setting as the cartoon experiment, but instead of rating cartoons prior to the experimental session, subjects were given a list of 100 common nouns and an alphabetical list containing 50 of those nouns. Their task was to cross out each word on the master list which also appeared on the alphabetical list. Thus each subject was required to scan the alphabetical list for each of 100 words and then either to cross out the word or to not cross out the word. This was the behavior which the subject was later asked to recall.

Each subject then went through the preliminary training session, described above, in which he learned to make true statements whenever the amber recording light was on and false statements whenever the green recording light was on. He was then required to make statements about the 100 nouns. Sometimes he was required to state aloud that he had crossed out a word and sometimes to state that he had not crossed out a word (e.g., "I did not cross out the word *tree*"). Half the statements he had to make were true, and half were false. Again the colored lights were connected to the tape recorder so that either the amber or the green light was illuminated as he made his "confession." After each statement was made and the recorder and light turned off, the subject indicated whether he recalled crossing out the word or not crossing it out. In addition, he indicated on a five-point scale how confident he was in the accuracy of his recall. The complete design for each subject was thus a $2 \times 2 \times 2$ in which the word had either been crossed out or not, the statement was either true or false, and it was made in the presence of either the "truth" light or the "lie" light. In addition, each subject was asked to recall his behavior on a set of control words about which no overt statements had been made.

The results confirmed the expectations of the self-perception hypothesis: In the presence of the "lie" light, the false confessions had no effect. Subjects were as able to recall their previous behavior just as accurately as they were for the control words not appearing in their confessions. But in the presence of the "truth" light, false confessions did produce significantly more errors of recall and less confidence in recall accuracy than either false confessions in the presence of the "lie light" or no confession at all. In addition, there was weak support for the complementary possibility that more recall errors would be produced by the "lie" light when the overt statement was true than would be produced by the "truth" light—where the light confirms rather than contradicts the validity of the statement.

In a replication of this experiment, Maslach (1971) reconfirmed the major finding that the truth light produced more errors of recall following false confessions, but failed to find that the "lie" light distorted recall for true statements. Instead, she reports that the "truth" light produced more errors of recall in both the false and true confession conditions, although the effect was stronger for false confessions. This opens up the possibility that the subjects are exercising more care in responding after a "lie" light statement, an hypothesis supported by auxiliary data. Unfortunately, because Maslach's design did not contain a set of control words, it is not possible to know which cells are deviating significantly from a recall baseline and hence which combination of independent variables is producing the effects. Nevertheless, her pattern of results casts a cloud over the false confession experiment as a pure demonstration of a self-perception effect.

C. THE PAIN PERCEPTION EXPERIMENT

Both the cartoon and false confession studies employed the overt behavior of self-persuasive statements and self-credibility cues as the independent variables. The pain perception study (Bandler, Madaras, & Bem, 1968) was designed to move beyond this conceptual paradigm and also to make contact with an extensive literature on pain perception. It has long been known that an individual's perception of pain is only partially a function of the pain-producing stimulus. This is apparent from the wide cultural differences in labeling stimuli as painful (e.g., childbirth; Melzack, 1961), from research on placebo effects (Beecher, 1959, 1960), and from the phenomena of hypnotic analgesia (Barber, 1959, 1963) and masochism (Brown, 1965).

Recent research has also revealed a number of "cognitive" operations which can influence an individual's inference that a particular stimulus is painful. For example, Nisbett and Schachter (1966) showed that the judged intensity of shock-produced pain and the willingness to tolerate such pain can be manipulated by supplying the individual with an alternative explanation for the physiological arousal he is experiencing. And, working within a cognitive dissonance framework, Zimbardo, Cohen, Weisenberg, Dworkin, and Firestone (1969) demonstrated that individuals who have volunteered to continue participation in an experiment using painful electric shocks and who were given little justification for volunteering to do so reported the shocks to be less painful and were physiologically (GSR) less responsive than individuals who were given no choice about continuing or who were given much justification for volunteering to continue.

As noted earlier, these parameters of choice and justification can be embraced within the self-perception framework. If an outside observer sees an individual choosing freely to continue enduring shocks with little justification, the observer might well assume that the shocks are not very painful. If on the other hand, the individual appears to have been given little or no option to endure the shocks, the observer could infer nothing about their painfulness from the individual's behavior. Again, if one places this hypothetical observer in the same skin as the subject, then the pattern of results displayed in the experiment by Zimbardo *et al.* (1969) is the result.

There is another kind of behavior which an observer can use to judge the painfulness of the shock: Does the individual attempt to escape from the shock or does he endure it? It seems reasonable to suppose that an observer would judge shocks from which the individual tried to escape as more uncomfortable than shocks the individual was willing to endure. Self-perception theory, then, predicts that the individual who observes himself freely choosing to escape a shock should rate it as more painful than a shock he chooses to endure. On the other hand, if he is not permitted to choose the action, but is simply instructed by the experimenter to escape the shock, he should not rate it as any more painful than a control shock. The study by Bandler *et al.* (1968) attempted to verify this hypothesis.

Each subject in the experiment received a series of shocks to his hand. Just after the onset of each shock, one of three colored lights was illuminated on a box in front of him. He was told that if the red light came on, he should press a button which he held in his hand and this would terminate the shock. In order to enhance feelings of choice, he was also told, "However, if the shock is not uncomfortable, you may elect to not depress the button. The choice is up to you." This condition was labeled the escape condition. In the green-light condition, subjects were instructed to not depress the button (the no-escape condition) unless the "shock is so uncomfortable that you feel you must . . . Again the choice is up to you." In the yellow-light condition, subjects were told that "we are interested in recording only the time that it takes you to press the button once the yellow light comes on. Therefore, please press the button as soon as the yellow light is illuminated. Your depression of the button *may* or *may not* turn off the shock."

Following each shock the subject rated the discomfort it produced on a 7-point rating scale. The 30 critical shocks were all of equal intensity, and, if not terminated by the subject, had a duration of 2 seconds. Thus, for 10 shocks paired with the escape light, the subject pressed a button and terminated the shock. For the 10 shocks paired with the no-escape light, the subject did not press the button. (Despite the implied choice, subjects overwhelmingly complied with the instructions.) And, finally, for the 10 shocks paired with the "reaction-time" trials, the subject pressed the button as soon as he could after the light was illuminated. For five of these trials, pressing the button terminated the shock. For the remaining five reaction-time trials, pressing the button had no effect on the shock. It should be noted that the subject's overt behavior was the same in the reaction-time condition as it was in the escape condition: He pressed the button when the light was illuminated. But the subject was not given the implied choice of pressing or not pressing and, as the instructions make clear, pressing the button did not necessarily terminate the shock. Thus in the reaction-time condition, the button press should no longer be seen by the subject as a self-determined escape response, and he should not infer his discomfort from it. Discomfort ratings should therefore be significantly lower in the reaction-time condition than in the escape condition.

The results supported the self-perception hypothesis. Subjects rated shocks as significantly more uncomfortable when they escaped them than when they endured them, the same inference an outside observer might have drawn. This was true even though the endured shocks were necessarily longer than the escaped shocks. (Within the reaction-time condition, the endured shocks were rated as slightly more uncomfortable than the briefer terminated shocks.) Moreover, the subject had to perceive that he had some choice in the matter. Pushing the button in the reaction-time condition was not used as a guide for inferring the discomfort of the shock. Ratings of shocks in the reaction-time condition were significantly lower than those in the escape condition and were not significantly different from ratings of shocks in the no-escape condition.

This experiment has since been replicated by Corah and Boffa (1970) using white noise as the aversive stimulus and a between-subjects design for the choice parameter. That is, half of their subjects were given the implied choice of escaping or not escaping, just as Bandler *et al.* had done, but the remaining subjects were not given such a choice. The results of Bandler *et al.* were confirmed. When given choice, subjects rated bursts of noise they escaped as significantly more aversive than bursts of noise they endured. When the choice was omitted, endured noise was slightly more aversive than the escaped noise, a replication of the Bandler *et al.* finding within the reaction-time condition.

A second replication of the Bandler *et al.* experiment was conducted by Klemp and Leventhal (1972), who controlled for stimulus duration by contrasting the shocks the subject "chose" to escape with the reaction-time shocks he escaped (i.e., without choice) and the shocks he "chose" to endure with the reaction-time shocks which were not terminated. These investigators found that the self-perception effect—chosen escaped shocks rated more painful than unchosen escaped shocks—held only for subjects who had a high tolerance for shock. An opposite pattern was found for low tolerance subjects: After choosing to escape a shock, they rated it as less uncomfortable than a shock which is escaped without choice. Klemp and Leventhal suggest, among other possibilities, that low-tolerance subjects may be more frightened, i.e., they may show more of the bodily components of fear, and fear might intensify the judged discomfort of shock. If being able to choose is critical in reducing this fear (as other research implies), then lower discomfort ratings in the choice conditions would be expected.

This finding is also consistent with an earlier finding by Nisbett and Schachter (1966), who actually manipulated fear in a self-attribution experiment involving electric shock. The predicted self-perception effect occurred only in the low-fear condition; there were no significant differences between conditions in the high-fear treatment.

It will be recalled that the basic self-perception postulate states that self-perception effects based upon observations of overt behavior occur "to the extent that internal cues are weak, ambiguous, or uninterpretable." The findings of Klemp and Leventhal and of Nisbett and Schachter would appear to exemplify cases in which the internal stimuli of fear override any information potentially available to the individual from external sources, including overt behavior.

III. The Reinterpretation of Cognitive Dissonance Phenomena

If a person holds two cognitions that are inconsistent with one another, he will experience the pressure of an aversive motivational state called cognitive dissonance, a pressure which he will seek to remove, among other ways, by altering one of the two "dissonant" cognitions. This proposition is the heart of Festinger's theory of cognitive dissonance (Festinger, 1957), a theory which received more widespread attention from personality and social psychologists during the decade of the Sixties than any other contemporary statement about human behavior.

In 1965, it was suggested that self-perception theory might be able to account for the major phenomena of cognitive dissonance theory (Bem, 1965), a suggestion which was elaborated more systematically in Bem (1967b). The basic theme of that reinterpretation has already been spelled out in Section I, B, with respect to the Festinger and Carlsmith (1959) experiment. Now that the experiments providing independent evidence for the self-perception postulates have been described, it is appropriate to return to the conceptual reanalysis of the various dissonance paradigms.

A. THE FORCED-COMPLIANCE STUDIES: THE PSYCHOLOGY OF
   INSUFFICIENT JUSTIFICATION

The Festinger-Carlsmith study exemplifies the experimental procedure known as the forced-compliance paradigm. In all of these experiments, an individual is induced to engage in some behavior that would imply his endorsement of a particular set of beliefs or attitudes. Following his behavior, his "actual" attitude or belief is assessed to see if it is a function of the behavior in which he has engaged and of the manipulated stimulus conditions under which it was evoked. Thus in the Festinger-Carlsmith experiment, subjects were induced for either $1 or $20 to tell a waiting fellow student that the repetitive tasks were fun and interesting, and then their own attitudes were assessed. As noted earlier, the low-compensation subjects expressed significantly more favorable attitudes toward the tasks than the high-compensation subjects or control subjects, the reverse-incentive effect.

Dissonance theory interprets these results by noting that all subjects initially hold the cognition that the tasks are dull and boring. In addition, however, the experimental subjects have the cognition that they have expressed favorable attitudes toward the tasks to a fellow student. These two cognitions are dissonant for subjects in the $1 condition because their overt behavior does not "follow from" their cognition about the task, nor does it follow from the small compensation they are receiving. To reduce the resulting dissonance pressure, they change their cognition about the task so that it is consistent with their overt behavior: they become more favorable toward the tasks. The subjects in the $20 condition, however, experience little or no dissonance because engaging in such behavior "follows from" the large compensation they are receiving. Hence, their final attitude ratings do not differ from those of the control group. It is the motivational force provided by the drive toward consistency or dissonance reduction which changes the attitudes of the low-compensation subjects.

As noted earlier, self-perception theory considers the subject in such an experiment as simply an observer of his own behavior. Just as an outside observer might ask himself, "What must this man's attitude be if he is willing to behave in this fashion in this situation?" so too, the subject implicitly asks himself, "What must my attitude be if I am willing to behave in this fashion in this situation?" Thus the subject who receives $1 discards the monetary inducement as the major motivating factor for his behavior and infers that it must reflect his actual attitude; he infers that he must have actually enjoyed the tasks. The subject who receives $20 notes that his behavior is adequately accounted for by the monetary inducement, and hence he cannot extract from the behavior any information relevant to his actual opinions; he is in the same situation as a control subject insofar as information about his attitude is concerned. Thus in the self-perception explanation, there is no aversive motivational pressure postulated. The dependent variable is viewed simply as a self-attribution based on the available evidence, which includes the overt behavior of the communication and the apparent controlling variables of that behavior. A similar analysis can be applied to other experiments conducted within the forced-compliance paradigm.

The advantages of the self-perception explanation emerge more clearly in forced-compliance experiments in which dissonance theory does not provide an applicable account of the findings. Three such experiments can be mentioned here.

1. Pro-Attitudinal Advocacy

Kiesler, Nisbett, and Zanna (1969) conducted a forced-compliance study specifically designed to rule out the dissonance explanation by inducing subjects into committing themselves to argue a position with which they initially agreed. Such a situation presumably does not arouse the "dissonance" produced by counterattitudinal advocacy. In addition, Kiesler *et al.* manipulated the "meaning" of the behavior by having a confederate subject express his willingness to argue the issue assigned to him because (*a*) he believed strongly in it (belief-relevant condition), or (*b*) the experiment was scientifically valuable (belief-irrelevant condition). The confederate's issue was not the same one assigned to the actual subject. The results produced a self-perception effect: Subjects in the belief-relevant condition were found to be more favorable to the position they were to argue than either belief-irrelevant subjects or control subjects who were not committed to the behavior.

2. Rejection of Alternative Action

A second study in which subjects were to give a speech advocating a position they already endorsed was conducted by Zanna (1970). This study was specifically designed to show that the individual's inferences about his beliefs may be based not only on acts he performs but also on alternative acts he rejects. After committing themselves to giving a speech which advocated a moderate position on an issue, subjects were given the opportunity to alter the speech so that it advocated a position more extreme, an opportunity which was arranged so that all subjects would nevertheless choose to reject it. Control subjects were not given the opportunity to alter the speech. A belief-relevance manipulation similar to that in the Kiesler *et al.* (1969) study was introduced for all subjects. The results supported the self-perception analysis: Subjects who had observed themselves decline a chance to make their speech more extreme attributed to themselves an attitude toward the issue less extreme than the self-attributions made by control subjects. In further support of the self-perception postulate that such self-attributions are like interpersonal attributions, Zanna also conducted a successful parallel experiment which showed that observers generate the same pattern of results as the actual subjects. This kind of study is now known as an interpersonal simulation (Bem, 1968c), and will be discussed at length in Section III, C.

Harvey and Mills (1971) conducted an experiment conceptually similar to the Zanna study in which subjects were given the opportunity to substitute a different speech for the one they had initially given. As in the Zanna study, the opportunity was offered in such a way that all subjects rejected it. Again the results showed that subjects who were given the opportunity and rejected it expressed final attitudes more in line with the speech they had given than subjects who were not given that opportunity. However, because the speech in this study was counterattitudinal, both dissonance theory and self-perception theory can predict this result (notwithstanding the contention of Harvey and Mills that this study favors dissonance theory over self-perception theory). A dissonance-theoretic prediction that attitude change would be greater if the subject's initial attitude were made more salient for him was not confirmed; in fact, the differences were in the opposite direction. As we shall see in Section III, D and E, self-perception theory suggests that making an initial attitude more salient should *diminish* the degree to which self-attributions can be altered by observations of overt behavior.

3. The Effects of Repeated Advocacy

Cohen (Brehm & Cohen, 1962, pp. 97–104) conducted an experiment to see what the effects of repeated "dissonances" might be on attitude change. Although dissonance theory might predict that dissonance pressure would build up, yielding greater final attitude change, Brehm and Cohen note that it is also possible for a "tolerance for dissonance" to build up at the same time. Thus they ventured no specific predictions. In this study, subjects in the predissonance conditions were required to write four separate essays against positions they currently held; subjects in the preconsonance conditions wrote four essays in favor of positions they currently held. All subjects were then induced to write a fifth essay which was counter-attitudinal. The fifth essay was preceded by a manipulation of justification. Half of the subjects were given little justification for writing the fifth essay; half were given a great deal of justification. Following the writing of the final essay, attitudes were assessed on that one issue.

The pattern of results did not lend itself to any simple dissonance or "tolerance" of dissonance interpretation. Within the predissonance conditions, there was no attitude change at all. But within the preconsonance conditions, the usual effect of justification was found: significantly greater attitude change when little justification was given than when a great deal of justification was given. Another way of stating the results is that attitude change occurred only in the preconsonance-low justification condition.

The self-perception analysis of this pattern of findings is straightforward. In fact, the experiment is remarkably like the cartoon and false confession experiments described in Section II. Each subject receives pretraining which informs him either that he can believe what he says (preconsonance condition) or that he cannot (predissonance condition). Thus preconsonance subjects arrive at the fifth essay with their self-credibility intact, a credibility which can be maintained (low justification) or destroyed (high justification) for the crucial fifth essay. The predissonance subjects arrive at the fifth essay with their self-credibility already destroyed, and hence further manipulations have no effect, and no attitude change is observed.

4. Combining Sources of Credibility Information

The experiment on repeated "dissonances" makes explicit an underlying assumption of self-perception theory concerning the way in which different sources of information combine. Self-perception theory states that if external contingencies seem sufficient to account for the behavior, then the individual will not be led into using the behavior as a source of evidence for his self-attributions. This suggests that if any elements of the situation imply that the behavior is not credible or is not otherwise relevant to his private views, then the presence of other cues implying credibility does not help. Thus, if either predissonance training *or* high justification was present in the repeated dissonance study, the behavior was not used as the basis for self-attribution. Another way of saying this is that the sources of self-credibility combine multiplicatively: If any source implies irrelevance or low credibility, then self-attributions will not occur.

More direct support for this combination rule is provided in an experiment by Linder and Jones (1969) which is a clever hybrid between a self-perception study and a dissonance study. Their subjects were trained to make true and false statements in the presence of two colored lights following exactly the procedures used in the cartoon and false-confession studies. Thus subjects learned that they could believe what they said in the presence of the "truth" light, and that they could not believe themselves in the presence of the "lie" light. All subjects then had to read counter-attitudinal essays in the presence of one of the two lights. Half of the subjects were permitted a "free" choice whether or not to comply; the remaining subjects were given no choice. Final attitudes were then assessed. The results show that significantly greater agreement with the position advocated in the essay appeared only when essays were read under free choice conditions in the presence of the "truth" light. In other words, if either the "lie" light was on *or* if the subject had no choice, self-attributions based upon the behavior did not occur. The rule for combining conflicting sources of credibility information appears to be multiplicative.

5. The Forbidden Toy Studies

One variation of the forced-compliance paradigm which has been employed with increasing frequency is the forbidden toy procedure. In this situation, children are asked not to play with an attractive toy and are given either a mild or a severe threat of punishment for disobeying. Following a period in which all the children do resist the temptation, children under mild threat have been shown to devalue the prohibited toy (Aronson & Carlsmith, 1963). Unlike the studies of counter-attitudinal advocacy, which frequently fail to replicate, the forbidden toy finding has proved extremely reliable, producing both verbal derogation of the previously forbidden toy (Aronson & Carlsmith, 1963; Carlsmith, Ebbesen, Lepper, Zanna, Joncas, & Abelson, 1969; Lepper, Zanna, & Abelson, 1970; Ostfeld & Katz, 1969; Turner & Wright, 1965) and actual behavioral avoidance of the toy up to 6 weeks after the initial session (Freedman, 1965; Pepitone, McCauley, & Hammond, 1967).

The dissonance theory account of this effect is that a severe threat provides high justification for the child not to play with the toy, rendering the temptation period nondissonant; the mild threat, however, is insufficient to justify his not playing with the toy, producing dissonance which can be resolved by convincing himself he really doesn't like the toy. The self-perception account is also straightforward. The child, when asked his toy preferences after the temptation period reviews his behavior toward the toy and the apparent controlling variables of his avoiding the toy. If he has refrained from playing with the toy under severe threat, he can still infer that he may like the toy, but if he has refrained under mild threat, then he could conclude that he must not like the toy. Again, it is as if subjects use the implicit self-selection rule, "What must my attitude be if I am willing to behave in this fashion in this situation."

Both theories can also handle certain variations of the procedure. For example, Lepper *et al.* (1970) show that if the child is told prior to the temptation period that other children did not play with the toy when asked, then mild-threat subjects no longer devalue the toy. Within the dissonance theory framework, this consensual information gives the child a "consonant" reason for not playing with the toy, and hence no dissonance is aroused. Similarly, in self-perception theory, the information prevents the subject from using the implicit self-selection rule; because everyone behaves the same way, the child cannot use such normative behavior to infer something unique about his attitudes from it. [Kelley (1967) has pointed out the importance to the self-attribution process of having subjects believe their behavior is distinctive if it is to be used as the basis of inference.]

But both theories require added assumptions to account for the second finding of Lepper *et al.*: Mild-threat subjects still do devalue the toy if the consensual information is given after rather than before the temptation period. This implies that the attitudinal attribution takes place during the temptation period and is irreversible. Dissonance theory does not commit itself with regard to when dissonance reduction takes place, but the implication that it is a continuing process which begins immediately and which, once accomplished, is resistant to reversal is consistent with the spirit of the theory. In self-perception theory, however, it has always been implicitly assumed that the attribution probably occurs when the experimenter asks the individual for his final opinion, at which time he reviews the immediate past for the answer. The Lepper *et al.* experiment implies that the child seeks an inferential account for his behavior earlier, during the temptation period. Something prompts him to ask, "How come I'm not playing with this toy?" But even if this assumption is added to the self-perception account, there is still nothing within the theory which would predict that the child's attribution should resist change when new information comes in (e.g., the consensual information). In this instance, then, self-perception theory requires more "patching up" to account for the results than does dissonance theory. Interestingly, however, the forbidden toy paradigm has simultaneously become the vehicle for demonstrating two nondissonance, self-perception phenomena (Lepper, 1971). These will be discussed in detail in Sections IV, A and B.

These, then, are the major phenomena which have emerged from the forced-compliance paradigm of cognitive dissonance theory. As we shall see in Section VII, there are hidden intricacies in these phenomena which outrun all current theories, including the present analysis. At this juncture, however, this section may be taken to constitute the psychology of insufficient justification as seen from the perspective of self-perception theory.

B. The Free Choice Studies

After the forced-compliance paradigm, it is the free choice paradigm which has received the most attention within dissonance theory (Brehm & Cohen, 1962). In these studies, a subject is permitted to make a selection from a set of objects or courses of actions. The dependent variable is his subsequent attitude rating of the chosen and rejected alternatives. Dissonance theory reasons that any unfavorable aspects of the chosen alternative and any favorable aspects of the rejected alternatives provide cognitions that are dissonant with the cognition that the individual has chosen as he did. To reduce the resulting dissonance pressure, the individual exaggerates the favorable features of the chosen alternative and plays down its unfavorable aspects. This leads him to enhance his rating of the chosen alternative. Similar reasoning predicts that he will lower his rating of the rejected alternatives. These predictions are confirmed in a number of studies (see Brehm & Cohen, 1962, p. 303; Festinger, 1964).

A number of secondary predictions concerning parameters of the choice have also been confirmed. In an experiment by Brehm and Cohen (1959), school children were permitted to select a toy from either two or four alternatives. Some children chose from qualitatively similar toys; others chose from qualitatively dissimilar alternatives. The children's postchoice ratings of the toys on a set of rating scales were then compared to initial ratings obtained a week before the experiment. The main displacement effect appeared as predicted: Chosen toys were displaced in the more favorable direction; rejected toys were generally displaced in the unfavorable direction. In addition, however, the displacement effect was larger when the choice was made from the larger number of alternatives. This is so, according to dissonance theory, because "the greater the number of alternatives from which one must choose, the more one must give up and consequently the greater the magnitude of dissonance [Brehm & Cohen, 1959, p. 373]." Similarly, the displacement effect was larger when the choice was made from dissimilar rather than similar alternatives because "what one has to give up relative to what one gains increases [p. 373]," again increasing the magnitude of the dissonance experienced.

Again, self-perception approaches the phenomenon by considering an observer trying to estimate a child's ratings of toys; the observer has not seen the child engage in any behavior with the toys. Now compare this observer with one who has just seen the child select one of the toys as a gift for himself. This comparison parallels, respectively, the prechoice and the postchoice ratings made by the children themselves. It seems likely that the latter observer would displace the estimated ratings of the chosen and rejected alternatives further from one another simply because he has some behavioral evidence upon which to base differential ratings of these toys. This is the effect displayed in the children's final ratings.

The positive relation between the number of alternatives and the displacement can be similarly analyzed. If an observer had seen the selected toy "win out" over more competing alternatives, it seems reasonable that he might increase the estimated displacement between the "exceptional" toy and the group of rejected alternatives. Finally, the fact that the displacement effect is larger when the alternatives are dissimilar would appear to be an instance of simple stimulus generalization. That is, to the extent that the chosen and rejected alternatives are similar to one another, they will be rated closer together on a scale by any rater, outside observer, or the child himself.

In sum, if one regards the children as observers of their own choice behavior and their subsequent ratings as inferences from that behavior, the dissonance findings appear to follow.

C. The Interpersonal Simulations of Cognitive Dissonance Studies

As we have seen, the reinterpretation of dissonance studies proceeds by utilizing the second postulate of self-perception theory: To the extent that internal cues are weak, ambiguous, or uninterpretable, the individual is functionally in the same position as an outside observer. In order to bolster the purely conceptual use of this postulate in the reinterpretation of the dissonance studies, an experimental methodology was devised for testing this notion more experimentally. The resulting experiments within this methodology have now become known as interpersonal simulations (Bem, 1965, 1967a, 1967b, 1967c, 1968a, 1968b, 1968c; Bem & McConnell, 1970). In these experiments, an observer-subject is either given a description of one of the conditions of a dissonance experiment or actually permitted to observe one of these conditions and then asked to estimate the attitude of the subject whose behavior is either described or observed. The prediction is that such observer-subjects should be able to reproduce the patterns of results generated by actual subjects in the original experiments. It should be noted that observer-subjects are not asked to play amateur psychologist and predict the results of the experiment; rather, each observer-subject attempts to infer the attitude of a single "other." In the simulation, he "stands in" for the actual subject.

For example, the free choice study described in the prior section was simulated by giving college students a sheet of paper which informed them that an 11-year-old boy in a psychology experiment was permitted to select one of several toys to keep for himself (Bem, 1967b). The sheet informed the observer-subject which toy the child had chosen and from which alternatives he was permitted to choose. Each observer-subject then estimated the child's ratings of the chosen and rejected toys. These observer-subjects were randomly assigned to one of four conditions corresponding to the combinations of number of alternatives (two or four) and similarity of alternatives (similar or dissimilar). The toys listed were selected from the list reported in the original experiment (Brehm & Cohen, 1959) and were rated on the same rating scales. A group of control observer-subjects simply estimated toy ratings of a typical 11-year-old boy. The results showed that observer-subjects not only replicated the main displacement effect (chosen toy enhanced, rejected toy devalued), but also replicated the effects of the number of toys (displacement effect enhanced with more rejected alternatives) and the effects of the similarity of the toys (displacement effect diminished with similar alternatives).

A somewhat more elaborate simulation was conducted for the Festinger and Carlsmith (1959) study in which, it will be recalled, subjects who had received $1 for telling a stooge that a series of tasks were fun and interesting subsequently gave the tasks higher ratings than either subjects paid $20 or control subjects.

Seventy-five college undergraduates participated in an experiment designed to "determine how accurately people can judge another person." Twenty-five subjects each served in a $1, a $20, or a control condition. All subjects listened to a tape recording which described a college sophomore named Bob Downing, who had participated in an experiment involving two motor tasks. The tasks were described in detail, but non-evaluatively; the alleged purpose of the experiment was also described. At this point, the control subjects were asked to evaluate Bob's attitudes toward the tasks. The experimental subjects were further told that Bob had accepted an offer of $1 ($20) to go into the waiting room, tell the next subject that the tasks were fun, and to be prepared to do this again in the future if they needed him. The subjects then listened to a brief conversation which they were told was an actual recording of Bob and the girl who was in the waiting room. Bob was heard to argue rather imaginatively that the tasks were fun and enjoyable, while the girl responded very little except for the comments that Festinger and Carlsmith's stooge was instructed to make. The recorded conversation was identical for both experimental conditions in order to remain true to the original study in which no differences in persuasiveness were found between the $1 and the $20 communications. In sum, the situation attempted to duplicate on tape the situation actually experienced by Festinger and Carlsmith's subjects. All subjects estimated Bob's responses to the same set of questions employed in the original study.

The results of this simulation showed that interpersonal observers were able to replicate the reverse-incentive effect. Observers of $1 subjects estimated "Bob's" attitude to be significantly more favorable toward the tasks than did observers of either $20 subjects or control subjects. Observers of $20 subjects did not differ in their estimates of Bob's attitude from observers of control subjects. An extended version of this same simulation (Bem, 1967b) replicated an interaction effect between the monetary compensation and the length of the communication found in the original study. Similar simulations conducted by the author (Bem, 1965) have replicated results from a forced-compliance experiment which utilized small compensations of 50¢ and $1 (Brehm & Cohen, 1962, p. 73) and results from an experiment on hunger ratings by Brehm and Crocker (Brehm & Cohen, 1962, pp. 133–136).

A particularly persuasive simulation was performed by Alexander and Knight (1971) in order to replicate a complex pattern of results found in a forced-compliance study by Carlsmith, Collins, and Helmreich (1966). In their experiment, Carlsmith et al. had shown that one obtains the classical reverse-incentive effect when the subject actually has a face-to-face encounter with the waiting stooge, but that an incentive effect emerges (more money, more attitude change) if the subject simply writes an anonymous essay stating that the tasks were fun and interesting. Alexander and Knight were able to simulate this interaction effect between the monetary inducement and the mode of counter-attitudinal behavior by modifying and extending Bem's use of tapes about "Bob Downing."[2]

There have also been several simulations which have failed to

[2] The successful interpersonal simulation of the Carlsmith et al. (1966) findings is actually the least important aspect of the Alexander-Knight article, and it trivializes their contribution to present it in this context. The simulation was actually the first step toward demonstrating their theory that the results of many experiments can be predicted from a knowledge of the most socially desirable response in the situation. Their interpretation of the forced-compliance studies in particular is an alternative to both the dissonance and self-perception analyses. For both methodological and theoretical reasons, the Alexander-Knight article is an important document for social psychologists.

replicate the original studies. Some of these failures have come from simulations specifically modified in ways designed to disconfirm the self-perception analysis (e.g., R. A. Jones, Linder, Kiesler, Zanna, & Brehm, 1968; Piliavin, Piliavin, Loewenton, McCauley, & Hammond, 1969). For reasons to be discussed below, such failures are not, in fact, informative with respect to the validity of the theory. Several other failures are also not informative in this regard because they yield only unsystematic noise rather than systematic differences between observer-subjects and actual involved subjects. (Most of these appear in unpublished manuscripts sent to the author over the years.)

The major reason such failures are uninformative is the unreliability of the dissonance phenomena themselves, particularly the reverse-incentive effect, the design most commonly simulated. Indeed, one has learned to fear that an experimenter's unintended belch might destroy or reverse the effect (for discussions, see Abelson et al., 1968, pp. 801–833). It is only semifacetious to suggest that serious doubts about the self-perception analysis could be raised if the simulations were too reliable or more robust than the phenomena themselves, that is, if the simulations were not also sensitive to unknown and uncontrolled parameters. For example, Harris and Tamler (1971a) have shown that one of the simulations fails if it is conducted the way most of the theory's critics have conducted their simulations, but it succeeds if the observer knows that the assessment of final attitudes was made by an experimenter different from the one who manipulated the independent variable, hardly a predictable contingency.

Such variability of outcome suggests that simulations should probably always be conducted directly in conjunction with the experiment being simulated, either simultaneously or with stimulus materials and consequent behaviors actually generated from the experiment itself. Only a few simulations have been conducted in this way.

For example, Harris and Tamler (1971a, 1971b) actually conducted the dissonance experiment which separated the attitude assessment from the initial experimental setting and confirmed that the dissonance effect could be obtained in this way. Materials for their successful simulation were then carefully patterned after the experiment itself. As noted above, they demonstrated that the simulation failed if this single item of information was omitted.

A second example is provided by Zanna (1970) who conducted both the original experiment reported in Section III, A, 2, on the rejection of alternative actions as a source of self-attribution and an associated interpersonal simulation. The simulation successfully replicated his finding that rejection of the opportunity to make a more extreme speech results in the attribution that the subject is more moderate. He also found, as predicted, that observer-subjects who were told that a subject rejected the opportunity to make the speech more moderate judged him to be more extreme than did control observer-subjects, a prediction that was not actually tested in the original experiment because of time limitations.

R. G. Jones (1966) has reported a study in which observer-subjects listened to tapes of the original sessions. Again observers' attributions replicated the inverse functional relation between monetary compensation and final attitude found with involved subjects.

The strategy of conducting both the original experiment and simulation simultaneously pays off even when the simulation fails. For example, in one study of this type, Wolosin (1969) uncovered some important systematic differences between observers and actors in their perceptions of the actor's freedom to comply with the experimenter's request. As we shall see in Section V, such a finding has important implications well beyond the controversy over the simulations, and Wolosin has wisely decided to follow up this auxiliary finding (Wolosin, 1971; Wolosin & Denner, 1970). At the same time, however, it should be noted that even the care and rigor of Wolosin's study did not guarantee that negative results on the simulation would provide an unequivocal disconfirmation of self-perception theory, because none of the main effects or predicted interactions on the *major* dependent variables (ratings of thirst, willingness to undergo water deprivation, and actual water consumption) were significant for the involved subjects themselves. Thus most—albeit not all—of the comparisons that Wolosin hoped to make between observers and involved subjects required him to argue that the columns of random noise generated by two types of observers do not fluctuate in harmony with the column of random noise generated by involved subjects.

D. The Controversy over the Interpersonal Simulations

Although there have been some simulations which have failed to reproduce the pattern of results found in the original dissonance experiments, the controversy surrounding the simulation methodology has focused on the simulations which are successful. In particular, the controversy has centered around the information that the observer-subject ought or ought not to be given concerning the original situation (Bem, 1967a, 1968c; Elms, 1967; R. A. Jones *et al.*, 1968; Mills, 1967; Piliavin *et al.*, 1969). Most of the critics have objected specifically to the fact that observer-subjects are not told the original subject's premanipulation attitude. The conceptual reason for this deliberate omission can be understood by considering some of the epistemological features of the simulation methodology.

Self-perception theory asserts that an individual's attitude statements and an observer's judgments about the individual's attitudes are "output statements" from the same internal "program." Both the individual and observer are assumed to use a self-selection rule: "What must my [this man's] attitude be if I am [he is] willing to behave in this fashion in this situation?" To test this isomorphism, we run a simulation of a self-judgment situation, the dissonance experiment, but instead of writing our own program, we plug in an interpersonal judgment program that the culture has written for us. This program is embodied in our interpersonal observer, who "stands in" for the original subject.

But before we can actually run such a simulation, we must first abstract the relevant "input statements" from the situation being simulated: we must decide how to describe the situation to the observer. This requires some theoretically guided assumptions. For example, if the dissonance experiment subject actually arrives at his final attitude by using the self-selection rule, as the theory implies, then it follows that any conflicting initial attitude he may have had prior to the experiment must no longer be very salient for him. That is, the self-perception analysis implies that the data of his incoming behavior "update" his information on his attitude, replacing any prior information to the contrary. Insofar as the individual himself is concerned, his postmanipulation attitude is, in fact, the same attitude which motivated him to comply in the first place; phenomenologically, there is no attitude "change" as such. If an interpersonal simulation is to constitute a valid test of the isomorphism between the subject and an observer, then the theory dictates that a conflicting "initial" attitude of the original subject must not be part of the "input" description for the observer any more than it is for the subject himself. The observer, too, is postulated to be using the self-selection rule to infer the original subject's postmanipulation attitude.

It should be noted that this set of assumptions about what input information an observer-subject in the simulations should receive is self-correcting. If the wrong input statements are selected, then the simulation will not succeed in producing output statements which match the output of the original experiment. Thus, R. A. Jones et al. (1968) reconfirmed that the simulations produce the "dissonance effect" outputs when the inputs dictated by the self-perception model are employed, but they found that the simulations fail when a conflicting "initial" attitude is introduced into the description given to the observer-subject. After an intensive analysis of observer-subject's inferential processes under several variations of the simulations, Piliavin et al. (1969) reported that when the "Bem" inputs are utilized, observer-subjects do, in fact, utilize the self-selection rule and replicate his results. But when additional information, including a reference to the subject's initial attitude, is introduced into the description, the observer-subjects become amateur psychologists and revert to hypotheses about attitude *change*. They are no longer stand-ins for the original subjects and, accordingly, they fail to reproduce the dissonance effects.

Such results underscore the importance of conducting simulations directly in conjunction with the experiment being simulated. For example, in the combined experiment and simulations of Harris and Tamler (1971a, 1971b) mentioned above, these investigators first verified that they could obtain the reverse-incentive effect even if the subject's initial attitude were made salient for him just prior to the forced-compliance manipulation (reinstatement condition) *and* if the final attitude was assessed by a different experimenter in a "different experiment" (separation condition). They then conducted a $2 \times 2 \times 2$ simulation in which two levels of monetary incentive were crossed with the reinstatement *vs.* nonreinstatement variable and the separation *vs.* nonseparation variable. Under nonseparation conditions [which parallel the R. A. Jones *et al.* (1968) and Piliavin *et al.* (1969) designs], these investigators obtained an incentive effect when reinstatement was employed, and a reverse-incentive effect when it was not. But under separation conditions, both reinstatement and nonreinstatement conditions generated the reverse-incentive effect predicted by self-perception theory. When the actual experiment was simulated exactly, the simulation worked.

It is important to note just what a successful simulation means. It implies the same thing that a successful computer simulation implies, namely, that the process model embodied in the "program" is functionally equivalent to the process being simulated, and, further, that the selection of the input statements was not in error. The simulation becomes a plausibility demonstration, a sufficiency test: The process model embodied in the program is sufficient—but not necessarily "true" or unique—for generating the output statements observed in the situation being modeled by the simulation.

But there are weaknesses in this methodology when it is applied to this context. Abelson (1968) has noted some of the validation problems connected with the simulation methodology in general, and his discussion of the "degrees of freedom" problem is particularly relevant to interpersonal simulations. Abelson stated the problem this way:

> If a simulation could be "right for the wrong reasons," that is, fit the data by virtue of compensating errors, then in what sense can a good fit be regarded as support for the theory underlying the simulation model? . . . Most cognitive simulations are so rich in qualitative detail that it is very easy for them to fail . . . Because it is so hard to obtain good data fits, anything which comes close is impressive, and any

cognitive model yielding an apparently perfect fit to a wide range of data would indeed deserve serious theoretical recognition.

> With social simulations, however, the issue is probably more cogent. If the outcome variables of the model are few while the number of parameters to be juggled is great, there can always be the lingering suspicion that a good fit was too easy to achieve and thus not strongly supportive of the model [pp. 343–344].

This, then, is the main reason why the interpersonal simulations provide only weak support for the self-perception theory. There are too many "degrees of freedom," input variables that can be "juggled" (like the initial attitude), while the complexity of the output predictions rarely exceeds a prediction about the ordering of two or three means. Abelson suggests some of the paths open for strengthening simulation arguments, however. The most obvious remedy, of course, is "to design the simulation so as to generate as large a number of outcome variables as possible. The more outcomes that can be validated, the merrier—and the more convincing the underlying theory [Abelson, 1968, p. 344]."

This path toward strengthening the self-perception theory of dissonance phenomena was followed in three interpersonal simulations (discussed in Section III, C) which not only replicated main effects of dissonance experiments but reproduced either an interaction effect which dissonance theory itself had not anticipated or the secondary effects of additional parameters in the experiments (Alexander & Knight, 1971; Bem, 1967b). Although these extended simulations do not go very far toward eliminating the "degrees of freedom" problem, they are illustrative of the method.

A second remedy is "to show, if possible, that the fit was not so easy by changing the model in various ways and demonstrating consistent lack of fit [Abelson, 1968, p. 343]." In effect, this is what some of the critics have done. They have altered some of the input assumptions of the model and demonstrated that the simulations fail (R. A. Jones et al., 1968; Piliavin et al., 1969). As Abelson has remarked:

> Ironically, what [Bem's] detractors should now really be doing if they must still simulate is to replicate [his] outcome with clearly bad descriptions to the observer, rather than to reverse [his] outcome with purportedly good descriptions [R. P. Abelson, personal communication, January 22, 1969].

The third and most important way of strengthening simulation arguments which suffer from the "degrees of freedom" problem, however, is to return to the original situation and demonstrate that the assumed isomorphism between the inputs of the original situation and the inputs of the simulation actually exists. This is what Harris and Tamler (1971a, 1971b) have done. This too, is what was done in an experiment by Bem and McConnell (1970) which demonstrated that subjects in dissonance experiments cannot, in fact, recall their initial attitudes at the time of the final attitude assessment, that they see their postmanipulation attitudes as the same attitudes which motivated them to comply in the first place, and that they do not experience any attitude change phenomenologically. Hence, initial attitudes are not salient for involved subjects, and should thus not be made salient for observers in the simulations.

This process of moving back and forth between the simulation and the actual situation is precisely the one which cognitive theorists have attempted to follow and, in fact, it is this interaction between simulation and direct experimentation which constitutes the heuristic utility of the simulation methodology. A simulation reveals an underlying assumption or implication of the model which was not originally observed or even anticipated. The theorist can then return to the original situation armed with a new hypothesis. Thus, the hypothesis that subjects in dissonance experiments would perceive their postexperimental attitudes to be identical to the pre-experimental attitudes came to light through the debate between the author and his critics over the simulations. Even though the hypothesis was logically implied by the original analysis, it remained unarticulated until the "countersimulations" of R. A. Jones *et al.* (1968) raised it explicitly. It is important to note, however, that once one of the isomorphisms is questioned, the issue can be resolved only by returning to the original situation. A simulation will not suffice: "No 'as if' methodology, including the technique of interpersonal simulation, is an adequate substitute for the intensive study of the actual situation being modeled [Bem, 1968c, p. 273]."

E. The Possibility of a Crucial Experiment

At the end of their experiment, Bem and McConnell (1970) state that "If the past history of controversies like this is any guide, it seems unlikely that a 'crucial' experiment for discriminating between [dissonance theory and self-perception theory] will ever be executed. At this juncture each theory appears capable of claiming some territory not claimed by the other, and one's choice of theory in areas of overlap is diminishing to a matter of loyalty or aesthetics (p. 30)." Admittedly, this was partially a ploy to bring the whole thing to a halt. But it didn't work, for the controversy over the salience of initial attitudes itself suggested a possible "crucial" test to Snyder and Ebbesen.

In the typical forced-compliance experiment, the subject's initial attitude is in conflict with the induced behavior. What should happen, Snyder and Ebbesen wondered, if the initial attitude is made more salient to the subject? Self-perception theory predicts that this will diminish the degree to which the final attitude attribution will be based upon the induced behavior and hence will diminish the amount of attitude change observed. Dissonance theory, however, predicts just the opposite: Making the initial attitude salient makes one of the two "dissonant" cognitions salient, thus increasing the amount of dissonance aroused. This in turn should produce *more* attitude change. If, on the other hand, the behavior is made more salient, then both theories predict more attitude change. For self-perception theory, this would make salient the very source of evidence upon which the final attribution is to be based; for dissonance theory, this is simply making the second of two dissonant cognitions more salient, again arousing more dissonance. Finally, consider the possibility that both the initial attitude and the behavior were to be made more salient. Under the multiplicative rule for combining different sources of credibility information (Section III, A, 4), self-perception theory predicts that this will be equivalent to making the initial attitude alone salient; hence, attitude change will diminish. Dissonance theory here predicts the greatest attitude change of all since both "dissonant" elements are made salient, thus maximizing the amount of dissonance aroused.

With these differential predictions in hand, Snyder and Ebbesen attempted the crucial test by duplicating exactly the experiment by Bem and McConnell (1970), a standard forced-compliance experiment in which subjects were given a choice or no choice to write a counter-attitudinal essay. First they verified that they could replicate the standard effect as Bem and McConnell had done: Subjects given their choice expressed final attitudes more in line with their counter-attitudinal essays than those expressed either by no-choice subjects or control subjects who wrote no essays at all.

When initial attitudes alone were made salient, choice subjects did not differ from no-choice subjects, and neither group differed from the no-essay control group. Considered alone then, this column of results supported self-perception theory and runs counter to the dissonance theory prediction. When the behavior alone was made salient—where both theories predict enhanced attitude change—the column of results looked like the standard condition: There was more attitude change in the choice than in the no-choice condition which, in turn, did not differ from the control condition, but the effect was not significantly larger than in the standard condition. Neither theory is supported strongly by this condition, but neither was this a condition designed to discriminate between the two theories. Finally, no attitude change was observed in either condition when both the attitude and the behavior were made salient. Again, this supports self-perception theory (multiplicative rule) and not dissonance theory.

A contrast applied to the entire pattern of results shows that self-perception theory accounts for more of the between-cells variance than dissonance theory. But on the other hand, both theories leave a significant amount of the variance unexplained. In particular, there were differential amounts of attitude change among the several no-choice conditions which neither theory anticipates. Snyder and Ebbesen propose a self-perception theory of their own to account for the pattern of results, a theory which proposes that the subject's perception of how counter-attitudinal his behavior appeared to him mediates the attitude change effects. Whatever the merits of the Snyder-Ebbesen theory turn out to be, the "crucial" test between dissonance theory and the original self-perception interpretation of forced-compliance effects remains equivocal. Nevertheless, contrary to the prediction of Bem and McConnell (1970), somebody did manage to force the two theories to confront each other.

It is particularly unfortunate that the Snyder-Ebbesen experiment is equivocal, for the remaining Zeigarnik is likely to tempt others to go forth and do likewise. There are many more interesting paths off the self-attribution road to be explored, and the demise of the precious controversy between dissonance theory and self-perception theory is a consummation devoutly to be wished. It is resolved that, henceforth, nothing more on this subject shall be heard from this quarter.

IV. Other Self-Perception Phenomena

In addition to the cognitive dissonance experiments and the initial studies specifically designed to provide support for self-perception theory, there are a number of other effects which have begun to emerge which fit more or less into the self-perception explanatory framework. Three of these will be reviewed here.

A. MISATTRIBUTION EFFECTS

Before self-perception theory had been enunciated, Schachter's (1964) work on emotional states was already providing evidence that a person's attribution of his internal states was a joint function of both internal physiological cues and external factors of the situation (e.g., Schachter & Singer, 1962). It follows from this fact that one can manipulate an individual's self-attributions by manipulating those external factors.

Valins (1966) took this possibility a step further when he showed that an individual's self-attributions could also be influenced by giving him false feedback about his autonomic arousal. Thus, as noted earlier, Valins was able to manipulate attitudes toward stimulus pictures of seminude females by giving his male subjects false auditory feedback which they could interpret as their heartbeat. Since then, a number of studies have adopted this general procedure. For example, Valins and Ray (1967) asked snake-phobic subjects to look at slides picturing snakes; subjects were given false feedback about their heartbeat designed to imply that they were not afraid of snakes. Subsequently, these subjects were able to approach the snake more closely than control subjects.

Berkowitz, Lepinski, and Angulo (1969) and Berkowitz and Turner (1972) have showed that they could influence the amount of instrumental aggression displayed by subjects by first giving those subjects false feedback about how angry they were. And finally, extinction of the GSR can be facilitated (Loftis & Ross, 1971) or retarded (Koenig & Henriksen, 1972) by giving subjects false information about their arousal. Although there are some intracacies in these studies to be discussed later, the general point to be made at this juncture is that false feedback concerning arousal can lead individuals to misattribute emotional states to themselves.

Misattribution can also be created by manipulating not only the apparent degree of arousal, but the apparent sources or causes of arousal (cf. Nisbett & Valins, 1971). For example, Nisbett and Schachter (1966) were able to obtain higher shock tolerance from subjects who believed that their arousal was produced by a pill rather than the shock. Using a very similar technique Ross, Rodin, and Zimbardo (1969) reduced fear of electric shock by persuading their subjects to attribute their arousal to loud noise. And finally, Storms and Nisbett (1970) gave insomniacs placebo pills and told them that the pills would produce either arousal or relaxation. As predicted, "arousal" subjects reported that they got to sleep more quickly than they had on nights without the pills—presumably because they attributed their arousal to the pills and, as a consequence, worried less about their insomnia, a worry which seems to exacerbate insomnia. Similarly, "relaxed" subjects reported that they got to sleep less quickly than usual—presumably because they worried that their emotions were unusually intense since their arousal level was high even after taking an arousal-reducing agent.

As Nisbett and Valins (1971) point out, all such studies can be seen as special cases of the underlying assumptions of self-perception theory even though the source of cues for the self-attributions are not the individual's overt behavior *per se.* But even this gap was closed in a study by Davison and Valins (1969), who actually manipulated the subjects' behavior and its apparent controlling variables to produce misattribution. In their study, Davison and Valins asked subjects to take a series of electric shocks of steadily increasing intensity and told them to report when the shocks first became painful and when they could no longer tolerate them. Following this series, subjects were given a placebo which they were told might change their skin sensitivity. A second shock series was then administered, but the intensity of all shocks was surreptitiously halved so that subjects ended up taking nearly double the number of shocks than in the first series before reporting pain or asking the experimenter to terminate the series. All subjects were then told that the experiment was over. Some subjects were merely thanked and told that in a few minutes, after the drug had worn off, they would participate in another experiment. Other subjects were told that the drug was really a placebo. Davison and Valins reasoned that the placebo subjects would thus have to attribute their high-shock tolerance on the second series to themselves, their actual ability to withstand shock, since they now knew the drug could not have been responsible, whereas the subjects who had not been "debriefed" would make no such attribution of ability to themselves. This hypothesis was confirmed when a third shock series was administered as part of a "different" experiment. Placebo subjects took significantly more shock on the third series than they had on the first, whereas subjects who continued to believe that their performance on the second series was due to the drug did not.

Bowers (1971) conducted an experiment conceptually quite similar to the Davison-Valins experiment, except that he altered picture preference rather than shock tolerances through misattribution of behavior. His subjects were shown pairs of postcard pictures and asked to state their preference for one of the two pictures in each pair. Each picture also had a four-digit code number printed on its face, and each paired comparison required the subject to choose between a landscape and a portrait. Immediately prior to the series of trials, subjects in two of the experimental conditions were hypnotized and told they should always select pictures whose code numbers contained the digit 7. They were then given amnesia for the suggestion and for the fact that they had been hypnotized. The series of paired comparisons was then begun.

As in the Davison-Valins experiment, three series of trials were given. The first 20 trials determined the subject's baseline for preferring either portraits or landscapes. None of the pictures in these trials had a code number containing the digit 7. During the next 90 (treatment) trials, 60 of the pictures contained the digit 7 paired with the type of picture (portrait or landscape) the subject had least preferred in the baseline trials. Thus, all previously hypnotized subjects saw themselves choosing either portraits or landscapes for at least two-thirds of the treatment trials with no explanation for their behavior. Bowers reasoned that these subjects would be led to infer that they must, in fact, now prefer their previously nonpreferred type of picture. But for half of these subjects, obvious explicit verbal reinforcement was administered during the treatment trials each time the subject expressed his preference for the nonpreferred type of picture. This, according to Bowers, should provide a suitable explanation to the subject for his preference change and thus prevent the self-attribution from taking place. Several types of control groups who had not been hypnotized were also run.

The test of this self-attribution hypothesis was sought in the subjects' preferences on a final set of 40 trials in which none of the pictures contained the digit 7. As predicted, subjects whose behavior had been manipulated through the hypnotic suggestion and who were left with no alternative explanation for their preference change persisted in choosing the initially nonpreferred type of picture significantly more than the reinforced group or any of several control groups.

It is clear why these various phenomena have earned the label of misattribution effects. On the other hand, it is easily overlooked that every effect discussed so far in this review is, without exception, a "misattribution" effect. If individuals actually accurately discriminated the variables controlling their behavior, then none of the predicted self-attributions would have occurred. For example, as Kelley (1967) has pointed out about forced-compliance studies, subjects in low-justification conditions must have an "illusion of freedom," must fail to apprehend the forces which induced them to comply, if they are to draw the predicted self-attributions from the behavior in which they engage. [The perception of freedom has itself now become a major research topic. For a review and analysis, see Steiner (1970).]

Self-perception theory may thus appear deficient because it does not attempt to account for this pervasive unawareness of the actual controlling variables. Or, as a Stanford colleague is fond of saying, self-perception theory appears to explain everything about why induced compliance leads to attitude change except why induced compliance leads to attitude change. But this apparent deficiency emerges only if one assumes that awareness is the normal state of things, and that unawareness is the phenomenon to be explained. As noted in Section I, A, the unique contribution of the radical-behavioral analysis of self-referring statements resides precisely in its explicit assumption that unawareness is the given and awareness the problematic. From this perspective, what needs to be explained—and what Skinner's analysis explains—is how individuals learn to respond to the apparent controlling variables we have purposely made salient in the laboratory, not why they fail to discriminate the actual controlling variables we have intentionally obscured. Under such conditions, the radical behaviorist's answer to the question, "Why do subjects have this 'illusion' of freedom?" is "Why not?"

It is consistent with Western man's fascination with the unconscious that misattribution seems somehow "sexier" and more mysterious than veridical attribution. There are, of course, problematic cases of unawareness involving repression and motivated distortion. But these are challenge enough without adding the extra theoretical burden of having to explain the pseudo-problem of why individuals are not also perfect information processors.

B. The Self-Attribution of Dispositional Properties

All of the studies reviewed so far in this article demonstrate that external sources of stimuli can exercise control over an individual's attributions of his transitory states or his attitudes. Some studies are beginning to be reported, however, which suggest that it might be possible to change longer-standing attributions that the individual might make about himself by manipulating his behavior and apparent controlling variables appropriately. Interestingly, the first real clue that this might be possible was discovered almost accidentally by Freedman and Fraser (1966), who were investigating the so called "foot-in-the-door" phenomenon in which a person who can be induced to comply with an initial small request is then more likely to comply subsequently with a larger and more substantial demand.

In their study, Freedman and Fraser had two undergraduate experimenters contact suburban housewives in their homes, first with a small request and later with a larger more consequential request. The housewives were first asked either to place a small sign in their window or to sign a petition on the issue of either safe driving or keeping California beautiful. Two weeks later, a second experimenter returned to each home, asking all subjects to place a large and rather unattractive billboard promoting auto safety on their front lawn for several weeks. The second request thus involved both an action and an issue which were either similar to or different from those involved in the first request. A control group was contacted only about the second request.

The results showed a very strong foot-in-the-door effect. Subjects who had complied with the earlier trivial request were much more likely to comply with the larger one 2 weeks later. The remarkable finding, however, was the striking generality of the effect. It did not matter which issue or action had been involved in the initial request; the compliance generalized equally in all four conditions to the later larger request. Thus, even the small action of signing an innocuous petition to "Keep California Beautiful" increased the subsequent probability of the subject's agreeing to place a large billboard reading "Drive Safely" on her lawn when asked to do so 2 weeks later by a second unrelated experimenter. In fact, the failure to find a generalization gradient as a function of similarity between the initial and final requests tends to rule out several plausible theoretical explanations of the effect. Thus, Freedman and Fraser (1966) arrive *post hoc* at what is essentially a self-perception explanation:

What may occur is a change in the person's feelings about getting involved or about taking action. Once he has agreed to a request, his attitude may change. He may become, in his own eyes, the kind of person who does this sort of thing, who agrees to requests made by strangers, who takes action on things he believes in, who cooperates with good causes [p. 201].

In thinking about the Freedman-Fraser study and self-perception theory, it occurred to Lepper (1971) that attributions of this kind might also be taking place in other experimental settings which had previously measured attitudinal attributions only. For example, in the forbidden toy paradigm it is found that children who comply under mild threat conditions devalue the forbidden toy. But the attribution, "I don't like that toy" is only one possible inference that a child in the mild-threat condition might draw. Lepper suggests that another inference might be that he is a particularly "good" boy, one who is able to resist temptation. Moreover, this is not an inference which would be drawn under conditions of severe threat. Such an attribution might then generalize so that the child would display increased resistance to temptation in a different situation, an exact analogue to the Freedman-Fraser finding.

Lepper tested this hypothesis in the classical forbidden toy setting. Two groups of second-grade children were forbidden from playing with an attractive toy under mild or severe threat of punishment, while a third, control group received no initial prohibition. Three weeks later, a second experimenter asked these subjects to play a game in which they could obtain attractive prizes only by falsifying their scores. As predicted from the self-perception analysis, subjects who complied with the initial prohibition under mild threat showed more resistance to temptation in this second situation than control subjects or subjects who had initially complied under severe threat.

Lepper also reports that subjects who had initially complied under severe threat tended to show even less resistance to temptation than control subjects. Although this finding is open to more than one interpretation, Lepper suggests that it might be an "overjustification" effect, wherein the child under threat of severe punishment infers that he resists temptation only because of strong external forces. Hence, when such pressures are subsequently withdrawn, he is even less resistant to temptation than before. We turn now to a more detailed consideration of such overjustification effects.

C. OVERJUSTIFICATION EFFECTS

The self-perception analysis of insufficient justification essentially states that a person will infer that he was intrinsically motivated to execute the induced behavior to the extent that external contingencies of reinforcement appeared to be absent. Thus he infers that he "wanted" to do the activity, that he believes in it, or that it reflects his true opinions. An overjustification effect is predicted if one is willing to assume that to the extent that external contingencies of reinforcement are strongly apparent, the individual infers that he did not want to perform the activity, that he does not believe in it, or that it does not reflect his true opinions. Because behavior is "consonant" with the initial attitudes in most overjustification studies, dissonance theory does not apply, and some writers (e.g., Nisbett & Valins, 1972) have looked to such effects as clearer instances of self-perception phenomena.

If overjustification effects do occur, then they provide a possible affirmative answer to the old question of whether or not extrinsic reinforcement for an activity reduces the intrinsic motivation to engage in that activity. Performing the activity under strong contingencies of reinforcement leads to the attribution that the activity must not be enjoyable in itself and then perhaps to decreased motivation to engage in that activity (deCharms, 1968; Deci, 1971, 1972; Deci & Cascio, 1971; Lepper, Greene, & Nisbett, 1971). For a number of reasons, early experiments with monkeys do not provide an affirmative answer to this question, discussions in elementary textbooks, and elsewhere (e.g., deCharms, 1968) notwithstanding. Accordingly, new attempts to confirm this overjustification effect have now begun to appear. For example, a series of studies by Deci (1971, 1972; Deci & Cascio, 1971) does suggest that intrinsic motivation to solve puzzles is reduced when the activity is executed under either monetary reinforcement or, possibly, threat of punishment, but not if positive verbal feedback is the reinforcer. It is clear that the "meaning" of the individual's self-observed behavior is going to be a function of his past history with the particular reinforcement contingencies used. Thus, money has probably acquired the discriminative property of "buying" compliance more than verbal praise.

The definitive experiment in this area, however, appears to be an elegant study by Lepper *et al.* (1971), who carefully divorced the measurement of intrinsic interest from the situation in which the rewards were administered in order to rule out alternative interpretations of the anticipated results. Children who met a criterion of intrinsic interest in a play activity during baseline observations in their classrooms were randomly assigned to one of three conditions. In separate individual sessions 2 weeks later, children in the Expected-Award condition engaged in the activity in the anticipation of receiving an extrinsic reward. Children in the Unexpected-Award condition engaged in the activity only for its own sake, but subsequently received the same reward. The No-Award control subjects neither expected nor received the reward, but otherwise duplicated the experience of the subjects in the other conditions. One to two weeks after the experimental sessions, the target activity was again introduced into the children's classrooms, and unobtrusive measures of intrinsic interest were again obtained. The results confirmed that children in the Expected-Reward condition now freely engaged in the activity less than did either children in the Unexpected-Award or No-Award conditions.

Although these effects have here been interpreted in terms of self-perception theory, there are some problems involved in doing so which will be discussed in Section VII where the role of other explanations (e.g., deCharms, 1968) will also be considered.

V. Some Differences between Self-Perception and Interpersonal Perception

Self-perception theory asserts that self- and interpersonal perception are similar in two ways. First, the processes of inference involved in attribution are the same, and second, both actors and observers share certain sources of evidence—overt behavior and its apparent controlling variables—upon which those attributions can be based. This leaves open at least four ways in which the self-attributions and interpersonal attributions can still differ.

The first difference is what might be called the *Insider vs. Outsider* difference. All of us have approximately 3–4 ft^3 of potential stimuli inside of us which are unavailable to others but which are available to us for self-attributions. The thrust of the Skinnerian analysis of self-attributions is not that we can make no discriminations among internal stimuli, but only that we are far more severely limited than we suppose in this regard because the verbal community is limited in how extensively it can train us to make such discriminations. Nevertheless, the Insider can often detect, for example, that he is "trying hard" to solve a problem, and can infer that the problem is difficult, whereas an Outsider lacking such internal information, might infer laziness and suppose the problem to be easy.

A closely related difference is the *Intimate vs. Stranger* distinction. Here it is our knowledge of our past behavior which guides our attributions, whereas others typically lack such historical information. If past experience has convinced the Intimate that he is intellectually capable, then he will dismiss an experimental task as unfair, irrelevant, or both when he fails it, but as fair and pertinent when he succeeds. The Stranger, however, might well infer that the individual is stupid if he fails but capable if he succeeds. The difference between Intimate and Stranger is that the Stranger does not have any past performance upon which to "anchor" a dispositional attribution, and hence, he is more likely to permit task performance to determine a dispositional attribution than is the Intimate for whom the present task is but a single datum point in a familiar history of intellectual competence. The individual himself has already achieved a relatively stable dispositional inference about his ability, and hence fluctuations in performance can more plausibly be attributed to the task. [This is essentially a partial restatement of Kelley's (1967) "analysis of variance" model for attributions.]

A third difference between self-perception and interpersonal perception stems from the *Self vs. Other* difference. It is here that motivational effects may enter as the Self seeks to protect his esteem or defend against threat. Presumably the several Freudian defense mechanisms are prototypic of processes which distort self-attributions so that they differ from interpersonal attributions. On the other hand, the jump to motivational explanations is probably made too hastily. For example, when subjects and observers differ in evaluating intellectual competence in success and failure conditions, it is tempting to infer that the subject is defensively trying to maintain his self-esteem. But he may simply be veridical. As the example in the above paragraph illustrates, such attribution differences can be frequently explained by looking at the Self's knowledge of his past history. In other words, the motivational *Self vs. Other* difference is probably too often invoked when it is the *Intimate vs. Stranger* difference which is operative.

Moreover, the evidence for esteem-maintenance processes in self-attribution is not nearly so strong as is often supposed. For example, Ross, Bierbrauer, and Polly (1971) conducted a study in which professional teachers and college students attempted to teach an 11-year-old boy the spelling of a list of commonly misspelled words. Contrary to theories of self-esteem maintenance or ego-defensiveness, participants tended to rate "teacher factors" as being more important when the child failed than when he succeeded, and "student factors" more important in success than in failure conditions. Moreover, this pattern of attribution was considerably more pronounced for professional teachers than for college students, a result which seems to challenge the frequent assertion that esteem maintenance and ego-defensiveness become factors when outcomes are important or central to one's self concept.

This is not to say that motivational distortions do not occur in self-attribution. But Self should be innocent until proved guilty.

There is, finally, the possibility that there exists an actual difference in perspective between *Actor vs. Observer*, in which different features of the situation are differentially salient to them. In an excellent article which seems likely to become highly influential, E. E. Jones and Nisbett (1972) suggest that an actor's attention is focused outward toward situational cues rather than inward on his own behavior. For the observer, however, the actor's behavior is the figural stimulus against the ground of the situation. E. E. Jones and Nisbett (1972) present a well-reasoned argument for the existence of this perspective difference and some preliminary findings relevant to it. It is clear, however, that some ingenuity will be required to isolate a pure perspective difference empirically, uncontaminated by the other differences discussed above. At the time of this writing, there appears to be only one study which comes close to accomplishing this feat (Storms, 1971).

The major thesis of the Jones-Nisbett article is that the several differences mentioned above, including the perspective difference, conspire to create a pervasive tendency for actors to attribute their actions to situational requirements, whereas observers tend to attribute the same actions to stable personal dispositions of the actor. It is, of course, too early to evaluate the validity of this proposition; but it is sufficiently rich in its implications, and it is so likely that the various actor-observer differences will pull in opposite directions in some situations, that the full exploration of this single hypothesis is likely to set the direction of research in this area for the next few years.

VI. The Shift of Paradigm in Social Psychology

During the Sixties, it will be recalled, all thinking beings were characterized by chronic drives toward consistency and uncertainty reduction, vigilant forces which coaxed us all toward cognitive quiescence. Our affects, cognitions, and behaviors were held in homeostatic harmony, and our "evaluative needs" initiated emergency information searches whenever any internal state broke through threshold without clear identification or certified cause. In contrast, we are emerging into the Seventies as less driven, more contemplative creatures, thoughtful men and women whose only motivation is the willingness to answer the question, "How do you feel?" as honestly and as carefully as possible after calmly surveying the available internal and external evidence.

There is, in short, a shift of paradigm taking place within social psychology, a shift from motivational/drive models of cognitions, behaviors, and internal states to information processing/attribution models of such phenomena. Self-perception theory is only one element in that shift, and thus it is appropriate at this juncture to place it within this larger context. We begin with a brief history of this transformation and the four separate lines of research which mark it.

First, of course, are the various cognitive consistency theories, whose formal history is usually traced to Heider's (1946) article, "Attitudes and Cognitive Organizations" (McGuire, 1966). The system Heider proposed employed the motivational constructs of Gestalt psychology, and he elaborated the theory in the well-known *The Psychology of Interpersonal Relations* (Heider, 1958), and explored the motivational aspects in a 1960 contribution to the *Nebraska Symposium on Motivation* (Heider, 1960).

During the decade of the Fifties, several other consistency formulations were developed, and collectively they set the dominant tone of the motivation/drive paradigm during the early Sixties. This era appeared to culminate with the publication of the massive source book of such theories in 1968 (Abelson *et al.*, 1968). Cognitive dissonance theory is the most prominent example of this paradigm.

The second research tradition involved in the paradigm shift is Schachter's (1964) work on the cognitive and physiological foundations of emotional states. Although Schachter's theorizing has not been associated with the cognitive consistency paradigm as such, it is rooted in the same tradition, and the major motivational concept "evaluative needs" rests upon Festinger's (1954) earlier theory of social comparison processes. This is the motivation which leads individuals to seek out an appropriate explanation and label for otherwise ambiguous internal states.

It is illustrative of the paradigm shift that this prominent motivational feature of Schachter's (1959) earlier work on affiliation and the initial research on emotional states (e.g., Schachter & Singer, 1962) has now receded very much into the background, and investigators who trained under Schachter tend increasingly to employ the vocabulary of self-attribution in their studies.

Some convergence between the cognitive consistency research and Schachter's work was achieved when dissonance-theoretic operations began to be applied to the manipulation of emotional and motivational states (e.g., Zimbardo, 1969).

The third relevant conceptual development has been self-perception theory. As noted in this review, the theory derives from the very different tradition of radical behaviorism. However, as the paradigm shift has developed, the Skinnerian parentage of the theory has been increasingly muted in successive translations. Indeed, one purpose of this review has been to repay homage to the origins of self-perception theory and, in Section VII, C, below, to restate the need for some of the heuristic advantages that the stubborn functional orientation can bestow when behavioral mysteries threaten to become behavioral-science muddles.

The ways in which self-perception theory has attempted to assimilate both the Schachter tradition and cognitive dissonance theory have already been reviewed in detail. It should be noted that self-perception theory lacks any motivational construct other than an implicit assumption that individuals are willing to answer inquiries concerning their internal states.

The fourth major development in the move to the attribution paradigm is attribution theory itself. Once again history begins with Heider, who stated the major ideas in *The Psychology of Interpersonal Relations* (Heider, 1958). During the "consistency" era, this book was cited primarily for its formal balance theory, while Heider's rich but less formalized observations about person perception and attribution were relatively ignored. This was remedied by E. E. Jones and Davis (1965), who added a number of testable propositions and explicated some specific empirical consequences of the attribution hypotheses contained within the book. The resulting research tended to focus on an observer's attribution of an actor's intentions and attitudes (e.g., E. E. Jones & Harris, 1967) and would probably have proceeded independently of the other three traditions discussed above had it not been for the influential essay, "Attribution Theory in Social Psychology" by Harold Kelley in the 1967 *Nebraska Symposium on Motivation*. This essay integrated the Jones and Davis formulation and self-perception theory into a single theoretical framework along with some propositions about attributional biases, errors, and illusions. These latter considerations also afforded Kelley the opportunity to make his observations about the "illusion of freedom" found in dissonance experiments, thus providing an added flourish to the convergence of these several distinct lines of research and theory.

If Kelley can be seen as a final step in this shift from drive models to information-processing models, as this brief intellectual history implies, then it is somewhat ironic that his essay appears in a symposium on motivation. For despite Kelley's valiant try, the motivational flavor is very bland indeed:

Consideration of attribution theory is relevant for a symposium on motivation in several respects. The theory describes processes that operate *as if* the individual were motivated to attain a cognitive mastery of the causal structure of his environment. Indeed, Heider explicitly assumes that "we try to make sense out of the manifold of proximal stimuli . . . " And Jones and Davis state, "The perceiver seeks to find sufficient reason why the person acted and why the act took on a particular form." The broad motivational assumption makes little difference in the development and application of the theory, but it gives the theory a definite functionalistic flavor . . . and affords whatever motivational basis might seem necessary to support the complex cognitive processes entailed in attribution.

More important for the student of motivation are the specific processes and their consequences. Attribution processes are assumed to instigate, under certain conditions, such activities as information-seeking, communication, and persuasion. Thus attribution theory plays an important role in describing the motivational conditions for these significant classes of social behavior. Equally important is the relevance of attribution theory to the *perception* of motivation, both in others and in one's self [From Kelley, 1967, p. 193, by permission of The University of Nebraska, Lincoln, Nebraska]. [Emphasis in the original.]

It is an admirable attempt, but the strongest motivation to emerge from this quotation appears to be Kelley's need to understand why he was there. Presumably his fellow participants were thus provided with "sufficient reason why the person acted and why the act took on a particular form."

It is, finally, Kelley's article which has now set the stage for the analysis of the differences between self- and interpersonal perception, discussed in the previous section, and this appears to be the next phase of research in this area.

This, then, is where the paradigm shift currently stands and where it appears to be going. But there are still some sticky problems left in what has gone before, as we shall now see.

VII. Some Unsolved Problems

Up to this point, this review has attempted to fit as many phenomena as possible into a single framework with a minimum number of loose threads. This pedagogically motivated elegance, however, must now come to an end, for it has been purchased at the price of some fairly glib legerdemain. It is time to sneak backstage and see what the performance looks like from the wings.

A. THE CONCEPTUAL STATUS OF NONCOGNITIVE RESPONSE CLASSES

If one has managed to alter an individual's attitude or self-attribution, it is not unreasonable to expect that this will induce consequent changes in other response systems. For example, if one has increased a person's favorability toward a dull task, he might be expected to work at the task more assiduously. Induce him to believe that he doesn't fear snakes and he will approach snakes more closely. Convince the child he is obedient, and he will resist temptation. Change a man's perception of his hunger, thirst, or pain, and he should consume more or less food or drink, or endure more or less aversive stimulation. Nor should such expectations be confined to instrumental or consummatory behaviors only, for there is a long history of evidence that beliefs, attitudes, and self-attributions can exercise influence over physiological responses as well (for reviews, see Frank, 1961; Zimbardo, 1969). It is therefore not unreasonable to expect physiological changes to follow upon induced self-attributions of internal states.

Happily, the experimental laboratory has blessed such expectations with some striking confirmations. Dissonance manipulations designed to enhance the perceived attractiveness of dull tasks do produce greater intensity of behavior on the task itself (for a review, see Weick, 1967). Behavioral observations of subjects in Schachter's experiments reveals them to be behaving "appropriately" in accord with their induced emotional states (e.g., Schachter & Singer, 1962; Schachter & Wheeler, 1962); and, dissonance manipulations designed to alter self-attributions of drive states like hunger, thirst, and pain do alter overt behaviors with respect to their respective stimuli and do produce striking physiological changes (Zimbardo, 1969).

In the present review, we have seen that false feedback designed to imply that subjects are not snake-phobic leads them to approach the snake more closely (Valins & Ray, 1967); feedback designed to manipulate self-attributions of anger produces changes in overt instrumental aggression (Berkowitz & Turner, 1972); and feedback designed to create misattributions concerning autonomic arousal alters resistance to extinction of the GSR (Koenig & Henriksen, 1972; Loftis & Ross, 1971). Attempts to encourage subjects to attribute fear-induced arousal to a pill or loud noise rather than shock produce greater shock tolerance (Nisbett & Schachter, 1966; Ross et al., 1969), as does self-observed behavior designed to imply that the subject has higher shock tolerance than he initially thought (Davison & Valins, 1969). Induced obedience which implies to the child that he is "good" produces greater resistance to temptation (Lepper, 1971); and finally, overjustification for performing intrinsically interesting activities diminishes subsequent engagement in those activities (Deci, 1971, 1972; Lepper et al., 1971).

But precisely because it has been "not unreasonable to expect" these phenomena to occur, and precisely because they have in fact occurred, the problematic nature of their conceptual status within the various theories has been insufficiently appreciated. Thus, the "theoretical" predictions or explanations of these phenomena that one finds in the literature are rarely more sophisticated than the "it-is-not-unreasonable-to-expect . . ." statement with which this section opened three paragraphs above. The lucky theory within which the particular investigator is working then gets gratuitous credit for the "derivation." A related practice, also encouraged by the fact that the response classes seem to "hang together," is to treat the response classes interchangeably as if they were functionally equivalent; the self-attributions and the noncognitive responses are simply grouped together as the "effects" of the stimulus manipulations. Such practices are unfortunate for they can easily obscure important gaps in our understanding by causing us to pretend to knowledge that we do not in fact possess. It is thus important to explore how the various theories account for these noncognitive response classes.

In attribution models generally—and in self-perception theory in particular—cognitions or self-attributions are the dependent variables. Instrumental behaviors, consummatory responses, and physiological responses (real or falsified) are among the variables which can serve as antecedent or independent variables, the stimuli from which self-attributions of beliefs, attitudes, or internal states can be partially inferred by the individual. Attribution models are thus very explicit about the direction of the causal arrow, and they remain mute about any phenomenon in which the noncognitive response classes play the dependent variable role; as *dependent* variables, such response classes are extratheoretical. To state this another way, attribution models do not treat cognitions, overt behaviors, and physiological responses as functionally equivalent response classes, but rather, spell out in detail the mechanisms through which the cognitive response class can be under the partial functional control of the other two. How do attribution models account for noncognitive response classes? They don't! Self-perception theory can get us from the stimulus manipulation to the attribution. It cannot get us from the attribution to anything beyond that.

The consistency paradigm is in much the same position as the attribution paradigm with regard to the physiological response class. Thus an early prediction that physiological phenomena might emerge from dissonance-theory settings was precisely a speculation in the spirit of "it would not be unreasonable to expect . . . [Brehm & Cohen, 1962, pp. 151–155]." The positive empirical results which followed and confirmed that early hunch (Zimbardo, 1969) in no way altered the theoretical status of the hypothesis within the formal theory itself, nor does the invocation of dissonance reduction as a motivational explanatory concept bridge the gap from the attribution changes to the physiological effects. It is, for example, no "explanation" to assert that an individual lowers his GSR in order to reduce dissonance until it is explained just how the individual goes about doing just that. Again, this gap is not to be confused with the prior gap from the stimulus operations to the attribution changes, a link with which the theory *is* prepared to deal. This is, of course, the same position in which self-perception theory finds itself; as noted above it, too, has a theory about the first link, but is reduced to handwaving about the second. Similarly, the effects of false feedback on GSR extinction reported by Koenig and Henriksen (1972) are *not* accounted for by any of the three theories they mention— modeling, Schachter's theory, or self-perception theory—and for the same reason: None of these theories contains the theoretical machinery for explaining physiological changes in a nontrivial way. For example, the "explanation" borrowed from Schachter's formulation, that "a state of arousal will be perceived as positive or negative depending upon the label which a person attaches to that state, and that he will then behave accordingly" (i.e., show higher resistance to extinction of the GSR) is, at best, a restatement of the data. It is in no sense an explanation of that second link. (See also Bem, 1972a.)

It is thus an important step forward simply to recognize that a detailed theoretical model is still needed to account for the cognitive control of physiological responses. One of the criteria for a successful theory in this domain will almost certainly be its ability to account simultaneously for the related physiological effects of placebo medication, hypnotically or cognitively induced anesthesia, and the associated phenomena of the "mind-body" problem. A start in this direction is provided by Zimbardo (1969, pp. 269–283) whose theoretical discussion at least outdistances the dissonance theory framework which guided the choice of stimulus manipulations.

When one turns from the physiological to the behavioral variables associated with self-attributions, the consistency paradigm appears to be on firmer ground. For example, although the theory of cognitive dissonance is, in literal terms, a theory about cognitions (like the attribution models), the concept of a general drive toward consistency extends itself more easily to instrumental and consummatory behaviors than to physiological responses. Thus, if an individual suffers inconsistency between something he believes and the cognition that he is not behaving in accord with that belief, a purely cognitive conflict, then it follows from the basic postulate of the consistency model that he can achieve drive reduction by altering either the belief or the behavior. The motivational construct within the theory provides a built-in "motor" force behind a change in overt behavior.[3] If a dissonance manipulation makes an individual more favorable toward a dull task, a higher rate of performance on the task is a reasonably legitimate prediction from the theory. It is important to note that the behavior in this formulation is necessarily mediated by a prior belief, attitude, cognition, or attribution with which the behavior is brought into harmony.

A similar kind of consistency principle is also invoked to explain behavioral effects by many investigators who employ Schachter's theory of emotional states. As already noted above, Koenig and Henriksen (1972) remark that Schachter postulates that an individual "will then behave accordingly" after he has labeled his emotional state. Similarly, Berkowitz and Turner (1972) interpret Schachter as saying that an individual interprets his state and "then acts in a manner consistent with this interpretation." And although Berkowitz and Turner go beyond the Schachter formulation in their own analysis of the stimulus variables leading to instrumental aggression, they too come back to the same mechanism in order to get from the self-attribution of anger to the act of aggression: "Looked at from a larger perspective, the findings also provide yet another demonstration of the search for cognitive consistency. We want our actions to be in accord with our emotions, as we understand them . . ."

Interestingly, however, Schachter himself does not invoke such a principle of consistency in his own writings on the topic [including Schachter (1964), which other writers most frequently cite in this connection]. Rather, he treats self-attributions and overt behaviors as separate "indices" of the underlying "mood" he set about to produce; that is, Schachter's conceptual analysis treats the two response classes as functionally equivalent. Thus, from the very beginning, Schachter and his colleagues have routinely collected behavioral observations along with, or even in lieu of, self-report data of emotional state (e.g.,

[3] It will be noted that we thus grant legitimacy to a motivational concept for explaining cognitive and behavioral responses, but deny it legitimacy in accounting for physiological responses. The distinction, however, is not based upon response class membership *per se*, but upon the individual's ability to directly control the response in question. A motivational construct is still, at bottom, a way of saying that the individual "wants to" perform some response, even if unconsciously; being motivated is not sufficient, however, if he "doesn't know which string to pull." As recent work demonstrates, physiological responses can be brought under direct conscious control; presumably they then fall subject to motivational explanations in the same way that instrumental responses do. Nevertheless, we are still avoiding here the deeper epistemological problems concerning the explanatory legitimacy of motivational constructs generally. As a sometimes radical behaviorist, I am inclined to the view that their explanatory power is, in general, illusory.

Schachter & Singer, 1962; Schachter & Wheeler, 1962). Similarly, self-attributions of hunger appear in some of the Schachter obesity studies (e.g., Goldman, Jaffa, & Schachter, 1968), but the dependent variable has now become eating behavior *per se*, and the word "hunger" has faded quietly from view (e.g., Nisbett & Storms, 1972). Although several new conceptual distinctions have been introduced into this important research to keep abreast of the new findings, there has been no comparable conceptual distinction introduced to parallel or accompany the *sub rosa* shifts from one response class to another.

In sum, pure attribution models presume only to deal with the cognitive response class; additional machinery must be added if they are to deal with behavioral or physiological responses as *dependent* variables. Schachter's model, hovering somewhere between the information-processing/attribution paradigm and the motivational/drive paradigm, does not distinguish on the dependent variable side between the self-attributions and the "emotional" behavior. Just as the attribution models do, Schachter's model places physiological responses in the role of independent variables only; they are stimuli which partially determine the individual's perception of his emotional state. Finally, theories within the motivational/drive paradigm, particularly the theory of cognitive dissonance, cannot handle the physiological response class in anything other than a trivial fashion, but they do have a conceptual device for predicting or explaining any overt behavioral changes that are mediated by prior cognitions, attitudes, or attributions. We turn now to a closer examination of this proposed sequence of events from stimulus manipulation to attribution change to behavior change.

B. Do Attributions Mediate Behavior?

Increase a person's favorability toward a dull task, and he will work at it more assiduously. Make him think he is angry, and he will act more aggressively. Change his perception of hunger, thirst, or pain, and he should consume more or less food or drink, or endure more or less aversive stimulation. Alter the attribution, according to the theory, and "consistent" overt behavior will follow.

There seems to be only one snag: It appears not to be true. It is not that the behavioral effects sometimes fail to occur as predicted; that kind of negative evidence rarely embarrasses anyone. It is that they occur more easily, more strongly, more reliably, and more persuasively than the attribution changes that are, theoretically, supposed to be mediating them.

For example, in a well-controlled study by Grinker (1969) on eyelid conditioning, it was predicted that ". . . the dissonance aroused by voluntary commitment to a painful stimulus will be reduced by lowering pain-avoidance motivation—that is, by perceiving the UCS to be less threatening or painful—and thus the conditioning level [will be less]." The study did obtain the predicted effects in conditioning, but "there were no significant differences between any groups on self-report measures of perceived pain, irritability, eye tearing, or apprehension, or on other questionnaire items designed to measure subjective response to the aversive aspects of the situation [Grinker, 1969, p. 132]." And in a closely related experiment, Zimbardo et al. (1969) were able to obtain predicted changes in learning performance, physiological measures, and pain perception. But the attributions of pain showed the weakest effects, and furthermore, the correlations between these cognitive attributions and the behavioral measures of learning they were supposed to be mediating were $-.01$ for one group and $+.11$ for the other.

Similarly, in the Davison and Valins (1969) shock study, experimental subjects were willing to take more shock than control subjects, as predicted, but they did not rate a set of sample shocks as any less painful than did controls. The snake study by Valins and Ray (1967) gives similar results: Experimental subjects were able to approach the snake more closely than control subjects, but they did not report themselves to be any less frightened of snakes than did the controls.

Finally, Weick (1967) reviewed all the studies designed to increase an individual's favorability toward a dull task. He found that increased effort on the task often occurred in the absence of the attitude change toward the task which was supposed to cause the increased effort. Weick concludes that

initial cognitive enhancement of the task followed by increased effort simply does not occur often enough for us to be convinced that this is a reasonable explanation. Instead, it appears that the phenomenon in which we are interested may involve just the opposite sequence of events, namely behavioral change followed by occasional attempts to summarize the experience evaluatively.

What is one to make of such failures? One possible explanation for them is that the measures of attributions are not well designed or appropriate to the self-attribution which actually mediates the behavior. Another possibility is that subjects are hesitant to admit to some states like anger (Schachter & Singer, 1962). Although these methodological explanations may account for some of the negative findings, the same pattern of results—behavior changes in the absence of equally strong attribution changes—is found in some of the best designed and carefully executed experiments in the field (e.g., Grinker, 1969).

Another possibility is that the attributions do change as predicted and do mediate the behaviors, but that the attributions themselves are unconscious (Brock & Grant, 1963; Zimbardo, 1969, p. 76). There have been arguments, of course, that inconsistency itself and the process of inconsistency reduction need not be represented in awareness (e.g., Tannenbaum, 1968), and the author himself has made a parallel claim that individuals need not be able to verbalize the cues they use in arriving at self-attributions (Bem, 1965, 1968b). But such claims can edge dangerously close to metaphysics, and the next retreat into invisibility—that one of the "dissonant" cognitions itself is unknown to the individual—should surely be resisted mightily until all other alternatives, save angels perhaps, have been eliminated. A related but more plausible explanation involving defensive denial processes has been proposed by Zimbardo (1969, pp. 269–273); his version of an unconscious cognition at least generates some empirical consequences, and there are some suggestive supporting data for such a process within the settings explored in that body of research.

A final lead is provided by Weick's suggestion, quoted above, that the attributions or attitudes may follow upon rather than precede the behaviors. This is, of course, the major postulate of self-perception theory and a phenomenon well known to dissonance theory. If this is, in fact, the sequence involved, then it would explain why the measured attribution changes are often less reliable and weaker than the behavioral changes since they are the third, rather than the second link in the chain, as originally assumed. For example, the self-reports of euphoria and anger in the classic Schachter and Singer experiment (1962) were obtained after the behavior had occurred and were, in fact, less reliable than the behavioral observations themselves.

A similar instance appears in the Berkowitz and Turner study (1972). The self-reports of anger were retrospective measures in which the subjects had to recall how angry they had been prior to engaging in the aggressive behavior. A study by Bem and McConnell (1970) would imply that such "recall" measures would be more highly correlated with the subject's current attribution (as altered by the intervening behavior) than they would be with the actual previous state he is attempting to recall. And in fact, the Berkowitz-Turner self-report data—designed to check the false feedback manipulation of anger—do appear to parallel the overt aggression displayed by the subjects more closely than they correspond to the meter readings themselves. Prophetically, Berkowitz (1968) himself has said elsewhere: "We generally assume as a matter of course that the human being acts as he does because of wants arising from his understanding of his environment. In some cases, however, this understanding may develop *after* stimuli have evoked the action so that the understanding justifies but has not caused the behavior [p. 308]."

Is, then, the Berkowitz-Turner study one of these cases of reverse sequence? Not necessarily, for it is still possible that the appropriate attributions were actually present prior to the behavior and did mediate it. All that can be said is that self-report measures collected after the behavior has occurred may not be a valid index of those attributions. The same holds true for the Schachter and Singer study (1962) and several other studies which have collected attribution data confounded by intervening behavior. This analysis, then, implies that some of the failures to find attribution changes may simply reflect the methodological practice of collecting the self-reports after other stimulus events, including overt behaviors, have intervened. But like the other explanations offered above, this cannot account for all the failures, for again some of the best studies are not subject to this criticism (e.g., Zimbardo et al., 1969), and they still do not find attribution effects as strong as the behavioral ones they are supposed to be mediating.

If we are thus forced to the conclusion that, at least in some settings, attribution changes do not mediate the observed behavioral effects, then we find that a phenomenon which had been previously accounted for within the consistency paradigm has become "unsolved." That is, we are still left with the task of accounting for the behavior changes themselves. Several attempts to do so are already under way.

For example, Nisbett and Valins (1972) have proposed that the stimulus manipulations themselves may be insufficient to actually alter the attribution, but that they do cause the individual to question his current attribution sufficiently so that he "tests" the new attributional hypothesis by engaging in behavior to find out. As a result of engaging in the behavior, the hypothesis about his attribution may be confirmed, and he will accept the attribution as valid. Or the hypothesis may be disconfirmed, leading him to reject the attribution, and leaving the investigator with a set of results showing a behavioral effect and no attribution effect. Thus, false feedback implying that one is not afraid of snakes is not sufficient to create a stable attribution of "I'm not afraid," but it is sufficient to motivate a test of this possibility by approaching the snake. The process of handling the snake can then stabilize the new attribution via the self-perception process. This intriguing scenario is spelled out in greater detail in Nisbett and Valins (1972).

With regard to the task enhancement studies, Weick (1967) has suggested that the behavioral effects in these experiments might be accounted for by propositions drawn from frustration theory and cue-utilization theory; again the attribution effects—when they do occur—can be handled as postbehavior phenomena by either self-perception theory or dissonance theory.

It may be that still other cases of behavioral effects such as the over-justification phenomenon will be "re-solved" by using variations of motivational constructs like the need to be in control of one's self and environment (cf. deCharms, 1968; Zimbardo, 1969). And, as suggested earlier, the physiological effects should probably be split off and reunited with other physiological phenomena under cognitive influence rather than being grouped according to their independent-variable manipulations as dissonance or attribution phenomena.

It is clear that the door has now been opened for many mini-theories, for it is unlikely that any single process will account for the diverse phenomena which found themselves grouped together when consistency and attribution models converged. It is, of course, painful to have to deny to self-perception theory some of the effects with which it has been gratuitously credited by other investigators. At least its heuristic value for such phenomena remains intact even if its explanatory power is more limited than its friends had realized. Similarly, it may seem a shame to abandon the parsimony which obtained during the reign of the consistency theories, but it is now clear that some of that parsimony was illusory and was purchased at the cost of obscuring some important gaps in our knowledge. The fact that everything seems to be falling apart should probably be taken as an index of scientific advance.

C. The Strategy of Functional Analysis

If there is an underlying moral here, it is that response classes should be given independent conceptual statuses from one another and analyzed separately for the stimulus variables which control them. If they are observed to covary, one should first inspect the stimulus manipulations for overlapping functional properties which produce that covariation. Any theory which assumes that one response class should vary as a function of another ought to spell out in detail the mechanism of control. What are the stimulus properties of the response class which is presumed to exert functional control over the other? Finally, response classes should not be treated as functionally equivalent unless the theory explicitly dictates that they can be and/or experimentation vindicates the merger.

These prescriptions form a part of a more general strategy known as functional analysis, the strategy associated with the radical behaviorism within which self-perception theory was initially enunciated.

A functional analysis of a complex behavioral phenomenon proceeds by first inquiring into the ontogenetic origins of the observed dependent variables—treated as response classes in their own right rather than as reflections of underlying structures, processes, or internal states—and then attempts to ascertain the controlling or independent stimulus variables of which those observable behaviors are a function.

In its purest form, such a strategy also assumes that the principles of behavior, that is, the most general orderly functional relations between stimuli and responses, are relatively simple and few in number. The complexity of human social behavior derives, it is assumed, from the complexity and variety of the environmental conditions under which these principles have been operative in the individual's past history. Thus, the radical behaviorist does not begin with the *a priori* expectation that he will discover new principles of behavior through the study of social behavior in its terminal complexity. Rather, he attempts to establish a complex behavioral phenomenon as a special case or a compound of previously substantiated functional relations discovered in the experimental analysis of simpler behaviors. The re-emergence from the analysis of the previously established functional relations becomes the vindication for the extrapolation into new domains and for the network of assumptions upon which the extrapolation rests. The spirit of the analysis, therefore, is frankly inductive, not only in its experimental execution, but in its formal presentation.

The radical behaviorist's usual insistence that the analysis also eschew any reference to internal physiological or conceptual processes, real or hypothetical is, of course, its most celebrated (and misunderstood) prescription. Whatever the heuristic value of such a restriction may be in other psychological areas, the tactic carries especial probative force in the analysis of self-perception precisely because the socializing community itself must necessarily train the individual's self-descriptive skills on the basis of observable stimuli and responses.[4]

Not all functional analyses comprise every one of these tactics, and orthodox radical behaviorists are not the only psychologists whose

[4] It is probably the relaxation of this restriction which has robbed latter-day self-perception theory of its radical behavioristic flavor. One does not remain a behaviorist in good standing with repeated references to "inferential processes" and hypothetical inner dialogues ("What must my attitude be if I am willing to behave . . ."). In order to reclaim membership, therefore, it should probably be said that such concessions to expositional clarity do not, in my view, add anything to the explanatory power of the theory; it remains formally equivalent to its earlier, albeit nearly incomprehensible, incarnation in the more rigid and arid vocabulary of radical behaviorism (Bem, 1964). But as this section is attempting to demonstrate, a choice of language is not without heuristic consequences. For private "thinking" purposes, functional analysis remains my preference; but for exposition purposes, English prose does not seem overly risky. Roman and arabic numeral systems are also formally equivalent, but performing long division in the former is reputed to be unwieldy.

analyses are informed by particular elements of the approach. For example, Leventhal (1970) has recently employed a similar strategy in analyzing the attitudinal and behavioral effects of fear-arousing communications, thereby bringing elegant order out of the chaotic and conflicting findings in this area. (In addition, Leventhal's analysis is another instance of a drive theory being replaced by an information processing orientation.) Berkowitz's (1965) analysis of aggression has a similar spirit and strategy behind it.

If it had been employed earlier, the functional approach would have led to very different kinds of analyses within the domain of self-attributions. For example, Schachter's (1964) own review of the literature on emotion reveals that physiological cues should have more functional control over the cognitive attributions than over "emotional" behaviors *per se*. Thus, sympathectomized animals continue to show emotional behaviors, and human "subjects with cervical lesions described themselves as acting emotional but not feeling emotional [p. 74]." These findings would seem to have implications for which response class is being used as the "index" of mood in the Schachter experiments. But as noted earlier, Schachter and his colleagues interchange the two response classes repeatedly and nowhere acknowledge a functional distinction between them.

A similar confounding of these same response classes appears in the insomnia experiment by Storms and Nisbett (1970), an experiment also conducted within the Schachter framework. As described in Section IV, A, insomniacs who thought the placebo pill would arouse them reported that they got to sleep more quickly than they had on nights without the pills, whereas subjects who thought the placebo to be a relaxant reported that they got to sleep less quickly than usual. The important point to note here is that the dependent variable is the subject's *report* of how much time had passed before he fell asleep. But when this experiment is cited, and even in the abstract of the article itself, it is reported that "arousal" subjects *got* to sleep more quickly and "relaxation" subjects *got* to sleep less quickly. And that's not the same thing! Estimates of time passage are themselves attributions which are subject to manipulation (cf. London & Monello, 1972). Perhaps the implied state of arousal is more interesting to introspect than the implied state of relaxation, making time appear to pass more quickly. If true, then "arousal" subjects would report getting to sleep more quickly even if it weren't the case. This alternative explanation is admittedly less plausible than the original, but the point to be made here is that the time it takes to fall asleep is a different response measure from the self-report of the time it takes to fall asleep, and both are subject to cognitive manipulations. Indeed, the therapeutic implications of this experiment could be quite different from those suggested by the authors unless we are prepared to assume that getting insomniacs to think they are falling asleep faster is the same as curing the insomnia.

For years, personality theorizing has been dominated by the "trait" assumption that there are pervasive cross-situational consistencies in an individual's behavior. After reviewing the literature, Mischel (1968) concludes that the empirical search for such consistencies or traits rarely generates a correlation above +.30, a finding of some disappointment if one's theory of human behavior anticipates +1.00. He, too, suggests a learning-theoretic functional analysis in which covariance of responses is sought in the overlap of situational conditions which evoke and maintain particular response classes. Under such a strategy, one constructs the consistencies from the ground up rather than assuming them *a priori,* and any increment over zero in the magnitude of the cross-situational correlations becomes a matter for some rejoicing (for discussion, see Bem, 1972b).

There is a parallel in social psychology. The decade of the consistency theories was dominated by the assumption that everything was glued together until proved otherwise (cf. Bem, 1970, p. 34). Since it is now proving otherwise, it is suggested that we try the opposite assumption that nothing is glued together until proved otherwise. It is a question of whether we should begin with expectations of +1.00 correlations or .00 correlations. The heuristic advantage of this strategy is not guaranteed, of course. But the difference in morale if +.30 correlations continue to come is in itself worth considering.

References

Abelson, R. P. Simulation of social behavior. In G. Lindzey & E. Aronson (Eds.), *Handbook of social psychology.* Vol. 2 (2nd ed.). Reading, Mass.: Addison-Wesley, 1968.

Abelson, R. P., Aronson, E., McGuire, W. J., Newcomb, T. M., Rosenberg, M. J., & Tannenbaum, P. H. (Eds.), *Theories of cognitive consistency: A sourcebook.* Chicago: Rand McNally, 1968.

Alexander, N. C., & Knight, G. W. Situated identities and social psychological experimentation. *Sociometry,* 1971, 34, 65–82.

Aronson, E., & Carlsmith, J. M. Effect of severity of threat on the valuation of forbidden behavior. *Journal of Abnormal and Social Psychology,* 1963, 66, 584–588.

Asch, S. E. *Social psychology.* Englewood Cliffs, N. J.: Prentice-Hall, 1952.

Bandler, R. J., Madaras, G. R., & Bem, D. J. Self-observation as a source of pain perception. *Journal of Personality and Social Psychology,* 1968, 9, 205–209.

Barber, T. X. Toward a theory of pain: Relief of chronic pain by pre-frontal leucotomy, opiates, placebos, and hypnosis. *Psychological Bulletin,* 1959, 59, 430–460.

Barber, T. X. The effects of hypnosis on pain. *Psychosomatic Medicine,* 1963, 25, 303–333.

Beecher, H. K. *Measurement of subjective responses: Quantitative effects of drugs.* London and New York: Oxford University Press, 1959.

Beecher, H. K. Increased stress and effectiveness of placebos and "active" drugs. *Science,* 1960, **132,** 91–92.

Bem, D. J. *An experimental analysis of beliefs and attitudes.* (Doctoral dissertation, University of Michigan) Ann Arbor, Mich.: University Microfilms, 1964. No. 64–12,588.

Bem, D. J. An experimental analysis of self-persuasion. *Journal of Experimental Social Psychology,* 1965, **1,** 199–218.

Bem, D. J. Inducing belief in false confessions. *Journal of Personality and Social Psychology,* 1966, **3,** 707–710.

Bem, D. J. Reply to Judson Mills. *Psychological Review,* 1967, **74,** 536–537. (a)

Bem, D. J. Self-perception: An alternative interpretation of cognitive dissonance phenomena. *Psychological Review,* 1967, **74,** 183–200. (b)

Bem, D. J. Self-perception: The dependent variable of human performance. *Organizational Behavior and Human Performance,* 1967, **2,** 105–121. (c)

Bem, D. J. Attitudes as self-descriptions: Another look at the attitude-behavior link. In A. G. Greenwald, T. C. Brock, & T. M. Ostrom (Eds.), *Psychological foundations of attitudes.* New York: Academic Press, 1968. (a)

Bem, D. J. Dissonance reduction in the behaviorist. In R. P. Abelson, E. Aronson, W. J. McGuire, T. M. Newcomb, M. J. Rosenberg, & P. H. Tannenbaum (Eds.), *Theories of cognitive consistency: A sourcebook.* Chicago: Rand McNally, 1968. Pp. 246–256. (b)

Bem, D. J. The epistemological status of interpersonal simulations: A reply to Jones, Linder, Kiesler, Zanna, and Brehm. *Journal of Experimental Social Psychology,* 1968, **4,** 270–274. (c)

Bem, D. J. *Beliefs, attitudes, and human affairs.* Monterey, Calif.: Brooks/Cole, 1970.

Bem, D. J. The cognitive alteration of feeling states: A discussion. In H. London & R. E. Nisbett (Eds.), *Cognitive alteration of feeling states.* Chicago: Aldine, 1972. (a)

Bem, D. J. Constructing cross-situational consistencies in behavior: Some thoughts on Alker's critique of Mischel. *Journal of Personality,* 1972, in press. (b)

Bem, D. J., & McConnell, H. K. Testing the self-perception explanation of dissonance phenomena: On the salience of premanipulation attitudes. *Journal of Personality and Social Psychology,* 1970, **14,** 23–31.

Berkowitz, L. The concept of aggressive drive: Some additional considerations. In L. Berkowitz (Ed.), *Advances in experimental social psychology.* Vol. 2. New York: Academic Press, 1965. Pp. 301–329.

Berkowitz, L. The motivational status of cognitive consistency theorizing. In R. P. Abelson, E. Aronson, W. J. McGuire, T. M. Newcomb, M. J. Rosenberg, & P. H. Tannenbaum (Eds.), *Theories of cognitive consistency: A sourcebook.* Chicago: Rand McNally, 1968. Pp. 303–310.

Berkowitz, L., Lepinski, J., & Angulo, E. Awareness of own anger level and subsequent aggression. *Journal of Personality and Social Psychology,* 1969, **11,** 293–300.

Berkowitz, L., & Turner, C. Perceived anger level, instigating agent, and aggression. In H. London & R. E. Nisbett (Eds.), *Cognitive alteration of feeling states.* Chicago: Aldine, 1972.

Bowers, K. S. An attributional analysis of operant conditioning: The problem of behavioral persistence. Unpublished manuscript, University of Waterloo, 1971.

Brehm, J. W., & Cohen, A. R. Re-evaluation of choice alternatives as a function of their number and qualitative similarity. *Journal of Abnormal and Social Psychology,* 1959, **58**, 373–378.

Brehm, J. W., & Cohen, A. R. *Explorations in cognitive dissonance.* New York: Wiley, 1962.

Brock, T. C., & Grant, L. D. Dissonance, awareness, and motivation. *Journal of Abnormal and Social Psychology,* 1963, **67**, 53–60.

Brown, J. S. A behavioral analysis of masochism. *Journal of Experimental Research in Personality,* 1965, **5**, 65–70.

Carlsmith, J. M., Collins, B. E., & Helmreich, R. L. Studies in forced compliance: I. The effect of pressure for compliance on attitude change produced by face-to-face role playing and anonymous essay writing. *Journal of Personality and Social Psychology,* 1966, **4**, 1–13.

Carlsmith, J. M., Ebbesen, E. B., Lepper, M. R., Zanna, M. P., Joncas, A. J., & Abelson, R. P. Dissonance reduction following forced attention to the dissonance. *Proceedings of the American Psychological Association,* 1969, 321–322.

Chapanis, N. P., & Chapanis, A. Cognitive dissonance: Five years later. *Psychological Bulletin,* 1964, **61**, 1–22.

Chappell, V. C. (Ed.) *The philosophy of mind.* Englewood Cliffs, N. J.: Prentice-Hall, 1962.

Corah, N. L., & Boffa, J. Perceived control, self-observation, and response to aversive stimulation. *Journal of Personality and Social Psychology,* 1970, **16**, 1–4.

Davison, G. C., & Valins, S. Maintenance of self-attributed and drug-attributed behavior change. *Journal of Personality and Social Psychology,* 1969, **11**, 25–33.

deCharms, R. *Personal causation: The internal affective determinants of behavior.* New York: Academic Press, 1968.

Deci, E. L. Effects of externally mediated rewards on intrinsic motivation. *Journal of Personality and Social Psychology,* 1971, **18**, 105–115.

Deci, E. L. Intrinsic motivation, extrinsic reinforcement, and inequity. *Journal of Personality and Social Psychology,* 1972, in press.

Deci, E. L., & Cascio, W. F. Changes in intrinsic motivation as a function of negative feedback and threats. Unpublished manuscript, University of Rochester, 1971.

Elms, A. C. Role playing, incentive, and dissonance. *Psychological Bulletin,* 1967, **68**, 132–148.

Festinger, L. A theory of social comparison processes. *Human Relations,* 1954, **7**, 117–140.

Festinger, L. *A theory of cognitive dissonance.* Stanford: Stanford University Press, 1957.

Festinger, L. *Conflict, decision and dissonance.* Stanford: Stanford University Press, 1964.

Festinger, L., & Carlsmith, J. M. Cognitive consequences of forced compliance. *Journal of Abnormal and Social Psychology,* 1959, **58**, 203–210.

Frank, J. *Persuasion and healing.* Baltimore: Johns Hopkins Press, 1961.

Freedman, J. L. Long-term behavioral effects of cognitive dissonance. *Journal of Experimental Social Psychology,* 1965, **1**, 103–120.

Freedman, J. L., & Fraser, S. C. Compliance without pressure: The foot-in-the-door technique. *Journal of Personality and Social Psychology,* 1966, **4**, 195–202.

Goldman, R., Jaffa, M., & Schachter, S. Yom Kippur, Air France, dormitory food, and the eating behavior of obese and normal persons. *Journal of Personality and Social Psychology*, 1968, **10**, 117–123.

Grinker, J. Cognitive control of classical eyelid conditioning. In P. G. Zimbardo (Ed.), *The cognitive control of motivation*. Glenview, Ill.: Scott, Foresman, 1969.

Harris, V. A., & Tamler, H. The effects of attitude reinstatement in bystander replications. Unpublished manuscript, State University of New York at Buffalo, 1971. (a)

Harris, V. A., & Tamler, H. Reinstatement of initial attitude and forced-compliance attitude change. *Journal of Social Psychology*, 1971, **84**, 127–134. (b)

Harvey, J., & Mills, J. Effect of an opportunity to revoke a counterattitudinal action upon attitude change. *Journal of Personality and Social Psychology*, 1971, **18**, 201–209.

Heider, F. Attitudes and cognitive organizations. *Journal of Psychology*, 1946, **21**, 107–112.

Heider, F. *The psychology of interpersonal relations*. New York: Wiley, 1958.

Heider, F. The gestalt theory of motivation. In M. R. Jones (Ed.), *Nebraska symposium on motivation*. Vol. 8. Lincoln: University of Nebraska Press, 1960. Pp. 145–172.

Jones, E. E., & Davis, K. E. From acts to dispositions. In L. Berkowitz (Ed.), *Advances in experimental social psychology*. Vol. 2. New York: Academic Press, 1965. Pp. 219–266.

Jones, E. E., & Harris, V. A. The attribution of attitudes. *Journal of Experimental Social Psychology*, 1967, **3**, 1–24.

Jones, E. E., & Nisbett, R. E. The actor and the observer: Divergent perceptions of the causes of behavior. In E. E. Jones, D. Kanouse, H. H. Kelley, R. E. Nisbett, S. Valins, & B. Weiner (Eds.), *Attribution: Perceiving the causes of behavior*. New York: General Learning Press, 1972.

Jones, R. A., Linder, D. E., Kiesler, C. A., Zanna, M., & Brehm, J. W. Internal states or external stimuli: Observers' attitude judgments and the dissonance theory—self-persuasion controversy. *Journal of Experimental Social Psychology*, 1968, **4**, 247–269.

Jones, R. G. Forced compliance dissonance predictions: obvious, non-obvious, or non-sense? Paper presented at the meeting of the American Psychological Association, New York, September 1966.

Kelley, H. H. Attribution theory in social psychology. In D. Levine (Ed.), *Nebraska symposium on motivation*. Vol. 15. Lincoln: University of Nebraska Press, 1967. Pp. 192–238.

Kiesler, C. A., Nisbett, R. E., & Zanna, M. P. On inferring one's beliefs from one's behavior. *Journal of Personality and Social Psychology*, 1969, **11**, 321–327.

Klemp, G. O., & Leventhal, H. Self-persuasion and fear reduction from escape behavior. In H. London & R. E. Nisbett (Eds.), *Cognitive alteration of feeling states*. Chicago: Aldine, 1972.

Koenig, K. P., & Henriksen, K. Cognitive manipulation of GSR extinction: Analogues for conditioning therapies. In H. London & R. E. Nisbett (Eds.), *Cognitive alteration of feeling states*. Chicago: Aldine, 1972.

Lepper, M. R. Dissonance, self perception, and honesty in children. Unpublished manuscript, Stanford University, 1971.

Lepper, M. R., Greene, D., & Nisbett, R. E. Undermining children's intrinsic interest with extrinsic reward: A test of the "overjustification" hypothesis. Unpublished manuscript, Stanford University, 1971.

Lepper, M. R., Zanna, M. P., & Abelson, R. P. Cognitive irreversibility in a dissonance reduction situation. *Journal of Personality and Social Psychology*, 1970, **16**, 191–198.

Leventhal, H. Findings and theory in the study of fear communications. In L. Berkowitz (Ed.), *Advances in experimental social psychology*. Vol. 5. New York: Academic Press, 1970. Pp. 120–186.

Linder, D. E., & Jones, R. A. Discriminative stimuli as determinants of consonance and dissonance. *Journal of Experimental Social Psychology*, 1969, **5**, 467–482.

Loftis, J., & Ross, L. Facilitation of GSR extinction through misattribution. Unpublished manuscript, Stanford University, 1971.

London, H., & Monello, L. Cognitive manipulation of boredom. In H. London & R. E. Nisbett (Eds.), *Cognitive alteration of feeling states*. Chicago: Aldine, 1972.

Maslach, C. The "truth" about false confessions. *Journal of Personality and Social Psychology*, 1971, **20**, 141–146.

McGuire, W. J. The current status of cognitive consistency theories. In S. Feldman (Ed.), *Cognitive consistency: Motivational antecedents and behavioral consequents*. New York: Academic Press, 1966. Pp. 1–46.

Melzack, R. The perception of pain. *Scientific American*, 1961, **204**, 41–49.

Miller, N., & Dollard, J. *Social learning and imitation*. New Haven: Yale University Press, 1941.

Mills, J. Comment on Bem's "Self-perception: An alternative interpretation of cognitive dissonance phenomena." *Psychological Review*, 1967, **74**, 535.

Mischel, W. *Personality and assessment*. New York: Wiley, 1968.

Nisbett, R. E., & Schachter, S. Cognitive manipulation of pain. *Journal of Experimental Social Psychology*, 1966, **2**, 227–236.

Nisbett, R. E., & Storms, M. D. Cognitive and social determinants of food intake. In H. London & R. E. Nisbett (Eds.), *Cognitive alteration of feeling states*. Chicago: Aldine, 1972.

Nisbett, R. E., & Valins, S. Perceiving the causes of one's own behavior. In E. E. Jones, D. E. Kanouse, H. H. Kelley, R. E. Nisbett, S. Valins, & B. Weiner (Eds.), *Attribution: Perceiving the causes of behavior*. New York: General Learning Press, 1972.

Ostfeld, B., & Katz, P. A. The effect of threat severity in children of varying socioeconomic levels. *Developmental Psychology*, 1969, **1**, 205–210.

Pepitone, A., McCauley, C., & Hammond, P. Change in attractiveness of forbidden toys as a function of severity of threat. *Journal of Experimental Social Psychology*, 1967, **3**, 221–229.

Piliavin, J. A., Piliavin, I. M., Loewenton, E. P., McCauley, C., & Hammond, P. On observers' reproductions of dissonance effects: The right answers for the wrong reasons? *Journal of Personality and Social Psychology*, 1969, **13**, 98–106.

Ross, L., Bierbrauer, G. A., & Polly, S. The attribution of success and failure in student-teacher interaction. Unpublished manuscript, Stanford University, 1971.

Ross, L., Rodin, J., & Zimbardo, P. G. Toward an attribution therapy: The reduction of fear through induced cognitive-emotional misattribution. *Journal of Personality and Social Psychology*, 1969, **4**, 279–288.

Ryle, G. *The concept of mind*. London: Hutchinson, 1949.

Schachter, S. *The psychology of affiliation*. Stanford: Stanford University Press, 1959.

Schachter, S. The interaction of cognitive and physiological determinants of emotional state. In L. Berkowitz (Ed.), *Advances in experimental social psychology*. Vol. 1. New York: Academic Press, 1964. Pp. 49–80.

Schachter, S., & Singer, J. E. Cognitive, social, and physiological determinants of emotional state. *Psychological Review*, 1962, **69**, 379–399.

Schachter, S., & Wheeler, L. Epinephrine, chlorpromazine and amusement. *Journal of Abnormal and Social Psychology*, 1962, **65**, 121–128.

Skinner, B. F. The operational analysis of psychological terms. *Psychological Review*, 1945, **52**, 270–277, 291–294.

Skinner, B. F. *Science and human behavior*. New York: Macmillan, 1953.

Skinner, B. F. *Verbal behavior*. New York: Appleton, 1957.

Snyder, M., & Ebbesen, E. B. Dissonance awareness: A test of dissonance theory versus self-perception theory. In press.

Steiner, I. D. Perceived freedom. In L. Berkowitz (Ed.), *Advances in experimental social psychology*. Vol. 5. New York: Academic Press, 1970. Pp. 187–248.

Storms, M. D. Video tape and the attribution process: Changing actors' and observers' points of view. Unpublished doctoral dissertation, Yale University, 1971.

Storms, M. D., & Nisbett, R. E. Insomnia and the attribution process. *Journal of Personality and Social Psychology*, 1970, **2**, 319–328.

Tannenbaum, P. H. The congruity principle: Retrospective reflections and recent research. In R. P. Abelson, E. Aronson, W. J. McGuire, T. M. Newcomb, M. J. Rosenberg, & P. H. Tannenbaum (Eds.), *Theories of cognitive consistency: A sourcebook*. Chicago: Rand McNally, 1968. Pp. 52–72.

Turner, E. A., & Wright, J. Effects of severity of threat and perceived availability on the attractiveness of objects. *Journal of Personality and Social Psychology*, 1965, **2**, 128–132.

Valins, S. Cognitive effects of false heart-rate feedback. *Journal of Personality and Social Psychology*, 1966, **4**, 400–408.

Valins, S., & Ray, A. A. Effects of cognitive desensitization on avoidance behavior. *Journal of Personality and Social Psychology*, 1967, **7**, 345–350.

Weick, K. E. Dissonance and task enhancement: A problem for compensation theory? *Organizational Behavior and Human Performance*, 1967, **2**, 175–216.

Wolosin, R. J. *Self- and social perception and the attribution of internal states*. (Doctoral dissertation, University of Michigan) Ann Arbor, Mich.: University Microfilms, 1969. No. 69–12,276.

Wolosin, R. J. Attribution of freedom to the self and others. Paper presented at the meeting of the Midwestern Psychological Association, Detroit, May 1971.

Wolosin, R. J., & Denner, B. Three studies of the attribution of freedom to the self and to others. Unpublished manuscript, Indiana University, 1970.

Zanna, M. P. Inference of belief from rejection of an alternative action. Unpublished manuscript, Princeton University, 1970.

Zimbardo, P. G. *The cognitive control of motivation: The consequences of choice and dissonance*. Glenview, Ill.: Scott, Foresman, 1969.

Zimbardo, P. G., Cohen, A., Weisenberg, M., Dworkin, L., & Firestone, I. The control of experimental pain. In P. G. Zimbardo (Ed.), *The cognitive control of motivation*. Glenview, Ill.: Scott, Foresman, 1969. Pp. 100–125.

FROM ACTS TO DISPOSITIONS

The Attribution Process in Person Perception[1]

Edward E. Jones   and   **Keith E. Davis**

DEPARTMENT OF PSYCHOLOGY
DUKE UNIVERSITY
DURHAM, NORTH CAROLINA

DEPARTMENT OF PSYCHOLOGY
UNIVERSITY OF COLORADO
BOULDER, COLORADO

Many social psychologists have expressed a central interest in the ties between person perception and interpersonal behavior. The writings of Fritz Heider have exerted a predominant and continuing influence on research designed to illuminate these ties. From his 1944 paper on phenomenal causality to his more recent (1958) book on *The Psychology of Interpersonal Relations,* Heider has persistently concerned himself with the cognitive aspects of social interaction. His writings are especially important for recognizing and identifying the major problems with which

[1] Much of the research reported herein was supported by National Science Foundation Grants 8857 and 21955 to the first author.

Reprinted from *Advances in Experimental Social Psychology,*
Volume 2, 219–266.

any theory of person perception must contend: causal attribution, cognition-sentiment relations, taking the other's perspective, and so on. Heider's comments are comprehensive, perceptive, and provocative. His exposition does not lend itself readily, however, to the formulation of interrelated propositional statements. Thus the research which has been done to date is largely demonstrational in significance and dismayingly sparse in quantity. While the studies which we intend to review in this chapter may be seen as islands in the same phenomenological sea, it is not very clear how one navigates between them.

We believe that the kind of systematic, conceptual structure that is needed must involve an analysis of phenomenal causality, or the determinants and consequences of attributing causation for particular actions. In the central portion of this chapter we shall attempt to review, and to some extent reformulate, much of the recent research concerning phenomenal causality and the attribution of intentions. Our first task, however, is to introduce the notion of explaining an action by assigning an intention and to set the stage for the theory of inference which follows.

I. The Naive Explanation of Human Actions: Explanation by Attributing Intentions

At the heart of Heider's analysis of naive or "common sense psychology" is the distinction between personal and impersonal causality. We assume that the person-perceiver's fundamental task is to interpret or infer the causal antecedents of action. The perceiver seeks to find *sufficient reason* why the person acted and why the act took on a particular form. Instead of the potentially infinite regress of cause and effect which characterizes an impersonal, scientific analysis, the perceiver's explanation comes to a stop when an intention or motive is assigned that has the quality of being reason enough. "He eats because he is hungry" would not ordinarily bring a request for further explanation. After all, eating is something one would do if one were hungry.

The cognitive task of establishing sufficient reason for an action involves processing available information about, or making assumptions about, the links between stable individual dispositions and observed action. Let us start with the case in which a perceiver observes an action and at least some of its effects. His basic problem as a perceiver is to decide which of these effects, if any, were intended by the actor. Let us first address ourselves to the problem of "if any." In order to conclude that at least some of the effects achieved by an action were intended, the perceiver must first believe that the actor was aware his action would have the observed effects. Thus a first condition in the inference process is the assumption of knowledge on the part of the actor. Consequences of an action which the actor could not have forseen do not qualify as candidates for what he was trying to achieve. The condition of knowledge is of critical importance within our legal system where it is customary to distinguish among levels of responsibility for a crime: (1) intentional (P did X to enjoy the immediate effects of X), (2) incidental (P did X as a means of getting to Y), and (3) accidental (X was a consequence of P's action that he neither intended nor expected).

In addition to assumptions about knowledge of consequences, decisions linking intentional attributes to the effects of action are also affected by the perceiver's judgments of the actor's ability to bring about the effects observed. Simply put, an actor cannot achieve his objectives solely by desiring to achieve them. He must have the capacities or skill to move from his present condition of desire to a subsequent condition of attainment and satisfaction. When a person's actions have certain consequences, it is important for the perceiver to determine whether the person was capable of producing these consequences in response to his intentions. Especially in the case where an actor *fails* to produce certain effects that might have been anticipated by the perceiver, there may be ambiguity as to whether the actor did not want to produce the effects, or wanted but was not able to.

Even when effects are achieved, however, the perceiver may have the problem of assessing the relative contribution of luck or chance. When a novice archer hits the bull's eye, we are more apt to attribute this to luck than to skill. There are other occasions when we do not assign intentions to correspond with effects achieved because we do not consider the actor capable of producing those effects at will. A jury is more likely to believe that a killing is accidental if the average person would have lacked the skill (the marksmanship, the strength, etc.) to bring about the crime deliberately. It was quite possible to believe that Oswald intended to kill President Kennedy and not Mrs. Kennedy or a secret service man, because he was known to be an expert marksman. For a further discussion of the problems involved in judging ability relative to difficulty and luck, the reader is referred to Heider (1958).

The perceiver may have certain information about knowledge and ability (he may be informed that Oswald knew the gun was loaded and that Oswald often practiced on a local rifle range), or he may merely assume that knowledge and ability were probably present or probably absent. Whether the perceiver's conclusion about such matters is correct or incorrect, the conclusion obviously will affect his decisions about the actor's intentions in the situation. Knowledge and ability are preconditions for the assignment of intentions. Each plays a similar role in enabling the perceiver to decide whether an effect or consequence of action was accidental. The assignment of intention, in turn, is a precondition for inferences concerning those underlying stable characteristics toward which the perceiver presses in attaching significance to action. As Heider (1958) argued, the perceiver ordinarily strives to discover the invariances which underlie manifest actions in order to stabilize the environment and render it more predictable.

We may attempt to summarize the foregoing remarks by the diagram presented as Fig. 1. It is assumed that the perceiver typically starts with the overt action of another; this is the grist for his cognitive mill. He then makes certain decisions concerning ability and knowledge which will let him cope with the problem of attributing particular intentions to the actor. The attribution of intentions, in turn, is a necessary step in the assignment of more stable characteristics to the actor.

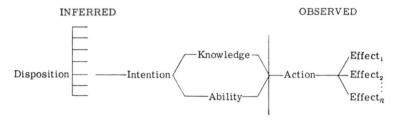

FIG. 1. The action-attribute paradigm.

Fig. 1 attempts to clarify the circumstances under which *any* intentions will be assigned to explain action. But we now seek to extend the analysis in order to account for the attribution of particular intentions and dispositions on the basis of particular actions. We shall here largely ignore the problems involved in imputing knowledge and ability and concentrate on specific linkages between effects achieved and intentions revealed. We assume that those consequences of action obviously neither intended by the actor nor within the range of his capabilities will be considered irrelevant by the perceiver.

II. A Theory of Correspondent Inferences

Our purpose is to construct a theory which systematically accounts for a perceiver's inferences about what an actor was trying to achieve by a particular action. In achieving this purpose we view the action as occurring within a particular situational context which defines, in large part, its meaning for the perceiver. In particular, as we shall attempt to show in greater detail below, the meaning of an action—its intentional significance—derives from some consideration of the alternative action possibilities available to but foregone by the actor. As perceivers of action, we can only begin to understand the motives prompting an act if we view the effects of the act in the framework of effects that other actions could have achieved.

Perhaps an example will further clarify our purpose and approach. Let us imagine ourselves as silent observers of an interaction episode in which A and B are working together on a task. We observe that A gives orders to B, monitors his performance, and shows his displeasure with the quality and quantity of B's work. The inferences about A we would most likely draw from this episode would depend critically on the action alternatives seen to be available to him. If A and B had come together in a free situation, we would be inclined to see A as quite arrogant and domineering. If we were informed that A had been given instructions to take a directive leadership role, we would be less likely to regard his dominating behavior as an indication of his personal qualities: that is, our inferences about dominance from his action would be much less *correspondent*.

Such role-playing instructions presumably limit A's freedom to behave in a "revealing" way, that is, in a way which is characteristic of *him* relative to others. The theory which follows attempts to imbed this consideration of perceived freedom of choice in a systematic framework. We will attempt to extract conceptual commonalities from empirical situations involving different varieties of environmental constraint. Our approach is to cast these "conceptual commonalities" in a form which is amenable to cumulative experimental research.

A. The Concept of Correspondence

When the perceiver infers personal characteristics as a way of accounting for action, these personal characteristics may vary in the degree to which they correspond with the behavior they are intended to explain. *Correspondence* refers to the extent that the act and the underlying characteristic or attribute are similarly described by the inference. In the example provided in the preceding section, the most correspondent inference is that which assumes with high confidence that domineering behavior is a direct reflection of the person's intention to dominate, which in turn reflects a disposition to be dominant. Thus, to anticipate the broad outlines of the theory to come, correspondence of inference declines as the action to be accounted for appears to be constrained by the setting in which it occurs.

To say that a person is dominant is to say that he is disposed to behave in a dominant fashion in a variety of settings. Of course, the perceiver in the above example would not infer such a dominance disposition if he had not first inferred an intention to dominate. The actor's intention may or may not be conscious and deliberate, but it is marked by some aspect of desire or volition which comes from the person and is not predetermined by environmental forces. Our theory assumes, in using the two concepts of intention and disposition, that correspondence declines as the perceiver moves from inferring intentions to more elaborate inferences about dispositional structures. If the perceiver, having observed a single action, infers intention X with moderate confidence, he cannot be more confident in inferring the underlying disposition X′ from the intention X. This would appear to be so because intentions are the data for inferring dispositions, and because an intention may reflect any of several dispositions.

Hopefully, the foregoing discussion has given the reader some general feeling for the meaning of correspondence in the present context. For the sake of theoretical clarity, however, more precise and formal explication is in order. Such an explication may provide a clearer path toward understanding the theory.

All actions have effects on the environment. From the perceiver's point of view, any effect of another person's action is a potential reason why this person had engaged in that action. To infer that the action occurred for X reason is to specify the actor's intention and, indirectly, an underlying disposition. Both intentions and dispositions are attributes of the person. The perception of a link between a particular intention or disposition and a particular action may therefore be called an attribute-effect linkage.

Let us now attempt a more formal definition of correspondence. *Given an attribute-effect linkage which is offered to explain why an act occurred, correspondence increases as the judged value of the attribute departs from the judge's conception of the average person's standing on that attribute.* Turning to the illustration used earlier, the inference that domineering action reflects an underlying trait of dominance is correspondent to the extent that the actor's dominance is seen as greater than that of the average person. This implies, incidentally, that the intention to dominate is out of the ordinary—somehow more intense and noteworthy than we would normally expect.

As a simple example of how the concept of correspondence can be put to use in a research setting, we may provide the perceiver with rating scales designed to measure the strength of the trait attributed to the actor and his confidence in making his rating. The perceiver's certainty that the actor is extreme on a trait which provides sufficient reason for the action's occurrence is, then, the level of correspondence of his inference.

B. ACTS AND THEIR EFFECTS

An act is conceived of as a molar response which reflects some degree of personal choice on the part of the actor (if only between action and inaction, though more typically between alternative courses of action) and which has one or more effects on the environment or the actor himself. *Effects* are distinctive (or potentially distinctive) consequences of action. Stated in the broadest terms, they are discriminable changes in the pre-existing state of affairs that are brought about by action. Delimiting the unit with which we shall be concerned is more a problem in theory than in practice. If we observe that a man leaves his chair, crosses the room, closes the door, and the room becomes less noisy, a correspondent inference would be that he intended to cut down the noise. One might ask whether the inference that the man intended to reach the door is not also a correspondent inference since "reaching the door" is an effect of crossing the room. But the subordinate parts of a meaningful action sequence do not have to be confused with the effects of an action. In this case, the perceiver is likely to "organize" the action in his mind as beginning with the decision to leave the chair and ending with the closing of the door. It is the effects of the terminal act in a meaningful sequence, then, that provide the grist for our theory.

An act may have only one effect, but usually has multiple effects. When the man closes the door this may reduce the draft, reduce the illumination in his office, and make two students talking in the hall feel a little guilty for interrupting his work. Thus, we are usually dealing with *choice areas* rather than single choices. Important implications for the theory are contained in the fact that "the bitter often comes with the sweet"—an action may be performed to achieve effect x, but effects m, p, t, and z are inextricably produced by the act as well. A choice between two choice areas, then, is a choice between two multiple-effect clusters. The multiple effects in one cluster may or may not overlap extensively with the multiple effects in the second cluster. That is, certain effects may be common to the chosen alternative and to the nonchosen alternative.

If the promising young psychologist Dr. Smedley accepts a position at Harvard rather than Yale, the following effects are obviously common to these two areas of choice: being in the Ivy League, living in New England, joining a university with high prestige and good salaries, living near the sea coast, etc. The theory assumes, then, that these common effects could not have been decisive in the choice, and thus do not provide information which could contribute to correspondent inferences. There are also, of course, distinctive differences between the setting at Yale and Harvard—especially if the perceiver were intimately knowledgeable about the psychology departments of the two institutions—and the perceiver's cognitive accounting of these differences would be the critical determinant of whatever inference was made.

For convenience in representing the structure of the situation in which action occurs, we shall from time to time diagram each perceived choice area as a circle within which the effects of the choice expressed as alphabetical letters may be circumscribed. Common effects may then be represented by the appearance of the same alphabetical letters in different "choice circles." Our hypothetical example of Dr. Smedley's dilemma might be diagrammed as in Fig. 2.

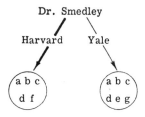

a. Ivy League
b. New England
c. prestige
d. good salary
e. close to New York plays
f. emphasis on interdisciplinary research
g. emphasis on experimental approaches
   to learning, etc.

FIG. 2. Smedley's choice.

C. THE ASSUMED DESIRABILITY OF EFFECTS

As the perceiver considers the multiple effects of action, he will usually assume that some of the effects were more desirable to the actor, and therefore more diagnostic of his intentions than others. In fact, it is almost always the case that some of the effects of the chosen alternative action are assumed to be undesirable to the actor and some of the effects of nonchosen action are assumed to be desirable. The two major effects of a man's buying a car, for example, are the acquisition of an automobile and the incurring of a substantial debt. The average perceiver, given evidence of such a purchase, will probably assume that the individual desired the car so much that he was willing to go into debt for it, not that he was willing to accept the burden of an automobile for the privilege of being a debtor.

These assumptions by the perceiver tend to operate as hypotheses which bias the inference process. Thus upon observing that an action leads to a normally desirable effect, the perceiver usually will believe that most persons, including the present actor, find that effect desirable. The achievement of this effect will therefore be regarded as the actor's most likely intention. The perceiver may, of course, be wrong in his assumptions about people in general. This particular actor may have intended to produce effects in the choice area that most people would be indifferent about or even feel negatively toward. Thus, cultural assumptions or social stereotypes may obscure the true significance of an action.

Let us take a closer look at the consequences for the inference process of assumptions about the desirability of effects. The first step is to distinguish clearly between effects which are assumed to be desirable and those assumed to be undesirable consequences for the average actor. Unless he has evidence to the contrary, the perceiver will assume that the actor has acted in spite of, rather than because of, any negative effects in the choice area. We may go beyond this to assert that any effects in the choice area which are not assumed to be negative will take on greater importance the more negative the remaining effects. Inferences concerning the intention to achieve desirable effects will increase in correspondence to the extent that costs are incurred, pain is endured, or in general, negative outcomes are involved.

Within the range of the supposedly desirable consequences, we still must recognize that effects assumed to be highly desirable are more likely to enter into attribute-effect linkages than effects assumed to be variable or neutral in desirability. However, it is also clear that attribute-effect linkages based on universally desired effects are *not* informative concerning the unique characteristics of the actor. To learn that a man makes the conventional choice is to learn only that he is like most other men. By the definition of correspondence stated above, an inference must characterize the actor's standing as high or low on an attribute relative to the average person, in order to qualify as correspondent. If a choice is explained on the basis of effects in the choice area which anyone would like to produce and enjoy, an attribute inferred to account for that choice will be low in correspondence. In general, we learn more about uniquely identifying intentions and dispositions when the effects of a chosen action are no more universally desired than the effects of a nonchosen action.

D. The Determinants of Correspondence

It may be helpful to divide the inference process into two aspects (which may in fact be seen as stages in the process). Given an act which leads to multiple effects, the perceiver implicitly attaches a probability value to each effect as a candidate for launching the inference process. In other words, the perceiver assumes that certain of the effects achieved are more likely to have been the goal of action than others. In certain cases the probability of all effects but one may be zero, indicating extreme confidence in attributing causation to a particular intention. In other cases, the probability values may be distributed among a range of effects, and since it is possible that the target person acted for more than one reason the probabilities may add up to more than 1.00. The probability value for any given effect should vary directly as a function of the assumed desirability of the effect and inversely as a function of the number of other effects competing for the perceiver's attention. If the perceiver is asked, then, "what was A trying to accomplish?"—his response should reflect this combination of assumed desirability and the number of noncommon effects.

The second aspect or phase is to attach personal significance to the effect or effects singled out as most probable courses of action. In short, what does the action reveal about this particular actor that sets him apart from other actors? By our definition of correspondence, relative extremity of perceiver rating is the crucial measure. Here it seems quite clear that assumed desirability and the number of noncommon effects have conflicting implications. The greater the assumed desirability of the effect in question, the less warrant there is for ratings of relative extremity. The smaller the number of effects in contention, on the other hand, the greater the warrant for extreme ratings. Assumed desirability, then, positively affects the probability of an attribute-effect linkage being chosen to begin the inference process and negatively affects the tendency to assign extreme values to personal characteristics.

The correspondence of an inference, which should directly reflect the amount of information revealed by an action, is thus a function of the two conditions covered by the following explicit formulation: An inference from action to attribute is correspondent *as an inverse function of (a) the number of noncommon effects following the action, and (b) the assumed social desirability of these effects.* This relationship may be stated in simpler terms as a near tautology: the more distinctive reasons a person has for an action, and the more these reasons are widely shared in the culture, the less informative that action is concerning the identifying attributes of the person.

It should be reiterated that correspondence has nothing to do, necessarily, with the accuracy of the inference. The actor may have had no intention of producing an effect which is seen by the perceiver as a prominent consequence of his action. Being able to predict the effects of one's own actions is an important precondition for being accurately perceived by others. The theory does not assume, then, that the perceiver and the actor agree on the effects of the latter's action, but focuses on those effects of which the perceiver assumes the actor was aware. The knowledge portion of the attribute-action paradigm (see Fig. 1) is relevant only in determining which effects the perceiver will include in the choice circle (see Fig. 2).

There is an interesting relationship between imputations of knowledge and actions leading to socially undesirable effects. We have already noted that when there are both desirable and undesirable effects of an action, more significance is attached to the desirable effects the more numerous and distasteful the undesirable effects "incurred." In a case where the actor produces solely negative effects, however, the situation

ASSUMED DESIRABILITY

		High	Low
NUMBER OF NONCOMMON EFFECTS	High	Trivial ambiguity	Intriguing ambiguity
	Low	Trivial clarity	High correspondence

FIG. 3. Effect desirability and effect commonality as determinants of correspondence.

is quite different. Here the perceiver has two obvious options: He may decide that the actor is truly a deviant type, that he desires those goals which are shunned by others; or he may decide that the actor was unaware of the effects of his action. It seems reasonable to propose, therefore, that in cases where the action-choice circle contains only effects judged to be socially undesirable, the more undesirable these effects the greater the perceiver's tendency to impute ignorance or lack of awareness to the actor. The possibility of imputing ignorance thus sets a limit on the degree of correspondence predicted when actions lead only to socially undersirable effects. (Note that this is quite different from what one would predict in the case where an action leads to effects which are undesirable *for the perceiver* but recognized by him to serve some purpose of the actor. We shall discuss this latter case below under the heading of Hedonic Relevance.)

It may be helpful in summarizing the theory to consider the joint operation of effect desirability and effect commonality as determinants of correspondence, and to do so in the framework of a fourfold table. Such a table is presented in Fig. 3. As the figure shows, actions which lead to effects deemed highly desirable to most persons cannot help but be trivial from an informational point of view. Also, when the number of noncommon effects is high, the perceiver cannot escape from the ambiguity of his data in making inferences either to common or idiosyncratic personal characteristics. In line with the stated theoretical relationship, the high correspondence cell is that in which assumed desirability and the number of noncommon effects are both low.

E. THE CALCULATION OF COMMONALITY

Since the theoretical statement refers to the number of noncommon effects in the chosen alternative, it is important to clarify how effects are identified and their commonality assessed. There are two rather different clusters of problems involved here. One cluster concerns identifying effects and determining whether or not two effects so identified are to be viewed as common. This will simply have to be a matter of cumulative research experience in fractionating and labeling consequences.

The other cluster of problems assumes that we can somehow achieve the necessary identifications and concerns the method of determining how the noncommon effects in the chosen alternative will be sorted out from all others in order to generate reasonably precise predictions. There are essentially three steps involved in sorting out the number of noncommon effects. The first is for the experimenter to lay out (for example, in the graphic manner of Fig. 2) the different action alternatives that the perceiver is likely to envision in the actor's situation. For each of these alternatives there will be a choice area, a circle containing the distinctive effects of that action. Having identified these circles and the effects they circumscribe, the second step is to pool all the effects associated with the nonchosen alternatives and to compare them with the effects in the choice circle of the chosen alternative. Having done this, one follows through on the assumption that effects which appear in both chosen and nonchosen alternatives cannot serve as a basis for inferences about personal dispositions. One is then left with effects which appear only in the chosen alternative and only in the nonchosen alternative(s). The third and final step is to view the noncommon effects in the nonchosen alternatives as effects which the actor may be trying to avoid. They may thus be transposed, with their sign reversed, and regrouped among the noncommon effects of the chosen alternative. The new total of noncommon effects now serves as the basis for making predictions about the level of correspondence.

In order to illustrate these three stages in the calculation of noncommon effects, let us invent a case involving the choice of a marital partner. We are informed that a Miss Adams, who is ripe for matrimony, has received proposals from three suitors, Bagby, Caldwell, and Dexter. All we know about Bagby is that he is wealthy, he has high status in the community, and he is physically attractive. Caldwell is also quite wealthy, he is physically attractive, and he has often expressed his longing for a houseful of his own children. Dexter is physically attractive like

Effects of marriage to be considered:

    a. wealth

    b. social position

    c. sexual enjoyment

    d. children

    e. intellectual stimulation

A. The Choice

Miss Adams

Bagby   Caldwell   Dexter

(a b c)   (a c d)   (c e)

B. Elimination of Common Effects (c)

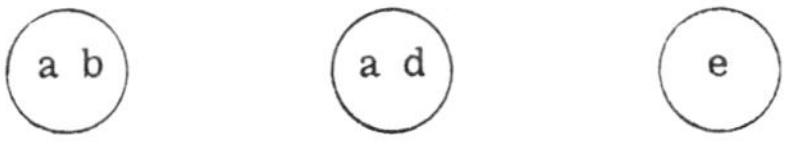

(a b)   (a d)   (e)

C. Regrouped Noncommon Effects

If choice is:

    Bagby   b wanted, d and e not important

    Caldwell   d wanted, b and e not important

    Dexter   e wanted, a not wanted, b and d not important

D. Inferences:

If Bagby, Miss Adams is a snob; if Caldwell, Miss Adams is the maternal type; if Dexter, Miss Adams is an intellectual.

FIG. 4. Miss Adams chooses a husband.

the others, and he is very much the intellectual—widely read and conversationally scintillating. These are the only characteristics of these men that we know anything about, and on the basis of this knowledge we may diagram Miss Adam's choice as in Fig. 4A.

First we lay out those effects presumed to follow from the choice of each man to the exclusion of the other. Then we notice that the three men are physically attractive so we rule out the common effect of sexual enjoyment—we have no information about the importance of this particular characteristic as a determinant of Miss Adams' choice. The remaining effects are regrouped after we receive information about which man has been chosen. The only further distinction is that between effects which are judged to have been wanted by Miss Adams, effects judged to have been unimportant to her, and effects judged to have been *not* wanted or actively avoided. The distinction between lack of importance and undesirability is new; it is based on the commonality of particular effects among the nonchosen alternatives. Thus, if Dexter is chosen, we have no more reason to assume that Miss Adams wanted intellectual stimulation than that she didn't want the responsibilities of wealth. After all, she has avoided two wealthy suitors in favor of one who is not wealthy. Our inference about not wanting wealth, then, would be more correspondent than an inference about not wanting children or not caring about social position. If it were just a matter of not having children, Miss Adams could just as easily have married Bagby. If she was anxious to avoid social position she could have accomplished this by marrying Caldwell. We say these these two effects were not *important* to her to suggest that she is willing to forego them in favor of intellectual stimulation, but our evidence that she wanted to avoid these effects is weaker than in the case of wealth.

A further complexity which must be acknowledged is the fact that some or all of the noncommon effects may be correlated or seen by the perceiver to express the same general purpose. At the present stage of developing the theory of correspondence, no formal provision is made for this possibility. To some extent, our flexibility in deciding what we shall call an effect reduces the magnitude of the problem. Thus, certain combinations of discriminable effects may be treated as a more general, unitary effect if each member of the combination has a common significance for the perceiver. The result would be to increase the correspondence and the generality or importance of the ensuing inference. We shall examine this possibility in greater detail when we consider, below, the contribution of hedonic or affective relevance of effects in the inference process and again when we consider sequences of action choices over time.

F. Conditions Affecting Desirability Assumptions

We have remarked that the perceiver's assumptions or hypotheses about which effects of action were most likely desired by the actor play an important role in the inference process. Those effects perceived to have been high in desirability (i.e., commonly desired by all persons or by all members of a particular cultural group) play a smaller role in the determination of correspondence than those effects which are less universally sought. Without going too deeply into the problem, there are a number of variables which might condition the perceiver's assumptions that the actor desires the same effects as most persons. Even if we restrict ourselves to the case in which the perceiver confronts the actor for the first time, there may be cues in the circumstances of their encounter and in the appearance of the actor which affect the likelihood of his being seen as desiring the same things most persons would in a given situation. If the situation is so structured that the actor and the perceiver are working for the same objectives, the perceiver may reflect on his own intentions to draw inferences about the most likely aspirations of the actor. Cues about shared perspectives should thus facilitate the formation of definite hypotheses about the actor's motives and desires. Other cues, perhaps reflected in the features of the actor's appearance, might lead the perceiver to assume similarity of intention and disposition before any action has occurred. Or the perceiver's stereotypes about the members of identifiable classes or cultural groups may be triggered by such appearance cues.

G. INFORMATION GAIN AND THE ROLE OF PRIOR CHOICE

We now come to one of the most frustrating sources of complexity in calculating noncommon effects in the chosen alternative, both for the individual perceiver whose actions the theory concerns and for the theory itself. A person who confronts certain behavior choices has often made previous choices which have brought him to his present decision. There is often a great deal of information contained, then, in knowledge about what alternatives are being considered, above and beyond the information revealed by the actual decision which is made.

Once again, this point can be clarified by an example. Let us consider Miss Adams again, this time caught between the options of going to medical school or to law school. She has been accepted for admission in the two professional schools of comparable universities and the choice is, in that sense, entirely up to her. In comparison, we come upon Mr. Bagby, poised before the choice of going to Duke or to Colorado for graduate study in psychology. Since the Duke and Colorado psychology departments would seem to have much more in common than medical school versus law school, our theory would seem to suggest that any inference we might make about Mr. Bagby after he has chosen would be more correspondent than any comparable inference about Miss Adams. There are many noncommon effects in Adams' chosen alternative, whereas the number of noncommon effects in Bagby's chosen alternative is unquestionably smaller. The hidden factor in this comparison is the fact that considerably more information is contained in the datum that Bagby had already ruled out everything besides psychology, than in the datum that Adams is still struggling with the choice between two basic professions, professions which differ from each other on many different dimensions. The example is thus misleading because Bagby is at a later stage of the choice process than Adams. In order to render them comparable we would have to have more information concerning Bagby's preceding choices, choices which have narrowed the field to psychology.

The example points up the importance of defining correspondence in terms of the information *gained* through the observation of behavior, not in terms of the confidence one has in drawing an inference which may be based on prior information or on knowledge of the culture. If all we know is that Bagby has chosen the Colorado Department of Psychology over the Duke Department of Psychology, we have learned nothing *from the choice itself* concerning the strength of his motivation to become a psychologist. On the other hand, we might be willing to make some rather confident statements about his love of mountains or the degree of his dislike for hot and humid summers. The facts that there are high mountains and low humidity in Colorado are certainly two of the noncommon effects in the Colorado versus Duke choice.

In dealing with cases of complex behavioral choice in the natural environment, the matter of prior choice is destined to create enormous difficulties in the application of the theory to individual cases. However, in the realm of experimental planning, prior choice presents opportunities for empirical exploration rather than disruptive trouble. The probability of imputing prior choice can either be held constant or systematically varied by suitable experimental arrangements. In the former case for example, subject-perceivers, starting from the same baseline of relative ignorance about a stimulus person, may be exposed to a choice made by that stimulus person under conditions which emphasize the stimulus persons's lack of control over the choice presented him.

H. CORRESPONDENCE, CHOICE, AND ROLE ASSIGNMENT

A recent experiment by Jones *et al.* (1961) exemplifies the reasoning which underlies the foregoing theory. It is worth reviewing this study before considering some of the more subtle and tentative extensions of the theory into interaction settings marked by personal involvement. The investigation's central purpose was to demonstrate that behavior which conforms to clearly defined role requirements is seen as uninformative about the individual's personal characteristics, whereas a considerable amount of information may be extracted from out-of-role behavior. In other words, inferences based on out-of-role behavior were predicted to be higher in correspondence than inferences from in-role behavior. The reasons for this will become more apparent after the procedures of the experiment are described.

Male undergraduate subjects were exposed to one of four tape recorded "job interviews" in which the interviewee was instructed (on the tape) to appear very interested in qualifying either as a prospective submariner or as an astronaut. The subjects were aware that the interviewee was being invited to play a role in a fictitious interview situation, but they were not told that the entire interview was carefully written as a prearranged script and was recorded by an experimental accomplice serving as the interviewee.

Those subjects who listened to the recording involving the submariner role, heard the interviewer describe the ideal submariner as obedient, cooperative, friendly, gregarious—in short, as "other directed." The remaining subjects listened to a description of the ideal astronaut as one who does not need other people, who has inner resources—in short, a rather "inner-directed" person. These two interview beginnings were spliced into two different endings, thus creating the four experimental groups. The interviewee either responded with a series of statements indicating extreme other-directedness or he responded with a series of inner-directed statements. On half of the recordings, then, the interviewee-accomplice behaved very much in line with the requirements of the occupational role (astronaut-inner condition, submariner-other condition). On the other half the behavior was distinctly out of line with these requirements (astronaut-other condition, submariner-inner condition).

After listening to these tape recordings, the subjects were asked to rate the interviewee ("what do you think he is *really* like as a person?") and indicate their confidence in the traits they evaluated on their rating scale. The results were striking and unequivocal (see Table I). After the two in-role recordings, the stimulus person was rated as moderately affiliative and moderately independent. In each case the confidence ratings were extremely low. On the other hand, the astronaut-other was seen as very conforming and affiliative, and confidently rated as such. The submariner-inner was seen as very independent and non-affiliative, again with high confidence. Thus the actual responses of the interviewee were clearly evaluated in the context of the structured setting from which they emerged. If other-directedness is called for, an inner-directed response is highly informative. Inner-directedness in the face of a situation which seems to require it, on the other hand, is difficult to interpret. The same kind of contrast applies to other-directedness in the two settings described, providing a replication of the basic hypothesis within the single experiment.

Now we may ask how the results of the Jones *et al.* (1961) experiment are to be explained in terms of the foregoing theoretical statement relating cultural desirability and the number of noncommon effects to the degree of correspondence of an inference about personal dispositions. In-role behavior does not lead to confident, correspondent inferences because such behavior has multiple consequences and many of these are high in cultural desirability. Most people want to avoid embarrassing others by not meeting their expectations, most people want to gain the rewards implicit in approval from authority figures, most people wish to manifest their intelligence by showing that they understand what is required of them, and so on. Each of these effects is a "plausible reason"

TABLE I

PERCEPTIONS OF AFFILIATION AND CONFORMITY[a,b]

	Astro-other (AO)	Astro-inner (AI)	Sub-other (SO)	Sub-inner (SI)	Comparisons Direction	t
N:	33	33	31	37		
Affiliation						
$\bar{X}$	15.27	11.12	12.00	8.64	AO > SO	4.02[d]
SD	2.92	3.81	3.53	4.73	AI > SI	2.12[e]
Conformity						
$\bar{X}$	15.91	13.09	12.58	9.41	AO > SO	4.02[d]
SD	3.22	3.42	3.39	4.95	AI > SI	3.65[d]

[a] Data from Jones et al. (1961).

[b] The higher the mean value, the greater the perceived affiliation or conformity. Comparisons between AO and SI are not tabled, but the differences between these conditions would of course be highly significant.

[c] $p < .05$.

[d] $p < .001$.

for in-role behavior in the experiment just described. On the other hand, plausible reasons for out-of-role behavior (i.e., those with a reasonable degree of assumed social desirability) are comparatively scarce. One of the few noncommon effects of behavior at variance with role demands is the satisfaction of expressing one's true nature. This effect is also a possible accompaniment of in-role behavior, but in that case it exists in the choice circle along with many other effects. Since there are fewer noncommon effects in the astronaut-other and submariner-inner choices, the effect of "being oneself" forms the basis of a more correspondent inference in these conditions and the interviewee's behavior tends to be taken at face value.

The implications of this study can probably be extended quite generally to cover behavior which is or is not constrained by a well defined social situation. When certain role requirements are salient, conformity is more rewarding to the actor, more likely to avoid embarrassment and social disapproval, than is nonconformity. The actor may conform for many other reasons as well. Thus, in the case of conformity to role requirements, we do not know the exact reason why the individual behaves the way he does, but there is really no particular mystery in his behavior. This is an example of "trivial ambiguity." On the other hand, behavior which departs from clearly defined role requirements cries for explanation. The fact that the effects of such behavior are presumably low in cultural desirability makes the behavior intriguing to the perceiver. The fact that there are few reasons why a person would behave that way (the action leads to a limited number of noncommon effects) provides the basis for a correspondent inference concerning the intentions and dispositions of the actor.

III. Personal Involvement and Correspondence

In the remaining sections of the chapter, we shall turn to those factors of personal involvement which affect the inference process in person perception. The theory of action implied in the discussion thus far obviously assumes that the actor is concerned with the consequences of his action. It is the very fact that his action choices have motivational significance for *him* that makes these choices informative for the perceiver. But a special and enormously important feature of many person perception settings is that the choice of an actor has significant rewarding or punishing implications for the perceiver. We turn to examine this feature and to consider its implications for our theory of correspondence.

A. THE HEDONIC RELEVANCE OF THE ACTION TO THE PERCEIVER

The actor's behavioral choices may or may not contain effects which have hedonic relevance for the perceiver. The hedonic relevance of an effect is a function of its motivational significance for the perceiver: does the particular action consequence promote or undermine the perceiver's values; does it fulfill or obstruct his purposes? Effects which fulfill a purpose have positive relevance; those which obstruct a purpose have negative relevance. For a *choice* to have relevance means that the algebraic balance of positive and negative effects in the chosen alternative is not equal to the algebraic balance of positive and negative effects in the nonchosen alternative(s). Simply put, the choice proved gratifying or disappointing to the perceiver.

An experiment by Steiner and Field (1960) is conceptually quite similar to the astronaut-submariner study but contains a strong dash of hedonic relevance as an added ingredient. In this study, University of Illinois students met in groups of three to "discuss the desirability of desegregation of public schools and . . . attempt to reach agreement among themselves." The major manipulation varied the extent to which the responsibility for presenting certain points of view was assigned by the experimenter. For half of the groups, a confederate of the experimenter was always assigned the role of "a typical Southern segregationist." In the other groups, subjects were encouraged to take into consideration the viewpoint of an N.A.A.C.P. member, a Northern clergyman, and a Southern segregationist, but no role assignments were made. In both cases, however, the confederate gave an identical, prosegregation performance. From the perceiver's point of view, he apparently chose to express prosegregation beliefs where no role assignment was made, whereas he had little choice *but* to express the same beliefs in the role assignment condition. Since the subjects themselves were all in favor of integration, the expression of prosegregationist beliefs would, we assume, be relevant in the negative direction.

The following results would be expected given the theoretical statement that we have developed thus far: (1) perceivers should attribute more intense prosegregation beliefs to the actor in the choice condition than to the same actor in the assignment condition; (2) perceivers should be more confident of their inferences in the choice condition; and, (3) they should evaluate the chooser less favorably than the actor who had the role assigned to him. The investigators do not report the data bearing on the first hypothesis, but the other data make sense only if it were supported. Hypothesis 2 was strongly supported, and both indices bearing on hypothesis 3 were in the predicted direction, though only one treatment difference was significant. In addition, while the fact is not particularly relevant in the present theoretical context, the subjects were apparently more influenced by the remarks of the actor when he chose the role than when he was assigned to it, even though he was better liked in the latter case.

The results confirm very well the expectation derived from the theory of correspondent inferences, and the subjects show the same uncertainty in the role assignment condition as was observed in the in-role treatments of the astronaut-submariner study. Since there are so many objectives served when the actor in the role assignment condition follows his assignment, and since most of these objectives are quite culturally desirable, the perceiver learns very little from the actor's compliance.

Hedonic relevance is involved because the position taken by the actor is contrary to the view held by all perceivers in the experiment. While the experiment does not manipulate the relevance of the action directly, it does alter the subject's evaluative response to the action by altering his interpretation of the act.

It is not as yet clear, however, precisely how relevance enters into the inference process. At the outset, it may be useful to distinguish between the effects of relevance on correspondence, and the joint effects of relevance and correspondence on evaluation by the perceiver. Let us consider each of these in turn. We propose that as relevance increases there is also an increase in the likelihood that inferences will be correspondent. This is because effects which might appear to have little in common in the eyes of most observers might be functionally equivalent to a particular perceiver. Thus, relevance may provide a potent criterion for grouping and packaging the effects of action, thereby reducing the number of unrelated or noncommon effects in the choice circle. The result is an increase in the correspondence of any inference based on that particular choice. This reasoning does not apply in the event that a nonrelevant effect is seen as the probable goal of the action. However, we may assume that the probability of launching the inference from a relevant effect increases directly as a function of the degree of relevance involved.

In addition to the packaging of effects in terms of their positive or negative significance for the perceiver, the number of noncommon effects may be further reduced by *assimilation to the predominant hedonic value*. When the actor makes a choice which is relevant to the perceiver, there will be a tendency for the remaining more or less neutral effects to take on the sign of other effects in the choice circle. This assimilation should operate in such a way as to increase the differentiation between chosen and nonchosen courses of action. The process may be illustrated by changes in the connotative meaning of attributed dispositions. Let us assume that we have identical information concerning the moderately high risk-taking tendencies of Adams and Bagby. If Adams does something which, on balance, goes against our interests, the assimilation hypothesis proposes that risk-taking proclivity might be construed as recklessness and irresponsibility. If Bagby does something that supports our interests and benefits us, riskiness might take on connotations of creativeness and inventive autonomy. This would seem to be an expression of Heider's (1958) general balance principle: Bad actions come from bad people and good is achieved by the good.

Turning now to the joint effects of relevance and correspondence on evaluation by the perceiver, the following proposition suggests itself: If the consequences of an act are predominantly positive, the perceiver will be more favorably disposed toward the actor, the greater the correspondence value of the action. The converse will be true of actions whose effects are negative. In general, ignoring direction for the moment, the evaluation of an individual will be more extreme as a joint function of increases in relevance and correspondence.

Since relevance increases correspondence, and since relevance and correspondence affect evaluation, it might seem reasonable to link relevance directly to evaluation. However, relevance may well affect only one condition of correspondence—the commonality of effects—and not the other, the cultural desirability of effects. For this reason it is possible to have high relevance and only moderate correspondence. When, for example, the Russian ambassador to the United Nations makes a speech accusing America of imperialistic ambitions, dollar diplomacy, exploitation of the worker, and so on, it is easy for us to put these remarks into a single package under the label of negative hedonic relevance. And yet, we are sufficiently aware of the norms of cultural desirability among Russian public spokesmen to recognize that none of the ambassador's statements departs very far from these norms.

In terms of the fourfold table presented as Fig. 3, we are dealing with a case of trivial clarity. Note that relevance is high—the statements chosen by the ambassador have effects almost all of which are an affront to our values as American perceivers. The number of noncommon effects is low—the disparate remarks may be readily packaged as anti-American; and assumed cultural desirability (for a Russian) is high. But, we would not predict a particularly intense negative evaluation in this case. Since this particular Russian is just saying what any other Russian would say under the same circumstances, it is rather hard to take special umbrage at his "negatively relevant" remarks. The example helps us to see, then, that a combination of relevance and high correspondence is prerequisite for extreme evaluations to occur. Relevance controls the direction of evaluation, but is only one of two contributing determinants of its extremity.

1. Relevance Increases Correspondence: Empirical Support

In order to test the hypothesis that relevance increases correspondence in the inference process, it is necessary to present the same action or series of acts in contexts of differing personal relevance for the perceiver. This was done in an experiment by Jones and deCharms (1957) and in another by Kleiner (1960), the results of which we shall briefly summarize.

Two separate experiments, sharing certain basic procedural features were conducted by Jones and deCharms (1957). In the first experiment a trained accomplice was the only member of a group, including four or five naive subjects, who failed the assigned experimental task. In one condition, *individual fate,* the relevance of this failure was minimized.

The subjects all received the rewards promised them for succeeding and this was in no way contingent on the accomplice's performance. In another condition, *common fate,* the accomplice's failure prevented anyone from reaping the rewards available. This was, then, a condition of negative hedonic relevance for the naive subjects. The subjects rated the accomplice twice; first, prior to the main experimental inductions and again after his failure was established. We would expect to find, in an index of change in ratings of the accomplice, indications of greater correspondence in the negative relevance than in the minimal relevance condition. In line with this prediction, the accomplice was regarded as being less competent, less dependable, and generally judged in less favorable terms in the common fate (negative relevance) than in the individual fate (minimal relevance) condition. Contrary to expectation, no differences in likeability or friendliness occurred as a function of relevance. Perhaps we may cite this pattern of findings to illustrate that relevance may affect certain attributions without necessarily affecting personal evaluation.

A study by Kleiner (1960) varied the positive relevance of constructive member actions by varying the probability of group failure. A previously instructed accomplice then facilitated group goal achievement by solving problems too difficult for the others. We assume that the degree of positive relevance varies directly with the degree of initial threat to the group. Unfortunately for our purposes, Kleiner did not get extensive impression ratings over a variety of traits, but he did get evidence concerning changes in perceived importance of group members. Consistent with the relevance-correspondence hypothesis, the greater the group's need for help, the greater importance attributed to the helpful confederate. Consistent with the second evaluation, the rated likeability of the confederate as both a teammate and as someone to socialize with was positively related to the degree of initial need for help.

While there are no other investigations (to our knowledge) that concern themselves directly with the relevance-correspondence hypothesis, there are several closely related studies which increase our confidence in its validity. These are studies in which conditions of *potential* relevance are created by the anticipation of further interaction, but in which impression ratings are taken before the direction of relevance has been established by final action. The general pattern of findings from these studies has been called "facilitative distortion" of perceived attributes—the stimulus person is assigned attributes that are consistent with the positive outcome hoped for in the interaction.

The classic study was done by Pepitone (1950). Variations in motivation (relevance) were established by having high school students think that their ideas about athletics would be instrumental in obtaining either very desirable championship basketball tickets (high relevance) or much less desirable tickets (low relevance). The three judges who evaluated the students' ideas were again accomplices of the experimenter. They varied their apparent approval of the subject in some conditions, and their apparent power to grant him a ticket in others. On the whole, there was a strong tendency for subjects to view the more favorable judges as more powerful than the less favorable judges, though power was ostensibly equated by instructions and the accomplices' careful attention to their prescribed roles. Similarly, when there was a deliberate attempt to vary the judges' power, the more powerful judges were regarded as more approving. We may only assume that such "facilitative distortion" would not have occurred in a no-relevance control group. It *was* true that the high relevance subjects saw the approving judge as more powerful than the low relevance subjects did, which provides direct support for the relevance-correspondence hypothesis, but the remaining differences which might test the hypothesis were not significant.

A similar pattern of facilitative distortions was found in one phase of Davis' (1962) study. Subjects were given preinformation about an individual with whom they were to engage in a series of either cooperative or competitive interactions. For half of the subjects, this information portrayed an essentially submissive person; for the other half, an essentially ascendant person. When the submissive person was to be a *partner,* she was seen as more active, outgoing, forceful, tough, and as less passive, shy, and uncertain of herself than when she was to be an *opponent.* These differential effects did not approach statistical significance in the condition of ascendant information. Perhaps the constraints of clear information were strong enough to inhibit distortion in the latter case.

Other studies also show both facilitative distortion effects and the absence of such effects, but in no study do "pessimistic" distortions occur. There seems little doubt that relevance may increase distortion by causing increases in correspondence which are not based on added information. What we now need is to determine other parameters which influence the relevance-correspondence relationship and thus affect the perceiver's reliance on the available data he obtains from observed action.

2. Relevance and Correspondence Determine Evaluation: Empirical Support

The second hypothesis concerning relevance was that evaluation is a joint function of the degree of relevance and the level of correspondence. Under a variety of different guises, this hypothesis has received greater empirical attention than the prior hypothesis linking relevance to correspondence. It is not difficult to find ample support for the proposition that people like others who benefit them in some way and dislike others who are harmful. But since we have already argued that relevance increases correspondence, this proposition is not a very precise rendition of the second hypothesis. The second hypothesis requires the demonstration that *both* relevance and correspondence are necessary conditions for evaluation, or at least that evaluation will be more extreme when both are present at a high level. Our reasoning implies that evaluation will become more extreme as a function of increases in either relevance or correspondence, as long as the other variable is held constant at some value greater than zero. If an action is expected to be positively or negatively relevant for a perceiver, for example, the perceiver's evaluations should become more extreme when the conditions of judgment give rise to high correspondence.

As one test of this hypothesis, we may return to the second experiment reported in Jones and deCharms (1957). Cross-cutting the common fate-individual fate variation which characterized both experiments, an additional instructional variation was introduced. Half of the subjects were led to believe that the task was such that failure should be primarily attributed to lack of ability. The remaining subjects were told that failure on the particular problems to be solved could only reflect a lack of motivation, a lack of willingness to try hard. In retrospect, we might now see the ability condition as involving less choice for the actor than the motivation condition. After all, if ability and not motivation is involved, then the subject may try heroically, knowing that others are dependent on him and that doing well is important—but still fail. In the ability condition, therefore, his failure would not provide a basis for correspondent inferences about his attitudes toward the group. The individual must have some degree of choice among action alternatives before one may begin to speak of noncommon effects in the chosen alternative.

The results bear out the prediction quite well. An evaluation change index was composed from the combined ratings of the accomplice made by each naive subject before and after the experimental variables were introduced. The traits involved were deliberately chosen to reflect an evaluative "halo effect": competent, intelligent, conscientious, likeable, dependable, and so on. When the accomplice supposedly had no choice (in the ability conditions), variations in personal relevance for the perceiver did not lead to differential changes in evaluation. Thus the evaluation change scores in the common fate-ability condition were almost identical to the evaluation change scores in the individual fate-ability condition (see Table II). When the accomplice was presumed to have a choice, on the other hand, relevance was a crucial determinant of evaluation. Subjects in the common fate-motivation condition were significantly more negative in their evaluation change scores than subjects in the individual fate-motivation condition.

It should be emphasized, of course, that the actual behavior of the accomplice was as nearly the same in all conditions as careful pre-training and periodic monitoring could make it. In conclusion, then, the accomplice was negatively evaluated if his failing performance prevented the others from obtaining rewards *and* he could have avoided failure by trying harder. Not trying hard in this case may have been equivalent to an attitude of indifference to the group, an attitude which (once inferred) would be resented by the group's members.

TABLE II[a]
CHANGE IN "HALO EFFECT," EXPERIMENT II

	Groups			
	Common fate		Individual fate	
	Motivation	Ability	Motivation	Ability
$\bar{X}$[b]	23.0	17.3	14.4	18.9
SD	10.68	6.27	2.12	9.53

[a] Data from Jones and deCharms (1957).

[b] The greater the mean change, the more negative the "after" evaluation.

Perhaps the most celebrated study linking causal attribution and evaluation is that of Thibaut and Riecken (1955). They conducted two separate experiments to explore the proposition that an act of benevolence which is "internally caused" is more appreciated than one which is the inevitable result of environmental circumstances. We would now view internal causation as another way of talking about the perception of choice alternatives available to the actor. A person "internally causes" certain effects in the environment only when he had the option of causing other effects and did not do so.

In each of the Thibaut-Riecken experiments, an undergraduate subject was introduced to two experimental accomplices or confederates, one of whom was apparently much higher in academic or social status than himself and one of whom was lower in status. The subject soon found himself in the position where he needed the help of at least one of the confederates. The experimenter encouraged him to ask for help and required only that he make an identical request of both the high status and the low status confederate. When both of the confederates eventually complied with his request, the subject was asked to explain the compliance and to evaluate each confederate. Since the differences in experimentally manipulated status were perceived as differences in the ability to resist persuasion, the high status confederate was regarded as having more choice in his decision about compliance. The low status confederate, on the other hand, was more likely to be viewed as complying because he felt "coerced" by the more powerful subject. The norms governing a low status position are such that compliance to those higher in status is often expected. In our terms, then, the behavior of the high status person should lead to more correspondent inferences concerning the intention to help the subject out of a disposition of spontaneous affection or good will.

As our hypothesis would predict, holding relevance constant (the subject is benefitted equally by the two confederates), as correspondence of inference (about spontaneous good will) increases, positive evaluation also increases. The benevolence of the high status confederate earns him a greater increase in attractiveness than does the benevolence of the low status confederate. Relevance in the positive direction, coupled with high correspondence in the form of perceived internal causation, results in more positive evaluation.

Incidental findings from two other studies may be mentioned as well. These findings also bring out the relationship between relevance, correspondence, and evaluation. In the study by Davis (1962) briefly referred to above, control groups were run in which subjects anticipated either cooperative or competitive discussions with each other, but no pre-information about the partners was provided beforehand. Each subject rated the other person prior to the interaction on traits which could be combined into an ascendance-submission index, and on likeability. In the competitive condition, the more ascendant one's opponent, the greater the probability of one's own failure; ascendance has negative hedonic relevance. In the cooperative condition, on the other hand, ascendance has positive relevance since it implies a greater probability of team success. Comparing individual differences in the tendency to assign high first impression ratings on ascendance, we should expect a positive correlation between perceived ascendance and likeability in the cooperative condition and a negative correlation between these two sets of ratings in the competitive condition. The correlational values were actually +.60 and −.18, respectively, reflecting a difference between conditions which is significant.

Finally, in an experiment by Jones and Daugherty (1959), some subjects were led to anticipate interacting with one of two persons about whom a fair amount of information was provided via a tape-recorded interview. Others received the same information about the two persons, but it was clear that no subsequent interaction would take place. One of the two interviewees was presented as a rather intellectual, somewhat diffident person, with moderately strong aesthetic interests. The other was presented as a rather opportunistic and conforming, but obviously sociable person. In the no-anticipation condition, in which we may assume that the characteristics of both persons were of minimal relevance, the diffident esthete was more highly evaluated on a variety of dimensions than was the sociable politician. In contrast, when the subjects were led to anticipate interacting with one of the two, making the relevance of sociability more salient, the subjects' evaluation of the politician markedly and significantly increased. These results, then, suggest that a particular personal attribute (sociability) was assigned approximately the same ratings in the two conditions (varying in the anticipation of interaction) but variations in the relevance of that attribute were associated with shifts in evaluation. If there had been no evidence that the "politician" was sociable, correspondent inferences about him would not have been drawn regarding that disposition and evaluation would not have varied with relevance. It should be emphasized that the obtained differences were not anticipated. However, we view the interpretation as the most plausible one available and are encouraged to think that a replication specifically addressed to the present hypothesis would show the same pattern.

In summary, there seems little question that variations in the relevance of an action to the perceiver have an effect on the process of inferring dispositions which explain the action. Our first hypothesis was that relevance tends to increase correspondence by reducing the number of noncommon effects in the action alternative chosen. We have presented some evidence in favor of this hypothesis, although it is clear that the strength of confirmation depends on other conditions, such as the ambiguity of available information about the actor and the consequent leeway for facilitative distortion. The second hypothesis, which states that personal evaluation varies as a joint function of relevance and correspondence, has received stronger support than the first. Here again, however, much of the evidence is indirect and circumstantial. Hopefully, the present theoretical analysis will point the way toward more precise tests of both hypotheses.

B. PERSONALISM: THE ACTOR'S INTENTION TO BENEFIT OR HARM THE PERCEIVER

An act or a choice may be hedonically relevant to the perceiver even though it is quite clear to the latter that the choice was not conditioned by his unique presence. An actor might express opinions which differ radically from the perceiver's without having any knowledge of the latter's views. Such a choice of opinions may have hedonic relevance for the perceiver, but may not have been offered with any intention to gratify or to spite him. The variable of *personalism* is introduced to distinguish between choices which are conceivably affected by the presence of the perceiver and choices which are not conceivably so affected.

It is usually difficult for a perceiver to judge whether a choice was affected by personalistic considerations. He may, in effect, experimentally arrange conditions of his own presence and absence in an attempt to detect differences in the choice made by the stimulus person. This is often done indirectly, as when the perceiver compares reports of choices made in his absence with his own observations of choices made in his presence. We may try, for example, to find out what others say about us and our beliefs behind our backs. When the actions of another person obstruct our interests, it becomes important for us to determine whether the other sets out specifically to make life unpleasant for us or whether we have been disadvantaged as a by-product of actions primarily directed toward other objectives. Similarly, when others go out of their way to help us, we have an interest in establishing whether they did this because of our uniquely attractive personality or because they would have helped almost anyone under the circumstances.

The distinction between relevance and personalism hinges on the perceiver's imputation of a certain kind of knowledge to the actor: the actor's awareness that the interests of the perceiver are positively or negatively affected by his actions. If such knowledge is *not* imputed by the perceiver to the actor, then we are dealing with a case of "impersonal hedonic relevance."

When a hedonically relevant action is produced in the presence of the perceiver, the latter's problem is to decide whether the act was uniquely conditioned by the fact that he was its target. When there is such evidence of a "unique conditioning," the perceiver is likely to draw strong inferences of malevolence or benevolence, stronger than he would as a bystander. He and only he is the target of the other's highly relevant action; therefore, it is assumed that the other has a special interest in making life easy or difficult for him as a person.

Since the perceiver is going to be so vitally concerned with relevant effects that were deliberately produced for his consumption, such effects should clearly play a special role in shaping his inferences about the actor. We propose that action which is both relevant and personal has a direct and dramatic effect on evaluative conclusions about the actor. One reason for this is that personalism clearly implies choice. If an actor benefits a perceiver, this is a personalistic episode only if it reflects the selection of that particular perceiver as a worthy beneficiary in the face of opportunities to select other targets or other actions. The combination of personalism and positive relevance, then, insures a positive evaluation simply by insuring a correspondent inference of focused benevolence. The special significance of such focused benevolence may lie in the fact that it satisfies the perceiver's needs for information about his worthiness, as well as other needs for security, power over others, and so on. In any event, the receipt of focused benefit or focused harm should generate "halo" effects in the inference process which go beyond the assimilation to hedonic value predicted in the case of impersonal hedonic relevance.

Personalism may, of course, be incorrectly assumed by the perceiver. The most extreme form of distortion along these lines may be seen in paranoia, where innocent actions and actions not conditioned by the perceiver's presence, become the data for inferences concerning ulterior malevolent motivation.

Surprisingly, there are few experiments which precisely assess the role of personalism in the inference process. The above proposition implies that hedonically relevant actions which the perceiver judges to be uniquely affected by his presence will give rise to correspondent inferences to all those attributes captured by a positive or negative "halo" effect. In an experiment specifically concerned with variations in personalism, Gergen (1962) arranged to have coeds receive uniformly positive, reinforcing remarks from another coed under personal versus impersonal conditions. Such remarks probably are hedonically relevant and positive as far as the first coed is concerned.

In the personal treatment, the girls had been previously introduced to each other, had engaged in a pleasant and informative interaction, and the reinforcing person (actually an experimental accomplice) had quite a bit to go on in expressing her positive feelings about the subject. In the impersonal treatment, on the other hand, the subjects were informed that the accomplice had been through some intensive training designed to help her establish rapport in a social interaction. In addition, and in clear contrast with the personal treatment, the accomplice never saw the subject, but interacted with her through a microphone-speaker system while the subject observed her through a one-way mirror. Each subject was ultimately asked to record her impression of the accomplice on a series of evaluative scales. From our proposition concerning the role of personalism in producing high correspondence for evaluative characteristics, we would expect a more positive halo effect in the personal than in the impersonal experimental treatment. There were, however, no significant differences between the subjects' evaluative ratings of the accomplice in the two conditions.

There was some evidence that the subjects felt sorry for the accomplice in the impersonal condition, since she had to operate under the rather embarrassing handicap of being seen by the subject without being able to see her. There was also some confusion about whether the subject was to rate the accomplice as she appeared to be or as she "really was." We do not feel, therefore, that the Gergen experiment is a crucial test of the personalism proposition, though some variation of Gergen's procedure would seem to have promise as a fairly direct approach to the problem. It is at least conceivable that the proposition only holds for harmful actions, and that persons are much less sensitive to variations in personalism when positive actions are involved. This may be especially true when these positive actions involve verbal compliments. The reluctance of subjects to assume that a compliment was not intended for them personally is discussed in detail by Jones (1964). In this same source the reader will find a fuller exposition of the Gergen experiment along with results of other dependent variable measures which were more central to his concerns.

1. Factors Mitigating One's Evaluation of an Aggressor

More indirect and yet more promising evidence on the role of personalism comes from experiments concerned with the factors which mitigate one person's reactions to being verbally attacked or insulted by another. The basic paradigm involves comparing perceivers' reactions to the same attacking action when it occurs in different settings. Typically, one setting is designed to bring out reciprocal hostility in the subjects (in the form of highly negative impression ratings) while other settings are arranged to check whether factors which theoretically should mitigate a hostile reaction in fact do. We are especially interested in those studies within this paradigm which exemplify variations in the perceived personalism of the attack.

a. Provocation by the perceiver. An obvious mitigating variable which comes to mind is the extent to which the attack is seen as justified by the target person. If the perceiver believes he has done something to earn attack, insult, or rejection, he will presumably be less inclined to appraise his attacker negatively than if the attack was unreasonable or arbitrary. For example, Deutsch and Solomon (1959) found that subjects who were led to believe they had performed poorly on a task were less negative in appraising a stimulus person who rejected them as future work partners than subjects who were led to believe they had performed well.

A similar point is brought out by the results of an experiment by Strickland *et al.* (1960) on the effects of group support in evaluating an antagonist. Each subject met first with two other subjects who shared his opinions (pro or con) about the role of big-time athletics in university life. He then privately chose a series of five arguments to support his position. These were to be transmitted to a person in the next room who was presumably neither for nor against big-time athletics. After this person had a chance to study the arguments, he was interviewed by the experimenter who probed his feelings about the person who sent the arguments. This interview was broadcast into the subject's room and it contained a strong attack on his intelligence and integrity.

However, prior to his exposure to the broadcast interview (which was actually a standardized tape-recording), the subject learned that his fellow group members would either have chosen the same arguments he did (group support) or would have chosen a very different set (no support). The subject's final ratings of the person in the next room—which tapped into such dispositional characteristics as intelligence, warmth, adjustment, conceit, and likeability—were affected by this variation in group support. These rating differences were corroborated by free response sketches in which each subject expressed his private feelings about the person. Those whose arguments were supported were more negative in their evaluations of the person in the next room than those whose arguments were not supported.

In neither the Deutsch and Solomon (1959) nor the Strickland et al. (1960) study was the potential for perceiver personalism particularly high. In each, regardless of the experimental condition, a very limited sample of the subjects' behavior was the stimulus occasion for attack or rejection. The subject did not, in other words, expose the full range of his personal characteristics as a preface to the attack received. Nevertheless, the attack was directed toward him ostensibly because of behavior for which he must bear at least some of the responsibility.

We now suggest that an attack in the face of good performance (or group support) is more apt to be viewed as an attempt to harm or to disadvantage the subject than an attack in response to poor performance, because after a poor performance (including the sending of arguments defined as inferior by the group), the attacker will be seen as more constrained to respond negatively. The correspondence value of his hostile action, in other words, will be lowered by the presence in the choice area of effects having more to do with fulfillment of task requirements, candor, and realism than with hostility. Since there are fewer reasons for the antagonist's attack in the good performance setting, and one of these is presumably the antagonist's desire to hurt the subject as a person, correspondence and therefore unfavorability of general impression are high in this latter case.

b. *Evidence of chronicity.* Another factor which mitigates a perceiver's evaluation of an antagonist is any evidence concerning the latter's general tendency to be indiscriminately aggressive. If the antagonist is known to be or gives fairly good evidence of being a chronically dyspeptic or uncontrollably negative person, his derogation will have less sting for the target person who bears its brunt.

Two recent experiments by Berkowitz (1960), conducted in quite a different framework from the one we are here proposing, shed some light on the effects of a perceiver's prior knowledge of a particular attack. Since only the first of the Berkowitz studies is particularly relevant to our present concerns, we shall confine ourselves to that.

Pairs of subjects were brought together for a study of first impressions. Through a bogus note exchange, the subject received information first, indicating that the partner was either generally hostile or generally friendly and second, indicating that the partner either liked or disliked the subject personally. The subject recorded his impression of the partner once at the outset of the experiment, once after the general information, and once after the personal evaluation from the partner.

The results showed that if the partner was perceived to be hostile initially, the partner's favorable evaluation of the subject had a decidedly ameliorating effect on the subject's impression, while the unfavorable evaluation changed this impression very little. Similarly, if the subject initially perceived the partner to be friendly, the unfavorable evaluation received from the partner created a striking change of impression in the direction of perceived unfriendliness, while the favorable evaluation resulted in minimal change.

It would appear, then, that the fact of prior knowledge concerning the hostility of the attacker reduces the personal significance of the attack. If we look more closely at the Berkowitz results, however, the point they make is actually rather different from the one we are presently pursuing. If a person who is already seen as generally hostile attacks the perceiver, there will be less of a *decline* (from the second to the third rating) than if a friendly person attacks the perceiver. However, the subject actually ends up liking the hostile attacker less than the friendly attacker, presumably because the evidence concerning the undesirable characteristic, hostility, summates: two hostility indicators are worse than one. The Berkowitz results really do not suggest that the perceiver is less bothered or upset by the attack if he has already decided that the attacker is generally hostile. They merely tell us that the attack is not as unexpected from a hostile person and therefore it contributes less to a change in impression from a point that is more negative to start with. We are dealing here, then, with the attempt on the part of the perceiver-subject to appraise the significance of a particular action choice against background information about different prior choices.

In order to confirm the significance of perceived general hostility as a prior choice factor mitigating the significance of the attack, the results would have to show that the generally hostile attacker is better liked by the recipient of the attack than the friendly attacker. However, such a finding might be difficult to obtain experimentally. After all, the fact that he is hostile does not make the attacker likeable to anybody. It merely means that the attack itself will cause less of a stir.

Evidence from a recent experiment does indicate that someone who starts out being derogatory and continues to act that way is better liked than someone who starts out being favorably disposed to the subject and becomes increasingly derogatory (Aronson and Linder, 1965). In this experiment the subject believed he was over-hearing a series of appraisals referring to him with short episodes of social interaction intervening; he was not the target of openly expressed hostility. This may be a critical difference between the Berkowitz design and the Aronson and Linder design. Another difference that may have been crucial is that the former study asked for an intervening rating (which might have "committed" the subject to a particular rating of the attacker) while the latter study did not.

If we return to the conditions of the Berkowitz experiment, it may be too much to expect the hostile attacker to be better liked than the friendly attacker. What is needed is a comparison between the target of the attack and an "innocent" bystander as regards their impressions of the attacker. Because of the general negative significance attached to being hostile, it does not make sense to predict that either the involved subject or the bystander would like the hostile attacker better than the friendly one. However, a more refined and promising hypothesis, still in the spirit of our earlier remarks on the role of personalism, is that the involved subject will dislike the hostile attacker less than the bystander, relative to the discrepancy between their impressions of the friendly attacker.

c. Emotional adjustment of the attacker. Such an experimental comparison has yet to be made, unfortunately, but the results of an earlier experiment by Jones *et al.* (1959) can be interpreted quite nicely in these terms. The procedures of the study by Jones *et al.*, were roughly as follows. At a given experimental session, a pair of female subjects listened to two female stimulus persons allegedly conversing about one of the subjects in an adjacent room. The conversation was actually a carefully written and skillfully acted tape-recording. The stimulus persons were allegedly enrolled in a "senior course in personality assessment" and it was their duty to observe a designated subject through the one-way mirror for a period of time and then to discuss their impressions of that subject. It was clear to them that their remarks would be overheard by the subjects in the adjacent room. One of the stimulus persons was generally neutral or mildly favorable in her comments, but the other stimulus person ("the derogator") was decidedly hostile and clearly had a low opinion of the subject. The subject whose characteristics were not being discussed was instructed to sit aside as a bystander and to pay close attention to the proceedings.

Prior to the attack, both the involved and bystander subject were given some information about the two students who would be observing them from the next room. It was clear upon reading this information that one of these students was quite maladjusted: She had an unstable home life, inadequate emotional resources, and underlying anxiety. The other student was presented as an effective, well-rounded, insightful undergraduate who had reached her present station from a home life that had been happy and rich with support and affection. For one group of subjects (the *derogator-mal* group), the data sheets presented the stimulus person who did not derogate as well adjusted. For a second group of subjects (the *derogator-well* group), the background information sheets were simply reversed.

After the involved and the bystander subjects listened to the tape-recorded discussion, including the derogatory remarks, they were each instructed to rate the two stimulus persons on a number of items. The items with which we are particularly concerned at the present are two reflecting the perceived likeability of the stimulus person. The subjects were asked to indicate the extent of their agreement with the two statements: "As a person, she is extremely likeable," and "I find it hard to like this person to any extent."

Thus the experimental manipulations created a standard situation in which a subject was derogated by a well-adjusted or a maladjusted person while another subject looked on. The variable of perceived maladjustment was included, in effect, to see whether it would serve as a factor mitigating the subject's response to the derogator. Jones *et al.,* reasoned that the involved subject would be less upset by an attack from a maladjusted person than by an attack from a well-adjusted one. The bystander, on the other hand, was expected to be less concerned in general with the derogation and its implications for inferences about the derogator's personality, and more inclined to prefer the well-adjusted person because she was probably more appealing and talented. The prediction, then, was that there would be a statistical interaction between role (involved versus bystander) and condition of the derogator (maladjusted versus well adjusted).

The data were analyzed in terms of each subject's relative preference for the nonderogator over the derogator, a procedure adopted to reduce that portion of rating variability due to individual differences in scale interpretation or style of responding to the scale items. (Some such device is usually essential in an "after-only" design.) The crucial results are summarized in Table III. It is evident that there is a general dislike for people who are derogatory and a general preference for people who are well adjusted. When these two factors work in the same direction (as in the first column of the table), the discrepancy scores are understandably large. Of greater theoretical interest, when the derogator is well adjusted, the involved subject obviously likes her much less than the bystander subject ($p < .025$). To a slight extent, the average bystander even prefers

TABLE III
JOINT EFFECTS OF DEROGATOR ADJUSTMENT AND SUBJECT INVOLVEMENT
ON "LIKEABILITY"[a,b]

	Condition	
	Derogator-mal	Derogator-well
Involved subjects		
$\bar{X}$	3.92	2.17
SD	(1.78)	(2.29)
Bystander subjects		
$\bar{X}$	4.33	−.57
SD	(3.17)	(3.96)

[a] Based on discrepancy between ratings of derogator and nonderogator. The larger the mean value, the greater the tendency to dislike the derogator *relative to* the nonderogator.
[b] Data from Jones *et al.* (1959).

the well-adjusted derogator to the maladjusted nonderogator (as indicated by the minus sign in that cell). When the derogator is maladjusted, however, the involved subject actually likes her better than the bystander does (though this difference does not approach statistical significance). The predicted interaction effect is minimally significant ($t = 1.877$; $p < .05$, one-tailed test).

In the context of the present discussion, we would argue that the personalistic significance of the derogation is obviously greater for the involved subject than for the bystander, and that it is greater for the involved subject when the derogator is well adjusted than maladjusted. When the derogator is maladjusted, the involved subject can take comfort in the hypothesis that the attacker's hostility is a symptom of her own problems and she would express similar insults to anyone who came within range. Perceived personalism should be fairly low. When the derogator is well adjusted, the involved subject will be more likely than the bystander to package the insulting remarks into one cluster of highly related hedonic effects, and therefore to assign more correspondent, personalistic meaning to the attack. There is no easy way to escape the inference that the derogator finds the subject personally offensive and is "against her."

The maladjustment treatment in the preceding experiment may be construed in terms of the reduction of freedom to choose which accompanies poor adjustment, and the perception of these restraints on choice by the perceiver. Perhaps the prevailing stereotypes of mental health and mental illness contribute to the tendency to perceive the maladjusted person as not responsible for the trouble he may cause others. Under the proper circumstances, however, he may be seen as *more* responsible for causing trouble than the normal, well-adjusted actor. At least such is the implication of some results from the experiment by Gergen and Jones (1963).

d. Amplification by ambivalence. Gergen and Jones set out to test a set of hypotheses deriving from the assumption that people are ambivalent toward the mentally ill. Many persons expect the mentally ill to have annoying characteristics but inhibit their annoyance because they acknowledge the fact that they are not responsible for their condition and its consequences. Gergen and Jones reasoned that the ambivalence toward a particular mentally ill person would be "split" if a situation were arranged in which his behavior had clear positive or negative consequences for the perceiver. Thus a perceiver should like a benevolent mentally ill person better than a benevolent normal person, and dislike a malevolent mentally ill person more than a malevolent normal person.

In order to test this hypothesis (which was loosely derived from psychoanalytic writings on ambivalence), 64 ambulatory V.A. hospital patients (nonpsychiatric) were given the task of predicting a series of hypothetical consumer choices being made by a patient in the adjoining room. The patient in the next room was alleged to be in the hospital either with a psychiatric illness or with a minor organic ailment. Actually there was no person in the next room, and all the information about him was conveyed by a combination of tape-recorded interviews and feedback through equipment controlled by the experimenter.

The choices of the patient in the adjoining room (hereafter called the stimulus person) were either very hard or very easy to predict. In the *low consequence* (i.e., low relevance) condition, the stimulus person (actually, by a ruse, the experimenter) provided corrective feedback by an informative signal light whenever a prediction error was made. In the *high consequence* condition, prediction errors called forth a raucous buzzer of unpredictable duration. The experimenter also made it clear that he found the buzzer very annoying, implying that it was up to the subject to keep him happy by making the correct predictions. Both before the prediction task and after it was completed, the subject filled out an impression rating scale indicating his current feelings about the stimulus person.

The experimental hypothesis was stated as follows: "Evaluative judgments of a mentally ill stimulus person vary little as a function of predictability unless affective consequences are attached to success and failure of prediction. The role of affective consequences is less important

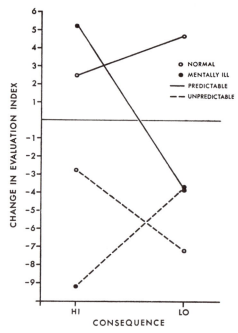

FIG. 5. Changes in evaluation as a function of mental status, predictability, and consequence. (Data from Gergen and Jones, 1963.)

in evaluative judgments of a normal stimulus person. Judgments of the normal should directly reflect variations in predictability, regardless of the consequences of judgment" (Gergen and Jones, 1963, p. 70).

The results presented in Fig. 5 quite strikingly confirm this complicated hypothesis. There is, as implied by the hypothesis, a significant statistical interaction between the three factors of normality, predictability, and consequence. The most striking thing to note is the extent to which consequence determines perceptions of the mentally ill person. When he is in a position to hurt the subject or to spare him pain—in short, when he is either benevolent or malevolent toward the perceiver—the mentally ill stimulus person is judged very favorably or unfavorably. When there are no such personal consequences for the perceiver, the stimulus person's predictability is not a relevant factor in judging him. (There is also an overall effect of predictability such that, across conditions, the predictable person tends to be evaluated more positively than the unpredictable person.)

Furthermore, it may be shown that the perception of benevolent versus malevolent intentions is involved in the subject's judgments of the high consequence-mentally ill person. A variation of the experiment was run in which the stimulus person had supposedly made his consumer choice days before and was not, as alleged in the main experiment, actually in the next room at the time and responding through his own actions to the subject's predictions. In other words, all feedback to the subjects (including the unpleasant buzzer) was openly controlled by the experimenter. The experiment was in all other respects a precise replication of the first version. In this variation, predictability again had a strong effect on average evaluations, but there were no main or interaction differences as a function of consequence or normality. There must, then, be some possibility that the stimulus person is deliberately hurting or sparing the subject for the complex effects noted in the first experiment to occur.

There are many questions raised by the Gergen and Jones experiment. There are also special problems involved in relating these results to the Jones *et al.* (1959) findings. In interpreting those findings we argued, in effect, that an attack by a maladjusted stimulus person was less devastating than an attack by a well-adjusted stimulus person, because the normal person is perceived to have greater freedom of choice. It is as if evidence concerning maladjustment acts as a damper on the intensity of personal feeling toward the maladjusted person. The Gergen and Jones results, however, seem to show that under certain conditions evidence concerning maladjustment (i.e., mental illness) *amplifies* rather than constricts the intensity of the perceiver's personal feelings. Does this mean that the mentally ill person is assumed to have greater freedom of choice than the normal person in the Gergen and Jones study?

In spite of certain superficial resemblances, the experiments are really quite different in several, crucial respects. In the earlier experiment the very meaning and intensity of the attack is presumably a function of the attacker's adjustment status. To be insulted by a pathetic, perhaps mildly paranoid person is hardly to be insulted at all. In the Gergen and Jones experiment, however, the consequences of the attack are embarrassing, painful, and irritating, regardless of their source. In this case, furthermore, the question of freedom to choose may actually exacerbate rather than mitigate the response to the mentally ill stimulus person.

While the data do not force this interpretation on us, there is at least nothing inconsistent in the rating or the post-experimental questionnaire results with the following speculations: When unpredictability hurts, the "why" of the unpredictability becomes a more important issue to the one who suffers. Two possible effects of "buzzing" the subject in the high consequence condition are especially salient, hurting the subject and being honest to one's true preferences for certain consumer objects. In the replication of the experiment, the first of these effects is ruled out by the change in information about the role of the stimulus person. Perhaps it is the case that when the stimulus person is normal, the most likely hypothesis is that he is making "normal choices" and, therefore, that the subject must take at least some of the blame for not being able to figure these out. When the stimulus person is mentally ill, on the other hand, the abnormal choice becomes an instrument of malevolence. Since the choice is a function of abnormality, it is difficult for the subject to maintain the feelings of sympathy which, in the low consequence condition, are sufficient to keep his impression a fairly neutral one. The impression of malevolence may be heightened by the feeling that since the mentally ill person is confused about his choices anyway, the least he can do is to go along with the subject's predictions and not lean on the error buzzer.

Such speculations are obviously no substitute for clear and compelling data on the role of perceived choice in the assignment of benevolent or malevolent intentions. The preceding review of studies involving the effects of personalism, studies mainly focusing on factors which mitigate a target person's response to being attacked, points up the need for additional research into the cognitive consequences of being singled out for benefit or harm. Those of us who have done research on this problem have lacked the kind of integrating framework which is needed to carry out a series of related studies. Perhaps the theory of correspondent inferences will help to provide a focus for the parametric experiments which are needed in clarifying the basic facts about personalism and its implications.

2. Personalism and Ingratiation

We have defined as personalistic those actions which are relevant to the perceiver's interests and, as far as the perceiver can tell, are deliberately carried out by the actor because of this relevance. The concept of personalism inevitably implies a certain degree of choice on the part of the actor which is not inherent in the concept of relevance. Since the condition of choice increases the likelihood of correspondent inferences, the coexistence of relevance and personalism should produce rather extreme evaluative judgments. It seems intuitively plausible that someone who helps us will be seen as more generous, helpful, friendly, etc., than someone who helps another in our presence. A comparable line of thought applies to the case of malevolent actions when we have been singled out as their target.

In an attempt to provide a more rational basis for this intuition, we suggest the following distinctions and their consequences. There are three basic decisions which lurk in the wings during an interaction episode: whether to approach the person further and open oneself to him, whether to avoid or ignore him, or whether he must be "coped with," i.e., attacked or fended off. When the effects of an action are relevant in the positive direction, the decision is typically made to approach further. Such a decision is likely to be made whether or not the action is personalistic in addition to being relevant. When the effects of an action are negative, however, the imputation of personalism means that coping may be necessary. In other words, if a person's actions happen to offend you, he can merely be avoided—unless he is intent on offending you and will go out of his way to accomplish this objective. To the extent that coping is required, we would expect greater hostility to be aroused toward the threatening person, and those characteristics associated with malevolence should be inferred with higher correspondence. This might be partly a matter of justifying the hostility and partly a matter of keeping it at a high enough level (through self-reminding instigations) to support coping behavior.

On the basis of this reasoning, it would appear that personalism plays a larger role when an action is harmful than when it is beneficial. The examples we have cited, along with most of the relevant experiments in the literature, describe the response of a perceiver to some form of attack or rejection. However, a number of experiments have recently been completed which deal with first impressions in response to beneficial gestures, compliments, and agreements. These studies raise a new set of considerations which we shall discuss in concluding our treatment of the role of personalism.

We have argued that negative actions lead the target person either to avoid the actor or to mobilize cognitive support for the actions involved in coping with him. Positive actions, on the other hand, lead to approach behaviors, personal openness, and reciprocation in kind. But a new and complicated problem arises with respect to positive actions. The perceiver must determine their credibility; to what extent does the beneficial act correspond with the intention really to improve the situation of the perceiver as an end in itself? As Jones (1964) has argued in his extended discussion of *ingratiation,* beneficial actions tend to be much more ambiguous than harmful actions when it comes to deciding on the actor's true intention or his ultimate objectives in the situation. The ambiguity of beneficial actions centers around the extent to which ulterior, manipulative purposes may be served by them.

We may now ask, what implications are contained in the theory of correspondent inferences for predicting the cognitive impressions of someone faced with beneficial action? First of all, it is clear that the ambiguity arises because there are at least two classes of effects following from those actions. Actions such as compliments, agreements, and favors may validate the perceiver's self-concept, reduce his uncertainties, offer support against antagonists. Alternatively, or in addition, such actions may have the effect of obligating the perceiver to benefit the actor in return. If the first class of effects is the most salient, the perceiver will attribute to the actor the intention to express his true feelings. From this starting point, correspondent inferences will be drawn to such dispositions as candor, friendliness, likeability, and generosity. In short, the perceiver's evaluation of the actor who has complimented him or agreed with him will be positive. If, on the other hand, the second effect, creating obligations to benefit, is salient and noncommon, the actor may be seen as manipulative, self-seeking, conforming, lacking in candor, etc.

Whether the inference process is tipped in the first, positive direction or the second, negative direction depends on the perceiver's reconstruction of the action alternatives available to the actor. This cognitive reconstruction will depend, in turn, on the perceiver's own role as one of the components in the actor's situation. Specifically, if the perceiver does not control any resources which are important to the actor, then the circle containing the effects of the chosen alternative will not contain the effect of "obligating the perceiver to benefit the actor in return." Presumably, then, some such effect as "validating the self-concept" will be salient and the perceiver will be seen as intending an honest compliment or expressing his genuine agreement with the perceiver's opinions.

If the perceiver does control resources important to the actor (i.e., if the actor is dependent on him), it will be hard for him to decide whether he is merely the target of an ingratiation attempt or the target of honest compliments. At the very least, the correspondence of inference to favorable dispositions will be reduced as a function of his own position as a dispenser of valuable resources. Depending on the circumstances, the perceiver may infer flattering or manipulative intentions and assign unfavorable dispositions, or he may infer benevolent intentions reflecting favorable dispositions.

Let us now consider three recent experiments which support the conclusions of the above line of reasoning. Jones *et al.* (1963) conducted an experiment in which upper classmen in a campus R.O.T.C. unit exchanged written messages with freshmen in the same unit. This exchange occurred in response to two different sets of instructions, constituting the major treatments of the experiments. In the *ingratiation* condition, both the high and low status subjects were given instructions concerning the importance of compatibility. The experimenter said he was trying to find a number of highly compatible leader-follower pairs to participate in some crucial studies on leadership later in the year. In the *control* condition, the message exchange was presented as part of a first impression study and the importance of "not misleading your partner" was stressed.

The messages that were sent concerned opinions on a variety of issues and eventually contained ratings by each subject of himself and his partner. These messages were actually intercepted and standard information about each subject was conveyed to his partner. Each found the other agreed with him on a variety of opinion issues, presented a rather modest view of himself, and expressed a complimentary view of his partner, the message recipient. On a post-experimental questionnaire (not to be seen by the partner) he was asked to rate the partner with respect

TABLE IV
PERCEPTION OF FLATTERY[a,b]

	Perceiver group						
	HS			LS			
	M	SD	N	M	SD	N	P_{diff}
Ingratiation	13.05	4.14	19	9.62	3.16	21	.01
Control	11.68	4.46	19	11.85	3.41	20	ns

[a] Mean post-experimental ratings in each condition and differences between them. The higher the mean score, the greater the perceived flattery.
[b] Data from Jones *et al.* (1963).

to the following trait dimensions: completely sincere—on the phony side, trustworthy—unreliable, and brutally frank—flatterer. Each pair of antonyms was separated by a twelve-point scale. By adding a subject's rating on each of the three traits, he could be given a score ranging from 3 to 36 with a "perceived average" value at 19.5.

The results are presented in Table IV. They show that high and low status subjects perceived each other to be equally sincere in the control condition, but that the low status subjects attributed significantly greater sincerity to the highs than the highs did to the lows in the ingratiation condition. Restricting our concern to the ingratiation condition, we would say that the inference concerning sincerity is more correspondent for the low status perceivers than for the highs. Relative to the hypothetical average value of 19.5, the empirical mean of 9.62 is more extreme than the mean of 13.05.

This could have been predicted from the theory of correspondent inferences on the grounds that fewer noncommon effects were involved in the high status person's decisions to compliment the low status person than vice versa. Since the low status person was, presumably, in greater need of approval than the high status person, the latter may have been more apt to include "reciprocation of approval" among the effects serving as grist for the inference process. This could, then, have led to reduced correspondence of inference, i.e., ratings of sincerity which were closer to the mean or, in effect, greater perceived flattery.

Such an interpretation is quite *post hoc* and we offer it to illustrate how the theory might account for such findings rather than as confirmation of the theory. The problem is that other assumptions (which we believe are plausible) must be introduced to account for the fact that low status subjects perceive the highs to be more sincere in the ingratiation than in the control condition.

A study by Jones *et al.* (1963) was more explicitly designed to test the hypothesis that positive, supportive behavior will be taken more at face value as a genuine indication of sincerity and good intentions when the actor is not dependent on the target person. The supportive behavior, in this case, was consistently high agreement with the latter's opinions. Dependence was manipulated in a manner simular to the preceding experiment. Unlike the conditions of that experiment, the subjects were not themselves the targets of agreement, but served in the role of bystanders. Their task was to evaluate a stimulus person who agrees very closely with another person on whom he is obviously very dependent *or* not dependent at all.

In general, when the agreeing person was presented as dependent for approval on the other, he was better liked and was assigned more positive characteristics when he did not agree too closely. When dependence was low, on the other hand, the degree of agreement did not affect the ratings to any significant extent. Once again, the actor's condition of dependence affected the significance attached to highly "ingratiating" behavior. The subjects felt neutral about the high dependent conformist, because they did not know whether he was conforming for strategic advantage or whether his opinion agreement was coincidental. The fact that he was dependent, thus, increased the ambiguity of his behavior by adding the granting of approval to those possible effects of action with which the perceiver had to come to terms in his evaluation.

A study by Hilda Dickoff (discussed in Jones, 1964) also showed quite clearly that an actor who consistently compliments the perceiver is better liked when he is not dependent on the latter. Dependence has no effect when the evaluation received is still positive but contains a few plausible reservations.

The obvious feature of all of these studies is the fact that the same behavior (actions which can be seen as ingratiating in intent) results in quite different inferences depending on the context in which it occurs.

More specifically, the studies on ingratiation which we have cited share a concern with the variable, dependence, as the contextual conditions whose presence or absence affects causal attribution. Our inference that a complimentary or agreeable person really likes us is apt to be stronger if we are unable to think of anything we have that he might covet. In other words, the compliments or expression of opinions will be taken at face value and correspondence will be high when the actor has no apparent reason to choose the compliment other than his belief that it applies to us.

Now let us return to the notion of personalism and note an apparent qualification of our proposition that personalism increases correspondence. It may appear that when we are dealing with actions that are potentially ingratiating, correspondence *declines* as a function of personalism. Compliments to one's face are harder to evaluate than the same positive statements said behind our back. Opinions which agree with our own are more apt to be taken at face value when expressed prior to our opinion avowals than after such avowals.

We would not argue with the above interpretations in these hypothetical cases. We would claim, however, that personalism is involved in quite different ways in the kind of face-to-face confrontation where ingratiation is an issue and in the case of negative or neutral information. In fact, ingratiation only becomes an issue in the absence of indications that personalism is involved. The person who receives a face-to-face compliment must decide whether that compliment was meant for him because of his unique personal qualities, or was meant for anyone who happened to occupy a position as a potential dispenser of resources. The high status person may have a difficult problem arranging conditions to test the reactions of his subordinates to him as a person; it may be hard for him to get certain kinds of self-validating information. The important point is that actions that may be seen as directed toward him as an occupant of a social position may therefore not be personalistic and the correspondence value of inferences derived from such ambiguous actions is apt to be low.

IV. Summary and Conclusions

In the present essay we have attempted to develop a systematic conceptual framework for research on person perception. We have been especially interested in specifying the antecedent conditions for attributing intentions or dispositions, having observed an action. Dispositional attributes are in a general way inferred from the effects of action, but not every effect is equally salient in the inference process. Even if we assume as perceivers that the actor *knew* what the effects of his action would be, we must still engage in the complex analytic process of selectively linking certain effects achieved to certain effects intended. This assignment of intentions can provide sufficient reason for (or explanation of) the action, so that the perceiver may go about his interpersonal business unfettered by a concern with ultimate or infinitely regressive causes.

Our most central assumption in considering the attribution of intentions is that actions are informative to the extent that they have emerged out of a context of choice and reflect a selection of one among plural alternatives. When we pursue the implications of this assumption in some detail, it is apparent that the distinctiveness of the effects achieved and the extent to which they do not represent stereotypic cultural values determine the likelihood that information about the actor will be extracted from an action. We have used the term "correspondence of inference" to refer to variations in this kind of informativeness. To say that an inference is correspondent, then, is to say that a disposition is being rather directly reflected in behavior, and that this disposition is unusual in its strength or intensity. Operationally, correspondence means ratings toward the extremes of trait dimensions which are given with confidence.

Having formulated the inference problem in these terms, an obvious research question arises. What are the factors which control the perceiver's judgment that the actor had a choice? Or, more precisely, what conditions influence his judgment concerning the number and distinctiveness (non-commonness) of effects? It is our hope that cumulative, perhaps even parametric, research will be stimulated by posing the inference problem in these terms. A study in which the stimulus person either went along with or resisted clearly stated role-demands, was presented to exemplify some of the more obvious implications of the theory. The results of the study may be interpreted as showing that a low degree of "psychological" choice is functionally the same thing as having many reasons for making a choice. In-role behavior is supported by too many reasons to be informative about the actor; out-of-role behavior is more informative because the effects of such actions are distinctive (few in number) and not to be dismissed as culturally desirable.

In the latter portions of the present essay we have considered the further complexities associated with perceiver involvement which affect theoretical predictions concerning inferred attributes. Our analysis distinguished between two levels of involvement: hedonic relevance and personalism. An actor's choice is hedonically relevant for the perceiver if, on balance, it promotes or thwarts his purposes. An action is personalistic, in the perceiver's view, if it was uniquely conditioned by the latter's presence: if conditions are such that the perceiver believes he is the intended consumer of the effects produced by the actor.

In discussing the various effects of relevance, we argued that correspondence generally increases with increasing relevance. Evaluation, in turn, is a joint function of both relevance and correspondence. A small number of studies were discussed which seem to shed some light on the impact of relevance. In particular, it was noted that if one holds relevance constant (at some value other than zero) and manipulates the variables alleged to increase correspondence, evaluation becomes more extreme. Similarly, by pegging correspondence at a particular level and increasing relevance, the same increase in evaluation extremity may be observed. It should be emphasized, however, that much of the research cited was only indirectly concerned with variations in relevance. More systematic research is needed to establish the conditions under which relevance calls forth positive or negative evaluations. In addition, we need to know much more about the relations between affective and cognitive processes implied by the linkage between relevance and correspondence.

In the final section on personalism, we discussed a study in which this variable was directly and dramatically manipulated, only to acknowledge that the effects were negligible. It will be important to establish the reasons for this curious result by designing other experiments which directly approach different facets of the complex personalism variable. There is, however, indirect or circumstantial evidence which encourages the conviction that personalism and hedonic relevance are not identical in their effects. Specifically, we discussed several experiments which were concerned with the mitigation versus amplification of hostility toward an attacker. Here it was seen that the intensity of hostile reciprocation was affected by factors in the situation which made it more or less likely that personalism was involved. Such factors as sufficiency of provocation and indiscriminateness of the attack, were shown to affect the recipient's evaluation of the attacker. These conditions could be, and were, discussed in terms of the correspondence-noncommon effect theory. Several experiments on ingratiation and the perception of flattery were also discussed in these terms. The main dilemma of the perceiver, when he becomes the target of actions which may be ingratiating in intent, is to determine whether he is being benefited because of his unique personal qualities or because of the resources which he may control.

This essay, long as it is, could have been much longer if we had hedged our statements with proper qualifications and dealt fully with the problems which remain in our formulation. We have no illusions that we have finally opened the main door on the mysteries of causal attribution. Our formulation has changed considerably since our work on this essay began, and it will undoubtedly change much more with further thought. We trust it is also obvious that the ability to accommodate old findings from complex experiments is an easy hurdle for any theory to jump. We remain optimistic, however, that the present framework encourages systematic thinking about inferring dispositions from actions and suggests some of the major variables that merit initial consideration.

REFERENCES

Aronson, E. and Linder, D. (1965). Gain and loss of esteem as determinants of interpersonal attractiveness. *J. exp. soc. Psychol.* **1**, 156–172.

Berkowitz, L. (1960). Repeated frustrations and expectations in hostility arousal. *J. abnorm. soc. Psychol.* **60**, 422–429.

Davis, K. E. (1962). Impressions of others and interaction context as determinants of social interaction and perception in two-person discussion groups. Unpublished doctoral dissertation, Duke Univer.

Deutsch, M., and Solomon, L. (1959). Reactions to evaluations by others as influenced by self-evaluations. *Sociometry* **22**, 93–112.

Gergen, K. J. (1962). Interaction goals and personalistic feedback as factors affecting the presentation of the self. Unpublished doctoral dissertation, Duke Univer.

Gergen, K. J., and Jones, E. E. (1963). Mental illness, predictability, and affective consequences as stimulus factors in person perception. *J. abnorm. soc. Psychol.* **67**, 95–104.

Heider, F. (1944). Social perception and phenomenal causality. *Psychol. Rev.* **51**, 358–374.

Heider, F. (1958). *The psychology of interpersonal relations.* New York: Wiley.

Jones, E. E. (1964). *Ingratiation.* Appleton, New York.

Jones, E. E., and Daugherty, B. (1959). Political orientation and the perceptual effects of an anticipated interaction. *J. abnorm. soc. Psychol.* **59**, 340–349.

Jones, E. E., and deCharms, R. (1957). Changes in social perception as a function of the personal relevance of behavior. *Sociometry* **20**, 75–85.

Jones, E. E., Hester, S. L. Farina, A., and Davis, K. E. (1959). Reactions to unfavorable personal evaluations as a function of the evaluator's perceived adjustment. *J. abnorm. soc. Psychol.* **59**, 363–370.

Jones, E. E., Davis, K. E., and Gergen, K. J. (1961). Role playing variations and their informational value for person perception. *J. abnorm. soc. Psychol.* **63**, 302–310.

Jones, E. E., Gergen, K. J., and Jones, R. G. (1963). Tactics of ingratiation among leaders and subordinates in a status hierarchy. *Psychol. Monogr.* **77**,

Jones, E. E., Jones, R. G., and Gergen, K. J. (1964). Some conditions affecting No. 3 (Whole No. 566). the evaluation of a conformist. *J. Pers.* **31**, 270–288.

Jones, E. E., Gergen, K. J., Gumpert, P., and Thibaut, J. W. (1965). Some conditions affecting the use of ingratiation to influence performance evaluation. *J. pers. soc. Psychol.* **1**, 613–626.

Kleiner, R. J. (1960). The effects of threat reduction upon interpersonal attractiveness. *J. Pers.* **28**, 145–156.

Pepitone, A. (1950). Motivational effects in social perception. *Hum. Relat.* **1**, 57–76.

Steiner, I. D., and Field, W. L. (1960). Role assignment and interpersonal influence. *J. abnorm. soc. Psychol.* **61**, 239–246.

Strickland, L. H., Jones, E. E., and Smith, W. P. (1960). Effects of group support on the evaluation of an antagonist. *J. abnorm. soc. Psychol.* **61**, 73–81.

Thibaut, J. W., and Riecken, H. W. (1955). Some determinants and consequences of the perception of social causality. *J. Pers.* **24**, 113–133.

Update of "From Acts to Dispositions: The Attribution Process in Person Perception"

Edward E. Jones

PRINCETON UNIVERSITY

More than 12 years have passed since the original presentation of correspondent inference theory. In the intervening period there have been numerous important developments in our theoretical under-standing of person perception, and the attributional approach has been extended to accommodate self-perception, interpersonal conflict, emotional experience, and divergent perceptual perspec-tives. Kelley's (1967) seminal paper had much to do with these exten-sions, as did the volume of original essays by Jones, Kanouse, Kelley, Nisbett, Valins, and Weiner (1972).

Flexibility rather than hypothetico-deductive rigor has been the strength of the attributional approach, and this adaptive flexibility has made possible the development of numerous attribution-based theories of important psychological phenomena. But in spite of the modish shift toward the attributional analysis of traditional problems in interpersonal relations, the growth of basic attribution theory itself has been somewhat stunted. In 1976 Jones and McGillis (in Harvey, Ickes, & Kidd, 1976) engaged in a tenth anniversary reexamination of correspondent inference theory in an attempt to shore up the weak-nesses of that theory and to integrate the Jones and Davis framework with the Kelley model. This brief account will attempt to summarize the major points of that reanalysis and to comment on some of the major empirical consequences of the 1965 paper.

Correspondent inference theory is essentially a theory of informa-

Cognitive Theories in Social Psychology

tion *gain*—it concerns changes in one's impressions, brought about by behavioral evidence. An expectation is to some extent violated, and the perceiver must come to terms with the new information reflected in this violation. Correspondent inference theory is an attempt to explain how the expectancy violation might be resolved. The earlier Jones and Davis formulation referred to these expectancies under the heading of cultural desirability, but I now view this as unduly restrictive. The more generic view of an expectancy may be phrased in terms of the prior probability that an actor would desire a certain effect. This prior probability is in turn determined both by assumptions of cultural desirability and by any specific knowledge the perceiver has concerning the actor and his prior behavior. For convenience we may refer to the former as *category-based* expectancies and the latter as *target-based* expectancies, although any given expectancy is very likely to be a combination of the two in the natural world. An exciting challenge for future research is to determine whether these different expectancy origins have different consequences in the event that the expectancy is violated by some act of the target person. In one such attempt, Jones and Berglas (1976) were unable to detect any systematic differences in the combining of action data with category-based versus target-based expectancies.

Whether the prior probability of the target person's desire for an effect or consequence derives from category-based or target-based expectancies, it seems useful to conceive of a valence attached to each of the effects of an observed action. Such a valence has a theoretical value ranging from a-1 to a $+1$. A maximally undesirable effect will have a -1, indicating the highest probability that the target person would seek to avoid that effect. A $+1$ valence would signify maximum desirability, either because the effect is universally sought, sought by all members of a category to which the target person belongs, or known to be sought vigorously by him in the past. From the point of view of information gain, pursuit of a low valence effect should lead to greater correspondence of inference, other things equal, than pursuit of a high valence effect.

This reformulation of the cultural desirability variable in terms of a valence measure of a prior probability is intended to extend the generality of correspondent inference theory. The theory can now better handle the problem of what is learned from the actions of a familiar other and is less restricted to the first impression case. The other major theoretical variable—number of noncommon effects—remains as originally stated. Each action is still conceived of as a choice between alternatives. Typically, some of the effects of action are common to the alternatives and should logically be uninformative. Thus, it is the *noncommon* effects that are crucial, and the more there are of these attendant on a given action, the more ambiguous is the meaning of that action. Research has hardly begun on the role of noncommon effect number, though McGillis's study (1974) represents an important step in this direction.

Questions concerning the number of noncommon effects are equivalent to those raised by Kelley's (1971) use of the "discounting principle." The greater the number of noncommon effects attendant on a chosen action, the more will any given effect be discounted as a plausible reason for that action. Kelley's augmentation principle also has equivalences in correspondent inference theory, in the notion of costs incurred. To the extent that some of the effects of a chosen act have negative valences, more emphatic or confident inferences will be drawn from the remaining positive effects. These intentional or dispositional inferences will thus be augmented by the presence of negatively valent effects.

The original subtitle of the Jones and Davis paper reads "From Acts to Dispositions," but the theoretical statement is actually more concerned with momentary intentions—inferred reasons for action—than with inferences to durable underlying dispositions. Kelley's (1967) theoretical framework may be more convenient for discussing how dispositions are inferred, because it includes explicit references to consistency over time and modality. When a stable disposition is inferred from a single action combined with an expectancy, this is probably the most tentative kind of hypothesis, one that the perceiver will be motivated to test in the course of further observations of the target person. A comprehensive theory of correspondent inference must eventually incorporate considerations of how behavioral information is combined over multiple observations.

Much of the research spawned by correspondent inference theory has used the theory as a rational baseline model. That is , the theory has been less valuable in pointing to how people actually function in drawing person-perceptual inferences than in providing a logical template for detecting various sources of bias or error. Both functions of the theory—the descriptive and the prescriptive—are illustrated in the research on attitude attribution. Here the basic paradigm has been to present subjects with essays, speeches, or interview comments favoring particular attitudinal positions and allegedly prepared by target persons under clearly specified conditions of choice or no choice. The subject's task is to infer the target person's "true attitude" by considering the position taken and its context of varying constraint.

The main results of this line of research are consistent with correspondent inference theory in that attitudes in line with behavior are
most strongly inferred when the actor has choice (few noncommon
effects) and the behavior is low in prior probability (expected effect
valence).

But it is also the case that behavior under no choice conditions
(numerous noncommon effects high in positive valence) leads to significant correspondence as well (Jones & Harris, 1967; Jones, Worchel, Goethals, & Grumet, 1971). Snyder and Jones (1974) have shown
that this finding does not derive from artifacts such as the particular
nature of the chosen essay or speech and that there is even an error of
imputing too much correspondence to actual essay writers in a high
choice condition.

This tendency for subjects to assess behavior and subsequently to
attribute too much causal significance for the particular behavioral
content to internal characteristics of the target person has been referred to by Ross (1977) as the "fundamental attribution error [p.
183]." The tendency also played an important role in Jones and Nisbett's (1971) speculations that observers of an action tend to attribute
to the actor what the actor himself attributes to the situation.

A recent paper by Snyder and Frankel (1976) has extended the
notion of a fundamental attribution error to the attribution of emotions. Specifically, these investigators found that observers of a silent
videotape showing a female actor supposedly in an anxiety-arousing
situation thought she was more likely to have a durable disposition of
anxiety than did observers who watched the same actor in a neutral
setting. Thus, information about a situational constraint leads to a
stronger dispositional inference rather than the more equivocal one
"required" by correspondent inference theory or by Kelley's model.
In this case, since the same results are not obtained when subjects are
told about the context *after* observing the tape, information about the
setting appears to induce perceptions of the (actually neutral) behavior as "anxious," which then gives rise to an inference that seems
to belie their origin.

The concepts of hedonic relevance and personalism have received little attention since the Jones and Davis paper. An exception
generally confirming our speculations therein is a study by Chaikin
and Cooper (1973) that presented in-role and out-of-role behavior
vignettes that were positive, neutral, or negative in hedonic relevance
for the subjects. The results showed that respect and admiration were
affected by the combination of correspondence and hedonic relevance, whereas liking and friendship choice were mediated by con-

siderations of hedonic relevance alone. Subjects disliked a member of the Ku Klux Klan whether he was the son of an Alabama millworker or a northern physics professor. They liked a medical student whether he was the son of a Puerto Rican custodian or the son of a Boston physician. Admiration and respect, however, varied with whether the behavior was in-role or out-of-role.

* * *

Jones and McGillis (1976) attempted to integrate correspondent inference theory with Kelley's analysis of variance model, emphasizing distinctiveness, consensus, and consistency. This integration suggests the comparability of distinctiveness and a violated target-based expectancy. When the expectancy is based on nearly identical past actions, we speak of inconsistency. Circumstance attributions are the equivalent of ignorance—reflected in the knowledge factor in the correspondent inference scheme—since the attributor uses circumstance as a residual category when neither "person" nor "entity" seem appropriate.

More generally, correspondent inference theory and the Kelley analysis of the variance cube make a number of similar or at least complementary distinctions. Both theoretical statements approach a lay version of experimental design and analysis. Both the experiment and the attribution episode involve an attempt to isolate distinctive causes for observed behavior. Each proceeds by a combination of comparison and control procedures. The experiment manipulates potential causal variables and compares the effects observed with those effects present in the absence of these variables. The attributor makes use of the experimental logic whenever possible but usually must cope with the natural confounding of potential causes that occurs in the real world.

Although they have much in common, correspondent inference theory and the Kelley cube are divergent in important respects. Correspondent inference theory focuses on the attribution of identifiable personal dispositions and addresses the case in which the attributor is trying to consider a dispositional cause for a perceived act by evaluating the strength of environmental constraints. Kelley, on the other hand, was more explicitly concerned with how personal biases in perception may be corrected or ruled out in the determination of the "true" nature of environmental entities.

I have already noted that Kelley's model incorporates the data from repeated observations in his consistency-over-time-and-modality variable. But Kelley's model has clear weaknesses on the dependent variable side. Combinations of distinctiveness, consensus, and consistency result in attributions that "something" about the person, stimulus, or environment caused the behavior. The noncommon effects analysis of correspondent inferent theory provides a mechanism for determining what specifically the "something" is. That is, specific causal factors are focused upon in the noncommon effects analysis, particularly specific causal factors residing in the person.

REFERENCES

Chaikin, A. L., & Cooper, J. Evaluation as a function of correspondence and hedonic relevance. *Journal of Experimental Social Psychology,* 1973, **9,** 257–264.

Harvey, J. H., Ickes, W. J., & Kidd, R. F. *New directions in attribution research.* Vol. I. Hillsdale, New Jersey: Erlbaum, 1976.

Jones, E. E., & Berglas, S. A recency effect in attitude attribution. *Journal of Personality,* 1976, **44,** 433–438.

Jones, E. E., & Harris, V. A. The attribution of attitudes. *Journal of Experimental Social Psychology,* 1967, **3,** 1–24.

Jones, E. E., Kanouse, D. E., Kelley, H. H., Nisbett, R. E., Valins, S., & Weiner, B. *Attribution: Perceiving the causes of behavior.* Morristown, New Jersey: General Learning, 1972.

Jones, E. E., Worchel, S., Goethals, G. R., & Grumet, J. F. Prior expectancy and behavioral extremity as determinants of attitude attribution. *Journal of Experimental Social Psychology,* 1971, **7,** 59–80.

Kelley, H. H. Attribution theory in social psychology. In D. Levine (Ed.), *Nebraska symposium on motivation.* Lincoln: University of Nebraska Press, 1967.

Kelley, H. H. *Attribution in social interaction.* Morristown, New Jersey: General Learning Press, 1971.

McGillis, D. A correspondent inference theory analysis of attitude attribution. Unpublished doctoral dissertation. Duke University, 1974.

Ross, L. The intuitive psychologist and his shortcomings: Distortions in the attribution process. In L. Berkowitz (Ed.), *Advances in experimental social psychology,* 1977, **10,** 173–220.

Snyder, M. L., & Frankel, A. Observer bias: A stringent test of behavior engulfing the field. *Journal of Personality and Social Psychology,* 1976, **34,** 857–864.

Snyder, M., & Jones, E. E. Attitude attribution when behavior is constrained. *Journal of Experimental Social Psychology,* 1974, **10,** 584–600.

THE INTUITIVE PSYCHOLOGIST AND HIS SHORTCOMINGS: DISTORTIONS IN THE ATTRIBUTION PROCESS[1]

Lee Ross

STANFORD UNIVERSITY
STANFORD, CALIFORNIA

[1] The author gratefully acknowledges the assistance of Teresa Amabile, Daryl Bem, Phoebe Ellsworth, Baruch Fischhoff, David Greene, Larry Gross, Mark Lepper, Richard Nisbett, Julia Steinmetz, Amos Tversky, and Philip Zimbardo, all of whom have contributed useful comments and suggestions concerning both the manuscript and the research and conceptual analysis it reports. The preparation of this chapter and reported research were supported by National Institute of Mental Health Research Grant MH 24134.

Reprinted from *Advances in Experimental Social Psychology,*
Volume 10, 173–220.

I. Introduction to Attribution Theory and
Attribution Error

A. ATTRIBUTION THEORY AND INTUITIVE PSYCHOLOGY

Attribution theory, in its broadest sense, is concerned with the attempts of ordinary people to understand the causes and implications of the events they witness. It deals with the "naive psychology" of the "man in the street" as he interprets his own behaviors and the actions of others. The current ascendancy of attribution theory in social psychology culminates a long struggle to upgrade that discipline's conception of man. No longer the stimulus–response (S–R) automaton of radical behaviorism, promoted beyond the rank of information processor and cognitive consistency seeker, psychological man has at last been awarded a status equal to that of the scientist who investigates him. For man, in the perspective of attribution theory, is an intuitive psychologist who seeks to explain behavior and to draw inferences about actors and their environments.

To better understand the perceptions and actions of this intuitive scientist we must explore his methods. First, like the academic psychologist, he is guided by a number of implicit assumptions about human nature and human behavior, for example, that the pursuit of pleasure and the avoidance of pain are ubiquitous and powerful human motives, or that conformity to the wishes and expectations of one's peers is less exceptional and less demanding of further interpretation than is nonconformity. The amateur psychologist, like the professional one, also relies heavily upon data. Sometimes these data result from first-hand experience; more often, they are the product of informal social communication, mass media, or other indirect sources. Moreover, the representativeness or randomness of the available data is rarely guaranteed by formal sampling procedures. The intuitive psychologist must further adopt or develop techniques for coding, storing, and retrieving such data. Finally, he must resort to methods for summarizing, analyzing, and interpreting his data, that is, rules, formulas, or schemata that permit him to extract meaning and form inferences. The intuitive scientist's ability to master his social environment depends in large measure upon the accuracy and adequacy of his hypotheses, evidence, and methods of analysis and inference. Conversely, sources of oversight, error, or bias in his assumptions and procedures may have serious consequences, both for the lay psychologist himself and for the society that he builds and perpetuates. These shortcomings, explored from the vantage point of contemporary attribution theory, provide the focus of the present chapter.

While the label "attribution theory" and some of the jargon of its proponents may be relatively new and unfamiliar, its broad concerns—naive epistemology and the social inference process—have a long and honorable history in social psychology. The Gestalt tradition, defying the forces of radical behaviorism, has consistently emphasized the *subject's* assignment of meaning to the events that unfold in the psychological laboratory and in everyday experience (cf. Asch, 1952). Icheiser (1949) explicitly discussed some fundamental social perception biases and their origins almost 30 years ago. Long before attribution theory's current vogue, Kelly (1955, 1958) brought an attributional perspective to the study of psychopathology and, in fact, explicitly suggested the analogy between the tasks of the intuitive observer and those of the behavioral scientist. Schachter and Singer (1962) and Bem (1965, 1967, 1972) further anticipated current attributional approaches in their respective analyses of emotional labeling and self-perception phenomena.

The broad outlines of contemporary attribution theory, however, were first sketched by Heider (1944, 1958) and developed in greater detail by Jones and Davis (1965), Kelley (1967), and their associates (e.g., Jones, Kanouse, Kelley, Nisbett, Valins, & Weiner, 1972; Weiner, 1974). These theorists emphasized two closely related tasks confronting the social observer. The first task is causal judgment: the observer seeks to identify the cause, or set of causes, to which some particular effect (i.e., some action or outcome) may most reasonably be *attributed.* The second task is social inference: the observer of an episode forms inferences about the *attributes* of relevant entities, that is, either the dispositions of actors or the properties of situations to which those actors have responded.

Causal judgment and social inference tasks have both been the subject of intensive theoretical and empirical inquiry and, until recently, had constituted virtually the entire domain of attribution theory. Lately, however, a third task of the intuitive psychologist has begun to receive some attention; that task is the *prediction* of outcomes and behavior. Episodes characteristically lead the intuitive psychologist not only to seek explanations and to make social inferences but also to form expectations and make predictions about the future actions and outcomes. Thus, when a presidential candidate promises to "ease the burden of the average taxpayer," we do attempt to judge whether the promise might have resulted from and reflected the demands of political expediency rather than the candidate's true convictions. However, we are likely also to speculate about and try to anticipate this candidate's and other candidates' future political actions. The psychology of intuitive prediction, is thus a natural extention of attribution theory's domain.

The three attribution tasks are, of course, by no means independent. Explanations for and inferences from an event are obviously and intimately related, and together they form an important basis for speculation about unknown and future events. Each task, moreover, can reveal much about the assumptions, strategies, and failings of the intuitive psychologist. Each, however, provides some unique problems of interpretation and methodology that we should explore before proceeding.

In describing causal judgments, researchers from the time of Heider's early contributions to the present have relied heavily upon a simple internal–external or disposition–situation dichotomy. That is, they have tried to identify those configurations of possible causes and observed effects that lead the observer to attribute an event to "internal" dispositions of the actor (e.g., abilities, traits, or motives) or to aspects of the "external" situation (e.g., task difficulties, incentives, or peer pressures).[2] While this seemingly simple dichotomy has undeniable intuitive appeal, it creates a host of conceptual problems and methodological pitfalls (see also Kruglanski, 1975). For instance, attribution researchers (e.g., Nisbett, Caputo, Legant, & Maracek, 1973) frequently require subjects to explain why a particular actor has chosen a particular course of behavior. These attributions are then coded as "situational" or "dispositional" on the basis of the *form* of the subject's response. Thus the statement "Jack bought the house because it was so secluded" is coded as an external or situational attribution, whereas "Jill bought the house because she wanted privacy" is coded as an internal or dispositional attribution. The rationale for such coding seems straightforward: The former statement cites something about the object or situation to which the actor responded while the latter statement cites something about the actor. However, when one attends not to the *form* of the attributer's statement but to its *content,* the legitimacy of many such situation–disposition distinctions becomes more dubious. First, it is apparent that causal statements which explicitly cite situational causes implicitly convey something about the actor's dispositions; conversely, statements which cite dispositional causes invariably imply the existence and controlling influence of situational factors. For instance, in accounting for Jack's purchase of a house the "situational" explanation (i.e., "because *it* was so secluded") implies a disposition on the part of this particular actor to favor seclusion. Indeed, the explanation provided is no explanation at all unless one *does* assume that such a disposition controlled Jack's response. Conversely, the dispositional explanation for Jill's purchase (i.e., because *she* likes privacy) clearly implies something about the house (i.e., its capacity to provide such privacy) that, in turn, governed Jill's behavior. Thus the content of both sentences, notwithstanding their differences in form, communicates the information that a particular feature of the house exists and that the purchaser was disposed to respond positively to that feature. In fact, the form of the sentences could have been reversed without altering their content to read "Jack bought the house because he wanted seclusion" and "Jill bought the house because it provided privacy."

Is there a more meaningful basis for a distinction between situational and dispositional causes? One possibility merits consideration. One could ignore the form of subjects' causal statements and, by attending to content, distinguish

---

[2] Most contemporary researchers have been concerned with attributional rules or principles that apply commonly to all social perceivers. However, a few investigators [most notably Rotter (1966)] have used a similar dichotomy in discussing individual differences in such strategies (see also Collins, 1974; Collins, Martin, Ashmore, & Ross, 1973; Crandall, Katkovsky, & Crandall, 1965; Lefcourt, 1972).

between (1) explanations that do not state or imply any dispositions on the part of the actor beyond those typical of actors in general, and (2) explanations that do state or imply unique relatively atypical or distinguishing personal dispositions. Thus the causal statements "I was initially attracted to Sally because she is so beautiful" and "I was initially attracted to Sally because her astrological sign is Libra" should be coded differently in terms of the proposed distinction despite their similar form. Specifically, while the former explanation conveys that I, *like* most men, am particularly attracted to beautiful women, the latter implies that I, *unlike* most men, am particularly attracted to women of one specific astrological sign. In a sense, the former statement constitutes a situational explanation because it invokes a widely accepted and generally applicable S–R law; the latter explanation, by contrast, is dispositional because it resorts to an individual difference or distinguishing personality variable.[3]

The interpretation of causal statements in the manner just described is obviously a difficult undertaking and many investigators may favor the second attribution task, i.e., the formation of social inferences. This task, at first glance, seems to offer a far less forbidding but no less rewarding research target. For instance, the subject who learns that Joan has donated money to a particular charity may infer that the relevant act reflected [or, in Jones and Davis' (1965) terms, "corresponded" to] some personal disposition of Joan. Alternatively, the subject may infer that Joan's actions reflected not her personal characteristics but the influence of social pressures, incentives, or other environmental factors. The attribution researcher, accordingly, can measure the subject's willingness to assert something about Joan's traits, motives, abilities, beliefs, or other personal dispositions on the basis of the behavioral evidence provided. Specifically, the subject could be required to characterize Joan by checking a Likert-type scale anchored at "very generous" and "not at all generous" with a midpoint of "average in generosity." An alternative version of the scale might deal with the degree of confidence the rater is willing to express in his social inferences.

Such measures of social inference are, indeed, simple to contrive and simple to score. Nevertheless, nontrivial problems of interpretation do arise. Most obvious is the fact that the meaning of a given point on these scales differs for different subjects. More importantly, that meaning may depend upon subtle features of research context and instruction, features often beyond the experimenter's knowledge or control.

---

[3] The reader should recognize, however, that the form or structure of a causal statement may have a significance that cannot be predicted from a logical analysis of its contents and meaning. Thus, Mary's statement that she loves John because of his qualities rather than her own needs may be an important reflection of her feelings and an important determinant of their subsequent relationship, notwithstanding the dubious logical status of the implied distinction.

Even subtler problems of interpretation may arise. One common format, for instance, asks subjects to indicate whether the specified person is "generous" or "ungenerous," or that they "can't say, depends upon circumstances." Superficially, the first two options indicate willingness to infer the existence or influence of a personal disposition, whereas the third option suggests unwillingness to do so. But a more careful examination of the rater's perceptions may reveal that the third option reflects the rejection only of a *broad* or *general* dispositional label. Thus, further interrogation might reveal that the rater judged the relevant actor to be unexceptional with respect to the behavioral domain in question, that is, like most actors behaving generously or not as situational pressures and constraints dictate. In such a case it seems that no disposition has been inferred (and that the rater has made a situational rather than a dispositional attribution of relevant behavior). On the other hand, the rater's reluctance to choose either trait label may convey his judgment that the actor is relatively more generous than his fellows in some specific circumstances but less generous in others, i.e., that his generosity is inconsistent or idiosyncratic (cf. Bem & Allen, 1974). In the latter case a disposition *has* been inferred, albeit a relatively specific one, for example, a tendency to be unusually generous to one's employees but not to one's family, or vice versa. In fact, several important papers in the attribution area (e.g., Jones & Nisbett, 1971; Nisbett *et al.,* 1973), have failed to distinguish adequately between the absence of trait inferences and the rejection of broad trait labels in favor of narrow or situation-specified ones. Inevitably, confusion and unwarranted conclusions have been the product of this failure.

The third type of attribution task, prediction of behavior (e.g., Nisbett & Borgida, 1975), permits simple unambiguous questions and produces responses that can be scored objectively. Thus the witness to an ostensibly generous act by Joan might be required to predict Joan's behavior in a series of other episodes that seemingly test an actor's generosity or lack of it. Alternatively, the question put to the social observer might be: "What percentage of students (or of people, or of women, or of Joan's socioeconomic peers, etc.) would have behaved as generously as Joan did?" The logical relationship of the prediction task to the tasks of causal judgment and social inference is worth reemphasizing [although the relevant empirical correlations between attribution measures may prove surprisingly weak; cf. Bierbrauer (1973)]. To the extent that a given action or outcome is attributed to the actor rather than his situation and that some stable disposition is inferred, the attributer should prove willing to make confident and distinguishing predictions about the actor's subsequent behaviors or outcomes. Conversely, to the extent that an act is attributed to situational pressures that would dispose all actors to behave similarly, and to the extent that no inferences are made about the actor's dispositions, the observer should eschew such "distinguishing" predictions; instead, he should invoke the "null hypothesis" and rely upon his baseline information or estimates about how "people in general" respond in the specified situation.

Prediction measures of attribution processes have a crucial advantage (beyond their simplicity and seeming objectivity). Unlike causal judgments or social inferences, predictions can often be evaluated with respect to their *accuracy*. That is, whenever authentic information is available about the behavior of various actors in more than one situation, the success of the intuitive psychologist's attribution strategy can be measured and the direction of biases can be determined. To illustrate this advantage, research on "nonconservative" prediction biases will be discussed later in this chapter (Section III,C; cf. also Amabile, 1975; Ross, Amabile, Jennings, & Steinmetz, 1976a).

B. LOGICAL SCHEMATA AND NONLOGICAL BIASES

Contemporary attribution theory has pursued two distinct but complementary goals. One goal has been the demonstration that, by and large, social perceivers follow the dictates of logical or rational models in assessing causes, making inferences about actors and situations, and forming expectations and predictions. The other goal has been the illustration and explication of the sources of imperfection, bias, or error that distort these judgments. We shall consider briefly the so-called logical or rational schemata employed by the intuitive psychologist and then devote the remainder of the chapter to the sources of bias in his attempts at understanding, predicting, and controlling the events that unfold around him.

1. Two Logical Schemata

Individuals must, for the most part, share a common understanding of the social actions and outcomes that affect them, for without such consensus, social interaction would be chaotic, unpredictable, and beyond the control of the participants. Introspection on the part of attribution theorists, buttressed by some laboratory evidence, has led to the postulation of a set of "rules" that may generally be employed in the interpretation of behaviors and outcomes. These "commonsense" rules or schemata are analogous, in some respects, to the more formal rules and procedures that social scientists and statisticians follow in their analysis and interpretation of data.

H. Kelley, E. E. Jones, and their associates have distinguished two cases in which logical rules or schemata may be applied: In the *multiple* observation case the attributer has access to behavioral data which might be represented as rows or columns of an Actor × Object × Situation (or Instance) response matrix. Typically, summary statements are provided rather than actual responses. Thus the potential attributer learns that "Most theatergoers like the new Pinter play," or "Mary can't resist stray animals," or "The only television program that Ann watches is Masterpiece Theater." In the *single* observation case the attributer must deal with the behavior of a single actor on a single occasion. For instance, he may see Sam comply with an experimenter's request to deliver a painful shock to a peer, or he may learn that "Louie bet all his money on a long shot at Pimlico."

The logical rules or principles governing attributions in these two cases are rather different (Kelley, 1967, 1971, 1973). In the multiple observation case the attributer applies the Covariance Principle; that is, he assesses the degree to which observed behaviors or outcomes occur in the presence, but fail to occur in the absence, of each causal candidate under consideration. Accordingly, the attributer concludes that the new Pinter play is a good one (and attributes praise to the play rather than the playgoer) to the extent that it is liked by a wide variety of playgoers, that it is liked by individuals who praise few plays (e.g., "critics"), and that it is applauded as vigorously on the ninetieth day of its run as on the ninth.

In the single observation case the attributer's assessment strategy involves the application of the Discounting Principle, by which the social observer "discounts" the role of any causal candidate in explaining an event to the extent that other plausible causes or determinants can be identified. This attributional principle can be restated in terms of social inferences rather than causal attributions: To the extent that situational or external factors constitute a "sufficient" explanation for an event, that event is attributed to the situation and no inference logically can be made (and, presumably, no inference empirically *is* made) about the dispositions of the actor. Conversely, to the extent that an act or outcome seems to occur *in spite of* and *not because of* attendant situational forces, the relevant event is attributed to the actor and a "correspondent inference" (Jones & Davis, 1965) is made, i.e., the attributer infers the existence and influence of some trait, ability, intention, feeling, or other disposition that could account for the actor's action or outcome. Thus, we resist the conclusion that Louie's longshot plunge at Pimlico was reflective of his stable personal attributes to the extent that such factors as a "hot tip," a desperate financial crisis, or seven prewager martinis could be cited. On the other hand, we judge Louie to be an inveterate longshot player if we learn that his wager occurred in the face of his wife's threat to leave him if he ever loses his paycheck at the track again, his knowledge that he won't be able to pay the rent if he loses, and a track expert's overheard remark that the favorite in the race is "even better than the track odds suggest."

It is worth noting that the application of these two different principles places rather different demands upon the intuitive scientist. The Covariance Principle requires the attributer to apply rules that are essentially logical or statistical in nature and demands no further insight about the characteristics of the entities in question. Application of the Discounting Principle, by contrast, demands considerable insight about the nature of man and the impact of such situational forces as financial need, alcohol consumption, and a spouse's threat of abandonment. In a sense, the Covariance Principle can be applied by a mere "statistician," whereas the Discounting Principle requires a "psychologist" able to assess the role of various social pressures and situational forces and even to distinguish intended acts and outcomes from unintended ones (cf. Jones & Davis, 1965).

Evidence concerning the systematic use of commonsense attributional principles comes primarily from questionnaire studies in which subjects read and interpret brief anecdotes about the responses of one or more actors to specified objects or "entities" under specified circumstances (e.g., McArthur, 1972, 1976). Occasional studies of narrower scope have also exposed the attributer to seemingly authentic responses, encounters, and outcomes (e.g., Jones, Davis, & Gergen, 1961; Jones & DeCharms, 1957; Jones & Harris, 1967; Strickland, 1958; Thibaut & Riecken, 1955). Such research has demonstrated that attributers can, and generally do, make some use of the hypothesized principles or rules of thumb. That is, manipulations involving information about either the covariance of causes and effects or the number of potential causes for a given effect have produced statistically significant effects upon subjects' judgments. Some studies have even provided evidence about the *relative* impact of various competing attributional principles or criteria (cf. McArthur, 1972, 1976).

What the methodologies employed to date have not assessed (and, logically, could never assess) is the accuracy of the attributer's judgments and the sufficiency of his judgmental strategies. As we have noted earlier, such determinations become possible only when attributers are presented with authentic information and are required to make predictions or other judgments that can be verified.

2. Motivational and Nonmotivational Sources of Bias

The central concern of the present chapter, and an increasingly important goal of contemporary research and theory, is not the logical schemata which promote understanding, consensus, and effective social control; instead, it is the sources of systematic bias or distortion in judgment that lead the intuitive psychologist to misinterpret events and hence to behave in ways that are personally maladaptive, socially pernicious, and often puzzling to the social scientist who seeks to understand such behavior.

In speculating about possible distortions in an otherwise logical attribution system, theorists were quick to postulate "ego-defensive" biases through which attributers maintained or enhanced their general self-esteem or positive opinion of their specific dispositions and abilities (Heider, 1958; Jones & Davis, 1965; Kelley, 1967). Attempts to prove the existence of such a motivational bias have generally involved demonstrations of asymmetry in the attribution of positive and negative outcomes—specifically, a tendency for actors to attribute "successes" to their own efforts, abilities, or dispositions while attributing "failure" to luck, task difficulty, or other external factors. Achievement tasks (e.g., Davis & Davis, 1972; Feather, 1969; Fitch, 1970; Wolosin, Sherman, & Till, 1973) and teaching performances (e.g., Beckman, 1970; Freize & Weiner, 1971; Johnson, Feigenbaum, & Weiby, 1964) have provided most of the evidence for this asymmetry. It has also been shown that actors may give themselves more credit for success and less blame for failure than do observers evaluating the same outcomes (Beckman, 1970; Gross, 1966; Polefka, 1965).

Critics, skeptical of broad motivational biases, however, have experienced little difficulty in challenging such research. [See D. T. Miller and Ross (1975) for a detailed discussion.] First, it is obvious that subjects' private perceptions and interpretations may not correspond to (and may be either less or more "defensive" than) their overt judgments. Second, asymmetries in the attributions of success and failure or differences in the judgments of actors and observers need not reflect motivational influences. As several researchers have noted, success, at least in test situations, is likely to be anticipated and congruent with the actor's past experience, whereas failure may be unanticipated and unusual. Similarly, successful outcomes are intended and are the object of plans and actions by the actor, whereas failures are unintended events which occur in spite of the actor's plans and efforts. Observers, furthermore, rarely are fully aware of the past experiences or present expectations and intentions of the actors whose outcomes they witness.

Challenges to the existence of pervasive ego-defensive biases have been empirical as well as conceptual. Thus, in some studies subjects seem to show "counterdefensive" or esteem-attenuating biases. For example, Ross, Bierbrauer, and Polly (1974), using an unusually authentic instructor–learner paradigm, found that instructors rated their own performances and abilities as more important determinants of failure than of success. Conversely, the instructors rated their learner's efforts and abilities as less critical determinants of failure than success. In the same study these seemingly counterdefensive attributional tendencies proved to be even more pronounced among professional teachers than among inexperienced undergraduates, a result which contradicted the obvious derivation from ego-defensiveness theory that those most directly threatened by the failure experience would be most defensive.

Researchers who insist that self-serving motivational biases exist can, of course, provide alternative interpretations of studies that seem to show no motivational biases or counterdefensive biases. Indeed, in many respects the debate between proponents and skeptics has become reminiscent of earlier and broader debates in learning theory and basic perception in which the fruitlessness of the search for a "decisive" experiment on the issue of motivational influences (i.e., one that could not be interpreted by the "other side") became ever more apparent as data multiplied and conceptual analysis sharpened. One approach favored by many researchers has been an attempt to specify relevant moderator variables that might determine when ego defensiveness will distort the attribution process and when it will not do so. An alternate and perhaps more fruitful strategy, however, may be to temporarily abandon motivational constructs and to concentrate upon those informational, perceptual, and cognitive factors that mediate and potentially distort attributional judgments "in general." A fuller understanding of such factors, in turn, might well allow us, ultimately, to understand and anticipate the particular circumstances in which attributions of responsibility will unduly enhance or attenuate an attributer's self-esteem (cf. D. T. Miller & Ross, 1975).

Unfortunately the existing attribution literature provides relatively little conceptual analysis or evidence pertaining to nonmotivational biases. The first identified (Heider, 1958) and most frequently cited bias or error, one which we shall term the *fundamental* attribution error, is the tendency for attributers to underestimate the impact of situational factors and to overestimate the role of dispositional factors in controlling behavior. The evidence for this error and its broader implications for our understanding of social psychological phenomena receive detailed consideration in Section II,A.

Our consideration of other previously cited nonmotivational biases shall be brief. Perhaps the most provocative contribution concerning nonmotivational biases has been Jones and Nisbett's (1971) generalization regarding the "divergent" perceptions of actors and observers (cf. also Jones, 1976). Essentially, it was proposed that actors and observers differ in their susceptibility to the fundamental attribution error; that is, in situations where actors attribute their own behavioral choices to situational forces and constraints, observers are likely to attribute the same choices to the actors' stable abilities, attitudes, and personality traits. An interesting and unusual feature of the Jones and Nisbett paper is its careful consideration of underlying processes—informational, cognitive, and perceptual in nature—which might *account for* these divergent perceptions of actors and observers (cf. also Jones, 1976). Another interesting line of investigation (one, incidentally, which promises to subsume Jones and Nisbett's actor–observer generalization) involves "perceptual focusing" (Duncker, 1938; Wallach, 1959). It appears that whatever or whomever we "focus our attention on" becomes more apt to be cited as a causal agent (Arkin & Duval, 1975; Duval & Wicklund, 1972; Regan & Totten, 1975; Storms, 1973; Taylor & Fiske, 1975).

Other attributional biases that have been proposed in the literature have been less systematically investigated. Our list, although incomplete, is perhaps representative. Jones and Davis (1965), for instance, proposed that actions directed towards the attributer, or having consequences for him, are more likely to be attributed to dispositions of the actor than are acts which do not personally involve or affect the attributer. Walster (1966) reported a questionnaire study suggesting that actors are held more responsible (and "chance" or "luck" less responsible) for acts that have serious consequences than for acts with trivial consequences. Finally Kelley (1971), summarizing the results of several prior questionnaire studies, observed that the actor is also held more responsible for acts which lead to reward than for acts which prevent loss or punishment.

II. Attributional Biases: Instances, Causes, and Consequences

A. THE FUNDAMENTAL ATTRIBUTION ERROR

Our exploration of the intuitive psychologist's shortcomings must start with his general tendency to overestimate the importance of personal or dispositional factors relative to environmental influences. As a psychologist he seems too often to be a nativist, or proponent of individual differences, and too seldom an S--R behaviorist. He too readily infers broad personal dispositions and expects consistency in behavior or outcomes across widely disparate situations and contexts. He jumps to hasty conclusions upon witnessing the behavior of his peers, overlooking the impact of relevant environmental forces and constraints. Beyond anecdotes and appeals to experience, the evidence most frequently cited for this general bias (e.g., Jones & Nisbett, 1971; Kelley, 1971) involves the attributer's apparent willingness to draw "correspondent" personal inferences about actors who have responded to very obvious situational pressures. For instance, Jones and Harris (1967) found that listeners assumed some correspondence between communicators' pro-Castro remarks and their private opinions even when these listeners *knew* that the communicators were obeying the experimenter's explicit request under "no choice" conditions. A more direct type of evidence that observers may ignore or underestimate situational forces has been provided by Bierbrauer (1973), who studied subjects' impressions of the forces operating in the classic Milgram (1963) situation. In Bierbrauer's study, participants witnessed a faithful verbatim reenactment of one subject's "obedience" to the point of delivering the maximum shock to the supposed victim. Regardless of the type and amount of delay before judging (see Fig. 1), regardless of whether they actually played the role of a subject in the reenactment or merely observed, and regardless of their perceptual or cognitive "set," Bierbrauer's participants showed the fundamental attribution error; that is, they consistently and dramatically underestimated the degree to which subjects in general would yield to those situational forces which compelled obedience in Milgram's situation. In other words, they assumed that the particular subject's obedience reflected his distinguishing personal dispositions rather than the potency of situational pressures and constraints acting upon all subjects. The susceptibility of observers to the fundamental attribution error has been noted

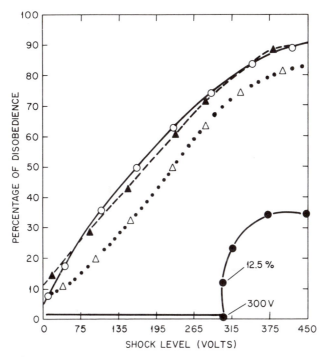

Fig. 1. Comparison of predicted and actual disobedience rates: *open circles,* no delay prediction; *black triangles,* distracted delay prediction; *open triangles,* undistracted delay prediction; *black circles,* rates obtained by Milgram (1963). From Bierbrauer (1973).

by many theorists (e.g., Heider, 1944, 1958; Icheiser, 1949) and disputed by few.[4] The relevance of this error to the phenomena and research strategies of contemporary social psychology, however, has been less widely recognized. To illustrate, we shall first discuss its critical role in mediating the effects of "forced compliance" or "role playing" upon attitude change; then we shall digress slightly to consider the *professional* psychologist's apparent susceptibility to this error.

1. Attribution Error and Forced Compliance Effects

Proponents of cognitive consistency and self-perception theories have regarded demonstrations of attitude change following forced compliance as impor-

---

[4] Insufficient attention, perhaps, has been given to the possibility that while many situational forces are typically underestimated, there may be others which generally are correctly estimated or even overestimated. Notably, an intriguing series of studies (Deci, 1971; Greene & Lepper, 1974; Lepper & Greene, 1975; Lepper, Greene, & Nisbett, 1973) suggest that actors, in certain circumstances, may inappropriately attribute intrinsically motivated behavior to the influence of salient extrinsic rewards and constraints.

tant evidence for their theoretical viewpoint. Upon closer examination, however, it becomes apparent that these theories "explain" the relevant phenomenon only to the extent that one additionally assumes the operation of the fundamental attribution error. Consider the classic Festinger and Carlsmith (1959) experiment in this regard. Why *does* the compliant actor in the "one dollar" condition experience dissonance? Or, in self-perception terms, why does he incorrectly infer that his compliant behavior reflects liking for the experimental task? Why don't the actors, or the observers in Bem's (1967) interpersonal "simulations," correctly identify the actual "external" causes of the actor's compliance and hence draw no inferences about the actor's attitudes from his counterattitudinal behavior?

The answer is clear: Actors and observers alike must systematically *underestimate* the sufficiency of the particular complex of situational factors in the Festinger and Carlsmith study to produce compliance and must *overestimate* the role played by personal dispositions in producing such behavior. "Correct" attributions, presumably, would produce little dissonance and certainly no erroneous "correspondent inferences" concerning the compliant actor's attitudes. (That is why the "twenty dollar" condition, which presumably facilitates "correct" attributions, produces no attitude change among actors and no tendency for observers to assume congruence between actors private attitudes and their public utterances.) In short, self-perception theory, attribution theory, and dissonance theory "explain" the Festinger and Carlsmith results only if one additionally recognizes the role of the fundamental attribution error.

2. *Fundamental Attribution Error by Psychologists*

The professional psychologist, like the intuitive psychologist, is susceptible to the fundamental attribution error. This susceptibility, in fact, is crucial to the strategy of designing so-called nonobvious research. Many of the best known and most provocative studies in our field depend, for their impact, upon the reader's erroneous expectation that individual differences and personal dispositions will overcome relatively mundane situational variables or "channel factors." Thus Darley and Batson's (1973) study of Good Samaritanism is noteworthy because it seems to contradict our intuition that an individual's ethical principles are more important determinants of bystander intervention than an experimental manipulation of the individual's earliness or lateness for an appointment. Similarly, Bavelas, Hastorf, Gross, and Kite (1965) earn our professional applause and recognition because they show that one can "overcome" those personal qualities which presumably propel the leader into his role through a banal manipulation of the amount of talking done by group members. Most notable of all, perhaps, are the now classic studies showing the vulnerability of actors to situational forces strongly challenging their judgments, preferences, or beliefs (cf. Asch, 1955; Milgram 1963). These studies were professional successes not because they showed that the relevant target behavior or perceptions could be influenced by a situational manipulation, but because they demonstrated control by a situational factor that the reader had previously assumed to be too weak to exert such control.

In this context it is instructive to consider the heated response of many professionals to Mischel's (1968) summary of evidence indicating that, for most behavior domains of interest to social psychologists, the degree of cross-situational consistency is very modest, making personality scales poor predictors of behavior. Adding insult to injury of the "trait theorists," Mischel and associates (Mischel, 1974; Mischel & Ebbesen, 1970; Mischel, Ebbesen, & Zeiss, 1972) have further demonstrated that in at least one paradigm of general interest—the "delay of gratification paradigm"—relatively subtle situational factors (i.e., the experimenter's suggestion concerning cognitive strategies) overwhelm any individual differences that might be anticipated. Why have Mischel's assertions and demonstrations proven so controversial and prompted such energetic rebuttal research? One reason may be that Mischel's work contradicted not only the formal theories of his critics but also the working assumptions that guide their everyday personal encounters.

The deep conviction that personal dispositions control and are reflected in everyday social behavior will no doubt continue to inspire research in personality theory and personality assessment. Similarly, successful social psychologists will continue to exploit the undue faith of their readers (and their subjects) in the impact of personal beliefs or standards relative to that of situational manipulations. In subsequent sections of this chapter we shall attempt to understand how erroneous trait inferences and trait theories survive or "persevere" in the face of logical challenges and empirical disconfirmations. We shall also explore further the relevance of attributional biases to the tactics and strategy of experimental social psychology.

B. THE "FALSE CONSENSUS" OR "EGOCENTRIC ATTRIBUTION" BIAS

The professional psychologist relies upon well-defined sampling techniques and statistical procedures for estimating the commonness of particular responses. Where such estimates are relevant to subsequent interpretations and inferences, he can proceed with confidence in his data. Intuitive psychologists, by contrast, are rarely blessed either with adequate "baseline" data or with the means of acquiring such data. To the extent that their systems for interpreting social responses depend upon estimates of commonness or oddity they must, accordingly, rely largely upon subjective impressions and intuitions.

The source of attributional bias that we shall consider next relates directly to the subjective probability estimates of intuitive psychologists. Specifically, we shall report research demonstrating that laymen tend to perceive a "false consensus," that is, to see their own behavioral choices and judgments as relatively common and appropriate to existing circumstances while viewing alternative responses as uncommon, deviant, and inappropriate. Evidence shall also be reported for an obvious corollary to the false consensus proposition: The intuitive psychologist judges those responses that differ from his own to be more revealing of the actor's stable dispositions than those responses which are similar to his own. Thus, we contend that the person who feeds squirrels, votes Republican, or drinks Drambuie for breakfast will see such behaviors or choices by an actor as relatively common and relatively devoid of information about his personal characteristics. By contrast, another person who ignores hungry squirrels, votes for Democrats, or abstains at breakfast will see the former actor's responses as relatively odd and rich in implications about the actor's personality.

The term *relative* is critical in this formulation of the false consensus bias and requires some clarification. Obviously, the man who would walk a tightrope between two skyscrapers, launch a revolution, or choose a life of clerical celibacy recognizes that his choices would be shared by few of his peers. It is contended, however, that he would see his personal choices as less deviant than would those of us who would *not* walk tightropes, launch revolutions, or become celibate clerics. Similarly, the present thesis concedes that for some response categories virtually all raters' estimates may be biased in the same direction. The incidence of infant abuse, for instance, might be underestimated by abusing and nonabusing parents alike. The relative terms of the false consensus hypothesis leads only to the prediction that abusing parents will estimate child abuse to be more common and less revealing of personal dispositions than will nonabusing parents.

References to "egocentric attribution" (Heider, 1958; Jones & Nisbett, 1971), to "attributive projection" (Holmes, 1968), and to specific findings and phenomena related to false consensus biases have appeared sporadically in the social perception and attribution literatures (cf. Katz & Allport, 1931; Kelley & Stahelski, 1970). Perhaps the most compelling evidence, however, is provided in a series of studies by Ross, Greene, and House (1977b) which we shall review in some detail.

1. Empirical Evidence and Implications

In the first study reported, subjects read descriptions of hypothetical conflict situations of the sort they might personally face. One of the four stories, for example, describes the following dilemma:

> As you are leaving your neighborhood supermarket a man in a business suit asks whether you like shopping in that store. You reply quite honestly that you do like shopping there and indicate that in addition to being close to your home the

supermarket seems to have very good meats and produce at reasonably low prices. The man then reveals that a videotape crew has filmed your comments and asks you to sign a release allowing them to use the unedited film for a TV commercial the supermarket chain is preparing.

The subjects then were asked to *(a)* estimate the commonness of the two response alternatives (e.g., signing or refusing to sign the commercial release in the supermarket story); *(b)* indicate the alternative they, personally, would follow; and *(c)* assess the traits of the "typical" individual who would follow each of the two specified alternatives.

The relevant estimates and ratings made by subjects strongly supported both the false consensus hypothesis and its corollary. For example, subjects reading the foregoing episode who claimed that they personally would sign the commercial release guessed that more than 75% of their peers would show the same response in the same circumstances; by contrast, subjects who reported that they personally would refuse to sign the release estimated that only 57% would sign. Furthermore, signers made more confident and extreme judgments about the distinguishing traits of the typical nonsigner, while nonsigners reported more confident and extreme impressions about the distinguishing dispositions of the signers.

A second questionnaire study by Ross *et al.* (1977b) dealing with a broad range of habits, preferences, fears, daily activities, expectations, and other personal characteristics greatly extended the apparent domain of the false consensus effect. That is, subjects' estimates of the commonness of the various responses and personal characteristics cited in the questionnaire were consistently biased in accord with their own responses and characteristics.

In a final demonstration by Ross, Greene, and House the hypothetical questionnaire methodology was abandoned and subjects were confronted with a real and consequential conflict situation: Subjects (in the context of a purported experiment on communication techniques) were asked to walk around campus for 30 minutes wearing a large sandwich-board sign bearing the message "EAT AT JOE'S." The experimenter made it clear to subjects that they could easily refuse to participate in the sandwich-board study but that he would prefer that they did participate and thereby "learn something interesting while helping the research project." Subjects were subsequently asked to make their own decision about taking part in the study, to estimate the probable decisions of others, and to make trait inferences about particular peers who agreed or refused to participate.

The results using this "real" conflict situation (Table I) confirmed the findings of earlier questionnaire studies dealing with hypothetical responses. Overall, subjects who agreed to wear the sandwich-board sign estimated that 62% of their peers would make the same choice. Subjects who refused to wear the

TABLE I

THE FALSE CONSENSUS EFFECT: RATERS' ESTIMATES OF COMMONNESS AND
TRAIT INFERENCES REGARDING TWO BEHAVIORAL ALTERNATIVES[a]

	Estimated commonness of:		Strength of trait inferences[b] about subject who:	
Raters	Agreement (%)	Refusal (%)	Agrees to wear sign	Refuses to wear sign
Subjects who agree to wear sign (n = 48)	62	38	120.1	125.3
Subjects who refuse to wear sign (n = 32)	33	67	139.7	106.8

[a]Summarized from Ross et al. (1977b).

[b]Sum of ratings for four traits: higher number indicates more confident and more extreme inferences by rater.

sign estimated that only 33% of their peers would comply with the experimenter's request. Furthermore, as predicted, "compliant" and "noncompliant" subjects disagreed sharply in the relative strength of inferences that they were willing to make about one peer who agreed and one who refused to wear the sandwich board. Compliant subjects made more confident and more extreme inferences about the personal characteristics of the noncompliant peer; noncompliant subjects made stronger inferences about the compliant peer.

Some broad implications of the Ross, Greene, and House demonstrations for our conception of the intuitive psychologist should be clear. His estimates of deviance and normalcy, and the host of social inferences and interpersonal responses that accompany such estimates, are systematically and egocentrically biased in accord with his own behavioral choices. More generally, it is apparent that attributional analyses may be distorted not only by errors in the intuitive psychologist's eventual analysis of social data, but also by earlier biases in sampling or estimating such data.

The present findings are interesting to consider in the light of Jones and Nisbett's (1971) contentions that (1) we see our peers' behavior as the product of broad consistent personal dispositions while attributing our own responses to situational forces and constraints, and (2) we are reluctant to agree that we ourselves possess the type of stable personality traits that we readily apply in characterizing our peers. To explain their results, Jones and Nisbett suggested important differences in the perceptual and informational "perspectives" enjoyed by actors and observers. The Ross et al. (1977b) results, however, lead one to speculate that attributional differences of the sort described by Jones and

Nisbett may arise, at least in some measure, simply from attributers' misconceptions about the degree of consensus enjoyed by their own responses and by the alternative responses of their peers.

The derivation is a simple one: To the extent that particular responses by one's peers differ from one's own responses in a given situation, such responses are likely to be seen as relatively odd or deviant—the product, therefore, not of situational forces (which, presumably, guide one's own *contrary* responses) but of distinguishing personality dispositions or traits. Moreover, since any peer responds differently from oneself in at least some situations, it is inevitable that one's peers be seen as the possessors of more numerous and more extreme distinguishing personal characteristics than oneself. The false consensus effect thus allows us to account for many of the phenomena and experimental results that have been mustered in support of Jones and Nisbett's thesis (cf. Jones & Nisbett, 1971; Nisbett *et al.*, 1973) without resorting to the "differing perspective" mechanisms they suggested.

2. Sources of the False Consensus Bias

Investigators who have discussed false consensus phenomena or egocentric attributional biases have typically emphasized their motivational status or function for the individual. Such biases, it is contended, both foster and justify the actor's feelings that his own behavioral choices are appropriate and rational responses to the demands of the environment, rather than reflections of his distinguishing personal dispositions. More dynamic interpretations (e.g., Bramel, 1962, 1963; Edlow & Kiesler, 1966; Lemann & Solomon, 1952; Smith, 1960) have stressed the ego-defensive or dissonance-reducing function of attributive projection, particularly as a response to failure or negative information about one's personal characteristics.

Several nonmotivational factors, more directly relevant to our present concern with the methods of the intuitive psychologist, may play some role in producing false consensus phenomena. Principal among these are (1) "selective exposure" and "availability" factors, and (2) factors pertaining to the resolution of situational ambiguity.

Selective exposure factors underlying false consensus are fairly straightforward. Obviously, we know and associate with people who share our background, experiences, interests, values, and outlook. Such people *do*, in disproportionate numbers, respond as we would in a wide variety of circumstances. Indeed, our close association is determined, in part, by feelings of general consensus, and we may be inclined to avoid those whom we believe unlikely to share our judgments and responses. This exposure to a biased sample of people and behavior does not demand that we err in our estimates concerning the relevant populations, but it does make such errors likely. More subtle, and more cognitive in character, are the factors which increase our ability to recall, visualize, or imagine paradigmatic instances of behavior. In a given situation the specific behaviors that we have chosen, or would choose, are likely to be more readily retrievable from memory and more easily imagined than opposite behaviors. In Kahneman and Tversky's (1973) terms, the behavioral choices we favor may be more cognitively "available," and we are apt to be misled by this ease or difficulty of access in estimating the likelihood of relevant behavioral options.

A second nonmotivational source of the false consensus effect arises from the intuitive psychologist's response to ambiguity—both about the nature and magnitude of situational forces and about the meaning and implications of various response alternatives. Attempts to resolve such ambiguity involve interpretation, estimation, and guesswork, all of which can exert a parallel effect on the attributer's own behavior choices and upon his predictions and inferences about the choices of others.

The biasing effect of ambiguity resolution perhaps is most obvious when the attributer's knowledge of a response or situation is secondhand and lacking in important specific details. Consider, for example, the subject who must decide on the precise meaning of such modifiers as *often* or *typically* or of any other potentially ambiguous descriptors encountered in the context of questionnaire items. It is obvious that both the response category to which that subject assigns himself and his categorizations of his peers will be similarly influenced by these decisions about the precise meaning of terms.

Similarly, the subject who reads about a dilemma regarding the signing of a release form for an impromptu television commercial [in Study 1 of Ross *et al.* (1977b)] is forced to imagine the interviewer, the physical setting, and a host of other situational details which might encourage or inhibit the relevant behavioral options. If these imagined details seemingly would encourage one to sign the release, then the subject is more likely to assume that he personally would sign, that a similar decision would be a common response among his peers, and that signing the release would reflect little about the distinguishing dispositions of any particular actor. By contrast, if the details imagined by the subject would inhibit signing of the release, the subject is more likely to assume that he personally would refuse, that his peers typically would do likewise, and that signing of the release would reveal much about the personal dispositions of the relevant actor.

In questionnaire studies this resolution of ambiguities in descriptions of situations and behaviors may seem a troublesome artifact. However, the same factor becomes an important source of bias in everyday social judgments and inferences where attributers may often respond to accounts of situations or actions that are vague and frequently secondhand. The intuitive psychologist constantly is confronted with statements like "Sally hardly ever dates short men" or "John refused to pay the painter's bill when he saw the paint job." In such circumstances he is forced to resolve ambiguities or uncertainties in the statement. Such resolutions in turn will exert parallel effects upon his assumptions about his own behavior, his impressions about consensus, and his inferences about the dispositions of those whose behavior has been loosely categorized or described.

The false consensus effect demonstrated in Ross *et al.* (1977b), it should be reemphasized, was not restricted to circumstances where raters relied upon ambiguous secondhand descriptions. However, even when attributers actually experience or have fully adequate descriptions of a choice situation, ambiguities remain which inevitably will be resolved differently by different subjects. Thus, subjects who anticipated and feared the ridicule of peers for wearing the "EAT AT JOE'S" sign and regarded the experimenter's wishes and expectations as trivial were likely to refuse to wear the sign, to assume similar refusals by their peers, and to draw strong inferences about the traits of any subject who chose to wear the sign. Opposite priorities, of course, would have produced opposite personal choices and opposite social estimates and inferences.

The false consensus bias, in summary, both reflects and creates distortions in the attribution process. It results from nonrandom sampling and retrieval of evidence and from idiosyncratic interpretation of situational factors and forces. In turn, it biases judgments about deviance and deviates, helps lead actors and observers to divergent perceptions of behavior, and, more generally, promotes variance and error in the interpretation of social phenomena.

C. INADEQUATE ALLOWANCES FOR THE ROLE-BIASED NATURE OF SOCIAL DATA

Interpersonal encounters provide an important informational basis for the intuitive psychologist's self-evaluations and social judgments. Often, however, the course of such encounters is shaped and constrained by the formal and informal roles that the various actors must play. More specifically, social roles typically confer unequal control over the style, content, and duration of an encounter; such control, in turn, facilitates displays of knowledge, skill, wit, or sensitivity, while permitting the concealment of deficiencies. Accurate social judgment, accordingly, depends upon the intuitive psychologist's ability to make adequate allowances and adjustments for such role-conferred advantages and disadvantages in self-perception.

In a recent paper, however, Ross, Amabile, and Steinmetz (1977a) have proposed that social perceivers may typically *fail* to make these "necessary" adjustments and, consequently, may draw inaccurate social inferences about role-advantaged and role-disadvantaged actors. In one sense the proposal of Ross *et al.* is simply a special case of the fundamental attribution error described in Section II,A: The fundamental error is a tendency to underestimate the impact of situational determinants and overestimate the degree to which actions and outcomes reflect the actor's dispositions. The special case proposed by Ross *et al.* deals with the intuitive scientist's underestimation of the effects of roles upon success in self-presentation. In another sense, the proposal of Ross *et al.* contends that the intuitive psychologist is insufficiently sensitive to the biased nature of the data provided by role-constrained encounters and, perhaps, insufficiently sensitive to the problem of sampling bias in general.

The particular roles dealt with in the empirical demonstration reported by Ross *et al.* (1977a) were those of "questioner" and "contestant" in a general knowledge quiz game. The questioner's role obliged the subject to compose a set of challenging general knowledge questions from his or her own store of information, to pose the questions to a contestant, and to provide accurate feedback after each response. Both of these participants (and, in subsequent reenactments, observers as well) were then required to rate the questioner's and the contestant's general knowledge.

The arbitrary assignment and fulfillment of these roles, it should be apparent, forced participants and observers alike to deal with nonrepresentative and highly biased displays of the questioners' knowledge relative to that of contestants. Indeed, the nature of the role-conferred advantages and disadvantages in self-presentation were neither subtle nor disguised. Questioners were allowed and encouraged to display their own wealth of general knowledge by posing difficult and esoteric questions to which their role guaranteed that they would know the answers. The contestant's role, by contrast, prevented any such selective self-serving displays and more displays of ignorance virtually inevitable.

The quiz game contrived by Ross *et al.*, in a sense, provided a particularly stringent test of the intuitive psychologist's proposed insensitivity to role-conferred self-presentation advantages and to corresponding biases in the data samples upon which social judgments frequently are based. For instance, the random nature of the assignment to advantageous and disadvantageous roles was salient and uncontestable. Furthermore, subjects were fully aware of the specific obligations, prerogatives, and limitations associated with each role. In short, subjects seemingly enjoyed an ideal perspective to overcome the proposed source of bias. Nevertheless, the unequal "contest" between questioners and contestants led to consistently biased and erroneous impressions (Table II). As predicted, questioners rated their own general knowledge higher than that of the contestants; moreover, this false impression was shared by the contestants themselves and by uninvolved observers of the encounter.

The narrower as well as the broader implications of the demonstrations of Ross *et al.* should not be overlooked. Indeed, the encounter between advantaged questioners and disadvantaged contestants has obvious parallels within academic settings. Teachers consistently enjoy the prerogative of questioners, and students typically suffer the handicaps of answerers (although some students leap at opportunities to reverse these roles). Consider, as a particularly dramatic in-

TABLE II
EFFECTS OF QUESTIONER–CONTESTANT ROLE UPON
SUBJECTS' PERCEPTIONS OF THEIR OWN AND THEIR
PARTNER'S KNOWLEDGE[a]

Subjects' role	Rating of self[b]	Rating of partner[b]	Self–partner difference
Questioner	54.84	51.66	+3.18
Contestant	40.24	65.16	−24.91

[a]Summarized from Ross *et al.* (1977a).
[b]Higher number indicates belief that the person rated is relatively high in general knowledge (1 = minimum; 100 = maximum).

stance, the role-constrained encounters that characterize the typical dissertation "orals." The candidate is required to field questions from the idiosyncratic and occasionally esoteric areas of each examiner's interest and expertise. In contrast to the examiners, the candidate has relatively little time for reflection and relatively little power to define or limit the domains of inquiry. In light of the present demonstrations, it might be anticipated (correctly so, in this author's experience) that the typical candidate leaves the ordeal feeling more relief than pride, whereas his or her examiners depart with increased respect for each others' insight and scholarship. Such evaluations, of course, may often be warranted. It is worth entertaining the possibility, however, that an alternative procedure for the oral examination, one in which the candidate first posed questions for his examiners and then corrected *their* errors and omissions, would yield more elated candidates and less smug examiners.

There are, of course, countless other contexts in which formal or informal social roles may constrain interpersonal encounters and, in so doing, bias both the data available to the intuitive psychologist and the interpersonal judgments that follow from such data. Thus the employer may dwell upon his personal triumphs, avocations, and areas of knowledge and may avoid mention of his failures, whereas his employee enjoys no such freedom. The physician, likewise, is relatively free to assume with his patient whichever role—stern parent, sympathetic friend, or detached scientist—he wishes. Similarly, the more dominant partner in a personal relationship can disproportionately dictate the rules and arenas for self-presentation and that partner's choice is likely to be self-serving.

If subsequent research confirms the generality of the present thesis, the implications may be all too clear for our understanding of social structures and of the forces that impede social change. Individuals who enjoy positions of power by accident of birth, favorable political treatment, or even their own efforts also tend to enjoy advantages in self-presentation. Such individuals, and especially their disadvantaged underlings, may greatly underestimate the extent to which the seemingly positive attributes of the powerful simply reflect the advantages of social control. Indeed, this distortion in social judgment threatens to provide a particularly insidious brake upon social mobility whereby the disadvantaged and powerless overestimate the capabilities of the powerful, who in turn inappropriately deem their own caste well suited to the task of leadership.

D. OVERLOOKING THE INFORMATIONAL VALUE OF NONOCCURRENCES

The astute Sherlock Holmes directs our attention to a rather subtle but potentially interesting and important shortcoming of the intuitive scientist. In the relevant episode (described in "The Silver Blaze" in *The Memoirs of Sherlock Holmes* by Arthur Conan Doyle) the great detective invites the faithful Dr. Watson to consider "the curious incident of the dog in the night-time." Watson, the conventional behaviorist, remarks correctly that "The dog did nothing in the night-time." Holmes, the inspired behaviorist, triumphantly observes, "That was the curious incident." For the premier practitioner of the science of deduction this *nonincident* or *nonoccurrence* furnishes the key to subsequent interpretations and inferences. (Specifically, Holmes recognizes that a barking dog would have provided no evidence but a silent one proved the intruder in question to be someone well known to the dog.)

The intuitive psychologist, it can more generally be postulated, is like Dr. Watson, a rather conventional behaviorist. He attends to actions or occurrences in forming inferences but neglects to consider the information conveyed when particular responses or events do *not* occur. The author can cite no research directly relevant to the postulated "behaviorist" bias. One source of indirect evidence, however, is provided by findings concerning subjects' use of the observations in a fourfold, presence–absence table. Specifically, Smedslund (1963), Ward and Jenkins (1965), Wason and Johnson-Laird (1972), and others report that only the "present–present" cell strongly influences subjects' inferences regarding covariation (for example, the covariation of diseases and symptoms). Logically, of course, frequency in this cell is no more relevant to the assessment of covariation than are frequencies in any of the other three cells (including the absent–absent cell, which, if our general contention is apt, should prove particularly difficult for subjects to use appropriately in forming impressions of covariation and causal inferences).

Although more directly pertinent research data may be lacking, there are a number of common social experiences which become more explicable in the light of our present speculations. Consider for example the following, rather common episode: Jack meets a new acquaintance, Jill, and after some personal interaction with her, he forms the vague impression that she does not like him.

Such impressions are rarely unfounded. Nevertheless, if Jack searches his memory for specific actions or responses by Jill that reveal her dislike, he will likely be frustrated in his search since, under normal circumstances, acquaintances do not express dislike in overt words or deeds. Thus, if Jack relies upon the sample of evidence he retrieves from memory, he may well conclude that his impression is incorrect and unjustified by the evidence; alternatively, he may cling to his impression but resort to "intuition" or "sixth sense" in order to justify it. If the peerless Mr. Holmes were available for consultation, he doubtless could end Jack's attributional dilemma by focusing his attention on what Jill did *not* do. Jack might well note that Jill did *not* deliberately prolong encounters, did *not* furnish positive nonverbal feedback, and, in general, did *not* show any of the responses that normally signal liking or interest.

In the encounter just described Jack has not been totally oblivious to the information conveyed by Jill's nonresponses—he has correctly discerned her sentiments; he has merely failed to process the information in a manner which facilitates accurate causal inferences or overt verbal expression. In other instances the attributer might even fail to detect or to store the relevant information and might entirely misjudge the sentiments of his acquaintance. The general contention is simply that nonoccurrences are rarely as salient or as cognitively "available" to the potential attributer as are occurrences. As a consequence, recognition, storage, retrieval, and interpretation all become less likely.

The difference between an occurrence and a nonoccurrence can, of course, sometimes be one of semantics. The absence of eye contact can be coded by the potential attributer as the presence of gaze avoidance (e.g., Ellsworth & Ross, 1975). The absence of sexual responsiveness similarly can be coded and interpreted as the presence of frigidity. These seemingly moot semantic distinctions, however, can have nontrivial consequences for the intuitive psychologist. Indeed, if present speculations are warranted, it should be possible to demonstrate that particular absences of response are more noted, more remembered, and more likely deemed as relevant by the attributer when he is provided with positive or active category labels to apply to such absences.

III. Attributional Biases in the Psychology of Prediction

Implicit expectations and explicit predictions are important products of the intuitive psychologist's collection, coding, storage, retrieval, and interpretation of social data. Often, such expectations and predictions are also crucial mediators of social responses. The attribution theorist, as we have noted earlier, has reason to be concerned with intuitive prediction not only because of its obvious connection to widely studied attributional processes, but also because of its unique potential for revealing the degree of attributional accuracy and the direction of particular biases. Nevertheless, it has not been attribution researchers but rather two cognitive psychologists, Daniel Kahneman and Amos Tversky, who recently have stirred social psychology's interest in prediction.[5]

A. THREE HEURISTICS GOVERNING INTUITIVE PREDICTION AND JUDGMENT

In a very impressive series of papers (Kahneman & Tversky, 1972, 1973; Tversky & Kahneman, 1971, 1973, 1974) these investigators have demonstrated that intuitive predictions and judgments made by typical social observers (and often those made by trained social scientists as well) deviate markedly from the dictates of conventional statistical models. Instead, such predictions seem to reflect the operation of a limited number of "heuristics," or informal decision-making criteria. Among these heuristics are "availability" (Kahneman & Tversky, 1973), "adjustment" (Tversky & Kahneman, 1974), and "representativeness" (Kahneman & Tversky, 1972, 1973). Each heuristic leads the intuitive psychologist to particular errors or biases in subjective estimates and predictions, and each is relevant to the concerns of this chapter.

Use of the *availability* heuristic leads the intuitive psychologist's estimates of the frequency or probability of events to reflect the ease of imagining or remembering those events. Since availability is often poorly correlated with frequency or probability, systematic errors and biases in judgment inevitably result. Thus subjects who heard lists of well-known personalities of both sexes subsequently overestimated the representation of that sex whose members were more famous. The false consensus bias, described earlier, and Chapman and Chapman's (1967, 1969) classic demonstrations of "illusory correlation" in clinical judgment, also seem to reflect the operation of the availability heuristic. Finally, we shall cite the role of availability in our subsequent discussions of impression perseverance and the effects of explanation upon expectation.

Use of the *adjustment* heuristic leads one to make estimates and predictions by "adjusting" either some salient initial value or the result of some partial computation procedure. Such adjustments, however, are rarely sufficient, and the result is typically an "anchoring effect." In one study (Tversky & Kahneman, 1974), for example, subjects were asked to adjust an arbitrary initial estimate of the percentage of African countries in the United Nations. Those starting with anchors of 10% or 65% produced adjusted estimates of 25% and

---

[5] Unfortunately, the scope of the present chapter forces us to neglect earlier contributions dealing with subjective prediction, expectation, and discrepancies between logical and "psychological" judgment (e.g., Alberoni, 1962; Edwards, 1968; Peterson &-Beach, 1967; Slovic & Lichtenstein, 1971; Wheeler & Beach, 1968). Much of this research is acknowledged and described in Kaheman and Tversky's papers and in a recent review by Fischhoff (1976).

45%, respectively. Tversky and Kahneman argue convincingly that overestimation of likelihood for conjunctive events (i.e., the likelihood of A *and* B *and* C *all* occurring) and underestimation for disjunctive events (i.e., the likelihood of at least *one* of A *or* B *or* C occurring) are further results of the intuitive statistician's failure to adequately adjust preliminary or partially computed estimates.

Use of the *representativeness* heuristic is easier to illustrate than to define. It is reflected in the intuitive statistician's tendency to predict that outcome which appears most representative of salient features of the evidence while ignoring conventional statistical criteria such as the reliability, validity, and amount of available evidence, or the prior baseline probabilities associated with the relevant outcomes.

A use of the representativeness heuristic that is particularly striking and pertinent to present concerns is reflected in the intuitive scientist's tendency to give too much weight to *predictor* variables and too little weight to central tendencies in the population distribution of the variable to be *predicted*. Indeed, a sample prediction problem may help the reader to recognize his or her own susceptibility to this bias: *I (the present author) have a friend who is a professor. He likes to write poetry, is rather shy, and is slight of stature. Which of the following is his field: (a) Chinese Studies, or (b) psychology?* The reader who has guessed Chinese Studies, or even seriously entertained the possibility, has fallen victim to the bias described so compellingly by Kahneman and Tversky. Let the unconvinced reader first consider his prediction in light of the number of psychology professors relative to the number of Chinese Studies professors in the overall population. Then let him further consider the more restricted population of the present author's likely friends. Surely *no* psychologist's implicit personality theory about the relationship among avocation, shyness, stature, and academic discipline is sufficiently strong to warrant overlooking such "baseline" considerations.

Errors in parametric prediction problems similarly reflect the use of the representativeness heuristic. Most obvious, perhaps, is the layman's shortcomings in dealing with problems of regression. People expect and predict behaviors and outcomes on variable Y to be as "distinctive" or deviant from the norm as the predictor variable X, and they are surprised and often disturbed by the phenomenon of "regression to the mean."[6] In fact, they are prone to invent spurious explanations for events that, in reality, are simple regression phenomena. Kahneman and Tversky (1973) describe a relevant anecdote: Israeli flight instructors, urged to make use of positive reinforcement, expressed skepticism. In their experience, they argued, praise of exceptionally good performance typically "led

---

[6] Nonregressive prediction is, in a sense, a special case of the intuitive statistician's inattentiveness to "baselines" or population distributions for the variable to be predicted. A regressive prediction minimizes error relative to a nonregressive one simply because the former is closer to more observations in the population than is the latter.

to" *diminished* performance on the next trial, while criticism of exceptionally poor performance typically "produced" an immediate *improvement* in performance. On the basis of such firsthand experience, in fact, the instructors concluded that, contrary to accepted psychological doctrine, punishment is more effective than reward.

B. USE OF CONCRETE INSTANCES VS. ABSTRACT BASELINES

The relevance of Kahneman and Tversky's work to the general concerns of attribution theory has recently begun to be appreciated (cf. Fischhoff, 1976). Nisbett and Borgida (1975), for example, were quick to note that the weak effects of base rate information on category prediction are analogous to the weak effects of consensus information on attributional judgments (e.g., Cooper, Jones, & Tuller, 1972; McArthur, 1972, 1976; A. G. Miller, Gillen, Schenker, & Radlove, 1973). Pursuing the implications of this observation, Nisbett and Borgida demonstrated that intuitive behavioral predictions, like category predictions, may be relatively impervious to consensus or baseline information. Specifically, subjects were given accurate baseline information about the behavior of previous participants in experiments involving such responses as altruistic intervention and willingness to receive electric shock. As the investigators anticipated, this authentic baseline information did not influence subjects' guesses about the behavior of particular participants in the original experiment. Similarly, this information did not influence subjects' attributions about the causes of such behavior, or their predictions about what their own behavior might be.

Nisbett and Borgida's research design also considered the opposite prediction task, that of estimating overall base rates for behavior on the basis of knowledge provided about the responses of particular individuals. The results were dramatic and consistent with yet another bias described by Tversky and Kahneman (1971). Nisbett and Borgida's subjects' previously demonstrated "unwillingness to deduce the particular from the general was matched only by their *willingness* to infer the general from the particular" (p. 939). Thus, given information that two subjects had behaved in an extreme and counterintuitive fashion (e.g., by taking the maximum possible shock level in a pain threshold experiment), raters predicted that such extreme behavior was *modal* for subjects as a whole.

In attempting to account for these seemingly contradictory but equally nonrational prediction biases, Nisbett, Borgida, Crandall, and Reed (1976) have contrasted the *concreteness* and vividness of specific cases with the pallid *abstract* character of statistical baselines. To illustrate, they invited their readers to participate in the following "thought experiment":

> Let us suppose that you wish to buy a new car and have decided that on grounds of economy and longevity you want to purchase one of those solid, stalwart, middleclass Swedish cars—either a Volvo or a Saab. As a prudent and sensible

buyer, you go to *Consumer Reports,* which informs you that the consensus of their experts is that the Volvo is mechanically superior, and the consensus of the readership is that the Volvo has the better repair record. Armed with this information, you decide to go and strike a bargain with the Volvo dealer before the week is out. In the interim, however, you go to a cocktail party where you announce this intention to an acquaintance. He reacts with disbelief and alarm: "A Volvo! You've got to be kidding. My brother-in-law had a Volvo. First, the fancy fuel injection computer thing went out. 250 bucks. Next he started having trouble with the rearend. Had to replace it. Then the transmission and the clutch. Finally sold it in 3 years for junk." [p. 129]

The logical status of this information, Nisbett *et al.* remind the reader, is that the frequency-of-repair record should be shifted by an iota or two on a few dimensions. As they contend, however, the reader's thought experiment is likely to suggest a more dramatic result. The implications of this thought experiment are also borne out in more formal empirical demonstrations. In a series of experiments Borgida and Nisbett (1977) gave undergraduate subjects course-evaluation information and invited them to state their own choices for future enrollment. Some students received summaries of the evaluations of previous course enrollees; others received the information through face-to-face contact with a small number of individuals. As anticipated by the investigators, abstract data-summary information had little impact on course choices, whereas concrete information had a substantial impact.

C. SOURCES OF NONCONSERVATIVE (NONREGRESSIVE) PREDICTION

Demonstrations of man's apparent failings as an intuitive statistician promise to capture the attention of attribution theorists. In attempting to clarify the implications of seminal research in this area by Kahneman and Tversky and by others (cf. Fischhoff, 1976), it is important to distinguish between two different sources of bias or error in judgment. Ross *et al.* (1976a) have termed these, respectively, shortcomings in intuitive *psychological theory* and shortcomings in informal *statistical methodology*. The former are misconceptions about the nature of objects and events in the domain of psychological inquiry; the latter are faulty applications of knowledge or information about that domain in making estimates, inferences, and predictions.

Ross, Amabile, and their associates have emphasized this distinction in a series of studies dealing with the intuitive psychologist–statistician's tendency to be "nonconservative" (i.e., nonregressive) in bivariate prediction tasks. In these studies (Amabile, 1975; Ross *et al.*, 1976a) the investigators made use of "authentic" data distributions derived from preliminary studies, student records, and self-report questionnaires. The use of such authentic data, of course, permitted direct assessment of the degree of accuracy and the direction of error in the subjects' predictions and estimates.

Amabile (1975) and Ross *et al.* (1976a) had little difficulty in replicating the basic phenomenon described by Kahneman and Tversky (1972, 1973). Subjects' predictions about the behavior, characteristics, and outcomes of their peers were clearly nonregressive and, by conventional statistical criteria, insufficiently "conservative." For bivariate distributions in which population or large sample correlations were in the range of $r = 0$ to $r = +.30$, subjects made predictions of one variable based on knowledge of the other variable that would have been justified only by correlations in the range of $r = +.60$ to $r = +1.00$.

As anticipated, two distinct sources of error were shown to underlie such nonregressive prediction tendencies. First, it was clear that the intuitive scientists in these studies typically held incorrect assumptions about the strength of the relationship among the observable characteristics and behaviors under consideration. Subjects were required to specify the degree of relationship they believed to exist between particular variables through a variety of "matching tasks" using scatterplots, bivariate charts of numbers, and figures portraying different degrees of covariation between simple physical properties. Using such procedures, subjects consistently overestimated the relevant correlation coefficients and, in so doing, consistently overestimated the degree of cross-situational consistency existing in the relevant behavioral measures and outcomes. This source of bias, accordingly, can be termed *correlation error*. In a sense, it reflects the intuitive psychologist's unwarranted adherence to simple broad "trait theories" of the sort that receive so little support in the systematic investigations of personality theorists (cf. Mischel, 1968, 1969, 1973).

A second source of bias reported by the investigators reflects the intuitive scientist's failure not as a psychologist but as a statistician. This bias, which we may term *regression error*, was reflected in predictions of variable Y from knowledge of variable X that were even less regressive than could be justified by the subjects' already-inflated estimates of population correlation. An example from the results reported by Amabile (1975) will help to illustrate the two different sources of nonconservative prediction. In one problem subjects dealt with the relationship between verbal Scholastic Aptitude Test (SAT) scores and subsequent GPA measures for Stanford freshmen. Through examination of a large sample of academic records the investigators estimated the relevant population correlation coefficient (Pearson r) to be $+.20$. The subjects' estimate for this relationship, indicated by their choice of appropriately labeled scatterplots, was a correlation coefficient of $+.60$ (i.e., correlation error). The subjects' predictions of GPAs from knowledge of SAT scores and vice versa, however, would have been justified by a population correlation not of $+.60$ but of $+.94$ (i.e., regression error). This pattern of results was replicated using a wide variety of authentic data matrices involving cross-situational consistency in outcomes, personal characteristics, and behaviors.

The data for individual subjects' predictions in the Ross and Amabile studies provide an interesting and more precise view of nonregressive prediction tendencies. Very few individuals rigorously and systematically applied a simple linear "prediction equation." Furthermore, it appears that subjects' departures from consistent linear prediction were governed by the strength of the relationship they believed to exist between X and Y. When the relationship was estimated to be strong, their individual predictions were well fit by a simple linear function. When the relationship was believed to be weak, subject's predictions varied widely about a best-fitting regression line. More specifically, the subjects who believed the relationship between X and Y to be relatively weak did *not* respond to extreme values of X with predictions of Y relatively close to the mean. Instead, they responded by *varying* their predictions (for example, by predicting one more extreme value of Y and one less extreme value of Y, given two identically extreme values of the predictor variable X).

The data on accuracy were also revealing. Group estimates of Y, "enlightened" by specific knowledge of X, consistently yielded a greater mean error (in terms of both absolute and square discrepancies) than would have resulted if the group had averaged across all of those estimates to produce one mean to be offered for all predictions. Similarly the vast majority of individual subjects in the various studies would have decreased the magnitude of their errors by simply repeating their average prediction for Y, never varying it on the basis of their knowledge of X. It is difficult to resist the blunt summary that, when it comes to predictions, a little knowledge (i.e., knowledge of a weakly related predictor variable) is a dangerous thing.

Before concluding our discussion of the intuitive psychologist's penchant for nonconservative prediction, a few qualifications, comments, and suggestions concerning future research directions may be in order. First, it is important to recognize that while the term *nonconservative* may be descriptive of the intuitive scientist's judgments in the contexts we have described,[7] it may not accurately describe his intent or his new view of his behavior. Indeed, he may be led to nonregressive prediction through a chain of inferences that seem impeccably conservative.

Consider, for example, a request to predict John's percentile score on a mathematics text in light of information that John scored at the ninetieth percentile in a reading test. The intuitive psychologist—statistician may begin by recognizing that academic abilities tend to be positively correlated and by reasoning that John's math score is likely to be better than average. He may then assume that, having no information about John's math score, he has no basis for predicting whether it will be higher or lower than John's reading score. From the

---

[7] There is ample evidence, in fact, that in certain judgmental contexts (those involving Bayesian probability) the intuitive psychologist is *overly* "conservative"; that is, he fails to extract sufficient information about population parameters from the data examples available to him (see Peterson & Beach, 1967; Slovic & Lichtenstein, 1971). Such conservatism, perhaps, reflects the operation both of the simple "adjustment" heuristic and of the more general "perseverance mechanisms" to be described later in this chapter.

intuitive scientist's viewpoint it may thus seem conservative to guess that the relevant scores will be equal (a judgment that would be justified, in conventional statistical terms, only by a *perfect* correlation) because such a guess seemingly represents the "middle course" between guessing either that X is greater than Y or that Y is greater than X.

A second conceptual issue involves the criterion for optimal prediction. It is entirely possible that subjects may be guided by considerations other than accuracy, or by criteria for accuracy very different from those adopted by the conventional statistician. We certainly have no a priori reason to assume that social observers are particularly concerned with minimizing average *squared* discrepancies, or even with minimizing average absolute discrepancies. Perhaps subjects are concerned with maximizing the number of "exact hits"; perhaps they are willing to increase their "average error" if it will help them to predict the few really deviant or extreme scores in the sample. Some subjects may even be concerned with criteria that are irrelevant to accuracy, for example, making their distribution of predictions reflect the range or variability of the sample scores to be predicted. Any of these nonconventional statistical goals or desiderata may characterize particular subjects or particular data domains (cf. Abelson, 1974). Indeed, one could readily suggest prediction contexts in everyday experience for which each objective would be highly appropriate.

Subsequent research could clarify these issues considerably by pursuing the following research questions: (1) What are subjects' own objectives and what are their criteria for good prediction—in the standard laboratory tasks that have been employed and in a wide range of judgment tasks outside the laboratory? (2) Do subjects recognize the costs of nonregressive prediction strategies, and do they labor under illusions about the possible benefits of such strategies? (3) What kind of feedback in a prediction paradigm, if any, could lead subjects to adopt and to generalize the use of more regressive strategies? Indeed, in what data domains, if any, may subjects already make use of such strategies, and why do they do so?

IV. Perseverance of Social Inferences and Social Theories

A. PERSEVERANCE IN SELF-PERCEPTIONS AND SOCIAL PERCEPTIONS

In the course of this chapter various biases in the sampling, processing, and interpretation of social data have been described. These biased strategies and procedures produce initial impressions about oneself or other people that typically are premature and often are erroneous. As long as they remain private and free of behavioral commitment, such first impressions may seem inconsequential, tentative in nature, and free to adjust to new input. A gradually increasing body of theory and research, however, can now be marshaled to suggest the contrary. We shall deal in detail with a pair of "debriefing" experiments reported by Ross, Lepper, and Hubbard (1975). These were designed to provide a simple and dramatic demonstration that errors in initial self-perceptions and social judgments are difficult to reverse and may survive even the complete negation of their original evidential basis (cf. also Walster, Berscheid, Abrahams, & Aronson, 1967; Valins, 1974).

The procedure in the experiments of Ross *et al.* was quite straightforward. Subjects first received continuous false feedback as they performed a novel discrimination task (i.e., distinguishing authentic suicide notes from ficticious ones). In the first experiment reported, this procedure was used to manipulate the subjects' perceptions of their own performance and ability. A second experiment further introduced observers who formed social impressions as they witnessed the false-feedback manipulation. In both experiments, after this manipulation of first impressions had been completed, the experimenter totally discredited the "evidence" upon which the actors' and/or observers' impressions had been based. Specifically, the actor (overheard in Experiment 2 by the observer) received a standard "debriefing" session in which he learned that his putative outcome had been predetermined and that his feedback had been totally unrelated to actual performance. Before dependent variable measures were introduced, in fact, every subject was led to acknowledge explicitly his understanding of the nature and purpose of the experimental deception.

Following this total discrediting of the original source of misinformation, a dependent variable questionnaire was completed dealing with the actors' performances and abilities. The evidence for postdebriefing impression perseverance was unmistakable for actors and observers alike. On virtually every measure (i.e., objective estimates of the actor's just-completed performance, estimates for performance on a future set of discrimination problems, and subjective estimates of the actor's abilities) the totally discredited initial outcome manipulation produced significant "residual" effects upon actors' and observers' assessments (see Table III).

In subsequent related experiments Ross, Lepper, and their colleagues have pursued the perseverance phenomenon using a variety of experimental settings and personal abilities. Although much of this research is still in progress, it is already apparent that the phenomenon is not restricted to the debriefing paradigm or to the suicide note task. For instance, students' erroneous impressions of their "logical problem-solving abilities" (and their academic choices in a follow-up measure 1 month later) persevered even after students learned that good or poor teaching procedures provided a totally sufficient explanation for their success or failure (Lau, Lepper, & Ross, 1976).

TABLE III

POSTDEBRIEFING PERCEPTIONS OF THE ACTOR'S PERFORMANCE AND ABILITY[a]

Measure	Actor's own perceptions			Observer's perceptions of actors		
	Success	Failure	t	Success	Failure	t
Estimated initial number correct	18.33	12.83	5.91[e]	19.00	12.42	4.43[e]
Predicted future number correct	18.33	14.25	4.23[e]	19.08	14.50	2.68[c]
Rated ability at task	5.00	3.83	2.65[c]	5.33	4.00	3.36[d]
Related abilities at related tasks	4.69	4.53	<1.00	4.69	4.11	1.76[b]

[a]Summarized from experiment 2 of Ross et al. (1975).
[b]$p < .10$.
[c]$p < .05$.
[d]$p < .01$.
[e]$p < .001$.

B. PERSEVERANCE MECHANISMS

1. Distortion and Autonomy

Two related mechanisms have been proposed by Ross and Lepper to account for perseverance phenomena. The first involves *distortion* in the process by which the intuitive psychologist assesses the relevance, reliability, and validity of potentially pertinent data. That is, the weight he assigns to evidence is determined, in large measure, by its consistency with his initial impressions. More specifically, he neglects the possibility that evidence seemingly consistent with his existing impressions may nevertheless be irrelevant or tainted; similarly, he too readily conceives and accepts challenges to contradictory evidence. As a result, data considered subsequent to the formation of a clear impression typically will seem to offer a large measure of support for that impression. Indeed, even a random sample of potentially relevant data "processed" in this manner may serve to strengthen rather than challenge an erroneous impression. The capacity of existing impressions and expectations to bias interpretations of social data is, of course, a well-replicated phenomenon in social psychology (e.g., Asch, 1946; Haire & Grunes, 1950; Hastorf & Cantril, 1954; Jones & Goethals, 1971; Zadny & Gerard, 1974).

The second proposed mechanism involves the *autonomy* achieved by distorted evidence. Once formed, an initial impression may not only be enhanced by the distortion of evidence, it may ultimately by *sustained* by such distortion. The social perceiver, it is contended, rarely reinterprets or reattributes impression-relevant data when the basis for his original bias in processing that data is discredited. Once coded, the evidence becomes autonomous from the coding scheme, and its impact ceases to depend upon the validity of that scheme. Thus an erroneous impression may survive the discrediting of its original evidential basis because the impression has come to enjoy the support of additional evidence that is seemingly *independent* of that now-discredited basis.

2. The Role of Explanation in Impression Perseverance

In accounting for the attributer's reluctance to abandon initial impressions, Ross *et al*. (1975) have emphasized the role of the intuitive psychologist's search for causal explanation. Individuals, they suggest do more than merely aggregate information consistent with their self-perceptions and social perceptions. They also search for antecedents that cause and account for events. These "causal schemata" play a particularly important role in impression perseverance. Once an action, outcome, or personal disposition is viewed as the consequence of known or even postulated antecedents, those antecedents will continue to *imply* the relevant consequence even when all other evidence is removed.

Consider, for example, a subject in the Ross *et al*. (1975) study who has attributed her success in discriminating suicide notes to the insights she gained from the writings of a novelist who committed suicide. Consider, similarly, an observer in that study who has attributed an actor's failure to that actor's manifestly cheerful disposition. Even after debriefing, these attributers retain a plausible basis for inferring the relevant outcome of the discrimination task. Neither participant, of course, has initially considered, or reconsidered after briefing, the many possible antecedents that might have caused and accounted for task outcomes opposite to that contrived by the experimenters.

A series of recent experiments reported by Ross, Lepper, Strack, and Steinmetz (1976c) have provided more direct evidence of the role that causal explanation can play in sustaining discredited impressions and expectations. In these experiments, subjects were presented with authentic clinical case histories. In various experimental conditions they were asked to use this case-study information to explain a significant event in the patient's later life (e.g., suicide, a hit-and-run accident, an attempt to gain elective office, or an altruistic act). In some conditions, subjects wrote their explanations believing that the event had actually occurred, only to learn afterward that the event was hypothetical and that absolutely no authentic information existed concerning the patient's later life. In other conditions, the event to be explained was presented as "merely hypothetical" from the outset. In both experimental conditions, subjects were ultimately asked to estimate the likelihood of the previously explained events and a number of other events as well. (In appropriate control conditions, subjects were given only this final prediction task.)

The results were unambiguous and compelling (Table IV). As hypothesized, the task of identifying case-history antecedents to explain an event increased the

TABLE IV

RESIDUAL EFFECTS OF "EXPLAINING" AN EVENT ON JUDGED LIKELIHOOD OF
THAT EVENT[a]

Event previously explained by subject[b]	Estimated likelihood[c] that patient will:		
	[A] Become involved in hit-and-run accident	[B] Seek election to City Council	Difference [A] − [B]
[A] Patient becomes involved in hit-and-run accident	+1.45	−2.47	+3.92
[B] Patient seeks election to City Council	−0.25	+0.66	−0.91
[C] None	−0.08	−1.55	+1.47

[a]Summarized from Ross et al. (1976c).

[b]Data are combined for subjects who explained event initially believing it to be real and for subjects who explained event knowing it to be hypothetical.

[c]More positive number indicates greater belief that the specified event is likely to have actually occurred in patient's life.

subjects' estimates of that event's likelihood. The relevant phenomenon was replicated across a variety of cases and predicted events and was demonstrated under both the "hypothetical" and "nonhypothetical" explanation conditions [see also Fischhoff (1975, 1976) and Fischhoff and Beyth (1975) for a discussion of the "certainty of hindsight knowledge," a phenomenon that may be closely related to the present demonstrations and may depend upon similar mechanisms].

C. PERSEVERANCE OF "THEORIES"

It should be apparent that the same biased attributional processes which sustain discredited individual inferences may also sustain the discredited attributional strategies that give rise to such inferences. Consider, for instance, the nonregressive or nonconservative prediction strategies discussed earlier. Why does the intuitive scientist continue to believe that correlations reflecting cross-situational consistency are strong when the evidence of his everyday experience will suggest that such correlations are weak? Why does he continue to make nonregressive predictions in a world that, presumably, better rewards more conservative strategies? The answers should be apparent from our foregoing discussion of impression perseverance. First, the intuitive observer selectively codes those data potentially relevant to the relationship between X and Y. Data points that fit his hypotheses and predictions are accepted as reliable, valid, representative, and free of error or "third-variable influences." Such data points are seen as reflective of the "real" or "paradigmatic" relationship between X and

Y. By contrast, data points that deviate markedly from the intuitive psychologist's expectations or theory are unlikely to be given great weight and tend to be dismissed as unreliable, erroneous, unrepresentative, or the product of contaminating third-variable influences.

Thus the intuitive scientist who believes that fat men are jolly, or more specifically that fatness causes jolliness, will see particular fat and jolly men as strong evidence for this theory; he will not entertain the hypothesis that an individual's jollity is mere pretense or the product of a particularly happy home life rather than obesity. By contrast, fat and morose individuals will be examined very carefully before gaining admission to that scientist's store of relevant data. He might, for instance, seek to determine whether the individual's moroseness on the day in question is atypical, or the result of a nagging cold or a disappointing day, rather than the reflection of some stable attribute. It need hardly be emphasized that even a *randomly* generated scatterplot or contingency table can yield a relatively high correlation if coded in the manner just outlined (cf. Chapman & Chapman, 1967, 1969). Indeed, the professional psychologist, like the intuitive one, can readily derive unwarranted support for almost any hypothesis if permitted to delete, post hoc, the data points that offend his thesis. Perseverant beliefs in extrasensory perception in the face of disconfirming experimental evidence may reflect such selective processing of data (see Gardner, 1975).

The autonomy enjoyed by distorted inferences may further contribute to the perseverance of nonoptimal theories and attributional strategies. The intuitive scientist detects more support for his general theory than is warranted and, having thus "coded" or summarized his findings, he is then disposed to maintain his theory in the face of subsequent logical or empirical attacks by "citing" the wealth of seemingly independent empirical support that it enjoys. It is through such means, perhaps, that the intuitive psychologist remains committed to concepts of broad, stable, heuristically valuable, personality traits and perseveres in the use of nonoptimal prediction strategies. Superstitious learning phenomena and the "partial reinforcement effect" similarly may reflect the subject's capacity to selectively attribute instances of reinforcement and nonreinforcement.

D. WHEN JUDGMENTS AND THEORIES CHANGE: OVERCOMING PERSEVERANCE MECHANISMS

An obvious question begins to emerge from our demonstrations of impression perseverance: Under what circumstances *do* erroneous or unwarranted personal judgments change? Clearly, none of us has exactly the same view of ourselves or of our fellows as he once did; personal experiences do have an impact upon such views. Therapy, education, persuasive arguments, and mass media campaigns also can alter our self-perceptions and social attitudes. Indeed, as we pointed out early in this chapter, psychology's broad view of man has changed and evolved in response to arguments and evidence presented by the field's vanguard. While a detailed examination of the requisites for such change is beyond the scope of the present discussion, a few observations may be appropriate.

First, it seems clear that neither challenges to specific bits of evidence confirming a belief (or theory) nor the addition of small amounts of contradictory evidence are likely to prove effective in producing overall change. Challenges and additions to data tend themselves to be "selectively" coded in accord with one's biased prior impressions. Such selective coding, in fact, generally is quite rational and reasonable: most of our personal impressions and beliefs *are* well founded, and confirming evidence usually *is* more valid, representative, and relevant than disconfirming evidence. But this rational selectivity in interpreting individual "bits" of evidence leads to an irrational result when a whole "batch" of evidence is considered; specifically, virtually any random sample of newly considered evidence processed in this manner will seemingly support the existing belief or theory. In the face of subsequent logical or informational challenges, furthermore, the random sample of newly "processed" data may even help to sustain the incorrect theory which dictated the processing bias. Consider, for instance, an apparently close friendship. Individual acts by either friend will be taken at face value by the other if they seem to reflect sensitivity, concern, affection, or interest. Conversely, particular acts that might seem insensitive, cold, or hostile in the eyes of some disinterested observer will *not* be taken at face value by the other—at least not without the presence of a good deal of corroborating evidence and the absence of potential alternative interpretations. Such biased attributional coding, it should be reemphasized, is not irrational. Our past experiences, and our global views of relationships, generally *do* promote more accurate attributions of specific acts and outcomes. By "rationally" giving our friends the "benefit of the doubt" in our inferences about individual acts, however, we risk irrational interpretations of larger samples of evidence. Specifically, we may be prone to overlook systematic evidence of indifference or resentment until it is overwhelming or until our peers explicitly interpret their behavior for us.

Erroneous impressions, theories, and data-processing strategies, therefore, may not be changed through mere exposure to samples of new evidence. It is not contended, of course, that new evidence can never produce change—only that new evidence will produce *less* change than would be demanded by any logical or rational information-processing model. Thus, new evidence that is strongly and consistently contrary to one's impressions or theories can, and frequently does, produce change, albeit at a slower rate than would result from an unbiased or dispassionate view of the evidence.

It seems clear that the effects of attributional distortion and autonomy can also be overcome without the brute force of consistently disconfirming data.

Dramatic religious and political conversions, for example, presumably are accomplished by other means. Specifically, these conversions seem to be the product not of new data nor attacks on old beliefs but, rather, involve assaults on whole belief systems. Typically, the target of the conversion attempt is not induced to reevaluate the evidence "objectively" or dispassionately. Instead, he is taught to make use of a new and encompassing attributional bias. Often he is also urged to reject all past beliefs and insights as the product of pernicious social, philosophical, or political forces. The attempt to induce a tabula rasa state in the individual and to provide a selective interpretation schema for both the consideration of new evidence and the reconsideration of old evidence is characteristic of strategies for ideological conversion. Insight therapies similarly attempt to overcome impression perseverance through global assaults on belief systems and through the introduction of new explanatory or inferential schemata (although the "working through" of isolated incidents and experiences responsible for perseverant feelings and perceptions is also an important aspect of many therapy regimens).

In a more limited vein, it is worth briefly considering one additional result reported by Ross *et al.* (1975). In one relevant experiment, two different types of debriefing conditions were employed. In the standard "outcome debriefing" condition, subjects were made aware that the prior success–failure manipulation

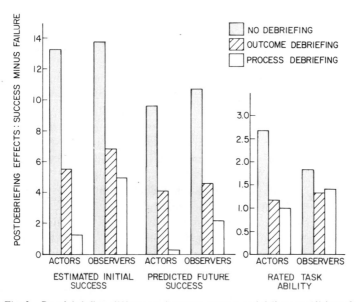

Fig. 2.   Postdebriefing differences between success and failure conditions for actors and observers. Summarized from Experiment 2 of Ross *et al.* (1975). Copyright 1975 by The American Psychological Association. Reprinted by permission.

had been a total deception and that their "outcome" had been assigned without regard to their real performance and ability. In special "process debriefing" conditions, subjects also received an explicit discussion of the perseverance phenomenon and of the distortion and autonomy mechanisms which might lead them, personally, to retain inappropriate or inaccurate self-perceptions. Figure 2 presents the relevant data. While the regular debriefing procedures could not eliminate postdebriefing effects of the original outcome manipulation, the special process debriefing conditions were almost totally effective for actors (although less effective for observers). This demonstration, at the very least, suggests process debriefing is an important requirement for the ethical conduct of deception research. It also hints that personal insight concerning one's attributional biases may hasten the achievement of therapeutic goals.

V. Attributional Biases and Social Science Research

A. THE RESEARCHER'S PURSUIT OF NONOBVIOUS PREDICTIONS AND RESULTS

Among social psychologists today there is an epidemic of critical self-evaluation and debate about the current status of the field's theory, research strategy, practical contributions, and prospects for the future. In such soul-searching appraisals, the issue of "nonobviousness" has figured prominently (cf. McGuire, 1973). Researchers feel compelled to defend the nonobviousness or counter-intuitiveness of their findings lest they be ridiculed as practitioners of "bubba psychology." Furthermore, results deemed subtle and surprising by the investigator may too often seem obvious to one reader (cf. Fischhoff & Slovic, 1976), gratituitous to a second reader, and simply wrong or misconstrued to a third. The issue of nonobviousness, and its relationship to research strategy, can be reconsidered in the light of our present concern with the shortcomings of the intuitive and the professional psychologist.

It is important, first, to distinguish nonobvious empirical results from non-obvious functional relationships. Rarely does the investigator, in his pursuit of nonobviousness, postulate a direct relationship between two variables that were previously considered to be unrelated or inversely related. The nonobvious nature of most predictions in social psychology, instead, relates to the specific context in which the relationship between variables is tested. By carefully contriving the balance of forces operating in a particular setting, the investigator attempts to prove a deficiency both in the intuitive commonsense psychology of the layman and in the existing conceptual analyses of the investigator's professional peers. The demonstration will be both successful and nonobvious to the extent that those factors identified or manipulated by the investigator are more potent determinants of behavior than are other factors which would justify the "intuitive," but wrong, hypothesis. In other words, the researcher proceeds from the assumption that his professional audience is prone to some attributional bias that leads it either to ignore the relevance or to underestimate the relative magnitude of a particular set of behavioral determinants. Typically, the investigator also introduces and makes salient in his description of the research setting other potential determinants which he believes will have less impact than his professional peers expect. If the attribution biases illustrated are genuine, and the relevant determinants and experimental context are of broad significance, the research is likely to become highly visible and controversial. If the investigator has incorrectly characterized the relative weightings assigned to behavioral determinants by his peers, or has dealt with very restricted failings in such weightings, then the demonstration will be dismissed as "obvious" or "too limited in its applicability and interest." Needless to say, the research strategy of capitalizing on nonobvious predictions may depend no less on the investigator's abilities as a stage manager and mystery writer than on his ability to recognize inadequacies either in contemporary psychological theory or in the informal attribution theories of his colleagues.

Earlier in this chapter we discussed the special relevance of the fundamental attribution error that leads the intuitive psychologist to underestimate the magnitude of situational factors relative to dispositional factors or individual differences. Now the argument can be generalized to suggest that the most "classic" experiments in social psychology are nonobvious in terms of the *relative magnitude*, rather than the existence, of the situational forces they manipulate or identify. Consider Milgram's (1963) provocative demonstrations of "obedience" or Asch's (1955) studies of conformity. The importance of such research clearly does not lie in the demonstration that subjects obey authority figures or that conformity pressures excited by peers have an impact. That *would* be dull, obvious, and scientifically unproductive. Rather, they demonstrate that these variables are important *relative* to other personal and situational influences that most of us had previously thought to be far more important determinants of behavior (see Ross, Bierbrauer, & Hoffman, 1976b).

In this connection it is worth noting that these celebrated demonstrations share a very unusual characteristic—they employ no control group. Typically, of course, a control group is necessary to establish some kind of baseline from which the experimental group deviates significantly. Asch and Milgram, however, were able to let our intuitions or expectations serve as the baseline condition from which deviations could be noted. Clearly, in their classic studies, the degree of deviation from expectations was sufficiently compelling *without* statistically contrasting the experimental conditions with some control condition. It is not surprising, furthermore, that each of the classic demonstrations cited has led critics to contend that the surprising effects demonstrated were the products of factors other than those proposed by the original investigators. Indeed, such truly nonobvious demonstrations become a continuing source of inspiration and a challenge for successive generations of scientists.

B. THE INTUITIVE PSYCHOLOGIST'S ILLUSIONS AND INSIGHTS

The same attributional biases that provide the basis for nonobvious research demonstrations by misleading the professional scientist may also mislead intuitive psychologists who serve as their subjects. Nisbett and Wilson (1977) recently have described several dramatic instances of the experimental subject's inability to identify accurately the nature and magnitude of the situational features or manipulations which influence his behavior. It is noteworthy that the subject in a nonobvious demonstration or experiment is typically surprised and dismayed to learn that his behavior is so susceptible to the set of situational factors under the experimenter's control. Conforming subjects in the Asch paradigm and obedient subjects in the Milgram paradigm reportedly were shocked, embarrassed, and prone to make inappropriate inferences about themselves, both during the demonstration and afterwards when the experimenter revealed his intent. It is not surprising, moreover, that they were not easily consoled by debriefing procedures, for the experimenter could not restore what the subjects had lost—a satisfying, albeit inaccurate, implicit theory about the relative impact of specific personal and situational determinants of their own behavior.

The intuitive psychologist, shielded by perseverance mechanisms, is no less likely outside the psychological laboratory to remain ignorant of the distortions and inadequacies both in his primary assumptions and in his methods of sampling, coding, and analyzing the data of everyday experience. Sometimes the results of such ignorance are benign or even benevolent, e.g., the social observer attributes his friendships to the particular personal qualities of his friends and overlooks the role of social ecology (Festinger, Schachter, & Back, 1950). At other times, the results may be harmful to the individual or the society, as unjust and maladaptive methods of resource allocation and social control are justified and perpetuated.

The intuitive psychologist, however, cannot be totally insulated from clashes between expectations and observations, between intuitions and evidence. From such clashes he may be led to cynicism, self-doubt, or disappointment. Alternatively, he may be led to new psychological insights and a willingness to reshape his own life and the institutions of his society.

REFERENCES

Abelson, R. P. Social psychology's rational man. In G. W. Mortimore & S. I. Benn (Eds.), *The concept of rationality in the social sciences.* London: Routledge & Kegan Paul, 1974.

Alberoni, F. Contributions to the study of subjective probability. Part I. *Journal of General Psychology*, 1962, **66**, 241–264.

Amabile, T. M. Investigations in the psychology of prediction. Unpublished manuscript, Stanford University, 1975.

Arkin, R. M., & Duval, S. Focus of attention and causal attributions of actors and observers. *Journal of Experimental Social Psychology*, 1975, **11**, 427–438.

Asch, S. Forming impressions of personality. *Journal of Abnormal and Social Psychology*, 1946, **41**, 258–290.

Asch, S. *Social Psychology*. Englewood Cliffs, N.J.: Prentice-Hall, 1952.

Asch, S. Opinions and social pressures. *Scientific American*, 1955, **193**, 31–35.

Bavelas, A., Hastorf, A. H., Gross, A. E., & Kite, W. R. Experiments in the alteration of group structure. *Journal of Experimental Social Psychology*, 1965, **1**, 55–70.

Beckman, L. Effects of students' performance on teachers' and observers' attributions of causality. *Journal of Educational Psychology*, 1970, **61**, 75–82.

Bem, D. J. An experimental analysis of self-persuasion. *Journal of Experimental Social Psychology*, 1965, **1**, 199–218.

Bem, D. J. Self-perception: An alternative interpretation of cognitive dissonance phenomena. *Psychological Review*, 1967, **74**, 183–200.

Bem, D. J. Self-perception theory. In L. Berkowitz (Ed.), *Advances in experimental social psychology*. Vol. 6. New York: Academic Press, 1972.

Bem, D. J., & Allen, A. On predicting some of the people some of the time: The search for cross-situational consistencies in behavior. *Psychological Review*, 1974, **81**, 506–520.

Bierbrauer, G. Effect of set, perspective, and temporal factors in attribution. Unpublished doctoral dissertation, Stanford University, 1973.

Borgida, E., & Nisbett, R. E. The differential impact of abstract vs. concrete information on decisions. *Journal of Applied Social Psychology*, 1977, in press.

Bramel, D. A dissonance theory approach to defensive projection. *Journal of Abnormal and Social Psychology*, 1962, **64**, 121–129.

Bramel, D. Selection of a target for defensive projection. *Journal of Abnormal and Social Psychology*, 1963, **66**, 318–324.

Chapman, L., & Chapman, J. The genesis of popular but erroneous psychodiagnostic observations. *Journal of Abnormal Psychology*, 1967, **72**, 193–204.

Chapman, L., & Chapman, J. Illusory correlations as an obstacle to the use of valid psychodiagnostic signs. *Journal of Abnormal Psychology*, 1969, **74**, 271–280.

Collins, B. E. Four components of the Rotter internal-external scale: Belief in a difficult world, a just world, a predictable world, and a politically responsive world. *Journal of Personality and Social Psychology*, 1974, **29**, 381–391.

Collins, B. E., Martin, J. C., Ashmore, R. D., & Ross, L. Some dimensions of the external-internal metaphor in theories of personality. *Journal of Personality*, 1973, **41**, 471–492.

Cooper, J., Jones, E. E., & Tuller, S. M. Attribution, dissonance and the illusion of uniqueness. *Journal of Experimental Social Psychology*, 1972, **8**, 45–47.

Crandall, V. C., Katkovsky, W., & Crandall, V. G. Children's beliefs in their own control of reinforcements in intellectual-academic achievement situations. *Child Development*, 1965, **36**, 91–109.

Darley, J., & Batson, C. D. "From Jerusalem to Jericho": A study of situational and dispositional variables in helping behavior. *Journal of Personality and Social Psychology*, 1973, **27**, 100–119.

Davis, W. L., & Davis, D. E. Internal–external control and attribution of responsibility for success and failure. *Journal of Personality*, 1972, **40**, 123–136.

Deci, E. Effects of externally mediated rewards on intrinsic motivation. *Journal of Personality and Social Psychology*, 1971, **18**, 105–115.

Duncker, K. Induced motion. In W. Ellis (Ed.), *A sourcebook of Gestalt psychology*. New York: Harcourt, 1938. Pp. 161–172.

Duval, S., & Wicklund, R. A. *A theory of objective self-awareness*. New York: Academic Press, 1972.

Edlow, O., & Kiesler, C. Ease of denial and defensive projection. *Journal of Experimental Social Psychology*, 1966, **2**, 183–191.

Edwards, W. Conservatism in human information processing. In B. Kleinmuntz (Ed.), *Formal representation of human judgment*. New York: Wiley, 1968.

Ellsworth, P., & Ross, L. Intimacy in response to direct gaze. *Journal of Experimental Social Psychology*, 1975, **11**, 592–613.

Feather, N. T. Attribution of responsibility and valence of success and failure in relation to initial confidence and task performance. *Journal of Personality and Social Psychology*, 1969, **13**, 129–144.

Festinger, L., & Carlsmith, J. M. Cognitive consequences of forced compliance. *Journal of Abnormal and Social Psychology*, 1959, **58**, 203–210.

Festinger, L., Schachter, S., & Back, K. *Social pressures in informal groups: A study of human factors in housing*. New York: Harper, 1950.

Fischhoff, B. Hindsight ≠ foresight: The effect of outcome knowledge on judgment under uncertainty. *Journal of Experimental Psychology: Human Perception and Performance*, 1975, **1**, 288–299.

Fischhoff, B. Attribution theory and judgment under uncertainty. In J. Harvey, W. Ickes, & R. Kidd (Eds.), *New directions in attribution research*. Hillsdale, N.J.: Lawrence Erlbaum Associates, 1976. Pp. 419–450.

Fischhoff, B., & Beyth, R. "I knew it would happen"—remembered probabilities of once-future things. *Organizational Behavior and Human Performance*, 1975, **13**, 1–16.

Fischhoff, B., & Slovic, P. On the psychology of experimental surprises: Outcome knowledge and the journal review process. *Oregon Research Institute Research Bulletin*, 1976, **16**, No. 2.

Fitch, G. Effects of self-esteem, perceived performance, and chance on causal attributions. *Journal of Personality and Social Psychology*, 1970, **16**, 311–315.

Freize, I., & Weiner, B. Cue utilization and attributional judgments for success and failure. *Journal of Personality*, 1971, **39**, 591–606.

Gardner, M. Concerning an effort to demonstrate extrasensory perception by machine. *Scientific American*, 1975, **233**, 114–118.

Greene, D., & Lepper, M. Intrinsic motivation: How to turn play into work. *Psychology Today*, 1974, September, 49–54.

Gross, A. Evaluation of the target person in a social influence situation. Unpublished doctoral dissertation, Stanford University, 1966.

Haire, M., & Grunes, W. F. Perceptual defenses: Processes protecting an organized perception of another personality. *Human Relations*, 1950, **3**, 403–412.

Hastorf, A. H., & Cantril, H. They saw a game: A case study. *Journal of Abnormal and Social Psychology*, 1954, **49**, 129–134.

Heider, F. Social perception and phenomenal causality. *Psychological Review*, 1944, **51**, 358–373.

Heider, F. *The psychology of interpersonal relations*. New York: Wiley, 1958.

Holmes, D. S. Dimensions of projection. *Psychological Bulletin*, 1968, **69**, 248–268.

Icheiser, G. Misunderstandings in human relations: A study in false social perception. *American Journal of Sociology*, 1949, **55**, Part 2, 1–70.

Johnson, T. J., Feigenbaum R., & Weiby, M. Some determinants and consequences of the teacher's perception of causation. *Journal of Experimental Psychology*, 1964, 55, 237–246.

Jones, E. E. How do people perceive the causes of behavior? *American Scientist*, 1976, 64, 300–305.

Jones, E. E., & Davis, K. E. From acts to dispositions: The attribution process in person perceptions. In L. Berkowitz (Ed.), *Advances in experimental social psychology*. Vol. 2. New York: Academic Press, 1965.

Jones, E. E., Davis, K. E., & Gergen, K. J. Role playing variations and their informational value for person perception. *Journal of Abnormal and Social Psychology*, 1961, 63, 302–310.

Jones, E. E., & DeCharms, R. Changes in social perception as a function of the personal relevance of behavior. *Sociometry*, 1957, 20, 75–85.

Jones, E. E., & Goethals, G. R. Order effects in impression formation: Attribution context and the nature of the entity. In E. E. Jones *et al.* (Eds.), *Attribution: Perceiving the causes of behavior*. Morristown, N.J.: General Learning Press, 1971.

Jones, E. E., & Harris, V. A. The attribution of attitudes. *Journal of Experimental Social Psychology*, 1967, 3, 1–24.

Jones, E. E., Kanouse, D. E., Kelley, H. H., Nisbett, R. E., Valins, S., & Weiner, B. *Attribution: Perceiving the causes of behavior*. Morristown, N.J.: General Learning Press, 1971.

Jones, E. E., & Nisbett, R. E. The actor and the observer: Divergent perceptions of the causes of behavior. In E. E. Jones *et al.* (Eds.), *Attribution: Perceiving the causes of behavior*. Morristown, N.J.: General Learning Press, 1971.

Kahneman, D., & Tversky, A. Subjective probability: A judgment of representativeness. *Cognitive Psychology*, 1972, 3, 430–454.

Kahneman, D., & Tversky, A. On the psychology of prediction. *Psychological Review*, 1973, 80, 237–251.

Katz, D., & Allport, F. *Student's attitudes*. Syracuse: Craftsman Press, 1931.

Kelley, H. H. Attribution theory in social psychology. In D. Levine (Ed.), *Nebraska symposium on motivation*. Vol. 15. Lincoln: University of Nebraska Press, 1967.

Kelley, H. H. Attribution in social interaction. In E. E. Jones *et al.* (Eds.), *Attribution: Perceiving the causes of behavior*. Morristown, N.J.: General Learning Press, 1971.

Kelley, H. H. The process of causal attribution. *American Psychologist*, 1973, 28, 107–128.

Kelley, H. H., & Stahelski, A. The social interaction basis of cooperators' and competitors' beliefs about others. *Journal of Personality and Social Psychology*, 1970, 16, 66–91.

Kelly, G. *The psychology of personal constructs*. New York: Norton, 1955. 2 vols.

Kelly, G. Man's construction of his alternatives. In G. Lindzey (Ed.), *Assessment of human motives*. New York: Holt, 1958.

Kruglanski, A. The endogenous-exogenous partition in attribution theory. *Psychological Review*, 1975, 82, 387–406.

Lau, R., Lepper, M. R., & Ross, L. Persistence of inaccurate and discredited personal impressions: A field demonstration of attributional perseverance. Unpublished manuscript, Stanford University, 1976.

Lefcourt, H. M. Internal vs. external control of reinforcement revisited: Recent developments. In B. A. Maher (Ed.), *Progress in experimental personality research*. Vol. 6. New York: Academic Press, 1972.

Lemann, T. B., & Solomon, R. L. Group characteristics as revealed in sociometric patterns and personality ratings. *Sociometry*, 1952, 15, 7–90.

Lepper, M. R., & Greene, D. Turning play into work: Effects of adult surveillance and extrinsic rewards on children's intrinsic motivation. *Journal of Personality and Social Psychology*, 1975, 31, 479–486.

Lepper, M. R., Greene, D., & Nisbett, R. E. Undermining children's intrinsic interest with extrinsic reward: A test of the "overjustification" hypothesis. *Journal of Personality and Social Psychology*, 1973, **28**, 129–137.

McArthur, L. A. The how and what of why: Some determinants and consequences of causal attribution. *Journal of Personality and Social Psychology*, 1972, **22**, 171–193.

McArthur, L. A. The lesser influence of consensus than distinctiveness information on causal attributions: A test of the person–thing hypothesis. *Journal of Personality and Social Psychology*, 1976, **33**, 733–742.

McGuire, W. J. The yin and yang of progress in social psychology: Seven koan. *Journal of Personality and Social Psychology*, 1973, **26**, 446–456.

Milgram, S. Behavioral study of obedience. *Journal of Abnormal and Social Psychology*, 1963, **67**, 371–378.

Miller, A. G., Gillen, B., Schenker, C., & Radlove, S. Perception of obedience to authority. *Proceeding, 81st Annual Convention, American Psychological Association*, 1973, **8**, 127–128.

Miller, D. T., & Ross, M. Self-serving biases in the attribution of causality: Fact or fiction? *Psychological Bulletin*, 1975, **82**, 213–225.

Mischel, W. *Personality and assessment*. New York: Wiley, 1968.

Mischel, W. Continuity and change in personality. *American Psychologist*, 1969, **24**, 1012–1018.

Mischel, W. Towards a cognitive social learning reconceptualization of personality. *Psychological Review*, 1973, **80**, 252–283.

Mischel, W. Processes in delay of gratification. In L. Berkowitz (Ed.), *Advances in experimental social psychology*. Vol. 7. New York: Academic Press, 1974.

Mischel, W., & Ebbesen, E. B. Attention in delay of gratification. *Journal of Personality and Social Psychology*, 1970, **16**, 329–337.

Mischel, W., Ebbesen, E. B., & Zeiss, A. R. Cognitive and attentional mechanisms in delay of gratification. *Journal of Personality and Social Psychology*, 1972, **21**, 204–218.

Nisbett, R. E., & Borgida, E. Attribution and the psychology of prediction. *Journal of Personality and Social Psychology*, 1975, **32**, 932–943.

Nisbett, R. E., Borgida, E., Crandall, R., & Reed, H. Popular induction: Information is not always informative. In J. Carroll & J. Payne (Eds.), *Cognitive and social behavior*. Potomac, Md.: Lawrence Erlbaum Associates, 1976.

Nisbett, R. E., Caputo, C. G., Legant, P., & Maracek, J. Behavior as seen by the actor and as seen by the observer. *Journal of Personality and Social Psychology*, 1973, **27**, 154–164.

Nisbett, R. E., & Wilson, T. D. Telling more than we can know: Verbal reports on mental processes. *Psychological Review,* 1977, in press.

Peterson, C. R., & Beach, L. R. Man as an intuitive statistician. *Psychological Bulletin*, 1967, **68**, 29–46.

Polefka, J. The perception and evaluation of responses to social influences. Unpublished doctoral dissertation, Stanford University, 1965.

Regan, D. T., & Totten, J. Empathy and attribution: Turning observers into actors. *Journal of Personality and Social Psychology*, 1975, **32**, 850–856.

Ross, L., Amabile, T. M., Jennings, D. L., & Steinmetz, J. L. Non-conservative and non-optimal prediction strategies: Experiments on the psychology of intuitive prediction. Unpublished manuscript, Stanford University, 1976. (a)

Ross, L., Amabile, T. M., & Steinmetz, J. L. Social roles, social control, and biases in social perception processes. *Journal of Personality and Social Psychology,* 1977, in press. (a)

Ross, L. Bierbrauer, G., & Hoffman, S. The role of attribution processes in conformity and dissent: Revisiting the Asch situation. *American Psychologist,* 1976, **31**, 148–157. (b)

Ross, L., Bierbrauer, G., & Polly, S. Attribution of educational outcomes by professional and non-professional instructors. *Journal of Personality and Social Psychology*, 1974, **29**, 609–618.

Ross, L., Greene, D., & House, P. The false consensus phenomenon: An attributional bias in self perception and social perception processes. *Journal of Experimental Social Psychology*, 1977, in press. (b)

Ross, L., Lepper, M., & Hubbard, M. Perseverance in self perception and social perception: Biased attributional processes in the debriefing paradigm. *Journal of Personality and Social Psychology*, 1975, **32**, 880–892.

Ross, L., Lepper, M. R., Strack, F., & Steinmetz, J. L. The effects of real and hypothetical explanation upon future expectations. Unpublished manuscript, Stanford University, 1976. (c)

Rotter, J. B. Generalized expectancies for internal versus external control of reinforcement. *Psychological Monographs*, 1966, **80**, No. 609.

Schachter, S., & Singer, J. E. Cognitive, social and physiological determinants of emotional state. *Psychological Review*, 1962, **69**, 379–399.

Slovic, P., & Lichtenstein, S. Comparison of Bayesian and regression approaches to the study of information processing in judgment. *Organizational Behavior and Human Performance*, 1971, **6**, 649–744.

Smedslund, J. The concept of correlation in adults. *Scandinavian Journal of Psychology*, 1963, **4**, 165–173.

Smith, A. The attribution of similarity: The influence of success and failure. *Journal of Abnormal and Social Psychology*, 1960, **61**, 419–423.

Storms, M. Videotape and the attribution process: Reversing actors' and observers' points of view. *Journal of Personality and Social Psychology*, 1973, **27**, 165–175.

Strickland, L. H. Surveillance and trust. *Journal of Personality*, 1958, **26**, 200–215.

Taylor, S. E., & Fiske, S. T. Point of view and perceptions of causality. *Journal of Personality and Social Psychology*, 1975, **32**, 439–445.

Thibaut, J. W., & Riecken, H. W. Some determinants and consequences of the perception of social causality. *Journal of Personality*, 1955, **24**, 113–133.

Tversky, A., & Kahneman, D. Belief in the law of small numbers. *Psychological Bulletin*, 1971, **76**, 105–110.

Tversky, A., & Kahneman, D. Availability: A heuristic for judging frequency and probability. *Cognitive Psychology*, 1973, **5**, 207–232.

Tversky, A., & Kahneman, D. Judgment under uncertainty: Heuristics and biases. *Science*, 1974, **185**, 1124–1131.

Valins, S. Persistent effects of information about internal reactions: Ineffectiveness of debriefing. In H. London & R. E. Nisbett (Eds.), *Thought and feeling: Cognitive modification of feeling states.* Chicago: Aldine, 1974.

Wallach, H. The perception of motion. *Scientific American*, 1959, **201**, 56–60.

Walster, E. Assignment of responsibility for an accident. *Journal of Personality and Social Psychology*, 1966, **3**, 73–79.

Walster, E., Berscheid, E., Abrahams, D., & Aronson, V. Effectiveness of debriefing following deception experiments. *Journal of Personality and Social Psychology*, 1967, **6**, 371–380.

Ward, W. D., & Jenkins, H. M. The display of information and the judgment of contingency. *Canadian Journal of Psychology*, 1965, **19**, 231–241.

Wason, P. C., & Johnson-Laird, P. N. *Psychology of reasoning: Structure and content.* London: Batsford, 1972.

Weiner, B. *Achievement motivation and attribution theory*. Morristown, N.J.: General Learning Press, 1974.

Wheeler, G., & Beach, L. R. Subjective sampling distributions and conservatism. *Organizational Behavior and Human Performance*, 1968, **3**, 36–46.

Wolosin, R. J., Sherman, S. J., & Till, A. Effects of cooperation and competition on responsibility attribution after success and failure. *Journal of Experimental Social Psychology*, 1973, **9**, 220–235.

Zadny, J., & Gerard, H. B. Attributed intentions and informational selectivity. *Journal of Personality and Social Psychology*, 1974, **10**, 34–52.

Some Afterthoughts on the Intuitive Psychologist[1]

Lee Ross
STANFORD UNIVERSITY

The *Advances* article reprinted in this volume was published so recently that this supplementary essay constitutes more of a postscript than a progress report. Nevertheless, the invitation to "update" is welcome because it gives the author a "second chance"—a chance not only to report a few key findings that just missed the last deadline but also to shift and sharpen emphases and offer some observations that limitations of time, space, or perspective had precluded last time.

Let me begin with a confession. The title and introductory section of the previous article may well have led the reader to expect a systematic exploration of the layperson–scientist analogy. If so, he was bound to be somewhat disappointed, for what was offered was largely a chronicling of specific attributional errors, with only occasional asides to suggest that parallel pitfalls exist for the professional scientist. This supplementary essay now seeks to remedy this deficiency, first by identifying some characteristics of human inference that are reflected in virtually all tasks of the lay scientist, and then by considering in more detail the performance of each task. Within this framework, the author will also update previous findings and interpre-

[1] Much of the research and conceptual analysis presented in this supplementary essay has been culled from a forthcoming book entitled *Human Inference: Strategies and Shortcomings in Social Judgment*, which was written in collaboration with Professor Richard Nisbett and will be published by Prentice-Hall.

tations and comment periodically on the normative status and implications of the layperson's "failings."

I. Three Sources of Influence and Error

A. THEORIES, SCRIPTS, AND OTHER COGNITIVE SCHEMAS

As Bruner (1957) noted over two decades ago, perhaps the most striking aspect of perception is the perceiver's tendency to "go beyond the information given." The intuitive psychologist, in other words, does not passively register the data of social experience. Rather, he assimilates what he observes to preexisting cognitive structures that are, in turn, residues of the interaction between his experience and his mental machinery for recording that experience. The previous essay placed considerable emphasis on the capacity of informal theories to bias the interpretation of social data and thereby draw unwarranted sustenance from such data. Increasingly, however, cognitive scientists, heavily influenced by the artificial intelligence tradition, have begun to emphasize the importance of mental structures that are more "schema-like" and less "propositional" than theories. Minsky's (1975) seminal paper on *frames,* described as abstract knowledge structures that serve to organize "generic expectations" about objects or situations, is one case in point. Abelson's (1976; Schank & Abelson, 1977) account of cognitive "scripts," postulated to represent familiar organized event-sequences or event-packages (for example, the "restaurant script" or the "Munich Conference script"), is another that promises to be particularly influential. Similarly, research dealing with schematic representation of actors—for example, Markus's (1977) work on "self-schemas" and Cantor's and Mischel's (1977, 1978) works on person "prototypes"—has begun to receive considerable attention.

The notion that the layperson's experience-organizing preconceptions arise from a great and varied store of both abstract and concrete knowledge-packages is intuitively satisfying. Following the arguments of the previous essay, it seems reasonable to propose that scripts, self-schemas, person-prototypes, and other members of the growing family of postulated cognitive schemas may themselves be influenced by the impact they exert on perception and memory. That is, like theories and other more propositional representations of knowledge, such schemas should systematically be strengthened and sustained by data samples that, processed in a more objective fashion, might not support or might even undermine the schemas. Indeed, it is reasonable to suppose that schemas may be even less amenable to logical or evidential challenges than are theories, and their biasing effects on data interpretation may therefore be all the more pernicious. The statesman who proceeds from a set of explicit assumptions and propositions about the goals and preferred tactics of his foes may at least recognize the relevance of new data to his analytic framework, however biased his interpretation of those data. By contrast, the statesman whose "Munich script" is recruited whenever a hostile and expansionist power seeks negotiations may never entertain the possibility that his script should be updated in the light of newer data.

A cautionary comment may be appropriate at this point. To date, our field's enthusiasm for schema-like concepts has served primarily to stimulate a proliferation of labels, distinctions, and definitions. Thus, although the current notion of a schema dates at least from the philosophical writings of Kant and has been familiar to psychologists since its use in the 1930s by Bartlett (1932) and Piaget (1936, see also Flavell, 1963), there still exists little consensus about the type of data that might clarify their properties or even definitively prove their existence. Related, and perhaps equally critical, is the need to begin clarifying the conditions of their instigation and use. In 1961, De Soto wrote of "our crippling ignorance of the dynamics of schema arousal [p. 22]," and a decade later Kelley (1972b) was obliged merely to repeat De Soto's complaint. Very recently, however, some progress has been made on both fronts. Markus' (1977) study, for instance, shows that the rapidity of information processing about the self may be predicted by several criteria indicative of the presence or absence of schema-like self-concepts. Similarly, Cantor's and Mischel's (1977, 1978) works have begun to document the biasing effects of prototypes on both interpretation and recall. At the same time, Langer (1977; Langer & Abelson, 1972) has used altruism as a target behavior in demonstrating the impact of script availability and script appropriateness manipulations. Despite such progress, however, the theoretical edifice in this area of investigation still rests on a very modest empirical framework.

B. JUDGMENTAL HEURISTICS

In the original *Advances* article, the availability and representativeness "heuristics" elaborated by Kahneman and Tversky (1972, 1973; Tversky & Kahneman, 1971, 1973, 1974, 1978) were introduced only in discussing intuitive prediction and were given relatively little emphasis. It is becoming increasingly clear, however, that any adequate portrayal of the intuitive psychologist and his shortcomings must bring these judgmental heuristics to center stage and assign them a leading role. Already, the number of references to them in the psychological literature, and the number of specific domains to which their application is being considered, is beginning to expand at an exponential rate. For example, an impressive body of studies by Taylor and her colleagues (cf. Taylor & Fiske, 1975, 1978; also Duvall & Wicklund, 1972; Storms, 1973) illustrates the role that availability (manipulated through systematic variation of perceptual distinctiveness or salience) may play in determining which individuals in a group will be perceived as potent causal agents. With regard to the representativeness heuristic, a soon-to-be-classic paper by Tversky (1977) has elaborated a formal theory of similarity judgment and in so doing has taken a major step toward clarifying the principal criterion underlying the use of this heuristic. Finally, an important and provocative paper by Nisbett and Wilson (1977) disputes the notion that the intuitive psychologist enjoys any direct or unique access to the cognitive processes that determine his behavior; the authors suggest, instead, that causal inferences regarding one's own behavior are governed by the same availability and representativeness factors that govern similar inferences about the behavior of others.

One can hardly doubt that our understanding of all of the various stages of intuitive scientific judgment, from data collection to theory-testing, will be informed by careful analysis of those factors that determine the availability of particular items of data as well as the availability of particular theories, schemas, and strategies for processing that data. Similarly, the list of inferential tasks in which feature-matching and other simple representativeness judgments replace more normatively justifiable strategies promises to be an ever-lengthening one in the decade ahead. Once again, the really challenging problem promises to be that of specifying the conditions of use. Exactly when are the various heuristics employed, and when do they yield to more conventional rules of inference? This question will doubtlessly try the skills and patience of our field's most talented contributors.

C. The Vividness Criterion

To this point in the essay, the intuitive psychologist may seem a prisoner of his preconceptions. But recent research has served to emphasize that the layperson is far from indifferent to the implications of data—provided, that is, that the relevant data are concrete, sensory, hedonically-relevant, or made "vivid" in some other fashion. This point was touched on only briefly in the *Advances* article and was discussed only in the limited context of the decision maker's penchant for overweighting concrete cases relative to abstract statistical baselines. Any systematic portrait of the lay psychologist must give greater emphasis to this point, for the intuitive psychologist may be misled by overreliance upon his senses as readily as by dogged adherence to his preconceptions.

Nisbett and Ross (1979) have recently amassed a wealth of anecdotal support for this point. They cite, for example, the inability of the professional reporters following McGovern in 1972 to give credence to public opinion polls in the face of the vivid and concrete "evidence" of the wildly enthusiastic throngs that constantly greeted the candidate. More generally, they remind readers of the impact on human affairs that vivid writing (e.g., *Uncle Tom's Cabin, The Jungle, All Quiet on the Western Front*) has exerted where dry statistics and rational disputations had previously failed. This broad contention has recently been buttressed by Hamill, Wilson, and Nisbett (1978), who demonstrated that a *New Yorker* article detailing the social pathology of a single "stereotypic" welfare case exerted more impact on subjects' attitudes towards welfare than did presentations of critically relevant summary data about overall welfare use. Also, an interesting study by Thompson, Reyes, and Bower (1978) shows that the impact of informational vividness may sometimes emerge only after a *delay*, so that the effects of memory can be felt. Specifically, subjects in the Thompson *et al.* study who read a brief transcript of a legal case initially judged the defendant no more harshly when details of the prosecution's case were presented vividly and those of the defense's case presented nonvividly than they did when the situation was reversed. After a 24-hour delay, however, the vividness effect had asserted itself (at least for a defendant of good character) and had swung the subjects' judgments in favor of whichever side had initially been presented in more vivid detail.

Extra-evidential vividness may be expected to influence a wide range of judgments, although, once again, a decade's research may be necessary before much can be said about the limits and range of the relevant phenomena. In a sense, of course, the study of vividness effects and the study of the availability heuristic are two sides of the same coin. Vivid events are, almost by definition, disproportionately available both in initial perception and again in recall; conversely, an understanding of the determinants of cognitive availability may depend upon a parallel understanding of the factors and processes that determine subjective vividness.

II. Tasks and Abilities of the Intuitive Psychologist

A. CHARACTERIZING THE DATUM AND THE SAMPLE

Perhaps the most basic of all scientific undertakings is that of characterizing or "coding" the individual datum. All higher-order inferences about the meaning of social experiences depend upon the adequate performance of this task. Thus, accurate inferences about the causes, correlates, and implications of smiles received across a crowded room depend upon one's ability to distinguish smiles from other facial expressions. Similarly, lay insights about the relationship between frustration and aggression are possible only to the extent that both the antecedent state and the response in question are coded accurately. No simple generalizations can be made about the intuitive psychologist's overall performance at data coding except, perhaps, for the assertion that expectations, whether based on propositional theories or on more schematic cognitive structures, obviously play a large and necessary role. The "theory" that our friends have our best interests at heart leads us to code as helpful a criticism that would be characterized as hostile if it came from a rival. By the same token, we code the attentive behavior of a waiter as professionally polite rather than obsequious when our perception of such behavior is guided by the "restaurant script" (cf. Schank & Abelson, 1977). In these, and probably in the majority of cases, such theory-biased coding undoubtedly leads to more accurate interpretation of events. It is only in domains where our preconceptions are likely to be seriously in error—for example, in domains where social stereotyping plays a role—that these coding biases are more apt to hinder than to help our overall accuracy.

A second, very basic, task of the intuitive psychologist involves characterizing the nature not of the single datum, but of the data *sample*. Everyday experience attests to the fact that people are often quite proficient at estimating frequencies, proportions, and averages, even when ordinary counting and computation are impossible. More important, perhaps, we expect the layperson's errors to be reasonably random, so that a large number of individuals estimating anything from their hamburger consumption to their sexual activities should produce mean estimates that closely approximate the relevant parameters. Indeed, this expectation is the article of faith upon which much of the survey researcher's trade is based. Early investigations, relying mainly upon laboratory presentations of samples of very simple stimuli, prompted a rather favorable assessment of the layperson's computational capacities (cf. Peterson & Beach, 1967). More recently, however, a rising tide of studies using richer and more complex stimuli, less clearly marked sample boundaries, and more stringent memory demands have produced far less flattering assessments (cf. Slovic, Fischhoff, & Lichtenstein, 1976).

Perhaps the most obvious biasing influence on sample description is that of event salience or availability and its resulting impact on memory storage and recall. In the previous *Advances* article, several illustrations of the point were provided—for example, Kahneman and Tversky's (1973) demonstration that subsequent to hearing lists of well-known personalities of both sexes subjects overestimated the representation of that sex whose members on the list had been more famous. A related study has subsequently been reported by Rothbart, Fulero, Jensen, Howard, and Burrell (1978), who showed that the *extremity* of the members of a class with respect to the defining attribute of the class can influence the perceived *size* of that class. Thus, subjects receiving information about the various individuals in a sample overestimated the percentage of criminals in the sample to the extent that the crimes committed by the criminal subset were *severe*. Still another provocative study was provided by Slovic *et al.* (1976), who reported some intriguing systematic errors in their subjects' estimates about causes of death. The investigators speculated that it was the tendency for local newsprograms to make fires and accidents disproportionately "available" that accounted for their subjects' consistency in estimating death from fire to be more common than death from drowning and accidental death to be more likely than death from stroke, despite actual mortality rates that are overwhelmingly to the contrary.

B. PARAMETER ESTIMATION

Many important social judgments essentially demand that the individual infer population parameters from knowledge about observations sampled from the population. Besides the various factors that bias such judgments through their influence on data coding and sample description, two further shortcomings of the intuitive scientist make their influence felt. Both, in a sense, reflect the layperson's tendency to rely upon simple representativeness judgments and to ignore other, more normatively important criteria. The first shortcoming involves insensitivity to the importance of sample *size*, and it is by now probably quite familiar to the reader through the work of Kahneman and Tversky (1972; 1973), extended by Nisbett and Borgida (1975; Borgida & Nisbett, 1977). The second, and related, shortcoming involves insensitivity to sample *bias* and is probably less familiar to the reader.

In the previous *Advances* article, a study was reported (Ross, Amabile, & Steinmetz, 1977) that suggested that social perceivers make inadequate allowance for the biasing effects of role-conferred advantages and disadvantages in self-presentation. A simpler, more decisive, and more disturbing demonstration of the layperson's insensitivity to sample bias has now been added by Hamill, Wilson, and Nisbett (1978). In one study, for example, subjects were presented with one of two videotaped "interviews" in which a person alleged to be a guard at a state prison discussed his job. In one condition, the guard was a model of decency who exuded compassion and concern for the rehabilitation of his charges; in the other, he was a veritable brute, scoffing at the idea of rehabilitation and characterizing the prisoners as "animals" responsive only to coercion. Crosscutting this manipulation was a systematic manipulation of the information available to subjects about the guard's "typicality." Some subjects were given no information about typicality, some were told in advance of seeing the videotape that the guard was quite typical of those at the prison, and the remainder were forewarned that his humaneness (or inhumaneness) was quite *atypical*—that is, that he was one of the three or four most humane (inhumane) of the sixty guards at the prison. Subjects in all conditions were ultimately asked to make judgments about American prison guards in general.

The results obtained were quite remarkable. The difference between the humane and inhumane guard conditions was *virtually identical, regardless of instructions about typicality.* Not only did subjects willingly generalize from a single guard in one prison to the entire universe of prison guards, they did so even when specifically warned that the guard was chosen because of his atypicality. Obviously, a great deal of research will be required before we can appreciate the full implications and limits of the Hamill *et al.* demonstration, but the departure from normative standards of statistical inference is too striking to overlook.

C. Covariation Detection, Causal Analysis, and Prediction

Intuitive scientists, like professionals, often must make judgments and inferences that involve *relationships* among variables. In particular, attempts at both causal analysis and prediction demand that the layperson first estimate the magnitude of covariations among observable events. Thus, the assessment of covariations between early symptoms and later manifestations, between behavioral strategies employed and subsequent outcomes, and between easily observable predictors and difficult or costly to observe criterion variables are all critical to the layperson's success in understanding his social world and responding adaptively to the opportunities and dilemmas it presents. Indeed, Kelley's (1973) "covariation principle," perhaps the cornerstone of contemporary attribution theory and the foundation of its fundamental optimism about the intuitive scientist's performance is essentially an assertion that the layperson can both recognize and make appropriate inferential use of covariation between events.

Nevertheless, most research that has dealt explicitly with covariation recognition and estimation has been less than flattering to the layperson's abilities. Even Peterson and Beach's (1967) generally positive evaluation of man as an intuitive statistician had little to say that was favorable about his capacity to appreciate statistical relationships. The previous *Advances* article briefly reviewed relevant research on this point, in particular the Chapmans's classic work (Chapman, 1967; Chapman & Chapman, 1967, 1969) dealing with the perception of relationships between clinical "symptoms" and "signs." Perhaps the simplest summary statement suggested by such studies (cf. also Golding & Roher, 1972, not cited in the previous article) is that reported covariation reflects true covariation far less than it does the reporter's representativeness-biased preconceptions about the nature of the relationship that "ought" to exist.

By showing the dominance of theories over nonsupporting or even disconfirming data, the Chapmans' studies offer further testimony to one of the broad sources of bias discussed early in the present essay. Careful consideration, however, should reveal that two separate questions or phenomena may be intertwined in such demonstrations. The first is essentially a psychophysical question involving the relationship between subjective judgment and objective measurements. It involves the layperson's capacity to assess covariation when he views the relevant bivariate distributions unencumbered by specific theoretical preconceptions. The second question involves the opposite case; it concerns the accuracy of covariation estimates when the relevant bivariate data are spotty, imprecise, or even nonexistent, so that the layperson's assessments of covariation are essentially "theory-driven."

The present author and his colleagues have pursued these two issues in a long series of studies that was in only its initial stages at the time of the previous article's publication. A more recent study (Jennings, Amabile, & Ross, 1978), however, has provided some interesting data that seems worth reporting in some detail. The procedure employed by Jennings *et al.* involved presenting subjects with two very different types of "covariation estimation" tasks. The first type of task was essentially the "psychophysical" one described above. Bivariate distributions about which the subjects held no prior theories (e.g., sets of number pairs, men of different heights holding walking sticks of different heights, and letters ranging from A to Z associated with tones of varying duration) were presented, and subjects were simply required to choose a number from 0 (no relationship) to 100 (perfect relationship) to describe their subjective impression for each distribution.

The results of these "theory-free" or "data-driven" estimation tasks can be summarized simply. First, regardless of the type of materials employed, the task proved very difficult; at least, that was both the subjective report of participants and the seeming implication of the very large standard errors associated with the group's covariation estimates for each distribution. Second, it became clear that the function relating subjective covariation estimates to objective covariation measures is a sharply accelerating one. Relationships in the range most frequently dealt with by students of personality traits and cross-situational behavioral consistency (i.e., $r = .2$ to $r = .4$) were barely detectable. Even relationship in the range considered quite strong by most social scientists (i.e., $r = .6$ to $r = .8$) prompted estimates that fell, on the average, on the bottom third of the subjective 100-point scale. In fact, only when the correlations began to approach the $r = .8$ to $r = 1.0$ range did raters begin to venture to the upper half of the scale. Overall, the subjects' judgments were best fit by a simple linear function not of r or even r^2 but rather of $1 - \sqrt{1 - r^2}$ (a statistic that some readers may recognize as the "coefficient of alienation," a measure of the reduction in the standard error in predictions of one variable that results from knowledge of the second, associated variable).

Treated in isolation, of course, such data could merely be suggesting what every statistician knows—namely, that the layperson's "subjective metric" for association is a very cautious one relative to that employed by most formal statisticians. The results of Jennings *et al.*'s second task, however, dispel any such benign interpretation. Pairs of variables were specified in this task, and the subject was simply required, in the absence of any immediately available data, to estimate the degree of relationship between each pair, using the same 100-point rating scale employed in the former task. The variable pairs employed were all such that correlation estimates existed from previous work undertaken either by the investigators or by previous researchers concerned with cross-situational consistency in behavior (e.g., Hartshorne & May, 1928; Mischel & Gilligan, 1964).

An examination of the relevant estimates revealed that, when subjects were unencumbered by immediately available data and were free to use their personal intuitions, they ceased to be "conservative." They willingly ventured to the middle and even to the upper regions of the subjective 100-point scales when their estimates were prompted by underlying theories about personal consistency. Thus, for example, subjects' estimates for two different measures of honesty and for two different measures of ability to delay gratification were both in the 55 to 60 range on the 100-point scale. When we consider the psychometric function that had emerged from the "data driven" covariation estimates, the meaning of such "theory-driven" estimates becomes apparent. Only bivariate distributions in the range of $r = .85$ to $r = .90$ had been strong enough to coax subjective ratings of this magnitude. In short, subjects' theory-driven estimates were an order of magnitude higher than any objectively sampled and processed data derived from actual experience could ever justify. Conversely, the underlying theories that prompted such estimates seem to have arisen and survived in the face of exposure to data that, viewed in the absence of any theory, would have prompted the assessment that very little, if any, relationship existed at all.

Given such limitations concerning intuitive covariation detection abilities, the implications for prediction and causal assessment should be all too clear. Preconceptions, representativeness criteria, vivid experiences, anecdotes, as well as other subtler sources of bias, are free to exert their influence on the layperson. The pattern of results presented by the Chapmans a decade ago becomes not a surprising symptom of the pigheadedness of clinicians but a predictable consequence of people's general inability to employ the processed data of experience to refute erroneous preconceptions.

D. Theory Testing and Theory Revision

At several points, this essay has discussed the capacity of a preexisting theory to guide, and sometimes distort, the layperson's response to social data. The same capacity, of course, protects the theory itself from logical or empirical challenges that, from the viewpoint of the individual who does not share the theory in question, might seem highly damaging or even decisive. Similarly, mildly supportive data processed in the light of the theory will disproportionately strengthen the theorists' confidence. Indeed, it is the vivid, highly "scriptal" contradicting datum, rather than the accumulation of disappointing data, that is likely to shake such confidence; and, when the theory fails, it is more likely to be at the hands of a new theory than because of decisively disconfirming data. As the reader is doubtlessly aware, these generalizations apply to formal as well as to informal science (cf. Mahoney, 1976, 1977; Mahoney & De Monbreun, 1978, for comprehensive recent reviews of anecdotal and empirical evidence dealing with the formal scientist's departure from normative standards in theory-testing).

In the previous essay, considerable attention was given to demonstrations of postdiscrediting perseverance of personal and social impressions and to the mechanisms that underlie such phenomena (Lau, Lepper, & Ross, 1976; Ross, Lepper, & Hubbard, 1975; Ross, Lepper, Steinmetz, & Strack, 1977). Now, there is some new evidence that can be added. For instance, Anderson, Ross, and Lepper (1978) have recently explored the perseverance of theories about functional relationships between variables. Specifically, Anderson *et al.* showed that theories about the relationship between success as a firefighter and prior "risk-taking" scores can survive the total discrediting of the data that originally gave rise to those theories. Furthermore, this theory-perseverance effect was greatly enhanced when the theorist was asked, prior to discrediting, to explain the logical basis for his theory. On another front, Snyder and his associates (e.g., Snyder, Tanke, & Berscheid, 1977) have further documented the self-fulfilling character of theories by demonstrating that one subject's preconceptions about the attractiveness of an unseen partner can alter that partner's behavior in such a manner that a *new* subject, listening to the recorded interaction, will rate the unseen partner's attractiveness in accord with the original subject's belief.

The weight of evidence now seems to have shifted so decisively against the intuitive scientist's capacity to alter incorrect theories that the need is becoming increasingly apparent to study the conditions under which impressions, beliefs, theories, or schemas *do* yield to evidence. Equally apparent is the need to focus more directly on the implications of the intuitive psychologist's fidelity to his theories. What is the normative status and the costs and benefits of such fidelity? When *should* the layperson reject or reinterpret the data rather than abandon his prior theory? The present essay concludes with some brief "afterthoughts" about this issue and the larger question it raises about the intuitive psychologists' overall performance.

III. In Defense of the Intuitive Psychologist

Several of my colleagues, particularly those with backgrounds in artificial intelligence and language comprehension, have responded to the original *Advances* article with a vocal defense of the intuitive psychologist. Indeed, in my own writing and research I have increasingly, if belatedly, come to share their conviction and to recognize how many of the layperson's apparent failings have their origins in strategies and processes that are highly functional and even normatively justifiable within broad domains of social experience (cf. Nisbett & Ross, 1979). In the same vein, it is important to recognize the many factors that shield the intuitive scientist from many of the potential costs of his failings. Most obvious is the fact that our mastery over the physical and social environment has not depended upon a stream of de novo inferences and intuitions. Knowledge is accumulated by entire cultures, not by individuals, and over the millennia it adds up to a rich heritage indeed. Also, when an issue is important enough, data are apt to be gathered in a fashion that does permit us to give up false beliefs and to adopt newer, less "obvious," but truer ones. Our species has learned to perform controlled experiments, to train and make use of statisticians and other experts schooled in the use of normatively appropriate methods of inference, and to employ advocates and agencies to keep an eye on those experts.

Let me therefore conclude with an attempt to balance the professional scientist's often uncharitable assessment of the amateur: Just as the most sophisticated of formal scientists, both in his work and in his everyday dealings with his fellows, manifests virtually all of the inferential failings that have been chronicled here, so the least sophisticated of informal scientists enjoys insights, interpretative capacities, and stores of practical knowledge that demand respect and a good deal of humility from those of us who study his behavior.

REFERENCES

Abelson, R. P. Script processing in attitude formation and decision making. In J. Carroll & J. Payne (Eds.), *Cognition and social behavior*. Hillsdale, New Jersey: Lawrence Erlbaum Associates, 1976.

Anderson, C. A., Ross, L., & Lepper, M. R. The perseverance of discredited theories. Unpublished manuscript, Stanford University, 1978.

Bartlett, F. C. *Remembering.* Cambridge, England: Cambridge University Press, 1932.

Borgida, E., & Nisbett, R. E. The differential impact of abstract vs. concrete information on decisions. *Journal of Applied Social Psychology,* 1977, **7,** 258–271.

Bruner, J. S. Going beyond the information given. In H. Gruber *et al.* (Eds.), *Contemporary approaches to cognition.* Cambridge, Mass.: Harvard University Press, 1957, Pp. 41–69.

Cantor, N., & Mischel, W. Traits as prototypes: Effects on recognition memory. *Journal of Personality and Social Psychology,* 1977, **35,** 38–49.

Cantor, N., & Mischel, W. Prototypicality and personality: Effects on free recall and personality impressions. *Journal of Research in Personality,* 1978, in press.

Chapman, L. J. Illusory correlation in observational report. *Journal of Verbal Learning and Verbal Behavior,* 1967, **6,** 151–155.

Chapman, L. J., & Chapman, J. P. Genesis of popular but erroneous diagnostic observations. *Journal of Abnormal Psychology,* 1967, **72,** 193–294.

Chapman, L. J., and Chapman, J. P. Illusory correlation as an obstacle to the use of valid psychodiagnostic signs. *Journal of Abnormal Psychology,* 1969, **74,** 271–280.

De Soto, C. B. The predilection for single orderings. *Journal of Abnormal and Social Psychology,* 1961, **62,** 16–23.

Duval, S., & Wicklund, R. A. *A theory of objective self awareness.* New York: Academic Press, 1972.

Flavell, J. *The development psychology of Jean Piaget.* Princeton: Van Nostrand, 1963.

Golding, S. L., & Rorer, L. G. Illusory Correlation and Subjective Judgment. *Journal of Abnormal Psychology,* 1972, **80,** 249–260.

Hamill, R., Wilson, T. D., & Nisbett, R. E. Ignoring sample bias: Inferences about collectives from atypical cases. Unpublished manuscript, University of Michigan, 1978.

Hartshorne, H., & May, M. A. *Studies in the nature of character, Vol. I: Studies in deceit.* New York: Macmillan, 1928.

Jennings, D., Amabile, T. M., & Ross, L. The covariation detection problem: Theory-driven vs. data-driven estimates of association. Unpublished manuscript, Stanford University, 1978.

Kahneman, D., and Tversky, A. Subjective probability: A judgment of representativeness. *Cognitive Psychology,* 1972, **3,** 430–454.

Kahneman, D., & Tversky, A. On the psychology of prediction. *Psychological Review,* 1973, **80,** 237–251.

Kelley, H. H. Attribution in social interaction. In E. E. Jones *et al.* (Eds.), *Attribution: Perceiving the causes of behavior.* New York: General Learning Press, 1972, Pp. 1–26. (a)

Kelley, H. H. Causal schemata and the attribution process. In E. E. Jones *et al.* (Eds.), *Attribution: Perceiving the causes of behavior.* New York: General Learning Press, 1972, Pp. 151–174. (b)

Kelley, H. H. The process of causal attribution. *American Psychologist,* 1973, **28,** 107–128.

Langer, E. J. The psychology of chance. *Journal for the Theory of Social Behavior,* 1977, **7,** 185–208.

Langer, E. J., & Abelson, R. P. The semantics of asking a favor: How to succeed in getting help without actually dying. *Journal of Personality and Social Psychology,* 1972, **24,** 26–32.

Lau, R., Lepper, M. R., & Ross, L. Persistence of inaccurate and discredited personal impressions: A field demonstration of attributional perseverance. Unpublished manuscript, Stanford University, 1976.

Mahoney, M. J. *Scientist as subject: The psychological imperative.* Cambridge, Massachusetts: Ballinger, 1976.

Mahoney, M. J. *Psychology of the scientist: An evaluative review.* The Pennsylvania State University, 1977.

Mahoney, M. J., & DeMonbreun, B. G. A comparison of confirmatory bias in scientists and non-scientists. *Cognitive Therapy and Research,* in press.

Markus, H. Self schemas and processing information about the self. *Journal of Personality and Social Psychology,* 1977, **35**, 63–78.

Minsky, M. A framework for representing knowledge. In P. H. Winston (Ed.), *The psychology of computer vision.* New York: McGraw-Hill, 1975.

Mischel, W., & Gilligan, C. Delay of gratification, motivation for the prohibited gratification, and responses to temptation. *Journal of Abnormal and Social Psychology,* 1964, **64**, 411–417.

Nisbett, R. E., & Borgida, E. Attribution and the psychology of prediction. *Journal of Personality and Social Psychology,* 1975, **32**, 932–943.

Nisbett, R. E., & Ross, L. *Human inference: Strategies and shortcomings in social judgment.* Prentice-Hall, 1979, in press.

Nisbett, R. E., & Wilson, T. D. Telling more than we can know: Verbal reports on mental processes. *Psychological Review,* 1977, **84**, 231–259.

Peterson, C. R., & Beach, L. R. Man as an intuitive statistician. *Psychological Bulletin,* 1967, **68**, 29–46.

Piaget, J. La naissance de l'intelligence chez l'enfant. Neuchatel et Paris: Delachaux et Niestle, 1936.

Ross, L. D., Amabile, T. M., & Steinmetz, J. L. Social roles, social control, and biases in social-perception processes. *Journal of Personality and Social Psychology,* 1977, **35**, 485–494.

Ross, L., Lepper, M. R., & Hubbard, J. Perseverance in self perception and social perception: Biased attributional processes in the debriefing paradigm. *Journal of Personality and Social Psychology,* 1975, **32**, 880–892.

Ross, L., Lepper, M. R. Strack, F., & Steinmetz, J. L. Social explanation and social expectation: The effects of real and hypothetical explanations upon subjective likelihood. *Journal of Personality and Social Psychology,* 1977, **35**, 817–829.

Rothbart, M., Fulero, S., Jensen, C., Howard, J., & Burrell, B. From individual to group impressions: Availability heuristics in stereotype formation. *Journal of Experimental Social Psychology,* 1978, **14**, 237–255.

Schank, R., & Abelson, R. P. *Scripts, plans, goals and understanding: An inquiry into human knowledge structures.* Hillsdale, New Jersey: Erlbaum Associates, 1977.

Slovic, P., Fischhoff, B., & Lichtenstein, S. Cognitive processes and societal risk taking. In J. S. Carroll & J. W. Payne (Eds.), *Cognition and social behavior.* Hillsdale, New Jersey: Erlbaum Associates, 1976, Pp. 165–184.

Snyder, M., Tanke, E. D., & Berscheid, E. Social perception and interpersonal behavior: On the self-fulfilling nature of social stereotypes. *Journal of Personality and Social Psychology,* 1977, **35**, 656–666.

Storms, M. D. Videotape and the attribution process: Reversing actors' and observers' points of view. *Journal of Personality and Social Psychology,* 1973, **27**, 165–175.

Taylor, S. E., & Fiske, S. T. Point of view and perceptions of causality. *Journal of Personality and Social Psychology,* 1975, **32**, 439–445.

Taylor, S. E., & Fiske, S. T. Salience, attention and attribution: Top of the head phenomena. In L. Berkowitz (Ed.), *Advances in experimental social psychology*. Vol. 11. New York: Academic Press, 1978.

Thompson, W. C., Reyes, R. M., & Bower, G. H. Delayed effects of availability on judgment. Unpublished manuscript, Stanford University, 1978.

Tversky, A. Features of similarity. *Psychological Review*, 1977, **84**, 327–352.

Tversky, A., & Kahneman, D. Belief in the law of small numbers. *Psychological Bulletin*, 1971, **76**, 105–110.

Tversky, A., & Kahneman, D. Availability: A heuristic for judging frequency and probability. *Cognitive Psychology*, 1973, **5**, 207–232.

Tversky, A., & Kahneman, D. Judgment under uncertainty: Heuristics and biases. *Science*, 1974, **185**, 1124–1131.

Tversky, A., & Kahneman, D. Causal schemata in judgments under uncertainty. In M. Fishbein (Ed.), *Progress in social psychology*. Hillsdale, New Jersey: Erlbaum Associates, 1978, in press.

THE INTERACTION OF COGNITIVE AND PHYSIOLOGICAL DETERMINANTS OF EMOTIONAL STATE[1]

Stanley Schachter

DEPARTMENT OF SOCIAL PSYCHOLOGY
COLUMBIA UNIVERSITY
NEW YORK, NEW YORK

I. Introduction

Many years ago, piqued by the disorderly cataloguing of symptoms which, in his time, characterized the classic works on emotion, William James offered what was probably the first simple, integrating, theoretical

[1] Much of the research described in this paper was supported by Grant MH 05203 from the National Institute of Mental Health, United States Public Health Service, and by Grant G 23758 from the National Science Foundation.

Reprinted from *Advances in Experimental Social Psychology*, Volume 1, 49–80.

statement on the nature of emotion. This well-known formulation stated that "the bodily changes follow directly the perception of the exciting fact, and that our feeling of the same changes as they occur *is* the emotion" (James, 1890). Since James' proposition directly equates bodily changes and visceral feelings with emotion, it must follow, first, that the different emotions are accompanied by recognizably different bodily states and second, that the direct manipulation of bodily state, by drugs or surgery, also manipulates emotional state. These implications have, directly or indirectly, guided much of the research on emotion since James' day. The results of such research, on the whole, provided little support for a purely visceral formulation of emotion and led Cannon (1927, 1929) to his brilliant and devastating critique of the James-Lange theory—a critique based on the following:

1. Total separation of the viscera from the central nervous system does not alter emotional behavior.

2. The same visceral changes occur in very different emotional states and in nonemotional states.

3. The viscera are relatively insensitive structures.

4. Visceral changes are too slow to be a source of emotional feeling.

5. Artificial induction of the visceral changes typical of strong emotions does not produce them.

Though new data have weakened the cogency of some of these points, on the whole Cannon's logic and findings make it inescapably clear that a completely peripheral or visceral formulation of emotion, such as the James-Lange theory, is inadequate to cope with the facts. In an effort to deal with the obvious inadequacies of a purely visceral or peripheral formulation of emotion, Ruckmick (1936), Hunt *et al.* (1958), Schachter (1959), and others have suggested that cognitive factors may be major determinants of emotional states. It is the purpose of this paper to spell out the implications of a cognitive-physiological formulation of emotion and to describe a series of experiments designed to test these implications.

A. The Interaction of Cognitive and Physiological Processes

To begin, let us grant on the basis of much evidence (see Woodworth and Schlosberg, 1958, for example) that a general pattern of sympathetic discharge is characteristic of emotional states. Given such a state of arousal, it is suggested that one labels, interprets, and identifies this stirred-up state in terms of the characteristics of the precipitating situation and one's apperceptive mass. This suggests, then, that an emotional state may be considered a function of a state of physiological arousal[2] and of a cognition appropriate to this state of arousal. The cognition, in a sense, exerts a steering function. Cognitions arising from the immediate situation as interpreted by past experience provide the framework within which one understands and labels his feelings. It is the cognition which determines whether the state of physiological arousal will be labeled "anger," "joy," or whatever.

In order to examine the implications of this formulation, consider the fashion in which these two elements, a state of physiological arousal and cognitive factors, would interact in a variety of situations. In most emotion inducing situations, of course, the two factors are completely interrelated. Imagine a man walking alone down a dark alley when a figure with a gun suddenly appears. The perception-cognition "figure with a gun" in some fashion initiates a state of physiological arousal; this state of arousal is interpreted in terms of knowledge about dark alleys and guns, and the state of arousal is labeled "fear." Similarly, a student who unexpectedly learns that he has made Phi Beta Kappa may experience a state of arousal which he will label "joy."

1. Physiological Arousal Not Sufficient

Let us now consider circumstances in which these two elements, the physiological and the cognitive, are, to some extent, independent. First, is the state of physiological arousal alone sufficient to induce an emotion? The best evidence indicates that it is not. Marañon (1924), in a fascinating study (replicated by Cantril and Hunt (1932) and Landis and Hunt (1932)), injected 210 of his patients with the sympathomimetic agent adrenaline and then asked them to introspect. Seventy-one % of his subjects reported physical symptoms with no emotional overtone; 29% responded in an apparently emotional fashion. Of these, the great majority described their feelings in a fashion that Marañon labeled "cold" or "as if" emotions; that is, they made statements such as "I feel *as if* I were afraid" or "*as if* I were awaiting a great happiness." This is a sort of emotional *déjà vu* experience; these subjects are neither happy nor afraid, they feel "as if" they were. Finally, a very few cases apparently reported a genuine emotional experience. However, in order to produce this reaction

[2] Though the experiments to be described are concerned largely with the physiological changes produced by the injection of adrenaline—which appear to be primarily the result of sympathetic excitation—the term physiological arousal is used in preference to the more specific "excitement of the sympathetic nervous system" because there are indications, discussed later, that this formulation is applicable to a variety of bodily states.

in most of these few cases, Marañon pointed out

> one must suggest a memory with strong affective force but not so strong as to produce an emotion in the normal state. For example, in several cases we spoke to our patients before the injection of their sick children or dead parents and they responded calmly to this topic. The same topic presented later, during the adrenal commotion, was sufficient to trigger emotion. This adrenal commotion places the subject in a situation of "affective imminence."

Apparently, then, to produce a genuinely emotional reaction to adrenaline, Marañon was forced to provide such subjects with an appropriate cognition.

Though Marañon was not explicit on his procedure, it is clear that his subjects knew that they were receiving an injection, in all likelihood knew that they were receiving adrenaline, and probably had some order of familiarity with its effects. In short, although they underwent the pattern of sympathetic discharge common to strong emotional states, at the same time they had a completely appropriate cognition or explanation as to why they felt this way. This, it is suggested, is the reason so few of Marañon's subjects reported any emotional experience.

2. The Need To Evaluate One's Feelings

Consider next a person in a state of physiological arousal for which no immediately explanatory or appropriate cognitions are available. Such a state could result were one covertly to inject a subject with adrenaline or, unknown to him, feed the subject a sympathomimetic drug such as ephedrine. Under such conditions a subject would be aware of palpitations, tremor, face flushing, and most of the battery of symptoms associated with a discharge of the sympathetic nervous system. In contrast to Marañon's subjects, he would, at the same time, be utterly unaware of why he felt this way. What would be the consequence of such a state?

Schachter (1959) suggested that just such a state would lead to the arousal of "evaluative needs" (Festinger, 1954). That is, pressures would act on an individual in such a state to understand and label his bodily feelings. His bodily state grossly resembles the condition in which it has been at times of emotional excitement. How would he label his present feelings? It is suggested, of course, that he will label his feelings in terms of his knowledge of the immediate situation.[3] Should he at the time be with a beautiful woman, he might decide that he was wildly in love or sexually excited. Should he be at a gay party, he might, by comparing himself to others, decide that he was extremely happy and euphoric. Should he be

---

[3] This suggestion is not new, for several psychologists have suggested that situational factors should be considered the chief differentiators of the emotions. Hunt *et al.* (1958) probably made this point most explicitly in their study distinguishing among fear, anger, and sorrow in terms of situational characteristics.

arguing with his wife, he might explode in fury and hatred. Or, should the situation be completely inappropriate, he could decide that he was excited about something that had recently happened to him or, simply, that he was sick. In any case, it is my basic assumption that emotional states are a function of the interaction of such cognitive factors with a state of physiological arousal.

B. THEORETICAL PROPOSITIONS

This line of thought leads to three propositions. One, given a state of physiological arousal for which an individual has no immediate explanation, he will "label" this state and describe his feelings in terms of the cognitions available to him. To the extent that cognitive factors are potent determiners of emotional states, it could be anticipated that precisely the same state of physiological arousal could be labeled "joy" or "fury" or any of a great diversity of emotional labels, depending on the cognitive aspects of the situation.

Two, given a state of physiological arousal for which an individual has a completely appropriate explanation (e.g., "I feel this way because I have just received an injection of adrenaline"), no evaluative needs will arise, and the individual is unlikely to label his feelings in terms of the alternative cognitions available.

Finally, consider a condition in which emotion inducing cognitions are present but there is no state of physiological arousal; an individual might, for example, be aware that he is in great danger, but for some reason (drug or surgical) remain in a state of physiological quiescence. Does he then experience the emotion "fear"? This formulation of emotion as a joint function of a state of physiological arousal and an appropriate cognition, would, of course, suggest that he does not, which leads to our final proposition. Three, given the same cognitive circumstances, the individual will react emotionally or describe his feelings as emotions only to the extent that he experiences a state of physiological arousal.[4]

II. Cognitive, Social and Physiological Determinants

The experimental test of these propositions requires (1) the experimental manipulation of a state of physiological arousal or sympathetic activation; (2) the manipulation of the extent to which the subject has an appropriate or proper explanation of his bodily state; and (3) the creation of situations from which explanatory cognitions may be derived.

In order to satisfy these experimental requirements, Schachter and

[4] In his critique of the James-Lange theory of emotion, Cannon (1929) made the point that sympathectomized animals and patients do seem to manifest emotional behavior. This criticism is, of course, as applicable to the above proposition as it was to the James-Lange formulation. The issues involved will be discussed later in this chapter.

Singer (1962) designed an experiment cast in the framework of a study of the effects of vitamin supplements on vision. As soon as a subject arrived, he was taken to a private room and told by the experimenter:

> In this experiment we would like to make various tests of your vision. We are particularly interested in how certain vitamin compounds and vitamin supplements affect the visual skills. In particular, we want to find out how the vitamin compound called "Suproxin" affects your vision.
>
> What we would like to do, then, if we can get your permission, is to give you a small injection of Suproxin. The injection itself is mild and harmless; however, since some people do object to being injected we don't want to talk you into anything. Would you mind receiving a Suproxin injection?

If the subject agreed to the injection (and all but one of 185 subjects did), the experimenter continued with instructions described below, then left the room. In a few minutes a doctor entered the room, briefly repeated the experimenter's instructions, took the subject's pulse, and then injected him with Suproxin.

Depending upon condition, the subject received one of two forms of Suproxin—epinephrine or a placebo.

Epinephrine or adrenaline is a sympathomimetic drug whose effects, with minor exceptions, are almost a perfect mimicry of a discharge of the sympathetic nervous system. Shortly after injection systolic blood pressure increases markedly. Heart rate increases somewhat, cutaneous blood flow decreases, muscle and cerebral blood flow increase, blood sugar and lactic acid concentration increase, and respiration rate increases slightly. For the subject, the major subjective symptoms are palpitation, tremor, and sometimes a feeling of flushing and accelerated breathing. With a subcutaneous injection, (in the dosage administered) such effects usually begin within three to five minutes of injection and last anywhere from ten minutes to an hour. For most subjects these effects are dissipated within 15–20 minutes after injection.

Subjects receiving epinephrine received a subcutaneous injection of ½ cc of a 1:1000 solution of Winthrop Laboratory's Suprarenin, a saline solution of epinephrine bitartrate.

Subjects in the placebo condition received a subcutaneous injection of ½ cc of saline solution.

A. MANIPULATING AN APPROPRIATE EXPLANATION

"Appropriate" refers to the extent to which the subject has an authoritative, unequivocal explanation of his bodily condition. Thus, a subject who had been informed by the physician that as a direct consequence of the injection he would feel palpitations, tremor, etc. would be considered to have a completely appropriate explanation. A subject who had been informed only that the injection would have no side effects, would have no appropriate explanation of his state. This dimension of appropriateness was manipulated in three experimental conditions which shall be called: (1) Epinephrine Informed (Epi Inf), (2) Epinephrine Ignorant (Epi Ign), and (3) Epinephrine Misinformed (Epi Mis).

Immediately after the subject had agreed to the injection and before the physician entered the room, the experimenter's presentation in each of these conditions went as follows:

1. Epinephrine Informed

"I should also tell you that some of our subjects have experienced side effects from the Suproxin. These side effects are transitory, that is, they will only last for about 15 or 20 minutes. What will probably happen is that your hand will start to shake, your heart will start to pound, and your face may get warm and flushed. Again these are side effects, lasting about 15 or 20 minutes."

While the physician was giving the injection, she told the subject that the injection was mild and harmless and repeated this description of the symptoms that the subject could expect as a consequence of the shot. In this condition, then, subjects had a completely appropriate explanation of their bodily state. They knew precisely what they would feel and why.

2. Epinephrine Ignorant

In this condition, when the subject agreed to the injection, the experimenter said nothing more about side effects and left the room. While the physician was giving the injection, she told the subject that the injection was mild and harmless and would have no side effects. In this condition, then, the subject had no experimentally provided explanation for his bodily state.

3. Epinephrine Misinformed

"I should also tell you that some of our subjects have experienced side effects from the Suproxin. These side effects are transitory, that is, they will only last for about 15 or 20 minutes. What will probably happen is that your feet will feel numb, you will have an itching sensation over parts of your body, and you may get a slight headache. Again these are side effects lasting 15 or 20 minutes." And again, the physician repeated these symptoms while injecting the subject.

None of these symptoms, of course, are consequences of an injection of epinephrine and, in effect, these instructions provided the subject with a completely inappropriate explanation of his bodily feelings. This condition was introduced as a control condition of sorts. It seemed possible that the description of side effects in the Epi Inf condition might turn the subject introspective, self-examining, possibly slightly troubled. Differences on the dependent variable between the Epi Inf and Epi Ign conditions might, then, be due to such factors rather than to differences in appropriateness. The false symptoms in the Epi Mis condition should similarly turn the subject introspective, etc., but the instructions in this condition do not provide an appropriate explanation of the subject's state.

Subjects in all of the above conditions were injected with epinephrine. Finally, there was a placebo condition in which subjects who were injected with saline solution were given precisely the same treatment as subjects in the Epi Ign condition.

B. PRODUCING AN EMOTION-INDUCING COGNITION

We initially hypothesized that given a state of physiological arousal for which the individual has no adequate explanation, cognitive factors can lead the individual to describe his feelings with any of a variety of emotional labels. In order to test this hypothesis, it was decided to manipulate emotional states which can be considered quite different—euphoria and anger.

There are, of course, many ways to induce such states. In this program of research, we have concentrated on social determinants of emotional states. Other studies have demonstrated that people evaluate their own feelings by comparing themselves with others around them (Wrightsman, 1960; Schachter, 1959). In the experiment described here, an attempt was again made to manipulate emotional state by social means. In one set of conditions, the subject was placed together with a stooge who had been trained to act euphorically. In a second set of conditions, the subject was with a stooge trained to act angrily.

1. Euphoria

Immediately[5] after the subject had been injected, the physician left the room and the experimenter returned with a stooge whom he introduced as another subject. The experimenter then said, "Both of you have had the Suproxin shot and you'll both be taking the same tests of vision. What I ask you to do now is just wait for 20 minutes. The reason for this is simply that we have to allow 20 minutes for the Suproxin to get from the

---

[5] It was, of course, imperative that the sequence with the stooge begin before the subject felt his first symptoms. Otherwise the subject would be virtually forced to interpret his feelings in terms of events preceding the stooge's entrance. Pretests had indicated that, for most subjects, epinephrine caused symptoms began within three to five minutes after injection. A deliberate attempt was made then to bring in the stooge within one minute after the subject's injection.

injection site into the bloodstream. At the end of 20 minutes when we are certain that most of the Suproxin has been absorbed into the bloodstream, we'll begin the tests of vision."

The room in which this was said had been deliberately put into a state of mild disarray. As he was leaving, the experimenter added apologetically, "The only other thing I should do is to apologize for the condition of the room. I just didn't have time to clean it up. So, if you need any scratch paper, or rubber bands, or pencils, help yourself. I'll be back in 20 minutes to begin the vision tests."

As soon as the experimenter left, the stooge introduced himself again, made a series of standard icebreaker comments and then went into his routine. He reached first for a piece of paper, doodled briefly, crumpled the paper, aimed for a wastebasket, threw, and missed. This led him into a game of "basketball" in which he moved about the room crumpling paper, and trying out fancy basketball shots. Finished with basketball, he said, "This is one of my good days. I feel like a kid again. I think I'll make a plane." He made a paper plane, spent a few minutes flying it around the room, and then said, "Even when I was a kid, I was never much good at this." He then tore off the tail of his plane, wadded it up, and making a slingshot of a rubber band, began to shoot the paper. While shooting, he noticed a sloppy pile of manila folders. He built a tower of these folders, then went to the opposite end of the room to shoot at the tower. He knocked down the tower, and while picking up the folders he noticed a pair of hula hoops behind a portable blackboard. He took one of these for himself, put the other within reaching distance of the subject, and began hula hooping. After a few minutes, he replaced the hula hoop and returned to his seat, at which point the experimenter returned to the room.

All through this madness an observer, through a one-way mirror, systematically recorded the subject's behavior and noted the extent to which the subject joined in with the stooge's whirl of activity.

Subjects in each of the three "appropriateness" conditions and in the placebo condition were submitted to this setup. The stooge, of course, never knew in which condition any particular subject fell.

2. Anger

Immediately after the injection, the experimenter brought a stooge into the subject's room, introduced the two, and after explaining the necessity for a 20-minute delay for "the Suproxin to get from the injection site into the bloodstream" he continued, "We would like you to use these 20 minutes to answer these questionnaires." Then handing out the questionnaires, he concluded: "I'll be back in 20 minutes to pick up the questionnaires and begin the tests of vision."

The questionnaires, five pages long, started off innocently, requesting face sheet information and then grew increasingly personal and insulting, asking questions such as:

"With how many men (other than your father) has your mother had extra-marital relationships?"

4 and under_____: 5–9_____: 10 and over_____.

The stooge, sitting directly opposite the subject, paced his own answers so that at all times subject and stooge were working on the same question. At regular points in the questionnaire, the stooge made a series of standardized comments about the questions. His comments started off innocently enough, grew increasingly querulous, and finally he ended up in a rage, ripping up his questionnaire, slamming it to the floor, saying "I'm not wasting any more time. I'm getting my books and leaving," and stomping out of the room.

Again an observer recorded the subject's behavior.

In summary, this was a seven-condition experiment which, for two different emotional states, allowed us (1) to evaluate the effects of "appropriateness" on emotional inducibility, and (2) to begin to evaluate the effects of sympathetic activation on emotional inducibility. In schematic form, the conditions were:

Euphoria	Anger
Epi Inf	Epi Inf
Epi Ign	Epi Ign
Epi Mis	Placebo
Placebo	

The Epi Mis condition was not run in the Anger sequence. This was originally conceived as a control condition, and it was felt that its inclusion in the Euphoria conditions alone would suffice as a means of evaluating the possible artifactual effect of the Epi Inf instructions.

The subjects were all male college students, taking classes in introductory psychology at the University of Minnesota. The records of all potential subjects were reviewed by the Student Health Service in order to insure that no harmful effects would result from the injections.

C. Measurements

Two types of measures of emotional state were obtained. Standardized observation through a one-way mirror was used to assess the subject's behavior. To what extent did he join in with the stooge's pattern of behavior and act euphoric or angry? The second type of measure was a self-report questionnaire in which, on a variety of scales, the subject indicated his mood of the moment.

These measures were obtained immediately after the stooge had finished his routine, at which point the experimenter returned saying, "Before we proceed with the vision tests, there is one other kind of information we must have. We have found that there are many things beside Suproxin that affect how well you see in our tests. How hungry you are, how tired you are and even the mood you're in at the moment—whether you feel happy or irritated at the time of testing will affect how well you see. To understand the data we collect on you, then, we must be able to figure out which effects are due to causes such as these and which are caused by Suproxin." He then handed out questionnaires containing a number of questions about bodily and emotional state. To measure mood the following two were the crucial questions:

1. How irritated, angry, or annoyed would you say you feel at present?

I don't feel at all irritated or angry	I feel a little irritated and angry	I feel quite irritated and angry	I feel very irritated and angry	I feel extremely irritated and angry
(0)	(1)	(2)	(3)	(4)

2. How good or happy would you say you feel at present?

I don't feel at all happy or good	I feel a little happy and good	I feel quite happy and good	I feel very happy and good	I feel extremely happy and good
(0)	(1)	(2)	(3)	(4)

D. THE EFFECTS OF THE MANIPULATIONS ON EMOTIONAL STATE

1. Euphoria

The effects of the several manipulations on emotional state in the euphoria conditions are presented in Table I. The scores recorded in this table were derived, for each subject, by subtracting the value of the point he checked on the "irritation" scale from the value of the point he checked on the "happiness" scale. Thus, if a subject were to check the point "I feel a little irritated and angry" on the "irritation" scale and the point "I feel very happy and good" on the "happiness" scale, his score would be $+2$. The higher the positive value, the happier and better the subject reports himself as feeling. Though an index is employed for expositional simplicity, it should be noted that the two components of the index each yield results completely consistent with those obtained by use of this index.

Let us examine first the effects of the "appropriateness" instructions. Comparison of the scores of the Epi Mis and Epi Inf conditions makes it immediately clear that the experimental differences are not due to artifacts resulting from the "informed" instructions. In both conditions the subject was warned to expect a variety of symptoms as a consequence of the injection. In the Epi Mis condition, where the symptoms were inappropriate to the subject's bodily state, the self-report score is almost twice that in the Epi Inf condition, where the symptoms were completely appropriate to the subject's bodily state. It is reasonable, then, to attribute differences between informed subjects and those in other conditions to differences in manipulated appropriateness, rather than to artifacts such as introspectiveness or self-examination.

TABLE I

SELF-REPORT OF EMOTIONAL STATE IN THE EUPHORIA CONDITIONS

Condition	N	Self-report scales
Epi Inf	25	.98
Epi Ign	25	1.78
Epi Mis	25	1.90
Placebo	26	1.61
Comparison		p values[a]
Epi Inf vs. Epi Mis		$< .01$
Epi Inf vs. Epi Ign		.02
Plac vs. Epi Mis, Ign or Inf		n.s.

[a] All p values reported throughout this paper are two-tailed.

It is clear that, consistent with expectations, subjects were more susceptible to the stooge's mood and consequently more euphoric when they had no explanation of their own bodily states than when they did. The means of both the Epi Ign and Epi Mis conditions were considerably greater than the mean of the Epi Inf condition.

Comparing the placebo to the epinephrine conditions, we note a pattern which repeated itself throughout the data. Placebo subjects were less euphoric than either Epi Mis or Epi Ign subjects, but somewhat more euphoric than Epi Inf subjects. These differences were not, however, statistically significant. The epinephrine-placebo comparisons are considered in detail in a later section of this paper, following the presentation of additional relevant data. For the moment, it is clear that, by self-report, manipulating "appropriateness" had a very strong effect on euphoria.

The analysis of the observational data was reported in detail elsewhere (Schachter and Singer, 1962). Here it is sufficient to note that on all behavioral indices devised—e.g. the amount of time the subject spent on stooge-initiated activity; "creative euphoria" (the extent to which the subject initiated euphoric activities of his own devising)— the same pattern of between-condition relationships held. Subjects in the Epi Mis and Epi Ign conditions behaved more euphorically than subjects in the Epi Inf condition. Placebo subjects again fell between Epi Ign and Epi Inf subjects.

2. Anger

In the anger conditions, we should again expect the subject to catch the stooge's mood only in those conditions where he was injected with epinephrine and had no appropriate explanation for the bodily state thus created. Subjects in the Epi Ign condition should, then, be considerably angrier than those in the Epi Inf or Placebo conditions. Data on behavioral indications of anger are presented in Table II. These figures were derived

TABLE II

BEHAVIORAL INDICATIONS OF EMOTIONAL STATE IN THE ANGER CONDITIONS

Condition	N	Anger index
Epi Inf	22	− .18
Epi Ign	23	+2.28
Placebo	22	+ .79
Comparison		p value
Epi Inf vs. Epi Ign		< .01
Epi Ign vs. Placebo		< .05
Placebo vs. Epi Inf		n.s.

from coding the subject's comments and behavior during the experimental session with the angry stooge. The nature of the index devised is described in detail elsewhere (Schachter and Singer, 1962). For present purposes, we can note that a positive value to this index indicates that the subject agreed with the stooge's comments and was angry. The larger the positive value, the angrier the subject. A negative value indicates that the subject either disagreed with the stooge or ignored him.

It is evident in Table II that expectations were confirmed. The value for the Epi Ign condition is positive and large, indicating that the subjects became angry; while in the Epi Inf condition, the score is slightly negative, indicating that these subjects failed to catch the stooge's mood at all. Placebo subjects fall between Epi Ign and Epi Inf subjects. On the self-report scales of mood, this pattern repeated itself, though on this measure

Placebo subjects do not differ significantly from either Epi Ign or Epi Inf subjects.

E. Discussion of Results

Having presented the basic data of this study, let us examine closely the extent to which they conform to theoretical expectations. If the hypotheses are correct, and if this experimental design provided a perfect test for these hypotheses, it should be anticipated that in the euphoria conditions, the degree of experimentally produced euphoria should vary in the following fashion:

$$\text{Epi Mis} \geq \text{Epi Ign} > \text{Epi Inf} = \text{Placebo}$$

In the anger conditions, anger should conform to the following pattern:

$$\text{Epi Ign} > \text{Epi Inf} = \text{Placebo}$$

In both sets of conditions, emotional level in the Epi Inf condition was considerably less than that achieved in any of the other Epi conditions. The results for the placebo condition, however, were ambiguous, for consistently the placebo subjects fell between the Epi Ign and the Epi Inf subjects. This is a particularly troubling pattern, making it impossible to evaluate unequivocally the effects of the state of physiological arousal and indeed raising serious questions about the entire theoretical structure. Though the emotional level was consistently greater in the Epi Mis and Epi Ign conditions than in the Placebo condition, this difference was significant at acceptable probability levels only on the behavioral indices in the anger conditions.

In order to explore the problem further, let us examine experimental factors which might have acted to restrain the emotional level in the Epi Ign and Epi Mis conditions. Clearly the ideal test of the first two hypotheses requires an experimental setup in which the subject has no other means of evaluating his state of physiological arousal other than the experimentally provided cognitions. Had it been possible to produce physiologically a state of sympathetic activation by means other than injection, one could have approached this experimental ideal more closely than in the present setup. As it stands, however, there is always a reasonable alternative cognition available to the aroused subject—he feels the way he does because of the injection. To the extent that the subject seizes on such an explanation of his bodily state, we should expect that he will be uninfluenced by the stooge.

It is possible, fortunately, to examine the effect of this artifact. In answers to open-end questions in which subjects described their own mood and physical state, some of the Epi Ign and Epi Mis subjects clearly attributed their physical state to the injection, e.g. "the shot gave me the shivers." In effect, such subjects are self-informed. Comparing such subjects to the remaining subjects in a condition, one finds in the Anger-Epi Ign condition that self-informed subjects are considerably less angry than the remaining subjects. Similarly in the Euphoria-Epi Mis and Ign conditions, self-informed subjects are considerably less euphoric than are their non-self-informed counterparts. If one eliminates such self-informed subjects, the differences between the Placebo and Epi Ign or Epi Mis conditions become highly significant statistically in both the Anger and the Euphoria set of conditions. Clearly, indications are good that this self-informing artifact has attenuated the effects of epinephrine.

Consider next the fact that the emotional level in Placebo conditions was greater than that in the Epi Inf conditions. Theoretically, of course, it should be expected that the two conditions will be equally low, for by assuming that emotional state is a joint function of a state of physiological arousal and of the appropriateness of a cognition we are, in effect, assuming a multiplicative function: if either component is at zero, emotional level is at zero. This expectation should hold, however, only if one can be sure that there is no sympathetic activation in the placebo conditions. This assumption, of course, is completely unrealistic, for the injection of placebo does not prevent sympathetic activation. The experimental situations were fairly dramatic and certainly some of the Placebo subjects must have experienced physiological arousal. If this general line of reasoning is correct, it should be anticipated that the emotional level of subjects who give indications of sympathetic activity will be greater than that of subjects who do not.

Since, in all conditions, a subject's pulse was taken before the injection and again after the session with the stooge, there is one index of sympathetic activation available—change in pulse rate. The predominant pattern in the Placebo conditions was, of course, a decrease in pulse rate. It is assumed, therefore, that in the Placebo conditions, those subjects whose pulses increase or remain the same give indications of sympathetic arousal, while those subjects whose pulses decrease do not. Comparing, within Placebo conditions, such self-aroused subjects with those who give no indication of sympathetic activation, we find in the Anger condition that those subjects whose pulses increase or remain the same are considerably and significantly angrier than those subjects whose pulses decrease. Similarly, in the Euphoria Placebo condition, the self-aroused subjects are considerably and significantly more euphoric than the subjects who give no indication of sympathetic activation. Conforming to expectations, sympathetic activation accompanies an increase in emotional level.

It should be noted, too, on the several indices, that the emotional

level of subjects showing no signs of sympathetic activity is quite close
to the emotional level of subjects in the parallel Epi Inf conditions. The
similarity of these sets of scores and their uniformly low level of indicated
emotionality would certainly make it appear that both factors are essential
to an emotional state. When either the level of sympathetic arousal is low
or a completely appropriate cognition is available, the level of emotionality
is low.

Let us summarize the major findings of this experiment and examine
the extent to which they support the propositions offered in the introduction of this paper. It has been suggested, first, that given a state of physiological arousal for which an individual has no explanation, he will label
this state in terms of the cognitions available to him. This implies, of
course, that by manipulating the cognitions of an individual in such a state,
his feelings can be manipulated in diverse directions. Experimental results
support this proposition, for following the injection of epinephrine, those
subjects who had no explanation for the bodily state thus produced, proved
readily manipulable into the disparate feeling states of euphoria and anger.

From this first proposition, it must follow that given a state of
physiological arousal for which the individual has a completely satisfactory
explanation, he will not label this state in terms of the alternative cognitions available. Experimental evidence strongly supports this expectation.
In those conditions in which subjects were injected with epinephrine and
told precisely what they would feel and why, they proved relatively
immune to any effects of the manipulated cognitions. In the anger condition, such subjects did not become at all angry; in the euphoria condition,
such subjects reported themselves as far less happy than subjects with an
identical bodily state but no adequate knowledge of why they felt the way
they did.

Finally, it has been suggested that given constant cognitive circumstances, an individual will react emotionally only to the extent that he
experiences a state of physiological arousal. Without taking account of
experimental artifacts, the evidence in support of this proposition is consistent but tentative. When the effects of "self-informing" tendencies in
epinephrine subjects and of "self-arousing" tendencies in placebo subjects
are partialed out, the evidence strongly supports the proposition.

III. Physiological Arousal and Emotionality

The pattern of data, then, falls neatly in line with theoretical expectations. However, the fact that it was necessary to some extent to rely on
internal analyses in order to partial out the effects of experimental artifacts
inevitably makes these conclusions somewhat tentative. In order further
to test these propositions on the interaction of cognitive and physiological

determinants of emotional state, a series of additional experiments was designed to rule out or overcome the operation of these artifacts.

The first of these experiments was designed by Schachter and Wheeler (1962) to test the proposition that emotionality is positively related to physiological arousal by extending the range of manipulated sympathetic activation. It seemed clear from the results of the study just described that the self-arousing tendency of placebo subjects tended to obscure the differences between placebo and epinephrine conditions. A test of the proposition at stake, then, would require comparing subjects who have received injections of epinephrine with subjects who, to some extent, were incapable of self-activation of the sympathetic nervous system. A class of drugs known generally as autonomic blocking agents makes such blocking possible to some degree. If it is correct that a state of sympathetic discharge is a necessary component of an emotional experience, it should be anticipated that whatever emotional state is experimentally manipulated should be experienced most strongly by subjects who have received epinephrine, next by placebo subjects, and least of all by subjects who have received injections of an autonomic blocking agent.

A. Procedure

In order to conceal the purposes of the study and the nature of the injection, the experiment was again cast in the framework of a study of the effects of vitamins on vision. As soon as a subject—a male college student —arrived, he was taken to a private room and told by the experimenter:

"I've asked you to come today to take part in an experiment concerning the effects of vitamins on the visual processes. Our experiment is concerned with the effects of Suproxin on vision. Suproxin is a high concentrate vitamin C derivative. If you agree to take part in the experiment, we will give you an injection of Suproxin and then subject your retina to about 15 minutes of continuous black and white stimulation. This is simpler than it sounds: we'll just have you watch a black and white movie. After the movie, we'll give you a series of visual tests.

"The injection itself is harmless and will be administered by our staff doctor. It may sting a little at first, as most injections do, but after this you will feel nothing and will have no side effects. We know that some people dislike getting injections, and if you take part in the experiment, we want it to be your own decision. Would you like to?" (All subjects agreed to take part.)

1. Drugs Used

There were three forms of Suproxin administered—epinephrine, placebo, and chlorpromazine.

1. Epinephrine. Subjects in this condition received a subcutaneous injection of $\frac{1}{2}$ cc of a 1:1000 solution of Winthrop Laboratory's Suprarenin.

2. Placebo. Subjects in this condition received a subcutaneous injection of $\frac{1}{2}$ cc of saline solution.

3. Chlorpromazine. Subjects in this condition received an intramuscular injection of a solution consisting of 1 cc (25 mg) of Smith, Klein and French Thorazine and 1 cc of saline solution.

The choice of chlorpromazine as a blocking agent was dictated by considerations of safety, ease of administration, and known duration of effect. Ideally, one would have wished for a blocking agent whose mechanism and effect were precisely and solely the reverse of those of epinephrine —a peripherally acting agent which would prevent the excitation of sympathetically innervated structures. Though it is certainly possible to approach this ideal more closely with agents other than chlorpromazine, such drugs tend to be dangerous, difficult to administer, or of short duration.

Chlorpromazine is known to act as a sympathetic depressant. It has a moderate hypotensive effect, with a slight compensatory increase in heart rate. It has mild adrenergic blocking activity, for it reverses the pressor effects of small doses of epinephrine and depresses responses of the nictitating membrane to preganglionic stimulation. Killam (1959) summarizes what is known and supposed about the mechanism of action of chlorpromazine as follows: "Autonomic effects in general may be attributed to a mild peripheral adrenergic blocking activity and probably to central depression of sympathetic centers, possibly in the hypothalamus." Popularly, of course, the compound is known as a "tranquilizer."

It is recognized that chlorpromazine has effects other than the sympatholytic effect of interest to us. For purposes of experimental purity this is unfortunate but inevitable in this sort of research. It is clear, however, that the three conditions do differ in the degree of manipulated sympathetic activation.

2. Emotion Induction

Rather than the more complicated devices employed in the previous experiment, an emotion-inducing film was used as a means of manipulating the cognitive component of emotional states. In deciding on the type of film, two extremes seemed possible—a horror, fright or anxiety-provoking film or a comic, amusement-provoking film. Since it is a common stereotype that adrenaline makes one nervous and that the tranquilizer, chlorpromazine, makes one tranquil and mildly euphoric, the predicted pattern of results with a horror film would be subject to alternative interpretation. It was deliberately decided, then, to use a comedy. If the hypothesis is correct, epinephrine subjects should find the film somewhat funnier than placebo subjects who, in turn, would be more amused than chlorpromazine subjects.

The film chosen was a 14-minute excerpt from a Jack Carson movie called "The Good Humor Man." This excerpt is a self-contained, comprehensible episode involving a slapstick chase scene.

Three subjects (one from each of the drug conditions) always watched the film simultaneously. The projection room was deliberately arranged so that the subjects could neither see nor hear one another. Facing the screen were three theatre seats, separated from one another by large, heavy partitions. In a further attempt to maintain the independence of the subjects, the sound volume of the projector was turned up so as to mask any sounds made by the subjects.

3. Measures

The subjects' reactions while watching the film were used as the chief index of amusement. During the showing of the movie an observer, who had been introduced as an assistant who would help administer the visual tests, systematically scanned the subjects and recorded their reactions to the film. He observed each subject once every ten seconds, so that over the course of the film 88 units of each subject's behavior were categorized. The observer simply recorded each subject's reaction to the film according to the following scheme: (a) neutral—straight-faced watching of film with no indication of amusement; (b) smile; (c) grin—a smile with teeth showing; (d) laugh—a smile or grin on face accompanied by bodily movements usually associated with laughter, e.g., shaking shoulders, moving head; (e) big laugh—belly laugh; a laugh accompanied by violent body movement such as doubling up, throwing up hands.

In a minute by minute comparison, two independent observers agreed in their categorization of 90% of the 528 units recorded in six different reliability trials.

The observer, of course, never knew which subject had received which injection.

B. RESULTS

The observation record provides a continuous record of each subject's reaction to the film. As an overall index of amusement, the number of units in which a subject's behavior was recorded in the categories "smile," "grin," "laugh," and "big laugh" are summed together. The means of this amusement index are presented in Table III. The larger the figure, the more amusement was manifest. Differences were in the anticipated direction. Epinephrine subjects gave indications of greater amusement than did

TABLE III

THE EFFECTS OF EPINEPHRINE, PLACEBO, AND CHLORPROMAZINE ON AMUSEMENT

Condition	N	Mean amusement index
Epinephrine	38	17.79
Placebo	42	14.31
Chlorpromazine	46	10.41
Comparison		p value
Epi vs. Plac		n.s.
Epi vs. Chlor		$< .01$
Plac vs. Chlor		$< .05$

placebo subjects who, in turn, were more amused than chlorpromazine subjects.

Though the trend is clearly in the predicted direction, epinephrine and placebo subjects do not differ significantly in this overall index. The difference between these two groups, however, becomes apparent when we examine strong ("laugh" and "big laugh") reactions to the film; we find an average of 4.84 such units among the epinephrine subjects and of only 1.83 such units among placebo subjects. This difference is significant at better than the .05 level of significance. Epinephrine subjects tend to be openly amused at the film, placebo subjects to be quietly amused. Some 16% of epinephrine subjects reacted at some point with belly laughs, while not a single placebo subject did so. It should be noted that this is much the state of affairs one would expect from the disguised injection of epinephrine—a manipulation which, as has been suggested, creates a bodily state "in search of" an appropriate cognition. Certainly laughter can be considered a more appropriate accompaniment to the state of sympathetic arousal than quiet smiling.

It would appear, then, that degree of overt amusement is directly related to the degree of manipulated sympathetic activation.

IV. Sympathetic Activity and Emotionality in Rats

A further test of the relationship of emotionality to sympathetic activity was made by Singer (1963) who, in a deliberate attempt to rule out the operation of the self-informing artifact, conducted his study on rats—a species unlikely to attribute an aroused physiological state to an injection. Among other things, Singer examined the effects of injections of epinephrine (an intraperitonial injection of epinephrine suspended in peanut oil in a concentration of .10 mg. per kg of body weight) and placebo on the reactions of rats to standard frightening situations. His technique was simple. In fright conditions, he placed his animals in a box containing a doorbell, a door buzzer, and a flashing 150 watt bulb. After a brief interval, a switch was tripped setting off all three devices simultaneously for a one-and-a-half minute interval. In nonfright conditions, of course, the switch was never tripped.

Singer's results are presented in Table IV. The figures presented in

TABLE IV
THE RELATIONSHIP OF EPINEPHRINE TO FRIGHT

Condition[a]	Epinephrine	Placebo	p value of difference
Fright	13.15	11.49	.025
Nonfright	7.47	7.17	n.s.

[a] $N = 12$ in each of the four conditions.

this table represent an index whose components are generally accepted indicators of fright such as defecation, urination and the like. The larger the figure, the more frightened the animal. Clearly there is a substantial drug-related difference in the fright condition and no difference at all in the nonfright condition. The drug $\times$ stress interaction is significant at better than the .01 level of significance. It would certainly appear that under these experimental circumstances the state of fear is related to sympathetic activity. Further evidence for this relationship is found in a study conducted by Latané and Schachter (1962) which demonstrated that rats injected with epinephrine were notably more capable of avoidance learning than were rats injected with a placebo. Using a modified Miller-Mowrer shuttlebox, these investigators found that during an experimental period involving two hundred massed trials, 15 rats injected with epinephrine avoided shock an average of 101.2 trials, while 15 placebo-injected rats averaged only 37.3 avoidances.

V. Discussion and Implications

Taken together, this body of studies does give strong support to the propositions which generated these experimental tests. Given a state of sympathetic activation, for which no immediately appropriate explanation is available, human subjects can be readily manipulated into states of euphoria, of anger, and of amusement at a movie. Varying the intensity of sympathetic activation serves to vary the intensity of a variety of emotional states in both rat and human subjects. Clearly the line of thought guiding these experiments is modified Jamesianism, for emotion is viewed as visceral activity in interaction with cognitive or situational factors. Let us examine the extent to which the addition of cognitive elements allows us to cope with the shortcomings of a purely visceral formulation. Since Cannon's critique (1927, 1929) has been the most lucid and influential attack on a visceral view of emotion, I shall focus discussion around Cannon's five criticisms of the James-Lange theory.

A RE-EXAMINATION OF CANNON'S CRITIQUE OF A VISCERAL FORMULATION OF EMOTION

1. Criticisms Overcome by Cognitive Considerations

a. Cannon's criticism that "artificial induction of the visceral changes typical of strong emotions does not produce them" is based on the results of Marañon's (1924) study and its several replications. The fact that the injection of adrenaline produces apparently genuine emotional states in only a tiny minority of subjects is, of course, completely damning for a theory which equates visceral activity with affect. This is, on the other hand, precisely the fact which inspired the series of studies described earlier. Rather than a criticism, the fact that injection of adrenaline, in and of itself, does not lead to an emotional state is one of the strong points of the present formulation; for, with the addition of cognitive propositions, we are able to specify and manipulate the conditions under which such an injection will or will not lead to an emotional state.

b. Cannon's point that "the same visceral changes occur in very different emotional states" is again damning for a purely visceral viewpoint. Since we are aware of a great variety of feeling and emotion states, it must follow from a purely visceral formulation that the variety of emotions will be accompanied by an equal variety of differentiable bodily states. Though the evidence as of today is by no means as one-sided as it appeared in Cannon's day, it does seem that the gist of Cannon's criticism is still correct. Following James' pronouncement, a formidable number of studies were undertaken in search of the physiological differentiators of the emotions. The results, in those early days, were almost uniformly negative. All of the emotional states experimentally manipulated were characterized by a general pattern of activation of the sympathetic nervous system but there appeared to be no clearcut physiological discriminators of the various emotions.

More recent work, however, has given some indication that there may be differentiators. Ax (1953) and Schachter (1957) studied fear and anger. On a large number of indices both of these states were characterized by a similar high level of sympathetic activation, but on several indices they did differ in the degree of activation. Wolf and Wolff (1947) studied a subject with a gastric fistula and were able to distinguish two patterns in the physiological responses of the stomach wall. It should be noted, though, that for many months they studied their subject during and following a great variety of moods and emotions, but were able to distinguish only two patterns.

Whether there are physiological distinctions among the various emotional states must still be considered an open question. Recent work might be taken to indicate that such differences are at best rather subtle, and that the variety of emotion, mood, and feeling states are by no means matched by an equal variety of visceral patterns—a state of affairs hardly compatible with the Jamesian formulation. On the other hand, the question of the physiological differentiability of the various emotions is essentially irrelevant to the present formulation, which maintains simply that cognitive and situational factors determine the labels applied to any of a variety of states of physiological arousal.

The experimental search for the physiological differentiators of emotional states has involved such substantial, long-time effort that the problem merits further comment. Viewed en masse, these experiments have yielded quite inconclusive results. Most, though not all of these studies have indicated no differences among the various emotional states. Since as human beings, rather than as scientists, we have no difficulty identifying, labeling, and distinguishing among our feelings, the results of these studies have long seemed rather puzzling and paradoxical. Perhaps because of this, there has been a persistent tendency to discount such results as due to ignorance or methodological inadequacy and to pay far more attention to the very few studies which demonstrate *some* sort of physiological differences among emotional states than to the very many studies which indicate no differences at all. It is conceivable, however, that these results should be taken at face value and that emotional states may, indeed, be generally characterized by a high level of sympathetic activation with few if any physiological distinguishers among the many emotional states. If this is correct, the cognitive-physiological formulation outlined here and the findings of the studies described may help to resolve the problem.

Obviously these studies do *not* rule out the possibility of differences among the emotional states. It is the case, however, that given precisely the same state of epinephrine-induced sympathetic activation, it has been possible, by means of cognitive manipulations, to produce in subjects the very disparate states of euphoria, anger, and amusement at a movie. It may, indeed, be the case that cognitive factors are major determiners of the emotional "labels" we apply to a common state of sympathetic arousal.

In *"Background to Danger,"* novelist Eric Ambler (1958) describes a fugitive who introspects this way:

Rather to his surprise, he found that being wanted for murder produced in him an effect almost identical to that of a dentist's waiting-room—a sense of discomfort in the intestinal region, a certain constriction in the chest. He supposed that the same glands discharged the same secretions into the blood stream in both cases. Nature could be absurdly parsimonious.

If these speculations are correct, nature may indeed be far more parsimonious than Ambler suggests.

c. Cannon's point that "the viscera are relatively insensitive structures" is again telling for a formulation which virtually requires a richness of visceral sensation in order to be able to match the presumed richness of emotional experience. For the present formulation, of course, the criticism is irrelevant. Just so long as there is *some* visceral or cardiovascular sensation, the cognitive-physiological hypotheses are applicable.

The introduction of cognitive factors does allow us, then, to cope with three of Cannon's criticisms of a purely visceral formulation. Let us turn next to Cannon's remaining two points which are quite as troublesome for the present view of emotion as for the Jamesian view.

2. Visceral Separation and Emotion

a. Effects of sympathectomies. Cannon's remaining criticisms are these: "Visceral changes are too slow to be a source of emotional feeling" (i.e., the latency period of arousal of many visceral structures is longer than the latency of onset of emotional feelings reported in introspective studies); and "total separation of the viscera from the central nervous system does not alter emotional behavior." Both criticisms make essentially the same point, for they identify conditions in which there are apparently emotions unaccompanied by visceral activity. The data with which Cannon buttresses his latter criticism are based on his own studies (Cannon *et al.,* 1927) of sympathectomized cats, and Sherrington's (1900) study of sympathectomized dogs. For both sets of experimental animals "the absence of reverberation from the viscera did not alter in any respect the appropriate emotional display; its only abbreviation was surgical." In the presence of a barking dog, for example, the sympathectomized cats manifested almost all of the signs of feline rage. Finally, Cannon notes the report of Dana (1921) that a patient with a spinal cord lesion and almost totally without visceral sensation still manifested normal emotionality.[6]

---

[6] More recent work supporting Cannon's position is that of Moyer and Bunnell (Moyer, 1958a,b; Moyer and Bunnell, 1959, 1960a,b) who, in an extensive series of studies of bilaterally adrenalectomized rats, have consistently failed to find any indication of differences between experimental and control animals on a variety

b. Prior learning. For either the Jamesian or the present formulation, such data are crucial, for both views demand visceral arousal as a necessary condition for emotional arousal. When faced with this evidence, James' defenders (e.g., Wenger, 1950; Mandler, 1962) have consistently made the point that the apparently emotional behavior manifested by sympathectomized animals and men is well-learned behavior, acquired long before sympathectomy. There is a dual implication in this position: first, that sympathetic arousal facilitates the acquisition of emotional behavior and, second, that sympathectomized subjects act but do not feel emotional. There is a small but growing body of evidence supporting these contentions. Wynne and Solomon (1955) have demonstrated that sympathectomized dogs acquire an avoidance response considerably more slowly than do control dogs. Further, on extinction trials most of their 13 sympathectomized animals extinguished quickly, while not a single one of 30 control dogs gave any indications of extinction over two hundred trials. Of particular interest are two dogs who were sympathectomized after they had acquired the avoidance response. On extinction trials these two animals behaved precisely as did the control dogs—giving no indication of extinction. Thus, when deprived of visceral innervation, animals are quite slow in acquiring emotionally linked avoidance responses and, in general, rapid in extinguishing such responses. When deprived of visceral innervation only after acquisition, the animals behave exactly as do the normal dogs—they fail to extinguish. A true Jamesian would undoubtedly note that these latter animals have learned to act as if they were emotional, but he would ask: Do they feel emotional?

c. Autonomic dysfunctioning in humans. This apparently unanswerable question seems on its way to an answer in a thoroughly fascinating study of the emotional life of paraplegics and quadriplegics conducted by Hohmann (1962). Hohmann studied a sample of 25 patients of the Spinal Cord Injury Service of the Veterans Administration Hospital at Long Beach. The subjects were divided into five groups according to the height of the clinically complete lesions as follows:

Group I, with lesions between the second and eighth cervical segmental level, have only the cranial branch of the parasympathetic nervous system remaining intact.

Group II, with lesions between the first and fourth thoracic seg-

---

of emotionally linked behaviors such as avoidance learning. The effects of adrenalectomy are by no means clearcut, however, for other investigators (Levine and Soliday, 1962) have found distinct differences between operated and control animals.

mental level, have in addition to the above, at least partial innervation of the sympathetically innervated cardiac plexus remaining intact.

Group III, with lesions between the sixth and twelfth thoracic segmental level have, additionally, at least partial innervation of the splanchnic outflow of the sympathetics remaining intact.

Group IV, with lesions between the first and fifth lumbar segmental level, have in addition at least partial sympathetic innervation of the mesenteric ganglia.

Group V, with lesions between the first and fifth sacral segments have, in addition, at least partial innervation of the sacral branch of the parasympathetic nervous system.

These groups then fall along a dimension of visceral innervation and sensation. The higher the lesion, the less the visceral sensation. If the present conception of emotion is correct, one should expect to find decreasing manifestation of emotion as the height of the lesion increases.

With each of his subjects, Hohmann conducted an extensive, structured interview which was "directed to specific feelings in situations of sexual excitement, fear, anger, grief and sentimentality, and the subject's attention was directed toward their feelings rather than to the concomitant ideation." Hohmann asked his subjects to recall an emotion-arousing incident prior to their injury and a comparable incident following the injury. They were then asked to compare the intensity of their emotional experiences before and after injury. Changes in reported affect comprise the body of data. I have adapted Hohmann's data for presentation in Figure 1. Following Hohmann's coding schema a report of no change is scored as 0; a report of mild change (e.g., "I feel it less, I guess") is scored -1 for a decrease and $+1$ for an increase; a report of strong change (e.g., "I feel it a helluva lot less") is scored as -2 or $+2$.

Hohmann's data for the states of fear and anger is plotted in Figure 1. It can be immediately seen that the higher the lesion and the less the visceral sensation, the greater the decrease in emotionality. Precisely the same relationship holds for the states of sexual excitement and grief. The sole exception to this consistent trend is "sentimentality," which, I suspect, should be considered a cognitive rather than a "feeling" state. It is clear that for these cases deprivation of visceral sensation has resulted in a marked decrease in emotionality.

If, in an attempt to assess the absolute level of emotionality of these cases, one examines their verbalized introspections, we note again and again that subjects with cervical lesions described themselves as acting emotional but not feeling emotional. A few typical quotes follow:

". . . it's sort of cold anger. Sometimes I act angry when I see some injustice. I yell and cuss and raise hell, because if you don't do it sometimes, I've learned people will take advantage of you, but it just doesn't have the heat to it that it used to. It's a mental kind of anger."

"Seems like I get thinking mad, not shaking mad, and that's a lot different."

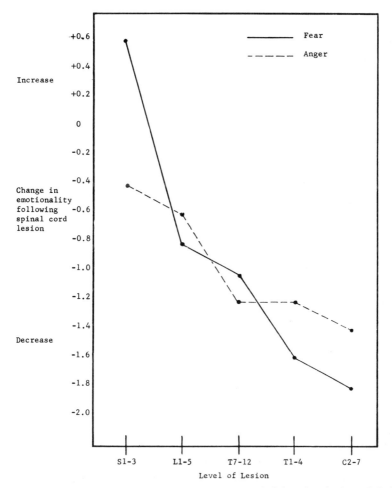

FIG. 1. Changes in emotionality as related to height of spinal cord lesion. (Adapted from Hohmann, 1962.)

"I say I am afraid, like when I'm going into a real stiff exam at school, but I don't really feel afraid, not all tense and shaky, with that hollow feeling in my stomach, like I used to."

In effect, these subjects seemed to be saying that when the situation demands it, they make the proper emotional-appearing responses, but they do not feel emotional. Parenthetically, it should be noted that these quotations bear an almost contrapuntal resemblance to the introspections of Marañon's subjects who, after receiving an injection of adrenaline, described their feelings in a way that led Marañon to label them "cold" or "as if" emotions. Many of these subjects described their physical symptoms and added statements such as, "I feel as if I were very frightened; however, I am calm."

The two sets of introspections are like opposite sides of the same coin. Marañon's subjects reported the visceral correlates of emotion, but in the absence of veridical cognitions did not describe themselves as feeling emotion. Hohmann's subjects described the appropriate reaction to an emotion-inducing situation but in the absence of visceral arousal did not seem to describe themselves as emotional. It is as if they were labeling a situation, not describing a feeling. Obviously, this contrasting set of introspections is precisely what should be anticipated from a formulation of emotion as a joint function of cognitive and physiological factors.

The line of thought stimulated by the Wynne and Solomon (1955) and Hohmann (1962) studies may indeed be the answer to Cannon's observation that there can be emotional behavior without visceral activity. From the evidence of these studies, it would appear, first, that autonomic arousal greatly facilitates the acquisition of emotional behavior but is not necessary for its maintenance if the behavior is acquired prior to sympathectomy; and, second, that in the absence of autonomic arousal, behavior that appears emotional will not be experienced as emotional.

VI. Some Effects of Cognitive Factors on the Appraisal of Bodily States

A. COGNITIONS AND RESPONSE TO MARIHUANA

Let us turn now to the cognitive component of this view of emotion and examine further implications of the formulation. The key cognitive assumption underlying the human experiments described is that "given a state of physiological arousal for which an individual has no immediate explanation, he will label this state and describe his feelings in terms of the cognitions available to him." Obviously, this proposition implies that a drive exists to evaluate, understand, and label ambiguous body states. It is suggested that Festinger's (1954) theoretical invention—the "evaluative need," which he employs as the conceptual underpinning of his theory of social comparison processes—is as necessary and useful for an understanding of emotion and the perception of bodily states as it has proven for understanding of the opinions. Given a new, strange, or ambiguous bodily state, pressures will act on the individual to decide exactly what it is that he feels and to decide how he will label these feelings. In the Schachter and Singer (1962) study the differences between the Epi Ign and Epi Inf conditions would certainly indicate that it is useful to apply this notion of evaluative needs to bodily states.

These cognitive assumptions as worded clearly imply applicability to bodily states other than the epinephrine induced state of sympathetic activation. If these ideas are correct, it should be expected that any novel bodily state will give rise to pressures to decide what is felt, to decide how these feelings are to be labeled, and, perhaps, to decide whether these feelings are pleasant or unpleasant ones. Though I know of no experiments directly designed to test these ideas for states other than that induced by epinephrine, the extensive literature on the effects of drugs provides constant hints and bits of data which suggest that these ideas do have wide applicability.

As an example, consider the effects of smoking marihuana. Following the pharmacological texts, marihuana or cannabis produces the following physiological effects:

> Marihuana usually causes an increase in pulse rate, a slight rise in blood pressure, and conjunctival vascular congestion; the cardiovascular system is otherwise unaffected. The blood sugar and basal metabolic rate are elevated, but usually not beyond the upper limits of normal. Urinary frequency without diuresis occurs. A marked increase in appetite (especially for sweets) and hunger are characteristic, and hypergeusia may occasionally be prominent. Dryness of the mouth and throat is frequent. Nausea, vomiting, and occasionally diarrhea may be noted.
>
> Tremor, ataxia, vertigo, tinnitus, hyper-reflexia, increased sensitivity to touch, pressure, and pain stimuli, pupillary dilatation with sluggish light reflexes, and a sensation of floating are also observed. . . . Tremulousness of the eyelids, lips, and tongue and nystagamus on lateral gaze are common. (Goodman and Gilman, 1958, pp. 172–173.)

These are the measured physiological changes caused by smoking marihuana. In and of themselves, are such bodily feelings pleasant or unpleasant? Given such symptoms, should the smoker describe himself as "high" or as "sick"?

In an absorbing study of fifty marihuana users, the sociologist Becker (1953) reports an invariable sequence in learning to use marihuana for pleasure. Once he has learned the techniques of smoking, the smoker must learn to label his physiological symptoms as being "high." In Becker's words,

> . . . being high consists of two elements: the presence of symptoms caused by marihuana use and the recognition of these symptoms and their connection by the user with his use of the drug. It is not enough, that is, that the effects

be present; they alone do not automatically provide the experience of being high. The user must be able to point them out to himself and consciously connect them with his having smoked marihuana before he can have this experience. Otherwise, regardless of the actual effects produced, he considers that the drug has had no effect on him.

An example of learning that he is high is provided by this quotation from a novice who gets high for the first time only after he learned that intense hunger is one consequence of smoking marihuana:

> They were just laughing the hell out of me because like I was eating so much. I just scoffed (ate) so much food, and they were just laughing at me, you know. Sometimes I'd be looking at them, you know, wondering why they're laughing, you know, not knowing what I was doing. (Well, did they eventually tell you why they were laughing?) Yeah, yeah, I come back, "Hey, man, what's happening?" and all of a sudden I feel weird, you know. "Man, you're on you know. You're on pot (high on marihuana)." I said, "No, am I?" Like I don't know what's happening.

An instance of more indirect learning is the following: "I heard little remarks that were made by people. Somebody said, 'My legs are rubbery,' and I can't remember all the remarks that were made because I was very attentively listening for all these cues for what I was supposed to feel like."

Obviously, these are instances where the novice must literally learn to notice his feelings. Given that a user is made aware of his symptoms and has learned that what he is feeling is being "high," Becker notes that one further step is necessary for continued use of the drug:

> He must learn to enjoy the effects he has just learned to experience. Marihuana-produced sensations are not automatically or necessarily pleasurable. The taste for such experience is a socially acquired one, not different in kind from acquired tastes for oysters or dry martinis. The user feels dizzy, thirsty; his scalp tingles; he misjudges time and distances, and so on. Are these things pleasurable? He isn't sure. If he is to continue marihuana use, he must decide that they are. Otherwise, getting high, while a real enough experience, will be an unpleasant one he would rather avoid.

Becker supports this analysis with numerous instances of novice smokers being taught, in social interaction, that their feelings were pleasant.

This study, then, indicates that new marihuana users must be taught to notice and identify what they feel, must be taught to label the state as "high" and must be taught that the state is "pleasant." The marihuana induced state of feelings appears to be another instance of a bodily state which takes its meaning and labels in good part from cognitive and social factors.

I would guess that the labels and hedonic valuation attached to an amazing variety of bodily conditions are cognitively determined.

Obviously, there are limits. It is unlikely that anyone with undiagnosed peritonitis could ever be convinced that he was euphoric, high, or anything but deathly ill. I suspect, though, that the limits are astonishingly wide. Vomiting to us may seem unpleasant, but to a banqueting Roman gourmet, it may have been one of the exquisite pleasures.

B. LABELING OF BODILY STATES IN OBESITY

As a final point, if it is correct that the labels attached to feeling states are cognitively, situationally, or socially determined, it becomes a distinct possibility that an uncommon or inappropriate label can be attached to a feeling state. Where such is the case, we may anticipate bizarre and pathological behavior. As an example of this possibility, consider the state of hunger. We are so accustomed to think of hunger as a primary motive, innate and wired into the animal, unmistakable in its cues, that even the possibility that an organism would be incapable of correctly labeling the state seems too far fetched to credit. The physiological changes accompanying food deprivation seem distinct, identifiable, and invariant. Yet even a moment's consideration will make it clear that attaching the label "hunger" to this set of bodily feelings and behaving accordingly, is a learned, socially determined, cognitive act.

Consider the neonate. Wholly at the mercy of its feelings, when uncomfortable, in pain, frightened, hungry, or thirsty, it screams. Whether it is comforted, soothed, clucked at, fondled, or fed has little to do with the state of its own feelings, but depends entirely on the ability and willingness of its mother or nurse to recognize the proper cues. If she is experienced, she will comfort when the baby is frightened, soothe him when he is chafed, feed him when he is hungry, and so on. If inexperienced, her behavior may be completely inappropriate to the child's state. Most commonly, perhaps, the compassionate but bewildered mother will feed her child at any sign of distress.

It is precisely this state of affairs that the analyst Hilde Bruch (1961) suggests is at the heart of chronic obesity. She describes such cases as characterized by a confusion between intense emotional states and hunger. During childhood these patients have not been taught to discriminate between hunger and such states as fear, anger, and anxiety. If correct, these people are, in effect, labeling a state of sympathetic activation as hunger. Small wonder that they are both fat and jolly.

REFERENCES

Ambler, E. (1958). "Background to Danger." Dell, New York.
Ax, A. F. (1953). *Psychosomat. Med.* **15**, 433–442.
Becker, H. S. (1953). *Am. J. Sociol.* **59**, 235–242.

Bruch, H. (1961). *Psychiat. Quart.* **35**, 458–481.

Cannon, W. B. (1927). *Am. J. Psychol.* **39**, 106–124.

Cannon, W. B. (1929). "Bodily Changes in Pain, Hunger, Fear and Rage." 2nd ed. Appleton, New York.

Cannon, W. B., Lewis, J. T., and Britton, S. W. (1927). *Boston Med. and Surg. J.* **197**, 514.

Cantril, H., and Hunt, W. A. (1932). *Am. J. Psychol.* **44**, 300–307.

Dana, C. L. (1921). *Arch. Neurol. Psychiat.* **6**, 634–639.

Festinger, L. (1954). *Human Relat.,* **7**, 114–140.

Goodman, L. S., and Gilman, A. (1958). "The Pharmacological Basis of Therapeutics." Macmillan, New York.

Hohmann, G. W. (1962). The effect of dysfunctions of the autonomic nervous system on experienced feelings and emotions. Paper read at Conference on Emotions and Feelings at New School for Social Research, New York.

Hunt, J. McV., Cole, M. W., and Reis, E. C. (1958). *Am. J. Psychol.* **71**, 136–151.

James, W. (1890). "The Principles of Psychology." Holt, New York.

Killam, E. K. (1959). *Natl. Acad. Sci.—Natl. Res. Council Publ.* **583**.

Landis, C., and Hunt, W. A. (1932). *Psychol. Rev.* **39**, 467–485.

Latané, B., and Schachter, S. (1962). *J. Comp. Physiol. Psychol.* **55**, 369–372.

Levine, S., and Soliday, S. (1962). *J. Comp. Physiol. Psychol.* **55**, 214–216.

Mandler, G. (1962). *In* "New Directions in Psychology" (R. Brown *et al.*, eds.), pp. 267–343. Holt, Rinehart and Winston, New York.

Marañon, G. (1924). *Rev. Franc. Endocrinol.* **2**, 301–325.

Moyer, K. E. (1958a). *J. Genet. Psychol.* **92**, 17–21.

Moyer, K. E. (1958b). *J. Genet. Psychol.* **92**, 11–16.

Moyer, K. E., and Bunnell, B. N. (1959). *J. Comp. Physiol.* **52**, 215–216.

Moyer, K. E., and Bunnell, B. N. (1960a). *J. Genet. Psychol.* **96**, 375–382.

Moyer, K. E., and Bunnell, B. N. (1960b). *J. Genet. Psychol.* **97**, 341–344.

Ruckmick, C. A. (1936). "The Psychology of Feeling and Emotion." McGraw-Hill, New York.

Schachter, J. (1957). *Psychosom. Med.* **19**, 17–29.

Schachter, S. (1959). "The Psychology of Affiliation." Stanford Univ. Press, Stanford, California.

Schachter, S., and Wheeler, L. (1962). *J. Abnorm. Soc. Psychol.* **65**, 121–128.

Schachter, S., and Singer, J. (1962). *Psychol. Rev.* **69**, 379–399.

Sherrington, C. S. (1900). *Proc. Roy. Soc.* **66**, 390–403.

Singer, J. E. (1963). *J. Comp. Physiol. Psychol.* **56**, 612–615.

Wenger, M. A. (1950). *In* "Feelings and Emotions" (M. L. Reymert, ed.), pp. 3–10. McGraw-Hill, New York.

Wolf, S., and Wolff, H. G. (1947). "Human Gastric Function." Oxford Univ. Press, London and New York.

Woodworth, R. S., and Schlosberg, H. (1958). "Experimental Psychology." Holt, New York.

Wrightsman, L. S. (1960). *J. Abnorm. Soc. Psychol.* **61**, 216–222.

Wynne, L. C., and Solomon, R. L. (1955). *Genet. Psychol. Monogr.* **52**, 241–284.

Second Thoughts on Biological and Psychological Explanations of Behavior

Stanley Schachter
COLUMBIA UNIVERSITY

Over the years, I have published various versions of the article
"The Interaction of Cognitive and Physiological Determinants of
Emotional State"—each time adding new bits of data, generalizing the
argument to bodily states other than that induced by adrenalin, hopefully sharpening the general line of thought—but in all versions making essentially the same point, that most complex behavior cannot as
yet be understood in purely biological terms. My most extreme statement of this position was the following:

> Any physiologically based formulation of emotion must specify the fashion
> in which physiological processes interact with stimulus, cognitive, or situa-
> tional factors.
>
> If we are eventually to make sense of these areas (i.e., emotion and
> motivation), I believe we will be forced to adopt a set of concepts with which
> most physiologically inclined scientists feel somewhat uncomfortable and
> ill at ease, for they are concepts that are difficult to reify and about which it
> is, at present, difficult to physiologize. We will be forced to deal with
> concepts about perception, about cognition, about learning, and about the
> social situation. We will be forced to examine a subject's perception of his
> bodily state and his interpretation of it in terms of his immediate situation
> and his past experience.
>
> In order to avoid any misunderstanding, let me make completely
> explicit that I am most certainly not suggesting that such notions as percep-
> tion and cognition do not have physiological correlates. I am suggesting that
> at present we know little about these physiological correlates but that we

433

Cognitive Theories in Social Psychology

can and must use such nonphysiologically anchored concepts if we are to make headway in understanding the relations of complex behavioral patterns to physiological and biochemical processes. If we do not, my guess is that we will be just about as successful at deriving predictions about emotion or any other complex behavior from a knowledge of biochemical and physiological conditions as we would be at predicting the destination of a moving automobile from an exquisite knowledge of the workings of the internal combustion engine and of petroleum chemistry [Schachter, 1971, pp. 54–55].

Given the banner-rallying quality of the quotation, I suppose it was inevitable that I became more and more absorbed by the perverse implication of this point of view—when we do finally know enough biology and biochemistry, psychological kinds of explanations become superfluous. Though for most behaviors this encyclopedic Utopia is hardly imminent, I do now maintain that there are areas about which we know sufficient biology to render the continued use of psychological explanatory constructs both superfluous and misleading.

To document this contention, I shall consider current research and theorizing on cigarette smoking—a behavior that, like most appetitive and emotional behaviors, would seem to involve both biological and psychological components. On the one hand, the smoker is a junkie. He's hooked, addicted, and whatever those words mean physiologically, he's got it. Some place, there is some set of cells that, when depleted, initiates signals to smoke.

On the other hand, almost any smoker can convince you and himself that there are major psychological components to smoking. They will convince you that smoking calms them; that they smoke more when they're anxious; that smoking helps them work; that they smoke more at a party; and so on. In short, smoking serves some psychological function; it does something positive for the smoker, and this is the reason he smokes. This emphasis on the functional properties of smoking is at the heart of virtually every serious psychological attempt to understand smoking. Presumably, nicotine or tar or some component of the act of smoking is so gratifying that, despite the well-publicized dangers, the smoker is unwilling or unable to give up the habit. Undoubtedly, the ultimate eulogy of the act is Marcovitz's (1969) suggestion that

as a psychological phenomenon, smoking is comparable to the ritual of the Eucharist. There the communicant incorporates bread and wine and in so doing symbolically introjects the Lord Jesus Christ. This is a conscious process, with the hope of identification, of attaining some of the attributes of Jesus. Similarly, the smoker incorporates the smoke introjecting in an unconscious fantasy some object which will confer on him its magic powers [p. 1082].

Among these magic powers, smoking serves to "delimit the body image in the quest for the sense of self," to "relieve the unconscious fear of suffocation," and to serve as "proof of immortality" [pp. 1082, 1083]. Though no one has matched Marcovitz's panegyric, almost all attempts to account for the habit have assumed that it does something positive for the smoker. And this is an assumption that is shared by the smoker himself, for questionnaire study after study (e.g., Coan, 1973; McKennell, 1973; Tomkins, 1968) indicates that heavy smokers report that cigarettes relax them or stimulate them, put them at ease, give them something to do with their hands, and so on. In short, for both the psychologist and the smoker, the act of smoking is functional, it does something for the smoker; and this is the reason he smokes. In this paper, I shall concentrate on just one of the presumed motivations for smoking. Smokers widely report that they smoke more when they are tense, anxious, or upset, and they also report that smoking calms them. Smoking, then, serves a respectable psychological function, and this presumably is one of the motivations for and explanations of smoking under stress.

Before worrying through interpretations of these facts, let us make sure that they are facts. First, does smoking increase with stress? The available evidence indicates that it does. In two almost identical experiments, Schachter, Silverstein, Kozlowski, Herman, and Liebling (1977) and Schachter, Silverstein, and Perlick (1977) manipulated stress within the context of experiments presumably designed to measure tactile sensitivity. In high stress conditions, such sensitivity was measured by the administration, sporadically over an experimental hour, of a series of intense, quite painful shocks. In low stress conditions, the shocks were a barely perceptible tingle. Between the testing intervals, the subjects, all smokers, were free to smoke or not to smoke, as they pleased. In both studies, the subjects smoked considerably more in high than in low stress conditions.

Turning to the effects of smoking on stress, we ask next if smoking reduces stress. The answer appears to be that it depends upon how you look at it. Silverstein (1976), in a modification of an experiment designed by Nesbitt (1973), attempted, within the context of a study of tactile perception, to answer the question by measuring how much electric shock a subject was willing to take. The procedure required that electrodes be attached to a subject's fingers, that he be exposed to a series of shocks of gradually increasing voltage, and that he report when he could first feel the shock, then when the shock first became painful, and finally when the shock became so painful that he could no longer bear it. Silverstein assumes that the more anxious and tense the subject, the less pain he will be willing to tolerate. There were four experimental groups—smokers who smoked high nicotine cigarettes during the experiment, those who smoked low nicotine cigarettes during the experiment, those who did not smoke at all during this time, and a group of nonsmokers who did not smoke.

The results of this experiment are presented in Figure 1. The ordinate plots the number of shocks the subjects endured before calling it quits. It is clear that smokers take more shocks when smoking high nicotine than when smoking low nicotine cigarettes, and they

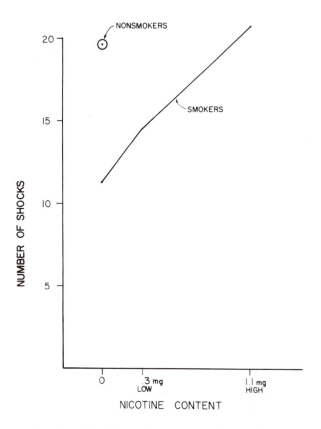

Fig. 1.   The effects of nicotine on tolerance of shock.

take the least number of shocks when not smoking. Given this pattern, one has a choice of interpretations: Either nicotine decreases anxiety, or lack of nicotine increases anxiety. The choice depends, of course, on the position of the group of nonsmokers who, as can be seen in the figure, take virtually the same number of shocks as smokers on high nicotine. It would appear, then, that smoking is not anxiety-reducing but, rather, that not smoking or insufficient nicotine is, for the heavy smoker, anxiety-increasing.[1]

Precisely the same pattern of results emerges in a study of irritability conducted by Perlick (1977). Within the context of a study of aircraft noise, subjects watching a television drama rated how loud and how annoying they found each of a series of simulated overflights. During the experimental session, heavy-smoking subjects were permitted to smoke at will high nicotine cigarettes in one condition, low nicotine cigarettes in another condition, and, thanks to a large "No Smoking" sign, were prevented from smoking in a third condition. Finally, there was a control group of nonsmokers. The results are presented in Figure 2, where it can be seen that smokers on high nicotine cigarettes are markedly less irritated by this series of obnoxious noises than are smokers restricted to low nicotine cigarettes or prevented from smoking. However, these high nicotine smokers are neither less nor more irritated than the group of nonsmokers. Again it would appear that smoking does not make the smoker less irritable or vulnerable to annoyance; it is nonsmoking or insufficient nicotine that makes him more irritable.

This same pattern appears to be characteristic of psychomotor as well as of emotional behavior. Heimstra, Bancroft, and DeKock (1967) examined the hypothesis that smoking facilitates driving performance by comparing ad-lib smokers with freedom to smoke at will, deprived smokers, and nonsmokers in a 6-hour simulated driving test. On a variety of measures of tracking and vigilance, the ad lib smokers do neither better nor worse than nonsmokers but do markedly better than deprived smokers.

[1] In the Nesbitt (1973) study, nonsmokers also took significantly more shocks than did deprived smokers but, in contrast to Silverstein's findings, the nonsmokers took fewer shocks than did smokers on high nicotine cigarettes. This difference between the two experiments is almost certainly explained by procedural differences. Nesbitt's study was couched as a study of the effects of smoking on Galvanic Skin Response (GSR), and his nonsmoker subjects knew, first, that following testing they would be required to smoke two cigarettes, and second, that they were required to puff at unlit cigarettes while thresholds were being taken. Both of these factors would almost inevitably make nonsmokers uneasy. In contrast, as far as the subjects knew, Silverstein's experiment had nothing to do with smoking, and no unlit cigarettes were used.

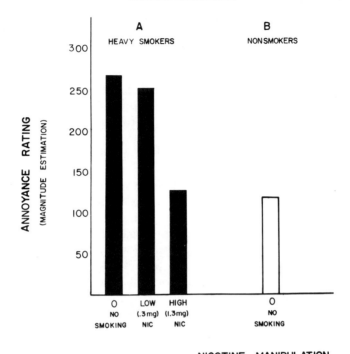

NICOTINE   MANIPULATION

Fig. 2.   The effects of nicotine on irritability.

Again and again, then, one finds the same pattern—smoking does not improve the mood or calm the smoker or improve his performance when compared with the nonsmoker. However, not smoking or insufficient nicotine makes him considerably worse on all dimensions.[2] Given this persistent fact, how, then, to account for the fact that the

[2] There is, of course, one alternative interpretation of this consistent pattern. Rather than indicating withdrawal, it is conceivable that people who become smokers are by nature more frightened of shock, more irritated by noise, and worse drivers than people who never become smokers and that for such people smoking is indeed calming and does improve psychomotor performance. Though nothing short of a longitudinal study could unequivocally settle the matter, it should be noted that there have been a formidable number of studies that compared smokers and nonsmokers on virtually every personality dimension imaginable. Smith (1970), in his review of this extensive literature, concludes that the *only* variables that with reasonable consistency discriminate between smokers and nonsmokers are extraversion and antisocial tendencies. And even on these variables the differences are all quite small. To this writer it seems particularly unlikely that selection rather than withdrawal can account for the numerous painful consequences of not smoking or inadequate nicotine, for to accept this interpretation requires that he concede that he was a thoroughly rotten, miserable human being before taking up smoking and would become so again were he to give up the habit.

smoker smokes more when he is stressed? One can, obviously, account for the generally debilitating effects of no or low nicotine by assuming that the deprived smoker is in withdrawal, but this assumption alone cannot account for the effects of stress on smoking rate unless one assumes that stress in some way depletes the available supply of nicotine. And this hypothesis, of course, can account for this pattern of data only if it is the case that the smoker, an addict, is smoking to keep nicotine at a constant level.[3]

I. Nicotine as Addiction

On the assumption that one manifestation of addiction is the regulation of nicotine intake, studies of the matter have either preloaded subjects with varying amounts of nicotine or have manipulated the nicotine content of the available cigarettes. Although the results of the many studies in this area are not wholly consistent (see Schachter [1977] for a review of the literature), the majority of studies do indicate that smokers will regulate nicotine, particularly if they are long-time, heavy smokers. A description of one study of such subjects will convey the magnitude of the effect. Schachter (1977) enlisted the cooperation of a group of subjects, all of whom had smoked a pack or more a day for at least 19 years. For the course of the experiment, these subjects agreed to smoke only the experimenter's cigarettes and, on alternating weeks, each subject was presented with cartons of specially prepared and packaged cigarettes that contained either 1.3 mg

---

[3] Another way of phrasing this same conclusion is that the heavy smoker gets nothing out of smoking. He smokes only to prevent withdrawal. I freely admit that this is a perverse conclusion to reach about a habit as costly and universally pervasive as smoking, but the existing data for humans do not encourage any other conclusion. Though my colleagues and I have found occasional hints that smoking may do something for the smoker when compared to the nonsmoker (Nesbitt, 1973; Silverstein, 1976), in general these differences have been small and usually seem explainable by some procedural artifact. In addition, Heimstra (1973) has presented tentative evidence that smokers may have somewhat less mood fluctuation than nonsmokers, and there have been numerous studies suggesting that smoking may affect one or another psychomotor or mental ability; but, in general, these have all been quite small effects, inconsistent from study to study (Larson, Haag, & Silvette, 1961, pp. 572–75). It should be noted, however, that almost all studies of the matter have used long-time heavy smokers as subjects. It may be that, in the early stages of the smoking habit, there are indeed major gratifications and effects, that the smoker gradually adapts to these effects, and that, by the time smoking no longer does anything for him, he is thoroughly addicted.

of nicotine per cigarette or .3 mg of nicotine per cigarette.[4] At bedtime the subjects noted the number of cigarettes smoked.

The effects of the nicotine manipulation are presented in Table 1. Obviously, the manipulation had a strong and consistent effect on these long-time heavy smokers; each of them smoked more low than high nicotine cigarettes. On the average, there was a 25% increase ($p < .01$) in smoking accompanying the manipulation of nicotine content.

It does appear, then, that heavy, long-time smokers do regulate nicotine. Given that the manipulation involved a four-fold difference in nicotine content, whereas smoking increased only 25%, it would appear to be at best crude and imprecise regulation. There is, however, reason to believe that nicotine regulation is considerably more precise than these data suggest. First, several studies (Ashton & Watson, 1970; Herman, 1974; Schachter, Silverstein, & Perlick, 1977) report that smokers puff more at low than at high nicotine cigarettes—clearly a mechanism for increasing nicotine intake. Second, given the range of nicotine content in this study, precise regulation was virtually impossible. For example, a subject who normally smoked 2 packs a day of 1.3 mg nicotine cigarettes would have to smoke almost 9 packs a day of our low nicotine cigarettes to get her customary dose of nicotine. Under these circumstances, virtually any theory of addiction would predict withdrawal for the subjects on low

TABLE 1

The Effects of Nicotine Content on Smoking

Subject characteristics					Smoking behavior (cigarettes per day)		
Subject	Age	Sex	Years as a serious smoker	Number of cigarettes per day (self-report)	Low (.3 mg nic)	High (1.3 mg nic)	Increase (%) (high to low)
J.A.	52	F	30	30	31.25	21.50	+45.3
S.S.	37	F	22	40	55.00	40.50	+35.8
R.R.	38	F	19	40	42.50	30.75	+38.2
R.S.	43	F	27	20	22.75	20.00	+13.8
D.R.	47	F	29	40–45	70.75	58.75	+20.4
R.A.	50	M	40	30	30.25	26.25	+15.2
J.E.	52	M	33	33	48.00	44.25	+8.5
Mean	45.6		28.6	33.6	42.93	34.57	+25.3

[4] Most of the currently popular cigarette brands have a nicotine content varying between 1.0 and 1.3 mg.

nicotine cigarettes. Though unfortunately no systematic provision was made in this study to measure withdrawal, there is dramatic anecdotal evidence that the subjects who were the worst regulators in this study were in states of marked irritability and explosive emotionality while on the low nicotine cigarettes. Supporting this observation, Perlick (1977) and Silverstein (1976) have both demonstrated experimentally that heavy smokers on low nicotine cigarettes are markedly more anxious and irritable than such smokers on high nicotine cigarettes.

It does appear, then, that heavy smokers do adjust smoking rate so as to keep nicotine at a roughly constant level. To account for this fact, one may suppose that there is an internal machine of sorts, one that detects the level of nicotine and regulates smoking accordingly. To begin consideration of the nature of such regulation, let us review some of the basic facts about the metabolic fate and excretion of nicotine. As summarized by Goodman and Gilman (1958):

> Nicotine is readily absorbed not only from the oral and gastrointestinal mucosa and from the respiratory tract but also from the skin . . . nicotine is chemically altered in the body, mainly in the liver but also in the kidney and lung. The fraction of nicotine which escapes detoxication is completely eliminated as such in the urine along with the chemically altered forms. The rate of excretion of the alkaloid is rapid and increases linearly with the dose. . . . When the urine is alkaline, only one fourth as much nicotine is excreted as when the urine is acid; this is explained by the fact that nicotine base is reabsorbed from an alkaline urine [p. 622].

The effects of the acidity, or the pH, of the urine on the rate of excretion of unchanged nicotine suggests that, given that smokers appear to regulate nicotine, the pH of the urine may affect the rate of smoking. Whether an effect of any consequence is to be anticipated, however, depends on the proportion of unchanged nicotine that is excreted. One can make reasonably accurate estimates from the work of Beckett and his associates. Beckett, Rowland, and Triggs (1965) have shown that subjects who smoke 20 cigarettes a day excrete an average of $1.0 \mu g$ nicotine per minute under normal conditions, $5.0 \mu g$ nicotine per minute when the urine was made acidic by the oral administration of ammonium chloride, and $0.1 \mu g$ after oral administration of the alkalizer sodium bicarbonate. In another study, Beckett and Triggs (1967) have demonstrated that smokers whose urine has been maintained acidic excrete in unchanged form about 35% of known quantities of nicotine that have been administered either by intravenous injection, inhalation of nicotine vapor, or smoking. Putting these facts together, it appears reasonable to estimate that the proportion of nicotine that will be excreted in unchanged form will vary with the manipulated acidity of the urine, as follows: If the urine is acid, 35% of the nicotine will be excreted; if normal, 7%; and if alkaline, less than 1%.

Obviously, the exact proportions will vary with the precise pH of the urine. However, one thing seems clear: Given the quite low proportion of unchanged nicotine excreted under normal or placebo conditions, increasing the alkalinity of the urine can at best have trivial effects on plasma level nicotine, whereas increasing the acidity of urine can potentially have substantial effects on plasma level nicotine. If, then, one assumes, first, that changes in urinary pH are reflected in circulating nicotine and, second, that the amounts smoked vary with changes in plasma level nicotine, it should be expected that experimentally increasing the acidity of the urine will increase the amounts smoked.

To test this guess, Schachter, Kozlowski, and Silverstein (1977) manipulated urinary pH by, in alternate weeks, administering to a group of 13 smokers substantial daily doses of placebo or of the acidifying agents vitamin C (ascorbic acid) and Acidulin (glutamic acid hydrochloride). The subjects were given cartons of their favorite cigarettes and kept count of the amount they had smoked each day of the study. The effects of these manipulations on smoking are presented in Table 2, where it can be seen that acidification is accompanied by increased smoking. During the period they were taking either of two different acidifying agents, subjects smoked 20% more cigarettes than during the time they were taking a corn starch placebo.

It should be specifically noted that, in keeping with the magnitude of the pharmacological effects (Beckett, Rowland, & Triggs, 1965; Beckett & Triggs, 1967; Haag & Larson, 1942), this 20% increase is not a

TABLE 2

THE EFFECTS OF VITAMIN C, ACIDULIN, AND PLACEBO ON CIGARETTE SMOKING

Condition	Cigarettes smoked per day	Mean percentage change from placebo
Vitamin C	26.7	+19.8
Placebo	23.1	—
Acidulin	28.1	+20.9
Comparison	Significance	
Vitamin C versus placebo	$p < .05$	$p < .05$
Acidulin versus placebo	$p < .01$	$p < .01$

large experimental effect. Judging from the work of Beckett and his colleagues on nicotine excretion, one would expect, at best, roughly a 30% increase in smoking with even a strongly effective acidifying manipulation, which ours was not. It seems clear that, of the body's two chief mechanisms for disposing of nicotine, enzymatic breakdown and urinary excretion of unchanged nicotine, the urinary excretion route plays by far the lesser role in the confirmed smoker. Nevertheless, acidification does affect smoking behavior, and this finding does at least raise the possibility that it may be useful to invoke this bit of pharmacological machinery in order to understand some of the presumed psychological and situational determinants of smoking rate. Conceivably, events that stimulate smoking may do so via their action on urinary pH.

In order to learn if this guess had any merit as a possible explanation of the stress–smoking relationship, Schachter, Silverstein et al. (1977) examined the effects of a variety of academic stressors on pH. In one study, subjects urinated immediately before an obviously stressful event, such as delivering a colloquium lecture or taking Ph.D. oral or comprehensive examinations. And, for control purposes, these same subjects urinated at precisely the same time on routine, nonstressful days. The results are presented in Table 3, where it can be seen that, for 9 of 10 subjects, the urine is considerably more acidic on stressful than on control days.

Precisely the same pattern is manifest in the urine of the undergraduate members of a seminar that normally was an intense, trying affair involving oral quizzing on assigned reading, enforced student participation in class discussion, and so on. On the experimental day things were probably more trying than usual for half of the class and considerably less so for the other half. Nine of the 20 students had been assigned to read highly technical material and to prepare 10–15 minute oral reports for class. For most of these students, this was the first time in college that they had been called upon to give an oral report. The remaining members of the class had no assignment and no reading; they were simply expected to provide an audience for the reporters.

An hour before class each of the students urinated and, following instructions, brought his urine to class. And, on a control day that was a business-as-usual class with no reporters or listeners, they did the same thing. The effects of these events on pH can be seen in Figure 3, where it is evident that, on the experimental day, the urine of students assigned to give reports was markedly more acidic than that of those students who for that day simply composed an audience ($p < .05$). In

TABLE 3

THE EFFECTS OF ACADEMIC STRESS ON URINARY pH

Subject	Stress day	Control day	Stress–control
A. Colloquium talk			
E.G.	5.50	6.35	−.85
H.T.	5.70	5.95	−.25
M.C.	6.70	6.90	−.20
H.K.	5.50	6.20	−.70
S.S.	5.40	6.45	−1.05
B. Ph.D. oral defense			
E.D.	5.40	7.10	−1.70
A.L.	6.00	6.20	−.20
C. Ph.D. comprehensive examination			
B.S.	5.85	5.80	+.05
I.S.	5.20	5.70	−.50
D.P.	5.40	5.70	−.30
All subjects (mean)	5.67	6.24	−.57

marked contrast, on a regular class day when both groups of students had equally good reason to be tense, pH for the two groups of subjects is virtually identical (interaction $p < .05$).

It does appear, then, that stress, at least of the sort endemic to academic life, acidifies the urine,[5]—a finding that at least encourages the exploration of a pharmacological interpretation of smoking behavior.

To review the line of argument so far: It has been widely reported

[5] It should be emphasized that I do not believe that pH changes are a quick and easy index of any sort of stress at all. In the data reported in this paper, an acid urine is associated with the chronic, long-duration sort of stress associated with preparing for and worrying about a public lecture or an important examination. In our experiments, Schachter, Silverstein, and Perlick (1977) succeeded in lowering pH over the course of an experimental hour during which a subject was repeatedly shocked. Silverstein (1976), using a similar procedure, failed to lower pH when the subject was shocked for only a 5-minute period and then urinated immediately thereafter. Similarly, a 10-minute horror film had little effect on pH. It may be that only chronic and intense stress affects pH. Alternatively, it may be that pH changes do accompany acute manipulations of stress, but for many possible reasons such changes are simply not reflected in urine samples taken immediately after the stressful event.

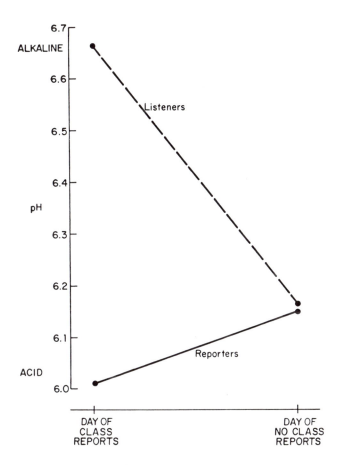

Fig. 3.   The effects of academic stress on urinary pH.

that smoking increases with stress and that smoking is calming—observations that appear to go hand in hand and to support the assertion that nicotine or tar or some component of the act of smoking is anxiety-reducing. The experimental facts are peculiarly at variance with this interpretation. Smoking does indeed increase with stress, but smoking smokers are neither more nor less calm than a control group of nonsmokers. They are, however, considerably calmer than groups of smokers who are either prevented from smoking or permitted to smoke only low nicotine cigarettes. This fact can be interpreted not as indicating that smoking is anxiety-reducing but as showing that not smoking or insufficient nicotine is anxiety-increasing. In effect, the smoker smokes more during stress because of budding withdrawal symptoms and not because of any psychological property of nicotine or of the act of smoking. Such an interpretation is plausible if one assumes that the smoker smokes in order to keep nicotine at some constant level and that there is something about the state of stress that depletes the body's supply of nicotine. A variety of studies have been described that, via the effects of urinary pH on the rate of nicotine excretion, suggest a biochemical mechanism that could account for this set of facts.

Although this elegant juxtaposition of facts makes almost irresistible the conclusion that the smoker's mind is in the bladder, obviously we are hardly yet in a position to rule out psychological explanations of smoking. Though "anxiety reduction" seems, by now, a particularly unsatisfactory explanation of the stress–smoking relationship, innumerable other purely psychological explanations are still conceivable. Ferster (1970), for example, has attempted to explain the relationship in these terms:

> With the increase in emotional symptoms there is frequently a major cessation in most of the ongoing repertoire the person might engage in. With such a temporary decrease in the frequency in most of the items in a person's repertoire, the relative importance of even the minor reinforcers increases enormously. Thus, the relative position of smoking in the entire repoertoire is increased considerably when other major items of the repertoire are depressed. Smoking becomes something to do when no other behavior is appropriate [p. 99].

In short, although the effect of pH on nicotine elimination is a well-established pharmacological fact, it may have little if anything to do with the effects of stress on smoking, for it is certainly conceivable that stress, with or without accompanying pH changes, will affect smoking rate. In order to learn if pH changes are a necessary and sufficient explanation of the stress–smoking relationship, it is clear that we must experimentally pit the mind against the bladder, and this Schachter, Silverstein, and Perlick (1977) attempted to do in an experiment that independently manipulated stress and the pH of the urine. If it is correct that pH changes are a necessary part of the machinery, we should expect more smoking in high than in low stress conditions when pH is uncontrolled and no difference between the two conditions when pH is experimentally stabilized. If, on the other hand, pH changes are irrelevant to the smoking–stress relationship, there should be more smoking in high than in low stress conditions no matter what the state of the urine.

In this study, too, stress was manipulated by use of electric shock. In fact, the experiment already described on the relationship of stress to smoking (Schacter, Silverstein *et al.*, 1977) was replicated with one major modification—in one pair of conditions, the high or low stress manipulation began 50 minutes after subjects took a placebo; in the other conditions, 50 minutes after subjects had taken 3 grams of bicarbonate of soda—an agent virtually guaranteed to quickly elevate urinary pH and to stabilize it for a time at highly alkaline levels. In Table 4, note first the effects of the manipulation on urinary pH. Examining first the two placebo conditions, it will be noted that pH decreases in the High Stress condition ($p = .02$) and tends to increase in the Low Stress condition. In the two bicarbonate conditions, in sharp contrast, pH increases markedly from the beginning to the end of the experiment, and the stress manipulation has had absolutely no effect on pH. If anything, the pH of High Stress bicarbonate subjects has increased more than the pH of Low Stress bicarbonate subjects.

Next, we note that, on a variety of self-report measures, the manipulation of stress was highly successful in both the placebo and the bicarbonate conditions. Obviously, then, the conditions necessary to pit the psychological against the pharmacological explanation of the effects of stress on smoking have been established. Subjects in High Stress conditions are considerably more tense than are subjects in Low Stress conditions, whether they have taken a placebo or a bicarbonate. In the placebo conditions in which pH is uncontrolled, however, stress acidifies, whereas in the bicarbonate conditions, it does not.

The effects of these manipulations on smoking are presented in

TABLE 4

THE EFFECTS OF THE MANIPULATIONS ON URINARY pH

Subjects:		Mean pH:			Number of subjects whose pH:		
Condition	N	Pre-stress	Post-stress	Pre–post	Decreased	Stayed same	Increased
High stress– placebo	12	6.00	5.83	−.17	8	3	1
Low stress– placebo	12	5.99	6.13	+.14	4	1	7
High stress– bicarbonate	12	6.08	7.44	+1.36	0	0	12
Low stress– bicarbonate	12	6.20	7.01	+.81	2	1	9

Figure 4, which plots the mean number of puffs taken by subjects in each condition once the stress manipulation had begun. It is clear that with placebo there is considerably more smoking in high than in low stress conditions, whereas with bicarbonate, stress has absolutely no effect on smoking (interaction $p < .01$). It does appear, then, that smoking under stress has nothing to do with psychological, sensory, or manipulative needs that are presumably activated by the state of stress, but is explained by the effects of stress on the rate of excretion of nicotine. The smoker under stress smokes to replenish nicotine supply, not to relieve anxiety.

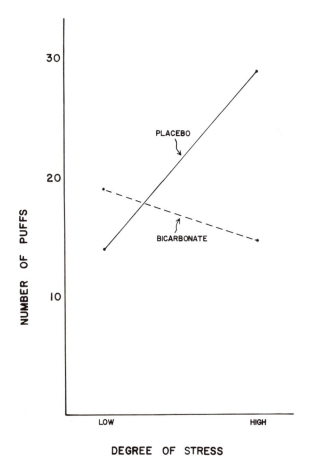

Fig. 4. The effects of sodium bicarbonate and placebo on smoking under stress.

Given these facts, a formidable case can be made for a purely pharmacological, addictive view of cigarette smoking. It must be admitted, however, that satisfactory though such a mechanistic view of smoking may be for understanding the behavior of many, perhaps most, smokers, the apparent exceptions to such a model are maddeningly various. There are smokers (see Schachter, 1977) who do not track nicotine content. Although it is known (Isaac & Rand, 1972) that plasma nicotine level is zero on awakening, there are smokers who find cigarettes distasteful in the morning and do not light up their first cigarette before lunchtime. Though withdrawal is a necessary component of virtually any model of addiction, some orthodox Jewish smokers, forbidden to smoke on the Sabbath, report that they can do so without a qualm. And so on.

Just how to cope with such blatant exceptions is problematic. Perhaps it is necessary to invent typologies (e.g., McKennell, 1973; Russell, 1974; Tomkins, 1968) to accommodate the distressingly apparent variety of smokers, but I find this an unsatisfying scientific stratagem. As a working hypothesis, I propose instead that virtually all long-time smokers are addicted and suggest that many, perhaps all, exceptions to an addiction model can be understood in terms of such notions as self-control, concern with health, restraints, etc. Certainly all smokers are aware of the dangers and the expense of smoking. To the extent that such concerns are prominent, the smoker probably inhibits his smoking by such devices as imposing an upper limit on his daily consumption, scheduling his smoking, and so on—devices intended to lower consumption and that would tend to mask such behavioral manifestations of addiction as tracking nicotine content.

If this is correct, we should expect to find other, less obvious indications of addiction and, of these, I would suggest that withdrawal is the key. Obviously, anyone can give up smoking, limit his daily intake, or restrict smoking to particular times or occasions if he is willing and able to put up with the withdrawal syndrome. If it is correct that virtually all long-time smokers are addicted, it should be anticipated that smokers who do not smoke in the morning will be more irritable at that time of day than in the afternoon; that smokers who restrain their smoking will be more volatile people than heavy smokers; and so on. To test such expectations, Perlick (1977), in the experiment described earlier, compared a group of heavy, unrestrained smokers to a matched group of highly restrained smokers, mostly formerly heavy smokers who, on a variety of indices, indicated that they were deliberately and successfully attempting to cut down, although not eliminate, smoking by a combination of devices such as

smoking cigarettes only halfway, smoking very low nicotine cigarettes, counting daily intake, and the like. On the average, these restrained smokers reported smoking at a rate less than half of their
former level. As described earlier, all subjects rated how annoying
they found the noise of each of a series of simulated aircraft overflights, when, depending on the experimental condition, they were
either prevented from smoking or permitted the smoking at will of
high or of low nicotine cigarettes. It should be noted first that in the
conditions in which they were permitted to smoke, restrained former
heavy smokers smoked only half as much as did current heavy smokers. They behaved in the laboratory, then, as they report they do in
life. The effects of these manipulations on the two groups of smokers
are presented in Figure 5. As noted earlier, the extent to which heavy,
unrestrained smokers were annoyed depends on the nicotine manipulation. When they did not smoke or smoked very low nicotine ciga-

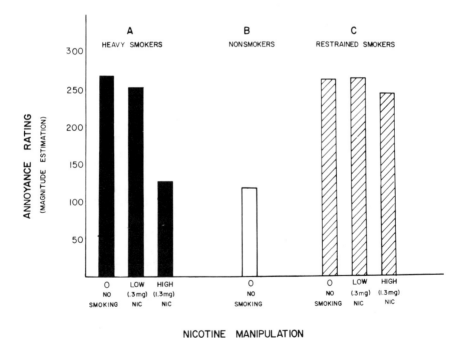

Fig. 5. The effects of nicotine deprivation on the irritability of heavy smokers,
nonsmokers, and restrained smokers.

rettes, they were markedly more annoyed than when they smoked high nicotine cigarettes. The restrained, former heavy smokers stand in fascinating contrast, for they were chronically annoyed—as they should be even in the high nicotine condition in which they are still getting considerably less nicotine than in former days was their wont. In other tests of the same hypothesis, Perlick (1977) demonstrates that such restrained smokers eat more than do heavy smokers when given free access to candy and also do worse at a proofreading task requiring concentration. Restrained smokers appear to be chronically more irascible, to nibble more, and to have poorer concentration than unrestrained smokers. It is possible to control and restrict smoking, but at a price—and the price appears to be a chronic state of withdrawal.[6] It does appear that one of the apparent exceptions to a purely addictive view of smoking is no exception. I suspect that this will be the case with most of these exceptions[7] and that by taking account of withdrawal we can understand those studies (Finnegan *et al.*, 1945; Goldfarb *et al.*, 1970) that fail to demonstrate nicotine regulation.

II. Psychological versus Pharmacological Explanation of Smoking

Let us review our conclusions so far. For the confirmed smoker:

1. The psychological and probably the sensory and manipulative gratifications of smoking are illusory. Serious smokers smoke to prevent withdrawal.
2. Smokers regulate nicotine intake.
3. Variations in smoking rate, which customarily have been interpreted in psychological terms, seem better understood as an attempt to regulate nicotine.
4. Apparent exceptions to a regulatory model of smoking seem understandable in terms of withdrawal. The smoker who fails to regulate suffers withdrawal.

[6] One alternative interpretation of these data must be considered. It is conceivable that naturally irascible people are more likely to restrain their smoking. If so, these results could be attributable to self-selection rather than to withdrawal. Acutely aware of this possibility, Perlick (1977) compared these groups on numbers of personality and demographic variables and found no differences between the two groups.

[7] With one exception—There are a small number of long-time, light smokers who give no evidence of nicotine regulation (Schachter, 1977) and no indication of withdrawal when deprived of nicotine (Perlick, 1977). What to make of such cases is at this time equivocal, but by any of the standard criteria of addiction they do appear to be genuinely nonaddicted smokers.

Given these facts, one is faced with a formidable question that, reduced to essentials, is this—so where is psychology? What's with the oral dependency needs or the habit strength or the misattribution if, as seems to be the case for stress, it all depends on the hydrogen ion concentration in the urine? Obviously, this has been an openly reductionist attempt to explain some of the effects of psychological variables without making use of the conceptual equipment of psychology. I believe that in the case of stress the attempt has been successful, for, given the facts outlined, attempts to formulate the stress–smoking relationship in terms of oral dependency needs (Marcovitz, 1969) or of attribution theory (Nesbitt, 1973; Schachter, 1973) or of learning theory (Ferster, 1970; Hunt, 1970) seem unnecessary, ad hoc constructions. Smoking increases under stress because that is the way the biological machine is built, and it makes as much sense to ask psychodynamically, cognitively, or situationally why the smoker smokes more under stress as it would to ask why psychologically the car speeds up when one presses on the accelerator.

REFERENCES

Ashton, H., & Watson, D. W. Puffing frequency and nicotine intake in cigarette smokers. *British Medical Journal,* 1970, 3, 679–681.

Beckett, A. H., Rowland, M., & Triggs, E. G. Significance of smoking in investigations of urinary excretion rates of amines in man. *Nature,* 1965, **207**, 200–201.

Beckett, A. H., & Triggs, E. G. Enzyme induction in man caused by smoking. *Nature,* 1967, **216**, 587.

Coan, R. W. Personality variables associated with smoking. *Journal of Personality and Social Psychology,* 1973, **26**, 86–104.

Eggleton, M. G. Urine acidity in alcohol diuresis in man. *Journal of Physiology,* 1946, **104**, 312–320.

Ferster, C. B. Comments on paper by Hunt and Matarazzo. In W. A. Hunt (Ed.), *Learning mechanisms in smoking.* Chicago: Aldine, 1970.

Finnegan, J. K., Larson, P. S., & Haag, H. B. The role of nicotine in the cigarette habit. *Science,* 1945, **102**, 94–96.

Goldfarb, T. L., Jarvik, M. E., & Glick, S. D. Cigarette nicotine content as a determinant of human smoking behavior. *Psychopharmacologia,* 1970, **17**, 89–93.

Goodman, L. S., & Gilman, A. *The pharmacological basis of therapeutics.* New York: MacMillan, 1958.

Haag, H. B., & Larson, P. S. Studies on the fate of nicotine in the body. I: The effect of pH on the urinary excretion of nicotine by tobacco smokers. *Journal of Pharmacology and Experimental Therapeutics,* 1942, **76**, 235–239.

Heimstra, N. W., Bancroft, N. R., & DeKock, A. R. Effects of smoking upon sustained performance in a simulated driving task. *Annals of the New York Academy of Sciences,* 1967, **142**, Art. 1, 295–307.

Heimstra, N. W. The effects of smoking on mood change. In W. L. Dunn (Ed.), *Smoking behavior: Motives and incentives.* Washington, D.C.: Winston, 1973.

Herman, C. P. External and internal cues as determinants of the smoking behavior of light and heavy smokers. *Journal of Personality and Social Psychology*, 1974, **30**, 664–672.

Hunt, W. A. (Ed.). *Learning mechanisms in smoking.* Chicago: Aldine, 1970.

Isaac, P. F., & Rand, M. J. Cigarette smoking and plasma levels of nicotine. *Nature*, 1972, **236**, 308.

Larson, P. S., Haag, H. B., & Silvette, H. *Tobacco.* Baltimore: Williams & Wilkins, 1961.

Liebert, C. S. The metabolism of alcohol. *Scientific American*, 1976, **234**, 25–33.

Marcovitz, E. On the nature of addiction to cigarettes. *Journal of the American Psychoanalytic Association*, 1969, **17**, 1074–1096.

McKennell, A. C. A comparison of two smoking typologies (Research Paper 12). London: Tobacco Research Council, 1973.

Nesbitt, P. D. Smoking, physiological arousal, and emotional response. *Journal of Personality and Social Psychology*, 1973, **25**, 137–145.

Perlick, D. The withdrawal syndrome: Nicotine addiction and the effects of stopping smoking in heavy and light smokers. Unpublished doctoral dissertation, Columbia University, 1977.

Russell, M. A. H. The smoking habit and its classification. *The Practitioner*, 1974, **212**, 791–800.

Schachter, S. *Emotion, obesity, and crime.* New York: Academic Press, 1971.

Schachter, S. Nesbitt's paradox. In W. L. Dunn (Ed.), *Smoking behavior: Motives and incentive.* Washington, D.C.: V. H. Winston, 1973.

Schachter, S. Nicotine regulation in heavy and light smokers. *Journal of Experimental Psychology: General*, 1977, **106**(1), 5–12.

Schachter, S., Kozlowski, L. T., & Silverstein, B. Effects of urinary pH on cigarette smoking. *Journal of Experimental Psychology: General*, 1977, **106**(1), 13–19.

Schachter, S., Silverstein, B., Kozlowski, L. T., Herman, C. P., & Liebling, B. Effects of stress on cigarette smoking and urinary pH. *Journal of Experimental Psychology: General*, 1977, **106**(1), 24–30.

Schachter, S., Silverstein, B., & Perlick, D. Psychological and pharmacological explanations of smoking under stress. *Journal of Experimental Psychology: General*, 1977, **106**(1), 31–40.

Silverstein, B. An addiction explanation of cigarette-induced relaxation. Unpublished doctoral dissertation, Columbia University, 1976.

Smith, G. M. Personality and smoking: A review of the empirical literature. In W. A. Hunt (Ed.), *Learning mechanisms in smoking.* Chicago: Aldine, 1970.

Tomkins, S. A modified model of smoking behavior. In E. F. Borgatta & R. R. Evans (Eds.), *Smoking, health and behavior.* Chicago: Aldine, 1968.

Do We Have to Believe We Are Angry with Someone in Order to Display "Angry" Aggression Toward That Person?[1]

Leonard Berkowitz
UNIVERSITY OF
WISCONSIN—MADISON

I. Introduction

Few conceptions have had as much of an impact on contemporary social psychology as has Stanley Schachter's cognitive theory of emotion. Known throughout the field, this formulation is accepted by many and ignored by virtually no one in the discipline. Even those who disagree with Schachter's theorizing in one or another respect often find that Schachter has defined the issues they must confront in their own discussions of emotionality.

The following comments also take off from Schachter's work. However, they are guided by a very different perspective and offer a different interpretation of the role of cognitive processes in emotional reactions. In a modified version of the James–Lange theory of emotions, a theory criticized by Schachter (along with Cannon), I suggest that an emotion-arousing event evokes a variety of relatively specific internal reactions—in the viscera, as James had emphasized, and throughout many other parts of the body and brain as well. The individual's awareness of these reactions gives rise to his emotional

[1] The research summarized in this paper was supported by Grant MH 17405 from the National Institute of Mental Health. Pierre Nunez conducted the first experiment, and Brian Schmitz carried out the second study. I am grateful to both men and their assistants for their skill and conscientiousness.

455

Copyright © 1978 by Academic Press, Inc.
All rights of reproduction in any form reserved.
ISBN 0-12-091850-1

experience. These internal reactions, furthermore, can also facilitate and stimulate specific overt responses consistent with the emotional responses. Thus, in the case of *angry aggression,* a person exposed to an aversive incident will have a spectrum of inner reactions, autonomic, motor, and even ideational in nature, which he may experience as "anger" (especially if situational cues lead his thoughts in this direction). If they are intense enough, these reactions can also facilitate and impel an attack on the perceived source of his displeasure. His belief that he is angry can affect the probability that he will show open aggression but is not necessary for this aggression to occur.

My remarks in this brief chapter are quite sketchy and certainly do not represent a definitive reply to Schachter's theory or a comprehensive analysis of emotional behavior. Rather they reflect a dialogue that I and others have with Schachter (in our own thoughts at least) as we consider his influential and provocative formulation.

II. Labels and Attributions

In the current social psychological scheme of things, the individual has to think of himself as having a particular emotional feeling if he is to show emotional behavior consistent with that feeling. Suppose someone has just blocked his attempt to reach a goal, thus causing him to be greatly aroused. Our prevailing theories tell us that he has to view himself as angry if he is to react with a violent outburst in which he tries to hurt the person who thwarted him. Stanley Schachter's well-known cognitive analysis of emotion has been exceedingly influential in shaping this conception. According to Schachter, the bodily (including neural) responses to a provocation do not in themselves provide stimulation specific to a given form of behavior or even to the qualitative feelings that are experienced. The outside occurrence presumably generates only a general arousal. How the individual feels about this event and what he does about it are theoretically dependent upon his interpretation of his internal sensations. He will strike out at the source of his arousal if he labels his sensations as "anger" but will feel "fear" and may run away if he thinks he is afraid. The specific experience and the concomitant behavior are supposedly shaped by the label attached to the feelings. Attribution theory has built on and extended this formulation. It maintains that the label given to the sensations is greatly influenced by the perceived cause of the event. The frustrated individual is most likely to regard himself as angry and then to attack his frustrater if he believes that that person had deliberately thwarted him. On the other hand, if he thinks that this other person had only accidentally impeded his goal-striving, he is theoretically less apt to see himself as angry and thus might not exhibit any aggressive reaction at all.

Experimental evidence indicates that cognitions about the cause of the arousal can indeed affect the subsequent aggression (Rule & Nesdale, 1976). In a study by Geen, Rakosky, and Pigg (1972), for example, a confederate gave the subjects electric shocks as they read a sexually exciting story. The participants were then led to believe that whatever sensations they were experiencing were due either to the shocks or to the story or to a drug they had taken. The people who were induced to attribute their arousal to something other than the confederate's shocks rated themselves as less angry than those who thought they were aroused by the confederate's treatment of them. Moreover, those who did not attribute their arousal to the confederate also delivered less intense shocks to him when they had an opportunity to retaliate. Zillmann has employed a version of Schachter's theory in his research on the consequences of physical exertion. He suggested that the individual will tend to attribute to salient events in his environment whatever excitation he feels. The young men in one of his experiments (Zillmann, Katcher, & Milavsky, 1972) were first either provoked or not provoked by their partners and then were required to work on either strenuous or easy physical tasks. Shortly afterward, when they had opportunities to punish their partners, they gave them the most intense shocks if they had been previously angered by them and had afterward engaged in strenuous activities. These subjects had presumably interpreted their relatively strong exercise-induced arousal as anger and then attacked their tormentors in accordance with this belief.

Although there are problems with these investigations,[2] I think, that their general thesis can be accepted. The aggressor's interpretation of his feelings and his beliefs regarding the cause of his arousal can

---

[2] For example, neither Zillmann in the study just mentioned nor Konecni (1975) in a conceptually similar investigation have any direct evidence that the provoked and then physiologically aroused subjects had actually misattributed their strong arousal to the provocation and thus regarded themselves as very angry. A simpler explanation of their findings, and one which I favor, is that the general arousal could not have "energized" aggressive responses if these responses had not been instigated beforehand. Only those subjects who had been provoked were relatively strongly disposed to be aggressive, and the general arousal then intensified this disposition. Geen and O'Neal (1969) demonstrated that a noise-engendered arousal similarly intensified the aggressive reactions that had been previously evoked by a violent movie, and in this study there is no reason to believe that the subjects had thought of themselves as angry.

influence the strength of his attacks upon the available target. I doubt, however, that impulsive aggression is totally dependent upon these interpretations and beliefs. There are several reasons for questioning the notion that our cognitions are all-important in shaping specific emotions out of an undifferentiated arousal state (see Leventhal, 1973). For one thing, why should we disregard the basic continuity of life processes in the higher animals? Other species and even very young human children show anger or fear and attack or try to get away, and it seems too much to assume that these differentiated responses are due solely to their interpretations of their internal sensations. Rather than making these cognitions all-important, I argue that they can facilitate or interfere with the development and display of specific emotional feelings and actions but are not entirely necessary for these reactions to occur. Our genetic inheritance creates a predisposition to respond in certain ways to particular classes of stimuli. As Leventhal (1973) put it, the precipitating incident, as perceived, gives "rise to distinctive central neural reactions and to distinctive body reactions and . . . these distinctive responses are necessary for feeling [p. 33]." My guess is that these specific, evoked internal reactions produce a disposition to certain kinds of actions as well as to particular feelings. In the case of angry aggression, the individual who is exposed to aversive stimuli (or who defines these stimuli as aversive) is inclined to become aggressive and may even experience anger, especially under certain conditions that we do not fully understand as yet. Moreover, he might lash out at the aversive stimulus (especially if he is not afraid of the consequences) even though he does not think of himself as angry.

III. Some Initial Research

The two experiments I will summarize here were designed to investigate this conception. Building on Zillmann's basic procedure, these studies also followed attribution-theory research in attempting to control the subjects' cognitions about either their feelings or the cause of the arousing event. But contrary to the thrust of attribution research, I wanted to determine whether frustrated men would display a relatively high level of aggression even though their cognitions did not call for this behavior.

A similar cover story was employed in both experiments. Each male participant was first required to pedal a stationary bicycle. He was informed that both he and his partner (who was supposedly engaged in the same task in the adjoining room) had to match their speeds of pedaling for 2 minutes. Signal lights on each bike would tell each person if his speed was too fast or too slow. Since his physiological reactions were ostensibly being recorded, the subject was also hooked up to various wires trailing out of the room.

A. EXPERIMENT 1

The men in some of the conditions in the first experiment were also told that each person in a pair would receive a $5 prize if the pair could maintain identical speeds over the entire interval. These people were then frustrated by the manipulation of the pedaling rate signal lights; after supposedly keeping their speeds together for almost the entire period, they and their fictitious partners evidently suddenly worked at different rates, so that they lost the prize in the last few seconds. The men could not tell who or what was the cause of the failure. In the nonfrustrated conditions, the task was minimized, and the subjects were not thwarted. These men were not told about any prize and were asked only to try to pedal at a certain speed. For another variation, half of the conditions required them to work hard as they rode, so that they would have a relatively high level of physiological arousal, whereas the remaining groups pedaled at a much slower rate and were therefore much less aroused physiologically. In sum, this initial experiment comprised a 2 × 2 factorial design: high or low arousal in the bicycle riding, and frustration or no frustration experience while engaged in this task.

There was also one other experimental manipulation. Shortly after the end of the bicycle-riding assignment, the experimenter entered the room with a complicated-looking computer printout purportedly representing the subject's autonomic measurements. He told each person that the patterns of his physiological reactions showed that he was physiologically exicted because of the physical exercise. This information, of course, presumably led the men to attribute whatever sensations they had to the exercise, so that the frustrated participants would not think they were angry. Our question was whether the thwarted subjects would display a fairly high level of aggression even though they did not believe they were in an angry mood.[3]

---

[3] I also tried to get other subjects in three separate experiments to believe their sensations were due to "anger." This feedback consistently led to less rather than to more aggression, apparently because of evaluation apprehension. Now more sensitive to the problem of aggression, they did not want to exhibit open aggression. For comparison

In order to determine how the subjects would act, a "communication situation" was established, in which each man had 20 opportunities to deliver either a punishment or a reward or no response to his partner as that individual worked on an "artillery game." In other words, the participants could choose among *three* kinds of reactions on each trial and did not have to punish the other persons if they did not care to do so.

Looking at the results, we can readily see that the subjects' rates of pedaling successfully produced the intended differences in physiological arousal. In comparison to their slowly pedaling counterparts, those given the more demanding requirement had significantly higher systolic blood pressures, lower diastolic pressures, and faster heart rates at the conclusion of the exercise period. The frustration manipulation did not have a significant effect on these physiological measures.

Much more important to us, the experimental conditions did not differ in the subjects' self-reported moods just after the experimental variations had been established. Presumably because they accepted the feedback about the meaning of their feelings, those who had been thwarted in their pursuit of the $5 did not rate themselves any more frustrated, irritated, or angry than those who had not been frustrated. This is a crucial problem in this research. Can we accept this absence of condition differences in reported mood as valid? Maybe the frustrated subjects were only reluctant to admit their negative feelings. However, my findings in the second study (to be reported later) indicate that thwartings can influence the men's reports of their moods. Why did this influence not show up in this initial experiment? Moreover, why were the present subjects also not reluctant to say bad things about their partners? As the results also indicate, the men who had not been able to win the $5 prize expressed significantly greater unwillingness to serve in another experiment with the same partners than did the nonfrustrated subjects. Awareness of one's own mood is different from one's attitude toward another. The subjects' interpretations of their moods were controlled by the attribution information,

purposes, I had in a high arousal–frustration condition subjects who were not given any information about the meaning of the physiological reactions. Seemingly due to the effectiveness of my feedback manipulation (attributing their sensations to exercise), these latter people reported themselves as significantly less excited than their counterparts who were provided with the exercise attribution. The lack of information about the meaning of their feelings seemed to make these men fairly cautious. They were relatively restrained in both their ratings and their actions. It is as if they were very unsure of themselves and held themselves back for safety. I will disregard this group in the remainder of this chapter.

but their attitudes toward their partners were not. Also unlike the mood reports, this questionnaire hostility was strengthened by the exercise-induced arousal, so that the participants were most negative toward their partners on this measure if they had worked hard in pedaling the bicycle.

Much the same pattern can be seen in the more behavioral measures. The participants were significantly more punitive to their partners after the frustration experience than after the nonthwarting effort and, moreover, administered the most punishments if they had been frustrated while working on the high arousing task. Again, the high arousal strengthened the aggressive reaction created by the frustration. Furthermore, the frustration had a selective effect; it led to more punishment and to a drop in the number of rewards.

All in all, the findings indicate that the frustration experience had evoked aggressive reactions even when the men had not regarded themselves as especially angry. They had no good reason to blame their failure on their partners and certainly had no cause to think that these people had deliberately blocked their tries at the prize money. But they still attacked them moderately strongly.

B. EXPERIMENT 2

I suggested earlier that cognitions regarding one's emotional state and the cause of this state are likely to facilitate or interfere with aggression but are not necessary for frustration-produced aggression to occur. This facilitation or inhibition can arise in various ways that I cannot go into here. It is fairly obvious, however, that these cognitions can affect the individual's judgment of what action he can appropriately show. He might believe that he is somewhat justified in behaving aggressively if he had just been thwarted undeservedly— and this therefore lowers his inhibitions. On the other hand, even though he has aggressive inclinations he might attempt to restrain himself if he thinks that it is no one's fault that he was frustrated.

The second experiment supports this conception. In this study each subject worked on our bicycle-riding task, pedaling hard. And, again, most of the men were frustrated by being led to think that they and their partners were not able to match their speeds, so that they could not get the $5 prize. In some cases, however, the experimenter explicitly attributed the failure to a malfunctioning of the bicycle apparatus, whereas the other participants were informed that their partners were at fault. In the third condition, they were not told about any prize and were not frustrated. We also employed the same "artillery game" as the behavioral setting for the second phase, but this time the subjects learned that they were dealing with people *other than* their first-phase partners. Whatever treatment they gave these new people could not be viewed as paying them back for their initial performances on the bicycle task.

The subjects' questionnaire ratings at the end of the first phase attest to the success of the experimental manipulation, as can be seen in Table 1. A subject expressed a greater unwillingness to serve in another experiment with the same partner if he thought that this person had caused the failure than if he believed the machine had been at fault or if he had not been frustrated. He did not want to avoid his first partner if the apparatus, not this person, had caused the failure. Nevertheless, *both* groups of thwarted subjects rated themselves as more frustrated and angrier and as having more negative feelings than the nonfrustrated participants. The perceived source of the failure did not matter much. The unpleasant experience led to bad feelings even when it could not be attributed to the initial partner's misconduct.

Now, how did the subjects treat their new partners in the second phase? The answer is that their behavior did not correspond with their reported feelings. Even though both frustrated conditions rated themselves as angrier than their nonthwarted controls, only the men who

TABLE 1

EFFECTS OF FRUSTRATION EXPERIENCE AND ATTRIBUTION OF CAUSE ON
MOODS AND TREATMENT OF SECOND PARTNER (EXPERIMENT 2)[a]

	Prior experience			
Measures	No frustration	Machine fault	Partner fault	F ratio
Unwilling to be in experiment with same partner (Partner 1)	5.67_b	6.67_b	10.57_a	7.89**
Change in heart rate	-6.3_b	-5.6_a	-5.8_{ab}	2.76*
Frustrated–satisfied	4.56_b	10.22_a	7.78_a	6.18**
Content–angry	16.83_b	12.67_a	12.61_a	5.13**
Negative–positive feeling	4.50_b	9.22_a	8.61_a	7.49**
Total number of punishments	14.94	15.06	20.06	.89
Total number of rewards	22.28	15.67	9.83	1.55
Total punishments–Total rewards	-7.34_b	$-.61_{ab}$	10.23_a	4.01**

* $p < .10$.
** $p < .05$.

[a]Cells not having the same subscript are significantly different ($p < .05$). $N = 18$ in each cell.

had been bothered by their first partners' supposed incompetence were much more likely to punish rather than to reward the other individuals as they worked on their assignments, and only in this condition was there a significant difference from the nonfrustrated group on this aggression measure. A frustrated participant evidently thought he could let himself go, so to speak, if he believed the earlier failure was his first partner's fault, but held himself back somewhat if he attributed the failure to the apparatus. Aggression was less justified in this latter case and had to be restrained even though he was angry.

IV. Conclusion

I cannot go into a comprehensive discussion here of the relationship between anger and aggression. Nonetheless, I would like to suggest that aversive incidents such as frustrations tend to evoke a variety of specific internal reactions in the brain, viscera, and periphery that dispose the individual to aggression. His awareness of this total pattern of reactions inside him leads him to think he is angry. Consistent with Leventhal's analysis (along with the James–Lange theory of emotions) and contrary to the Schachterian conception, I hold that the aggressive reactions (implicit as well as overt) generated by an unpleasant event actually parallel or even precede conscious experience. As a consequence, a frustrated person can display a relatively high level of overt aggression even when he does not regard himself as "angry."

References

Geen, R. G., & O'Neal, E. C. Activation of cue-elicited aggression by general arousal. *Journal of Personality and Social Psychology*, 1969, **11**, 289–292.

Geen, R. G., Rakosky, J. J., & Pigg, R. Awareness of arousal and its relation to aggression. *British Journal of Social and Clinical Psychology*, 1972, **11**, 115–121.

Konecni, V. J. The medication of aggressive behavior: Arousal level vs. anger and cognitive labeling. *Journal of Personality and Social Psychology*, 1975, **32**, 706–712.

Leventhal, H. The emotions: A basic problem in social psychology. In C. Nemeth (Ed.), *Social psychology*. Chicago: Markham, 1973.

Rule, B. G., & Nesdale, A. R. Emotional arousal and aggressive behavior. *Psychological Bulletin*, 1976, **83**, 851–863.

Zillmann, D., Katcher, A. H., & Milavsky, B. Excitation transfer from physical exercise to subsequent aggressive behavior. *Journal of Experimental Social Psychology*, 1972, **8**, 247–259.

OBJECTIVE SELF-AWARENESS[1]

Robert A. Wicklund

DEPARTMENT OF PSYCHOLOGY
UNIVERSITY OF TEXAS AT AUSTIN
AUSTIN, TEXAS

I. Introduction

A. DEVELOPMENT OF THE THEORY

In 1972 Duval and Wicklund proposed a theory of objective self-awareness that purports to explain numerous behaviors falling within

[1] Much of the research reported in this paper as well as the writing of this paper were supported by NSF Grant GS-31890. Sharon S. Brehm, William J. Ickes, Michael F. Scheier, and Melvin L. Snyder are acknowledged for their suggestions and insightful criticisms.

Reprinted from *Advances in Experimental Social Psychology,*
Volume 8, 233–275.

the domains of social psychology, personality processes, and human performance. At the core of the theory is a concept we have called "objective self-awareness," a state in which the person takes himself to be an object. It would not be far wrong to substitute "self-focused attention" for our theoretical term. As we originally postulated the theory, we assume that the person in self-reflection will typically find shortcomings in himself. If the dimension of occupational success is the focus of attention, discrepancies will be found between attainment and aspiration. Similarly, when the obese individual focuses on his eating habits he will discover that his gluttony falls short of the ideal abstinence. Our original theory also proposed that attention focused on an intraself discrepancy would result in negative affect in proportion to the size of the discrepancy. This negative affect is the core behind the theory's application, and the motivational theme will be taken up in detail shortly.

What of this state of self-focused attention? How does it operate, and what produces it? The Duval and Wicklund (1972) statement of the theory assumed that attention at any given instant is directed either wholly toward the self, or wholly toward external events. The possibility of a state of attention divided between self and environment was ruled out of the theoretical framework. However, we allowed that attention could oscillate, however rapidly, between the self and the nonself, and this allows one to speak in terms of "increased" or "decreased" objective self-awareness. An increase simply means an increment in the proportion of time spent in self-focus.

Conceptually, the antecedents of change in the proportion of time spent in objective self-awareness are extremely simple. Stimuli that remind the person of his object status will increase objective self-awareness, while all other stimuli will tend to draw attention outward. Theoretically, any symbol or reflection of a person will cause a shift of his focus inward, and experimentally we have often used mirrors and tape recordings of the person's voice for this purpose. Not only should symbols of oneself create self-focused attention, but the knowledge of being attended to by others should also create a set toward self-observation. Strictly speaking, the sight of an audience does not provide a symbol or reflection of oneself, but the self readily comes to the fore when the person realizes that the attention of the audience is on some feature of self.

Stimulators of self-focus are not the exclusive determinants of the degree of objective self-awareness. Those stimuli that draw attention away from the self play an equal role in determining the direction of attention. Most obvious are simple distractions—sounds and sights that impinge upon our senses and demand immediate attention. It is not the purpose of the theory to delineate all possible stimuli according to their distraction value, but the point here is that such distractions as a fight between two neighbors or a captivating movie can easily distract conscious attention away from the self.

There is one final determinant of the degree of self-focused attention, called "deindividuation." If a person's surroundings make it problematic for him to discriminate himself from the immediate environment, it then becomes difficult for him to focus on himself as an object. There is a real sense in which the surroundings have obliterated his uniqueness or object status. Such examples as a Ku Klux Klan meeting come to mind, in which culturally and physically each member is virtually indiscriminable from the group as a whole.

Thus far the theory addresses itself to a dichotomizing of conscious attention and to the conditions basic to the rising and falling of self-focused attention, but there is one more vital element. Objective self-awareness theory is a motivational theory, and Duval and I assumed that negative affect would result whenever attention became fixed on a within-self dimension. The reasoning was straightforward. The objectively self-aware person was assumed to find shortcomings within himself no matter what self-related dimension became the focus of attention. Discrepancies between aspiration and attainment were assumed to be negative in general—across virtually all people and all traits—with the consequence that self-focused attention was postulated to be an aversive condition. At this point it may be instructive to illustrate these rudiments of the theory in an example, at the same time introducing the "salience" concept.

Suppose that a 13-year-old male has been raised protectively and has never been subject to much criticism. Then, as part of his initiation into manhood, he suddenly falls subject to intense and unabated ridicule from his peers and elders. They come down particularly hard on his timidity, citing numerous embarrassment-provoking instances of his chicken-heartedness. All of this comes as a surprise to him, and the feedback immediately engenders a good deal of self-criticism. At this point we might reasonably assume a high degree of objective self-awareness, and the manipulation of the state is an obvious one. Certainly a person attends to a trait when others bring it forth for direct comment.

After this rite of criticism the young initiate recedes into solitude, and the question now is this: What happens to the objective self-awareness that was so obviously generated while he was criticized? The theory views the direction of conscious attention as determined by the complex of stimuli that impinge upon us, and such stimuli may be divided into two classes: those that remind the person of his object status, and those serving to pull attention away from the self. Therefore, as the young man gains solitude his attention will inevitably be drawn away from the self and toward whatever takes place in his immediate surroundings. This is not to say that all his subsequent time will be spent in attention directed outward, but objective self-awareness will be minimized to the extent that the necessary activities and distractions of his existence demand attention. However, during those moments of self-focused attention, the theory would have it that his attention will turn toward that salient trait on which he was recently berated.

What happens to the focus of attention when a self-focusing stimulus, such as a mirror, is encountered? Initially our youthful subject sees himself as a physical fact, but the theoretical analysis is now just beginning. The mirror does more than stimulate attention toward one's face, for as soon as the face, or any other reflection of the self, receives attention, attention will then shift to whatever self-related dimension is most salient. This means that the young initiate's cowardice will receive an increase in attention due to the mirror, and that the attention given to that trait will be greater than it would be without the mirror's presence as a self-focusing stimulus. How do we know that this personality dimension would be more salient than some other dimension? In this example that is a guess, and in experimentation to follow stricter precautions have been taken to ensure that one trait will be salient above others.

What follows from the postulated negative affect? In the first statement of the theory we indicated that either avoidance of self-focusing stimuli or discrepancy reduction would result. At that time Duval and I did not stipulate clearly which of these should be primary or preferred, but in re-examining the theory there is good reason for assuming that these two reactions would fall into an order of preference. This is because negative affect is postulated as the motivating force, and whatever eliminates such affect most quickly should be preferred. Certainly a successful averting of self-focused attention would eliminate the negative affect, however temporarily; thus an individual's immediate reaction to objective self-awareness should be an avoidance of self-focusing stimuli and/or efforts to find distractions. If elimination of objective self-awareness is impossible, the alternative affect-reducing response will involve discrepancy reduction, which typically will entail efforts to bring a trait or behavior into line with a standard or aspiration. More generally, discrepancy reduction involves eliminating internal discrepancies, meaning any variety of within-self contradiction or shortcoming.

Early reactions to the negative affect postulate of the theory were skeptical, if not occasionally hostile. For example, we were asked, "Why do people seek out training groups and psychoanalysis if they are trying to avoid self-awareness?" There were also frequent testimonies of narcissistic phenomena, and I gathered from some of these observations that most of us do not like to think that self-observation reveals only the shortcomings within us. More important, there is no doubt that most of us frequently enter into situations that stimulate self-focused attention, but there is reason to question whether or not man enters training groups, psychoanalysis, or a room of mirrors purely out of a motivation for self-focused attention. More likely these activities are initiated out of yearnings for self-improvement, whether improvement of the mind or of the facial expression and grooming.

We continued to operate on the assumption that self-focused attention was invariably aversive, and the assumption appeared to lead to theoretically consistent results. But the story does not end here. There is recent evidence that objective self-awareness is occasionally a state to be desired, and a state in which a person feels especially favorable toward himself. The evidence shows that a recent and potent success experience seems to be sufficient for transforming objective self-awareness into a desirable state of affairs. If someone meets with unequivocal success on a dimension and then proceeds to rate himself on the same dimension, ratings are more positive when undertaken in the presence of self-focusing stimuli.

At this time a small theoretical revision is called for, of the following nature. A success experience can often exceed a person's aspirations or standards, and although aspirations will in turn accelerate, there will at least be a fleeting moment during which the person can be characterized as possessing a *positive* discrepancy. It is presumed here that positive affect will prevail to the degree that conscious attention is turned toward such discrepancies, and mirroring the earlier postulate about negative discrepancies, it is further presumed that positive affect increases with the size of the positive discrepancy. There are further questions having to do with the frequency and longevity of positive discrepancies, but these will be reserved for the following discussion of research.

B. The Theory Summarized

The theory of objective self-awareness as it stands presently is this: Conscious attention is viewed as dichotomous, having the property of being directed either toward the self or toward the environment. The direction of attention is guided by events that force attention inward, such as reflections of the self, and events that pull attention outward, such as distracting stimuli outside the self. Under objective self-awareness the person will experience either negative or positive affect, depending on whether attention is directed toward a negative or a positive discrepancy. The degree of affect is a joint function of the proportion of attention (over a time interval) focused on the discrepancy and the size of the discrepancy.

The initial reaction to the onset of objective self-awareness is postulated to be self-evaluation. If the salient discrepancy is negative, the person will be increasingly cognizant of that discrepancy, owing to self-focused attention. In terms of operations, the discrepancy will loom larger. The converse should hold for positive discrepancies: The onset of objective self-awareness will create a heightened positive self-evaluation on the salient positive discrepancy.

In trying to anticipate whether a person's discrepancy on some specified trait will be positive or negative, an atheoretical guideline will be useful. From all available evidence, especially in the area of achievement motivation, it is a reasonable assumption that virtually all naturally occurring discrepancies are negative. They can be rendered positive by a *recent* success experience, but it is also likely that the impact of such successes will dwindle with time. This is because aspirations rise and eventually surpass the individual's recently attained successes, re-creating negative discrepancies.

Finally, there are two possible reactions to self-focused attention in addition to the initial reaction of self-evaluation. The first is of the nature of an avoidance or approach response. If the discrepancy in focus is positive, the person will welcome stimuli that bring on the objective state, and will tend to seek out self-focusing circumstances. If the salient discrepancy is negative, there will be an active avoidance of such stimuli, including efforts to create distractions. Further, and only in the case of negative discrepancies, an inescapable objective self-awareness will result in attempted discrepancy reduction.

II. Self-Evaluation: The Initial Reaction to Objective Self-Awareness

The theory we are dealing with is foremost a theory of self-evaluation. All effects stemming from self-focused attention, whether efforts to avoid or seek out the state, or to reduce discrepancies, are presumed to be motivated by the person's affective reaction to his degree of completeness, goodness, or inner consistency.

A. Self-Criticism

What does self-criticism have to do with discrepancy reduction? This is an important question to consider as a prologue to research on self-criticism, and an example will be helpful in understanding the interrelationship. Consider a simple case of apparent hypocrisy. Thirty years after World War II a draft dodger of that war takes a hawkish position on amnesty, assenting to the notion that everyone who left the United States during the Viet Nam conflict should have to suffer the consequences. Everyone around this individual is easily cognizant of the hypocrisy, but the person himself does not sense a contradiction. If this man is forced to examine himself, with attention turned particularly to his opinions and behaviors relevant to the issue, there should be an increased chance of his discovering the contradiction. With attention forced toward the discrepant elements (his World War II behavior vs. present opinion), there will be an immediate negative affect together with a correlated negative self-evaluation. The basis of this self-criticism is simply the discrepancy between prior behavior and present opinion, and if the present theory is correct, there should be an admission of the discrepancy to the degree that focused attention is directed to it. But there is a second process that should also be engaged. Assuming that our hypocrite cannot escape self-focused attention, he should quickly attempt to eliminate the discrepancy, and in this case discrepancy reduction can be carried out with expediency. All he need do is change his current opinion to coincide with his earlier behavior; once this is accomplished there will no longer be a basis remaining for negative affect and self-criticism—on that dimension. And if asked about the extent of the discrepancy, the former hypocrite who has changed his opinion would have none.

Continuing this line of thought, should induced objective self-awareness be expected to increase, or decrease, the admitted size of discrepancy? The answer depends completely on the progress of discrepancy reduction. If the hypocrite's perceived discrepancy were measured just as his attention is focused toward the discrepancy, there should be a greater admission of discrepancy than there would be in the absence of self-focused attention. However, this direction of difference will reverse itself as discrepancy reduction proceeds. Therefore, in order to maximize the possibility of using objective self-awareness to bring on an admission of discrepancy (self-criticism), the measurement of self-criticism should be immediate and the elements of the discrepancy should be made as resistant to change as possible.

1. Self-Esteem

The following research on self-esteem was conducted with the intention of finding self-criticism, or lowered self-esteem, as a function of self-focused attention. That such effects have been found is presumably due largely to the inflexible nature of the dimensions involved. For example, experimental subjects are asked to examine the extent to which they fall short of their aspirations on traits such as intelligence, skill, and industriousness. Subjects' conceptions of themselves on these traits are the product of a lifetime of experiences and reinforcements, and it is not an easy matter in these cases either to improve oneself instantaneously or to lower aspiration levels. Accordingly, the initial self-critical reaction due to self-focused attention should be measurable, as there is not a great likelihood of the individual's eliminating the discrepancy with dispatch.

a. *Lowered self-esteem from a tape-recorded voice.* The first two studies reported by Ickes, Wicklund, and Ferris (1973) took the tack of asking female undergraduates to complete what may be called a "real-ideal self-discrepancy" questionnaire. On each of several dimensions (e.g, creative–unimaginative) the subject was asked to indicate her ideal self as well as her real self, and the discrepancy was taken to be a measure of self-criticism, which we may equate with low self-esteem. Half of the subjects responded to the scale while listening to their own tape-recorded voices, and half heard another female voice. The results, in terms of discrepancy scores, are shown in Fig. 1. Note that the own-voice (High OSA) treatment elevated discrepancy scores for the first several items, after which time the two groups were similar. The difference between conditions for the first five items was significant, substantiating our expectation that focused attention toward the self generates self-criticism. Since the order of presentation of the twenty questionnaire items was counterbalanced, the sequential effect cannot be attributed to type of item, and we suggest that the declining impact of the own-

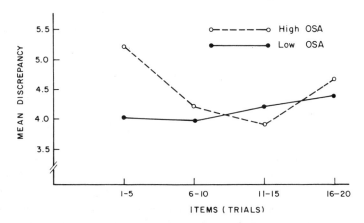

Fig. 1.   Mean discrepancies for the twenty items.

voice treatment is just that—an adaptation effect. Certainly the theory does not talk about adaptation, but in implementing the theory it is valuable to know that self-focusing stimuli may have their maximal impact on first being presented.

Because this is the first experiment described here, a visible feature of most of the self-awareness research should be reviewed. Presumably the tape-recorded voice initially brought subjects' attention to their voices, but then, as each self-esteem trait was given salience by subjects' examining the questionnaire, self-focused attention turned toward the trait in question. Theoretically, the subject's attention to each trait was more intense in the "own-voice" condition than in the "other-voice" condition, accounting for the self-critical effect.

Why is this "cross-modal" approach taken in the research? Certainly it would be possible to deal within one mode, simply by instructing a person to think about his intelligence, and then ascertaining changes in self-criticism of own intelligence. But this approach allows experimental artifacts that we have preferred to try to avoid in these early stages of developing the theory. For example, it is difficult to instruct a person directly to think about his I.Q. (or any other trait) without imparting some implicit demand that he should be self-critical, or even self-aggrandizing.

b. Lowered self-esteem from a mirror image. In part of the third study reported by Ickes *et al.* we attempted to induce in male subjects a strong negative discrepancy prior to subjects' self-ratings. Subjects were first given a bogus "surgency" test, and were told nothing about the trait except that it was important and, further, that high surgency is desirable. Some of the subjects were then given negative feedback on surgency. Second, and shortly after the feedback, subjects rated themselves on several self-esteem items and on the trait of surgency. Half of them were confronted with their mirror images during this interval, and half were not. The dependent measure was simply the goodness of the self-rating, and, unlike the previous two experiments, only the real self was measured this time. On the self-esteem items there was a clear self-criticism effect such that ratings were lower when a mirror was present. However, there was no effect whatever on surgency ratings.

This latter finding appears to make good sense if the reader will recall the earlier discussion of resistance to change. The self-esteem traits we used in this study should have had considerable resistance due to subjects' histories with each trait (e.g., success, intelligence); thus a defensive or imagined discrepancy reduction would be difficult. However, the surgency trait was contentless as far as subjects were concerned, and this may have enabled subjects in the Mirror condition to avert self-criticism by convincing themselves that the trait was trivial, that they didn't care about being high on the trait anyway, or any other cognitive work that would minimize the negative affect of the discrepancy.

c. Reducing self-criticism by supplying a distraction. Not only should there be a self-critical reaction to objective self-awareness-inducing stimuli, but it should also be possible to mute a self-critical reaction by forcing a person's attention elsewhere. An experiment was conducted by C. Brian Ferris and Wicklund on the assumption that a television program would serve this purpose. Female undergraduates were asked to examine thirteen rug samples on the pretext that home furnishings make a difference in a person's feelings about himself. After each rug was inspected the subject pressed a button to record her present level of self-like–self-dislike, and the series of thirteen samples was considered three times by each subject. Under the guise of assisting a second experimenter (a common and workable ruse in much of our research), the subject was given blatant exposure to three television images while making her ratings. These images were presented in order, such that she witnessed her own face during one 1–13 series of ratings, a test pattern during another series, and a television western program for the third series. The order of this within-subject variable was of course counterbalanced.

The results are shown in Fig. 2. Statistically, there was a main effect across the three levels of self-focused attention ($p < .01$), and with respect to the distraction hypothesis, the television-western condition differed reliably ($p < .05$ or better) from each of the other conditions. Distraction in the form of a television program does seem to operate as the theory would suggest.

d. Changing the ideal self. In research discussed thus far, the effects were accounted for entirely by shifts in the real, as opposed to the ideal, self. But what would happen to discrepancies if the real self were prevented from changing? It seems possible that a widened within-self discrepancy would then be manifested by a heightened ideal self. This idea was explored in a study by Michael F. Scheier and Wicklund, part of which will be described here.

Female subjects were told that they scored poorly on a test of psychological mindedness. Then they filled out a real-ideal self questionnaire which included a dimension of psychological mindedness. On that dimension the experimenter filled in the real self for all subjects. This real-self mark was near the low end of the scale, and the subject was free to fill in her ideal on that dimension, either under conditions of a mirror or without a mirror. Given that the real self was a fixed entity,

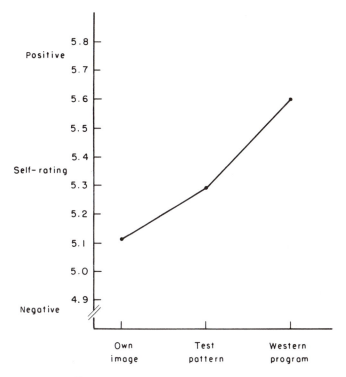

FIG. 2.   Self-ratings in the presence of a television monitor.

subjects who rated in the presence of a mirror indicated a significantly higher ideal self for psychological mindedness than did no-mirror subjects ($p < .01$). The result is clear, and allows us to make a general point regarding the objectively self-aware individual's admission of discrepancies. Evidently the aspiration level, or ideal self, is typically not moved when the subject focuses on a dimension, but ideals can shift upward if the real self is firmly anchored.

2. Attribution

If we may presume that people generally aspire not to bring about unwanted events, it becomes a simple matter to extend the negative discrepancy analysis to attribution of causality. Suppose that a man is not sure whether he, or his wife, is responsible for their economic downfall. The ideal in this case is to be free of responsibility, and a discrepancy exists when felt actual responsibility falls short of the ideal—that is, when there is some perceived responsibility. The greatest possible discrepancy would result when the man found himself to be totally liable for the economic problem. What is the impact of self-focused attention on this discrepancy? Just as with the self-esteem items, there should be an exaggerated negative discrepancy—and hence admission of greater responsibility—given the onset of objective self-awareness.

Paralleling the self-esteem analysis, it should be noted that self-focused attention has two potential outcomes when that attention is inescapable. First comes a self-critical reaction, manifested in an increased sense of responsibility for unwanted outcomes. But there should be an accompanying motivation to reduce this discrepancy, and if there is a viable means of accomplishing this, objective self-awareness may ultimately result in *decreased* self-blame. This, of course, would follow the initial reaction, which is one of *heightened* self-blame. How do we know that our measurements of self-blame are taken prior to successful discrepancy reduction? As with self-esteem, it is a guess that the elements of the discrepancy are highly resistant to change. It is conceivable that a person might convince himself of an absence of responsibility by examining the entire situation more closely, or if given sufficient time he might even eliminate the negative outcome. Given these considerations, it should be realized that the self-blame effects of the following attribution experiments are not necessarily the only effects that can accrue from self-focused attention. Given sufficient time to reduce the discrepancy, by whatever means, the effects noted here might conceivably be turned backward.

a. A mirror image and self-attribution. Part of the second experiment reported by Duval and Wicklund (1973) is relevant for our discussion of attribution as self-criticism. Female undergraduates were either confronted with their mirror images or not throughout the experimental session, and the experimenter read to them five hypothetical situations. These hypothetical situations were such as the following:

> You're driving down the street about five miles over the speed limit when a little kid suddenly runs out chasing a ball and you hit him.

After each item was read the subject indicated in percentages the degree to which she was causal and the degree to which the other party (i.e., the child) was causal for the negative event in question. The results were entirely consistent with the assumption that subjects were not actively involved in discrepancy reduction—i.e., the self-criticism effect appeared. In the Mirror condition subjects assigned an average of 60.2% of the total causality to themselves, while this figure was 51.1% in the No-Mirror condition.

b. Distraction and self-attribution. One of the primary reasons for conducting the first of our attribution studies was to inquire into the hunch that some kinds of motor activities can take attention away from the self and direct it toward the goal of the activity. Certainly not all motor behaviors would serve the purpose of reducing objective self-awareness, for numerous unfamiliar, awkward, or inappropriate behaviors would only bring attention toward a fumbling and embarrassed self. But if the activity is simple and relatively free from the possibility of failure, the necessity of concentrating on the products of one's motions can draw attention away from intraself discrepancies. Even if the behavior does not demand constant monitoring by the performer, the motivation to reduce objective self-awareness should result in attempts to devote increased attention to trivial tasks.

Wicklund and Duval (in Duval & Wicklund, 1972, pp. 193–205) conducted three experiments, all of which took a similar form. The subjects were asked to portion out responsibility for a hypothetical negative outcome between themselves and another possible perpetrator, and while they responded with percentage estimates half of them were physically active. In the first experiment subjects squeezed a handgrip, and in the second and third experiments subjects rotated a turntable with one hand. Suffice it to say that the results of all three studies were highly similar: attribution of blame to the self was diminished with physical activity.

Thus far there is a close parallel between self-esteem and attribution of blame to self as reflections of self-criticism. No matter whether objective self-awareness is relatively high owing to self-focusing stimuli, or to the absence of distractions including physical activity, the subject heightens his self-criticism. At this point we shall leave self-criticism, which is evidently the most likely initial reaction to self-focused attention, and move on to an opposite kind of reaction that occurs under very special circumstances.

B. Self-Exaltation

This section is for the purpose of illustrating the operation of a principle that is new to the theory. As was discussed in the Introduction, it has become necessary to recognize the concept of a positive discrepancy and the consequent self-aggrandizement accompanying self-focused attention. The reasoning is hardly different from that for negative discrepancies. When a person's behavior, or real self, exceeds his aspiration, the resulting positive discrepancy plus focused attention will produce a positive affect. Accompanying the positive affect will be a heightened realization of that discrepancy, and in terms of operational definitions, this means an inflated self-rating under objective self-awareness. There are three studies relevant to this new proposition—two on self-esteem and one on attribution.

1. Self-Esteem

a. Self-aggrandizement from favorable feedback. The third study by Ickes *et al.* was discussed only partially in the preceding section. In addition to what was described there, the study also included a condition of extremely positive feedback on the surgency dimension, and the feedback was at such a level that most subjects certainly would not have expected such a favorable result. When self-rated surgency was measured, a positivity effect for self-focused attention was obtained (Fig. 3), a result that surprised us at first and that led to the theoretical revision just discussed.

It may be recalled that the experiment also incorporated several questions as a general measure of self-esteem, and there was evidence that the surgency feedback generalized to the self-esteem items. The evidence is this: Figure 3 depicts a slight (although not significant) positivity effect due to self-focused attention with the self-esteem items, while the opposite effect occurred when feedback was negative, resulting

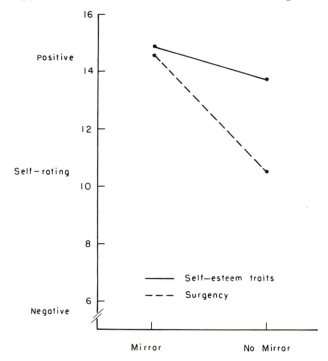

FIG. 3. Self-ratings among subjects given positive feedback.

in an interaction between feedback and self-focused attention. Although the results for the surgency item leaned toward a similar form of interaction, it was not significant, owing to the absence of a self-critical effect given negative feedback. But the important point is this: In terms of self-rating of a personality dimension, this study offers a strong suggestion that a recently created positive discrepancy can bring about an increased appreciation for oneself.

b. *Self-aggrandizement from substitution of standards.* In a study by Charles S. Carver there was an experimental substitution of low standards for the subject's own preexisting higher standards. A self-esteem scale comparable to that of Ickes *et al.* was used, with one important variation: On each self-esteem dimension an **X** had been marked in the center, and this **X** was described as the place where the average person would be located. Assuming that most subjects would think of themselves as better than average, and that the new comparison level became more salient than their previous ideals, a positive discrepancy should have been created for most subjects on most of the self-esteem dimensions. In fact, there was such a positive discrepancy. When subjects were not in the presence of a mirror they almost inevitably rated their real selves as higher than the average, and, consistent with Carver's argument, the introduction of a mirror exaggerated that effect $(p < .05)$. This is potentially an extremely important study, for it suggests that standards of correctness function as such only to the degree that the person attends to them. If attention is drawn to alternative standards, whether higher or lower, the degree of positive or negative affect in objective self-awareness can be altered considerably.

2. Attribution

Included in the Duval and Wicklund (1973) study of attribution were two conditions (Mirror and No Mirror) involving *positive* hypothetical situations. For example, the subject was told to imagine a circumstance in which there was some ambiguity regarding who was responsible for her A on a term paper. Just as with the negative items, the subject was asked to assign a percentage responsibility to herself and to the other person (her friend in this example). The results showed subjects taking more credit (60.0%) in the Mirror condition than in the No Mirror condition (49.9%). If the receipt of an A on a term paper consists in a positive discrepancy for our subjects, it becomes easy to interpret these results as a magnification of that discrepancy. When the person feels some degree of positive affect by virtue of a success experience, that affect apparently can be magnified by focusing attention onto the relevant dimension.

C. SUMMARY

The self-criticism phenomena noted in this section on self-evaluation may be the most difficult to obtain of all objective self-awareness effects, and for good theoretical reason. To reiterate, although self-criticism is postulated to be the immediate result of attention focused on a salient negative discrepancy, the resulting motivation to eliminate that discrepancy may well result in a decreased discrepancy. In our research we have apparently managed to take measurements before the onset of such discrepancy reduction, and it is also likely that the self-esteem discrepancies are difficult to reduce, a possibility that enhances the likelihood of obtaining decrements in self-esteem given objective self-awareness. When discrepancies are positive, the initial reaction of enhanced self-evaluation is not countered by discrepancy reduction, for there should be no such motivation. This means that it should be relatively easy to exaggerate a person's self-aggrandizement with a self-focusing manipulation.

One issue that is not dealt with specifically by the theory is the longevity of positive discrepancies. Certainly Durkheim (1897) had an answer to this question, which is that man has no limits to his appetites for well-being, comfort, luxury, and other nonphysiological requirements. More recently, analyses of achievement motivation are in agreement that man's appetites are seldom within the reach of what is attainable with certainty. The conclusion seems to be that positive discrepancies are necessarily fleeting phenomena, and if the self-focused attention experimentalist were to wait too long before bringing the person's attention to success experiences, the anticipated self-aggrandizement may slip into a self-criticism as aspirations again rise beyond level of attainment.

III. Escaping Objective Self-Awareness

A. THEORETICAL OVERVIEW

Except for those rare instances in which a salient discrepancy happens to be positive, the theory indicates that the onset of objective self-awareness will set off efforts to avoid that state. Self-criticism, the initial reaction, will persist only as long as the individual is under duress to continue in self-focused attention. Similarly, discrepancy reduction, the topic of the next section, will lose its vigor if the objectively self-aware person can easily shuck off the state.

What actions serve to eliminate self-focused attention? The clearest route to avoidance, and the first to be considered in the following summary of research, is a simple physical avoidance of self-awareness-provoking stimuli. Given that a person is attuned to a negative discrepancy, the theory clearly would predict an aversion to mirrors, the focus of others, cameras, and any comparable stimuli. These aversions would be in proportion to the magnitude of the negative discrepancy. Another possibility is the attempt to create distractions for oneself. By shifting attention to a cacophony of stimulation as might be found in a situation comedy or live rock performance, the danger of turning attention to one's own flaws is abated. Finally, there is overt motor action, and in the popular literature this approach to avoidance of objective self-awareness has no doubt received the most thorough treatment. We might mention just a couple of examples here.

In *The true believer* (1951) and *The passionate state of mind* (1954), Hoffer has interpreted passionate activity as the outcome of the loser's desire to eliminate consciousness of himself. Relentless creative work, dedication to a fanatical cause, and all other passionate behaviors are seen as motivated out of self-dissatisfactions. Hoffer also postulates an interchangeability of passions; since their function is to rid the person of consciousness of an unwanted self, any passion will do. Similarly, Rudin's *Fanaticism* (1969) sees a direct relationship between personal void and fanatic activity as well as an interchangeability of fanaticisms.

Why does motor activity take focused attention away from salient within-self discrepencies? When an operation demands that attention be given to the end point of one's actions, as in driving a nail, it seems clear that attention will move in a direction away from oneself. There is a subject–predicate relationship between the self and the nail being hammered, whereby the force of the person's bodily movements, plus his conscious attention, are directed toward the object. At the same time there are feelings within the body that correspond to these movements—feelings in the arm and in the palm of the hand—but at best there is only a "subsidiary awareness" of these feelings (Polanyi, 1958, p. 55). It is Polanyi's suggestion that the subsidiary awareness of bodily feelings is qualitatively different from the focal awareness (conscious attention) given to the object of a person's labors, and, further, that the subsidiary awareness even merges into the focal awareness of the nail being driven.

But what happens to the direction of attention when the nail springs back into the person's face? Composure is lost, there is a sudden forced interruption, and the subject–predicate relation just noted should reverse itself. Now the task is "attacking" the would-be nail driver, and conscious attention turns inward.

In order to best serve as a distraction a motor activity should carry little potential for unexpected disruption, failure, and surprise, for as soon as the person is thrown into a necessary evaluation of his abilities, the distraction function will cease. Finally, the activity must be "natural" in the context. This is an especially vital consideration when others are present, for a good many potentially distracting activities also have the quality of bringing forth attention and evaluation from others. We shall return to the topic of objective self-awareness and motor activity after several pages, but first some research on related topics will be discussed.

B. RESEARCH

1. Direct Avoidance of Self-Focusing Stimuli

a. Avoidance of a mirror given a large negative discrepancy. The theory indicates that avoidance will be a function of the magnitude of salient discrepancies, a proposition that Duval, Wicklund, and Fine (in Duval & Wicklund, 1972, pp. 16–20) set out to test. Subjects first received either favorable or unfavorable evaluations on creativity–intelligence, and subsequently they were placed in a room such that they would either have to view their mirror images, or would not. The measure of avoidance was simply the number of minutes that elapsed before they left the room; the results are shown in Fig. 4. Given a high discrepancy (unfavorable feedback) there was a clear and significant avoidance effect, while the mirror had no impact when the discrepancy was low (possibly even positive).

b. Avoidance of own tape-recorded voice as a function of discrepancy. While the results of Duval *et al.* show a definite avoidance phenomenon given a large discrepancy, the interaction in that experiment was not significant. Given the experimental design, an interaction would have been necessary to make the point that focus of attention and discrepancy size act multiplicatively. This problem was corrected in an experiment by Frederick X. Gibbons and Wicklund. Male subjects received either a highly accepting, or a rejecting, first-impression response from a female confederate. Then the subject was given a 12-minute task of listening to his own tape-recorded voice as well as to the voice of another male. Approach vs. avoidance of self-focused attention was ascertained by the relative amount of time spent by the subject in listening to his own voice, and the results were strong and consistent with the theory: When subjects had been accepted by the confederate, they

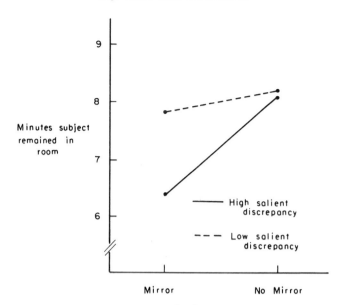

FIG. 4. Latencies for leaving room.

listened to their own voices considerably longer than did subjects who were rejected ($p < .02$). In short, avoidance of a self-focusing stimulus is the product of an inflated negative discrepancy.

2. Selectivity in Recognition and Use of Self-Related Symbols

a. Selectivity in recognition of self. Given a configuration that might stand for the self but is ambiguous in that respect, the theory would propose a reluctance to recognize the configuration as self-related, and this should be especially true given a salient negative discrepancy. Further, the longer that stimulus is presented, the more likely it is to create objective self-awareness and motivate the person to refuse to admit it as a self-reflection. For example, when subjects' tape-recorded voices were played back immediately (Rousey & Holzman, 1967), there was a tendency, although nonsignificant, toward poorer recognition of own voice given a 5-second playback than given a 1-second playback. A similar phenomenon was noted by Schumacher, Wright, and Wiesen (1968), but only among subjects who had been threatened with electrical apparatus. We might conjecture that the threatened subjects were attempting to avoid focusing on their fear state, certainly a negative discrepancy, although it is difficult to draw any definite conclusions from the results of Schumacher *et al.* because the statistical analysis is not sufficient for our purposes.

b. Selectivity in use of self-related symbols. Although there is as yet no strong evidence for the selective perception hypothesis just discussed, there are two experiments by Davis and Brock (1974) that make a similar point in the realm of deciding when to implement a self-related symbol. In the first study subjects were given either positive, negative, or no feedback on a test of creativity. This can be treated as a dimension of salient within-self discrepancy, running from negative to positive. Following the feedback a television camera was trained on half the subjects, and the experimenter indicated that the subject would from that point on be monitored by several members of the faculty. The subject's task, while being monitored or not, was to read a passage printed in a foreign language and to fill in the blanks where they appeared. He was led to think that a pronoun was always called for, and he was to guess which pronoun would be correct for each blank. Theoretically, the person with a negative discrepancy should avoid the use of first-person pronouns, especially while objectively self-aware, while someone with a positive discrepancy might show the opposite.

The results, in terms of mean number of first-person pronouns used, are shown in Fig. 5. The intrusion of a camera and its associated monitoring produced a significant increment in number of first-person pronouns within both the Positive Feedback and No Feedback conditions. It is evident that no effect appeared within the Negative Feedback condition. Further, the overall interaction was significant, as was the main effect for the camera variable. The pattern of the interaction is consistent with what we might expect from the avoidance–approach tendencies postulated by the theory, but the surprising effect is the overall high number of first-person pronouns obtained in the Camera condition.

This latter finding is seen by Davis and Brock as a direct reflection of self-focused attention. It makes sense that subjects in the Camera condition, who are thinking about themselves, would tend more to project self-references when asked for pronouns. This is a general process that may simply reflect the presence of self-focused attention, and the implication is that the existence of self-focused attention may generally be detectable by means of projective techniques similar to the Davis and Brock procedure. The avoidance tendencies given a high negative discrepancy would tend to interfere with such a process, as suggested by the absence of a difference in the Negative Feedback condition.

In a second and quite similar experiment Davis and Brock substituted a mirror manipulation in place of the television camera, and the neutral condition was not run. The results, again in terms of number of first-person pronouns (Fig. 6), are virtually identical to those of the first study.

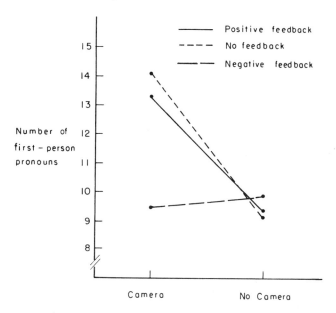

FIG. 5. First-person pronouns and self-focused attention.

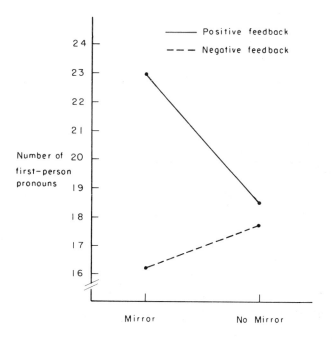

FIG. 6. First-person pronouns and self-focused attention.

3. Objective Self-Awareness and Nervous Habits

Lord Chesterfield (1774) remarked upon the nervous and awkward habits engaged in by people who are in the presence of others. He noted that such actions as putting the fingers to the nose or twirling a hat are likely to be manifested when a person feels ashamed in company. The present theoretical approach would agree with Chesterfield's observation, except to note that the conditions for hat twirling, etc., are more general than feeling ashamed in company. Focused attention toward *any* negative discrepancy can lead to actions whose function is to distract.

Liebling, Seiler, and Shaver (1974) have conducted a study of objective self-awareness and smoking which is perfectly amenable to the distraction analysis. Smokers were asked to sit in a room for two separate 30-minute intervals, one time in the presence of a conspicuous mirror, and the other time without the mirror. If objective self-awareness brings forth activities with potential for distraction, we should expect an increased rate of smoking, or at least of playing with cigarettes. The results showed exactly this: Considering the mean number of puffs taken, the mean time spent holding cigarettes, and the number of flicks, there was more cigarette-related activity when subjects were confronted with a mirror.

Before resting the theoretical case on this one experiment, a potential difficulty should be discussed. Liebling *et al.* originally predicted that the mirror would *decrease* cigarette smoking, on the assumption that to decrease was a standard of correctness for their sample of subjects. This was clearly a possible prediction in light of evidence they gathered about subjects' standards, and the difficulty is that two opposing predictions are possible in this context—one from the distraction thesis and the other from the discrepancy reduction thesis. In a reply to Liebling *et al.*, Wicklund (1975) has gone into more detail, and some methods of averting the ambiguity are explicated. For the present, it will suffice to say that the distraction prediction becomes unequivocal when standards are not present, or when the potential distracting actions are irrelevant to the dimension on which negative affect is experienced.

4. Distractions and Disfluency

There is a good deal of thought, and some evidence, within the world of speech therapy that points to self-evaluation as one of the critical antecedents of stuttering. For example, there is an "anticipatory struggle hypothesis," propounded by Brown (1945) and others, whereby stuttering is said to occur at those points in communication where meaning is highly important, the speaker's emphasis is high, and the listener is closely attuned to what is said. The anticipatory struggle notion suggests that the stutterer becomes apprehensive to the degree that an important error is possible and when conditions are conducive to self-focused attention. In line with this thinking, Bloodstein (1969) has listed several situations that have high potential for stuttering, such as an audience with high potential for evaluation or the speaker's need for approval. When the audience cannot evaluate, as in the case of an audience of animals, or when the stutterer stands little chance of stating an incorrect proposition, stuttering decreases markedly.

Bloodstein cites numerous anecdotal examples of the temporary therapeutic value of distractions, although systematic research that varies available distractions has been weak or nonexistent. Some of this research will be mentioned shortly, but first we shall examine the thesis that the stutterer, or even the speaker in general, makes active attempts to keep focused attention away from himself.

a. Sidetracking of stuttering by "starters." Swift and Hedrick (1917) compiled a list of postures, gestures, and "nervous habits" that appear to accompany the onset of a stutterer's speaking. They propose that the "starter" is an action that facilitates the flow of verbiage, and their reasoning is the following:

> The sole and only reason for employing a starter is for the obvious reason of diverting the attention from the throat contraction and throat spasm and the accompanying mental strain that prevents utterance [Swift & Hedrick, 1917, p. 84].

To elaborate on their thesis, it is proposed here that self-focused attention, when turned to evaluation of individual elements of the speech pattern, has a disruptive effect. By evaluating the potential quality of each forth-coming word, the stutterer inevitably inhibits a smooth flow of speech. It also seems reasonable that a pattern of speech, such as a clause or phrase, will sustain an absence of self-focused attention once it is underway. The activity of delivering a group of words that belong together should serve to distract attention from oneself. But once there is an interruption or disfluency it is again necessary to undertake an effort to remove attention from the self as speaker. A study by Dittmann and Llewellyn (1969) is entirely consistent with this thinking. They found their subjects, who were not chronic stutterers, to produce a disproportionate number of bodily movements at the beginning of phonemic clauses, and immediately after disfluencies.

   b. Recall of poetry and opportunity for movement. If self-focused attention breaks up the smooth flow of speech, it also makes sense that recitation of a memorized passage would suffer in proportion to the amount of objective self-awareness. Not only should the delivery become increasingly awkward, but the chaining of words that is fundamental in memorization is likely to break down, with resultant loss in performance. This thesis was tested in a study by Wicklund, Peter Dorflinger, and Susan Morris. Subjects were first asked to memorize two poems ("Stopping by Woods on a Snowy Evening" and "Casey at Bat"), then to deliver the poems in a cubicle where an experimenter, who did not fix his gaze on the subject, tape-recorded the delivery. For recitation of one of the poems the subject was asked to stand still with her hands at her sides, and for the other she was free to move about as she pleased. The order of "active–passive" and of the two poems was of course counterbalanced. The results, in terms of number of words recalled of the poems, indicated significantly better recitation ($p < .05$) when subjects were allowed free movement.

C. SUMMARY AND COMMENT

   The final study in this section is a logical outgrowth of the previous reasoning on the function of physical activities. If it is true that people engage in motions that function to reduce objective self-awareness, as is implied by the Dittmann and Llewellyn study, then it should be possible to affect verbal performance by giving subjects differential opportunity for action. The final study illustrates this application, and the results may be seen as parallel to a series of experiments on attribution by Wicklund and Duval, reported above, in which physical activity reduced self-blame. There is one important disqualifier in extending the notion that activity reduces objective self-awareness and self-criticism. If the activity is forced upon the person in such a way that it is "unnatural," or in any way causes a concern about correct or appropriate performance, the technique should backfire. In fact, during pretesting of the experiment on memorized poetry we attempted an activity manipulation whereby subjects paced regularly around the room, and this tended to debilitate performance. Evidently the most beneficial kinds of activities to foist onto self-critical subjects are activities they would be likely to perform in the situation, such as hand movements (Dittmann & Llewellyn, 1969) or smoking (Liebling *et al.*, 1974). Even then, it is important to ensure that the person does not feel estranged from the activity or evaluated on the basis of his performance. If these conditions are met, imposed activity should have beneficial effects.

IV. Coming to Terms with Discrepancies

A. THEORETICAL OVERVIEW

If behaviors, attitudes, or traits can readily be altered, focused attention toward a salient discrepancy should result in discrepancy reduction provided that avoidance is impossible. In most instances of application of the theory, the change, whether in attitude or in behavior, is in the direction of a specifiable, personal standard of correctness. But even where a standard is less than obvious, the theory at the very least predicts a reduction of within-self contradictions. For example, if someone says "A is the case" on one occasion and "not-A is the case" on a second, self-focused attention should lead to efforts to eliminate this contradiction, although the direction of discrepancy reduction would not be predictable from the theory unless more were understood about the person's standards. We shall resume discussion of this point in extending the theory to cognitive dissonance phenomena.

B. RESEARCH

1. Self-Consistency and Test Validity

Based on reviews by Mischel (1969) and Wicker (1969) there is ample reason to take a dim view of using self-report measures to predict behavior. Often such measures are totally invalid, as evidenced by surprisingly low correlations between tests and whatever criterion behavior is to be predicted. Viewing this difficulty in the context of objective self-awareness theory, we might think that the inconsistency between test and test-predicted behavior is due to an absence of motivation to bring the two into consistent relation. If a person could be forced into self-focused attention while taking a test, there is theoretical reason to think that there would be attempts to reduce discrepancies between self-report and behavior, and enhanced test validity would be the consequence.

John B. Pryor, Frederick X. Gibbons, and Wicklund designed an experiment to show that self-focused attention could raise the validity of a simple, face-valid measure of sociability. The scale, written by Pryor, consisted of sixteen items such as "I have difficulty in making new friends," and was administered to a sample of undergraduate males at the University of Texas. During the administration approximately half of the subjects were simultaneously forced to view themselves in a mirror. After a few days had lapsed the subject returned, ostensibly to take part in another experiment, and at that time he was asked to wait in a cubicle with a female undergraduate who was described as another subject. During the ensuing 3-minute interval the confederate spoke only minimally when spoken to, and at the end of the interval she rated his extent of overt sociability on a six-point scale. Another measure of overt sociability was provided via a hidden tape recorder, allowing a measure of number of words spoken by the subject.

The two indices of sociable behavior, confederate's evaluation and number of words, were then combined after being converted to z scores, and the resultant index was correlated with initial scale score. In the control condition, where self-focus was not prompted, the correlation between test and the combined behavioral index was .16, while the analogous figure was .62 in the Mirror condition. The correlations were reliably different ($p = .05$), supporting our contention that test validity can indeed be bolstered by a simple self-focusing device.

2. Aggression

a. Nonaggression as a standard. Scheier, Fenigstein, and Buss (1974) have conducted two experiments in which it is reasonable to assume that the objectively self-aware subject would invoke a personal standard against administering electric shock. The subjects were males, the victim a female, and the shock was administered by the subject as part of his role as teacher. In the first experiment half of the subjects were obligated to view their mirror images while shocking the victim, and the remainder were without mirror. In the second experiment self-focused attention was created through the presence of a small audience, with whom the subject was forced to have frequent eye contact. The audience manipulation is not completely free of a possibly confounded demand-characteristic, but nonetheless it is informative that the two objective self-awareness inductions operated similarly, both having an inhibiting effect on level of shock intensity.

b. Aggression as a standard. In an attempt to show that aggression follows personal standards no matter what the standard, Carver (1974) designed an experiment much like the first experiment of Scheier *et al.*, with two important changes. Subjects were instructed that a high level of shock would facilitate the victim's learning, and to bolster that manipulation the victims were males, who presumably would be weaker stimuli to inhibition than would females. The results were exactly as predicted, and exactly opposite to those of Scheier *et al.*: Subjects confronted with their own mirror images gave the more intense electric shock. (See Fig. 7 for a comparison of Carver's results with the experiment I results of Scheier *et al.*)

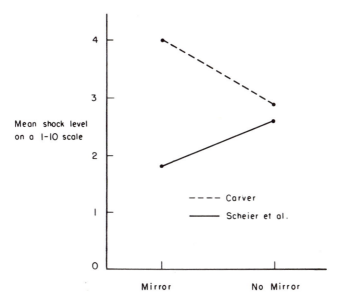

Fɪɢ. 7.   Contrasting two aggression-mirror experiments.

c. *Deindividuation and aggression.* One method of preventing attention from moving toward the self is deindividuation, a circumstance
where individual identity is swallowed up by the environment. This
variable was first studied systematically by Festinger, Pepitone, and
Newcomb (1952), and then by Singer, Brush, and Lublin (1965). The
latter investigators found increases in cursing during the experimental
session among subjects who had been deindividuated by donning lab
coats. Although cursing might be interpreted as a mild form of aggression, parallels to the lab coat technique have been adopted by Zimbardo
(1969) and then Baron (1971) to demonstrate that deindividuation can,
under certain conditions, loosen inhibitions against the more blatant
aggressive response of using electric shock against a victim. In interpreting this research in the framework of the present theory it would, of
course, be necessary to assume personal standards of opposition to strong
physical aggression.

d. *Prior activity and aggression.* It will be recalled that "starters"
are the various motions speakers initiate when beginning a phrase or
following a disfluency. Starters were interpreted in this paper as serving
to take attention off the self, allowing a reduction in self-evaluation
during speaking. By analogy the same technique could be effective in
disinhibiting aggressive behaviors. To the extent that self-focused attention restrains aggressive actions, various "starters" performed just prior

to aggression might loosen restraints. A study by Diener (1974) fits such an analysis. Some of the subjects were first asked to hurl bottles and rocks against a concrete wall, while others merely painted an ecology sign. Then all subjects were given the opportunity to harass physically a victim who sat on the floor in an experimental room. Subjects who had engaged in the prior rock and bottle throwing exhibited substantially more aggression toward the victim, and in addition to the aggression measure Diener provides additional evidence from questionnaires that the rock-and-bottle subjects were less focused on the propriety of aggression: For one, these subjects indicated less self-consciousness during the aggression session than did control subjects, and second, they were poorer at estimating the number of times they were aggressive toward the victim.

Although this is a lively experiment with a convincing manipulation, it should not be taken as unequivocal evidence for the theoretical position of this paper. Certainly the invitation to throw objects against a wall might have been taken as an implicit invitation to act uncivilized throughout the study.

3. Performance on an Experimental Task

To reiterate a very important point: As long as the person's present state, or behavior, can be altered easily with no complications, the theory allows that self-focused attention will facilitate performance. In a simple test of this idea Wicklund and Duval (1971, Experiment III) asked subjects to copy as much German prose as they could during two consecutive 5-minute intervals. One group of subjects was confronted with a mirror during the second interval, and in examining the amount of increased copying from the first to the second interval, objectively self-aware subjects were significantly more productive. A similar effect with Swedish words was obtained by Liebling and Shaver (1973), whose research will be discussed in more detail below.

4. Information Seeking

A theory of choice certainty by Mills (1965, 1968) implies that people hold standards whereby they desire to make wise choices. Mills argues that a common reflection of the desire for choice certainty (i.e., certainty of deciding correctly) is the predecisional seeking of information. Taking Mills' comments at face value, Wicklund and Ickes (1972) offered subjects a tentative choice between two academic courses on sex; then the subject was asked to indicate how much information she wanted to read about the courses before deciding. Some of the subjects heard their own tape-recorded voices played back while trying to determine how much information to read. Consistent with the assumption that exposure to relevant information is instrumental in arriving at a wise decision, subjects who heard their own voices showed a greater desire than other subjects for items of relevant information.

5. Cognitive Dissonance

Probably any within-self disparity could be classified as an instance of cognitive imbalance, but there is a particular variety of such discrepancies that seems to be resolved in accord with specifiable theoretical rules. These rules are the essence of Festinger's cognitive dissonance theory (1957) and are explicit about the direction to be taken in change of cognitive elements. The explicitness derives from an analysis of resistance to change of cognitive elements. Most of the cognitive dissonance research entails the subject's creating for himself a discrepancy between some previous attitude and a more recent behavioral commitment. Given the nature of this within-self discrepancy, or hypocrisy, the dissonance analysis typically assumes that cognitions about behavior are highly resistant to change, whereas attitudes that conflict with behavior, and that are not clearly anchored in behavior, are less resistant to change.

In applying objective self-awareness theory to dissonance phenomena, it is sufficient to say that self-focused attention to the salient dimension should motivate discrepancy reduction. There should first be an awareness of the discrepancy, with negative affect, and discrepancy reduction should then proceed provided that self-focused attention cannot be diverted elsewhere. (There is evidence for such a sequential process in a study by Walster, reported in Festinger, 1964.) The standards of correctness in this case are supplied by the dissonance analysis: If cognitions about behavior are indeed highly resistant to change, discrepancy reduction will consist in shifting the prior attitude in the direction of the behavioral commitment.

a. Self-focusing stimuli and dissonance reduction. Wicklund and Duval (1971, Experiment II) requested subjects to write five counterattitudinal essays, each one in strong opposition to subjects' beliefs on five college-relevant issues. During this session half of the subjects were confronted with a television camera which was described as operating for the purpose of testing out new equipment. An important feature of this study was the position of the camera: It was aimed directly into the subject's face, and never down at her questionnaires or essays. This was an attempt to eliminate any possible demand-characteristics that would result from the subject's inference of being monitored. Opinion measures on the five topics were taken both before and after the essay-writing, and the results showed discrepancy reduction to occur only when a camera was present: Subjects in that condition showed shifts of attitude in the direction of the essays for all five issues, while virtually no attitude change was observed among control subjects.

Insko, Worchel, Songer, and Arnold (1973) conducted a similar study, although they introduced additional dissonance-arousing factors. Subjects who were opposed to the legalization of LSD were asked to write essays in opposition to their opinions. This commitment was elicited from some subjects under conditions of high choice, and others were given no choice. Further, half of the subjects were informed that they would have to ride an exercycle for four miles before composing the essay, while others expected just a quarter mile of exercise. Arguing from dissonance theory, dissonance arousal should have been maximal among subjects who were given high choice and who anticipated the lengthy ride. Arguing from objective self-awareness theory, a self-focusing stimulus should make the greatest difference when a large discrepancy exists, and this is what the results indicated: Subjects who thought they were being videotaped showed an increment in attitude change in the direction of their behavioral commitment, and this effect occurred only when both of the other variables were at optimal dissonance-arousing levels.

These two studies make a simple conceptual point: Leaving to dissonance theory the rules by which a person will eliminate discrepancies, a television camera trained on the subject facilitates the dissonance-reduction process. This is an appropriate place to note that there are parallels to these studies. In experiments by Brehm and Wicklund (1970) and by Zanna, Lepper, and Abelson (1973), it was possible to heighten dissonance reduction by forcing subjects' attention directly to the dissonant elements. The interesting contrast between these latter studies and the objective self-awareness experiments has to do with the cross-modal operation of objective self-awareness. Even when the subject is confronted with a camera, which has no direct bearing on the dissonance, focused attention appears to transfer to the salient, dissonance-arousing dimension.

b. Distraction and dissonance reduction. Given the preceding results, it should be possible to eliminate the discrepancy reduction resulting from dissonance arousal by forcing attention away from the self. In a study by Allen (1965) subjects chose between two art prints; then either 2 or 8 minutes elapsed before dissonance reduction in terms of rating change was assessed. Within each of the temporal variations half of the subjects were provided with an absorbing technical task throughout the time interval. The results showed that dissonance reduction increased with time elapsed following the decision, but, more important, the distracting task totally eliminated dissonance reduction effects.

In summary, this diversity of research provides quite good support for the thesis that discrepancy reduction in the form of dissonance reduction (or avoidance) is dependent on the direction of attention. If attention is turned toward the self, whether directly to the dissonant elements or to some physical feature of the self, attitudes are shifted in the direction of behaviors. Although the theory of objective self-awareness does not stipulate that discrepancy reduction would necessarily take such a form, the theory does allow us to predict discrepancy reduction per se with certainty. In this case the standard of correctness, which is the most resistant element of the discrepancy, is pointed out by assumptions surrounding dissonance research.

6. Conformity

One of the many conceivable variations of within-self discrepancy arises when a person finds his opinion to be at variance with the opinions of a valued reference group. In a detailed analysis of conformity Duval and Wicklund (1972) have spelled out some determinants of the person's tendency to attribute a divergence of opinion to his own error, but for now it will suffice to say that a standard of correctness can reside in the homogeneous opinion of one's peers, or in the opinion of a highly credible communicator. Given objective self-awareness and the salience of a self–other opinion divergence, the motivation to eliminate the discrepancy should result in conformity.

a. Deindividuation. Perhaps the first relevant investigation was by Singer *et al.* (1965), in which deindividuation was instituted through groups of subjects wearing identical lab coats. Conformity in the "Asch situation" created by Singer *et al.* was found to be reduced by the deindividuation treatment, a result that is quite consistent with the present theoretical reasoning. Two additional studies that bear on this point have been conducted specifically to test the present theory, both of which employed self-focusing stimuli and which are described below.

b. Conformity and one's own tape-recorded voice. In the first experiment reported by Wicklund and Duval (1971), subjects' opinions on several social-political issues were measured before the experiment. During the actual session the subjects were asked to fill out the measure once more, but this time they were first furnished with knowledge of the modal opinions of undergraduates at their university. Other subjects were led to think that the modal opinions belonged to prison inmates. Just prior to completing this questionnaire, half of the subjects were exposed to the sound of their own voices for approximately 15 seconds, a decidedly weak manipulation. Nonetheless, it was effective: Given that the modal opinion was predicated of a positive reference group (students), the own-voice treatment facilitated conformity toward the mode, but this same effect was not present when the reference group was prisoners.

c. *Conformity, uniqueness, and one's own video image.* A more elaborate experiment was subsequently conducted by Duval (1972). The conformity measure was derived from subjects' estimates of the number of objects in a visual field. Each subject was asked to give an estimate without knowledge of others' opinions; then a second estimate was given with knowledge, enabling a measure of conformity. Two manipulations of self-focused attention were performed independently. The first of these used a television monitor, such that some subjects saw their own images throughout the conformity trials, while others saw no image on the screen. The second manipulation may be entitled "uniqueness"; it was established by informing the subject by means of diagrams that she was highly unique, moderately unique, or not unique with respect to a number of important opinions. Theoretically a person should become increasingly aware of his object status as uniqueness increases.

Using the amount of conforming change in estimate as the dependent measure, there was greater conformity when the subject was confronted with her own image ($p < .05$), and conformity also increased with experimentally heightened uniqueness ($p < .001$).

The conformity studies examined here provide good support for the theoretical reasoning, and this is the place to underline the reason for the relative ease of obtaining these results. Attitudes such as those considered here are highly flexible and readily changeable. Certainly the theory would hold that there would be an initial realization of discrepancy on discovering the disparity between one's own opinion and that of a homogeneous peer group, but it is not likely that this realization of discrepancy is easily measured. That is because discrepancy reduction can be immediate, with few anchors and obstacles, in the case of social, political, or judgmental opinions. Such measurements are in contrast with our research in self-esteem, where the elements of the discrepancies are not so readily changeable, where the likelihood of tapping into the heightened awareness of an existing discrepancy seems considerably greater.

7. When Does Objective Self-Awareness Interfere with Discrepancy Reduction?

a. *Distraction from task.* Successful performance of a task typically calls for both motivation and attention, unless the task is of an automatic or overlearned nature. Objective self-awareness can serve to enhance motivation by making discrepancies between performance and aspiration salient, but at the same time it is necessary that attention revert to the elements of the task in order for performance to proceed. In the majority of the discrepancy reduction experiments discussed thus far there was very little chance of objective self-awareness being so intense that the process of discrepancy reduction was debilitated. This is because changes in aggression level, intentions to read decision-relevant information, and attitude change require virtually no concentration. The subjects in those experiments could easily have devoted 95% of their attention to concerns about discrepancies while successfully reducing those same discrepancies. But in other contexts an overload of self-focused attention would interfere. For example, in the prose-copying task of Wicklund and Duval (1971) it was necessary that self-focused attention be sufficient to motivate faster work, but not so great that concerns with the self would interfere with performance.

Within the context of that prose-copying paradigm, Liebling and Shaver (1973) demonstrated that increases in self-awareness beyond a certain point can result in diminished performance level. The original Wicklund and Duval experiment was conducted with "relaxed" instructions, with no hint that the person was being evaluated in any significant way. Liebling and Shaver replicated this procedure, but they also introduced a high-evaluation set in which task performance was said to correlate with intelligence. Presumably such a set would make for increased self-focused attention, and if enough additional self-focusing factors were introduced, attention might be diverted from the task to the point of interference with performance. Figure 8 implies that Liebling and Shaver created such a level of objective self-awareness in their Mirror–High Evaluation condition. The interaction between variables tells us that the mirror served to slow the rate of copying, given that subjects were already self-focused through evaluation instructions.

The experiment offers an important commentary on one derivation from objective self-awareness theory. Even though the theory always predicts that self-focused attention will enhance the *motivation* to eliminate discrepancies, the theory cannot offer such a blanket statement about the end result of that motivation. If attention is seldom directed toward the self, then a self-focusing stimulus is likely to bring forth increased performance only if it is not too extreme. This line of thought might best be summarized by saying that the relationship between self-focused attention and task performance almost has to be curvilinear, and, further, the simpler the task (attitude change being one extreme of simplicity), the more that attention can be turned to the self before reaching the point at which that attention comes to interfere with performance.

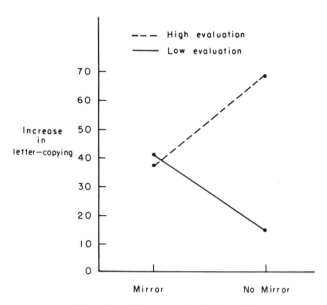

FIG. 8.   Effects of evaluation and self-focused attention.

b. Automatic acts. Much of human performance consists of behaviors that are carried out without the benefit of attention. In their cogent analysis of automatic acts, Kimble and Perlmuter (1970) refer to such performances as driving an automobile. When first learning the sequence of behaviors called driving, close attention is given to each of the several component behaviors, with subsequent evaluation of correctness. Further practice leads to an eventual automatization, whereby the volitional nature of each element of driving vanishes. The driver no longer entertains the question of whether to brake or accelerate, or whether to shift gears—the actions simply happen as a function of the immediate stimulus conditions. Kimble and Perlmuter also note that attention is redirected to the component acts only when behavior is blocked. Finally, they summarize experimental results which demonstrate the debilitating effect of attention turned toward automatic acts. Evidently the smooth functioning of these acts is disrupted when the focus of attention reanalyzes the behaviors into their components.

This latter point of Kimble and Perlmuter is similar to the assumptions underlying the preceding approach to disruptions of speech. Speech, in large part, consists of chains of automatic acts, and to focus on individual elements serves to destroy the desired fluency. This is true even when the person's intentions are to produce greater fluency. The behaviors dealt with in this section on discrepancy reduction have by no means been automatic to the degree that self-focused attention would serve to interfere, and the selection of these behaviors made it possible for the motivational consequences of self-focused attention to have beneficial effects.

It is not the purpose here to enumerate behaviors that are automatic, which should thereby suffer due to self-focused attention. Kimble and Perlmuter have suggested several (overlearned motor skills, conditioned reflexes, conditioned instructed responses), and the point is simply this: At the earlier, preautomated stages of behavior, the motivational impact of objective self-awareness on performance should be positive. Later, once a sophisticated automatization has taken place, self-focused attention will serve only to interfere.

V. Methodological Questions, Comparisons, and Conclusions

A. METHODOLOGICAL QUESTIONS

In the course of perusing the theoretically relevant research described here, the reader may have wondered about the exclusion of certain paradigms or methodologies, and this is the place to point out the reasons for such exclusions.

First, virtually no research has been reported here that has used an audience as the source of objective self-awareness. The reason is simple. The subject's inferences about what is desirable from the standpoint of others can easily create experimental demand properties, and we have preferred to avoid these problems as best as possible by using impersonal stimuli to bring about self-focused attention.

Second, nothing has been said about checks on manipulations of self-focused attention. Such checks have been tried on occasion, but there is quite good reason to believe that they are worthless in objective self-awareness paradigms. To understand this statement it will help to review the theoretical processes involved. For example, a person is first confronted with his mirror image. Second, it is assumed that attention shifts to whatever trait or behavior is salient; and third, a self-evaluative reaction, avoidance tendency, or discrepancy reduction is said to develop. Now, if the manipulation is going to be checked, at what level should the check probe? Ideally, and if we were psychic, we should like to know if the subject's attention has moved on to the salient dimension. Therefore, after the primary dependent measure is complete, the person could be asked to indicate his degree of self-consciousness with respect to that dimension. But this seems futile, for the theory most certainly would predict that a direct question of this kind would bring attention directly to bear on that dimension, and the result would be a washing-out of the prior manipulation. A question of more general nature ("How self-conscious are you?") has the same washing-out difficulties, compounded by the problem of the investigator's not knowing where the self-consciousness is directed. There is one more flaw in using these kinds of questions as checks on differential self-focus: In describing the extent of his self-consciousness the subject might simply be using the experimental manipulations as cues for an appropriate answer; thus a high self-consciousness score could reflect either actual differences in self-focus or a mere perception of the camera or mirror.

How about returning to the experimental operations for a check? For example, "Did you notice the mirror that was placed directly before you?" This would make approximately as much sense as asking subjects in social facilitation experiments if they noticed the audience. In short, these kinds of direct questions as checks on manipulations do not seem well-founded, and should anyone be interested in knowing about the direct effect of a manipulation, a possibility is suggested in the projective measure of pronouns developed by Davis and Brock (1974), discussed above. Their measure seems to be influenced considerably by the tendency to avoid self-focused attention, but if any reliable check of manipulation were to be developed, a projective device would be the most likely candidate for success.

Third, how about individual differences in susceptibility to objective self-awareness? In developing tests of the theory we have attempted to avoid the potential ambiguities associated with measures of self-consciousness, since it is difficult to know whether those measures are relevant to actual differences in self-focused attention, differences in types of personal standards or styles of discrepancy reduction, differences in ability to avoid self-focusing stimuli, or even theoretically irrelevant differences that would have a bearing on the results. This is not to say that an individual difference approach is "invalid," but it is to say that we have preferred to work with stimuli that are clearly relevant to self-focused attention, rather than with somewhat more ambiguous individual difference measures of direction of attention.

B. COMPARISONS WITH RELATED THEORIES

Mead (1934) and Piaget (1966) were drawn upon heavily by Duval and Wicklund in our original statement of the theory, but there are a number of other conceptualizations that are probably as germane. These other notions deal at least implicitly with the impact of variations in self-focused attention, and, although the domain of application of these other statements does not overlap completely with that of objective self-awareness theory, there are some interesting points of contact.

1. Actor–Observer Differences in Attribution

Jones and Nisbett (1971) proposed that two people, the actor and the observer, will differ systematically in their explanations of the actor's behavior. The actor leans toward interpretations based in environmental contingencies, but the passive observer is likely to see behavior as stemming from the actor's dispositions. In our own research on attribution (Duval & Wicklund, 1973) we have made the actor and the observer the same person, simply by varying the extent to which the actor becomes an observer of himself. For theoretical reasons different from those of Jones and Nisbett, we have indeed found greater attribution to self to the extent that the actor is turned into a self-observer. Similar phenomena have been noted by Storms (1973), who generated his research from the Jones-Nisbett conception; thus there is considerable overlap with Jones and Nisbett in this one area of application of objective self-awareness principles.

2. Attitude Polarization

An idea fostered by Tesser assumes that an attitude about any object will become polarized to the degree that thought is directed to that object. Sadler and Tesser (1973) and Tesser and Conlee (1975) have accumulated convincing evidence for this position in the context of evaluations of a negatively or positively valenced other. The more thought devoted to that other person, the more extreme the evaluation, whether negative or positive. This process bears a definite similarity to objective self-awareness derivations dealing with self-evaluation: If a person focuses on a negative discrepancy it appears even more negative, and positive discrepancies operate similarly. The parallel between Tesser and objective self-awareness theory is intriguing, since there is some hint that the exaggeration of affect, or evaluation, due to focused attention may apply to all objects of evaluation, the self being just one case in point.

3. Self-Concern

Berkowitz (1972) has noted that altruism can be adversely affected by concern with one's own self-worth. When a person has encountered failure or is under the scrutiny of others who intend to evaluate him, the resultant self-preoccupation can inhibit empathy. Presumably this is because the person who thinks only about himself fails to attend to the needs of others, or because the bad mood resulting from self-concern directly interferes with altruistic responses.

Berkowitz also suggests conditions under which self-concern can promote altruism. Self-concern carries with it a need for self-improvement, and if it becomes evident that the person can reduce his doubts about himself through helping, he will proceed to help.

In Berkowitz' proposals are some parallels to objective self-awareness theory. First, the self-concern postulated by Berkowitz evidently has a considerable self-focused attention component, suggesting that self-concern will bring forth a self-critical reaction. If Berkowitz is correct in assuming that a bad mood will inhibit altruistic efforts, then objective self-awareness with its accompanying self-critical state should reduce altruistic behavior. On the other hand, if the person can be made to realize that discrepancy reduction can be had through altruism, self-concern (and self-focused attention) should engender an increase in helping. Perhaps one of the tricks here is in bringing the objectively self-aware person's attention to the plight of the other. Self-focused attention generally might be expected to interfere with empathy, but if the person could be made aware of the discrepancy between his own present helping behavior and the needs of the other person, an increment in self-focused attention might then promote altruism. It should be kept in mind that this is largely guesswork, since empathy as a precondition for discrepancy reduction is a case we have not yet explored in research.

4. Self-Observation and Inference of Emotion

Bem (1965, 1972) would argue that a person's inferences about the funniness of a cartoon are based on his own laughter, but in a recent and provocative paper Cupchik and Leventhal (1974) argue that this inference process will break down when the person attends too carefully to his own mirth responses. Theoretically, attention to the mirth response changes that response into a discrete event and thereby interferes with the affect ("the cartoon is funny") that would normally follow from responses of smiling and laughing. Although this reasoning is independent of the premises of objective self-awareness theory, the Cupchik and Leventhal notion has some definite implications for the impact of objective self-awareness on emotional states.

5. Uniqueness

Citing Fromm (1941, 1955), Horney (1937), and Maslow (1962), who imply that man requires a separate identity, Fromkin (1968, 1970, 1973) has developed a body of research on the assumptions that individuals respond adversely to finding that they are not unique and, further, that they will seek after uniqueness when so deprived. His research has been consistently supportive of the central assumptions, and Fromkin (1973) finds additional support for his thesis in the conformity experiment by Duval (1972), discussed above. Considering just Duval's uniqueness variable, Fromkin's reasoning is straightforward: The subject who initially finds her attitudes to be widely shared by others should be experiencing a desire for increased uniqueness. This desire could be satisfied in Duval's experiment by showing relatively high disagreement on the subsequent conformity task, and of course this is precisely what happened.

Fromkin's interpretation of that experiment raises an interesting question. Does uniqueness operate in two different directions? Might a person on some occasions seek out a unique status, and on others avoid the possibility of standing out? There is no way to decide this question in the case of Duval's experiment, since the self-awareness notion and Fromkin's idea make identical predictions in that study. But in general, the following can be said about distinguishing the two theoretical approaches. First, self-focused attention is a different concept from uniqueness, and can be operationalized independently from it. For example, two individuals might differ radically in the extent to which they are unique, but independently of that fact each person could easily focus attention alternately toward himself or toward the environment.

Second, uniqueness has a value component in many instances, as is assumed within Fromkin's framework. For example, many people are not pleased to discover that they do not stand out, since the implication is one of mediocrity (Fromkin, 1973, p. 112). Thus in numerous instances of deprivations from uniqueness the person is effectively deprived of a success experience at the same time. This would explain why at least some kinds of uniqueness would be sought after.

Finally, in light of the latter point, is uniqueness a viable method of inducing objective self-awareness? Not always, for there are two prior considerations: (a) Some kinds of uniqueness would more effectively create self-focused attention than others, and it would be important to consider a variation in uniqueness carefully before treating it as analogous to a mirror or other definite reflection of self. (b) Although many kinds of uniqueness may create self-focused attention, the discovery that one is unique may at the same time constitute a success experience, and this discovery would operate against the avoidance tendency resulting from self-focused attention. If success–failure can be distinguished effectively from uniqueness, the uniqueness approach then has more definite applicability within a self-awareness context.

6. Egoism and Anomie

In a monumental analysis of suicide, Durkheim (1897) antedated the theoretical thinking of this paper with his concepts of *egoism* and *anomie. Egoism* was said to result from the absence of strong, ever-present group ties and norms that dictate the individual's mode of existence. If group structure is loose, without intense and repeated group obligations, the individual is then left to his own devices to contemplate and undertake his existence. This condition, Durkheim proposed, is one precursor of suicide.

Taking a more generalized view of egoism, we arrive at a distinction of self-focused attention vs. outward-focused attention. Presumably the person subject to egoism examines himself, becomes aware of his own rules for existence, and evaluates his unique approaches to the world. In contrast, the member of an intense group has no opportunity to reflect upon himself. The constant circulation of common group values forces individual thought processes to deindividuate—or to melt into the commonly shared group thought processes. Under such conditions it seems entirely likely that conscious attention would be focused on events other than the self. It was Durkheim's contention that nineteenth-century Catholicism and Judaism, as opposed to Protestantism, offered the intensity of group life that led to what we currently call deindividuation. In his archival searches he also concluded that marriage and war offer intensified action within the group, with a resultant prophylactic effect on suicide.

Anomie was viewed as a condition of ends, or goal states, outdistancing the available means to attain such ends. It was Durkheim's view that humans have a distinct capacity for continuously finding themselves short of their desired aspirations, and, according to his analysis, an acute or especially severe case of anomie predisposes the individual to suicide.

In addition to egoism (approximately equivalent to self-focused attention) and anomie (equivalent to negative within-self discrepancy), there is another parallel between Durkheim and self-awareness theory, this one having to do with the motivational state postulated by each system. Our theory deals with unhappiness or negative affect, and, analogously, Durkheim dealt with the conditions that precede suicide. This analogy to Durkheim, however, is not quite exact. He allowed that suicide could follow from either egoism *or* anomie, while the present conception argues that it is the combination of these two factors that produces an aversive psychological state.

C. CONCLUSIONS

The evolved theory of objective self-awareness has ramifications for three conceptual phenomena: (*a*) The initial reaction to self-focused attention is self-evaluation, which can be either favorable or unfavorable, depending on the nature of the salient within-self discrepancy. It has been assumed that discrepancies are negative except in those instances where a standard of correctness (aspiration) has recently been exceeded. (*b*) The onset of self-focused attention will generate attempts to avoid mirrors and similar stimuli given that salient discrepancies are negative, and in experimentation we have seen that attention can be taken from the self through passive diversions as well as through motor activities. (*c*) If there is no escape from self-focusing stimuli, discrepancy reduction will then follow. The research summarized here has addressed itself to a sample of the potential myriad of such discrepancy reductions, and has included both lowering and raising of aggression, improved rate of performance on simple tasks, dissonance reduction, and conformity.

REFERENCES

Allen, V. L. Effect of extraneous cognitive activity on dissonance reduction. *Psychological Reports,* 1965, **16,** 1145–1151.

Baron, R. S. Anonymity, deindividuation, and aggression. Paper presented at the convention of the Western Psychological Association, 1971.

Bem, D. J. An experimental analysis of self-persuasion. *Journal of Experimental Social Psychology,* 1965, **1,** 199–218.

Bem, D. J. Self-perception theory. In L. Berkowitz (Ed.), *Advances in experimental social psychology.* Vol. 6. New York: Academic Press, 1972. Pp. 1–62.

Berkowitz, L. Social norms, feelings, and other factors affecting helping and altruism. In L. Berkowitz (Ed.), *Advances in experimental social psychology.* Vol. 6. New York: Academic Press, 1972. Pp. 63–108.

Bloodstein, O. *A handbook on stuttering.* Chicago, Ill.: National Easter Seal Society for Crippled Children and Adults, 1969.

Brehm, J. W., & Wicklund, R. A. Regret and dissonance reduction as a function of postdecision salience of dissonant information. *Journal of Personality and Social Psychology,* 1970, **14,** 1–7.

Brown, S. F. The loci of stutterings in the speech sequence. *Journal of Speech and Hearing Disorders,* 1945, **10,** 181–192.

Carver, C. S. Facilitation of physical aggression through objective self awareness. *Journal of Experimental Social Psychology,* 1974, **10,** 365–370.

Chesterfield, Earl of (Philip Darmer Stanhope). *Letters to his son.* (W. M. Dunne, Ed.) New York: Wiley, 1901. (Originally published: 1774.)

Cupchik, G. C., & Leventhal, H. Consistency between expressive behavior and the evaluation of humorous stimuli: The role of sex and self observation. *Journal of Personality and Social Psychology,* 1974, **30,** 429–442.

Davis, D., & Brock, T. C. Heightened self awareness, self esteem, and egocentric thought. Unpublished manuscript, Ohio State University, 1974.

Diener, E. F. Prior destructive behavior, anonymity and group presence as antecedents of deindividuation and aggression. Unpublished doctoral dissertation, University of Washington, 1974.

Dittmann, A. T., & Llewellyn, L. G. Body movement and speech rhythm in social conversation. *Journal of Personality and Social Psychology,* 1969, **11,** 98–106.

Durkheim, E. *Suicide*. New York: Free Press, 1951. (Originally published: 1897.)

Duval, S. Conformity as a function of perceived level of personal uniqueness and being reminded of the object status of self. Unpublished doctoral dissertation, University of Texas at Austin, 1972.

Duval, S., & Wicklund, R. A. *A theory of objective self awareness*. New York: Academic Press, 1972.

Duval, S., & Wicklund, R. A. Effects of objective self awareness on attribution of causality. *Journal of Experimental Social Psychology*, 1973, **9**, 17–31.

Festinger, L. *A theory of cognitive dissonance*. Stanford, Calif.: Stanford University Press, 1957.

Festinger, L. *Conflict, decision, and dissonance*. Stanford, Calif.: Stanford University Press, 1964.

Festinger, L., Pepitone, A., & Newcomb, T. Some consequences of deindividuation in a group. *Journal of Abnormal and Social Psychology*, 1952, **47**, 382–389.

Fromkin, H. L. Affective and valuational consequences of self-perceived uniqueness deprivation. Unpublished doctoral dissertation, Ohio State University, 1968.

Fromkin, H. L. Effects of experimentally aroused feelings of undistinctiveness upon valuation of scarce and novel experiences. *Journal of Personality and Social Psychology*, 1970, **16**, 521–529.

Fromkin, H. L. The psychology of uniqueness: Avoidance of similarity and seeking of differentness. Unpublished manuscript, Purdue University, 1973.

Fromm, E. *Escape from freedom*. New York: Farrah & Rinehart, 1941.

Fromm, E. *The sane society*. New York: Rinehart, 1955.

Hoffer, E. *The true believer*. New York: Harper, 1951.

Hoffer, E. *The passionate state of mind*. New York: Harper, 1954.

Horney, K. *The neurotic personality of our time*. New York: Norton, 1937.

Ickes, W. J., Wicklund, R. A., & Ferris, C. B. Objective self awareness and self esteem. *Journal of Experimental Social Psychology*, 1973, **9**, 202–219.

Insko, C. A., Worchel, S., Songer, E., & Arnold, S. E. Effort, objective self awareness, choice, and dissonance. *Journal of Personality and Social Psychology*, 1973, **28**, 262–269.

Jones, E. E., & Nisbett, R. E. *The actor and the observer: Divergent perceptions of the causes of behavior*. New York: General Learning Press, 1971.

Kimble, G. A., & Perlmuter, L. C. The problem of volition. *Psychological Review*, 1970, **77**, 361–384.

Liebling, B. A., Seiler, M., & Shaver, P. Self-awareness and cigarette-smoking behavior. *Journal of Experimental Social Psychology*, 1974, **10**, 325–332.

Liebling, B. A., & Shaver, P. Evaluation, self-awareness, and task performance. *Journal of Experimental Social Psychology*, 1973, **9**, 297–306.

Maslow, A. H. *Toward a psychology of being*. Princeton, N.J.: Van Nostrand-Reinhold, 1962.

Mead, G. H. *Mind, self, and society*. Chicago, Ill.: University of Chicago Press, 1934.

Mills, J. The effect of certainty on exposure to information prior to commitment. *Journal of Experimental Social Psychology*, 1965, **1**, 348–355.

Mills, J. Interest in supporting and discrepant information. In R. P. Abelson, E. Aronson, W. J. McGuire, T. M. Newcomb, M. J. Rosenberg, & P. J. Tannenbaum (Eds.), *Theories of cognitive consistency: A sourcebook*. Chicago, Ill.: Rand McNally, 1968. Pp. 771–776.

Mischel, W. Continuity and change in personality. *American Psychologist,* 1969, **24,** 1012–1018.

Piaget, J. *Judgment and reasoning in the child.* Totowa, N.J.: Littlefield, Adams, 1966. (Originally published: 1924.)

Polanyi, M. *Personal knowledge: Towards a post-critical philosophy.* New York: Harper, 1958.

Rousey, C., & Holzman, P. S. Recognition of one's own voice. *Journal of Personality and Social Psychology,* 1967, **6,** 464–466.

Rudin, J. *Fanaticism.* Notre Dame, Ind.: University of Notre Dame Press, 1969. (Originally published: 1965.)

Sadler, O., & Tesser, A. Some effects of salience and time upon interpersonal hostility and attraction during social isolation. *Sociometry,* 1973, **36,** 99–112.

Scheier, M. F., Fenigstein, A., & Buss, A. H. Self awareness and physical aggression. *Journal of Experimental Social Psychology,* 1974, **10,** 264–273.

Schumacher, A. S., Wright, J. M., & Wiesen, A. E. The self as a source of anxiety. *Journal of Consulting and Clinical Psychology,* 1968, **32,** 30–34.

Singer, J. E., Brush, C. A., & Lublin, S. C. Some aspects of deindividuation: Identification and conformity. *Journal of Experimental Social Psychology,* 1965, **1,** 356–378.

Storms, M. D. Videotape and the attribution process: Reversing actors' and observers' points of view. *Journal of Personality and Social Psychology,* 1973, **27,** 165–175.

Swift, W. B., & Hedrick, J. Sidetracking of stuttering by "starters." *Journal of Applied Psychology,* 1917, **1,** 84–88.

Tesser, A., & Conlee, M. C. Some effects of time and thought on attitude polarization. *Journal of Personality and Social Psychology,* 1975, **31,** 262–270.

Wicker, A. W. Attitudes versus actions: The relationship of verbal and overt behavioral responses to attitude objects. *Journal of Social Issues,* 1969, **25,** 41–78.

Wicklund, R. A. Discrepancy reduction or attempted distraction? A reply to Liebling, Seiler and Shaver. *Journal of Experimental Social Psychology,* 1975, **11,** 78–81.

Wicklund, R. A., & Duval, S. Opinion change and performance facilitation as a result of objective self awareness. *Journal of Experimental Social Psychology,* 1971, **7,** 319–342.

Wicklund, R. A., & Ickes, W. J. The effect of objective self awareness on predecisional exposure to information. *Journal of Experimental Social Psychology,* 1972, **8,** 378–387.

Zanna, M. P., Lepper, M. R., & Abelson, R. P. Attentional mechanisms in children's devaluation of a forbidden activity in a forced-compliance situation. *Journal of Personality and Social Psychology,* 1973, **28,** 355–359.

Zimbardo, P. G. The human choice: Individuation, reason, and order versus deindividuation, impulse, and chaos. In W. J. Arnold & D. Levine (Eds.), *Nebraska symposium on motivation.* Vol. 17. Lincoln: University of Nebraska Press, 1969. Pp. 237–307.

Three Years Later

Robert A. Wicklund
UNIVERSITY OF TEXAS

The work of the parent chapter was accomplished within the period 1971–1974. Since that time, significant developments have taken place, both in terms of new implementations of the theory and in terms of the theoretical notion itself. The following section sketches out a sample of these recent endeavors.

I. Individual Differences

A. A SCALE FOR MEASURING PRIVATE SELF-CONSCIOUSNESS

The research reported earlier, and most of that to be reported here, has dealt exclusively with experimental manipulations of self-awareness (self-focused attention). Though it is interesting to document the rise and fall of self-awareness as a result of situational variables, it is also true that some people may be more-or-less chronically self-aware. These individuals, if identifiable, should behave in a manner much like people confronted with their own mirror images. A scale by Fenigstein, Scheier, and Buss (1975) was designed with this purpose in mind. Their scale can be factor-analyzed into three dimensions: private self-consciousness, public self-consciousness, and social anxiety. It is the relatively short private self-consciousness sub-

509

scale, with items such as "I reflect about myself a lot," that concerns us here. It has been noted repeatedly (e.g., D. Buss & Scheier, 1976; Carver & Scheier, in press; Scheier, 1976) that subjects high in private self-consciousness behave much as subjects in the familiar "mirror" conditions, whereas individuals low in private self-consciousness behave more like subjects not confronted with mirrors.

B. VALIDATING THE SCALE

A series of studies already exists that seeks to validate mirrors and cameras as self-focusing devices (Davis & Brock, 1975; Geller & Shaver, 1976). The purpose of a study by Carver and Scheier (in press) was to accomplish something similar with the private self-consciousness measure, that is, to validate it as a self-focusing device. Though there is little room to doubt the scale's face validity, the study is extremely useful in pointing to a simple method of assessing the existence of self-awareness.

Subjects were asked to complete in any way they saw fit each of 30 incomplete sentences. For example, an incomplete sentence such as "It's fun to daydream about. . ." might be answered in a variety of ways, such as "my success" or "giving a party for friends." If subjects answered with a strong self-orientation ("my success"), they were credited with a *self-focus* answer, and if the answer showed an external orientation ("giving a party"), they were credited with an *external world focus*. In examining the proportion of self-focus versus external-world focus answers, the results were clear: Subjects high in private self-consciousness showed a preponderance of self-focus answers, whereas the opposite was true for subjects low in private self-consciousness. Carver and Scheier also varied the presence of a mirror in the procedure, and the incomplete sentences index successfully discriminated the mirror from the no mirror condition.

Another approach to validating the scale may be taken in terms of the attribution-of-responsibility paradigm discussed earlier. Assuming that the psychological processes in the attribution phenomenon are relatively simple, and given that the paradigm seems highly replicable, a self-consciousness effect on the hypothetical attribution items would strongly suggest that the scale is dealing with the same state created by self-focusing stimuli. D. Buss and Scheier (1976) followed such a procedure, employing some of the negative and positive items from Duval and Wicklund (1973). To be sure, there was a very powerful effect for the scale, such that high private self-conscious subjects attributed more responsibility to the self. To make the point even more salient, Buss and Scheier also introduced a mirror manipulation that operated in a fashion parallel to the self-consciousness scale. Thus, at this point there seems every reason to think that self-awareness theory can be studied in terms of the individual difference approach.

II. Attribution and Defensiveness

A. ATTRIBUTION AND THE FOCUS OF ATTENTION

The analysis of attribution given above was rather complex, dealing with exaggeration of within-self discrepancies. An alternative analysis, and one that has a degree of simplicity to recommend it, can be found in Arkin and Duval (1975), Duval and Wicklund (1973), Jones and Nisbett (1971), Pryor and Kriss (1977), and Taylor and Fiske (1975). The essence of this explanation is that the focus of attention determines attribution and that any potential cause, including one's self, will be charged with responsibility to the degree that it is salient or accessible to attention.

B. DEFENSIVENESS: A VIOLATION OF THE FOCUS-OF-ATTENTION RULE

Though the foregoing attention-leads-to-responsibility notion has received broad support, the support has characteristically been found in personally uninvolving situations. For instance, the hypothetical situations of D. Buss and Scheier (1976) and Duval and Wicklund (1973) were anything but ego-threatening. What might happen if an element of personal involvement were added?

It was suggested before, in the introduction to the theory, that self-critical phenomena might be fleeting, given that the self-aware individual has a salient discrepancy to reduce. As long as the discrepancy is only hypothetical, there is virtually no motivation to deal with discrepancies; thus, the self-blame accruing from self-focused attention can easily become manifest. But when there is personal investment in a situation such that the self might be responsible for a real negative outcome, it is likely that the person will undertake self-esteem-protecting maneuvers, the most obvious of which is a denial of responsibility. The implication of this line of thought is clear: To the degree that an outcome is ego-threatening, self-awareness should result in a *decrease* in self-blame.

Federoff and Harvey (1976) gave subjects a brief training in the administration of therapy, then asked them to attempt to deal with a patient with a phobic problem. Some of the subjects were given a strong reason to expect success in this initial attempt to play therapist, and, among this group, half met with success and half with failure. It is the failure subjects who concern us, for the effect of self-awareness (produced by an apparently functional 16 mm camera on a tripod) was an *increase* in blame addressed to the phobic patient. In other words, under self-awareness conditions, when the subject failed in playing therapist, the subject leveled blame at the patient.

A highly analogous result was obtained by Hull (1977). Subjects took a test of cognitive abilities, and those who failed were less inclined to admit that abilities were involved when they were confronted with a mirror. Furthermore, self-aware subjects who failed were also more reluctant, relative to non-self-aware subjects, to characterize the performance outcome as failure.

As a further note, subjects in both studies tended to take more credit for success when in the presence of self-awareness-provoking stimuli, which means that there was a definite overall ego-enhancement process underway. The crucial lesson of these two studies, of course, stems from the failure conditions, for it is under conditions of ego-threat that the elegant rule of attention-leads-to-responsibility encounters an exception.

III. Progress in Discrepancy Reduction

A. SELF-REPORT VALIDITY: SELF-AWARENESS DURING TESTING

The study by Pryor, Gibbons, and Wicklund reported earlier showed that the predictive validity of a face valid sociability test can be enhanced substantially when subjects respond to the test while confronted with a mirror. That finding is now accompanied by two studies of *post*dictive validity (Pryor, Gibbons, Wicklund, Fazio, & Hood, 1977), both of which deal with extremely simplified individual difference measures. The first of these simply involved asking subjects, via a questionnaire, to indicate their combined verbal and math SAT scores, either in the presence of a mirror or without a mirror. This estimate was checked against their previously recorded actual score, and discrepancies between reported and real score were then examined. The results showed the predicted effect for self-focused attention: Subjects who responded in the presence of a mirror were significantly more accurate. This corrective effect was especially strong among subjects whose actual scores were low, owing to their propensity (in the no mirror condition) to exaggerate positively their SAT performance.

The second postdictive validity experiment employed a "Bemian" procedure (cf. Bem, 1965) in which subjects were asked implicitly to infer their attitudes from their free behaviors. Subjects first worked numerous problems from among five different types of intellectual problems. Each subject was free to work on whatever test-types she wished; thus, after the 10-minute working period, subjects characteristically had established rather definite behavioral preferences. During a second phase, subjects rated the attractiveness of each of the five types of problem. According to Bem (1965), subjects would be inclined to infer their attraction to the various tests on the basis of their prior behaviors. Accordingly, if a subject had worked primarily on Test A, she should rate it the highest, and so on. In order to examine the consistency between prior behavior and subsequent attractiveness ratings, a correlation was computed for each subject between the amount of work devoted to each problem type and the corresponding attractiveness scores. Indeed, in the no mirror condition the Bemian thesis was not supported: The average correlation for these subjects was a mere .13. However, if a mirror was present during the attractiveness ratings, the average correlation leaped to .74, and the two figures were significantly different.

In summary, the theoretical principle evidently operated the same way no matter whether the self-report referred to sociability, a single SAT score, or preferences among different kinds of tests. In every case, the self-report was only minimally related to a criterion behavior under control conditions but quite strongly related when the self-report was administered in a context of mirror-confrontation.

If a mirror can have these effects, then individuals who are chronically self-conscious should show analogous results. Groups of high and low private self-conscious subjects were selected by Scheier, Buss, and Buss (in press) and were administered the Buss–Durkee Hostility Inventory (Buss & Durkee, 1957). We would expect, of course, that high self-conscious subjects would answer the inventory with a high degree of attention on the self. Such attention should lead to self-report accuracy, resulting in a strong correlation between that inventory score and subsequent aggressive actions. The aggressive action in this case was behavior in a later situation in which the subject had the opportunity to shock another student, a procedure developed by Buss (1961). Aggression in this experiment was defined as the shock intensity delivered to the other student.

The results were just as predicted: The correlation between self-report and subsequent aggressive behavior was only .09 for low self-conscious subjects but a substantial .66 for the high self-conscious group. It seems clear once again that self-focusing stimuli and high chronic self-consciousness have similar effects on behavior—the effect in this instance being the all-important relationship between tests (or other self-reports) and behavior.

Given that the self-report validity paradigm has to do with accuracy of self-knowledge, the self-aware person should also have a more veridical understanding of his own arousal states. For example, it should be relatively difficult to fool the self-aware individual into thinking that a certain level of arousal is due to a cause that is in actuality false. In recent years it has become increasingly popular to study cognitive labeling of arousal states by means of the "misattribution" approach, which simply means that a subject is led to think that a certain experimentally administered drug (or placebo) is a source of arousal (e.g., Nisbett & Schachter, 1966; Storms & Nisbett, 1970). Given the above findings of accuracy of self-description, it might be expected that subjects who are self-aware would have a clearer picture of the sources of their arousal and, as a result, would be less inclined to believe that a pill (placebo) is generating arousal.

Gibbons (1977) asked subjects to drink a glass of bicarbonate of soda. Half of the subjects were correctly informed that it was simply bicarbonate of soda, which has no noticeable physiological side effects. The other subjects were led to think that they were drinking a drug that would produce an increase in heart rate, sweating, and a tight chest. Each of these conditions was then divided into mirror versus no mirror, such that half of the subjects remained in front of a mirror during the entire procedure. The results were highly informative regarding the impact of the mirror on subjects' suggestibility: Among the no mirror subjects, the type of instruction had a profound impact, such that "drugged" subjects reported considerably greater heart rate increase, sweating, and chest tightness *as a result of the ostensible drug.* In sharp contrast, the "drug" instructions had very little impact upon mirror subjects. In short, the mirror had the effect of virtually eliminating the subjects' suggestibility, implying that self-focus does give the person a more veridical picture of the causes and noncauses of arousal states.

B. TEST VALIDITY: SELF-AWARENESS DURING BEHAVIOR

The theoretical principle behind the foregoing studies is potentially simple. The person who is self-aware becomes motivated to bring his self-report into line with behaviors. But, alternatively, behaviors might be brought into line with self-reports. Thus far we have examined just the former of these two possibilities, in that the consistency-seeking effects of self-awareness were present just during the self-report. It should be an easy matter to reverse this procedure, such that the self-report is given external to the experimental session, and self-awareness is varied while the person behaves. The prediction is straightforward: The self-aware person should attempt to guide his behavior in a direction congruent with prior self-reports.

The first test of this idea was in two experiments by Carver (1975), who measured subjects' favorability toward using aggression to teach. Extreme subjects were selected, so that some were positively disposed toward teaching–aggression, whereas others were strongly opposed. Later in the semester all subjects had the opportunity to play the role of a teacher within the Buss (1961) shocking paradigm, and it was during this session that Carver manipulated the presence/absence of a mirror. The results of two highly similar experiments were striking: If subjects were not confronted with a mirror while they "taught," there was no relationship between previously measured attitudes toward aggression and the aggression that was subsequently administered. Given a mirror during the aggression session, there was a marked effect for attitude toward aggression, with proaggression subjects shocking significantly more than antiaggression subjects. In short, the scale had predictive validity only when the predicted behavior was enacted under self-awareness-provoking conditions.

An analogous procedure was followed by Gibbons (in press) using sex guilt instead of aggression. Subjects began by filling out a standard sex-guilt inventory (Langston, 1975; Mosher, 1968). Later in the semester they were asked to read an erotic passage and then to rate the degree to which the passage appealed to them. Just as in Carver's experiments, there was virtually no relationship between sex guilt score and reported enjoyment of sexually explicit literature. But as would be expected, the predictability of the sex guilt measure was much stronger when the second session was conducted with the benefit of a mirror.

C. HELPING AND SELF-CONCERN

The potential relationship between self-concern (Berkowitz, 1972) and self-awareness theory within the helping context was noted in the earlier published section of this writing. It was suggested that self-focused attention might generally interfere with empathy and hence with helping. A further idea was also proposed: If a person could be made aware of the discrepancy between his own helping behavior and the norm of responding to the needs of another, self-awareness might then promote helping. The issue then becomes one of salience. If the potential helper's personal needs or problems are salient, self-focused attention will not be effective in bringing forth altruism. However, if attention can be turned toward the other's plight, self-awareness might then facilitate the giving of help.

A series of five studies by Gibbons, Wicklund, Karyłowski, Rosenfield, and Chase (1977) has been brought to bear on the focus-of-attention-and-helping issue, with the following general findings: When the request comes in a relatively abstract, impersonal form, such that the need for help is not highly salient, self-focused attention then inhibits helping. This effect has held in three studies and is independent of subjects' gender and of the specific mode of self-awareness arousal (mirror/tape-recorded voice).

In a fourth study, subjects were first given either a failure or a success experience, with the idea in mind that success-experience subjects would be relatively free of immediate self-concern. The two conditions were then divided into mirror/no mirror, and subjects were confronted with a highly salient emergency situation. Latency to help was strongly *reduced* by the mirror among subjects who had just succeeded, and the opposite tendency was observed among subjects who had failed. Thus it appears as if people who are rendered relatively free of self-concern, and who are given a highly salient cue for helping, become faster helpers when self-aware.

The final study in this series did not vary self-concern. It did, however, involve a highly salient equity norm as the basis for helping. Some subjects found that they had, by a given time, performed an equitable amount of work. Other subjects found that their output had been short of an equitable amount. The results showed that the latter group increased volunteering to help when confronted with a mirror, whereas the former group, which had already reached equity, manifested no increase.

In summary, it now appears possible to say something about the conditions under which self-aware people will show prosocial behavior. If there is freedom from self-concern, and *especially* when the cue for helping is a prominent feature of the situation, self-focused attention acts to bring behavior into line with the norm of helping.

IV. Affect and Emotion

A. Intensification of Angry Aggression and Hostility

The human who has thus far been studied from a self-focused attention perspective is a civilized, moral, self-consistent, and self-critical being. Provided there is self-awareness on a salient self-relevant dimension, the individual can be shown to align his behavior with rules or standards, as exemplified by increments in altruistic behavior (Gibbons *et al.*, 1977), reduction in aggression (Scheier *et al.*, 1974), and alignment of behavior with personality traits (Pryor *et al.*, 1977; Scheier *et al.*, in press). All of these analyses have assumed, at least implicitly, that a moral dictate or internalized rule has been the mediator between self-focused attention and behavioral outcome. But what is the effect of such morals when the person is in an emotional state?

Scheier (1976) has addressed this question by introducing the idea that a strong state of affect can overshadow the functioning of a rule. For example, if a person is sufficiently angry, self-focused attention will move toward that state of angry affect, rather than to a rule about the appropriate way to deal out aggression. The implication is intriguing: Conceivably, the well-behaved subjects of Scheier *et al.* (1974), who inhibited their aggression toward women when self-aware, would not have been so chivalrous had they first been roused to anger. Indeed, according to Scheier's argument exactly the contrary might have been evidenced, with increased aggression stemming from the combination of an angry state and self-focused attention.

In the familiar Buss (1961) shock machine paradigm, male subjects either were or were not provoked to anger by a male confederate. Subjects then were asked to play the role of a teacher, giving them ample opportunity to retaliate via administration of electric shock to the anger provoking confederate. Subjects had been divided into high versus low private self-consciousness, and the results of this variable among provoked subjects were clear: Higher shock intensities were administered by high self-conscious than by low self-conscious subjects, and, furthermore, there was an opposite tendency among nonangered subjects. To paint an even clearer picture of the phenomenon, Scheier showed the same results for a mirror versus no-mirror variation.

An internal analysis sheds a degree of light on the question of "What happened to standards?" Subjects had earlier been tested on their values about angry aggression—a measure patterned after Buss and Durkee (1957). It will be recalled that Carver's self-aware people acted upon their values, whereas non-self-aware subjects did not. However, this coordination of behavior to values was conspicuously absent in the Scheier experiment—a definite suggestion that the all-salient state of anger simply outweighed the otherwise salient standards for behavior.

A phenomenon similar to Scheier's aggression results was found by Gibbons (1976), where liking for the confederate was measured; thus it begins to look as though the state of affect (anger) becomes more focal and more extreme when the person is subject to self-focusing. The aggression in Scheier's experiment may be viewed as a direct outcome of an increment in hostility.

B. OTHER AFFECT STATES

Is this exaggeration phenomenon unique to anger, or might it be found in general when affect is potentially high? Scheier and Carver (1977) have addressed this question, alternately using the self-consciousness individual difference and the mirror manipulation. For example, male subjects who viewed pictures of nude females found the nudes to be more pleasant when self-focused attention prevailed, no matter whether defined in terms of private self-consciousness or the presence of a mirror. In a related procedure with opposite content, subjects were shown a number of photographs of highly disgusting events, and again the self-aware individuals showed an exaggeration in reaction (this time negative).

Not only should affective reactions toward the external world be strengthened by self-awareness, but simple mood states would also be expected to work toward extremity under the influence of self-directed attention. Scheier and Carver (1977) followed the procedure of Velten (1968) and induced positive or negative moods in subjects by asking them to read a long series of depression-inducing or elation-inducing statements. The results were highly supportive of this line of reasoning: Both positive and negative moods were carried toward their respective extremes by self-focused attention.

V. Questions and Issues

In the midst of the accumulation of this diverse pattern of self-awareness studies, a few questions very general for the theory have arisen. These questions have largely to do with the notion of salience and also with the question of cognition versus affect.

A. ATTRIBUTION VERSUS DEFENSIVENESS

We have seen above that a "cold" model of attributional processes is a perfectly adequate description of a wide range of phenomena. Specifically, there is a good deal of evidence that attributions simply follow the focus of attention and that, when attention is directed toward a specific element (e.g., the self), causality is then seen to reside in that element. However, a crucial and distinguishing characteristic of the self is overlooked if this model of attribution is held forth as the only possibility. Federoff and Harvey (1976) and Hull (1977) have shown that attribution to the self for failure is greater when attention is *not* turned inward. This defensive phenomenon appears to go into effect when the attribution is based on a highly ego-involving experience, for when there is no failure experience, or when the failure is merely hypothetical, attributions then seem to follow with some regularity the focus of attention.

B. CONFORMITY VERSUS SELF-CONSISTENCY

Duval (1976) and Wicklund and Duval (1971) have demonstrated in a variety of settings that self-focused attention promotes conformity to group standards. One explanation given for this effect is that the self-focused individual finds himself to be in error vis-à-vis the group and thus adjusts his opinions or behaviors to match those of the group standard. The crucial question arises when we compare these conformity findings with the host of self-consistency results that has now accumulated (Carver, 1975; Gibbons, in press; Pryor *et al.*, 1977; Scheier *et al.*, in press). Whereas none of the studies mentioned earlier has created the appropriate conflict, it would be highly informative to place a strong individual standard alongside an opposite group standard and then determine the direction taken by the self-aware person. Would self-awareness bring out conformity or self-consistency? The question may well hinge upon the relative salience of these two alternative standards, and, in any case, the issue needs a good deal of exploration.

C. AFFECT VERSUS COGNITIVE RULES

The conflict just proposed was interindividual, but an analogous conflict—this one being intraindividual—is posed by the experiment of Scheier (1976) and by related research on affect states (Gibbons, 1976; Scheier & Carver, 1977). Thus far that line of research has intimated that affects run roughshod over the more civilized, moral bases for behavior, but to be certain about such a conclusion it would be necessary to place strong and salient personal standards into conflict with affect states of varying strengths. Again, the outcome may hinge upon the question of relative salience of rules versus affects. In summary, it seems highly likely that important modifications of the theory of self-awareness will lead the theory in the direction of becoming a notion about salience.

REFERENCES

Arkin, R. M., & Duval, S. Focus of attention and causal attributions of actors and observers. *Journal of Experimental Social Psychology*, 1975, **11**, 427–438.

Bem, D. J. An experimental analysis of self-persuasion. *Journal of Experimental Social Psychology*, 1965, **1**, 199–218.

Berkowitz, L. Social norms, feelings, and other factors affecting helping and altruism. In L. Berkowitz (Ed.), *Advances in experimental social psychology*, Vol. 6. New York: Academic Press, 1972. Pp. 63–108.

Buss, A. H. *The psychology of aggression*. New York: Wiley, 1961.

Buss, A. H., & Durkee, A. An inventory for assessing different kinds of hostility. *Journal of Consulting Psychology*, 1957, **21**, 343–349.

Buss, D. M., & Scheier, M. F. Self-consciousness, self-awareness, and self-attribution. *Journal of Research in Personality*, 1976, **10**, 463–468.

Carver, C. S. Physical aggression as a function of objective self-awareness and attitudes toward punishment. *Journal of Experimental Social Psychology*, 1975, **11**, 510–519.

Carver, C. S., & Scheier, M. F. The self-focusing effects of dispositional self-consciousness, mirror presence, and audience presence. *Journal of Personality and Social Psychology*, in press.

Davis, D., & Brock, T. C. Use of first person pronouns as a function of increased objective self-awareness and prior feedback. *Journal of Experimental Social Psychology*, 1975, **11**, 381–388.

Duval, S. Conformity on a visual task as a function of personal novelty on attitudinal dimensions and being reminded of the object status of self. *Journal of Experimental Social Psychology*, 1976, **12**, 87–98.

Duval, S., & Wicklund, R. A. Effects of objective self awareness on attributions of causality. *Journal of Experimental Social Psychology*, 1973, **9**, 17–31.

Federoff, N. A., & Harvey, J. H. Focus of attention, self esteem, and the attribution of causality. *Journal of Research in Personality*, 1976, **10**, 336–345.

Fenigstein, A., Scheier, M. F., & Buss, A. H. Public and private self-consciousness: Assessment and theory. *Journal of Consulting and Clinical Psychology*, 1975, **43**, 522–527.

Geller, V., & Shaver, P. Cognitive consequences of self-awareness. *Journal of Experimental Social Psychology*, 1976, **12**, 99–108.

Gibbons, F. X. Self-focused attention and the enhancement of response awareness. Unpublished doctoral dissertation, University of Texas, 1976.

Gibbons, F. X. Misattribution of arousal and self-focused attention: A reexamination of the placebo effect. Unpublished manuscript, University of Texas, 1977.

Gibbons, F. X. Sexual standards and reactions to pornography: Enhancing behavioral consistency through self-focused attention. *Journal of Personality and Social Psychology*, in press.

Gibbons, F. X., Wicklund, R. A., Karyłowski, J., Rosenfield, D., & Chase, T. C. Altruistic responses to self-focused attention. Unpublished manuscript, University of Texas, 1977.

Hull, J. G. Objective self-awareness and defensive attribution. Unpublished manuscript, Duke University, 1977.

Jones, E. E., & Nisbett, R. E. *The actor and the observer: Divergent perceptions of the causes of behavior*. New York: General Learning Press, 1971.

Langston, R. D. Stereotyped sex role behavior and sex guilt. *Journal of Personality Assessment*, 1975, **39**, 77–81.

Mosher, D. L. Measurement of guilt in females by self-report inventories. *Journal of Consulting and Clinical Psychology*, 1968, **32**, 690–695.

Nisbett, R. E., & Schachter, S. The cognitive manipulation of pain. *Journal of Experimental Social Psychology*, 1966, **2**, 227–236.

Pryor, J. B., Gibbons, F. X., Wicklund, R. A., Fazio, R. H., & Hood, R. Self-focused attention and self report validity. *Journal of Personality*, 1977, **45**, 513–527.

Pryor, J. B., & Kriss, M. The cognitive dynamics of salience in the attribution process. *Journal of Personality and Social Psychology*, 1977, **35**, 49–55.

Scheier, M. F. Self-awareness, self-consciousness, and angry aggression. *Journal of Personality*, 1976, **44**, 627–644.

Scheier, M. F., Buss, A. H., & Buss, D. M. Self-consciousness, self-report of aggressiveness, and aggression. *Journal of Research in Personality*, in press.

Scheier, M. F., & Carver, C. S. Self-focused attention and the experience of emotion: Attraction, repulsion, elation, and depression. *Journal of Personality and Social Psychology*, 1977, **35**, 625–636.

Scheier, M. F., Fenigstein, A., & Buss, A. H. Self-awareness and physical aggression. *Journal of Experimental Social Psychology*, 1974, **10**, 264–273.

Storms, M., & Nisbett, R. E. Insomnia and the attribution process. *Journal of Personality and Social Psychology*, 1970, **2**, 319–328.

Taylor, S., & Fiske, S. Point of view and perception of causality. *Journal of Personality and Social Psychology*, 1975, **32**, 439–445.

Velten, E. A laboratory task for induction of mood states. *Behavior Research and Therapy*, 1968, **6**, 473–482.

Wicklund, R. A., & Duval, S. Opinion change and performance facilitation as a result of objective self awareness. *Journal of Experimental Social Psychology*, 1971, **7**, 319–342.

SUBJECT INDEX

responsibility and blaming, 109–110
and self-perception, 110–111
and social judgments, 112–115
Cognitive dissonance
interpersonal simulation studies of,
243–251
and self-concept, 206–217
and social psychology, 215–216
theory of, 182–184, 493
Commitment
behavioral, 369
complexity of, 202–204
and volition, 198–200
Commonality calculation, 294–296
Common sense psychology, 284
Communication
constraints, 108–109
personal, 78, 164
Comparative judgment models, 20–21
Compliance effects, forced, 349–350
Confession experiments, false, 230–232
Conflicts, interpersonal, 331
Conformity, factor of, 495–496, 505, 519
Congruity
combination of strategies, 139–140
and informational consistency, 163–164
and persuasion in information processing, 160–166
principle of, 127–129, 133
Consensus, concept of, 105–107, 351–357
Consistency
concept of, 105–107
informational, 163–164
model of, 65–66
theory of, 128–130
Correspondence
concept of, 287–291
determinants of, 291–296
and personal involvement, 301–327
and relevance, 303–310
Correspondent inferences, theory of,
286–301
Covariance principle, application of,
344–345
Credibility, sources of, 27–28, 239–240

D

Decision making
applied, and probability models, 117–
118

integration theory in, 3
pioneering work in, 66–68
Defensiveness and attribution, 511–512,
519
Deindividuation and aggression, 491, 495
Denial treatment, 134–136, 142–144, 147
Derogation source combination, 136, 147
Deservingness, models for, 41
Desirability
assumptions affecting, 296–297
social, 13, 300–301
Determinants, cognitive, social, and physiological, 405–416
Developmental studies, 115–116
Discounting principle, application of,
344–345
Discrepancies
coming to terms with, 489–499
function of, 482
negative, 501
Discrepancy reduction, factor of, 470–476,
480, 494–497, 505, 512–516
Dispositional attribution, 261–262, 340–
342
Dissonance
and conflict, 192–193
reduction theory of, 493–495
and reward-incentive theory, 200–204
self-concept of, 216–217
self-focusing stimuli, 493–494
and self-judgment, 194–196, 216–218
tolerance for, 238–239
Distinctiveness, concept of, 105–107
Distortion and autonomy, 370–371, 374
Distractions
and disfluency, 486–488
and dissonance reduction, 494–495
and self-attribution, 476–477
from tasks, 496–497
Drugs, use and effects of, 401, 406–407,
417–423

E

Ecology, importance of, 378
Egocentrism, 351–357
Ego-defensiveness, 261–262, 345–347
Egoism and anomie, 503–504
Electric shocks, use of, 190–191, 232–235,
254–255, 364, 435–436, 447, 457, 490,
517

A 8
B 9
C 0
D 1
E 2
F 3
G 4
H 5
I 6
J 7